THE
ALASTAIR CAMPBELL
DIARIES

THE
ALASTAIR
CAMPBELL
DIARIES

Volume 1

PRELUDE TO POWER

1994–1997

Edited by
ALASTAIR CAMPBELL
and
BILL HAGERTY

HUTCHINSON: LONDON

Published by Hutchinson 2010

5 7 9 10 8 6 4

Copyright © Alastair Campbell 2010

Alastair Campbell has asserted his right under the Copyright, Designs
and Patents Act, 1988, to be identified as the author of this work

First published in Great Britain in 2010 by
Hutchinson
Random House, 20 Vauxhall Bridge Road,
London SW1V 2SA

www.rbooks.co.uk

Endpaper photographs: Election Campaign Meeting, Manifesto Launch, Speech
Writing on Bus copyright © Tom Stoddart Archive/Getty Images; Newspaper Headlines
copyright © Johnny Eggitt/AFP/Getty Images; Blair with Members of the Shadow
Cabinet copyright © Sean Dempsey/PA Photos; Blair at 1994 Labour Party Conference
copyright © Malcolm Croft/PA Photos; all other images from author's private collection.

Addresses for companies within The Random House Group Limited can be found at:
www.randomhouse.co.uk/offices.htm

The Random House Group Limited Reg. No. 954009

A CIP catalogue record for this book is available from the British Library

ISBN 9780091797263

The Random House Group Limited supports The Forest Stewardship
Council (FSC), the leading international forest certification organisation.
All our titles that are printed on Greenpeace approved FSC certified paper
carry the FSC logo. Our paper procurement policy can be found at
www.rbooks.co.uk/environment

Typeset in Palatino by Palimpsest Book Production Limited,
Grangemouth, Stirlingshire

Printed and bound in Great Britain by
CPI Mackays, Chatham ME5 8TD

In memory of Richard Stott, friend and editor

Contents

Acknowledgements

Sadly, the first person whose role in this book I would like to acknowledge is not here to read it, familiar though he was with every word that follows. In my journalism days, Richard Stott was my editor both at the *Daily Mirror* and at *Today* newspaper, and the obvious choice to be the editor of my diaries. He brought to that task the same enthusiasm, professionalism and attention to detail that made him an outstanding newspaper editor. It was a joy to work with him, first as we started to go through the whole diaries, then, after I decided to publish *The Blair Years* to coincide with Tony Blair leaving office, as we sought to reduce a vast body of words into a single volume of extracts. For much of the time we worked together, Richard was seriously ill with pancreatic cancer, but not even that would prevent him playing his full part. His final contribution was the so-called 'running feet', the little line at the bottom of each page which sets out the date and gives a flavour of what the page is about, a device also used in *Prelude to Power*. 'I'm very happy with the running feet,' he told me from his hospital bed. 'I just wish I could get my own bloody feet to run.'

By the time *The Blair Years* was published, he had been sent home to die. I was both humbled and deeply moved when I took the finished product to him, at his home in Kingston-upon-Thames, and I had rarely seen him so proud, sitting up in bed looking at our handiwork. I think both of us knew, as did Richard's loving wife Penny, that it might be our last meeting, and so it turned out to be. He died shortly after the book was published. He was a great friend and a superb editor, and I will never forget the role he played in my life, nor the contribution he made to this and future volumes.

Bill Hagerty was the first person I asked to take over, and I was delighted that he agreed to do so. He too was a close friend of Richard, who spoke very movingly at his funeral, and had also been my boss before I made the switch from journalism to politics. He shares

Richard's interest in, and passion for, Labour politics, and has developed the same enthusiasm for the task in hand. Richard was a hard act to follow, but I could not have asked for anyone better to take up the reins when he did.

Mark Bennett has been a tremendous support to me, starting in Downing Street, from where he resigned his civil service position to work on the 2001 election campaign for Labour. Since then he has combined his own career as a Labour politician with continued work for me, including the transcription of my diaries and tireless work at each stage of the editing process.

My literary agent Ed Victor has been a constant source of support and good counsel as I have contrived to become what he calls 'my most complicated client'. I owe thanks to him, to his PA Linda Van, and to his excellent team.

Both through my diaries and the two novels I have published, I have come to appreciate the professionalism and kindness of many people at Random House. I would like to thank Gail Rebuck, Susan Sandon, Caroline Gascoigne, Joanna Taylor, Charlotte Bush and her team of 'spin doctors', Martin Soames for his legal advice, Tess Callaway, David Milner, Alison Tullett, Vicki Robinson, Helen Judd, Sue Cavanagh, and Jeanette Slinger in reception for always ensuring one of my books is at the front of the display cabinet downstairs – at least when I am visiting the building.

I want to thank Tony Blair for giving me the opportunity he did, and thank the many friends and colleagues who have helped me in good times and bad.

Finally, thanks to my family: my mother Betty, still going strong and thanking me for every day I am not in the news, my brothers Donald and Graeme, my sister Liz, and my 'common-law mother-in-law' Audrey Millar; but more than anyone I owe thanks to our wonderful children Rory, Calum and Grace, and to Fiona, who not only had to live through it all but has had to read it all several times too.

Acknowledgements

Introduction

Is it really sixteen years since John Smith died, thirteen years since Tony Blair became prime minister, and three years since he left office, giving way to Gordon Brown?

I have a fairly vivid recollection of those three momentous days, each of them a turning point in British political history. But, perhaps especially when leading the kind of frenetic, full-on existence that modern politics has become, the memory can hold only so much. It is perhaps one of the reasons I keep a diary. Even for me, the author of these diaries and centrally involved as both witness and participant in the events they record, transcribing them was something of a voyage of discovery. Scenes described in sometimes intimate detail and often emotional mood at the end of a day came back to me, often differently from how I had remembered them. Some, indeed, I had completely forgotten. The memory can and does play tricks. My diary is as close as I will get to a full and accurate, if inevitably also partial and personal, account of a life lived witnessing history in the making.

Whereas *The Blair Years*, edited extracts of my diaries, opened on the day TB asked me to work for him in late July 1994, *Prelude to Power* begins several weeks earlier, on May 12, the day John Smith, his predecessor as Labour leader, died following a heart attack. The opening forty or so pages of hitherto unpublished material record the difficult days leading up to TB becoming leader, as he and GB argued over which of them should stand, and which of them step aside. From that first, grief-laden day, relationships between the key players were tested, and continued to be so at many stages in the months and years to follow.

At Tony Blair's top table was a disparate group of talented, driven individuals. Getting them to work together was never straightforward. Because of what happened three years later – a Labour landslide beyond all our expectations – the impression is sometimes now given of an almost effortless glide to power for a man blessed with luck. It was never easy. There were many disagreements and difficulties along the way, many moments of setback and exasperation, and fear to the end that a likely victory could still slip away. It was partly the dread fear of defeat that made TB and his team so determined to do all that was required for victory when prime minister John Major finally got round to calling a general election.

Could we have been more successful without some of the divisions and personality clashes described on these pages? Possibly. Indeed, almost certainly. But politics is a passionate business. It attracts people of strong beliefs and often large ambitions, sometimes with egos to match. At its best, it is all about principle and policy. But personalities are important, too, and perhaps a diary, much more than a memoir, in which the author is able to stand back from the day-to-day and put everything in a larger context, will reflect that. That may especially be the case when the person writing the diary, because of the co-ordinating role I was playing, was at the nexus of some of the key political and personal relationships which shaped New Labour and therefore recent British political history. But standing back from it all these years later, I believe any fair-minded person will agree that there are two inescapable political truths from the Blair era: under his leadership, one of the most successful electoral teams in British history was put together; and as a result of his three election wins, and all that flowed from them, Britain is a changed country – in my view, a country changed substantially for the better.

From the opening pages of *Prelude to Power*, the relations between the four people often cited as architects of New Labour – TB, GB, Peter M and myself – form a fundamental part of the narrative. Every single one of those relationships – some more than others – has endured bad times amid the good and the more productive, and these pages offer often dramatic testimony to that. Likewise we have all had our ups and downs with John Prescott, as we did at times with Robin Cook and other senior members of the Shadow Cabinet. Yet despite the tensions which were never far below the surface, and which sometimes exploded into the open, the bonds which tie us together are somehow stronger than the difficulties which sometimes drove us apart. Who would imagine, as they read some of the rows between Gordon Brown and Peter Mandelson in the early years of New Labour, that they would perhaps save the closest phase of their working relationship for the period which followed Peter's unexpected return to government many years later? There is definitely something called the Labour family.

Fiona, my partner of thirty years, regularly reminds me of the time Gail Rebuck, Philip Gould's wife and now my and Tony's publisher, asked us if Philip and I had ever had a conversation in which TB and GB's names were not mentioned. The answer, almost certainly, is no. I left Downing Street seven years ago, but for most of my adult life, aside from my immediate family, the leading figures in the Labour Party have been the central people in my life, just as they are the central people in this book. And though I now lead a different sort of life, they remain among the central people in the diaries I still keep today. As I write this, Tony Blair has just sent me an email asking to be kept informed about the arrangements for Michael Foot's memorial service, and to discuss how he might best help GB in the forthcoming general election. Gordon Brown is on a TV monitor to my left, giving evidence to the Chilcot Inquiry into the Iraq War, several weeks after I did so myself. John Prescott's office has called asking whether I can do a Go Fourth campaign rally with him in the near future. And I will shortly be taking a break to have a call with Peter Mandelson and Philip Gould to discuss Labour's planning for the election of May 6, 2010, which will include my pretending to be Tory leader David Cameron in GB's preparations for the first ever leaders' TV debates, a concept we negotiated about for the 1997 election but which only finally happened a full thirteen years later.

If transcribing the diaries was a voyage of discovery, so too the process of publication has had its own twists and turns. Initially, I had assumed that I would publish nothing until all the key players were safely off the main political and diplomatic stage. When the time came for Tony Blair to step down after a decade as prime minister, however, I decided I wanted to be part of the debate about his legacy. *The Blair Years* and an accompanying TV series were part of my contribution to that. I am pleased that I did publish that book, and happy with the way it was received, not least in the Labour Party for which it has raised many tens of thousands of pounds in various events since publication. As I said in the introduction to *The Blair Years*, I intended to publish the full diaries in chronological order at a later date and I have decided to publish my full account of the opposition years now, with campaigns and elections fresh in the public mind. Further volumes will follow, though I have yet to decide when.

In the paperback version of *The Blair Years*, we printed a small selection of the many reviews. One of my favourites came from Conservative foreign affairs spokesman Keith Simpson MP who said the diaries 'should be required reading' for all Tories, adding 'They demonstrate the focus, hard work, ruthlessness and imagination displayed by a group of men and women who wanted to win, and having won, to keep hold of power and make a difference . . . A lesson for us all.' I don't believe the Conservatives fully learned those lessons. As Peter Mandelson said in his Labour Party Conference speech last year, the Tories read the New Labour executive summary, but they did not read the whole book. In other words, they changed the presentation. But they did not fundamentally change their party. It was only because of fundamental change to the Labour Party that we were able to win as big and as often as we did, and deliver so much change to the country. These words may read oddly, if my hopes of a fourth Labour win have been dashed, as the polls continue to suggest they will be as I write this, but whatever the result, I do know that the Tories failed to transform their party with anything like the energy, conviction and courage that Tony Blair showed in leading the creation of New Labour. Cameron 2010 is not Blair 1997. George Osborne 2010 is not Gordon Brown 1997.

This volume, given the job I did as TB's press secretary, focuses a good deal on my and our dealings with the press and the broadcasters at a time when the media age was becoming a reality. But contrary to one of the things most regularly said about me, I was not 'obsessed' with every headline per se. My obsession was ensuring that the British people heard from us on our terms, and not on the terms of a media that was changing more quickly than any of us fully realised – in my view, for the worse. It was always for me about reaching the public, and clearly the media was an important vehicle. But whilst my constant, often round-the-clock efforts to deal with the media are recorded here, it is the politicians and their staff who dominate these pages. People are fond of saying that politics does not produce the characters it once did. I think a brief look through the cast of characters in this book shows that view to be a triumph of nostalgia over reality. Tony Blair, John Prescott, Gordon Brown, Robin Cook (the so-called 'Big Guns' of the Shadow Cabinet through the period covered here) – these are four very different, in their own ways very complicated, but endlessly fascinating characters, all of them big people who left their mark on UK history. Peter Mandelson, Philip Gould, Neil and Glenys Kinnock, Derry Irvine, Charlie Falconer, Mo Mowlam, Margaret Beckett, Donald Dewar, David Blunkett, Clare Short . . . there are plenty more and, whether liked or not, deemed competent or not, I think my diaries will confirm there are many strong and interesting characters in the New Labour story.

Of course the two who became prime minister are the two whose contribution to history will be greatest, and the most analysed. Much of that analysis thus far has been conducted through the prism of the sometimes difficult relationship between them that in some ways can be traced back to the events of the opening pages. In the days immediately before John Smith's death, a poll of MPs and Labour supporters on who was likely to be the next Labour leader would almost certainly have named Gordon Brown. Yet almost immediately after the news of the tragedy broke, a sense quickly developed that Tony, not Gordon, would be John's successor. Gordon, and to some extent Peter Mandelson, who my diaries suggest started out closer to GB than TB in the wake of John Smith's death, resented my articulating that thought in an interview that day. I did so accidentally, as it happens, though GB's team would not immediately believe that. But I was in no doubt, as these pages record, that TB becoming leader was inevitable. He was the right man, at the right time, as GB has since stated publicly. Alongside that thought, I had the certain feeling that I would work for him, though we had never discussed it before. I am glad that I did, despite the pressures it brought to bear upon me and my family, and proud that I was able to play a role in helping to get Labour back into power, so that power could be used to bring about change in a country desperately in need of it.

I hope these diaries will aid the understanding of both Tony and Gordon. Like all major historical figures, they are complex individuals, and I believe this and future volumes will show the many and varied aspects to their characters. It is true that I became much closer, personally and politically, to TB. That was perhaps inevitable given how closely we worked over so many years. I came to like him more, and respect his leadership skills more, as I watched him manage the myriad difficult issues and events that form the lot of the modern leader, even one with a keen and constant eye on his own objectives and strategy. But in some ways I went back further with GB. Though a journalist, I used to help him with his speeches, strategies and articles as far back as 1984, the year after he was elected to Parliament for the first time. He was charming, funny, hugely energetic, and clearly destined for senior positions in Labour politics. Though we fell out from time to time, usually when he and TB were not getting on or, as I recorded in *The Blair Years*, because of the behaviour of some of his supporters and staff, my post-2003 diaries will record that I was closely involved in the process that led to his taking over from TB, and have sought to help and support him in different ways since. This stopped short, however, of going back full-time, as at various points he asked me to, including by becoming a minister in the House of Lords as Peter Mandelson did. I took a decision, when I left Downing

Street in 2003, that whilst I always hoped to be able to make a contribution to Labour politics and Labour campaigns, I did not want to go back to a 24/7 job in the middle of the Westminster bubble. I felt I owed that to my family, not least a mother who extracted a promise to that effect, and a partner who had never wanted me to do the job in the first place. I now lead a different, more varied sort of life in which politics is important, but not the only thing I do. People often ask me if I miss the never-ending cut and thrust, and the sense of being right at the centre of the major events shaping the direction of the country and the world. The answer is that I do, but not enough to want to go back and do it all over again.

It would certainly not be true that I loved every minute of it. At times, I hated it. A natural tendency to depression was not always helped by the work rate required, or my dealings with the media, or trying to resolve political and personal differences, sometimes within my own home. But I am nonetheless pleased that I ignored the advice of friends and family, and took the job when I did. I thought I knew a lot about politics before I made the jump from the media side of the fence. But I think it is only when you really are part of the political process – a good one for all its faults – that you realise not just how important it is, but how hard it is too. It is why I ended my days with TB liking and respecting him even more than I did at the beginning. This first volume tells the story of how he took a party used to losing elections and made it one that became used to winning elections. In some ways, it could be the story of any organisation wrestling with change. The big difference in top-level politics is the scale of the decisions which sometimes have to be taken, and that fact that, especially now, it is a life lived in the eye of unrelenting and often hostile 24-hour scrutiny.

So for those who want to see politics as being all about personality, ego, ambition and process, they will find plenty to interest them in *Prelude to Power*. But there is a lot more to it than that, and I do tend to the Keith Simpson view of my diaries – that what comes through above all is our absolute determination to do all that was required to get Labour back into power, so that instead of raging in opposition we could make changes for the country, in government. As I said in the introduction to *The Blair Years*, it is a diary, not a paean of praise. It records without hindsight what I saw, said, heard, thought, felt and did during many of the key moments. Along the way, there were plenty of bad days amid the good, things going wrong as well as things going right, people falling out as well as pulling together. But we never lost sight of our core objectives, and by and large we met them.

I liked, too, the review in the *Financial Times* by John Lloyd, a man with views on relations between politics and media that are worth listening to. He said *The Blair Years* had 'inspired a thousand head-lines and hundreds of columns. But their real virtue, so far largely unrecorded, is that they picture people who differ widely in ability, evenness of temper and maturity of behaviour, working under huge strain and constant observation, with immense workloads seeking to achieve large goals. The proper headline drawn from Campbell's memoir would be "Top politicians make mistakes, have arguments, don't do everything they say they will, might lose power: insider's shock revelations." Blessed is the country run by such people: and we will be wiser if we recognise that this is the real story.' *Prelude to Power* tells the early years of that story in full, the 180 pages of the opposition period in *The Blair Years* extended to the 744 pages here.

On the morning after the 1992 election, as John Major returned to Downing Street to run the country, and Neil Kinnock returned to his house in West London to rest and reflect, I was on College Green outside Parliament, being interviewed about the result by the BBC with Peter Jenkins, the veteran commentator who has since died. Peter said something which immediately ate into my soul: he said that if Labour could not win in the circumstances of the election they had just lost, the likelihood was that they would never get power again, that they were finished as a political force.

This book tells the story that proved him wrong just five years later. It is the story of how Tony Blair became leader, how New Labour was created, how a formidable election team was forged, an incred-ible landslide won, which put the Tories out of power for so long. It is a story of great tensions, and clashes, but also of great achieve-ments, and advance. It is an everyday story of politics, and political change. I am proud of where that story leads in this volume: to a happy ending, the great victory recorded on the final pages; proud of so much of what we went on to do; and privileged to have been a part of it, able now to share my account with others, and with history.

Alastair Campbell
London, Friday March 5, 2010

Who's Who

May 1994–May 1997

Shadow Cabinet

Tony Blair	Leader of the Opposition (referred to throughout as TB or Tony)
John Prescott	Deputy Leader (JP, John P)
Gordon Brown	Shadow Chancellor of the Exchequer (GB)
Robin Cook	Foreign Affairs (RC, Robin C)
Margaret Beckett	Health 1994–95, Trade and Industry 1995–97 (MB, Margaret B)
Donald Dewar	Social Security 1994–95, Labour Chief Whip 1995–97 (DD, Donald D)
Jack Straw	Home Affairs (JS, Jack S)
David Blunkett	Education (DB, David B)
Harriet Harman	Employment 1994–95, Health 1995–96, Social Security 1996–97 (HH, Harriet)
Andrew Smith	Shadow Chief Secretary to the Treasury 1994–96, Transport 1996–97
Frank Dobson	Environment 1994–95, Environment and London 1995–97 (FD, Dobbo)
George Robertson	Scotland (GR, George R)
Mo Mowlam	Northern Ireland (Mo)
Chris Smith	National Heritage 1994–95, Social Security 1995–96, Health 1996–97
Jack Cunningham	Trade and Industry 1994–95, National Heritage 1996–97 (JC, Jack C)
Michael Meacher	Transport 1994–95, Employment 1995–96, Environment 1996–97 (MM)
Ron Davies	Wales
David Clark	Defence
Joan Lestor	Overseas Development 1994–96
Gavin Strang	Agriculture

Ann Taylor	Shadow Leader of the Commons 1994–97
Derek Foster	Labour Chief Whip 1994–95, Shadow Duchy of Lancaster 1995–97
Clare Short	Shadow Transport 1994–96, Overseas Development 1996–97
Lord (Ivor) Richard	Shadow Leader of the Lords
Lord (Derry) Irvine	Shadow Lord Chancellor

Leader's Office

Tim Allan	Press officer
John Burton	Blair's constituency agent
Alastair Campbell	Leader's press secretary (AC)
Hilary Coffman	Press officer
Jon Cruddas	Trade union liaison
Kate Garvey	Personal assistant to TB
Bruce Grocott MP	TB's parliamentary private secretary
Anji Hunter	Head of office (AH, Anji)
Peter Hyman	Speechwriter, policy adviser
Sue Jackson	Head of administration
Liz Lloyd	Policy adviser
Pat McFadden	Policy adviser
David Miliband	Head of policy (DM, David M)
Sally Morgan	Political secretary (SM, Sally M)
Geoffrey Norris	Policy adviser, trade and industry
Jonathan Powell	Chief of staff
Roz Preston	Adviser to Cherie Blair
James Purnell	Policy adviser
Derek Scott	Policy adviser, economics
Terry Rayner	Driver (Government Car Service)

Key Advisers outside the Leader's Office

Charlie Falconer	Barrister, close friend of Tony Blair
Philip Gould	Pollster and strategist; adviser to Tony Blair (PG)
Peter Mandelson	Labour MP for Hartlepool

Conservative Ministers 1994–97

John Major	Prime Minister 1990–97 (JM)
Michael Heseltine	Trade and Industry to 1995, Deputy Prime Minister 1995–97 (Hezza)
Kenneth Clarke	Chancellor of the Exchequer
Michael Howard	Home Secretary

Malcolm Rifkind	Defence to 1995, Foreign Secretary 1995–97
Michael Portillo	Employment, 1994–95, Defence 1995–97
Stephen Dorrell	National Heritage to 1995, Health 1995–97
Gillian Shepherd	Education and Employment
Brian Mawhinney	Conservative Party chairman 1995–97
John Redwood	Wales, to 1995

Gordon Brown's Office

Douglas Alexander	Adviser
Ed Balls	Economic adviser
Ed Miliband	Adviser
Sue Nye	Assistant to Gordon Brown
Charlie Whelan	Brown's press spokesman (CW, Charlie W)

The Labour Party

James Callaghan	Labour Prime Minister 1976–79, Labour Leader 1976–80
Michael Foot	Labour Leader 1980–83
Neil Kinnock	Labour Leader 1983–92, European Commissioner from 1995 (Neil, NK)
John Smith	Labour Leader 1992–94 (JS)
Nick Brown	Labour MP for Newcastle upon Tyne East
Alistair Darling	Labour MP for Edinburgh Central
Anna Healy	Press officer
David Hill	Chief spokesman for the Labour Party
Joy Johnson	Director of campaigns, elections and media 1995–96
Tessa Jowell	Labour MP for Dulwich
Gerald Kaufman	Labour MP for Manchester Gorton
Fraser Kemp	Labour Party election co-ordinator
Michael Levy	Businessman, Labour Party fundraiser
Jack McConnell	Scottish Labour Party general secretary
Margaret McDonagh	Senior campaign organiser
Jo Moore	Press officer
Tom Sawyer	Labour Party general secretary 1994–98
Dennis Skinner	Labour MP for Bolsover
Brian Wilson	Labour MP for Cunninghame North
Rosie Winterton	Head of John Prescott's office

Trade Union General Secretaries

| Rodney Bickerstaffe | UNISON |

John Edmonds	GMB
Bill Morris	TGWU
John Monks	TUC

Family, Friends and Others

Fiona Millar	Campbell's partner (FM)
Rory, Calum and Grace Campbell	Children of Campbell and Fiona Millar
Betty Campbell	Campbell's mother
Donald Campbell	Campbell's father
Audrey Millar	Mother of Fiona
Bob Millar	Father of Fiona (died 1994)
Paddy Ashdown	Liberal Democrat MP, Lib Dem leader
Martin Bell	Journalist and independent parliamentary candidate
Cherie Blair	Wife of Tony Blair (CB)
Sir Robin Butler	Cabinet secretary and head of the Civil Service
Carole Caplin	Friend and adviser to Cherie Blair (CC)
Charles	Prince of Wales
Alan Clark	Conservative politician and diarist, friend of AC
Bill Clinton	US President 1992–2000 (Bill C, BC)
Gavyn Davies	Economist, husband of Sue Nye, unofficial adviser to TB
Diana	Princess of Wales
Molly Dineen	Film-maker
Murray Elder	Former chief of staff to Labour leader John Smith
Alex Ferguson	Manager, Manchester United Football Club
Joe Haines	Former press secretary to Harold Wilson
Neil Hamilton	Conservative MP for Tatton
Matthew Harding	Businessman and Labour supporter (died 1996)
Roy Hattersley	Deputy Leader of the Labour Party, 1983–92
Alan Howarth	Tory MP who defected to Labour
Glenys Kinnock	Labour MEP from 1994, wife of Neil Kinnock
Mike McCurry	Bill Clinton's press secretary
David Mills	Lawyer, husband of Tessa Jowell
Pauline Prescott	Wife of John Prescott
Queen Elizabeth II	UK monarch
Maggie Rae	Lawyer advising Diana, Princess of Wales
Gail Rebuck	Publisher, wife of Philip Gould

Alan Sugar	Businessman
Margaret Thatcher	Conservative Prime Minister 1979–90

The Media

Tony Bevins	*Observer* political editor to 1996, then *Independent*
David Bradshaw	*Mirror* deputy political editor
Michael Brunson	ITN political editor
Paul Dacre	*Daily Mail*
Sir David English	Chairman and editor-in-chief, Associated Newspapers
Sir David Frost	*Breakfast with Frost* presenter
Andrew Grice	*Sunday Times* political editor
Phil Hall	Editor, *News of the World*, 1995–2000
Tony Hall	Chief executive, BBC News
Stuart Higgins	Editor, *Sun*, 1994–98
Les Hinton	Executive chairman, News International
John Humphrys	BBC *Today* presenter
Trevor Kavanagh	*Sun* political editor
Donald Macintyre	Independent political commentator
Andrew Marr	Independent political editor 1992–96, editor 1996–98
David Montgomery	Chief executive, Mirror Group plc
Piers Morgan	Editor, *News of the World*, 1994–95, then *Daily Mirror*
Rupert Murdoch	Chairman, News Corporation
Robin Oakley	BBC political editor
Peter Riddell	*Times* political commentator
Alan Rusbridger	Editor of the *Guardian*
John Sergeant	Chief political correspondent, BBC
Jon Snow	*Channel 4 News*
Jon Sopel	BBC political correspondent
Irwin Stelzer	Economist and journalist, adviser to Rupert Murdoch
Peter Stothard	Editor of *The Times*
Richard Stott	Editor of *Today* newspaper, 1993–95, personal friend of AC
Jeremy Vine	BBC political reporter
Philip Webster	*Times* political editor
Michael White	*Guardian* political editor
Patrick Wintour	*Guardian* political correspondent

The Diaries

Thursday, May 12, 1994

Up at 4.15 and off to the BBC to review the papers. I was getting driven to the office in Wapping by one of the regular drivers, Louie, when I got a call from Hilary Coffman [press officer in John Smith's office] that John Smith[1] was in hospital. 'How bad is it?' I asked. 'Bad,' she said. He had had a heart attack at his flat in the Barbican and was rushed to hospital, but I sensed from the tone of her voice that they already knew he was dead, or at least sensed it was going to happen. It was one of those moments that you knew mattered. We had just come off the Westway and were going down the slip road towards Paddington. I told the driver to head to the Commons instead. I called Richard [Stott, editor of *Today*] and warned him what was happening. The rumour mill was in full swing already. The news desk were calling saying he was in hospital and it looked like it was really serious. I'd seen John yesterday, and he was his usual affable self. And last night, we'd been out with Derry [Irvine, Shadow Lord Chancellor], Neil and Glenys [Kinnock] and Hugh Hudson [film-maker] and been talking about John, probably around the same time he was keeling over. The phone was going crazy now. The first person I bumped into at the Commons, just down the corridor from the entrance to John's office, was Jack Cunningham [Shadow Foreign Secretary]. He had tears welling up in his eyes. 'He's dead,' he said. 'What, confirmed, dead?' 'Yes,' he said. 'It's impossible to take in, isn't it?'

Everywhere you went, there was a gloom now descending on the place. There were little knots of people both spreading and taking in the news, and a genuine sadness that was palpable not just with the

[1] Hugely popular leader of the Labour Party, thought to be able to bring the party back in to power.

Labour politicians, but all of them, and not just with the politicians but the people who worked there too. I was getting bids to do loads of media. I went over to Millbank and was due to do ITN down the line first. It hadn't been confirmed he was dead yet, and as I waited to do the interview, I heard Dermot Murnaghan [broadcaster] in the studio saying 'God, Campbell looks really miserable, does he know something we don't?' The news was confirmed not long afterwards. I called TB [Tony Blair, then Shadow Home Secretary] who was up in Aberdeen, and said the speculation is going to start straight away. He sounded pretty cut up. He said anyone who was seen to be campaigning, or even thinking about the leadership, would get punished. I said I know, but he needs to understand that once the shock is absorbed, the speculation will begin. He said he had the media around him today, and would find a way of making a tribute, and then probably try to head back to London. It really was hard to take in. Even though John had had health problems before, he had been looking pretty fit and in good form and it just had not been an issue of late. All the tributes were stressing his decency, his Commons oratory, and his intellect. Most of the interviewers avoided the succession issue or if they didn't, I avoided answering. But the mood was definitely for TB. I saw Neil who had been talking to Charles Clarke [head of Kinnock's office, 1983–92] and Patricia Hewitt [Kinnock's former press secretary], and he said it was all moving for Blair. Brian Wilson [Scottish Labour MP] said it was a myth that all the Scots would go for GB [Gordon Brown, Shadow Chancellor]. The feeling was TB was the man for the moment. Gerald Kaufman [Labour MP, minister under former prime ministers Harold Wilson and James Callaghan] said there was a mood and a momentum and no amount of campaigning was going to change that.

I bumped into Charlie Whelan [GB's press officer] and Sarah Macaulay [PR consultant, later GB's wife] at Rodin's cafe in the basement at 4 Millbank. We had a sandwich together. Charlie said there was no way Blair would get unions behind him. I said the question for me was: who do the Tories fear most? I had done a TV thing with Norman Tebbit [former Conservative Cabinet minister] earlier, and he was in no doubt TB was the one the Tories did not want because he had an appeal that went beyond traditional Labour leaders, including JS. I did a pre-record with Mark Mardell [BBC journalist] for *Newsnight* and right at the end, he asked who was going to be the next leader and I just said it: 'Tony Blair.' I bumped into TB later as he was leaving the Commons to go home. 'This is all very difficult,' he said. 'What do you mean?' 'Relationships.' He and GB had had a couple of conversations, he said, and it was clear both were coming under pressure to stand, but both agreed it would not be good to stand against each other. He said to call him at home later. I did, and he said he was being inundated with calls and messages saying he had to stand. He was pissed off that JP [John Prescott, Shadow Employment spokesman] and RC [Robin Cook, Shadow Trade and Industry spokesman] were already making noises that suggested the campaign had begun. He didn't know what GB was up to, but he did feel they had to come to some kind of agreement about which one of them should do it. I said for what it's worth, virtually every single person I have spoken to, apart from committed GB people, are saying you have to go for it. I said the Tories are hoping we go for GB. I told him what Whelan said re the unions, to which he said 'That is rubbish. Some won't, some will.' We agreed his strength was the appeal he was thought to have to the broader public, and that would become more apparent in the coming days. Both he and GB were worried that Labour had not really been pushing on hard enough recently. Whichever one of them went for it, it had to be on a platform of faster change and modernisation. Again, that said TB rather than GB. As well as the stuff for the paper I was doing telly and radio all day, right up to midnight and was knackered heading home. Tessa [Jowell, Labour MP] paged me to call her. She said I must watch out not to get too tired. She said 'Your role in the next few weeks will be crucial, and you must stay fit and strong.' She then added '. . . for Tony.' She said he is going to need looking after, but he has to go for it. We agreed to have lunch tomorrow. The papers really did John Smith proud, fantastic tributes and many of them capturing the mood that seemed genuinely to have fallen upon the country.

Friday, May 13

TB called after he had left the house, angry that he was doorstepped on the way out. I said there will be more of that until it becomes clearer what is happening. He said GB had worked for this moment all his life, and he was not going to step aside easily. He said 'I only want to do what is right.' I said if we are talking about doing what is right, then you have to ask who would be better placed to take Labour from where we are to where we need to be: winning. I could tell he felt that was him, but it was a big psychological step to reverse the general position as perceived, namely that GB was the main man. He said he was surprised at some of the names who had been urging him to go for it, including Scots and people thought to be more leftist than he was. I said what John's death has done has focused people on the key question – who is more likely to win – and that was driving a lot of this. Up till now, people had not really had to think about it, because John had been there and we fully expected him to be there at an election. But his death means people have to face a different future and a question, when it becomes real, can throw up different answers to when it is a hypothesis. Even reading the papers, and listening to the broadcasters, you could see and hear the different tone for TB – the sense that GB would be what people might expect to happen, but TB was the one that people felt could win. 'I really don't want to fight Gordon,' he said in a later conversation. 'I don't think that would do anyone any good, not us and certainly not the Party.' We spoke several times during the day and he kept saying how difficult it all was. And it is. But the important thing was he had not just rolled over and said 'over to you Gordon'. They were going to have to tough it out between themselves, and at least TB sounded like he was beginning to marshal a few arguments.

I called Jo Moore [Labour press officer] to get briefed on the rules of a contest, and she said there was a real feeling in the press office it was moving to TB. TB was not sure what Peter [Mandelson, Labour MP] was up to, and nor was I. He did not return my calls today, which was really unusual, and I was hearing he was pissed off at my *Newsnight* interview, as doubtless GB would have been. TB said 'I think he is genuinely torn. This is going to be quite grim, because friendships are going to get mangled in all this.' I said he was going to have to show a bit of steel and strength. He said he had been talking to Elizabeth [Smith, John's widow] which had been really upsetting. He said it must be bad enough dealing with the death, and trying to grieve, but to do it when everything was so public, and surrounded by all the speculation about the future, cannot be nice. I asked him if he had any skeletons in his cupboard – women, drugs, that kind of thing – and he said no.

I had lunch with Tessa at Rodin's. She was adamant that it had to be TB and I had to be part of the team that persuaded him to stand. I said I don't think he will need much persuading, but he will want to do it with minimum damage to the party and maximum protection of key relationships. She too was confused about what Peter was up to. We both felt instinctively Peter would know it had to be TB, yet he was if anything looking inclined towards Gordon, and it was odd he was not returning calls. It was clear my *Newsnight* interview had gone down badly with GB's people, one or two of whom were staring daggers as I left the restaurant. Robin Cook looked like he was trying to set himself up as potential kingmaker rather than stand

May '94: 'I don't want to fight Gordon' – TB

himself. I did a stack of interviews during the day and was working on a piece for the *Sunday Telegraph* as well as doing more for *Today*. Alan Clark [maverick Conservative politician, diarist and friend of AC] phoned. 'Blair is the John Moore [former Tory Cabinet minister, tipped for prime minister but who faded] of the Labour Party.' I said you don't believe it. He said, I know, but that is the best line we can go on. He was clear the Tories would want to stop TB getting the job if they could.

Saturday, May 14

I called Peter and asked why he didn't return my calls yesterday. 'You know why.' 'No, I don't.' He said he was incandescent at my *Newsnight* interview. 'Why?' 'It was like a John Edmonds [general secretary of the GMB union]-style endorsement of the new leader, muscle-flexing.' I said that was ludicrous. I had not planned on saying it, but when the direct question came it was the obvious direct answer. He said, you are not just a pundit in all this and you know it; he said the TB media bandwagon will work against him if he is not careful. I asked if he was going to support GB and he said I had been wrong to be so unequivocal, and it had been deeply unhelpful. Everything he was saying suggested he was backing GB yet he didn't answer directly. 'Do not imagine GB will just walk away from this. He is a formidable politician and he cannot be ruled out lightly in the way you did.' I said all I did was answer the direct question: who did I think would be the next leader? He said the media wave for TB at the moment was 'froth' and would quickly be blown away. When I went through what I had said in a *Sunday Telegraph* piece, he said 'Sounds like a Blair briefing to me.' Fiona [Millar, AC's partner] said 'Is Tony aware how devious Peter can be?' I remembered John Smith's description, during some shenanigan or other, when he said Peter was so devious there was a danger that one day he would disappear up his own backside. TB was equally confused as to what Peter was up to, and even thought he [Mandelson], as well as Charlie Whelan, might be briefing against him. He was if anything even more torn than yesterday. He said if a clear mood developed in the party he would have to respond to it. 'I am only going to do this thing if I am sure it is the right thing.' He said he was sure the mood was moving his way, and said 'If I was Gordon, I would like to think I would know what to do. He can't win and deep down he must know that.' He felt that if it came to a contest, and he was desperate for it not to, he would win the MPs and the members and he was not sure GB would have quite the union support he imagines.

The problem was GB was so long seen as the number one out of the two of them and was having to adjust quickly to a changing reality. TB said he was worried about the effect on the children if he went for it, and got it. He knew how big a transformation this would be. I called Kim Howells [Labour MP] who said he was still gutted about John's death. But for the future, he said, it had to be Tony, no contest. I felt that whoever stood, of TB and GB, would win, so the question became who would be best against the Tories. Peter Kilfoyle [Labour MP and whip] felt that TB's 'new era' stuff might backfire, that it would just play to the idea he was not very experienced.

TB was calling fairly regularly, both to go over the stuff I was writing and broadcasting, and also just to run the same thoughts over and over again. He said, I'm talking to you all the time because I'm not sure who else to talk to. He said it was weird not to be able to have the constant dialogue with GB he normally had, and he knew that neither of them was being totally open with the other. Equally, he was suspicious of Peter M at the moment. He had the poll figures from *The Sunday Times* and *Sunday Telegraph* which showed the momentum with him. 'I cannot step down in the face of that,' he said. 'Even I would call myself a flake if I did that.' He said 'What I cannot understand is how GB cannot see how straightforward it all is, when most other serious people see it clearly. If there is to be only one contender, then it has to be me.' He said JP had called him and he was unsure of his intentions. I said I suspected JP would go for both jobs and hope he ended up with deputy, using the leadership election for profile as much as anything.

Peter called again, more emollient than earlier. I told him what I was planning to do for my *Today* column on Monday. 'Sounds like another Blair briefing,' he said. I said people would think it very odd if he ended up not backing TB, who was so clearly the leading moderniser. He told me again not to underestimate GB. I called JP in Hull but just missed him, as he was heading down to London to do *Breakfast with Frost* tomorrow. He returned the call later, and I told him I would definitely be backing him for deputy, but so far as the leadership was concerned, it had to be TB. I said we would be fair to him in the coverage but when it came to it, we were backing Blair. He said he liked TB, he was decent and fair and felt he could trust him in a way he couldn't trust [Robin] Cook. He thought Robin had made a fool of himself in saying he was standing and then pulling out. I relayed the [leadership] poll figures to him and he said 'Oh how my heart goes out at this moment to Peter and Harriet [Harman, Shadow chief secretary to the Treasury, GB's deputy]. How those poor souls must be suffering.' And he laughed. He did not buy the line that GB would get all the unions behind him. He said OMOV[1] had taken him to a different level. Equally, TB had a lot of respect among the union leaders for the way he stood up to them over the closed shop and other difficult policy stuff. He said if GB listened to the polls, he would pull out for him, but he will find it hard to do that. He has felt for too long this was like his right. I asked him if he thought he could win the leadership. He said no, 'But you never know, I guess, strange things happen.' Peter called again to discuss the papers as he was due to be doing them on *Frost*. I said did he realise JP would be there too? He hadn't till then.

Sunday, May 15

I was up early to do my *Today* and *Tribune* [left-wing political weekly] columns to get them out of the way so I could head off to Burnley for the first leg of the play-off semi-final against Plymouth. TB called at 7.30, wanting me to take him through the papers. He was worried there was already a bit of a backlash, much as Peter had predicted, but actually he was in pretty good shape media-wise. I got the 8.30 to Leeds and for once both Mum and Dad wanted to come to the match, which was exciting, albeit 0-0, so all down to the second leg. I finished my *Tribune* column on the train, and again was pushing lines most useful to TB I guess, without actually dumping on GB. Peter called after *Frost* to say JP had basically just snubbed him, cut him dead really. TB called later and said it was a nightmare and getting worse. He was worried about the kids who even now were picking up on the extra profile and the extra pressure. He also felt GB and some of his people were starting to fight back, and hoping that TB might cave in and let GB go for it. I had spoken again to JP who was moving towards the deputy leadership, using the leadership campaign as a vehicle. He was even thinking Margaret Beckett [deputy leader, acting leader] might stand down. I told TB re that and also re JP being vile about Cook – 'Untrustworthy bastard' – and even more vile about GB. JP seemed to have worked out that Margaret could be challenged and he would use the argument that one contest was better than two. What he really wanted was the deputy leadership. He thought there could be a simultaneous contest and the pressure to challenge Margaret would

[1] 'One Member One Vote' in leadership and deputy leadership elections, a much-debated change to Labour's constitution in 1993 in which Prescott had played a crucial promoting role.

be strong. I said if she did well as stand-in, it could get tricky. He felt sure there would be the two contests alongside each other and he would do fine. He knew he could get the nominations and once a contest started properly, all these questions would be forgotten. That, said TB, is very interesting. They arranged to meet each other at the House.

I had a slight worry JP might be talking to others in the same vein. I explained to TB that there have been times with Neil when I had got to a position where I knew things but was being told them on the assumption of not writing about them. It felt a bit like that with this. Was Prescott talking to others in the same way? TB felt Margaret might have to be talked to. She was in something of a different league. It was in some of the papers that he had spoken to Cook. 'Well it certainly didn't come from me.' He said it was a nightmare and a real problem that the two people he would normally talk to about the politics of all this – Gordon and Peter – he couldn't talk to. He was due to speak to GB later. I said he had to be firm and explain to him that he [TB] would be a laughing stock if he stood down when there was such momentum for him. I had a chat with Cherie [Blair] who felt the kids were fine with what was going on. She said the phone never stopped over the weekend with people saying he had to go for it.

Monday, May 16

I woke up and decided to go to Betty's funeral [Betty Parry, mother of Glenys Kinnock]. It meant a long drive to Bangor. First on the phone was Peter to record his amazement that JP had called him the night before to apologise for being so rude to him when they bumped into each other at *Breakfast with Frost*. JP confirmed when I spoke to him later. Peter was now giving every impression of being with the Blair camp, but Anji [Hunter, head of Blair's private office] was not so sure. She felt he was playing a very Peterish game. She sounded a bit overemotional. She said she didn't know who to trust. 'Can we really trust you?' She said it was getting nasty, that Nick Brown [Labour MP, GB ally] put Kevan Jones [GMB union official] on the *Today* programme to talk down TB. They were also putting it around that Peter was running Tony's campaign to get backs up. Anji called again later and said I had to keep talking to TB, and telling him he had to go for it. Spoke to Peter, and I was still trying to work out exactly where he was on all this. Had a good laugh when he said Nick Brown was devious. I called JP who said he had called Peter to say there was no point carrying on with all the old enmities. He still felt Margaret might stand down as deputy leader in exchange for a big job. She could do a stint as acting leader now, oversee the transition, and step down as a heroine, with TB leader and JP deputy. He said there was 'no way' Gordon was going to stay as Shadow Chancellor. He was constantly going on about Harriet and how upset she must be about having to decide which of the two of them to back.

He said if Gordon became leader it would be back to all the old stuff, who's in, who's out, aides whispering and doing people in, whereas TB is able to work with everyone. He reckoned Margaret would win her place in the history of the movement if she stepped down. He felt he and TB together best represented what JS was about and TB added the appeal to people we didn't normally reach. It was a pretty stressful journey and I spent most of it on the phone. I got really bad chest pains at the funeral, probably just the usual inability to cope at funerals. Felt really faint. Very moving event, very Welsh. At the do afterwards, Adam Ingram [Labour MP] said it was nonsense that most Scots and most of the unions would support GB. The journey back was more of the same, people phoning the whole time. I called Hilary [Coffman] who was up in Edinburgh organising John Smith's funeral. She got the impression TB was the only one not actively campaigning.

Tuesday, May 17

Anji called and said Tony had been pretty tough with GB. She was beginning to think GB would step aside, and it was important I did what I could to talk him up when that happened. I was due to do a load of radio and TV interviews and the general theme that had taken hold was that a media bandwagon had got behind TB. Fiona called as I was on the way back to the House to say that Bob [Millar, her father] had got cancer. Totally gobsmacked. Gerald Kaufman called and asked me to be on TB's 'little team'. He said he hoped I was talking to GB through all this and could make him see sense. He said he believed he had got Peter on board for TB 'as long as he's not playing a double game'. Gerald said that would be rather silly as we are almost certainly talking about the next prime minister here. Ann Taylor [Shadow Education Secretary] made very similar noises about GB seeing sense when I bumped into her in the lobby. Hilary Armstrong [Labour MP, John Smith's parliamentary private secretary 1992-94] said TB had gone to see Elizabeth Smith and had a clear sense of pressures from GB's people [to play a role] re the funeral. After PMQs, David Hill [chief spokesman for the Labour Party] said that I was being invited to the funeral as a family friend, and Paul Wilenius [*Today* political editor] would represent the paper with other political editors. Tessa [Jowell] called from the States, said she was worried about me. She said she had spoken to Harriet who was trying to work out how she could back Gordon without alienating herself from TB.

Wednesday, May 18

I called CB who sounded very down. She joked that if she could shoot Gordon she would, as it must be obvious to him by now that he's not going to get it. But he won't stand aside. TB had seen Elizabeth Smith yesterday. He saw GB, who was very difficult. Cherie said she had no doubt TB would win in a contest but what good would it do anybody to have one? I called TB later. I don't know how many times he said it was a nightmare. Lots. They had spoken again in Scotland yesterday and Gordon claimed he had a lot of support, e.g. 40 of the Scots MPs. He said he didn't believe it. What made this so hard for GB was that up until now, it had all been so clear. Now it wasn't. TB said he liked to think that if the evidence was stacked the other way, he would know to bow out. I worked on my column, which included a whack on Nick Brown, which I mentioned to Anji. She must have told TB who paged me to ask me not to have a go at Nick. I said that's how these people get away with it. And lo and behold, the *Evening Standard* got a phone call from Nigel Griffiths [Labour MP, GB ally] who called on the record to say they were furious that Mandelson was running TB's campaign. He later phoned to retract it, presumably on GB's orders. Peter paged me to say Nick Brown and Nigel Griffiths had gone mad and had been excluding him. He said the useful thing was that he was now back in charge. I was more confused than ever about whether he was working for TB or GB. I asked him who he was working for when he said he was back in charge. He said he was the peacemaker who was caught in the middle as always. Now he felt he could get back in and make a difference. I went for a cup of tea with Neil. He was desperately torn between TB and GB. But he felt the only questions were these: who can win a general election, and who can win it regardless of who the Tory leader is? That has to be TB. He felt that some of the people surrounding GB were giving him bad advice. But the truth was TB and GB had to sort it out themselves. He said he worried that the party had not fully grown up yet. Burnley won the second leg in the semis of the play-offs which means a trip to Wembley next Sunday. Bob seemed OK, considering.

May '94: I could shoot Gordon, jokes Cherie

Reviewing the papers for the BBC, then a lift in to Westminster to record *The Week in Westminster*. Did a discussion with Alex Salmond, Dennis Canavan and Phil Gallie [SNP, Labour and Conservative MPs in Scotland]. Over at the House, considerable support for my column against GB's sidekicks. PMQs was a little bit back to normal after all the tributes of last week, and then we had a statement on the Post Office from Hezza [Michael Heseltine, Conservative Trade and Industry Secretary]. Afterwards I went for a cup of tea with Peter M in the Pugin Room. He asked me to be totally honest with him. I said I felt he had got himself into a bad position. I guessed he was genuinely torn between GB and TB, whereas I had been clear from the start. His instincts in many ways said Gordon but his head had said Tony. That, allied to the Machiavelli reputation, was what had landed him in it. It meant he was loathed more than ever by some. I had discussed what to say with TB beforehand. He felt Peter had behaved honourably and it would all end fine. Peter said by and large he agreed with my analysis, that it had all been difficult and messy. He felt Gordon genuinely thought he could win, and TB thought he could, and they both looked to him for advice. I said GB was only being given information likely to lead him to think he could win. Peter agreed with that. Said if it came to a contest between them both, he had to keep out of it.

Friday, May 20

Up at 6 and the car came shortly afterwards to head for Heathrow. John Monks [general secretary of the Trades Union Congress] was across the aisle on the flight up, so inevitably the talk turned to the leadership. He was worried about whether the unions could manage a ballot. He sensed a lot of support for GB, JP and TB but felt the PLP [Parliamentary Labour Party] would dictate the shape of the overall vote. In which case, I said, it will go to TB. [Sir] Robin Butler [Cabinet Secretary and head of the Civil Service] was on the same plane, plus lots of trades union leaders and a smattering of hacks. There were buses laid on to the church service [at Cluny Parish Church, Edinburgh, attended by some 900 people], pretty big crowds lining the streets. Nice service, very JS. John Major [Conservative Prime Minister] appeared to be in row seven and Neil was not exactly prominent. There were a lot of media lined up as everyone filed out and a lot of focus on TB and GB. I bumped into GB on the bus, but he didn't say a word, despite me saying hello. TB was also on the bus and Gerald Kaufman said to me he already had an aura of leadership that set him apart.

Derry and Alison Irvine were chatting away, quite the thing, with Donald [Dewar, Labour MP and formerly husband of Alison]. At the reception, Joan Lestor [Labour frontbencher] told me she had been mistaken for Cherie on the way in. Had a long chat with Elizabeth, Sarah and Catherine [JS's widow and two of their three daughters] who had really handled themselves well but looked tired. Catherine said they were getting through it just by having lots of things to do. They were heading to Iona afterwards for a private family funeral on the island following the Edinburgh service. Neil told me he wanted to come to the play-off finals. Major looked a little bit out of place, and cut me dead as usual.

GB was moving and grooving, really working the room. JP was making jokes about the Brown camp and how any fight with them would be 'handbags at dawn'. I got a cab to the airport, filed, and, then flew back with Sue Nye [GB's assistant]. 'Can't you just stop writing?' she asked me. I said it was a bit difficult when it was a newspaper that paid my salary. We agreed not to talk about the contest, which wasn't terribly easy, and didn't last for long. She felt GB could win and, more important, so did he. I said Peter had suggested that I don't speak to Gordon but if he wanted to talk, we could. She said it had been obvious from the off who I supported because I had said so publicly. I said saying what I thought did not rule out the possibility of a conversation if he wanted to have one. I did *The World Tonight* from a radio car then Anji called, asking me to think who they could get as a press officer. She said she and I had to be like rocks for Tony, as there were a lot of things and people unsettling him at the moment. On the media front, she said that as I was the first and only one who had ever suggested to him that JP was becoming a serious figure who could make a difference in all this, he trusted my judgement.

Saturday, May 21

We went to Georgia's and Grace's [Gould, daughters of Philip, political pollster and strategist] joint birthday party. Patricia Hewitt was there, very pro Tony but unsure about how it would end. She thought Cook was still a possible runner. Philip was worried that the people round TB were not up to it without Peter in there. He felt if he didn't have Peter, he'd be in trouble. I called TB later at home. He said he still didn't really know what Peter was up to, and he didn't really know what GB's intentions were. I said it may be that Peter is still playing a double game. The Sunday papers arrived. I told him they weren't great. There was definitely a bit of an anti-Blair bandwagon. I briefed him on the *Observer* story about GB being pro union, which was a fairly blatant and very tactical pitch. He had promised he would stick to his guns as pro change, pro modernisation. He sounded very depressed. I said he had done himself a lot of good by not getting too involved last week but it did mean he now had to catch up and inject something into the whole campaign via his speech on Tuesday. There can be no trimming, he said. He was particularly worried by the notion getting out there that he didn't stand for anything at all. He asked if he could keep Neil onside. I said I thought so, though I think Neil is genuinely torn between the two of them. I told him not to worry, that one day's bad press meant nothing. He said I'm going to need your help.

Sunday, May 22

Mo [Mowlam, Labour MP] called early to ask whether I thought people like her should be out doing something straight away on TB's behalf. I said yes, even if just a few bullet points to trail Tuesday's speech. Worryingly, she said she had spoken to TB himself but she had to speak to me about doing anything with the media. I was getting more and more sucked into this. TB called on his way to church. Tuesday's speech was going to have to be something of a 'credo' event. There was no doubt there was a bit of a GB bandwagon rolling, partly a response to the early build-up for TB, partly because they had organised it. Do you think Gordon has just been buying time? Yes, I said, so has Peter. Perhaps TB should have done more earlier. Margaret Beckett was on *Frost*, and said there should be a contest. Philip [Gould] said he had been there when she briefed Isabel Hilton [*Independent* journalist] that she would run. All the contestants will run, she said.

Tessa was back from the States. She was fascinated by Peter's position and like all of us trying to work out what it was. TB called later, worried about GB's speech. It was clear he was pushing for the union vote. TB felt it was a mistake, too obvious, and said his speech on Tuesday had to be about Labour being a modern party. It had to be consistent with where he had always been. I told him Brian Wilson was backing him and thought a good majority of the Scots would, and he said Roger Poole [assistant general secretary of UNISON, the public sector union] and Tom Sawyer [UNISON's deputy general secretary] were backing him. Ditto John Monks. 'I really feel bad about the idea of not working with Gordon,' he said.

Monday, May 23

GB was getting good coverage for his speech, though Chris Mullin [Labour MP] said it was disingenuous, he was presenting himself differently to how he had been conducting himself. I bumped into Gerald Kaufman. 'What a waste of the man's breath,' he said. 'Tony has it.' Then to the House via a cup of tea with Tessa. We chatted mainly about the leadership and her desire to work properly for TB. She said I had to run TB's campaign. I said that was a bit difficult when I had a job on a newspaper. Once at the House, I learned from various people that Gordon had gone nuclear about my column, with its obvious view that TB was the man. Peter later told me that it had been drawn to GB's attention by Derek Draper [Mandelson aide] who told him 'I think your problems are very adequately set out in Alastair's column.' He seemingly hadn't seen it till then. But when he did, according to Peter, he went crazy. Kim Howells told me GB's speech went down OK but it was too long and there was a feeling the message and the tactics were all a bit too obvious.

Tuesday, May 24

Mum was down for three days, partly to help out with Audrey [Fiona's mother], who was probably worrying a lot more than she let on. TB was in the office early, working on his speech. He called to go over the main themes again. I suggested a headline in the area of family and community being the keys to national revival. He said won't that be seen as an implicit attack on Gordon? I said maybe, but only because of the speech he made. In any event, he has to accept before too long that it's all over. Labour has to be the party committed to restoring the social fabric, but it's not going to be done in the old ways. Peter was seemingly very down about GB. PG [Philip Gould] called to tell me he had just spoken to him and he was very fed up with life. I called Peter who said he was at the end of his tether. I did a leader on TB's speech, and at [the *Today* editorial] conference, when I said Radio 5 were on strike, Richard said, to general merriment, but making a point 'So you might spend an hour with us then?' Mo had fucked up talking to John Patten [Conservative Education Secretary] on the train to Eastleigh.[1] She had said something about TB being worried about bringing up the children in the Number 10 flat. Silly woman, just can't resist gabbing. Patten was unapologetic about using it in a press conference.

I spoke to Peter Kilfoyle who reckoned TB had around a hundred MPs at least, totally solid already. He said TB was a bit naive about

---

[1] The death of Conservative MP Stephen Milligan by auto-erotic asphyxiation had caused a by-election in Eastleigh. The facts of the death undermined John Major's moralistic 'Back to Basics' initiative. The Liberal Democrats would win by 9,239 votes, Labour pushing the Conservatives into third place.

some things, e.g. taking Jack Cunningham's support for granted when Jack might still be thinking about standing. Kilfoyle said Nick Brown was rapidly exposing as a myth the notion of his alleged political skills. Said he had been completely useless. I did an interview for Scottish TV, and was introduced as a Blair supporter. I said I was a supporter of no contest, and also that GB was getting bad advice. I had a cup of tea with Sam Galbraith [Scottish Labour MP] who thought a lot of Scots would vote for GB if they had to, but they would rather he didn't stand. Peter called as I got home. He said he had spent two hours with GB and was exhausted. They knew it was ridiculous for both of them to stand but GB was too proud to pull out. Peter still believed they would get to a position where only one would stand. I called TB, warned him that Mo's gaffe, which was sheer gabbiness, would take the shine off the coverage of his speech, which had gone down well, was seen as serious and hitting the right notes. He said he had given her a bollocking. I felt her problem was she wanted to be loved too much. It all looked too much like a game, and he had to be ruthless.

Wednesday, May 25

I did the *Today* programme with Austin Mitchell [Labour MP]. He said Cook hated Gordon which was a bit over the top. Took the kids to school. I wrote my column at home with the main piece on Mo but later changed it after Margaret Beckett announced there would be a deputy leadership contest at the same time as the leadership contest. Interesting move, necessary I suppose for her to be able to run for the leadership, and it meant JP could go for both without being seen to cause a lot of trouble. Gordon's office, doubtless at Sue Nye's prompting, rang me later to sing 'Happy Birthday' to me down the phone. Went to Luigi's for lunch, then to the lobby, hanging around picking up reaction on Beckett's move. Interesting how many people said both that TB was obvious as next leader, but also that they didn't know enough about what he really stood for. Took Mum to the *House Magazine* party in the Speaker's state rooms and introduced her to lots of people, Kim [Howells], Peter Bottomley [Conservative MP], Charles Clarke, Betty [Boothroyd, Speaker] herself who was really nice and warm. Peter M came round later. He felt Beckett would be more of a danger to the new leader than Prescott.

Thursday, May 26

TB pretty clear that Margaret was intending to stand for the leadership. Cherie was getting lots of media bids and I was advising against.

TB had done another little speech and I told him I felt he should have done more to get attention for it.

Friday, May 27

Up at 4, to the Beeb, doing the papers. Bob Wheaton [*BBC Breakfast* editor] said he would like to do panel interviews with all the leadership contenders. TB called. He said Cherie was keen to do an interview with the *Observer*, because they were definitely doing a profile. I said she should point them in Fiona's direction because she would give them the right line, and I thought they needed to think really carefully before actually doing interviews. He said JP had called him and was a bit worried, because the press were clearly seeing his speech as being really left wing, when it wasn't meant to be. JP was clearly trying to signal how much he thought he would work with TB. Cherie called Fiona and just about bought the line that if she started to push herself out, it would simply fuel it all, give the impression she was actively seeking a profile, which long term wouldn't be good for her.

I briefed TB on the stuff in the *Mail* about his 'secret grandfather'. He was amazed at some of the stuff they had found out, said even his dad didn't know about the sister.[1] I had far too much on, what with column and leaders, *Tribune*, telly, radio and interviews for the book [co-writing, with David Bull, *Football and the Commons People*, on politicians and football]. Did Ken Clarke [Conservative Chancellor of the Exchequer] today. Called Neil, who said he was still unsure what GB would do. He told Beckett he thought what she did was a real act of leadership. I still couldn't work out whether there was a more selfish motive, that it was a way of getting into the leadership election. Popped round to TB's office. Pretty manic in there. Clearly too much to do and not enough people. Liz Lloyd [policy adviser in Blair's office] wanted him to do more on race. Managed to get away for the boys' sports day. Rory and Calum both won their races.

Saturday, May 28

Peter M called and I was more confused than ever. In one breath, he would be speaking as a fully fledged TB person, giving the analysis on what TB had done, why it had gone well, and then, doing much

[1] It had emerged that Blair's father, Leo, was the illegitimate son of unmarried music hall entertainers and had been fostered (later adopted) by James and Mary Blair of Glasgow as a baby. Leo's unknown half-sister had now been discovered.

the same from the GB perspective, with the same conviction, and then saying how ghastly everyone else was.

Sunday, May 29

TB called 8am to discuss his *World This Weekend* interview, but I wasn't that interested given today was the [second division] play-off final at Wembley. He said the media were asking for him today because of Major saying something about beggars [Major had launched an attack on the 'menace' of begging]. I said you should start stressing the line that Major is a pygmy, constantly going on the wrong issues. TB said there was a poll coming out which had him way ahead in all sections, MPs, members and unions. I knocked off my *Today* column and sent it as Neil arrived just after 12. Both he and Bob [Millar] were impressed at the Burnley turnout, less so possibly at my behaviour, but it was unbelievably tense. The place went berserk when we took the lead. I thought my lungs were going to give out. When the final whistle went, it dawned on me that the woman in front was [Burnley manager] Jimmy Mullen's mother, because he charged up through the stands to see her. Fantastic day, can't quite believe that we did it [Burnley beat Stockport 2-1].

Monday, May 30

It was a bank holiday so worked from home and Peter M came round, really fed up. He said Gordon had told him that he felt he had betrayed him. So he was in a position where the people working for TB thought that he had been playing a double game, whereas GB thought he had been supporting TB all along. He said all he had been trying to do was to help them both reach a decision which did not end with them fighting each other. TB called re his press release on drugs and also a row with the *Today* programme who were trying to wind up a non-story on benefits. We agreed he should tell them to get lost.

Tuesday, May 31

Peter phoned in a dreadful state because TB was 'blaming him' for a line in the *Guardian* about GB losing the Shadow Chancellorship. He said he was at the end of his tether and wanted nothing more to do with either of them. He calmed down during the day, but was still pretty fed up with it. He felt he had tried to do his best by both of them, but it clearly hadn't worked. I said the problem was that GB tends not to do halfway measures. If you'd said to them both at the start you were not going to choose, you were not going to campaign actively, but you would help in any way you could to help them towards a decision, the chances are even that he would see that as a hostile act. He only does for or against. Maybe it's easier for me because I'm a journalist, not a politician, and whatever happens I'll have a role writing about it. But it felt blindingly obvious to me from the word go that it would be TB, and all this agonising was really just messing around. GB was clearly moving towards pulling out. TB had said he was seeing him for dinner this evening and hoped they would have something to say tomorrow. Peter said he had sacrificed himself for GB, who now would not even speak to him, and for TB, who had bollocked him over something he hadn't done. I was working on the [Tory MP Marcus] Fox interview for the *Spectator* and doing a *Today* leader on Alan Clark and his coven, the story having broken about him shagging a mother and daughter. I spoke to him. He said, unconvincingly, that he was full of remorse and, rather more convincingly, that Jane [Clark's wife] was bearing up.

Wednesday, June 1

TB called first thing. He said the dinner [at the Granita restaurant, Islington] had gone fine, and GB was going to make an announcement today that he was not standing. He said it would be very important what I write about it because people knew I was close. He said it was vital I talked up GB, and tried to get others in the media to do likewise, and it was also important I talked up the importance of the TB-GB partnership, that they remained good friends and would continue to work together, and the two of them working together was crucial to Labour's future success. He also wanted me to say that as they were both relatively young still, this was a selfless act which left open the chance of him getting the leadership at a later date. It was pretty clear GB had finally conceded, but driven a hard bargain along the way. That, or TB was just desperate to keep him onside and avoid a fight. In that first call of the day, he was almost exclusively concerned with GB getting what he called a soft landing. Then he called to talk about how to stage the photo of the two of them together, walking up from the Commons. I said they both had to be as natural as possible, but there is nothing natural about walking purely for the purposes of being filmed doing so. It didn't look too bad, but given it would be shown many, many times in the future, it was a shame it didn't look more natural. I saw them both briefly before they went out, and it was tense. GB was clearly pissed off with me, and the role I had been playing in recent days, but I felt this was ending where it was always going to end, from the moment JS died. Tony looked OK about it all, but he was constantly fussing re GB and how he was going to come out of it.

Then later he was a bit more concerned about himself. He called me when I was writing my column in the office in the afternoon and said straight out 'How do you reckon I will come out of today?' I said I think there will be quite a lot around about you showing a bit of steel, maybe being a bit more ruthless than people thought. He said it would not be at all unhelpful if a right-wing newspaper or two ran pieces along those lines. 'What, "Bambi gets tough" kind of headlines?' I said.[1] That kind of thing, he said, laughing. I went to the Tory press conference, which was a complete waste of time, Major at his worst. I called Peter who said GB was now not speaking to him at all, literally, not a word. He said Nick Brown was still going round the national media with the line that Gordon would have won, while telling his regional telly in the North-East that it would be great to have a leader from the region. I left at 6 to go and see Bob [Millar] in St Mary's at Paddington. He didn't look too great and was coughing a lot, but we chatted away about all kinds of things, including obviously the political scene. He said I was ideally positioned to be the absolute expert on the whole Labour scene now.

Thursday, June 2

Reviewing the papers for the Beeb, mainly on the reaction to GB pulling out, so another opportunity to talk him up a bit. Also doing a round of radio interviews. JP called, and was pretty caustic about the whole thing. 'Forgive me if I have total contempt for these press people writing all this shit about Brown. He pulled out for one reason only – because he finally realised he could not get the votes. End of story. So to have all this bollocks about it being selfless and all for the party, come off it, it's rubbish.' He was also on the warpath about the idea TB had made a guarantee GB would stay in charge of economic policy. 'If he thinks he is going to be in charge of all economic policy, then they both have a fight on, I'm telling you.' JP had decided that even though he wanted the deputy leadership, he had to go for both. 'Amazing, isn't it – Brown pulls out and he's a hero. If I pulled out, it would be Prescott's a coward.' He was effing and blinding the whole time, said there was no way we were going into an election with Brown in sole charge of fucking economic policy. He said Robin would be making a push on this too. It is true that the papers were kinder to GB than they would have been to JP, but it was a different situation. TB and GB were seen as friends and now rivals and that is what made it such an interesting situation. Also TB had showed a bit of

[1] Some of Blair's opponents had nicknamed him Bambi.

steel. 'He's definitely got a bit of steel behind the smile, but let's have no more of this "let's all love Brown" bollocks, it's not on.' He said TB was a lot tougher and a lot shrewder than people think. At the moment all the focus is on the pretty boy superficial stuff, family man, middle class, lawyer, clever, blah blah, but there is a lot more to him than that.

That's why it's the right decision, he said. He will also grow in the job. It was interesting how, even though there was to be a contest, and JP was to be involved in it, he was already talking of TB as though he were leader. He said he knew that there was a large part of TB that would prefer Margaret as his deputy, but he reckoned he and TB could work together well. He also realised there was a possibility that TB had offered GB precisely nothing. So Robin would definitely be on the lookout. I said I would be amazed if TB had anyone other than GB as Shadow Chancellor. JP said that does not automatically mean you are in charge of economic policy. You can work in committees, you can work in groups and in the end the leader has to decide. He was still thinking RC might throw his hat in the ring, but there was no sense of any real support for him, so there was a risk he would be humiliated. I assumed he was telling me all this not so that I wrote about it, but because he assumed it would all go back to TB, especially all his warm words and respect for him, which of course it did. I also warned him that as well as today's piece as part of the soft landing for GB operation, I was now working on another one. 'I can't work you lot out,' he said. 'He can't get the votes, so he's pulled out. Tony saw him off. That is the only possible interpretation.'

Friday, June 3

To Millbank for the *Week in Westminster*, then over to the House and went to see TB's team in the office. Anji was out so I was chatting to Tim [Allan, press officer], Kate [Garvey, TB's personal assistant] and Liz [Lloyd]. They looked so incredibly young, but they also looked and sounded like they knew what they were doing.

Sunday, June 5

John Burton [TB's agent in Sedgefield] called to say I must talk TB out of letting Mo run his campaign. It was what she was after but she didn't have the attention to detail or the understanding of what a campaign like this needs. He said JP had called apologising for cracking jokes about 'Bambi' re TB in a speech a couple of days ago. TB called, said he wanted to have a brainstorm with Peter and me. He needed to sit down and go through all the tough questions that were likely to come up during the campaign, and also start to think beyond. He said he hoped MB stood for the leadership, as it would give him a different approach to allow his proper positioning within the debate, and he wouldn't at all mind if RC stood either. He felt Margaret was in many ways to the left of JP, and he needed some of the old left arguments out there so that he could set out a different approach more convincingly. I asked who was going to be his campaign manager, and he said 'What's wrong with Mo?' When it comes to campaign management, everything, I said. She is indiscreet and it will become a danger to him. Look at the silly incident with Patten. That would just be the start. She has a lot of skills and he should think how to use them, but not as his campaign manager. He needed someone much more rigorous for that. But it didn't really matter, he said, because he and one or two others would be setting the direction and calling the shots. I said once you appoint a campaign manager, that person has the capacity to do good or bad to the campaign, and it matters who it is. 'People do say that about Mo,' he said – John Burton had been at him too – 'so who?' He said could it be Jack Straw [Shadow Environment Secretary]. He would certainly be better than Mo. Alan Clark called for advice, with the latest on his sex life having simmered away and now calming down a bit. I got a sneaking feeling though that he was enjoying the attention again, and the notion of himself as a great womaniser forever getting into major scrapes. He said he had hired George Carman [QC, top libel lawyer]. I said these people are really just posh Max Cliffords [PR man]. Brilliant, he said, posh Max Cliffords! More expensive too, I dare say. I said be careful, because your interest is in getting this thing buried and forgotten. A lawyer might see the benefit of getting the whole thing to court. Good advice, he said, toodle-pip, and off he went.

Monday, June 6

Did the *Today* programme, discussion with Peter Riddell [*Times* journalist]. Mainly on the Euro elections. Europe was just an unmitigated disaster for Major, and he showed very little sign he knew how to deal with it. I felt like I was doing three jobs at the moment – the *Today* job, all the outside media commentating, which in theory Richard didn't mind because it got a bit of free publicity for the paper, but which in practice meant I wasn't really focusing on the main event as much as I should. But then I was also spending as much time on TB as anything else probably. He was no longer talking to me as a journalist, more a member of his team. It was the same for his staff. I was going to have to work out how to balance all this out. Home via St Mary's to see Bob. He was looking OK but clearly not enjoying being holed up in there.

Out for dinner with Peter M and Hugh Hudson at the White Tower. Peter said I had upset TB's equilibrium with what I had said re Mo, because clearly he had been planning to ask her to run the campaign. Peter suggested that in reality he would run the campaign, Jack would be campaign manager and Mo could be campaign organiser, whatever that meant. It sounded like a bit of a mess, and also I think he underestimated how much opposition there would be, fairly or not, to him having that kind of role. He had not exactly emerged out of recent events with the TB MPs singing his praises overly. He said he had just been trying to help them make a difficult decision and he had as ever been hit in the crossfire. He said I had to be careful in how I spoke to TB. 'You have the capacity to trouble him, the same as you have the capacity to trouble me.' I said I just said what I thought. He said yes, and then maybe we overanalyse it but at the moment TB is a bit vulnerable and not sure about the lie of the land. This is all new and we all have to be careful. I said we also have to be as clear as we can be. Hugh asked who Tony really listened to. Peter said himself, me, Barry Cox [TV executive, friend of Blair] and Derry Irvine. I said you would have to add GB, but we would have to see whether that remained the case now that he had stepped aside. Hugh felt there was bound to be bad blood, but also that it was obvious it had to be TB.

Tuesday, June 7

Worked on the *Today* leaders in the morning, column pm, also sorting out tonight's Radio 5 show. Bill Cash on again – he loved it, and he was pretty good so long as he didn't bang on ALL the time about Europe, and didn't stop other people talking. Tessa was coming on again, which was good, plus Barbara Follett [Labour supporter, future parliamentary candidate], Lord Russell [Liberal Democrat peer]. Peter called to say that Margaret Beckett was claiming she could get sixty MPs to nominate her, so JP needed to know whether some of his supporters were facing both ways. Peter was with me that JP on balance would be a better deputy for TB, but he felt if MB was right in what she said, JP might be underestimating her support and overestimating his own. He said TB would much prefer JP as deputy, but John needed to handle himself carefully. I called JP and said, why don't you just stand for deputy, and really make that the focus, all the old stuff you did in past campaigns about making it a different kind of role? He said he was too far in now, that he would have to do both. He said he knew TB would rather deal with him than MB.

He was pissed off at the journos who did the 'Bambi' jokes, because it made it look more serious than it was. I said he had to be more careful, because they would be looking for every little slip now. He said he was always sure MB would stand for the leadership, because she had got a little taste of it now and would want to hold on to that. And she would be thinking that if the momentum for TB becomes unstoppable, she will get the deputy as a consolation, because she's done it before, because she stood in and because there will be a lot of people thinking it should be a woman.

TB called and said Mo had been a bit upset, and had fought hard to be campaign manager, but he was going to give that title to Jack, and ask her to focus on MPs and CLPs [Constituency Labour Parties]. I was a little worried that it had even got that far. I was worried what it said about his judgement that he really thought Mo could have done that job in a coherent and professional way. On the programme, we did Euro elections – Cash rampant – Germany, tax and shopping. All fine, if a bit heavy in parts. Tessa gave me a lift home. She had seen Robin for an hour earlier and he was definitely not standing. He was clearly going to angle for the Shadow Chancellorship. He claimed – and she thought there was something in this – that there were a lot of people who would happily support TB, but who would not support TB-GB as a team. I said my hunch was there was no chance at all that TB would make RC Shadow Chancellor. For one, he would be a bit worried about his politics on it. But also, he simply was not going to countenance anyone but GB in that position. She said he would have to give Robin a top job though. Clearly, but not that one.

Wednesday, June 8
Tessa called, said she thought she had been terrible on the programme. It is true that she had been a bit hesitant. She said she felt she should only do it when it was about subjects she really knew about. The problem with that was that we tended to get the guests around one or two obvious subjects they were suited to, but some were last-minute topical. I did the leaders and my column, which wasn't brilliant. I didn't feel I was on form at the moment, probably because I was thinking much less about all that than I was about the TB situation, not least because he and the people close to him called the whole time. Sloped off early to see Bob at the hospital.

Thursday, June 9
Doing the papers at the Beeb. Came off air and the first pager message was from Peter. 'Why aren't you wearing my tie?' He had given me

a tie for my birthday [May 25] but it was so not me I can only assume he gave it as a joke, or in the hope I would give it back to him. It was the kind of thing he would get away with, but I wouldn't. It was just too brash. But at least we were back to a bit of fun and banter in the exchanges, which had all gone out of the window immediately following John's death. I remembered John's old line about Peter being so devious that one day he would wake up and find he had disappeared up his own backside. When I told Peter, he laughed his head off, but I still didn't really know what he had been up to re TB/GB. He has good judgement and he must have sensed, as everyone did, that things were moving to TB. Yet he had seemed to be working for GB. And yet, GB and his people seemed to think he was working for TB. Was it because of the reputation that he just got blamed for stuff, even when in fact he had done no wrong? Or had he been playing both off against each other and trying to make sure he was in a position of strength with whoever emerged? I dunno. TB called later, and his view was that Peter had just been genuinely torn and when it came to it, got himself in a bit of a muddle. But he was a good political mind and TB was determined to have him around, whatever the objections of some of the MPs.

He had been filled in on Robin from various sources and, as I thought, he was absolutely clear that GB would stay as Shadow Chancellor. I asked if he was speaking much to GB. Not as much, he said, certainly not like before. He said it could be difficult for a while. It was quite a big thing for him to do, and he will be hurting. JP called. He was in a room somewhere with Ian McCartney [Labour MP, Prescott supporter] and was basically conducting two conversations at once, and only occasionally were they related to each other. He said he thought Beckett was a bit stronger, in terms of support, than he had first thought, and it wasn't just 'the sisters'. I could hear that Rosie [Winterton, head of Prescott's office] had arrived, and now he was talking to me about Margaret, Ian about the figures, and Rosie about some visit he was meant to be doing tomorrow. I couldn't begin to imagine what chaos it must be like in there.

Friday, June 10

JP and Margaret were doing their press conferences today, TB doing his big speech tomorrow, which was fine. Peter called to go over Tony's statement for tomorrow. The themes were fairly straightforward and in a way he had to bring together a lot of the things he had been saying and doing in the past, and then throw forward to ideas about the future. Peter felt TB should say he welcomed the contest. TB called and we went over much the same ground. He wanted to know which of all the themes he was putting out there I thought he should stress. I felt he had to make a rounded argument which had them all out there. Socialism, and a different view for the modern world, party reform, go big on family and community. He said he felt excited by the whole thing, but was too busy to think properly. He needed a bit more space around him and at the moment didn't really know how to get it there. He said the office team was doing fine but there was so much to do and a lot of it was falling on him. I said he should not have to be worrying too much about the detail of organisation, and the more he delegated the better. He had to be out there all the time now, saying what he thought in ways that connected. He wanted my take on what interviews to do first. He was keen on the *FT* as a way of signalling this was not just an internal debate for *Guardian* readers, but something that was trying to reach out to new areas.

Richard [Stott] wanted me to fix three interviews for the paper, with the three contenders, and I was also getting feelers from different parts of the Beeb re doing the same kind of thing. JP's press conference was at 11, and he was OK, all the familiar stuff, but he had a fair bit of energy and drive in there. He was asked if he was to the left of Beckett. 'Pass,' he said. Margaret's press conference was a bit more staid and low-key but she spoke well. What wasn't really clear was a strong strategic pitch that she could make her own. There was a very good profile of TB on *Newsnight*. Fiona thought I had missed a trick in letting him do the *FT* as his first paper interview. I agreed some quotes I could use simultaneously for *Today* but she was right. I was falling between two stools at the moment, not really proper journalist, not really campaigner and fixer for him, but a bit of it all, and none of it being done as well as maybe I could if I was properly focused. I was also so weighed down by work, and the never-ending phone calls, that I had pulled out of the Keighley Clarets [an event for the Burnley FC supporters' club in AC's home town] and even though they said they understood, they were not surprisingly pissed off at the short notice, and I felt dreadful about it.

Saturday, June 11

I was still in bed when TB called to go over his address, which was excellent. He read through the main bits, which were strong and ought to cut through. He said he had got into all sorts of bother re the *FT* interview. I said so had I, and I was also pissed off that the *Guardian* had been given a lot more than I had expected. I explained the difficulty re *Today* at the moment. He said we would find ways to make it up to them. He also felt he didn't have a clear media message at the moment, and wanted me to work on that. He faxed through some initial thoughts, which were a bit airy. But the message from the speech was strong and would get him in the right place media wise, and it would play through to the party fine. There was no merit in pretending he was something he wasn't. In fact, I think GB made a mistake when he started looking like he was tacking a bit to the left with all that pro-union stuff. TB was where he was now because people thought he was a bit different to your usual Labour politician, and needed to play that up, not down. JP was making a lot of noises about full employment. I later spoke to Ian McCartney who was full of how well JP and TB were getting on, and how it all boded well if they won the respective positions. It was not entirely clear who was running Margaret's campaign but it appeared to be Clare [Short, Labour MP], which was good news for TB. I called JP re fixing interviews and maybe a day out on the road with him. He said he had hired Gez Sagar [press officer]. I was not sure he was right for him, but we'd see.

I took the kids to see Bob and the boys were great with him. I think he enjoyed it even if it was all a bit stressy. I called Peter M to say how pissed off I was at the *Guardian*, who clearly had a lot more than a few 'TB will say' quotes. He said I mustn't take it out on Tony, who had told him I was on strike for the day. I said we were going to have to work out very clearly what was fair game for reporting and what was not. Stuff that I was providing by way of strategic advice, and words, was finding its way into other papers, which put me in a difficult position. TB called later, clearly prompted by Peter M. 'Are you pissed off with me?' I said I was a bit, because it put me in a difficult position when things I knew about were appearing in other papers when I could have written them earlier myself. He said we had to sit down and agree a proper modus operandi. And then he was straight on to discussing plans for *Panorama* and his interview tomorrow on *Breakfast with Frost*.

Out for dinner at Ian and Andrea's [Kennedy, family friends]. Donald McCormick and Liz Elton [broadcasters, married couple] were there and Liz said Bob Wheaton was a big fan of mine, and if I wanted to go into full-time telly, now might be the time. I said I wasn't sure I did. She said that at the second part of the JS funeral in Iona, Donald and Derry had talked properly for the first time in ages.

Sunday, June 12

TB did well on *Frost*. Looked the part, spoke well, nothing untoward came out of it. I called Peter M who agreed, but felt he could have been stronger on specific policy areas. I felt that could wait, that what it was about was showing in a well-known TV setting that he did not look out of place talking about the possibility of being a leader and a prime minister. I thought he passed that easily. TB called later and said he didn't think he had done that well. [David] Frost was tougher than he had expected him to be, and he didn't think he handled the tougher questions that well. I said he had to remember he was the clear front-runner in many ways so they were bound to want to give him a bit of a rougher ride, and let the others make the weather a bit, and create the environment for him to be questioned, but it was not that tough and in any event the main messages from his speech came through fine. He asked what JP was up to re full employment. I said I didn't know but TB should just stick to his line that we should only promise what we can deliver and that people were tired of false promises. He said it was important JP did not get himself into a position where he felt he had to make really leftist noises and then be expected to press TB to deliver on things that had not been part of his pitch for the leadership. Far better to set the targets low, and meet them, than to set them high, and deliver nothing but disappointment.

Monday, June 13

Did *Tribune* column, then a *Today* page 6, then the leaders, then pages 4 and 5 on the reshuffle. Major did his press conference in the garden at Number 10. Unbelievably hot. He's looking more and more like somebody who says quite well things that you can tell he wished he wasn't saying. Nick Guthrie [BBC] called to commission films on Glenys and John Monks. I called them both, John after his full-employment conference and Glenys at home, still on a high after going to the EPLP [European Parliamentary Labour Party] meeting. Watched TB, JP and MB on *Panorama*, where they were interviewed by Jim Naughtie [BBC], Mike White [*Guardian*] and Ann Leslie [*Daily Mail*]. Leslie was ghastly. TB looked a bit too tense, and didn't really answer the question about experience. Beckett was good on the sterility of political debate, very calm and clear. JP was good on tax. TB came out with a couple of decent lines on crime and put Leslie in her place pretty well, but overall not one of his best.

Tuesday, June 14

I called Peter to say I was pissed off at the TB interview in the *Mirror*. He said he thought I knew about it. TB called when I got to the office. Bastard, traitor, I said. He said he had no idea he was doing it, which was ridiculous. I said we had to work out proper ground rules. We discussed *Panorama*, which he agreed was pretty awful. The problem was they were constantly trying to jazz things up, and serious debate was the victim. Went to see Glenys to discuss the little film we were doing. Tea with Tessa in the Pugin Room. John Burton called and said he wanted me to speak to TB and get him to speak more the language of the common man. 'He talks *Guardian* and *FT*, there needs to be more *Mirror* and *Today*.'

Wednesday, June 15

Got in for the end of JP's press conference, then to his office to fix a date for interviews. He was pretty chuffed with himself. He had a few moans and groans about the nomination system and the hustings, but he was happy enough with the way things were going. He thought he came off best out of *Panorama*. There were rumours flying around that Margaret was thinking of quitting, which I didn't believe. His one problem might be the number of people who would go for Beckett either because she was a woman or, because JP was trying hard to stick fairly close to TB, because she was thought to be more on the left. I bumped into Dennis Skinner [Labour MP] on the way back to Members' Lobby. He told me he was backing Beckett because JP had sold out over One Member One Vote, and because when the pressure came on, he wasn't sure how he'd handle it. Lunch at the Savoy Grill with Richard [Stott] and Peter M. Richard on good form, but was echoing John Burton's view that TB was coming over as a bit hoity-toity, that he needed to speak more the language of people and illustrate with flesh and blood. He was regaling us with stories from when he covered Margaret and Leo [Beckett, her husband] getting together. Hard to think of her as a sex symbol now, he said, but it was quite something at the time.

Thursday, June 16

Reviewing the papers [on *BBC Breakfast*]. Jennie Bond was presenting, introduced me first time round as resident dreamboat and the second time, after an item about shirts, said 'From wrinkle-free shirts to wrinkle-free men.' And I thought Jill Dando [TV presenter] flirted. Chat with Bob Wheaton about possible format for interviews with the Labour leadership candidates. Then driven to the Hilton Mews Hotel where TB was having a TV training session with Greville Janner [Labour MP]. Peter had called last night asking me to help out. I got there just after 9. TB looked a bit sceptical about it all, but Greville was pretty good with him. He said his basic belief about interviews was to say what you were going to say, say it, then say that you've said it. Peter said there were elements of TB's interviews that weren't right. I made the point that he does seem to be speaking to *FT* and *Guardian* leader writers when he needed to connect more with real people and their daily lives. Too often, he sounded a bit theoretical in his language. We went over various questions that he might get at the TGWU [Transport and General Workers' Union] hustings such as why did you become a socialist; are you a socialist? – he smiled at that – how would you get unemployment down? We were trying to press him with short, sharp questions that lent themselves either to a line or a long argument. In his answers, there was too much throat clearing – I think, I believe, the first thing to say is, on the one hand. We were trying to get him to clearer, more concrete positions. Greville did a lot of pacing up and down, and when TB talked, even with just four of us in the room, he spoke as though making a speech to an audience of halfwits. But he did seem to get stronger. He was weak on tax, and there was too much 'We'll have to see how the books look.' I asked him how he could defend someone on £70,000 a year paying only forty per cent tax and he waffled on about loopholes. Waffle was a problem, particularly on unemployment.

We looked at some of the answers and he agreed that some of them were poor and waffly. He said he was tired. This was all going on in the basement of the hotel. We had a break to discuss his *Panorama* failure. He said he had been told that he would get the first minute to make a statement, but the questions were about something else. He agreed he had not been good. We got back to interviewing him. On the question of his background, we suggested he say something like you don't have to be a woman to see that women are not treated equally. You don't need to be black to know that blacks suffer. He had to start injecting a bit more passion into his language and a bit more normality. He came over either as a lawyer, or as someone who was talking to a classroom full of kids. Peter called me later and said he had not been that impressed. TB felt the same, but claimed he was tired. Peter was worried that GB was quietly promoting Margaret Beckett as a way of getting back at Tony. Nominations were published. The word from the TGWU hustings was that Tony did OK but was tired. He called to say he thought he did fine and that today's session had helped. Bob Wheaton called to say that one or two people internally were raising objections to me doing the Labour interviews as I was so clearly campaigning to get TB elected. I said provided JP and MB were OK, and accepted I'd be fair, there shouldn't be a problem. David Miliband and James Purnell [policy specialists from the Institute of Public Policy Research, later members of TB's team] had drafted an election address, which Peter wanted me to look at because he thought it was crap. There was a little drama going on to do with someone who knew TB at Fettes [public school attended by Blair] trying to spread dirt about him.

Saturday, June 18

Peter came round for dinner after the Fabian Society conference. He said it had been very well organised, but he was in a bad state re TB. He was having a dreadful time of it. 'People are constantly winding him up about me,' he said. 'But he has become part dependent on me and is terrified of having to push me out, which is clearly what some of the other people round him want.' They had ended up having a yelling match over various things in the papers that he was getting blamed for. People were constantly telling TB that Peter was 'undermining' his campaign and he clearly believed it at times. He looked pretty wretched about the whole thing. I advised him to disengage for a day or two. He said he had done that on Friday and immediately Tim [Allan] had been on, saying that he couldn't deal with everything going on without Peter to give advice. Also, when he read the draft election address, he realised how weak the operation was.

TB called after he had gone. He said thanks for the help on the election address. I asked him what was going on with Peter. He said one day the Labour Party will be ready to accept Peter and appreciate his talents, but he's not there yet. He said one day he would be in the Cabinet. Peter was fed up with only being seen as a spin doctor. He wanted to be seen as a politician, but a lot of the politicians weren't ready for it.

Sunday, June 19

Tony phoned at 8 and said what's wrong with Peter? He had just spoken to him on the phone and said he sounded awful. I said I thought there was nothing in particular but he was fed up with the non-person thing, getting all the flak but none of the credit. It then seems that TB went round there, because Peter called later and said they'd had another dreadful scene. Peter had told him that he couldn't operate in an atmosphere where some of TB's supporters thought he was being disloyal, but Tony said he wasn't prepared to listen, said simply 'This is wearying me.' Peter said he felt wretched, that it was as if TB was questioning his support. 'After all I've done.' E.g., I said, being disloyal to Gordon? Again, I advised him to disengage fully for

June '94: 'One day Peter will be in the Cabinet' – TB

a while, just not be available, make him realise who he could count on and who had sound advice more often than not. I called TB later and said he'd be daft not to use Peter, that he couldn't really afford not to. He said he knew that but wished he could find a way of him working in a way that was acceptable to those who didn't like or trust him.

Monday, June 20

Took the kids to school, did the leaders then down to the Commons to work on my column. Peter warned me about the story doing the rounds about TB's kids possibly going to the Oratory.[1] TB was working out a line that he would only do what was best for the kids and that he was looking at lots of different schools. I warned Peter it would be difficult if he went ahead. I had a cup of tea with Tristan [Garel-Jones, Conservative FCO minister]. He said if he were Major he would send Neil [Kinnock] to Brussels as a Commissioner, but he thought George Robertson [Labour MP and Shadow Scottish Secretary] might be a better bet. He said it was by no means certain that [Jean-Luc] Dehaene [Belgian Prime Minister] would get the top Europe job, because Britain, Italy and Portugal were still going for him. I had a good chat with Kate Garvey and Liz Lloyd in TB's office about language, and the need to get him speaking more like a fully paid-up member of the human race. Neil went to see Bob in the hospital, which cheered him up.

Tuesday, June 21

Out to see Glenys to fix filming an interview. TB called and wanted me to read his 'credo' which he sent through on Glenys' fax. I told Liz [Lloyd] it was far too long, repetitive and it felt like there were too many different authors at work. She said that was because half the Shadow Cabinet had been at it. I visited Bob on the way home from Ealing, then called TB and said he had to get a grip of it, cut it at least in half, iron out all the different voices and really say what he thought. I said it wasn't a manifesto, and it needed a bit more anger at the state of Britain, a sense of forward vision and also point up the theme that he was rejecting both the old left and the new right. 'Can I get away with saying that?' he asked. He said he was convinced

[1] The London Oratory School, a Roman Catholic grant-maintained school in West London. Grant-maintained (GM) schools had opted out of local authority control, receiving a direct grant from the Conservative government overseen by an independent governing body – an anathema to many Labour supporters.

that was where he had to get to, the question was whether now was the right time to say it. I felt he was best saying what he thought. He said he was convinced this was the path for Labour and that if we weren't careful the smarter Tories would start to move on to that territory. I raised the Oratory, and said it could become a running sore. He said the school the boys went to was a feeder school. I stressed again that his strength was an ability to connect, but a combination of some of the language he was using and a big thing about his choice of school would set him back.

Wednesday, June 22

The Blair/Fettes saga rumbling on. Day taken over with broadcast stuff, *Week in Westminster* interviews and also down to SE23 to interview John Monks for the Beeb profile. Really liked him, and his wife Frankie, who is Dutch, was a great laugh. I sensed he had a really strong understanding of what they needed to do, but he was obviously having difficulty with the TGWU and the GMB.

Thursday, June 23

Went straight to the House for Tony's manifesto launch at Church House. He looked pretty good, if a bit earnest, and the speech and the leaflet were both a lot stronger. I was mildly pissed off that having spent a fair part of the last few days helping him knock it into shape, it was illustrated by a picture of TB reading the *Mirror*. I had a chat with Peter M afterwards and we agreed he was still a bit waffly in Q&A. But the general feeling was that it had gone well. Liz Lloyd was trying to get me to say nice things about his leaflet, clearly not knowing I'd rewritten it for him. I met Peter M and we went out for tea on the Terrace. He seemed in better shape, but was still clearly annoyed that whilst TB wanted him around, and called on him the whole time, so many of the others felt they could do it without him, and wanted it that way.

Friday, June 24

To the Ivy for a Ken Follett [bestselling author, husband of Barbara] lunch organised by Julia Hobsbawm and Sarah Macaulay [PRs]. All a bit odd. Robert Crampton [journalist] was there doing a piece for *The Times*, and I told him I thought that while Labour needed people to raise money, the luvvie thing was damaging. Odd mix of people – Jon Snow [broadcaster], Gill Morgan, Katie Bravery, John Barton [journalists], a bloke from *Have I Got News For You* asking if I would do the programme.

Saturday, June 25

Played golf with David [Mills, husband of Tessa Jowell] and got back to their place to discover the car was completely knackered. They took us into Stratford, where we hired a car, then on to the wedding [AC family nanny, Anna Birch, was getting married]. David was helping keep our spirits up with lots of funny pager messages on the theme of the nightmare of the nanny's wedding. But then a bleep to call Gavin [Millar, Fiona's brother]. We were eating in the marquee and I said to Fiona I had to make a phone call. She asked who it was and I didn't tell her. I had a feeling it was bad news. I called him from a little room at the side and he said Bob was dead. Fiona guessed as soon as she saw my face. Telling the boys, who were playing on a little bouncy thing, was pretty grim. We told Anna and set off feeling absolutely wretched. I could barely speak when I told Dad, then Neil. Told Peter, then Tony called, which was nice of him. The drive back seemed to last for hours, even though the traffic wasn't that bad. Fiona said she could only cope if I stayed strong, but it was hard. Calum and Grace slept most of the way back but Rory was clearly taking it all in. It was the first time anything bad had really happened in his life.

Sunday, June 26

Woke up crying. Fiona already awake, also crying. The kids were being pretty amazing but both the boys were discombobulated. The phone was going the whole time which was both nice and irritating at the same time. Audrey wanted me to look through all Bob's old cuttings to sort out stuff to use at the funeral.

Monday, June 27

Went out for a swim, took the boys to school, then mainly pottering around, helping Audrey sort a few things. Mark Seddon [*Tribune* editor] asked for an obit, which I agreed to do instead of my column. Audrey and Fiona also asked me to do the funeral address so I started to sketch that out too. It was looking like Friday but then we got a message it would be Thursday at 3.15. Both of us kept bursting into tears, which was probably helping neither of us, at least not when we did it at the same time. I'd arranged to do an interview with Margaret Beckett for *Today* at 5pm, so went out for that. Felt a little bit like I was going through the motions. Then I was paged by Bob Wheaton. He explained that Beckett's people had complained about me being on the interviewing panel for *BBC Breakfast* because I was too close to Blair.

Tuesday, June 28

In at 10am to do JP interview for *Today*. Fiona not in good shape when I left, but it had been so difficult to fix times for these interviews, I didn't want to pull out. He was in quite feisty form, and decided he didn't want his picture taken while speaking. I called Fiona afterwards and she asked me to go home and help sort out readings, printing etc. I did my column from home and went to pick up Mum at 5.20 with Calum. The train was late so we sat in Burger King, Calum clearly wanting to talk about Bob. Out late for the radio programme, which was OK but not brilliant. And I was still feeling pretty wretched.

Wednesday, June 29

I got my eulogy in reasonable shape. The interview with TB wasn't great. I wasn't really up for it, and nor was he. I was doing these interviews with Lorraine Butler [*Today* journalist] and she didn't take to him terribly much.

Thursday, June 30

Took the kids to school, then went to get a prescription for Valium. Quite a lot to get through still before we went over to Abbey Road and then to the undertakers. Valium definitely worked. I managed to get through the address but broke down in the very last sentence when I caught sight of the kids. There was a good turnout and a nice atmosphere afterwards, and Audrey seemed to be holding up pretty well. TB called later but by then I was totally zonked out. I could see why some people get hooked on these pills. I was in bed by 9.

Friday, July 1

I wrote a letter to Dad saying how much I appreciated everything he'd ever done for us, then took Mum to the station. Spent a lot of the day writing up the leadership interviews. None of them were great, but they were OK.

Sunday, July 3

Up at 6.40 to finish the column, out for a swim, then took the kids to see *The Lion King*. Peter came round later and chatted about who might be TB's chief of staff. The two favourites were Julian Priestley [Secretary General, Socialist Group, European Parliament] and Jonathan Powell [FCO diplomat] who TB had met on one of his visits to Washington.

July '94: Who will be TB's chief of staff?

Monday, July 4

One of the worst things was how quickly everything else just slipped back to a kind of normality. To the TUC party to film Monks and interview various people. TB called me and I made the mistake of telling him that Lorraine Butler preferred JP to him. He called me over for a chat. He thought this was about people who don't really support Labour backing an image of the Labour Party as it should be. I thought that was nonsense and said so. I said the first thing is not to take it too seriously as it's just one person's subjective opinion. Secondly, he should never let it get to him, because there will be an awful lot more of it. He just hadn't been on very good form, but it was hardly the end of the world. He clearly worried what people thought of him, which was fine, so long as he didn't let things like this get to him. I often thought that Neil, who got far worse press than TB, let it get to him too much, and he stopped being himself. We chatted about JP, and whether he would be loyal. TB said that the argument for Margaret as deputy was that she would operate as she had with JS, be a figure in the background. JP was not like that. I said the argument for JP was that he would give him something additional, that at times he would need. TB agreed with that intellectually, but said he still had concerns.

Tuesday, July 5

Monks was addressing the TUC conference on employment so I went to that and did a few interviews. Fiona paged me. Cherie had called her to say she had been getting very worried about TB re the office. He was never home, he was tired and irritable and he was getting a bit imperious. She said Anji was telling him that he had to make all the decisions about the office now. I spoke to CB later. She said 'Can I enlist you in persuading him to take a holiday and do nothing by way of personnel decision-making till he gets back from it?' She clearly thought Anji was forcing the pace on personnel to try to cement her own position early on.

Wednesday, July 6

Swim, took the kids to school, then out to the airport for the flight to Brussels. Filming mainly in the Parliament building, meetings with Glenys, chatting to a few people. One or two impressive people in the EPLP, though there was an obsession about some of the issues that was a bit alarming, and a lot of it was just internal politicking.

Thursday, July 7

Was filming Glenys, but TB was there too for a meeting with Jacques Delors [EU President], so I had a little chat with him. I sensed he shared some of my irritation at the Eurobollocks side of things. Got some good stuff from Glenys. She was clearly worried though that Neil wasn't going to get the commissionership. Flew back pm.

Friday, July 8

To the BBC for a planning meeting on the interviews for the leadership candidates. All very relaxed. Bob Wheaton keen on quite a big international element. Matthew Parris [former Conservative MP, political commentator] obviously wanting opportunities to show off his wit.

Saturday, July 9

To Viceroy of India [restaurant] for Glenys' birthday party. Mainly chatting to Steve and Rachel [Kinnock children], who were brilliant. GB was there. It was the first time I had really seen him since the whole leadership thing and he was quite curt, just said he was very sorry that Fiona's dad had died. Had a good laugh with TB about how many people in the room were likely to be hoping that some time in the future he would be putting them up for a peerage.

Monday, July 11

The first of the BBC interviews. Margaret B. She arrived with literally a minute to spare, and appeared to be the only one who wasn't flustered about it. She did pretty well. She has a calm way about her, listens to questions, pauses and answers. Afterwards we had a little debrief to go over what we thought was good, and what bad. Then out to White City to edit the film on Glenys. Incredibly hot. TB paged me to call him in Sedgefield. He said he was really worried about whether JP was controllable.

Tuesday, July 12

TB second up on the Beeb. It was obvious that part of the tension in the dynamic he was dealing with was the sense that really he had already won. It was a bit odd interviewing him in this format, though I like to think I was as rigorous with him as with Margaret. I asked if he thought he was tough enough, felt he looked strong but sounded weak. Hilary Armstrong told me later she thought we were much softer on TB than Beckett. The general feedback was pretty good though. On the deputy front, things definitely seemed to be moving

JP's way. [Roy] Hattersley [Labour Party deputy leader, 1983-92] said he was voting for JP 'firmly but reluctantly'. Gerald K said we had to get Peter to vote for JP.

Wednesday, July 13

Got Matthew Parris' education details for JP, so he could throw them at him if the occasion arose. JP was a bit brittle, and needs to calm his temper, but on substance, I thought he was pretty good. He had breakfast with us, called Pauline [Prescott, JP's wife] and put me on to her. 'Wasn't he brilliant?' she said. 'I am so proud of him.' Saw Bryan Davies [Labour MP] who said he was definitely going for Prescott. Listened to the debate in the Commons, where I was attacked by George Galloway and Rupert Allason.[1]

Thursday, July 14

John Smith's memorial service at Westminster Abbey. Brief chat with Elizabeth, the whole thing seemed a bit overwhelming. TB was looking really odd, like he didn't quite know what he was supposed to be doing. He could sometimes look incredibly nervous for someone who would soon be spending virtually every minute being looked at in a different way. I didn't feel the service quite captured John in a way the funeral had. It was a bit impersonal, didn't feel like it had his character stamped on it.

Friday, July 15

Flew to Glasgow for the Scottish launch of *Today*. Doing lots of radio. Chatted with GB. He was in a better mood.

Saturday, July 16

Glenys called, and said the vibes were moving towards Neil becoming commissioner. Peter M came round for tea. We chatted over possibilities for TB's press office. Both he and TB thought I would be best, but assumed I wouldn't do it. They were thinking about Andy Grice [*Sunday Times* journalist]. Peter MacMahon [*Scotsman* journalist] had offered himself. I said what about Colin Byrne [former Labour chief

---

[1] Conservative MP Allason and Labour MP Galloway were referring to an article printed in the *Daily Mirror* in November 1992, which stated that Allason had been challenged by fifty MPs to demonstrate his concern for pensioners swindled by Robert Maxwell by giving them the estimated £250,000 libel damages he had won from the *Mirror* over articles concerning the publisher. Allason was later to sue the Mirror Group, Campbell and the paper's former political correspondent Andy McSmith for malicious falsehood.

press officer]? He agreed that the JS service hadn't quite captured him. He said Elizabeth had been really keen for the Archbishop of Canterbury to do the address.

Sunday, July 17

TB called re his press office. I knew what he wanted to ask, but he never did. I said I thought Andy Grice was OK. He should definitely keep Hilary [Coffman] on because she was strong and solid. I recommended Peter Hyman [speechwriter, policy adviser]. We talked about his acceptance speech. I suggested he quote something from one of John's big speeches, something from Neil's. Above all Smith on the 'journey' to eliminate poverty. TB said 'You won't believe this but guess who wrote that? It was Gordon and I.' I said he really had to hit the emotional buttons more than before, create some excitement, give a sense that it was a historic moment for party and country. It was another opportunity to flag up the big themes of community, social justice. He expressed concern about JP again. His worries kept coming back. I said there would be all kinds of tossers who wanted to get into him for a pound of flesh once he was leader, and I was sure that though JP might give him problems from time to time, he would be fundamentally loyal.

Tuesday, July 19

Out to see Neil and Jan [Royall, Kinnock aide], chatting about Brussels. Then an interview with Channel 4 on TB. He had asked me to help him write a passage for his speech, starting with 'Socialism is . . .' so worked on that for a while.

Wednesday, July 20

TB called first thing. He wanted me to go round to Richmond Crescent [Number 1, Blair family home, 1993–97] and work on his speech. There were some good themes in there but they were clashing into each other a bit – hope, service, change, renewal, duty. I gave him a few options on different beginnings and endings, including what I thought was the best one, worked around right and wrong. He said you really like this right and wrong, don't you? I said I did. He said he felt it was a bit too 'back to basics'. Fiona was working on a piece about Cherie. She was around and looking quite confident, whereas he had the look of a worried man. Peter M phoned while I was there, asking for help with a *Sun* article, and wondering if the *Mirror* would go mad. Liz Lloyd, Peter Hyman and James Purnell came round and we now had another draft to work on. I spent an hour or so with him in his little study, which was cluttered. He was scribbling frantically both over the draft and on blank sheets of paper, then saying what do you think, what do you think? I couldn't work out how much of it was about self-reassurance. At one point he just said 'It's awful, absolutely awful, not what I need at all.' He was really anxious about the right and wrong stuff.

Later, at the House, we went to see Neil who said he should keep detailed policy out of it, make it about direction and international renewal. On the right and wrong stuff, Neil felt he was in a better position to do it convincingly because everyone knew he had religion. He said you don't need much more than the Bible and Shakespeare for a speech like tomorrow's. It's not about policy. He said if you are confident, you can do it, but you have to feel comfortable with the words and the strength of the language.

Thursday, July 21

Labour leadership day. To the BBC to review the papers. Neil there, had a brief chat re the day, and he seemed in OK form. The only question now was how much TB was going to win by, and whether JP was definitely in as deputy, and by how much. Neil not instinctively keen on JP, but he seemed in a pretty good mood about things. The duty editor asked me to tone down the anti-Tory stuff in my review. I went to the House before heading down to Logan Hall [University of London], where the results were going to be announced. The *Mirror* was being handed out to people as we arrived. Took several, and put them in the bin. Peter M asked me to have a word with JP, and remind him today was about the new leader, not the deputy. I bumped into GB on the way in, and the word 'curt' does not really do justice to the curtness. He clearly felt he had to say something, but it was a single, rather indistinct 'hello'. He looked fed up to be there. He was seated next to Neil and even when he was in full flow, his anger and irritation were pretty clear. The mood generally though was good, a real buzz even though the results were more or less known. I had a nice little chat with Cherie who gave me a big hug and said 'Was Fiona's piece OK? I wanted to do something special for you for all the help you have given Tony.' She looked terrific, though her eyes were a bit manic and she was bouncing around a bit.

When the figures were announced, the buzz feeling went up to another level. JP was scribbling furiously. TB looked very calm, overdid the serious statesman stiff bottom lip thing a bit, but spoke well. I felt something somewhere between pride of authorship and humility of service or duty in hearing him say the bits I had written, particularly the reference to John Smith, May 11, 1994, and also the 'right and wrong' section, especially as I knew how much he had worried about it. He did not indicate the nervousness at all, and it came over well. There was a real excitement around the place afterwards and a lot of people saying he looked and sounded like a PM-in-waiting. I bumped into GB again who did one of his slightly forced smiles, and just walked on. I caught a quick word with JP as he came off the stage. 'I suppose I should say thanks,' he said. I said I thought he won because he deserved to.

I filed my copy and then headed to TB's bash at Church House [Westminster]. It was mainly friends and people who had been involved in the campaign. Good mood. Gerald Kaufman said it was the greatest day since 1963 when Harold Wilson was elected. TB made a little speech and it was interesting watching the different way people were looking at him, some with a little smile, some as though they were listening to something of enormous import. I chatted a bit with Philip and Gail [Rebuck, publisher, wife of Philip Gould], Clive Hollick [Labour-supporting businessman] and Tessa. TB came over and said thanks. He said he had been worried about the speech but it worked and the little touches had made the difference. He said we would have to work out a proper modus operandi.

I then went off to JP's do at Tattersall's. Such a different atmosphere. Like moving from a rarefied hotel to a working men's club. Noisier, more boisterous, more boozy. JP arrived, lots of applause and cheers and he looked a bit embarrassed. Made a good little speech. I did a few media bids at Millbank, then met Liz Lloyd for a drink at the Red Lion. I don't think they realised yet just how much their lives were going to change. Anji Hunter joined us, said she had just seen me on *Channel 4 News* and 'I thought you of all people could have been a bit more helpful!' What on earth was she talking about? I think the help I gave on his speech was help enough, without worrying too much about whether or not I went OTT on the telly. Home by 9 and I made the tail end of the party at the boys' school, then back to catch the news. All pretty good for TB. Peter called to discuss the press secretary's job. He had clearly kyboshed Hilary Coffman and was pro Colin Byrne. He said what about you? That is who he wants. I said I'd love to in many ways, but the salary cut was a bit severe and I would really worry about never seeing the children. 'Mmmm,' he said, 'and then there's your temper.'

Friday, July 22

Peter called first thing to go over a few things. Agreed yesterday went fine and the press was pretty good for him. He was not terribly happy that TB had referred to him as 'Bobby' yesterday [some of Blair's team had called Mandelson 'Bobby' through the campaign as a way of concealing his central role], said it was bound to get out and it all adds to this idea that he can only do the backroom stuff. Into the office for conference and they asked if I could get a TB piece for *Scotland Today*. Managed to fix it via Peter Hyman, who is good news. He did a draft which we then redid over the phone. We went to Neil and Glenys' for dinner. Usual up and down re JP, Neil saying it was only a matter of time before we regretted it, as he was a disaster waiting to happen. He thought TB's speech was 'OK', but said if he was as religious as TB, he would use the Bible a lot more. People will take it from him, he said, and it gives him not just wonderful material but conviction. He also thought he should have said something about Cherie and the kids as it would have made him more the regular guy. He said TB was bound to want me to work for him and he thought I would be mad to do it. He reckoned I could do as much good for him on the outside as on the inside. It was a dog's life, he said. He was angry that Hilary might be getting the boot while Murray Elder [Smith's chief of staff] was being retained.

Sunday, July 24

Barney Jones [editor and producer, *Breakfast with Frost*] called at 6.15, asked if I could go on and do the papers. It was with Martyn Lewis [newscaster] rather than Frost himself. Peter was calling regularly. First call was about TB/GB/JP. He said if we can get those relationships basically working, everything else ought to work its way into place. There was also a bit of a kerfuffle in Scotland re TB's piece. He called later to say TB was worried about JP again, and they looked to me to work on JP, as I seemed to be one of the few people close to TB that he quite liked and would talk to properly.

Monday, July 25

I went to see Neil again and he was more adamant than ever that I should not work for TB. He said he could not stress enough how bad he thought it would be for me and for the family. However bad you ever thought it looked from the outside, he said, multiply by ten and then ten again. It is the worst job there is. Peter M called, livid at a 'Bobby' piece in the *Guardian*. He said he sometimes despaired at the way he was perceived, but this could have been avoided. He said he just didn't understand why TB said it. He had another go at me re the press secretary's job.

TB called re the education policy launch. He wanted to get out there fast to emphasise education as key and he wanted to signal that he was up for change on it. He asked what he could do to pre-empt the Tory press turning on him. He said he was a bit surprised to see [Richard] Littlejohn [*Sun* columnist] turning against him so soon. I said it was bound to happen a bit now he was at the top, and a lot of papers and journos are basically very right wing. I spoke to Littlejohn later who said it wasn't a question of turning against anyone, it was just a bit of fun. I told TB he shouldn't worry about individual papers and journalists. There was definitely a mood to give him a fair wind and if he got his message right, and he carried on coming over as he had been, it would be very hard for them to do to him what they had done to Neil. And any day he thought he had it bad, he should take a look at Major, who had a mad and unmanageable party, and a press that was becoming more and more contemptuous.

Tuesday, July 26

Bob Wheaton called and said there were a few people in the Beeb wondering whether I would think about doing more and more broadcasting. Meanwhile the TB situation was beginning to weigh on me. Peter directly, and TB indirectly, had been building the pressure re working for him. Peter turned up at 9, clearly ratcheting up the pressure re working for TB. Straight to the point. Peter had told him it was undeliverable, but he had asked him to try. He said there wasn't anybody in politics who did not think I would be the best at it and they had to get the best if they could. I went through the objections – money, the kids, not suffering fools, saying what I thought, my temper. He said he accepted my temperament was likely to get me into trouble from time to time, 'But that's in part why TB wants you – he'll need people who say it as they see it.' TB clearly thought that was worth it for the other things I could offer. Peter felt my under-standing of the media, particularly the tabloids, was important, but what TB really wanted was political judgement and toughness. I found myself trying to suggest other names. Peter said I would also know how to deal with the politicians. And I was key to JP.

Fiona was hovering, and throwing in objections of her own. She said I could do as much good on the outside, helping with strategy and speeches, like I was doing already, but also doing public stuff on telly and radio and in print. That was Neil's view too. Peter said TB thought Neil should have taken me on too, that what I could do as a journalist is very limited. Fiona said 'Who else ever goes on TV and radio and defends Labour as well as he does?' Peter said what I could do on the inside dwarfed any of that. I said did he not worry that sometimes I might be too combustible even for TB? I said money was a problem and I really did not want a job where I never saw my kids. I chatted to Tessa later. She was keen for me to do it as well but accepted there would be a big impact on the family.

TB called very late, just asking for my take on things, but I knew where it was heading. You'd have thought about it a few years ago, wouldn't you? Yes, I said, I would, but Neil never asked and now I'm on a roll. A lot of the time we were talking about JP. TB was still rolling the doubts about John as deputy leader around his mind, and going over the same arguments, asking me to explain, again and again, why I thought he was the right man for the job. If something is on his mind he works it through by having the same conversation repeatedly. It's irritating if you're the other part of the conversation, but it's his way of doing things, and I'll get used to it.

Wednesday, July 27

TB called me and asked me to go and see him in the Shadow Cabinet room. I arrived at 1.30 and into the kind of turmoil you normally associate with moving house. Boxes and crates of John Smith's papers and possessions on the way out, TB's on the way in, and nobody quite sure where everything should go, and all looking a bit stressed at the scale of the task. Anji Hunter and Murray Elder were in the outer office, and I got the usual greeting from both, Anji all over-the-top kisses and hugs, Murray a rather distant and wary smile. He said Tony was running a bit late. He went in to tell him I was here. A couple of minutes later John Edmonds came out, and looked a bit miffed to see me. Tony's own office was in even greater chaos than the outer office so he was working out of the Shadow Cabinet room. He turned on the full Bunsen burner smile, thanked me for all the help I'd given on his leadership acceptance speech, and then, still standing, perched his foot on a packing case and got to the point, rather more quickly than I'd anticipated. He was going on holiday the next day, and he still had a few key jobs to sort out. He was determined to get the best if he could. He needed a really good press secretary. He wanted someone who understood politics and understood the media, including the mass-market media. They don't grow on trees. He said it had to be somebody tough, and confident, someone who could make decisions and stick to them. Historically the Labour Party has not been blessed with really talented people in this area of politics and political strategy but I think we can be different. Gordon is exceptional, so is Peter, so are you, and I really want you to do the job. It's called press secretary but it's much more than that. He'd assumed I didn't want to do it because I was doing so much media now, and really branching out into broadcasting. He'd sounded out Andy Grice at the *S Times*, who had said no. But really, he said, I would like to get the best I can and that has to be you. I know you've got reservations but I just ask you to think about it over the holiday. Even though I expected it, and had thought about it, I didn't quite know how to react. I'd gone in there with a list of names to suggest, and a raft of arguments against the idea. I said I'm not sure I'm suited to it. I've got a big ego of my own and a ferocious temper. I can't stand fools and I don't suffer them. I'm hopeless at biting my tongue. He said, I've thought about that, but I still think you're right for it. I said money might be a problem. I would be earning way into six figures this year, and it's not easy to take a big cut. Also, I could do lots for you from the outside, like I did on your leadership speech. It's not the same, he said. I agreed to think about it. Even as I left the office, though I'd raised all the reasons against, I had a feeling I would end up saying yes. I bumped into David Hill as I left who was none too happy because he reckoned Tony would move to get rid of Hilary [Coffman, his partner]. I told him I would put a word in, and I did.

Glenys Kinnock phoned to say that Neil had got the Brussels job (as European commissioner) and did we want to go round for dinner? Fiona and I were both thrilled. Neil had done so much, and taken so much, and was desperate for a real job that could make a difference. He was up in Salford doing an interview with Ryan Giggs [footballer], who was a lovely bloke but it sort of summed up the drift in Neil's life since he gave up the leadership. We all went round to Ealing [Kinnock's home] to celebrate after Neil had taken the call from Major. I told Neil about my chat with Tony, and he said I'd be absolutely mad. You've got a great number at the moment. You're in total control of your own position, you can make it big in broadcasting if you want, and you'll be giving it up for one of the shittiest jobs known to man. Cherie called, said TB was desperate for me to do the job and we had to work out how best to do it without wiping out family life.

Saturday, July 30 [holiday in France]
The day before we left to go on holiday, I told Richard Stott [editor of *Today*]. He had been so good to me when I went bonkers (in 1986) and when I was pushed out of the *Mirror*, that I felt bad at the thought of leaving him just when it looked like *Today* was on the move a bit. He said he hoped I didn't go, but I could tell from the tone of his

voice – the usual jocularity was gone – and the look in his eye that he reckoned I had probably written my last piece for him.

Sunday, July 31

I drove down to France while Fiona and the kids flew, the kind of luxury we would probably have to knock on the head if I did the job. As I drove down, I played over a number of scenes in my head: the phone ringing while I was fast asleep and some ghastly story had broken in the papers; Tony with a big speech to do and he was looking to me to write the key bits; a briefing when the press were in full cry; a difficult colleague that Tony wanted me to talk to and persuade to change position. The scenarios kept coming, and I felt confident there were none I wouldn't be able to deal with. Then I worried about whether the press would go for me personally, all the things they knew about but because I was one of them kind of went unsaid: the breakdown, the drink problem, the violence, the writings for *Forum*.[1] They would do it all, but so what? The pros began to feel heavier than the cons. I had two images which kept coming into my mind. In one, Tony is standing on the steps of Number 10, he's won the election, I'm in the pen on the other side of the street covering the great day and I'm thinking: I could have been part of that. In the other, Tony is conceding defeat to John Major and I'm surrounded by people crying, and I'm thinking: I could have made a difference. I was worried about the kids, and seeing less of them, but even on that, I felt it would be a fantastic experience for them to grow up as witnesses to the people and the events that their own children and grandchildren would one day study in their history lessons.

Thursday, August 4

I phoned Tony as planned, and said I still had a lot of misgivings and intended to take the whole month to think about it. He said we should meet up. He was down near Toulouse, which was a good four or five hours from Flassan. I mentioned that Neil and Glenys were coming over next week, and I could sense he was worried. 'Neil will be opposed to you doing this, and for genuine reasons of friendship, because he knows how tough it will be. But it will be different. I promise you. If I can get the best people around me, it will be different.'

[1] At twenty-one, AC had written a number of pornographic stories for the men's magazine *Forum*, including 'Riviera Gigolo' and 'Busking with Bagpipes'.

Tuesday, August 9

Cherie called to say they were on their way. Tony felt it was important we thrashed it all out and tried to reach a decision. Some holiday this was turning out to be. Neil and Glenys were arriving in a couple of days, and I'd have Neil and Fiona in one room trying to talk me out of it and Tony and Cherie in the other trying to talk me into it. And God knows where everyone was going to stay. I had to drive down to Avignon to meet them, and pack them and all their bags into the Espace while they dumped their battered old Citroën. Their ability to withstand chaos had already made an impression on me when I'd been helping Tony with his leadership leaflet and speeches, but this was something else. They were travelling with a few battered old cases and a black bin liner into which Cherie had thrown the last-minute stuff, including, Fiona noticed, some old carrots. We got home at 1.30.

Wednesday, August 10

The kids were getting on fine, and Tony, Cherie, Fiona and I sat down in the sitting room, with the overhead fan forcing us to speak up, to go over the pros and cons. Tony said that in opposition, what you said, how you said it, and how it was reported, was a large part of your armoury. Governments can do things. They can set the agenda with their actions. Our words are going to be vital, and I want your help in that. He said tactical minds are two a penny, but strategic minds are hard to come by and you've got a strategic mind. You will be a key adviser, answerable only to me, part of the inner team with JP, GB and Robin C. We discussed his conference speech. I said he had to make clear he was of the centre left, but where he could make progress for Labour in a way nobody else could was through emphasis on centre, not left. He started to lay the themes out: said he wasn't impressed with the way Jack Straw kept bashing the Lib Dems, they could be useful tactically in hitting the Tories, but also strategically in trying to forge a progressive alliance. Said he liked to think Owen, Jenkins, Williams[1] could support most of what we do. Went over thoughts on a reshuffle, RC to the Foreign Office, Jack Cunningham to DTI, maybe Mo for education, but she'd done some silly piece of nonsense in the *Mail on Sunday* about privatising Buckingham Palace so there was still some growing up to do around

---

[1] David Owen, Roy Jenkins and Shirley Williams, former Labour Cabinet ministers who, with Bill Rodgers, defected to form the breakaway Social Democratic Party in 1981.

August '94: Blair turns on the charm

the place. We stopped after lunch and went to play football with the kids at Bedoin. Then back to it, more on the Libs, more on the strategy for the Tories, and also started to discuss salary. He reckoned he could push it to £75,000, which he'd defend on the basis he wanted the best, but it was still a big drop. We went for a long walk up through the hills behind the village and he ran through his view of the main papers and the main opinion formers. He wanted to know whether I was capable of building bridges with Montgomery.[1] I reminded him that the day I got the heave from Montgomery's *Mirror*, Neil and Roy Hattersley led a major parliamentary attack on MGN, and he (TB) did a piece for the *Mirror*. I said that was when I first realised there was a bit of steel behind the smile. I said I wasn't good at grovelling. The *Mirror* needed Labour more than Labour needed the *Mirror*. Mmmm, he said. Not so sure. He said he was hoping to recruit Tom Sawyer [to become general secretary, 1994–98]. He told me GB thought I was hostile to him. I said he shouldn't. I used to work very closely with him, and I think he thinks that when I went on *Newsnight* the day that John died, and said you'd be leader, that was some thought-through strategy to get a head of steam up. It wasn't. I'd actually said to *Newsnight* I just wanted to do a tribute but they threw me the question at the end, who'd be next leader, and I said you. It was pretty obvious by then. Tony said he still believed GB was in many ways a superior politician. We had dinner at the restaurant down the hill, and while the kids played football Tony regaled us with stories of him and JP getting sworn in as privy councillors, JP agitating at the flunkies telling him what to do.

Thursday, August 11

Neil and Glenys arrived. Glenys was in a different place to Neil on whether I should do it. She said Neil was totally opposed but she felt that I was dedicated to the Labour cause, we'd got a new leader, he'd asked me to do the job, he was obviously determined that I should do it, and it was hard to say no. Neil kept saying things like – why live your life at the beck and call of a bunch of shits (the press) when you could be the new [Brian] Walden [former Labour MP and TV presenter], the next Jeremy Paxman [TV news journalist], the next Michael Parkinson [chat-show host], whatever you want? Cherie's mum was due to leave and I had to drive her to Marseille airport. TB came along and again we chatted over the issues. Gale [Booth, Cherie's mother]

[1] David Montgomery, chief executive of Mirror Group Newspapers, 1992-97. AC departed acrimoniously as political editor in 1993.

was clearly worried about the whole thing. She'd told me a while back she was scared for Cherie and the children. It was just such a big thing, one step from being prime minister, and then the family might as well say goodbye to normality. On the way back, I told Tony in graphic detail about my breakdown. I said I thought it was important he knew, because I had to assume that ultimately I had cracked because of pressure, and the pressure was as nothing compared to what we would face if I did the job. I said I was sure I was a stronger person than ever, but he needed to know there was a risk. He said he was happy to take it. By now, he had also let me know, and sworn me to secrecy, that he was minded to have a review of the constitution and scrap Clause 4.[1] I have never felt any great ideological attachment to Clause 4 one way or the other. If it made people happy, fine, but it didn't actually set out what the party was about today. It wasn't the politics or the ideology that appealed. It was the boldness. People had talked about it for years. Here was a new leader telling me that he was thinking about doing it in his first conference speech as leader. Bold. I said I hope you do, because it's bold. I will, he said. And he had a real glint in his eye. He knew that in terms of the political substance, it didn't actually mean that much. But as a symbol, as a vehicle to communicate change, and his determination to modernise the party, it was brilliant. He'd first mentioned it in our walk up the hill yesterday. On the drive back from Marseille, a hint became an intention, and he asked me to start thinking about how best to express it, and how best to plan the huge political and communications exercise that would follow. Whether it was deliberate or not, I don't know, but he had found the way to persuade me, and I told him that I would do the job.

I phoned Peter M in the US. It was obvious that Peter's judgement was largely trusted by Tony and indeed it had been Peter who

[1] This was in essence a rerun of the argument after the 1959 defeat, when Hugh Gaitskell proposed amending Clause 4 of the party's 1918 constitution in a vain bid at modernisation. The clause, close enough to Labour's heart and history to be reprinted on membership cards, proclaimed the aim of 'Common ownership of the means of production, distribution and exchange'. Wholesale nationalisation, in other words. Gaitskell lost out because questioning Clause 4 was, in the words of one Labour historian, like trying to 'persuade Christian fundamentalists that they need not believe in God'. Gaitskell's attempt at modernisation not only failed, but deepened the divisions in the party that by the 1983 election debacle had become a chasm. Effectively Labour had become two parties, one of the centre left, the other hard left. Nevertheless, to Blair such a high-risk, resonant symbol was the example he needed. Clause 4 had to go to show a new Labour Party was being forged and it meant business.

August '94: Campbell tells Blair of breakdown

first sounded me out on his behalf, when he came round for dinner, spent a couple of hours skirting round the issue, finally blurted it out and I said no way. I told him Tony had talked me into it. He said he was pleased. It was the right thing for the party, and he was sure it was the right thing for me. He said I hope we don't fall out, which I thought was a very odd thing to say, but on reflection maybe not. I suppose people working closely together often do end up falling out and there was bound to be tension from time to time in that we would often be advising Tony from different perspectives on the same issues. He said I should consider him as an extra mind I could call on whenever I wanted, but equally I could always tell him to get lost. Later, he spoke to Tony and said he wasn't sure about keeping on Hilary Coffman. I told Tony that I was sure and she had to stay, and it was important that I could decide, provided he was happy, who worked for me.

Went to the local restaurant for dinner. Neil said to Tony, 'A piece of advice, which I wish I had been able to do myself – don't be afraid to take speech drafts from other people.' Tony said he was the same, big speeches he had to write himself, which made me smile when I thought of the bits I'd done for his leadership speech.

Friday, August 12

As part of the Blairs' chaotic travel plans, we had to set off at 4am so that I could get them to Marseilles railway station. Fiona and I, and Neil and Glenys, couldn't believe the way they went from place to place on holiday. Why can't they settle in one place? We arrived at the station at 5.35 and the train wasn't due to leave, so we thought, till 6.15, so I started to get the half-asleep kids and the assortment of bags sorted while Tony went to check where the train was going from. With Euan still asleep and refusing to wake up, Tony came charging out, said they'd got the times wrong, it was about to go. He looked very odd in a pair of holiday shorts and what looked like a suit jacket. He picked up Euan and as many bags as he could carry. I did the same with Kathryn and Cherie hustled Nicky along and we just made it as the platform attendant started to blow his whistle. It turned out it wasn't their train at all, but an earlier one which had been delayed but they decided to stay on board and hope they could find seats. Then just before the doors closed, Tony and I had one of those leaving-train conversations loved by film directors in need of a device. I said I still had huge misgivings but I would do it, and I would never give him and the party anything less than one hundred per cent. He said I was right to feel nervous, but together we could change the face of

British politics for a generation, and change the world while we're at it. At which point, as he was right in the middle of this momentous statement, the door shut automatically, angrily, forcing our dear leader to jump back. All of a sudden he looked bewildered. He gave me a little wave, the big smile, and off he went.

I drove back to Flassan, wondering what on earth I was letting myself in for. I got home as everyone was getting up and over breakfast agreed we could not cope with chaos like Cherie seems able to. Neil asked me outright if I was going to do the job. I said yes. He said it's good for Tony, bad for you and the family, and I'm totally opposed. You'll hate the crap, the detail, the wankers you have to be nice to. Glenys said Neil, don't do this, he's made up his mind and we should support him. I said I've told him I'll do it, Neil. 'Have you shaken on it?' 'No.' 'Well don't.' I said he was really serious about winning, but he would need help and I felt I had to help when he asked me like that. Neil even asked if I wanted to be his chef de cabinet but I said no, I'd made my mind up.

Tuesday, August 16

Spoke to TB in Italy. Said he was furious that Neil was trying to talk me out of it. I said it was for good reasons. Neil is a real friend, and he loves my kids like his own. He's worried for us. I'd read an interview with Rupert Murdoch in *Der Spiegel* in which he said he could see himself backing Blair. TB said he was probably messing around. I wasn't so sure. The right wing have had it with Major, and I think we can really make inroads. The aim should be to keep the left press on board, neutralise the Mail and if possible get the *Sun* to back us.

Saturday, August 20

Neil was relentless. As I was fiddling to get the BBC World Service for the Burnley score, he said 'That's the nearest you'll ever get to Burnley in your new life, pal.' Fiona was also joining in, saying that Peter M would want to be doing the job at the same time as me, and it would become impossible. I said I was perfectly capable of looking after myself and doing the job as it should be done and in any event Peter had a lot to offer, whatever the problems he caused. She had a point though. It was why I had to hold absolutely firm re Hilary, because I sensed Peter was just trying it on a bit. Spoke to Anji who said she was thrilled I was joining, and that I was just what Tony needed. Also, everyone else is a bit scared of Peter and you won't be and that will give everyone a bit more strength and confidence. She said she couldn't believe how much I was being paid. I said it's half what I would get if I stayed where I was. She said 'It's three times what I get though.'

Tuesday, September 6

David Hill called and said the *Mirror* was on to the fact I was doing the job, and running something tonight. Not much we could do about it. I was doing my Radio 5 programme at midnight with Roy Greenslade [media commentator], Julie Kirkbride [*Telegraph* journalist, later Conservative MP] and others. Once the papers came in, Julie started teasing me on air about the job.

Wednesday, September 7

There was a lot more media interest than I thought there would be. I discovered that tomorrow's party strategy meeting in the New Forest wasn't at a private house but a country hotel, which was daft, and that JP was not invited. Madness.

Thursday, September 8

Anji called with a change of plan. Only TB, Peter and Philip Gould would go for the evening discussion in the New Forest. I assumed this was Peter's response to a row we'd had yesterday, when I'd said I was adamant that Hilary be employed. I'd also told Peter that it was brain dead to exclude Prescott from this meeting. These things do not stay quiet, and he will feel very pissed off, and rightly so. You're talking about the kind of hotel where editors probably take their mistresses so someone is bound to see us; it'll get in the papers and JP will hit the roof. I said to TB that Peter M was one of my oldest and closest friends but if I was going to do the job properly, I could not be second-guessed and I had to know all the advice that was going his way. Peter is good, but he's not infallible.

Lunch with Richard Stott who said he reckoned Murdoch might stay neutral. Pat McFadden [political adviser, Leader of the Opposition's office] came in and said should Tony see Ian Paisley [MP, Democratic Unionist leader] and I said yes, provided John Hume [MP, nationalist SDLP leader] was happy enough. I spoke to Stuart Higgins [editor, *Sun*] who was very friendly. Also got the first calls – from the *News of the World* – re the breakdown and the porn. Didn't take long. Took Hilary for a cup of tea in the Pugin Room at the Commons and explained the background. She seemed pleased and grateful. Hilary was one of those people you just know you need on your side. Not flash, but solid and steady and totally reliable. Alan Clark called. 'Congratters old thing. Bloody great news. Be great to see all the arse lickers in the media moving your way now. How does Monty [David Montgomery] feel about it? Pig sick I bet.' He said it was a shrewd move by Blair and he was coming round to the view there was an awful lot more to him than met the eye.' I bumped into Ken Baker [former Conservative Cabinet minister] in the evening and he said something similar. 'You've got something good to sell. We haven't.'

Friday, September 9

Chewton Glen. Beautiful hotel. We were meeting in a conference room that was too big for the numbers. Also wondered why these conference rooms always had Fox's Glacier mints on the table. It was an OK meeting but because people were in some ways relatively new to each other, I got the sense they were holding back. I certainly was. I felt Gordon was too. When he spoke, he was strong, and clear, but you kind of felt he'd say most of it in public. There was no real insight there, though you knew he had it, but was holding back.

Sunday, September 11

I'd been pre-booked to do the papers on *Breakfast with Frost* with Bernard Ingham [former press secretary to Margaret Thatcher]. Over breakfast, with [David] Frost, [General Sir Peter] de la Billière, Mo, [Tory Chairman Jeremy] Hanley et al, Barney Jones [editor and producer, *Breakfast with Frost*] said to Bernard: 'What would you advise Alastair to do with Mandelson?' Bernard stopped stuffing his face for a moment and said 'Slit his throat.' De la Billière looked like he approved. I said this struck me as being over the top. Bernard was adamant: you can't have two voices going out from the master. There was far too much kitchen-cabinet stuff in the Sundays and the fact that Hilary appeared to have been excised made everyone assume it was Peter M. I said to TB he has to stop briefing the press. Peter Kilfoyle called and said I had to sort Peter M out. He's loathed in the party. I said you have to balance that against his ability, which is real. Peter K said he was not convinced. I asked Peter M if he had briefed the *Sunday Times* and he said don't be ridiculous, why on earth would I? For heaven's sake don't get ridiculous. This is like John Underwood [briefly Labour's campaigns and communications director, 1990–91]. What are you doing, sitting there with you and Fiona sticking pins in effigies? Hold on a minute, I said, I just asked if you briefed the *Sunday Times*. 'No, I did not.' I said good, because the best thing for him, and incidentally for me, would be for him to stop being a spin doctor. He said he agreed, but I had to understand that I could faze him and I mustn't.

Tuesday, September 13

TB was meeting Rupert Murdoch. He phoned me from the car as he was heading home. Said he didn't feel it went terribly well.

Wednesday, September 14

Gus Fischer [chief executive of News International, 1994-95] called. Murdoch had been hugely impressed by Blair. Gus said he could easily see Murdoch backing him. Blair had been very impressive. Gave nothing away but made a really strong impression. I interviewed TB for a party political in the Shadow Cabinet room. He was on good form, then persuaded him to do *World at One* re [Michael] Howard [Home Secretary] on jails. He was always keen to do the big crime stuff and stop the Tories getting back the ground they had lost. But he was worried the party still didn't universally get why we had to have this new stance on crime. Tomorrow's Shadow Cabinet was important. He wanted to give them a big no complacency message, a unity message, and set out the main themes for the conference.

Meeting at 3.45 with Peter M, Philip [Gould], Pat [McFadden], Anji and [David] Miliband to go over conference problems. The planned slogan was 'Labour's New Approach', which was fine as far as it went, and it was a good enough umbrella but it didn't really do the business as far as I was concerned. It was difficult spelling out why we had to be ultra bold, when some in the meeting didn't know what TB was planning, but I emphasised that he would never get as big an opportunity to use a single conference to reshape the party, and to signal his commitment to change. PG said that's what New Approach was about. It would allow the main spokesmen to set out the new approach – on education, on health, on crime etc. I said fine, but we're looking for something bigger and bolder. I said what we were talking about here was a new leader who wanted to change the party. We were talking about New Labour, and the clearer we were about that, in strategic terms, the better it was. Left early to see Burnley at Millwall – brilliant, won 3-2 – but had started the debate about the backdrop. I knew there would be opposition because it was so bold. But if he was going to dump Clause 4, we had better make the most of it. And New Labour was a big, bold message that would give us real direction and momentum.

Thursday, September 15

Shadow Cabinet meeting, Brunswick Square. TB certainly delivered on his no complacency message. He didn't buy the John Smith line that governments lost elections. He believed Oppositions had to go out and win. The public needed to know what we stood for, and above all needed to know we could be trusted on the economy. GB did a very strong presentation on the whole tax and spend scene. It was my first Shadow Cabinet and got the feeling that many of them spoke simply because they felt they had to, rather than because they were taking part in a discussion. But one or two surprises: Clare Short was ultra loyal and orthodox. So was [Michael] Meacher, which was odd as well. Very different to how they spoke to journalists. Dobbo [Frank Dobson] made a couple of insightful observations, including the fact that the press and media was now more sprawling and it was not so easy to get a message through. We had to keep it simple. And repeat our basic messages the whole time. TB told me later he'd sounded out JP for the first time on the constitution. He didn't explode. Said he would think about it. I'd been scribbling some thoughts on a slogan for conference. 'New Labour, New Britain' was the best. It was bold, it was clear and it would give us momentum. And if he did Clause 4, it would really drive through. TB expressed some of the nervousness the others had. The problem was that New had an opposite, and you couldn't guarantee there wouldn't be a lot of hostility.

Monday, September 19

Met JP and tried out New Labour on him. Not overwhelmed. But not totally hostile. I didn't know how far TB had gone re his discussion on Clause 4, and I sensed JP didn't know everything, so we didn't really get to the point. But I was relieved he didn't just say no. He agreed that TB had a short window during which he could really make the kind of impact that would basically set us up for the election. But everyone else was wobbling on 'New Labour, New Britain'. Pat and Jon Cruddas both said it could backfire. Peter M and Philip were really worried about it. The speech was really coming on. We already had the basic argument and some great passages, and if he did Clause 4, it could be sensational. I can't believe we're having a great argument about whether we can stick NEW Labour on a backdrop. New Labour, New Britain. We're changing the party to show we're fit to be trusted to change the country. It's obvious, but I was worried even Peter and PG were baulking at it.

Tuesday, September 20

More trouble re the slogan. JP had been on to Anji and he was not happy either with mine, or with 'Labour's New Approach'. He thought there was a danger they looked presidential. I called him, and said I was convinced we should go for 'New Labour, New Britain', but it wouldn't work if he felt he couldn't sign up to it. He said he was worried we were saying to the party, you've always failed and we're only going to succeed if we change everything. What's new? The leader. But are we saying more than that? I said we were making clear the party had changed, and it was going to carry on changing as it became fit for power. I went through the speech and said there was nothing as it stood that should upset the party, but as far as the public was concerned, they had to know the party had changed, and New Labour was a clear expression of that. Then we'd have the big bold changes to make it clear this was real. I said it's not different to his traditional values in a modern setting, but it brings it home more clearly to the non-political audience. He said he didn't want the party thinking we were saying they were failures. They had to know this related to what they believe in. 'This kid has got some agenda and it's exciting and all the rest but maybe my role at times will be to be the cautious one saying are we sure? Like his Clause 4 plan, how do you know it won't cause a two-year riot in the party? Is it worth it? Now I know why he wants to do it but we have to think it through. Last year we rowed about One Member, One Vote, now Clause 4.' I said the OMOV row was worth it. So would this be if we won the argument. I asked if he was totally against 'New Labour, New Britain'. He said, I'm not but it's a risk and we have to weigh it up carefully. I then got a message that everyone at Walworth Road [Labour Party headquarters] was against it. Probably an exaggeration but it was not going to be easy. The only way to do it would be to get TB and JP on board, and force it through.

Thursday, September 22

Met JP to go over his speech for tomorrow when he was kicking off his tour. He was fine about the slogan, at least more than he had been. TB asked me if JP was really hostile on the constitutional change plan. He says he's not totally opposed but thinks you must be off your head. OMOV last year, Clause 4 this, when are we going to get on to things people care about? TB said he needed something big and symbolic that people would notice, then they would hear us on the other policy areas too. This was the route to doing what John wanted. The public had to know we were serious about change. He signed up finally to 'New Labour, New Britain', and gave me the go-ahead to get it signed off.

Friday, September 23

Office meeting, Pat taking us through some of the difficult outstanding issues. He was worried Tony had said drop 'The Red Flag'. He said even Fraser Kemp [Labour's election co-ordinator, 1994–96] thought we might be going too fast for our own good. I said by the way, the slogan is agreed. TB and JP are both up for it, so it's 'New Labour, New Britain'. Pat did his best Private Fraser from *Dad's Army*: we're all doomed. Cherie's fortieth birthday party at Frederick's. Odd kind of do. Didn't feel right being photographed going in, by Alan Davidson [celebrity photographer] of all people, and I couldn't quite work out the guest mix. Family, a bit of politics, law, and friends that didn't always seem like Tony's kind of people. Maybe he is a lot more eclectic than we are. Cherie had certainly been given a makeover. She looked great, but it was an odd do.

Saturday, September 24
TB wanted to know why Major was getting great coverage out of [Boris] Yeltsin [visiting Russian President]. I said it didn't matter a damn. If he got a decent speech by Tuesday, who would ever remember a few nice pictures of JM and Yeltsin?

Sunday, September 25
David Miliband and I went round to Tony's to carry on work on the speech. He was down about it again, also floating the idea of New Socialism. I said he wouldn't need it if he did the Clause 4 thing. Everyone would get the message, and New Labour was clearer. He said JP was coming round, but Robin was the one to watch if I fall over in trying to move the party too quickly. Robin won't like this, but I'm clear I need to do this, for its own reasons, but above all to show we're serious about breaking the mould, and doing whatever it takes to modernise.

Tuesday, September 27
Conference meeting with TB and JP. JP not great about the brochure we were doing. Said he was getting worried about new, new, new. Agreed he would do the 'New Labour, New Britain' speech but just wanted to urge a bit of caution. As things stood, he was against doing Clause 4 in Tony's speech. He thought Tony had all the momentum he needed, and it was OTT. TB and JP had a private session and as JP came out, I asked whether we were being too gung-ho. He said he's just got to be careful he doesn't blow up. He was off to see Robin, who was the person Tony was really wary of on this one. David and I talked about it as we worked on the speech. Agreed Tony's lack of roots in the party was both an asset and a disadvantage. An asset because he could reach parts the others couldn't but he would need

September '94: John Prescott urges caution

the party and there would be suspicions there. The question was whether he worried about them, or ignored them and did what he thought was right. I had another chat with him about JP. TB said once we do this, people will wonder what the fuss is all about. I said all people like JP are saying is be careful – to some people this is like going into church and taking down the cross. Oh for heaven's sake, he said, people believe in God, and they believe in Christ. Name me a single person who actually believes in what Clause 4 says.

Wednesday, September 28
Everyone talking about GB's 'gobbledegook'.[1] JP in to see TB and this time we could hear the raised voices. That was not always a bad sign with John. Sometimes meant he was getting something off his chest before coming round. Or it meant he was negotiating. We had a new draft of the speech. Took it home, showed it to Fiona who said it was a lot worse than the last one she saw. There was too much in there now and it was all getting muddled.

Thursday, September 29
GB was doing a speech tonight and Tony had told him to get a hold of the note I'd done on greed, which we might be putting into TB's speech. Sent it to GB and he swallowed the whole thing for his own speech. Amazing. Round to Richmond Crescent for yet another speech meeting. TB was getting irritated, saying he couldn't understand why it was going to be so difficult to persuade people to do the blindingly obvious.

Friday, September 30
GB's speech, much of it nicked from my draft, all over the papers. Up to see Steve Hardwick [Prescott aide and speechwriter] in JP's office. His press release on the speech had a few odd lines in it, including a perpetual Maoist revolution. Chatted to JP in Hull and we agreed an approach for the weekend. TB called, said he had read JP the form of words we agreed last night, with no reference to the constitution, and he was just about OK. But TB felt without reference to the constitution, it would be odd. Back to Richmond Crescent. Another draft. Went through the Clause 4 section, and it didn't work. He said what do you think? Is this madness we're even considering it? I said no, definitely worth doing, but we've got to get it right. He said there has to be a signal to the outside world that we're serious

[1] Brown had spoken about 'post-neoclassical endogenous growth theory'.

about change, and this is it. Peter Hyman suddenly chipped in: did you know there are more Indian waiters in Britain than there are coal miners? Blank faces all round. Tony was beginning to look exasperated. His hair was wild, two big prongs of it heading off towards the ceiling. He folded his arms across his chest, put his head down, and groaned. 'I cannot believe this is so difficult. It's ridiculous.' He went out to the garden to work on the rest of the speech and asked me to have another go at Clause 4. He called me out half an hour later, said was I worried about Peter M? I said I was, and once I was fully *in situ*, his briefing had to stop. You can only have one HMV [His Master's Voice] when it comes to the press and Peter has to accept that.

Saturday, October 1

Felt bad leaving home because Rory had been sick during the night. Up to Tony's and chaotic scenes. Photographers gathering outside. TB had added a whole lot more to the speech overnight. We worked in separate rooms on separate drafts and then met to compare notes. Derry called and said he'd read the latest draft and there was an awful lot of verbiage in it. Derry was something of a mentor/father figure to TB, so I felt this was probably the last thing he needed to hear whilst he was adding rather than subtracting from the speech, so I waited till later before telling him the great man's view. TB locked himself away in his little study, his desk a mass of papers, earlier discarded drafts, papers with his own handwriting, lines straight through it, rejected even before it became a draft. He had a new A4 pad, a red pen, and off he went, with a Do Not Disturb sign etched on his face. I left him and went downstairs to make a cup of tea. Carole [Caplin, friend of Cherie Blair] was there. She had made a strong impression on me when I first met her a couple of days earlier, and had been troubling me. She was pretty and odd in equal measure. I'd asked her where she fitted into the whole Blair scene, and she'd said she was just an old friend that Cherie had called on to give her a hand. I took from that she was a lifelong friend, so I said I was surprised I'd never met her before. In fact she'd known CB before but then went to the US and came back just after John Smith died. She said she was into holistic healing, and I confessed I didn't know what that was. You could tell in one look that she was big into health and fitness. She looked great. She made lunch, which was a great mix of different salads. Cherie said Carole would be going with them in the car and on the plane and I said the press would be straight on, asking who this strange woman was. Carole said she didn't want any attention, but my instinct said otherwise. It was hard to dislike her,

October '94: Carole Caplin makes Campbell uneasy

but she made me feel very uneasy. Set off at 3, worked on the speech in the VIP lounge, again on the plane, then he and I went through it line by line in the car on the way into Blackpool. Arrived at 7, and he did a little doorstep. JP said he agreed the 'New Labour, New Britain' document was pretty good, and he'd felt OK talking about it. Anji told me Carole had introduced herself as TB and CB's guru. Weird.

Sunday, October 2

JP's interview had gone badly, *Indy* and *Observer* were bad and the right-wing press more than usually hostile. Also, lots of niggling little bits re Peter M. I went through to see TB who was sitting in his pyjamas surrounded by papers strewn all around his chair. He was in a terrible mood, both re the press, which he felt was ridiculous, and the state of the speech. He said, something is missing and I'm not sure what it is. We went through it line by line and then took away a few changes which David M and I put into a new draft. I had to disappear for a while to do my *Today* column. It was odd being both journalist and speechwriter but not long left now. I also felt bad that I was sitting on a huge political story, but the new role meant I could tell nobody about it. Surprise was a vital part of the package and we had to keep it very tight.

I went to see JP in his suite. He was fuming because Gordon had put forward yet another document to the NEC that he wasn't happy with. Although we'd had our differences when I was a journalist, I'd always got on OK with JP and TB had asked me to make sure he was kept in the loop and onside re the speech on Tuesday. It wasn't easy. John instinctively knew what the plan was, but he had to be persuaded bit by bit. I think if we'd have said from the day Tony became leader: by the way, John, he's going to stand up and scrap Clause 4 in his first conference speech, we might have ended up with a disaster. But the thing about JP is that he is open to persuasion if the argument is strong and this argument was strong. He knew he'd not done great on *On the Record*. The press were on to the fact he hadn't said yes when asked if he agreed with TB and didn't want to put more taxes on the middle classes. There was some thought about putting out a clarifying statement but we agreed that might just make matters worse. Then there was a little block-vote flurry because [Bill] Morris [general secretary of the TGW] and Edmonds both said their delegates would be voting en bloc and TB went out and did a little organised doorstep saying the old block-vote days were gone. He thought he'd got agreement from the two of them not to cause trouble. The problem was that once they got to

Blackpool they got the whiff of publicity in the nostrils and the reality of our media was that they were only likely to get noticed if they had a pop at the leadership, so away they went. It also hardened TB in his determination to do Clause 4. He was still working through the consequences and whilst it's pretty clear by now he'll do it, it is not one hundred per cent certain. He said it's stuff like this that makes people think we're not a serious party. We had a decent draft by now, with or without the Clause 4 change, but TB was still not sure. Meanwhile I was telling him that we had to keep Carole C out of the public eye.

Monday, October 3

Woke up at 5, nervous and tired. Got the papers and read them in the bath. JP stuff pretty bad. I went to see him before he did *GMTV* and then in to see TB, who was pretty fed up. I said this stuff is all froth and it'll get blown away if you do a decent speech tomorrow. I had another session with JP to go through the draft again, then wandered over to the Winter Gardens. We had a good speech but now Derry had thrown in a spanner. Derry is not your obvious natural politician but he has a big brain and, more important in this context, Tony thinks Derry has a brain the size of a melon. So when Derry gets on to him and says he doesn't think it's a good speech – no, worse, he thinks it's a BAD speech – Tony listens and there's a danger we're going back to square one. I was really pissed off with Derry. We had less than a day to go and he's saying go back to scratch. We asked him for detailed comments and when they came through, they were fairly marginal so Tony realised he'd been exaggerating. It wasn't that bad. It just wasn't brilliant, but we had a bit of time left yet.

At lunch JP came up and read the speech, said it was fine, have a debate, blah blah blah, and TB said let's be clear what I'm saying: Clause 4 is not an adequate expression of what we stand for, and I'm saying this debate is about what goes in its place, something around which we can all unite. I said, right, John, we're doing an interview tomorrow night and I'm asking you: So, Mr Prescott, this new statement Tony Blair talks about, could that go in the party's constitution? And JP doesn't look wild about it, but he says yes, if it's agreed by the party, it could. But as we leave, he says, I'm not sure this is what we need right now, a bloody great row through the party, but let's see. I showed the first twenty pages of the speech to Neil, who liked it. I then did a briefing of the political editors, which was weird, me still a working journalist spelling out the purpose of the speech they'd be covering tomorrow. Nobody had a whisper of the Clause 4 plan. So far so good. Tom Sawyer was in the loop and seemed pretty relaxed, said he thought he could get some union guys out in favour tomorrow, and was confident we could carry the party OK.

Back at the hotel, Tony met Neil and set out what he intended to say in detail. Bloody great, said Neil, right thing to do. The last time the three of us had talked together, we were in France, TB and NK on different sides of the argument. I felt a real sense of privilege, in terms of witnessing history, to be in the room with one leader of the Labour Party explaining to another why and how he was changing the party's constitution as a means of giving real power and symbolism to the modernisation process the older man had started. Neil said: I never had a conference speech as good as this the night before I made it. Don't mess around with it too much. TB to NK: I knew you said these speeches were a nightmare, but I didn't realise how big. NK to TB: You'll feel great tomorrow night, I promise you. That is a helluva speech. Neil left and then TB asked me to rewrite the economic and investment sections while he worked on the middle. I gave him Neil's changes, which he liked. He gave me Derry's, which I didn't like. TB had to go out to Scots night and Peter M came up to see me. He said it was strong but it lacked clarity. It would be bad if he said something, the meaning of which we all knew, but which had to be explained in a TV studio afterwards. I agreed, always best to call a spade a spade. But if he stands up and says I'm scrapping Clause 4, you cannot guarantee the right reaction. If he makes a passionate but rounded argument about New Labour, what we stand for in the modern world, and then says let's argue and agree a new definition of what we stand for, you can win the whole hall round. One slow handclap halfway through this and we're over before we begin. TB came back and had another mini explosion about the state of the ending of the speech. He asked why I wasn't working on it. I said because I'm in here listening to you complaining about it. Can I go now please? And I went. Back to the word processor in the little room down the corridor, where the pile of uncleared-away room-service trays was growing.

Time to widen the loop. We had a meeting in my room with Peter M, David Hill, Hilary C, Peter Hyman, Anji, Tim [Allan], Murray, Philip G. Some of them knew the full story. Others had picked up the vibes. I told them straight out that the headline from the speech would be Blair scraps Clause 4. I thought Hilary's eyes were going to fall out. David gulped and then whistled. Murray looked ill. I read them the current draft re the constitution, and I said very few people knew what was going on, but I said JP was one of them and he was basically on board. Murray pressed me repeatedly what basically on board meant. I said he was on board. He would be fine, and supportive, and would say that Clause 4 was too narrow a definition of modern socialism. Philip suggested a joint TB-JP press conference after the speech to show they were together on it. It was vital the party knew they were together on it. The only remaining question was whether, within the speech, he actually said, in terms, this is about ditching Clause 4. Murray and David felt it risked being too provocative. The boys were in favour. But it was a tough call. Saw TB later and said the only way to do it is to put the word 'constitution' in there. So we're not just talking about a debate about what we stand for, but we're clear that we're going to debate a new constitution. That is enough. David M and I rewrote that section and I took it to JP. Before I showed him the text, he said 'If you're talking about a new constitution, you've got to say so.' I couldn't believe it. He'd got there at exactly the same point as the rest of us did. I showed him the words. He tested the arguments to destruction and the arguments held up. He said he could live with it. I said great, but could you go ten rounds in the TV studio defending it? Course I can. He wasn't exactly delirious but, like me, he liked the boldness and he liked Tony's style. Went back to tell TB who had gone to bed. Philip was still up. He said there is a twenty per cent chance TB will explode over this, that the party will think he's pushing them too far, and he's finished before he even gets going. On the other hand, it could be a massive step forward.

Tuesday, October 4

About an hour and a half's sleep. Peter M came round about 7 and said he was really nervous. There is a small chance Tony will end up dead in the water as a result of this. Tony asked me what the chances were that he'd be out of the job if he went through with it. I said about ten per cent. JP remained the key to this. I went to see him again. Pauline [Prescott] was in bed still. I said can we be clear that you will put your name to a new statement of objectives and that you're happy for TB to use the word constitution in that part of the speech? He said, I'm not pretending I'm totally comfortable with it but he's the leader and I'm the deputy and I can see why he wants to do it. I can see the ups as well as the downs on this and I'll support him on it. I borrowed his red pen and he and I went through another round of it, and got a final agreed version which I took to TB. Later he came up to see TB and said, you've got your agenda and I'll back you on it, but there are things I want us to do as well, and I want your backing for them. JP was a very canny operator and was likely to be using this to press for his own position in a future government. Tony now had to get on with telling other key Shadow Cabinet people.

Robin Cook came in, and sat down in the chair by the fireplace. They spent a couple of minutes on small talk before Tony got to the point. Robin deflated visibly, paused, then said: Tony, you're making a terrible mistake. 'Why?' Because it is divisive, people will not want this debate, it will cause you nothing but problems. 'Are you telling me people will fight to save a piece of language that no longer represents what any of us stand for?' Yes. 'Who?' Dennis Skinner. In any event, it's an emblem. You don't need to change it. 'Well, you may think me crazy but I intend to do it. It is my strong instinct that it's the right thing to do.' You may well win but by the time the blood is cleared from the carpet, I doubt you will think it was a fight worth having. 'Nobody, if they are presented with a better alternative, should feel the old Clause 4 is worth spilling blood for.' TB said JP and GB were on board and it was obviously important RC supported it too. Robin started from a very negative position but TB said he hoped he could win him around. RC went straight to see JP. I got JP to come back up to see TB, who asked me to leave. TB was now seeing Clare, [David] Blunkett, some of the others. It was widening but amazingly not a whisper leaked out. I briefed the evening regionals and felt that even without the Clause 4 bombshell, it was a strong speech. I sent through word that the last couple of pages were not to be put in the press-release version. Got all the press officers together to go through the Q&As. There were still concerns that it would not be clear enough but I said we were at the limit of JP's tolerance and we had to go with it.

I was confident it would go well now. I had a last run through the whole text with TB and then the disk was taken through for autocue rehearsal. Even though he did it in a very soft whisper, stopping only to check points or correct literals, by the time he got to the bit that mattered, even in that room, with the half a dozen or so people in there, you could feel hairs standing on necks. Anji said it was the first time she'd seen the whole speech and it was brilliant. As first leaders' speeches went, this would be unforgettable. We were driven over. I was clutching the original, driven by Neil's old driver Mike Joy. Caution won't win elections. Courage will. Any doubt I had that it was the right thing to do finally went.

TB had spoken to a few more people, Margaret B, [John] Edmonds, [Bill] Morris, and still not a whisper. I walked up with him to the point where he was being held before going on. 'Oh well, here goes,' he said, smiled and walked on. There was a ballsiness to his enthusiasm which I liked. I wandered round the side to watch and there was a real buzz of excitement. There was a real warmth towards him.

I was standing next to Tim Allan and when they laughed really loud at one of the jokes we'd not been sure about, I said to Tim: this is going to be fine. When it came to the moment, George Robertson summed it up brilliantly later when he said that as the applause died, you could hear the sound of pennies dropping all around the hall. It had worked. The hall was electrified, and so were the media. David English [chairman, Associated Newspapers] was in raptures. We regrouped briefly in the little office behind the stage, to go through the joint press conference. Neil came in, really enthusiastic, told Tony it was brilliant, loved it. NK and JP never the best of friends, and JP cooled a bit, but was still on for what was to follow. We'd arranged for TB/JP to do a joint briefing in the press room. I told them to follow the cops. We went through but some fucker had moved the lectern and the police just marched on. Ended up doing it on the top of the stairs, all a bit messy but the content was fine. The press centre was as excited as I have never known a conference press centre to be, and that included some of the Thatcher split and the Thatcher demise conferences. [Tony] Bevins [*Independent* political editor] said it was the most brilliant conference speech he'd ever heard. Tony and Cherie effusive in their thanks. I said I'd really enjoyed it. Anji was close to tears, said I just feel we're going to win now, I'm sure of it.

Wednesday, October 5

Up early and skimmed through the papers. Took them through to TB and said you might as well have a read of them because you will never get a better press than this for a speech. I know, he said. There was a terrific atmosphere around the place. I also had my first public media spat. Anna Healy [Labour press officer] told me Nick Jones [BBC political correspondent] was reporting that JP had been unhappy and that he had not been kept in the loop throughout. It was an obvious story to go for, but it misrepresented the situation. I bawled him out publicly, and said I wanted it corrected on air. He did. I went early to the *Mirror* lunch, another weird experience. It's fair to say these people had effectively given me the boot, and I felt they were taking the political heart out of the paper, but I stayed pretty shtum, TB did the talking and he was on form.

George Pascoe-Watson [deputy political editor of the *Sun*] came up to me, and said they had some topless pictures of Carole Caplin. He said they'd got a reporter up to the hotel-room door and Carole had said she was a personal secretary. They were asking what her role was. I got Anji to get a message to TB and filled him in when he came off the platform. I said it was probably handleable but if she was a gold digger, or a media plant, heaven knows where this could lead. She and Cherie were obviously friendly and presumably she'd confided all sorts of things. TB didn't exactly look happy but he said he did not believe this would be being done with Carole's knowledge. I spoke to Carole who at first denied doing topless pictures but then said maybe topless, nothing else, a long time ago. I said she might as well tell me the truth because we would have to deal with it. These papers would be into her big time and we needed to know what they would find. We prepared a statement for me to give to the *Sun*, which distanced Tony from the whole thing, and I spoke to Stuart Higgins who said they were not doing it as a big deal, and agreed he would keep it distant from Tony. When I'd said earlier she hadn't done topless, he said 'Why am I staring at her tits then?' I didn't think Carole had been candid and told her so, and I said it would be better for everyone if she left Blackpool. Burnley were at home and I'd been hoping to go and was stuck dealing with this. Once the *Sun* appeared there was a mini frenzy. Peter M and I tried to play it light, chucking out the *Sun* vendor in the foyer, overlooking the irony that Murdoch was still paying my wages. Pauline Prescott was worried for Cherie, said you just never know where people are coming from, and whether there is some other motive there. It may be innocent but you just don't know.

Thursday, October 6

Sat down with TB, CB, Peter, Carole and went over the kind of confidentiality agreement everyone would have to sign. Carole said no problem, but she did come out with all manner of mumbo-jumbo. TB was clear to CB that she had to be very careful. Up to three working on the JP speech. When he was happy-ish with it, he rehearsed it at full volume booming out to the sea through open windows. God knows how Pauline managed to sleep.

Friday, October 7

The Carole problem was worrying me. Papers on Clause 4 defeat not as bad as they might have been. People knew that the ground had moved on Tuesday and the debate would change. Said to TB that I understood why CB felt angry that we were trying to say who her friends ought to be, but it was important she got from the outset that the honeymoon wouldn't last for ever, and the press would be after her if they could, and Carole had the potential to be a real problem for all of us. It may be fair or unfair but there we are. He said he knew that. Cherie had been incredibly warm up to now but it all changed. I spoke to CB and said I was sorry I'd had to be so direct but this had the potential to do real damage. I may be overreacting but I may not be. I'd pencilled out the kind of thing a confidentiality agreement might cover and went over it all with Derry. He agreed there may be nothing to worry about but equally that it could be calamitous if she was not in fact a friend. I called home and TB also spoke to Fiona who said they should really learn from this. People will be after them from all sorts of angles and they just had to be ultra careful. Carole signed the agreement. Flew back with Anji who felt we'd been right on Clause 4, and right to be tough re Carole. Had been a great week for TB. JP too had risen to it. GB speech didn't really do the business. Robin had undermined himself with his initial opposition on Clause 4 but would find a way back. The Shadow Cabinet had seen Tony move up, the press knew that we had changed the weather, and they were reporting that to our advantage.

Saturday, October 8

Robin C more on board. Took the boys to play football with Neil. Back to find Fiona and Glenys talking about how much the *Sun/News of the World* would pay for Carole's story if she was as close as she was saying. I suppose what was happening was that Cherie could see Tony having to become more and more absorbed with the job, the absolute determination to win, and there would be less space for her and the family, and she was looking around for support. Glenys said the same as Derry, that Cherie had had a rough childhood and because we saw her as a sophisticated lawyer, maybe she found it all a lot harder than we thought. I remembered what Joe Haines [former press secretary to Harold Wilson and ex-political editor of the *Mirror*] said when I called to ask whether he thought I should do the job. He said make sure you think about Fiona. It is very hard to be married to these all-consuming jobs. Neil seemed to have come round re the job, said things would not have gone as well if I hadn't been there, but exploded when I said JP had been constructive, said he had a long memory and he wouldn't forget some of the things JP said and did when Neil was leader.

Monday, October 10

Hilary felt I had been over-brutal re Carole, and I said maybe, but we shouldn't underestimate the potential damage to Tony. It was important everyone got the message we were in a different league. I could tell TB was wondering if I'd overreacted too and it's true I was probably thinking worst-case scenarios, so maybe going over the top. I said he and Cherie were big figures, and there were various types of people: people they could trust, who were likely to be people they had known for some time; people they would have to get on with, because it went with the job; people who would want to know them because of who they were; and among them would be people on the make, for money, for association, for the kick of saying they were close. You're far more trusting, and you have a much sunnier disposition than I do, but I think you have to be ultra careful about new people coming in. TB said that he felt Carole was probably more sinned against than sinning, and that she had been a great help to Cherie who suddenly found everyone writing about her, scrutinising her and what have you. TB was seeing Jonathan Powell [soon to be Blair's chief of staff] at 11 and I had a brief chat with him afterwards. Really bright, and eager, and struck me as someone who wouldn't easily get fazed. Meeting with JP to go over strategy for the Tory conference. Had to push them to the right. TB keen that we build up [Michael] Portillo [Conservative Employment Secretary and aspiring Tory leader]. I then had to leave for Bournemouth for the Tory conference.

Tuesday, October 11

I was amazed they hadn't withdrawn my pass. Yes, I'd be filing pieces every day, but the reality was I was working as a Labour press officer. The *Mail* had a story saying Tories wanted me banned, and *The Times* diary said [Jeremy] Hanley had a picture of me on his desk. I went up to the Highcliff Hotel for the Major-Thatcher arrival and amid the fiasco that followed, I was the only person Major made a point of talking to, usual mix of small talk and mickey-taking. Thatcher looked awful. Spoke to TB as he was heading home in the car. He said he thought Major was looking pretty cocky about things.

Wednesday, October 12

Did some TV, then spoke to JP re Portillo, worked out a very strong line which I took round the press centre. Bizarre that they were letting me do this. Maybe they'd just lost the will to live. TB wanted me to push a very pro-Europe line. Watched Hezza who got them going a bit but it was a very dispirited conference. Met up with Richard Stott for a drink, and was dreading the evening because he'd asked me to go with him and Lloyd Turner [*Today* executive] to a dinner for Kent Tories at Chewton Glen. He'd been so good to me I couldn't say no but it wasn't my idea of fun. In fact it turned out to be a surprise farewell from *Today*. [Nicholas] Soames [Conservative minister, friend of AC] was there, said he'd tried to get Alan Clark to come along but he was probably getting his leg over somewhere, then lo and behold there he was. My friendship with Soames and Clark had always fascinated Richard, and appalled the Tories, but what I like about them both is that they are funny, larger than life, and they believe politics is about having fun as well as being serious business. Alan said there was a whiff of auto destruct around the place. Couldn't see any way back for Major now that 'your boy' is stealing the show.

Thursday, October 13

TB told me Cherie had taken a knock re Carole. I had to understand this was all new and difficult for her, she was actually quite shy, and to find that even your friends are being approached and written about, it takes a bit of getting used to. He said again he thought I'd been harsh, but JP agreed with me that you were unlikely to make new friends once you got into a job like his.

Meeting with Peter M, Peter Hyman, Miliband and Pat Hewitt who is chairing the Social Justice Commission. Main focus child benefit, welfare to work, higher education. Pat said real difficulties. We were talking about targeting. I said you could easily mount the argument that it was socialism, helping most those who need it most. But Peter was worried whether the sums we were talking about – £300m – justified the political price of breaking universality. David M was nervous about it. Pat H wanted to go further, said this should only be the start of the process. Felt it crazy that the rich parent got the same child benefit as the poor parent. I'd only ever known Pat as Neil's press person, which was never her real thing. But she was really impressive on policy and on policy detail. The commission could be a big thing for us. There was a lot of talk about Shadow Cabinet shake-up. Robin's people were putting it round that he would be the best Shadow Chancellor, lot of interest in Margaret B. Drove back to Bournemouth and went to the BBC party. Lots of whingeing about the way we treated them last week. Dinner with John Monks at a Law Society bash. He reckoned my problems were: 1. Mandelson; 2. Unions/Edmonds; 3. Shadow Cabinet; 4. JP. He said if you can keep all of them basically in line, you've cracked it.

Friday, October 14

TB on early, making sure we had everyone lined up to deal with Major's speech. JP and others were on standby. But Major was not at his best. Not one of those speeches that would cut through to the public. You really had the sense of the party's head leaving the body.

Saturday, October 15

TB called asking why *Indy, Guardian* and others had given JM a good press. Probably sympathy, I said. I really wouldn't worry. That was a speech that will be forgotten by Monday. We talked over the article I'd drafted for the *News of the World*. He was keen on emphasising that Major was unable to hold firm in the centre ground, partly because of his record, partly because his party won't let him. He was in no doubt Major being pushed to the right was in our interests, and the conference had clearly helped on that. It was a huge strategic error because the issues that mattered were on the centre ground – economy, health, education. I had another go at dissuading him from sending the boys to the Oratory. I said that line in Major's speech about people doing the best for their own children was laying down a line of attack. What did he gain from going to the Oratory? You get all the grief politically, Euan will get attention he won't want or need, and is it really that much better than the school down the road? Discussed Shadow Cabinet. He was moving towards Jack Straw to Home Office.

Sunday, October 16

TB a lot happier about JM speech. Re Shadow Cabinet he was settling on GB Chancellor, RC Foreign Secretary, JS Home.

Monday, October 17

Finally started full-time. Fiona drove me in, and I said TB's a lovely bloke, but he is so relentlessly modernising I feel myself getting more traditional by the day. I didn't feel at all like I was going in for the first day at a new job. Bumped into TB on the stairs as he was leaving for the NEC/general secretary's meeting and he said he was getting worried re PMQs. He rushed off without waiting for Gordon who I think was hoping for a lift. Office meeting, Jonathan Powell's appointment confirmed, then a discussion of what we do after Shadow Cabinet elections on Thursday. TB was now going into circular conversation mode re PMQs, and also worrying re Shadow Cabinet. Fiona angry that CB was still so hostile to me over Carole. Can't she see you're just doing your job and trying to protect TB?

Tuesday, October 18

PMQs. TB had decided to go on Europe and the question of a referendum. He decided it should be just two questions if possible. I wondered about him maybe doing something on Ireland at the top, to signal it wouldn't just be gladiatorial combat the whole time. There was a push for him to do something more obviously domestic, but he felt this was where the Tories' main fault line was, it was the reality of their conference. PMQs day was obviously going to be stressful. He cleared the diary, and I was like a yo-yo up and down from my office up the stairs from his. 'Can you pop down and see Tony?' and we'd have pretty much the same conversation as before. He said: If you knew how I felt inside you would feel more sympathy. PMQs went fine. Anji was sitting with Cherie in the officials' box. I was up on the Opposition's bench in the press gallery, which was a good view of Major but not of Tony, but it seemed to go fine. As I walked out, Jon Craig [political editor, *Daily Express*] said 'Nil-nil' which was about right. I was surrounded by the hacks as we came out. Why Europe? Why Ireland? How did he prepare? Who helped him? Process, all they were really interested in. The reality was there was more interest in Tony than in Major and we had to capitalise on that.

Meeting with TB, Donald D, David M and Peter H re Social Justice Commission report. A problem. Went through it line by line but DD against the idea of line-by-line rejection/acceptance. Should say welcome contribution to debate but not Labour policy. Said GB had costed it at £20bn worst-case scenario. TB asked if it was really as modernising a document as being said, and DD thought not. TB agreed we welcome but don't allow to be taken as Labour policy. I said we had to guard against big rows running through the weekend, hype machine in full flow. DD said he felt John Smith would have rejected most of it. I said we'd get considerable credit if we were committed to looking at radical options re child benefit, pensions. DD said it was anti means test. Said GB was in a deep and dismal gloom about it. DD always managed to sound happy about other people's glooms, but gloomy about his own. I went up to the press gallery to see where they all were on it. 'Friends of Robin' I was told – i.e. Robin, I assumed – had been making clear that he was not too chuffed about the idea of being moved to Shadow Foreign Secretary. TB could scarcely believe it when I told him. Is he really saying the Foreign Office job [moving from Trade and Industry] is a demotion? I've only just persuaded Jack Cunningham to go to DTI. The only other possibility was that it was coming from JP because he didn't want RC there, but that was doubtful. If RC, TB said, a big mistake. He'd be good at it, what's more. PMQs impact was fine. Best thing being said was that it did not look at all odd for him to be there.

Wednesday, October 19

TB speech to PLP went pretty well. GB was beginning to get to TB over the Social Justice report. TB said he keeps telling me there's a problem but doesn't seem to have a solution. It's as if I set this whole thing up so as to give us a problem. I felt we were as well placed as we could be and Patricia [Hewitt] was clearly on for being sensible and co-operative. 6pm meeting fine, largely because Donald was brilliant, and held the thing together. GB was at the gloomy end of the market, saying that if we mishandled this, it could be the difference between winning and losing the election, and quoting liberally from the £20bn costing of the report. Tried to calm him, and he liked the idea of doing a briefing on Jonathan Powell's appointment and slipping in a partial welcome of the report. Pat H OK about that and would be briefing on wage subsidies and international labour markets. Pat flared up at one stage because DD, GB and Ed Balls [economic adviser to GB] insisted the proposals on child benefit and pensions were crude targeting. GB was so down about the whole thing we ended up wondering whether the strategy we had worked up was going to work at all. He said by Tuesday the Tories would be on spend, spend, spend. Maybe he was right, but we couldn't just wish the report away.

TB got the Shadow Cabinet election results around 8. MB did well, Jack S not as big a vote as expected. Press line was record number of women. Had to say young generation knocking on door, because the sense in the media was of dead wood. TB back from the women's committee, said, I didn't know Alice Mahon [Labour MP and leading light in the Socialist Campaign Group] was a fan of yours. Kept going on about how you speak her language and now you're on the payroll there's no need for Peter M. TB was dreading reshuffle. Everyone always had the highest hopes for themselves and most would be disappointed. Margaret B didn't seem too happy. Ditto RC which I couldn't understand. He can't seriously have thought TB was going to make anyone other than GB Shadow Chancellor. Jack C not delirious either.

Thursday, October 20

I'd only ever seen reshuffles from the media side of the fence, and could never understand why they always took so long. Surely the PM or Leader of the Opposition just did his list and told people what was what. Er no. First he had to decide what HE wanted. Then he had to find out whether that is what THEY would be prepared to do. And he had to get buy-in from the other big beasts, and if anyone said no to something, or started to negotiate, it was back to the drawing board. Plus there was all the planning going on around the junior jobs, which the Shadow Cabinet people themselves may not want. It was like a big jigsaw puzzle, but the shape of the puzzle kept changing.

Margaret felt that she ought really to be one of the big four jobs, having stood in as leader following John's death. And Mo was really not keen on N Ireland. I couldn't understand why anyone would not jump at NI. It had the potential to be about as interesting, and as important, as any other job. But I think she thought she was in for one of the big domestic jobs. MB eventually agreed to health, which in Labour terms was a big job, but she was clearly disappointed not to be in one of the top four. Robin making clear not happy. Phones going all day, like I used to ring, and now I understood why press officers always sounded so irritated. But they had the Neil Hamilton-Tim Smith sleaze story[1] to be going on with, which kept the heat off a little. PMQs. I saw something of the actor in TB, the careful preparation, the rehearsal, the need for time to compose himself, the need for assurance and reassurance. But it paid off. He looked and sounded the part, and the Tories were troubled by him.

Ian Greer [former Conservative agent and lobbyist], who was at the centre of the latest Tory sleaze story, was putting it round that his company, Ian Greer Associates, had funded a TB trip to the US. Went to see TB who was appointing middle-ranking spokesmen. Looked perplexed by it. Said check with Anji but he went on all-party lobbying delegation in 1985 on behalf of government and business, to lobby James Baker who was then Treasury Secretary. They were lobbying on unitary taxation. He could remember the withering look from Baker when TB 'gave him a piece of my mind'. TB almost done reshuffle. Kevin McNamara [Labour MP, relieved of the Northern Ireland brief] was almost in tears as he came out and when I went in TB looked really drained and upset. 'That was a really hard thing to do, telling a decent man doing a job he's really committed to that I didn't want him to do it any more. This reshuffle business is ghastly.'

My farewell do at the Reform. Mum said she couldn't believe all those Labour party leaders were there – Tony, Neil, Jim [Callaghan]. Richard [Stott] made a hilarious speech, his basic theme that it was really nice and noble of Tony to give up everything to be my press officer. Said the real reason Fiona had never married me was that, like so many other women, she was waiting to see if Peter M changes his mind. Cecil Parkinson[2] was there, and Richard gave no quarter

[1] Neil Hamilton, Conservative MP and junior Trade and Industry minister. Tim Smith, Conservative MP and junior Northern Ireland minister. Both resigned over the Mohamed Al Fayed 'cash for questions' scandal.
[2] Former Conservative MP. Resigned as Trade and Industry Secretary in 1983 after it was revealed his former secretary, Sarah Keays, was bearing his child. Went to the House of Lords after standing down as an MP in 1992.

to him either. Good turnout from the Tories – Alan Clark, Tristan Garel-Jones, David Davis – considering it was now officially my task to try to get rid of them. Really pleased that Frank Teasdale [Burnley chairman] and Jimmy Mullen [Burnley manager] made it. Lot of earbashing re the reshuffle, Clare, Brian Wilson devastated re [Michael] Meacher at transport.[1] Totally impossible job, Tony's, but interesting that it was my ear they were bashing, not his. I lost it with Brian, but then apologised because the reality was I'd had my fill of seeing all the egos at work and play, and I took it out on one of the few who was not as ego-driven as most of them. Real mix of my two lives. I had no doubt I was now on the right side of the fence. Mum and Dad enjoyed it.

Friday, October 21

TB called several times during the day, starting to get angry that the Social Justice speech wasn't up to the mark. He wanted Peter H and me to work on it. I said Anji was suggesting David M go up to Sedgefield and work with him on it, and he said he was fed up of being accompanied everywhere. He needed to have a bit of space from time to time. I was doing a briefing on it this afternoon, alongside Powell announcement for Sundays. Did Radio Lancashire double act with Leighton James [former Burnley footballer]. Told him he was the only real hero I ever had. Sunday briefing, had a row with Paul Routledge [*Daily Mirror* journalist] because he quoted back something at me that I hadn't said. He said no need to be rude. Said I'm not being rude but I'm not wasting my fucking time and breath on people who can't take down what I say and quote it accurately, rather than twist everything to their own agenda. Peter MacMahon [*Scotsman*] and David Wastell [*Telegraph*] called me later to say I shouldn't be so grumpy with them all.

Saturday, October 22

Martin Kettle's column in the *Guardian* was a pain because it claimed a TB bunker mentality was setting in already and Peter M had advised on reshuffle. Neil K came round 12.30 and we set off for Charlton vs Burnley, Rory going to be mascot. NK reasonably happy re reshuffle. Doubts re DB at education, and Joan Lestor [Overseas Development]. Generally OK though. Told him what a nightmare it was. He said he

[1] Michael Meacher held the Shadow transport brief 1994-95 before being moved to environment. Brian Wilson, Labour MP from 1987, had held the transport brief 1992-94 and would hold it again when Meacher moved on.

was often driven close to physical violence, once with Eric Heffer[1], and once when David Clark [Labour MP] didn't want the environment brief. Burnley players surprised to see Neil wandering into the dressing room. Great game, nice atmosphere, and the Burnley fans singing about Neil – 'Only one Neil Kinnock' – which was nice. Lots of good wishes for Tony as well. Fiona was still very steamed up that Cherie, having been one of the people most keen for me to work for Tony, was now so angry with me for doing what I thought was right. I said to her there really was no point falling out about it. As long as Tony knew that whatever I was doing, I had his interests at heart, we'd get over the odd spat and difficulty.

Sunday, October 23
TB sounded very chirpy, said he'd really enjoyed being able to work on his own for a few hours. I said I was a bit worried about him saying he was already feeling he needed space. What did he think it would be like being PM? You'd get no space at all. You can't even go out for a walk without a great palaver. He said maybe that's why I want to hang on to more space now.

Monday, October 24
Surprised to find Peter M at Tony's. Cherie very chilly. Went over the basic message for today, and made some last-minute changes to the Social Justice Commission speech. TB not sure whether this was going to be seen as too radical or not radical enough. I was dealing with Jack S who was up on a sleaze story, and Margaret B up on health. Meanwhile an interesting interlude when I got a call from Neil Wallis [deputy editor, the *Sun*] who said they were doing a major investigation on Carole's past, and in particular her links with the Exegesis cult. I said I didn't know she had any. Oh yes, he said. He said they would say it called into question Tony's judgement. I said this was a story about Carole Caplin not Tony Blair, and they should not make too much of it. Told TB whose concern was whether they would think this reflected badly on him and Cherie. I said we should be reasonably cool about it, but it underlined the need to be cautious about company. DD and GB sent over changes for the speech, GB wanting more focus on Better Off with Labour. Neil Wallis went through what they intended to run, and I said the statement that Cherie should have known about CC's

[1] Eric Heffer (1922-91), former left-wing MP who famously walked out of Neil Kinnock's 1985 conference speech when Kinnock savaged Liverpool's Militant leadership under Derek Hatton.

links to a cult was actionable. Why should she have known?

Got to the Connaught Rooms and could see TB was distracted. 'I hate it when the press get into the family.' I said that's why they do it. Speech went well, but in the car on the way back, he looked fed up. People were staring at him through the window and he was smiling, but his face wasn't happy. 'Do you like it when strangers come up to you like that?' Sometimes I do, sometimes I hate it, he said. But I know there's no way back from it now. I just console myself with the thought that one day it will be someone else, but hopefully I'll have done a fair bit with the time I get. He asked if I was glad I'd done the job. I said up to a point. It was hard work, harder even than I thought it would be. He said he was worried I worked too hard, and I needed to relax whenever I could. In the office got the *Sun* questions, which I went over with TB and then called CB who could barely bring herself to speak to me or Anji at the moment. It struck me as odd that they weren't asking if CB was still going to Carole C exercise class. Seemed an obvious question. Perhaps they just assumed CB had dropped her because of the fuss in Blackpool. Anji and I could scarcely conceal our exasperation that their basic posture was still to defend Carole. Spoke to Derry, who agreed it might be better if Carole was out of their lives, but it may be better to leave things until the story had calmed down. Also, he said, I know you have a job to do, but there have to be areas of their lives that Tony and Cherie are allowed to treat as totally private.

Tuesday, October 25

Didn't sleep well. The Cherie situation was a problem. I thought about writing to her, to point out that she more than anyone but Tony had fought for me to do the job, and I was only doing what I thought was best for them. Decided against. The *Sun* was grim but it was barely followed up, so I think we had been right not to overreact. Major called TB and said he would be making a statement and setting up an inquiry into the conduct of public life. Several times, Tony said 'right' with that upward lilt to the end of the syllable, which was usually his way of saying I've got the point, let's end the conversation, but JM kept going on and on. TB didn't like the sleaze issues. Said reality was our politics was probably least corrupt of anywhere in the world, and while the party advantage was there, the trouble was it ended up tarring all politics. He was excellent in the Chamber and the Tories seemed bewildered. TB spoke to Jim Callaghan who we originally thought might sit on the committee, but eventually settled on Peter Shore [former Labour Cabinet minister under Wilson and Callaghan]. TB there till midnight working out the last bits of the reshuffle. Ann Clwyd [Labour MP, foreign affairs frontbencher] being very difficult. Felt very sad watching Peter Pike [Labour MP] leave after TB had asked him to leave the job [as a frontbencher on housing].

Wednesday, October 26

TB said he hated the reshuffle. Peter H said his friends had said TB far too soft yesterday. TB to Walworth Road for renaming as John Smith House. Tories started trying to put round one or two sleaze stories re Tony, e.g. whether all his media payments declared. Didn't fly though. I just don't think people felt he was in it for money. Threatened the *Guardian* with a writ if they hinted at wrongdoing. TB said this was why he hated the focus on sleaze. Once that became the currency of politics, the media would love it, and if you try hard enough, you can make Mother Teresa look sleazy, if you manage to establish there is something wrong in the motives of the people who want to help her. *Observer* offered 1,500 words for TB. Got Tim [Allan] to start drafting and went to meet Jane Proctor of *Tatler*. She said *Tatler* readers were flocking over to Labour so she would like to do something with us. Anna [Healy] and Hilary [Coffman] said that there was a buzz Peter was to be a whip, and TB said if he was the story, rather than women into big jobs, he'd be livid. Went to the gallery to try to explain names being touted as whips were absurd.

Thursday, October 27

PMQs meeting, sleaze again. Big story in the *Guardian* re Jonathan Aitken/Ritz hotel bill.[1] Obvious line that Hamilton was being kicked out when they were saying he'd done nothing wrong, and Aitken was being kept in when it was clear he had. Main point re JM was his inconsistency and the inadequacy of the inquiries. Bruce Grocott said the PLP was up in arms at the idea of Peter being a whip. The neuralgic effect Peter had on the PLP was extraordinary. It was unfair in many ways as he was a real political talent, and they had a lot to thank him for. But he made a lot of enemies and he had the capacity to produce

[1] Jonathan Aitken, Conservative MP for South Thanet, had resigned from his Cabinet job as Chief Secretary to the Treasury to fight accusations that while Minister of State for Defence Procurement he violated ministerial rules by allowing an Arab businessman to pay for his stay at the Ritz Hotel in Paris. Aitken sued Granada TV's *World in Action* and the *Guardian* but his case collapsed when they countered his claim that his wife had paid the hotel bill by producing evidence that she had in fact been in Switzerland at the time. Aitken was subsequently charged with perjury and was in 1998 jailed for eighteen months.

unreason in people's responses to him. Bruce said the media put me and Peter in the same bracket, but that 'The PLP basically see you as Labour, but they worry about our Pete's basic politics.'

Robin Butler came over at 12.30 to brief TB on membership of Major's new committee. TB had seen him yesterday too and said if we keep meeting like this, I might as well be in government. The press were trying to get some non-story going about Barry Cox's son Buster being in Cherie's chambers because Barry had raised money for TB's leadership campaign. Tim was worried the Aitken story might not stack up and we shouldn't get too involved until we knew that it did. Feeling in the press gallery was mixed. TB was not sure it would work, Major was desperate to get down into the gutter and make it nasty. TB held up well, did three questions for the first time and general feeling among the hacks was that he got the better of it and JM was poor. TB not at all sure. He really didn't like this terri-tory. Mike Brunson [ITN political editor] said he won on points. Then we heard they were all doing stories on Cherie, including ITN. I called Brunson who was waiting for their arrival at the *Tribune* dinner, and asked how they could justify it as a story. He said it would only be a glancing reference to illustrate how ridiculous it was all becoming. I said we were saying nothing and if ITN wanted to be in the same category as the *Sun* and the *Star* who were chasing this story, carry on without our help. The Peter/whips thing was still doing the rounds, and the word was that Don Dixon [Labour deputy chief whip] didn't want to work with him. The Buster Cox story was contained to the *Mail*, and ITN's passing reference, so had a mild shouting match with Brunson. Good speech by TB.

Friday, October 28

TB constantly reanalysing his approach yesterday, which meant he wasn't happy about it. I said even the *Mail* were going at Major, and the news for him yesterday was bad. I just hate all this, he said. It is not what politics should be about. And I think the public just end up thinking all politics is bad. He was also worried that Cherie was now being targeted as a way of getting at him. She is as tough as old boots, he said, but it does unnerve me. Derek Foster [Labour chief whip] told me he was having a real problem with Don Dixon over Peter. He said in the end a lot of the opposition to Peter was probably down to the fact he was gay. The demonology went deep, beyond reason, considering the role he'd played in getting us to where we were. JP came in a bit worried because he'd been late declaring a Concorde trip. Sundays chasing all manner of stories re Tony's campaign funds and Register of Members' Interests. We had to emphasise the word actionable to a number of them.

Sunday, October 30

JP working on his speech in the office, and sorting out his Concorde problem. Said re Peter that if the PLP thought he was back to being 'Bobby' or being treated differently, TB would have a problem. The *Observer* ran a troublesome story that Don Dixon would resign if Peter was made a whip. Peter said Don was fine.

Monday, October 31

I alerted Derry to the [Oratory] school problem. He said, again, that you had to be careful about crossing the line on what were in the end personal decisions. I said sure, but where there were political implications, it was as well to be open about them. TB called re today's debate on the privileges committee, and agreed to meet to get line right for JP. Both not happy that all politics focusing on this at the moment, and keen to get on to Post Office privatisation tomorrow. JP asked me to work on a flourish at the end which would be what was used on TV, but we toned it down after hearing the Speaker was going to criticise the *Guardian*. Chat with TB re Cherie. He said he thought we should get it written about that she was being targeted by the Tories, which was fair enough. I used it to raise again my view that he was leading with his chin in sending Euan to the Oratory. I couldn't see the point of generating all the fuss it would cause. He said they'd decided it was the right school for Euan and that was that. I felt it would give him a political problem, and put Euan in the spotlight in a way I thought they wanted to avoid. The press would say it made the kids fair game. He was adamant that grant-maintained or not, it was the right school for him, and he was going, and he felt the public would understand he wanted the best for his kids. 'I am not going to sacrifice my kids' education for political correctness. It is not as if it is a private school, for heaven's sake. It is a state comprehensive.' Up to a point, I said. I asked him to imagine the Heseltine speech on the Labour leader who expected ordinary kids to go to the local sink school but shipped his own kids across London to a GM school the likes of which his party opposed. He said Tories sent their kids to private schools. I said they believe in private education, we don't. I asked if the local schools were really that bad, and he said all he knew was the Oratory was the best school for Euan. I said imagine the boost to the morale of the local school if you did send your kids there. He said that was the first persuasive argument I had put, but he was still not budging. Their minds were made up.

JP was getting into a rage before the debate, saying he couldn't find the right words and the right tone. He did fine. Afterwards we came back and tried to sort the whips business. Derek had the list but Don Dixon was making it clear Peter M was different, and his real job was liaison between the Whips Office and JP's office. Derek and I agreed it would inflame the situation but Don was adamant. By 6.30, with Don still effing and blinding, and the press sensing something was up, we decided just to put out the list, and I would brief the *Guardian* re the liaison role. Don shouted at one point: I didn't create Peter Mandelson. TB warned him he would only make matters worse if he went round saying Peter was a special case.

Tuesday, November 1

TB called to say JP had done well, and that he was doing Post Office for PMQs. I said I thought it was a mistake to clear the diary for PMQs days. He didn't need all morning to prepare. He said it's OK for you, but I have to do it. Until he felt totally on top of it, he wanted to keep the diary relatively free Tuesdays and Thursdays. Toured gallery after PMQs, general feeling Tony hadn't 'zinged' today. Met Christopher Hitchens [US-based British journalist working for *Vanity Fair*] who was doing a piece on New Labour, who was up, who was down, what Blair was all about. JP had a little party for Joyce's birthday [his secretary] and straight away asked me if I was responsible for the *Guardian* story re Peter. I said I was. It was Don's demand and if I hadn't done it we would not have had a list of whips to put out. JP said to Alan Meale [Labour MP, Prescott's parliamentary private secretary] it was Don's way of saving face after saying he would quit if Peter was made a whip. Kilfoyle said the PLP were pleased at my appointment but there were worries about some of the advice going to Tony, and the whips list was part of that. JP said he was going to be linking the whips to various campaigns.

Wednesday, November 2

Lunch with TB and a group of twelve women's mag editors. They were so different to our usual customers who were always just looking for the word out of place that might give them a story. TB was terrific with them.

Thursday, November 3

TB asked me if I was enjoying it. I said mostly, but it was a problem that the job was so all-consuming and Fiona didn't feel involved, and of course by the time I got home the last thing I wanted to do was go over all the same ground again. He said one thing I know is that you've made a massive difference to the operation and I need your energy and commitment. Philip G had been doing some focus groups – really impressed with TB, JP was doing well, but still no sense of strength in depth and also no real sense of party identity. PG said he'd shown a group of women some of TB's PMQs and they liked the way he spoke and they felt he was speaking up for them. He'd also presented some of the Tory messages and the only ones that got anywhere near working were the negative ones, so he was sure the Tories would be putting together a nasty negative campaign. That gave TB the opportunity to be above it. He had a positive approach that people liked.

Friday, November 4

TB on from Sedgefield. He said he needed a rest. Anji came back from a lunch with Charles Clarke who said the PLP were convinced Peter was basically running the office. I wish we could get them to be less obsessed about Peter. Anji was wound up about it but we agreed we just had to ignore the tittle-tattle stuff as best we could. As long as the PLP and the Shadow Cabinet felt we ran a tight, competent ship, we would keep their basic support. And so far, they were not questioning our basic competence and professionalism.

Saturday, November 5

JP on *Today* programme, said MPs should only have one job. Went to Reading vs Burnley, good 0–0 draw. Chatted to some of the players while they were warming up. Felt they were pretty onside, asking what TB was like etc., though [Adrian] Heath [Burnley FC player] was more interested to know if the chairman and the manager got pissed at my leaving do. He said Jimmy Mullen looked a bit knackered the next day.

Sunday, November 6

David Hill called saying RC had been on about a report about Labour trying to provoke a Maastricht 2 crisis over the European Contributions Bill. I said the line would combine our basic pro-Europeanism with troublemaking for the government. Then Robin called and his protestations made me feel he was trying to fuel the story. This was in keeping with what David said, and earlier GB, namely RC feeling TB too cautious. I said we had a perfectly good holding line pending the meeting of the economic committee, but felt RC was trying to bounce us. He said a holding line would not hold for very long in the face of a sustained interview. He agreed, in that very offhand way of his which makes you realise he doesn't agree at all, that he would do nothing proactive and if asked he would simply say discussions go on. He said he thought Tony would have difficulty avoiding a position of all out troublemaking for the government. Briefed TB, who had not read the story, but agreed 'Roberto', as for some reason he called him, was causing trouble on this. He said, I hope you were firm. We are pro Europe, anti government, and with maximum flexibility.

Monday, November 7

Meeting with TB, Geoff Norris [policy adviser], Miliband and Pat McFadden re Scotland. West Lothian Question[1] and how best to answer. He did an interview with the *Daily Record* and Pat identified three problems: 1. Did not push Scottish Parliament as first Queen's Speech priority; 2. Compared devolution politics with N Ireland; 3. Didn't go as far as George Robertson re sacking quango bosses. Didn't seem disastrous to me but you could never tell with the Scottish press. TB said he really wanted me to make efforts to get on with GB and Peter M. Said you three are the key to a real strategic capability and you have to work together. You are the least prima donnaish and you tend not to have your own angle. But I really want you all working together. TB was wanting GB to chair election planning which was not universally popular because GB could be very cautious when it came to decisions, which often meant last-minute planning. And of course JP had to be happy with whatever set-up we had. TB agreed the big picture was not clear at the moment, because there was no overall agreed strategy between the big players. He said the Tories were in real trouble but there was no automatic jump to Labour and that worried him. Peter M called and said he felt inhibited in his dealings with the office, and there were more than the usual knives out for him. I said we had to legitimise his role and have it accepted and part of a proper structure. He said fine, but there were an awful lot of people, and not just GB's people, blaming him for lack of strategy whilst also insisting he shouldn't be involved. I agreed the demonology was out of control, but some of it he fed. He couldn't deny that he partly thrived on the sense that he was

---

[1] First raised by Tam Dalyell, Labour MP for West Lothian, a dilemma of Scottish devolution. Dalyell asked how it could be right for Westminster MPs from Scotland to have no power to affect issues of their constituents taken over by the Scottish Parliament, yet be able to have the power to vote on issues affecting England.

scheming and at the centre of things. He said all he wanted was to have a set of working relationships that allowed him to work to the best advantage of TB and the party. Long chat with GB who was trying to persuade me that he really could make something of the tax loopholes. David Montgomery called asking if I would help broker a deal between MGN and the NUJ over the Paul Foot case.[1] TB said he had no objection provided it was done privately.

Tuesday, November 8

Peter M still expressing ignorance at why he was currently so un-popular. He said he'd stopped talking to journalists. Agreed that was sensible, and key to him being 'normalised'. The other key was JP and he had to work at that. Getting the structures right was going to be difficult. TB was settled so far on a weekly meeting of 'Big Guns' (TB, JP, GB, RC) plus myself. GB chairing election committee. But he also wanted weekly meetings with me, Peter, PG. I said we had to get to Peter's role being open. Peter operating hidden was not sensible and wouldn't be effective. I said everyone had to understand how draining it was, the time and energy we spent dealing with the issue, working round it, persuading people Peter was not as bad as his enemies said. He should be out in the open, and operating in a way that everyone can defend. Meanwhile we were trying to make sense of GB's tax reform press release. He sometimes managed to make things sound so complicated. TB had one of his 'would Robin be better?' moments, but it passed quickly. He said the election would be fought largely on tax, trust, the economy, and for all that he could be difficult to work with, GB had a great mind and operated at a far more strategic level than anyone else in the Shadow Cabinet. Didn't feel great, strangely unmotivated and I woke up with chest pains, feeling very stressed all of a sudden.

Wednesday, November 9

Midterm elections a disaster for [Bill] Clinton [US President]. In early for Queen's Speech meeting. DM had done an excellent outline. Derek Scott [Blair's economic adviser] was appallingly pro the Tory line on economic recovery. TB keen as usual for a mass of facts and figures to be gathered. He went to the *Q.Magazine* Awards, which I'd advised against, but they were clearly a success. Pat and I were working on two draft speeches for Scotland. A discussion on the Clause 4 situation.

[1] Foot was suing the *Daily Mirror* for constructive dismissal following the arrival of David Montgomery as chief executive. The case was settled.

We'd let things slip a bit. Pat's draft consultation paper had been seen by most of the big players now, but there remained a lot of opposition out there and we hadn't really taken the debate forward. I was worried that if we didn't press on with the TB/JP draft we would be accused of retreat. Pat warned that there could be more opposition to Tony's review than he thought. JP came down and agreed with the strategy of bringing the process forward but we wanted a real consultation based upon the clear themes we had laid out. TB said Bill Morris wanted a special conference. JP said it was a device to avoid him having a TGWU conference on it. TB said he was keen on an advisory referendum. JP: why bother when there will be a vote? TB was castigating himself that we let the grass grow under our feet. It went so much better than we expected at Blackpool that we sat back a bit. That was a mistake. Now we needed to motor. Clearly opponents were organising proper campaigns aimed at the CLPs and we had to get our arguments out there. Trying to lift the mood a little, I asked if TB would have to resign if he lost the vote. JP laughed and said it was all part of his master plan to become leader. We agreed I should start to brief up the consultation paper early next week. TB said he wanted a draft of his Queen's Speech debate speech by Friday. Left at 5.30 to meet up with Philip to go to a focus group in Edgware, all Con/Lab switchers. Hilarious moment when one woman said she thought Ian Lang [Conservative Scottish Secretary] ought to be Labour leader.

Thursday, November 10

TB/CB seeing the Queen. Briefed him on the groups before he left. He and JP strong, but remarkable levels of ignorance about anyone else. He raised GB again. Said it was difficult because he obviously felt his old allies were against him and yet if only he could be fully harnessed, he is brilliant. We are going to have to sort it out. Also emphasising the need for us to be the party of living standards. I heard from Philip that Peter had spent four hours with JP the night before, went to see JP. I asked how it went. He was in total grump mode. 'Presume he reported back?' No, I only found out by chance he'd been. He said the jigsaw was falling into place and it was obvious Gordon was carving him out of the election because he wanted to be in charge of strategy. So I've given up a front-bench portfolio but now I don't do the big election job. I said I didn't think it was all finalised. He said Harriet Harman had told Ian McCartney [Labour front-bencher] that Ed Miliband [policy official, later special adviser to GB, younger brother of David] was leaving her to work on GB's election strategy team, and GB's off to the States etc., etc., it all fits. I said he knew he was essential to everything we did, and he said he was tired of being told nothing could happen without him. He said he would not rock the boat but if GB was in charge of election strategy he found that hard to support. He looked crestfallen, said he was disappointed. He had a relationship of trust and he valued that. I said I would report back he was not happy. Re Peter, JP said he could work with him OK, but he sometimes felt Peter almost enjoyed being unpopular and he certainly enjoyed everyone thinking he was all-powerful. He went round the place behaving like a chief staff officer. Rosie [Winterton] asked if I minded Peter having a role in campaigns. I said I was not bothered; I wanted TB to have the structures he wanted and if I felt Peter got in my way unreasonably, I would deal with him. JP said TB felt he owed Gordon, because he stepped aside, and he owed 'Bobby', because he helped him, and we all have to accommodate that. I said it was also true that they had talent. Also, TB was as aware as anyone of the difficulties they brought with them, and JP was in a very strong position with TB. He had a veto on a lot of this. But I could tell both he and Rosie were pissed off. He said if someone in this is going to get a black eye, me or Gordon, then it's not going to be me. I called Anji as they arrived in Scotland to tell her just how pissed off he was. She spoke to TB and he got her to assure Rosie no final decisions had been taken and wouldn't be without his approval. Peter called, felt his meeting with JP went well. JP certainly sounded better disposed to him but there was a long way to go. I assumed TB had promised the role to GB but JP effectively had power of veto.

Friday, November 11

Anji called at 8 to say TB was in a real state re the Queen's Speech debate. He called as I was taking the kids to school and he went over the same ground. He said you sound irritated I'm raising all this. I said I get irritated when we have the same conversation. I know, he said, but it's how I work these things through. I'm not happy with the basic arguments. So we went round it again, education, tax, do we say it this way or that way. Went to see JP. Dudley [visit] had gone well.[1] Re GB he said: who knows what else he's been promised. He reminded me again of the time at Blackpool when he'd made the point that he was happy to support TB but he had to get support

---

[1] A by-election was being held in Dudley West, after the death of Conservative MP John Blackburn.

in return, and that meant for a proper role in opposition and in government. Harriet called re unemployment, and I seemed to upset her by asking her not to upset JP. She said it wasn't her fault if GB said he was in charge of elections but JP wasn't told. Then JP did his speech in Brighton where he aroused the interest of the press by appearing to question Gordon's economic conservatism. Felt a bit disaffected all day, partly at missing the Newspaper Press Fund do, where Jim Rodger[1] was on great form, organising celebs and dignitaries like clockwork, wheeling them in for one picture after another with TB.

Sylvie [driver] took the Queen's Speech [draft response] to meet him at the airport. Anji said the visit to Scotland had gone well, and it was the right thing to tell him none of us were yet happy with the speech because he really had to focus on it now. He'd admitted to her that he should have spoken to JP more about GB's role. He wanted GB and Peter M involved in strategy and maybe the best way to involve Peter was through JP. I told TB of JP speech and the way it was being interpreted. He asked if it was a mistake or a warning shot. I said probably the latter. JP was very pissed off at the way this had been handled and feeling he'd been excluded. TB said JP had not wanted the strategy job when they discussed this before. That's why he felt he should take a portfolio. GB was the best strategic mind we had. He said I can't be doing with all this, the time and energy I have to use on psychology. He'd had a session with GB in Scotland and had obviously been getting it from him too. I said well, we have to sort it, because the feeling at Walworth Road is that there is no clarity. Someone talked about strategic planning being a two-headed monster and it won't be long before the press are asking about it.

Saturday, November 12

TB fed up with the JP situation. He said he'd asked him at one point if he wanted the campaign planning role, and JP said he wasn't bothered. Now I want Gordon to do it, he's doing all this. He was complaining about his diary, particularly having so many speeches. He had a youth rally and a dinner today and of course the Cenotaph tomorrow. Out with the kids when TB called and spoke to Fiona. She said he sounded exhausted. He'd asked her if I was OK, and she said don't worry about him, he always gets fed up after he's started a new job.

[1] Legendary Scottish sports journalist and tireless worker for the NUJ and journalists' charities.

Monday, November 14

Tony sitting on his own on the sofa in the office, working in the near dark. 'Put some bloody lights on and stop looking so depressed,' I said. He said, I don't know what's wrong with me. I said you're tired, you're fed up with some of the problems you're dealing with, if you're like me you're feeling guilty about not seeing your kids enough and it's cold and miserable outside. Also, you're worrying about the QS speech which is the right thing to do because it's important and it's not there yet. He said he'd read some of Thatcher's in opposition and she was at her best when she had one clear message. I'd seen JP who was also fed up, and TB said that if JP simply refused to have GB chairing election strategy, he (TB) would have to do it. JP was even suspicious GB and Peter M were in cahoots on it. It's pretty incredible if you think about it – GB thinks I'm cutting him out of things; JP thinks I'm cutting him out of things; and what I really want is all of us just working together. He commissioned a load of work and then went off to see Derry for a father-figure chat. It was odd how sometimes the media would be saying things were all going wrong when in fact they weren't and at other times, like now, we'd all be feeling down but the media felt everything was going pretty well.

Tuesday, November 15

Met JP with Philip Gould. JP in jocular form: 'Advance, friend or foe, whichever thou art.' He was finally signed up to the idea that maybe we could learn something from focus groups. It was odd how polls were accepted as part of the political scene but there was something somehow wrong about actually sitting with a small group of individuals and trying to find out in depth what they really thought about politics. JP said he had mistrusted polling before because he felt at the last election it had been tailored to a pre-planned strategy. He was obviously pleased at his own position, which was strong. He connected with people in a way that most politicians didn't. PG tried to emphasise the nature of the real change that was taking place. People were coming over because they sensed we had changed. JP said in the end though it's about policy. Fair wages, of course they like that message. But what matters is whether we do the minimum wage, and how much it is. It was a positive, upbeat meeting and we agreed he should go to a group himself and just observe it.

After PG left I said to JP, re his friend or foe joke, that he had to understand the extent to which I fought his corner downstairs, and tried to make sure the others bore him in mind too. I wasn't

November '94: Voters switching because they sense change

daft and nor was he, and there was a political reality in his position which I was alive to. He might remember that when I agreed to take the job, I asked TB to make sure JP was happy with it. He said he valued our relationship which was very different to the days when I was slagging him off in print. This was a reference to a vicious piece I wrote for the *Mirror* during one of his deputy leadership challenges. He'd called to demand a right of reply and I said fine, and he said, can you help me write it, and I did. He said, I know your first loyalty is to Tony, that it was difficult for me with GB, and I had to play a deep game re Peter, but he hoped I could be straight with him and he was worried that last week I was holding something back. I said he had to see it from TB's perspective. He knew the people he rated and trusted and he just wanted to get them working together properly. You may not rate GB the strategist as highly as Tony does, but he does, and that's that. And you may think he overrates Peter, but he wants him involved and we have to find a way.

Wednesday, November 16

Queen's Speech. Up at crack of dawn and in with TB to go through the speech line by line. John Pienaar [BBC political journalist] called to say Number 10 were saying Major would threaten a general election if the EU Contributions Bill was defeated. TB went off for the Lords procession and when he came back was worried about it. RC of course had been on urging a vote against it and clearly if JM was turning it into effectively a vote of confidence, it would be odd if we supported him. But there were worries that some of the populist stuff was being lost and that the only story out of today would be Europe. That was fine on the Westminster village level, but there was a wider audience on which we needed to be heard about other things. TB spoke to RC, said that if JM had not made it the issue it was, we would not be opposed to the bill, we would table an amendment. If there was a genuine prospect of removing the government, it would be our duty to do that but if it is a big charade, we need to rethink our tactics. We should keep options open until we see if it is a genuine vote of confidence. We have to be careful they are not laying a trap for us. We tried to turn to our advantage by saying this was an attempt to create a diversion from such a threadbare programme. TB had really prepared but found it tough. If there is a worse nightmare than this, I've never had it, he said. He started nervously, but warmed up after taking a few interventions. Did OK, but it tailed off too much and he murdered some of the best lines. I think his hopes of what you could do in a speech like that were inflated. The general view was not great. David Bradshaw [*Mirror*] thought he was off form, Peter Riddell said TB was 'competent but not commanding.'

I felt he had not hit them as hard as he should have done, and he should have laid into [Norman] Lamont [former Conservative Chancellor of the Exchequer] and Ken Clarke, but TB felt he didn't just want to be seen as negative, the yah-boo stuff, but try to get over a positive message. He was down because he'd put a huge amount into it and it didn't really work. Trouble is, he said, it's always a triumph or a disaster. I said that was neither but because you've hoped for triumph, it feels like disaster. TB had a discussion with [Paddy] Ashdown [Liberal Democrat leader] re the EU bill. TB saying to Bruce G it was important to keep the Liberals involved. Bruce insistent that there would be trouble if we didn't vote against the bill. He also felt TB should be less worried about media reaction, and more about the PLP on this. He said he wished he hadn't played into the Europe thing, needed to be there speaking for the people in Parliament and it didn't work. He'd cut out the wrong bits, didn't hit them hard enough on the domestic agenda. He went home pretty downcast.

Thursday, November 17

TB on the phone after RC on *Today*. RC had not returned my calls last night and though he and TB had spoken, he went further than TB would have wanted. Led to Huw Edwards saying on the news that we'd virtually decided to vote against the second reading of the EU bill. TB asked me to get Robin in to see him. Bleeped RC who came back and said though he was busy preparing his speech for the debate, he could always find time for a chat with Tony. I said TB felt RC went further than they had agreed he should. RC said not. TB told him he should make clear we only vote against if there is a genuine prospect of bringing down the government. He felt the whole thing was a ploy. Agreed Robin should call Huw Edwards to put the story straight. Huw later complained (gently) that I'd set Robin loose on him. RC said Huw had told him the Treasury team was the source for his story, not RC's interview. He said he thought we'd given him a 'bum rap' earlier but all was now well. TB agreed to do *World at One* to set the position straight.

Then doing PPB [party political broadcast] filming where he took an age getting his hair sorted. Then an interview with the *Western Mail* which threw up another little mini drama. Ron Davies [Labour MP and Shadow Welsh Secretary] had apparently told the *Western*

Mail he would scrap the Cardiff Bay project [a huge regeneration initiative] which was not our policy. Hilary [Coffman] sorted that out and then TB, based on a chat with Ron we assumed, said he would play all that down, but say he wouldn't mind if the Welsh Assembly was called a 'Senedd' – Welsh for senate. What a lot of nonsense. Anyway, TB duly said it and David Cornock [*Western Mail* journalist] got very excited by it. As he left, Hilary asked why and he said because the feeling is that Senedd means more powers than Assembly. Our sense was that Ron had done a deal with Cornock, that he would get him off the Cardiff Bay story if he could get TB to say Senedd. Had to persuade Cornock he should not read any plan for beefed-up powers into that.

Clause 4 meeting. TB really getting seized of this now. He also wanted a post-mortem on yesterday's speech. He said both Cherie and Peter M had volunteered that they felt it lacked a single clear message. I liked the way he was big enough to admit mistakes and then try to learn from them. He said he wanted me to take charge of the party media operation as well as his. I said I was dreading the workload just growing and growing. Learn to delegate, he said. That seemed to contradict what he'd just said, but he disagreed. First meeting of the Big Guns, or *Les Grands Fusils*, as Anji and I called them: TB, JP, GB, RC, AC. Neil was in seeing TB so it started late. Agreed would put down a reasoned amendment, as the rebels were being brought off, and then maybe abstain on the bill. GB went over some of his pre-Budget thinking. RC seemed to be going out of his way to agree with TB. Clause 4, TB re plans to put it to NEC. JP worried we were seen as too pro Europe and GB said we should challenge JM to take part in the debate, if they were saying it was a motion of confidence. Gavin [Millar] popped in to see us later, said he had just been to a lawyers' conference, and everyone was slagging me off.

Friday, November 18

Calls started coming through that ministers were to get 4.7 per cent pay rise on the same formula to which TB was tied. Hilary and I convinced TB he should refuse as others in the public sector were being asked to accept a pay freeze. TB sceptical, felt it was one of those gestures that would backfire among what he called grown-up people, whilst those who thought it was a good idea would soon forget. I felt the background was a growing sense that politicians were loathed, and it wasn't just a matter of setting a party divide, it was about being a different sort of politician. PG felt strongly the same way, felt TB would go close to the same bracket as JM if he did take it. TB keen for Peter's view. I said Peter was a politician and would look at it from the politician's point of view which missed the point. By 4pm he agreed.

Went for lunch with Paul Potts [deputy editor, *Daily Express*] and Matthew Harding,[1] who had helped rescue Chelsea and said he wanted to help Labour. Fund-raising not really my thing, I said, but he could either help the office, pay a small private donation or make a large public donation to the party. Got the impression of a very likeable rogue. Back for Budget strategy meeting, but TB was a bit distracted, not happy with the pay rise decision, felt it was a gesture that would backfire. Another problem emerged, *Western Mail* had splashed exactly as we feared, TB promising a Senedd with beefed-up powers, alongside what looked like Ron Davies briefing on how this fucking thing would work. It looked like a Ron set-up and this was the result. I told Cornock it was his first and last interview; it was the opposite of what we'd said yesterday. He said he got the detail from elsewhere. I said the headline said it was proposed by Blair. Did a letter to the editor making clear I was aware of the 'deal' Cornock had done with Ron, but TB felt it was too strong. Anji felt it wouldn't have happened if one of us had been in for the meeting with Ron. TB said it comes to something if I can't trust my own Welsh spokesman to brief me for an interview with the *Western Mail*. News coverage of TB's non pay rise was brilliant, but TB still very sceptical. JP told him he thought it was crazy too – where do you stop? Called JP who was pissed off at TB's populist gesture.

Saturday, November 19

Brilliant press re pay. TB called after listening to Tony Newton [Conservative MP, Leader of the Commons] trying to defend Tories taking the rise. Accepted on balance the pay decision worked, but he felt long term may not have been right. I said he could feel free to blame me at any point in the future. He was on his way to the Unions 94 conference in Cardiff and said he wanted coverage for his labour market plans. I said what, from the Sunday papers? He was doorstepped on the wretched Senedd story. Philip and Gail came round for lunch and we spent much of the time talking about how

---

[1] Multimillionaire businessman who made his money in the reinsurance business. Ploughed cash into Chelsea FC of which he was vice chairman. Prominent supporter of New Labour.

November '94: Blair not to take pay rise

on earth to legitimise Peter so that he could work with us properly. Gail felt the whole operation had to run much less like a court and more like a business organisation with TB as chief executive. Dinner at the Brackenbury [restaurant] with John Humphrys [BBC presenter], Valerie Sanderson [BBC TV news presenter, Humphrys' partner], Neil Pearson [actor in TV news satire *Drop the Dead Donkey*] and his girl-friend Siobhan [Redmond, actress]. Humphrys and Pearson both said GB was awful and he had to come up with more detail on tax, not just play the gramophone record. Papers came. Someone had briefed Andy Grice (*Sunday Times*) on the Clause 4 consultation papers which was deeply irritating. Pearson interesting on luvvies for Labour; felt we would be better off with footballers. Humphrys and VS said I'd have no trouble getting back in at the Beeb after I finished with TB, and that Jenny Abramsky [controller, BBC Radio 5 Live] was a great fan of mine.

Sunday, November 20

In to see JP after reading papers and watching Blunkett on *Frost*. JP had travelled back from Cardiff with TB, and was a bit agitated re the *Sunday Times* Clause 4 story. Clearly someone had briefed Grice way beyond the content of TB's speech. Neither of us had much doubt it was probably Peter. We got Peter M on the speakerphone. JP had had a blast at GB earlier for leaving Cardiff straight after his speech and now he was having another one because Peter referred to another GB document JP didn't know about. Peter referred to the *S Times* story as 'accurate', thereby confirming our suspicions he put it there, but he denied it outright when I called him later, said Grice had spoken to him about Europe and the Civil Service, that Andy had mentioned the Clause 4 story but he hadn't been able to help him. I said you could have told me he was working on it and I could have put him right. I felt strongly enough about it to bother TB with it and pointed out there were direct quotes from the Clause 4 paper just shipped direct to the press, and not in a way that helped anyone. We could not have a separate briefing operation going on. He said he couldn't be bothered with this and I said nor can I but we have to grip it. He said he was more worried that even though things felt OK, there was a lack of the big picture, and we did not yet have the right overall political strategy that everyone understood and signed up to. Went to LWT to see Burnley vs Sheffield Utd on the live feed. 4-2. Brilliant. David Hill called at 10 re a *Financial Times* story about a John Maples [Conservative Party deputy chairman] memo to Major saying they should set their 'yobboes' on TB, which delighted us because it confirmed they were getting just about everything wrong at the moment.[1]

Monday, November 21

The *FT* 'Tory yobboes' story was brilliant, running pretty well on the news and I spent most of the day trying to fuel it. TB was keen we push two lines: 1. it shows how desperate they are; 2. that on the strategic questions they are getting it wrong and we are getting it right. TB doing *Standard* drama awards at the Savoy and we organised a doorstep on the Maples memo which was even better in full than David Hill's edited highlights last night. In the car TB said what it exposed was the total lack of a political strategy at Central Office. He did a word-perfect clip on the way in. TB and Richard Wilson [actor and Labour supporter] had a chat about what it was like dealing with sudden fame. Joan Collins [actress] made a beeline for TB but he was taken through to have his picture taken with [Dame] Maggie Smith [actress], who was pretty offhand, and Tom Courtenay [actor] who was really nice. Said his dad would be really proud of him meeting TB. At the lunch I was sitting with David Hare[2] and his wife and told him I would never have let him have the access he did for *Absence of War* and I didn't think he used it well. Also suggested to Stephen Glover [media commentator] that he return to his planet and find the other three beings who thought Major was wittier than TB during the Queen's Speech debate. What a deeply unpleasant man. If I had all that blackness inside me, I really would want to get off the planet. I had a really nice chat with John Oates, vicar of St Bride's [Fleet Street], who said he often talked about the address I did at John [Merritt]'s[3] memorial service.

Tuesday, November 22

Meeting at 4 with Philip and Peter M in W6 [Commons meeting room, off Westminster Hall] in which PG started re his strategy paper. I said before that we needed to sort out exactly who was doing what and

[1] Maples wrote a memo saying that the Tories should not discuss the NHS as it was a discussion they could never win. The Speaker, Betty Boothroyd, would promise to take action against Tory 'yobboes' who were being incited by Maples to disrupt speeches by Blair.

[2] Playwright. In the run-up to the 1992 election Neil Kinnock had allowed Hare close access for the writing of his play about a fictionalised Labour leader.

[3] *Daily Mirror* and *Observer* journalist. Campbell's closest friend from their days on the *Mirror* training scheme together. Died from leukaemia at the age of thirty-five in August 1992.

November '94: 'No Central Office political strategy' – TB

how it all fitted into the structures TB wanted. PG knew what I was talking about, Peter feigned ignorance. I said he should not be briefing the press on anything to do with TB or strategy. He said he was not at all sure TB would agree with that. I said I spent a good deal of my time defending him to his colleagues on the basis that he was no longer all over the press, but it was hard to keep doing that. It was always difficult having these conversations because he tended to deny outright that he was briefing the press, as with the Grice story. Also, he was so witty with it that we usually ended up having a great shouting match and then the meeting would end perfectly amicably. As we walked through Westminster Hall, and I headed off back to the office, he startled onlookers by suddenly yelling out, in the campest voice he could muster: 'Love you lots.' It is impossible not to like him, but I told TB that if Peter wasn't reined in and just part of the team, it would be a problem not just for me but for him as well. Anji was totally with me that it was intolerable if Peter was briefing. I said I'd never done a job I didn't enjoy and I could easily walk away from this, and I would if it was not possible to do on my terms. She spoke to TB who then spoke again to Peter. Anji called later to say that TB had said he wanted both of us working for him, but if he was forced to choose, he would keep me. I said there was no need to cut off Peter at all, and I didn't want that. I just wanted the thing sorted out. Got home, Fiona said TB had called and that I was upset re Peter. I said I wasn't upset, I was just determined to get everything sorted out and running properly. Peter was resisting proper executive structures because then he could float around being seen to be influential. It should not be difficult to work together. Had another chat with TB re the Oratory. I'd asked Kilfoyle to talk to him, which he did, but it was obvious he was not going to change his mind.

Wednesday, November 23

TB called at 8, and reiterated what he said re Peter. Work together, but understand you're in charge of the media operation. He asked me to contact RC and ask him to negotiate directly with the Tory rebels on the EU bill. Also had to work out what he would say at pre-Budget press conference tomorrow. There had been a meeting yesterday, which I missed, at which he and GB agreed to do it in two parts. TB/GB Thursday, GB Friday on the strong welfare-to-work plan. Good deal of confusion through the day, as TB felt it better to do it all in one go, but GB didn't. Agreed with David Hill and Jo Moore that TB should only do it if strong enough. Bruce said he was worried re the Oratory. I was also conscious, however, remembering something Derry had said, that I was getting too close into real family matters for comfort. Peter M called to say he'd won a *Spectator* magazine award as the member to watch – 'presumably by you' – and was I going to the lunch? Nice do, chatted with Tebbit and Cecil Parkinson re the old days. Back to the House and TB agreed to do press conference tomorrow. He'd just seen the union barons re Clause 4 and JP was in full flow when I arrived. Tom Sawyer looked exhausted, pretty obvious the meeting had not been great. Euro story was running hard re [Eurosceptic Conservative Party vice chairman] Patrick Nicholls' attack on France and Germany and Clarke's fiddled figures on the EU Budget. Did final changes to the PPB, then had to tell Jack, Harriet and Andrew [Smith, Labour MP, Shadow chief secretary to the Treasury] that only TB/GB would be speaking at the press conference. Jack Cunningham absolutely fine. Went upstairs to work on the *Tatler* piece, which was a bit of light relief. The obvious thing to do was a TB piece but I'd suggested they'd get an even bigger hit out of it if JP did it. JP in the *Tatler*. They liked it and we had a lot of laughs putting it together.

Left for Swindon vs Burnley. Bleeped by Anji during the match that Patrick Nicholls had quit. Spoke to a few Burnley fans at the station and suddenly it dawned on me there was a real danger JM might have to quit before an election, and the Tories could regroup and relaunch. 'He's a total goner,' one of them said. There was a contempt for him.

Thursday, November 24

Picked up by Terry [Rayner, driver], to TB's. He was still in his pyjamas getting Nicky his breakfast. Radio blaring out the Tory revolt. On the way in, going over PMQs, he wanted to do a specific question on the EU Budget, one on why he wasn't doing the debate, and a wrap on the various disasters – Maples, Nicholls, Clarke, and hitting them as an ill-disciplined rabble. To Church House for the press conference. We were worried it would all be overtaken by Europe. Jo Moore mentioned RC had done an interview on Europe for *News at One*. GB glowered at me and snapped: You've got to sort this out. I should be up on Europe because it's Clarke. I said I didn't think it mattered because it was likely we could get two packages on the news. GB shook his head then went off into a huddle with Whelan. He was giving the sense that everything was about to go wrong, whereas we had the dynamic with us at the moment, which meant more likely than not things would go right. Press conference was fine. TB did very strong statement at the top. Most of the questions were Budget-related. At the PMQs meeting we persuaded TB to drop the detailed money question and instead go on whether JM would lead for the government on the bill as it was now agreed by the Cabinet that it was a motion of confidence.

Probably TB's best PMQs yet. Our side loved the first question which got a huge roar and JM didn't look comfortable at all, and every time they were on Europe, you could see the divide on his benches, some heads shaking, some nodding. Meeting with TB and Tom S who felt the Clause 4 document wasn't clear enough on the economy. Then Big Guns. GB surly. JP went straight in on documents being circulated to the press before the politicians. GB defended himself, said the documents were not complete, Harriet and Donald had not cleared them. TB assured JP there was no attempt to exclude and there should be the widest possible disclosure but you could not always guarantee things would not leak to the press. Discussed Europe and agreed to table amendment forthwith, TB having lined up Ashdown's support. Agreement Clause 4 paper wasn't right and worry it would leak over the weekend as though an agreed document. GB had to leave early after which RC, pointedly, said to TB how useful these meetings were and how he appreciated the inclusive nature of the leadership. TB said it was important that whenever possible the Big Four were together on the big issues. JP said to me he couldn't fathom Gordon at the moment. TB said later he found GB's body language extraordinary. 'It's as if he thinks I shouldn't be talking to JP and Robin about what's going on.'

Friday, November 25

Papers brilliant post PMQs but Tony said he wasn't happy with it all because he was worried he'd come over as Old Labour. What utter balls. Edmonds came on to Pat McF with several late suggested changes to the Clause 4 document. Went for lunch with Tom Sawyer at Rodin's. He wanted to discuss general election teams. Agreed all the structures had to be open and above board, that TB may have to change what he wants if he can't sort JP and GB, that Peter has to be either in or out. He said he and TB had discussed the idea that I would be in overall charge with DH working effectively to me. He was worried re the JP/GB scene. Six months ago he would never have believed JP could chair a campaigns team but now he thinks he could but GB was clearly feeling he'd be left with nothing. JP is a ruthless operator and he was pretty determined on this. If that happens it's hard for Gordon. It's like a marriage and another woman just moves in. So he feels hurt and bruised. Tom said he'd always taken Neil's line on JP but he'd changed. He said he wanted to present an election structure to TB soon. He felt David Hill was good and as for Peter, his talents had to be weighed against the problems he caused because of the way people reacted to his personality. He felt the main team ought to be TB, JP, TS, AC, DH, PG. But TB wanted GB and Peter for their strategic minds. He wanted me alongside him, Peter standing back thinking strategy, DH possibly as the main press person working to us. TB came up to the office for a chat later and GB called. Only heard one side of the conversation but it was fairly obvious GB was complaining. 'For heaven's sake, Gordon, see it in perspective. I get criticised all the time. It's part of the job. I am not appeasing Prescott, but he is deputy leader of the party and he is a big player.' And he gets votes from certain quarters, I said, and he is the only one who is willing to do the *Today* programme tomorrow to beat up Angela Rumbold [Conservative Party deputy chairman]. TB to GB: 'We should all be doing what we have to do. JP is working on membership. You should be focusing on economic message and strategy, Tom should be sorting the organisation.' Later had the first warm and friendly chat with Cherie for ages. She even made a joke about him not taking the pay rise.

Sunday, November 27

A quiet day enlivened by some very Robinesque shenanigans over a Grice story saying there had been a TB/RC rift over Robin's non appointment to the Economic Policy Commission. TB asked me to convey to Robin that he was not very happy at what his 'friends', who were widely assumed to be Robin, were saying to the press. I loved these chats with Robin, because he managed to combine innocence, wit and political dexterity. First he professed total ignorance about the story. Not seen it. Not heard about it. I read it to him. 'It's garbage,' he said. 'I AM on the commission.' Oh, said I, knowing – or certainly assuming – he was not. He called me back within an hour to say he'd opened his NEC papers and it did indeed appear that it was not intended he was on it. Given the news management problem we now had, he said, and the suggestion of a rift with Tony, which none of us want, might it not be sensible if we said that he was, as chair of the National Policy Forum, entitled to attend the Economic Policy Commission? I ran it by TB, who was fine. Spoke to Charlie Whelan, who said GB would not be happy with that. TB said he was fed up having to sort out egos. Robin claimed GB had specifically asked him to be on the commission. TB said he was sure GB always intended he shouldn't be on it. 'I'm perfectly relaxed,' said RC, sounding anything but, 'but I think my formula helps us out of the problem.'

Monday, November 28

Got a cold. Tube in. Strategy meeting was hopeless. TB wasn't focused, JP was doing his pro heavy government thing, and Peter was pretending to support it. Tom S said nothing, and Rosie W chipped in with 'Are we clear about what is new about New Labour?' PG and I stressed our complaint that we always abandoned populist messages just when the public were starting to hear them. TB asked the five of us to draft out a proper written strategy. He said afterwards he thought people were a bit intimidated by JP when he went into full-on mode. It was a hopeless meeting largely because we were speaking different languages and TB wasn't clear what he wanted from it. The key people were too individualistic, doing their own thing without proper regard to the bigger strategic picture. Very dispiriting meeting, and it was almost a relief to get away for [*Mirror* journalist] Ron Ricketts' funeral, and back to my old milieu. Beautiful music and of course lots of people remembering John [Merritt] as well as Ron.

Back for another long and at times tedious meeting, this time chaired by JP, of his campaign management team. JP determined to get Shadow Cabinet more proactive on campaigns front. He wanted to know why the roadshow press conference cost £3,000. I said because we had a proper sound system, which was important. I said he should judge the cost against the coverage. Good sound, good pictures. David Hill said, rightly, that we still didn't focus enough on living standards. Back to watch the Clarke-Brown speeches on the EU finance bill. Clarke awful. GB good. One had prepared properly, one hadn't, though it was hard for Clarke with a mad party behind him. Media had a different take, and Brunson not great about GB. I joined a TB/GB/Andrew Smith meeting and TB asked how news was going. I made the mistake of telling the truth, said I thought GB had beaten Ken but Brunson said he thought GB gave a bad speech. It sent GB into a real tailspin, seething, though I wasn't sure whether the anger was directed at me for telling him or Brunson for saying it. He was going to have to get a thicker skin when it came to criticism. He clearly couldn't concentrate after that, and the meeting sort of fizzled out. Murray [Elder] told me he was leaving to work for Richard Faulkner [Labour-supporting lobbyist]. It hadn't really gelled, but I wondered if it was an Old Labour/New Labour thing.

Tuesday, November 29

TB read through his Budget speech again. He asked me to draft a 'tale of two Budgets' section, the people's Budget and the politician's Budget. I'd already done a Mr and Mrs Smith passage. TB said again if there was anything more nightmarish than these big parliamentary

November '94: GB must develop a thicker skin

set pieces, he didn't know what it was. Said we had no idea how nerve-racking it was. We worked away at it until just before 3 when the official Budget press pack came in. GB very impressive. We had precious little time to work out everything that was likely to be in it, but GB was hoovering the paper, tearing out the pages we should focus on, and running his black felt pen hard and thick up against the main points. Best lines were the VAT Budget, Mr and Mrs Smith passage, clear dividing lines. We had the Shadow Cabinet room packed full of helpers and advisers and we were number crunching as fast as we could. Clarke did OK though his delivery was unbelievably dull. TB was excellent, all the worry and the circular conversations paid off and he was applauded back into the office. Pat meanwhile was worried re Clause 4, feeling that Tom S and Jon Cruddas were not happy with where it was going, and things would be exacerbated by Murray's departure.

Meeting of the Big Guns minus GB who was busy on the Budget. Main focus Europe and whether to have a referendum. The general view was that the Tories would only be able to use a referendum as a way of quelling the issue short term. RC was foxing around. I felt instinctively he was against the single currency but they were all edging towards a referendum position. Robin said if we did it, better to do it sooner rather than later, possibly as early as Friday. Surely there was some mileage in being the first to pledge it. JP not so sure. RC was. TB said there was something that held him back re a referendum right now. RC said we were already pledged to referendums on Scotland, maybe N Ireland, and we could have an umbrella Referendum Act. He also raised the draft Clause 4 paper, saying there was no mention of unions in a positive light. Tom Sawyer came over for a meeting and we agreed yesterday's meeting was hopeless. Too many generals.

Wednesday, November 30

Murray called to say TB should call Tom Sawyer. Last night's meeting with the unions had gone badly and it was clearly not going well and the special conference on Clause 4 could get voted down at the NEC. I went to Walworth Road where David Hill said the atmosphere was really bad, even good people saying it had all been badly handled and if there was a vote on a special conference, we would get defeated. TB finally emerged with a furious-looking JP who said what a disaster area it had been. We just about managed to pretend it was a great win, 20–4, decision through, but already [Dennis] Skinner and [Diane] Abbott [Labour MPs] were briefing there was a delay to the special conference. TB did a consummate performance, at the end of which, however confused, people thought he must have won. We went back to Tom's office and though it was recoverable, TB was pretty exasperated at the lack of work done, and the state of the NEC. It's just not serious politics this. Back to the press gallery and most people were focused on the unions blocking conference line, and it was hard to push them off it.

Then we set off for Dudley. Walking across the concourse at Euston, got a message to call Hilary. The *Mail* had been on about Euan going to the Oratory. They had it as a fact and wanted our comment. We put together a short statement on the train and got it to David Hughes at the *Mail* via Hilary. Then heard it was the splash, which seemed to surprise TB, for all the discussion we'd had. Got to Dudley, fish and chips in the car, then the bleeps started coming through re the Oratory. I called Cherie to warn her and said it was important the kids didn't get too caught up in it. 'I didn't know you cared about these things,' she said, not without sarcasm. I said you'd be surprised. I said it was always bound to come out, it did not surprise me it was the *Mail*, they and the Tories would play it for all it was worth, and I'm simply alerting you. I had to phone Robin to get a line on what was going on re Bosnia. He said: My advice is to look serious and sober, look straight ahead and say something unutterably pompous. He did make me laugh, sometimes intentionally.

Thursday, December 1

Up just after 6, Oratory story going big. Agreed with *Breakfast News* they could do one question on it but otherwise we'd stick to what we discussed yesterday. I went in to see TB, who was standing stark naked reading the *Mail*. He said they hadn't carried our side of the story. There's a surprise. No, come on, he said, I know what you think but it's a Catholic comprehensive school and Euan's primary school is a feeder school. I said they're not interested in facts. They're interested in inflicting political and personal damage and this is the first thing they've got. He said his real concern was the effect on Euan but he was also asking what the effect on the public would be. I said it would be a lot worse in the party. Lots of people would support the idea you put your kids before politics, but if the Tories can make the hypocrite charge stick, and the party helps them just by keeping it as a running sore, it could be bad. It was also the case that the press were bored with kicking Major and praising you and this would let them get stuck into you a bit more. The Tories were going mainly on the fact it was a GM school. If I was them, I'd go more on Mr Community shipping his kids across London because the Labour community schools weren't good enough for them. He and I had been over the same argument so many times but now it was here and we were having to deal with it so we just had the arguments again. I tried my best to help, got a script done to make the best of the facts, and suggest he urge the Tories not to turn his children into a political football. He worked out what he was going to say on the school, said it, nothing more, nothing less, and moved on.

Dudley was full of Labour switchers and he got a fantastic reception. Only one reporter tried to doorstep him on the school, but we saw that off. As we left, he said: What a formidable operation we've got. I said: Apart from you, and he looked a bit hurt. That was a joke, I said. TB did *Anne and Nick* [daytime talk show] at Pebble Mill, during which Downing Street announced talks with Sinn Fein. Anne Diamond pushed him on the Oratory and he used a line that made the bulletins, and sent Fiona on the rampage, about not being prepared to do what was politically correct with his children. Tim called with [Conservative Education Secretary] Gillian Shephard's statement on it which took it on to a different level, and clearly Major will have given the go ahead for her to do it. We worked out the best way to deal with it but it wasn't easy. On the way into the press gallery, Jonathan Haslam [Major's press secretary] said: 'For once you've got the pads on.' I can't say I felt much like defending the whole thing.

Jacques Arnold [Conservative MP] asked JM the question that let him off the leash and they were really going for it. It was a blessed relief afterwards when the press surrounded David [Hill] rather than me, because he'd been more on top of the detail. I went downstairs and found TB with Hilary, GB, Peter, Bruce, and all pretty down. There had been a thought TB should put out a statement, which I thought was too defensive and better Blunkett do it. DB was up for being supportive. We had to cancel yet another meeting with PG. He said the worry was if this became a defining moment. TB asked again what was the public reaction. I said again, mixed. Some would support you. Others will say hypocrite. The damage comes if the party really helps the Tories keep it going, and you have hypocrisy and division rolled into one, and it all gets to you more than the usual because the family is involved. Not that I told you so. DB did an excellent interview but the news was awful. TB said the whole thing was ridiculously overblown, and we should be doing more to push back. This was difficult, because he knew I disapproved and he knew I wasn't very good at doing things if my heart wasn't in it. And we'd been arguing about it for weeks. He went potty when I said he should calm down. Bruce and I were pretty much in despair and feared a read-over into the Clause 4 situation. Pat [McFadden] felt it gave the party the sense he wasn't of them, his strength and his weakness. Fiona and Glenys both livid. I was through the anger on it, now working out how best to contain it. I was amazed the Tories, for all their strong words, hadn't actually got on to the biggest point of vulnerability on it, a Labour leader shipping his kids out of a Labour area because he thought the schools weren't good enough.

Friday, December 2

Papers grim. Peter called saying he hadn't realised this was coming now, but he thought we could turn it to our advantage. Nice try, but bollocks. The office was getting dozens of calls from party members really pissed off, some asking what they were meant to do with their local anti-GM campaigns. TB said up to them. Sue Jackson [head of support services in Blair's office] was virtually in tears. In truth, I told TB, the papers could have been worse, and he thought there would be a difference between the press and the public on this. I said it was the party that was the problem. They felt let down and confused by it. It was a big dent in the halo and the press would now feel they could pile in a lot harder. Plus the community message was blunted. I told him Fiona was barely speaking to me about it, let alone him. He called her and she was reasonably supportive but said she found it very hard to defend. Tim [Allan] was at the other end of the scale, saying TB should do a piece defending his decision as a parent in the *Mail*. I was worried that would just inflame the party further. TB said the problem was that I didn't think his decision was justified. True, but I said I was happy to make the best possible case. Peter M had persuaded him he should do a *Mail* piece, that we had to get his case out, so Peter, Tim and I drafted something.

Cherie had phoned and was angry that it was in the papers that she was keener on the Oratory than TB. We chatted for a while and after some polite talk, not really getting to the point, I sensed she was suggesting I had put that out. I said if she really believed that, she ought to have some evidence, and she ought to realise if she was that suspicious it would be quite difficult for me to carry on working for her husband. She said she thought I'd been giving TB too negative a picture of the school because I was personally opposed and it was actually none of my business. I said it was only my business in so far as Tony expected me to deal with the media and political flak, and I felt it was my job to warn him the flak would be considerable, which indeed it was. She said TB was really upset at the coverage. I said I can't be blamed for that. She seemed to think I had some kind of magical powers over the press, that I could somehow control what they did report and what they didn't. She was angry the *Sunday Times* were doing a profile of her and I said did she want me to speak to them and she said not on her behalf. At one point she appeared to suggest I was personally hostile because she was a Catholic or a barrister. I said I had never heard such an absurd statement. I understood why she was angry and upset but this was ridiculous. We hung up on pretty bad terms.

She called back ten minutes later to say sorry. I said I really did understand why this was difficult. She said she felt there was a hostility between us. I suggested the four of us went out and talked it all through. I reminded her that one of the reasons she'd been so keen for me to do the job was that she saw me as someone who would always tell him what I thought. She couldn't just turn because she didn't like what I was saying. She didn't want TB and Fiona involved at this stage. I told TB and he said she was upset but she did not mean to be hostile and she was probably feeling bad about it. 'It is difficult for Cherie and she doesn't have the same support I have.' I suspected she thought I was allowing my own views to colour my advice on this. Then we heard the *Mail* weren't running the piece, which probably meant they didn't think they could do much damage with it. Fiona was in a foul mood all night, as if it was me sending our kids there. This was turning into a fucking nightmare. I spend all day arguing one way telling him he's wrong, then get home and I'm sort of trying to defend him. Tim told Anji after hearing my conversation with CB that he wouldn't like to get on the wrong side of me. My big worry was that there would be a backlash in the party that would spill over into other issues like Clause 4, and that the press would now turn.

Saturday, December 3

Chat with Neil who said his real anger at the Oratory was the position it put Euan in. It also gave the press a way in to go at others over their kids' schools as a way of driving a wedge. In his job, you can't divorce the personal choice from the political any more. Tough but there it is, the reality of our times. I went to get the Sunday papers and they were grim. The *Observer* and the *Indy* were on exactly the points I'd been warning about, choice, community. If we were not careful, this would be a bridge to a 'what does he stand for?' campaign. Trouble in the *Sunday Times* too, with Jack Straw's 'slimmed-down monarchy.'[1]

[1] Shadow Home Secretary Straw had said the monarchy was 'caught at the crossroads between whether it continues at the apex of a very hierarchical class system in our society, or whether it moves over to be a symbol, a figurehead of a much more classless society.' Many believed this reflected Labour's views on the Royals.

Chat to TB and both of us pretty glum. Told him Hattersley's piece exactly as expected. 'Very helpful.' I said he was saying what a lot of our people would be thinking. He spoke to Fiona, who as ever was softer on him than she was on me for defending him. She said she could live with his personal choice so long as the policy focused on ensuring kids at the lower end got a decent chance, but if they changed policy to suit his decision, she'd probably leave the party.

Sunday, December 4

I didn't think TB fully grasped the potential damage being caused by the Oratory. He said, anyone would think I'd sent him to Eton. I said we had to watch a kind of revenge crossover to Clause 4. Glenys had said it would drain goodwill. At least he could laugh about himself still. 'Not much chance of persuading the country if I can't persuade my press secretary and his missus.' I said I'd had to stop Fiona pinning the *Indy on Sunday* editorial to the front door for Neil and Glenys to read on arrival. We were all going for a party at Helena Kennedy's [QC and civil liberties campaigner] but Rory, Calum and I left to watch Chester-Burnley on Sky then went back and the whole place was arguing about the bloody Oratory, because the Kennedys were sending their son there too. I left them to it, went upstairs and called JP, who was also getting flak. He said you did all you could but his mind was made up. You warned there would be damage and there is. He said he'd been wary about being too heavy on it because you've got to be careful pushing too hard on family/personal. Watched *Spitting Image* [topical TV satire], which had a field day on the Oratory.

Monday, December 5

TB was far more up than at the weekend. I'd noticed that he didn't need that much rest time to get rested. He said he'd recovered his equilibrium and we should never have lost it. We were far too flaky over the opt-out issue. On the Oratory we should have been clearer, stronger and had a strategy ready to go. He said I had got very down and hangdog about it, and I was the linchpin of the operation and everyone weakened. Whatever my views, I had to be professional about these things. I couldn't really deny I'd allowed my views to get in the way of doing what he felt should be done. But I felt every new line of defence opened new lines of attack against him. Better maybe to shut up and get the policy right as it affects most schools. We had two central problems strategically: communications were not strong or clear enough; and we were not in control of the Clause 4 debate. TB wanted a detailed week-by-week month-by-month strategy up to the spring. Basic 'on your side', 'party of the people' messages were key, but the policies, the arguments, the events had to drive them home. TB also clear that we had to ensure we were not getting cluttered up, e.g. as Jack had done on the monarchy. Discussed Euro referendum. JP keen but I was worried to do it right now would look opportunistic.

Tuesday, December 6

TB still pretty dreadful re school. 'Why are they still going on about it?' he said. Because they know it hurts us.

Went through PMQs mainly with Gordon, also discussed Clause 4 and Euro referendum, and in between times dealing with some story the *Mail* were chasing about TB's bloody haircut.[1] GB put strong case against a referendum announcement, let alone pre-empting them now. In principle everyone agreed but TB felt if the Tories were going to end up doing it, which they were, and we would probably have to do the same, then there was something to be said for being out front with it. I argued it might be better to wait and try to create conditions that made it harder and harder for them to be able to do it, because JM would not want to look like doing it out of weakness. GB and I also arguing still for special conference on Clause 4. He warned the Scottish party conference might defeat us on Clause 4 just before a special conference. Meanwhile another set-to with Peter because having persuaded TB against going for the referendum now, he was in there now trying to persuade the opposite.

4.45 meeting with RC, Murray and Nick Sigler [Labour's international officer] re the Essen summit and PES.[2] JP came in towards the end for a Big Guns meeting and took umbrage that TB and Robin were discussing Essen without him. Called out by Anji to deal with Cherie and the Oratory headmaster, John McIntosh, who was being hassled by the *Guardian*. I had a perfectly polite chat with CB then called McIntosh advising him to stress working-class children were there, how Labour education policy was not a matter for him and he was not some right-wing loony on the subject. I didn't feel he and I were on the same wavelength. 6.45 meeting with TB, GB, Peter re referendum; nothing right now, keep it under review. TB arguing that if the Tories went for it, it would be hard to stand aside. GB argued we could hold the line for some time. He was at his most impressive when he had thought through a position and really powered the argument through. I think he was right on this.

[1] The *Mail* accused Blair of having a £60 haircut from an elite hairdresser at home.
[2] Meeting of the Party of European Socialists at the European Council in Essen.

Out to a dinner for Norman Pearlstine [editor-in-chief, Time Inc.] at the Savoy. In the car Cherie asked, almost in jest, if I'd managed to get Euan expelled yet. I kept getting called out by people following up the *Mail* story about TB's hair. Left the dinner at 9.30 to go back to the House for the vote on VAT. For all the hype everyone had been expecting the government to win so when the result came through all hell broke loose.[1] I watched Major and Clarke heading back to JM's office looking utterly dejected. We put out a few words to PA [Press Association] about a dying, discredited government unfit to govern. There was a sense this was an important moment, and I also felt it might help GB get his confidence back, and stop being so down about everything.

Wednesday, December 7

Left at 6.30 to get to Tony's and plan for *Today*. In the car, going over all the points we needed to get over, a historic win for a Labour Party reconnecting with the public.

Robin Butler and Stella Rimington [director general of MI5] were coming to see TB. He called me in, and looked pretty alarmed, said he was only telling me this because I may have to deal with it. It was that a book was coming out[2] alleging Michael Foot [Labour Party leader 1980-83] and Jack Jones [former general secretary of the TGWU] helped the Russians and that Richard Gott [left-wing journalist] of the *Guardian* was a KGB agent. JP came in later and volunteered that he thought GB did well yesterday and had got his confidence back. Meanwhile interest rates had gone up and GB came over to agree how we react. Vital to distance from the VAT vote, all about the weakness of the fundamentals. TB said Harriet had told him I'd slagged off Helena Kennedy re the Oratory and I said it's true. I found it very difficult.

Then into a meeting on Clause 4 with Sawyer, Cruddas, Pat, Rosie, etc. TB dead set on a special conference but Cruddas had the

---

[1] Clarke's Budget proposal to increase VAT on domestic fuel from 8% to 17.5% was defeated 324-297 by a Labour motion supported by smaller parties and seven Conservative rebels.

[2] The book, published the following year, was *Next Stop Execution*, by Oleg Gordievsky, a former London bureau chief of the KGB. It claimed that Michael Foot was a KGB agent 'of influence', with the codename 'Boot', and Foot successfully sued the *Sunday Times* after the paper repeated this in an article derived from the book. The book also alleged that Jack Jones had provided intelligence to the Soviet Union in return for money – denied by Jones – and named Richard Gott as a KGB agent, an accusation he denied. After publication of the allegation in a magazine, Gott resigned from the *Guardian* in December 1994, confessing he had failed to inform his editor of trips abroad to meet KGB officials.

figures on the way a vote might go and there was a real risk we could lose a vote at a special conference. TB said it was important people understand that if we lost a vote on Clause 4, he would have to quit as leader. He also believed that if we lost a vote on Clause 4, we would lose the election because the public would conclude we were not a serious party. 'People need to understand if we lose on this, we might as well pack up.' TB said we basically had to go on to an election-type footing for this. He was on great form, refusing to accept what he saw as illogical arguments, determined to challenge them and win the party round.

Then late meeting Fiona at Camden Brasserie. She was saying I had no time for anything but the job.

Thursday, December 8

I was pretty upset re last night's discussion with Fiona, took the boys to school then in to see TB re PMQs. He was on the phone to Derry who had come round to my/GB's view that there was no great mileage in being ahead of them on a referendum. We should be making it harder for JM so that when he did it, it was a sign of weakness, a device to unite his party for a while, whereas when we did it, nobody would be shocked. PMQs was fine, the Tories did a number on school and hair. Then Clarke statement. GB did fine but Clarke came back brilliantly, culminating in 'Silly Billy.' GB was a bit downcast but I kept trying to explain that the story was taxes up. Another Clause 4 meeting, TB clear that 'these fuckers need to understand if we lose on this, we might as well pack up'.

Friday, December 9

TB in Sedgefield. Government talks with Sinn Fein so very little demand for us. The *Guardian* said they hadn't run my letter [on the Oratory] because it was too personal. They love giving it, these people, but can't take criticism at all. Briefing the Sundays that Blair was ordering election alert. Lunch with Nick Guthrie [BBC] who would be doing election night. He said they needed more archive material and could do with a day on the road with TB.

Sunday, December 11

Watched Portillo on *Frost*. Fascinating. Seemed to be against a referendum because he didn't think it would be about Europe and they needed to change the policy to make it more Eurosceptic and therefore they wouldn't need a referendum. Papers fine, especially Clarke/Hezza against a referendum. Suggested to TB we go to Dudley on Wednesday.

Worried re turnout. Tim called to say RC very sniffy about not going further than TB re referendum. He felt we could not hold the line much longer which was total balls. He was due to do *On the Record* and said to TB he would need to speak to him, which he did. Peter and I had a discussion about whether TB should go on a winter holiday. Peter/PG thought it was fine but I feared an own goal, TB sunning himself while pensioners froze, we could do without it. Peter pointed out that TB had to be fit and rested for the road into the election, and he needed some sun and a break. A few calls during the day on referendum, RC having gone a little bit further than he should have done after TB spoke to him. Philip and Gail came for lunch. Got the feeling Gail felt pretty much the same as Fiona about how much we had to put into the job. PG and I both felt we were getting close to a proper strategy. JP called on his train from Hull to Dudley and kept cutting out. He said he'd had Daddy Blair on asking what he was going to be saying in his interviews tomorrow. I said we were all a bit knackered and just limping to Christmas really. TB had had his first bloody nose and he needed to reconnect with the party. I said I know you do a lot, but TB has to do more than any of us. He agreed but said on the education policy there was no way we could change the policy to suit his personal circumstances. Not on. I said to TB that JP was finally seized of his status and significance and occasionally he would use it but he was basically on board. But he should never be taken for granted. And we needed to be aware that it was possible for him to be popular at TB's expense and with this Clause 4 thing unpredictable, it was really important to keep him involved and on board.

Monday, December 12

Up to hear JP on the *Today* programme. I'd briefed him on the 'options open' line on Europe last night but he virtually committed us to a referendum. TB was straight on the phone. 'Did you speak to him or not? That was a pretty extraordinary interview. That was JP saying he would go his own way. It's almost OK on this but what if we were dancing on pins on interest rates.' He was also worried because it went further than we'd agreed with GB. I said I would immediately brief that it was all part of an open-options policy, aimed at unsettling the Tories, and meanwhile he should speak to JP in Dudley, and make clear when he said 'definitely' we meant we would definitely consider a referendum not that we would definitely have one. JP called after TB spoke to him and said 'What did you put in his porridge this morning?' so he must have left no doubt. JP agreed he would emphasise open options and no final commitment to anything. Fraser Kemp called after the press conference, said JP did fine, slightly rowed back, options open. TB pretty steamed up about it though and he had a proper chat with JP, said we just about got away with it today but imagine that kind of thing under the heat and pressure of an election campaign. He said to JP he had to decide if he was George Brown [Labour Party deputy leader 1960–70 and notorious drinker] or Ernie Bevin [Labour movement titan, Foreign Secretary 1945–51]. JP clearly took it to heart because at the Shadow Cabinet party he took me aside and said he knew he'd ballsed it up, and his problem was he sometimes forgot the league we were in, and that sometimes it was as well to say no as yes. He didn't need to do that programme. I briefed that it was all part of a strategy to confuse the opposition. GB pushing for Joy Johnson [BBC political journalist] for Walworth Road. TB impressed she was willing to leave the BBC but not convinced she was a moderniser. We persuaded TB that he should go to Dudley overnight to put his stamp on the by-election. Anji came in with the *Standard* – 'LABOUR POLL PLEDGE' – from JP. I spoke to the *Standard* and PA and pushed the options open line to try to calm it down.

Up to the gallery by which time the *Telegraph* were on to the Sue Jackson incident she'd phoned me about on Friday when she found three young Tories in TB's office. The story spread like wildfire and I was briefing away on it. Then the *Sun* got a bit heavy that we were saying this without letting them speak to Sue. Got them to call her. Noreen Taylor [*Mirror* journalist] called to say she'd been at a *Sunday Times* lunch where a Mirror Group freelance journalist and columnist, who didn't seem to realise Noreen and I were friends, was telling all and sundry that I beat up Fiona and she was always turning up at school with black eyes. Some people are utter poison. My instinct, and Tony's when I discussed it, was to slap a writ on her, but Fiona and Derry thought ignore it. I made sure Montgomery knew one of his columnists was wandering round the place smearing people and talking drivel.

Tuesday, December 13

Papers were extraordinary, if not ridiculous. 'BLAIRGATE' the splash in several papers, including *The Times*. Second story on BBC. Textbook case of setting something off gently, then letting the media just drive it on through their own enquiries and momentum. Didn't look good for the Tories though. I called the office to discover Betty Boothroyd had been to look at the 'scene of the crime'. TB was worried about being away again on PMQs day. Also asked me whether I thought I picked too many fights with journalists. And whether I thought it was too late for JM to recover. I felt that unless they came up with a set of strategies that could get real buy-in from the Tory Party, he was a goner, but we had to assume he could do that. I felt it was part of my job to imagine the worst-case scenarios including the Tories getting their act together.

TB did a fascinating meeting with a group of switchers, which was like a focus group with media present. Even though the media did the usual 'carefully stage-managed' bollocks, I noticed one or two of them clocking that it was genuinely interesting to hear real-people explanations in real-people language about why they were switching. In the car with TB and the candidate, Ian Pearson, I said it was important on Friday morning that he emphasised it was a victory for TB and New Labour. Poll in the local paper had us on 71, Tories 18. Ridiculous. On the train back he decided to do rail at PMQs.

Got to Euston with Blairgate running well on the news. PMQs fine, then a statement on the intruders, Betty saying they were having their credentials [security passes] withdrawn. As I went downstairs for TB meeting with our 300,000th member, TB was talking to JP. He said: 'You won't believe this. As we came out of the chamber, the prime minister took us both aside and said John, I hear Alastair had to go round the gallery to clear up your mess yesterday.' Once a whip, always a whip, I said. Classic Major. I briefed a little on NEC Clause 4 tomorrow, on a knife-edge. Got a lift home with TB. He said he couldn't believe the NEC sometimes. He said he was going to meet Ashdown soon and we had to think carefully about how we handle the Littleborough and Saddleworth by-election.[1]

Wednesday, December 14

Terrific press from Dudley, though the big picture of me in the *Guardian*, looking like a bulldog, worried us both that I was getting too much coverage. NEC. TB was irritated that Jack [Straw] and Robin focused on pedantic points. We won the NEC vote 20–3 but the mood was sullen rather than positive. TB and I left for lunch with Lord Hanson [Thatcherite businessman] and his board, which I enjoyed more than I thought I would, chatting to Hanson mainly about Yorkshire, while TB worked his charm on the rest of them, and they seemed impressed. I couldn't imagine him backing us, but he barely mentioned JM. Big Guns meeting. TB felt we had to get our economic message tighter and that we had to get more disciplined in our approach to speeches so that we

[1] Conservative MP Geoffrey Dickens would die in May 1995 after a long fight against cancer.

were all working to an agreed strategy. RC said it was hard to get coverage for a positive agenda. I said the only way was to keep at it, not to give up on honing the basic messages, and keep going in pushing those messages out. GB said we needed broader access to the polling.

Thursday, December 15

TB had had dinner with Roy Jenkins, said he liked his company, and for the first time I can recall he said he had a bit of a hangover. He said we were working him too hard and yet again he asked Anji to try to get a better grip on the diary. Anji said to him: 'Have you any idea how hard we work for you, and how much we do to keep things out of your diary?' She felt there was nothing there that wasn't either politically essential, or something he'd asked to do, and she asked whether he'd noticed that most days, when he went home to see his kids, she, I and some of the others were still there working for him. I was drafting reactions to the by-election in advance, including a piece for the *Sun* for later editions. When I was going through it with TB he said I should watch my own back with the press; at some point they would turn on me and I should try to avoid giving them the ammunition. I said it was inevitable, but frankly while we were in such a strong position, I was keen to change the terms of the debate, and make them understand that we would decide how we interacted with the media, not them. Alan Clark called to say he was backing Gillian Shephard for leader. I couldn't quite work out whether he was serious.

TB on form at PMQs, JM got into the gutter again with a planted question on the Oratory.[1] TB was really irritating the staff at the moment, incredibly demanding and complaining. He was constantly asking for updates from Dudley, and the sense of a big win rose as the day wore on. Stayed up for the by-election. 20,694 majority for Labour – almost a thirty per cent swing to us from the Tories.[2] JP terrific on the box, even talking about it being a great win for NEW Labour. When I spoke to him he said he only did it because Stephen Dorrell [Conservative Heritage Secretary] tried to wind him up when the cameras were off, saying 'You don't believe in all this NEW Labour nonsense.' Ian Pearson delivered our message word-perfect.

[1] Conservative MP Bob Dunn asked Major if he had any advice for the people of Islington, given that education in the borough was not good enough for the Leader of the Opposition. Major responded: 'We need the highest quality of education in Islington not just for the Right Honourable Gentleman, of course, but for every Islington resident whose children attend schools there.'
[2] The largest swing since World War Two, demonstrating Blair's revival of Labour fortunes.

December '94: TB warns AC about press

Friday, December 16

Terry arrived at 6.45, off to TB's, Cherie welcoming, and asking me to help with Euan's homework. In the car we agreed he should stress no complacency, not too upbeat, hard work goes on. Got to Millbank, TB did *Today* then nine other interviews before 8.55. His best was *GMTV* because Eamonn Holmes [TV presenter] got him relaxed. TB then off to Belfast to see the troops and do some visits. Clause 4 was more important than ever now. We won because the Tories were useless, but we won big because people sensed the change was real. Clause 4 would make that unchallengeable, and the sense of a battle helped, provided we win.

Saturday, December 17

TB called saying Mo and others were saying the Clause 4 scene wasn't great. Fiona and I went to David and Janice Blackburn's [family friends of AC] party. Peter M there. [Andreas] Whittam Smith [founding editor of the *Independent*]. Carole Stone [PR consultant and networker]. I spent a lot of the time talking to Tom Bower [author and journalist] who wanted to do a book on TB, *The Making of a Premier*. Er, no thank you.

Sunday, December 18

Up at 6, got briefed re *Frost*, then over to TB's. Chatted over the various issues likely to come up, mainly Europe. Lots of 'friends of Blair' briefing in the papers, which TB thought may have been George Robertson. I said it was time he started going a bit ballistic at all the chatter. It was always bad at Christmas, but we had to get a grip. *Sunday Times* was saying JM may go for a referendum as a way of uniting the Tories, which was clearly going to be the story of the day. Arrived, and he got very irritated with the make-up woman who kept trying to fiddle with his hair. When Frost asked re the referendum story, TB said that an attempt to restore party unity was the worst possible reason to do it. Alan Clark, who had been reviewing the papers with Helena Kennedy, was sitting a couple of seats away from me at the back of the studio and he nodded so hard I thought he was going to fall out of his chair and land on the floor. Throughout the interview he would look over to me, and either nod sagely or raise a thumb in a 'Your boy's doing well' signal. And indeed at the end, said 'Your boy did well.' His liking for TB was matched only by his growing disregard for his own boy. TB did well but in the car afterwards, I said I didn't much like the answer where he joked about being a Tory.

Monday, December 19

Late in after taking boys to school. Strategy meeting a bit tired and vague. We agreed that living standards should be the theme for the next three months, tied in to privatisation. TB wanted JP to do a party 'head and body' piece for the *Guardian* or *Indy*. Peter M was talking about auditing all Tory statements for the lies they told. Very poor meeting, unfocused, though Karen Buck [campaign strategy co-ordinator] was quite impressive. DH emphasised to TB that we would not be able to move forward on living standards without real and enthusiastic commitment from GB. The looks around the room did not ooze confidence it would be forthcoming. To Neil's party, which was at a room in the Treasury. Mainly chatting with Charles Clarke and Dick Clements [former *Tribune* editor and aide to Kinnock], who felt I was sending off too many letters to the press. It was nice to see Neil in a good office, and looking in his element. Then up to JP's party for Ian Pearson. Fraser [Kemp] was there, soon to take over as Tom Sawyer's special projects man. Then Murray's farewell and our office party for the press, with them all swarming round TB. I chatted to Tony Bevins then had to deal with a mini flurry because some of them had gone off with the impression TB had signalled a shift on devolution. These parties are nothing but trouble. Everyone is pretending to be nice to everyone else but basically the politicians loosen up and the journos are just hoovering up stories, some of them even true.

Tuesday, December 20

Another run round the block on education. TB said they'll have Euan on *Spitting Image* next. Another little flurry when Hilary was sent what purported to be an account of what Major said to the Central Office Xmas party. We gave it to the *Standard*, Robin Oakley [BBC political editor] and Mike Brunson making clear we couldn't vouch for the accuracy. Central Office denied it was his words which should have been that, but Mike B did a big Labour dirty tricks number on the 12.40. As Hilary said, if it was a Labour dirty tricks job, it wasn't very effective. But it was a pain, and showed how careful we have to be, and how much the media likes going on about dirty tricks if they can. Big Guns at 2.30 prior to which TB had had an hour with GB and Peter M trying to get them to work together better. The atmosphere by the time I got back suggested the meeting had not been entirely fruitful. TB then had a private session with GB and by the time JP and I trooped in the mood was not great. Mainly discussing economic message, devolution, Europe. TB started by venting his anger

December '94: Big Guns must work together better – TB

on all the leaking and briefing going on and RC said TB really must lay down the law, which made me chuckle. RC and JP protested (gently) that they felt they were not seeing all the relevant papers on Europe. GB looked very defensive. He said he'd sort it, but he had his arms folded into his stomach, his eyes looking down. GB had to leave early, then JP and RC, sensing TB was pretty down at the moment, told him they thought he was doing really well and the PLP was a bit bemused that he had been so downbeat after Dudley. TB said there was too much complacency around. We chatted re Clause 4, JP saying that any covert campaigning would backfire, and RC saying we had to broaden out from the usual voices of support. Took the kids to see *Babes in the Wood*, came out to find the car window smashed in.

Wednesday, December 21

Just about got away with 'Hilarygate'. I wanted a big push on Clause 4, but TB felt he had to be majoring on education, wanting to take the argument to the Tories. We had a little flurry when TB, back from his three-hour briefing at MI6, realised he'd left some of the papers at home, and Terry had to be despatched to retrieve them. TB called later after his homeless visit to say some of the press had complained that they weren't destitute enough! 'These people are unbelievable.' We had our staff party at the Gay Hussar and TB was mildly annoyed he hadn't been invited. I said these events were to talk behind the boss' back, not sit around talking to him.

Thursday, December 22

TB had breakfast with Max Hastings [editor, *Daily Telegraph*] and got the sense that the right-wing press were fed up with JM and warming to TB's leadership. He thought we could neutralise most of the right-wing press and even get some of them over. TB also met Tony Hall [head of BBC News] and we started to get into his mind the importance of the UK press as an ISSUE, and the need for the BBC not to be driven by its methods or its agenda. Then Piers Morgan [editor, *News of the World*], who was insistent that the *Sun* couldn't go back after all they said about Major, and also going on about Murdoch non-interference (apart from insisting Woodrow Wyatt stayed, despite Piers' best efforts). TB sent Anji out to get Xmas presents for the staff then we all trooped over to Walworth Road for the staff party. TB and JP made speeches, a bit platitudinous, doing a great job, long way to go, etc. I got a lift back with TB and he said we had a hell of a team. He said he was worried about Gordon, who seemed to think everyone was working against him, which was ridiculous. He asked me if I thought the Tories could get their act together. I said it's hard but yes, I do. 'That's what I think,' he said.

Friday, December 23

Did some Christmas shopping then met Fiona to go to Charles Moore's [editor, *Sunday Telegraph*] extraordinary party in Islington. Never have so many right-wing loonies been crammed into such a small space. It was full-blown, red-waistcoated, cigarette-holding ultra-libertarian Thatcherism at its most extreme. Charles delighted in showing me off as a token left-wing friend. Someone introduced me to the author Peter Ackroyd as Tony Blair's valet, which became a running joke for the evening. I mentioned GB and Ackroyd said 'Who is Gordon Brown?' Peter Lilley [Social Security Secretary], standing nearby earwigging, leant over and said: 'He's the next Chancellor of the Exchequer.' I got the sense these people knew how to have a party but politically, they had lost the will to live.

Saturday, December 24

Peter M turned up for dinner unexpectedly, as usual our run-ins ignored and forgotten. We went over all the obvious – Clause 4, TB relations with the Shadow Cabinet, how Jonathan Powell would fit in. He asked if I was enjoying the job and it took me a little aback. I'd been doing it so much I'd stopped thinking about whether I actually enjoyed it. I said there were some great moments. I'd enjoyed conference. I liked the preparation for the big moments and the big speeches. I liked strategy but I felt we were not at the races yet on that because it was so hard to get buy-in and understanding. We also talked about whether I was too honest and abrasive with TB. I said I felt it was important that I said what I thought and didn't do the sycophantic adviser bit. He said that was fine, but I should not underestimate my ability to faze and unsettle people and it might be better if that particular quality was more directed towards our opponents. It was very Peter. For all that he could be infuriating, at least he was clever and witty.

Sunday, December 25

We went to Neil and Glenys' for dinner after doing all the presents, etc. Neil was in one of his rages, not helped when there was a two-hour power cut whilst Glenys was cooking. I got through most of the day without interruption but late on there was a rash of calls in response to a *Times* splash on our election fund. Another Christmas party story they had saved up.

December '94: Peter M invites himself to dinner

Monday, December 26

I'd left my coat at Neil's so went to pick it up and had a chat to find out why he was in such a mood. He said it was mainly because the press in Brussels was starting to get its teeth into him. Checked out the *Times* splash as best I could but not surprisingly most of the key people were less keen to work than the duty hacks who kept phoning desperate for anything to fill space.

Wednesday, December 28

TB pissed off at the lack of grip and the stories seeping out all over the place, e.g. graduate tax, and a 'trad' health policy story we didn't like. I said it always happened at Christmas, a combination of loose-tongued politicians and hacks who save up stories for the quiet days. He said how come they're all Labour stories? I said they're not. He kept telling me to delegate more and take off more time, yet usually in the same sentence as asking me to do something else. I asked who would be drafting the New Year message. He said, I assumed you would.

Thursday, December 29

TB had shifted in his view of Joy Johnson having spoken to her. Something about her he liked. The NY message went down OK but rather lost in the mass of Tory Euro division. Martin Jacques [deputy editor, the *Independent*] called re a piece he was writing on TB/Murdoch and Labour/News International relationship. He didn't have much but I must have fucked up and been too expansive because by the time we'd finished he said he thought he could get something on the front. I also muddled the dates about TB/Murdoch meeting. Cherie's diary to the rescue. TB said we should be aggressive about this. Why should we have to defend seeing Murdoch or trying to get our case heard in newspapers read by millions of people?

Friday, December 30

One of those nightmarish, stressed-out bitty days that make me wish I'd stuck to banging out columns and wandering round TV studios saying what I thought. Good coverage for the NY message though hostile pieces in the *Sun* and the *Mail*, focusing on U-turns and the comparison with Harold Wilson, which was the latest Central Office line of attack. The *Guardian* splashed on the new Clause 4 campaign, but spoke of 'humiliation' which was presumably what they were hoping for. TB had not seen the *Guardian* when I spoke to him but needless to say he fulminated. I said the important thing was that he killed the story without giving them another story about 'splits'. Mo called and said she had assumed that all these stories that had been appearing were part of a plan. I wish. Several chats with TB re tomorrow's *Today* programme interview. As usual he was complaining about being filmed while doing the interview. I felt this let him kill two birds with one stone, but he felt radio was different to TV, required a different style and it was harder to relax and open up if everything was being filmed. He has a point. The phone never stopped, capped by TB late on saying he'd forgotten his private line number and could I remember it because he was going to get the *Today* programme to wake him up.

Saturday, December 31

TB still complaining that I'd agreed to cameras. Strong interview, and he did well on devolution. Bit worried about rail/public ownership. I did my usual Sunday paper ring round and felt the end of year reviews were in good shape. Mike Prescott [*Sunday Times*] said he'd spoken to Blunkett re education policy. He may have mentioned, as later he said he did, VAT on school fees but if he did, it didn't register. By now I was on the train to Preston heading for the Burnley game. Great game, won 5-1 and felt brilliant as Frank Teasdale [Burnley chairman] drove us back to Preston. Nightmare journey back. The train was delayed. Then it stopped at Crewe and after an age they announced it was clapped out and we'd have to wait for another one. And then the calls from the Sundays started, first about some nonsense story in the *Telegraph* that TB wanted to call the head of the Scottish Parliament the 'premier'. I knocked it down as best I could, bollocked David Wastell (the reporter) but he held his ground. When I spoke to George Robertson I realised why. George said he may have mentioned it as one of the options. Then the Blunkett stuff, *S Times* splashing on Labour plans to tax school fees. I hated doing these calls on the train, with people listening and the signal forever coming and going but this one had the potential to go neuralgic. TB would go berserk. Which indeed he did when I told him. By now I was at David and Anita Miles' [friends] New Year Party. 'Are you telling me,' said Tony, 'that one of our own people has done an interview and as a result of it we are going into the New Year with a story about Labour taxing people to educate their children?' I said I am, and the exasperated silence spoke volumes. He went into one of his 'will we ever get serious' tirades. Do we care about what a few activists think, or do we care about what millions of people think?

As midnight neared, I was still on the phone to him, and at the stroke of midnight itself was on to David Hill, who had been trying to track down DB. Jo Moore told me that to make matters worse Bryan Davies, one of DB's team, had told the PA [Press Association] it was being considered. I called PA to make sure they got the difference between charitable status and VAT. TB said he was sorry I'd had yet another day of my holiday buggered. I said we had to stop all this loose talk all over the place. He'd just got away with an interview with the *Guardian* so why does he need to do one with the *S Times*? It meant we were starting the New Year not on Tory turmoil but on Labour/tax, Labour/chaos, Labour/split, Labour/education mess. I said sorry to go on about the Oratory, but I reckon this one was born of David [Blunkett] feeling the need to protect his left flank because he'd taken a hit in standing up for you over the school. TB said the Tories would be behind this somewhere. It looks like he's just fallen for a question. At about 1.20, after our umpteenth call and with us still failing to find DB, we eventually wished each other a Happy New Year. I relayed to him my conversation with Frank Teasdale earlier. He said what people found impressive, particularly given Labour's history of division, was that we so obviously had a really tight control over all of the key players in the team. TB said it didn't feel like it tonight.

Sunday, January 1, 1995

Woke up early anxious about the DB situation. Fiona was determined I get some rest, so unplugged all the phones upstairs. I just lay there listening to them ring in the rest of the house so got up to begin another crap day. TB also said he thought this was potentially serious, and could give the Tories the beginnings of a way back. He was never off the phone. He asked me to persuade the BBC it wasn't a story. I said it's hard to maintain that when your education spokesman has said on the record that he is thinking about it. Short of him going out and denouncing himself, we can't pretend it didn't happen. He said it is so unnecessary and it's so damaging. I said I know it is, but we don't get very far just because you keep telling me that. We have to decide what to do. He said I can't believe this is New Year's Day and I am having to spend the day dealing with a total own goal. 'And you are,' he added, as something of an afterthought. GB also went berserk, saying DB should not be opining about taxation at all. Eventually I spoke to DB and said we'd spent the whole of last night and today picking up the pieces, that TB had gone ballistic, that we had to knock VAT on the head, and stay only with the review of charitable status. I got TB to call him to emphasise the point and clearly he did because when DB called me he said that when he said Happy New Year, TB just about grunted the reply. At TB's behest, David Hill called the BBC explicitly to disown the VAT policy just before the news. DB said to me later he was 'flabbergasted' when he heard it. Nick Jones said TB and GB had forced DB to backtrack against his will. I was feeding Grace at the time and dropped the spoon. TB said he'd be shocked if DB was still defending the policy. As well as this, we also had Martin O'Neill [Labour MP and energy spokesman] on *The World This Weekend* effectively rewriting energy policy. TB was now on overdrive. 'This just isn't a serious party. Until we face up to the scale of change needed to make it serious, we might as well not bother. We're finished.' I then had a rash of calls from press keen to follow up the backtrack line and I didn't disabuse them. GB called and said he was 'very, very angry'. He was fed up being portrayed as the cautious conservative one getting in the way of the great radicals Blunkett and Cook. 'Here we are, we've just won a great VAT campaign, we've got VAT likely to be an issue at the election, food and books and the rest, and thanks to Blunkett the issue is now LABOUR and VAT. It is a disaster.' I've rarely heard him as angry as he was today. 1. He should not be getting into tax at all; 2. this is just playing to the party. He said you have to put the fear of God into these people, or they will do it again and again. You should brief that DB has been disciplined and he should feel it in the press, otherwise nothing will change.

I did some of that with the *Indy*, the *Guardian* and the *Express*. When I told TB, he said I hope you haven't gone too far. I agreed with GB though. There was just too much of this going on and we had to get some order and discipline back. The story was raging until news that Fred West[1] was found dead in his cell. JP called. He was on a mini break in a hotel near Grantham, which he said was filled with people who seemed to enjoy trying to wind him up. Re DB he said: How do we get into these messes? He accurately summarised that DB felt vulnerable on GM schools so was playing to the left a bit with this and didn't think maybe it would go so big. I called DB to warn him the papers would be grim, without confessing I had been responsible for some of the grimness. He said he was prepared to accept he made a mistake and we should learn from it and now get on with the job of sorting the policy.

Monday, January 2

TB due to go on holiday (Prague). He phoned in the morning to go over the damage. Lots of 'Blair gets tough', and even the odd supportive editorial, though the *Sun* was savage for the first time in a while. TB was sure we'd done the right thing and stopped it being even worse. It died away pretty quickly. TB called again from Heathrow, said yet again he was sorry my holiday had been ruined, which was becoming tedious, and could I speak to GB. GB's mood was not much improved, despite the slap-down headlines. He said

[1] Fred West, a builder, and his wife had been charged with multiple murders after the discovery of bodies at their home in Cromwell Street, Gloucester. West hanged himself in jail as he awaited trial. Rose West was tried and jailed for life after being convicted of ten murders.

he was just not going to be used again by anyone as the right-winger who stood in the way of the others' so called radicalism. He repeated they needed the fear of God put into them. DB was playing to the left and so would RC and others. Out for Fiona's birthday lunch then briefed *Times* and *Guardian* on TB's planned discipline bollocking of the Shadow Cabinet. DB called when I was trying to have a nap to say he owed me a drink. He accepted we had to knock it down and felt we'd done it reasonably.

Tuesday, January 3

First day back in office having had no rest at all. Jonathan Powell's first day so went to see him downstairs in the basement to give him my take on the various challenge areas: Clause 4, sorting education policy, the Big Guns [TB, JP, GB, RC] relationships, TB's informal style, short-termism, the relative inexperience of the office. Powell struck me as professional but I wondered if he quite knew what he was in for re the ways of the party. Maybe that was an asset. I was going over how important JP was when a call came through from an incandescent GB who'd heard JP on the radio say DB had never been informed of the 'decision' not to put VAT on school fees. GB said this was another piece of the effort to paint him as the forces of evil getting in the way of progress, when all he was doing was trying to get some discipline and solidity into our approach to tax and the economy. The JP interview meant we were drawn into briefing on it again, that DB fucked up and GB was being unfairly treated in this. I asked JP why he said it and he said he said nothing more than TB had said. GB was full of foreboding, saying unless we filled the vacuum there would be ten days of Labour chaos before Parliament came back. JP said we'd handled it badly. Yes. DB had fucked up but you can't treat him like that. We had a half-hour mutual whingeing session. I said count up the self-inflicted wounds recently. We both felt TB was leaving the party work too much to JP. He said he was happy to support us on NEW Labour because it gave TB the authority to make the changes he needed to make, but we had let things slip and TB needed to get more engaged with the party. Did a round of the press gallery, spoke to GB again then lunch with Anji and Jonathan to go over the problem areas. Jonathan was flabbergasted when Anji said TB still more or less defended Carole Caplin.

Wednesday, January 4

Sort of day off. Stayed in bed till 10.15 which was wonderful. Jonathan called to go over possible forward strategy. I asked how was Day

Two. He said it felt like Day Ten. We agreed a press conference when TB returned could help get us back on the front foot. I spoke to GB who was in a dark gloom, saying it was all building up as a left-right thing and Blunkett, far from being the villain, was seen as the hero. I said short of removing his legs, I'm not sure I could have done more. Jonathan came round for dinner. Fiona was unrelentingly hostile re TB, about which we had cross words after he left. He was clearly bright, focused and there was something likeable if distant about him. He'd already got up to speed on the personalities of the main players and some of the problems we were dealing with. He said he felt TB was a genuine values-based politician, an optimist, and someone who knew why he wanted to be in government. He felt sure he'd enjoy working for him. He was totally up for New Labour but was savvy enough to know Clause 4 would require some very basic connection with Old Labour too.

Thursday, January 5

Pat [McFadden] showed me JP's draft Clause 4 article for *Labour Party News* which was far too heavily public ownership. Pat and I drafted a balancing paragraph which I took to JP and he was fine about it.

Friday, January 6

Jonathan's first office meeting. We went through the various problems: complacency, ill discipline, the need for greater unity and co-ordination. He had a nice easy manner and made a point of saying how impressed he was with the people there. We had some good media plans for the weekend, both on devolution and Clause 4. Our main problems were Clause 4 and education and the two were becoming linked. It meant that the Clause 4 campaign could not be all-out New Labour but would need some very traditional messages alongside. I also felt, re PMQs strategy, that we had not really delivered on our aim of using it to lay down people vs privilege dividing lines because TB often shied away from populism.

I called Gordon. Aggressive straight away. 'What are you doing about Blunkett?' And he wasn't happy about the format of the press conference and starting to get iffy about living standards as the theme. We agreed to confer over the weekend but it was so hard to get him to commit to any idea that wasn't his own from the off.

Home to put the kids to bed, then down to Fiona telling me Gerry Malone [Conservative MP, health minister] had been on TV saying Labour education policy was written by TB, Peter M and myself to suit the Sunday papers. She said it not as if he were a lying Tory politician shit trying to make a point, but as if he were the sole purveyor of truth on earth. So it provoked another great row. She said it was damaging my 'street cred' to defend TB on schools. I said nobody argued with him more than I did but in public it is my bloody job to defend him, whatever the damage to my alleged street cred. She said that one day there would be something that even I could not defend.

Sunday, January 8

Blunkett called to say he was fed up with the briefing against him, which he assumed was coming from GB and his people. He said he accepted he'd made a mistake but it was a week ago and it was surely time to move on. Anji and I had a bet on how soon after landing TB would call. He landed at 13.55 and at 14.20 called to say he was exercised that the DB story was still rumbling away and was becoming a TB/GB vs the rest situation and he was not sure of the purpose of tomorrow's press conference. I said it was to get back with a message of our own, rather than being driven by mistakes, leaks and all the rest. And on DB, I said you couldn't get away from the fact it was being fuelled by the party anger over the Oratory. He was having none of it. GB did an excellent interview responding to Major on *The World This Weekend*. He called to say he was unsure about the press conference, as was I. I said we just had to be out there the whole time, confident, setting the agenda, leading from the front, laying down the big messages then later following through with the detailed policy work. TB apologetic I'd had no break. Fiona going mad at the constantly ringing phone, as were the kids. Watched Newcastle vs Blackburn with Rory then the fourth-round draw which threw up Burnley vs Liverpool. At last some decent news. TB found a way of linking Clause 4 to the idea of a national crusade for renewal, and it worked really well. Tessa called to say the phone permanently engaged. I said that was because people kept phoning.

Monday, January 9

Terry picked me up and drove me over to TB's. He was back on a no-coffee kick. The break had not done much good as far as I could tell. What is the point of the press conference? What are we trying to say? Aren't we just giving them the chance to set a different agenda? And so on. Jonathan got his first taste of the circular conversation when he watched TB and I have an obvious repeat of the conversation we'd had in the car. At the pre-meeting the atmospherics between JP and GB weren't great. It went fine, then TB did *Five Live, World at*

One, and he was back on form. Strategy meeting turned into a post-mortem of some of the holiday mistakes and how we better correlate the TB/JP offices. TB had a private session with JP and I joined them to go over JP's *Newsnight* interview. At one point, JP became quite emotional. He said that people were very supportive of Tony, they wanted him to do well, they even backed him on Clause 4 because they knew it would give him authority with the party and that was a route to authority with the public but they had worries too, and he had to be alive to them, and education had given them the thing to worry about. JP said it's because a lot of them thought it was wrong, and it's important you see that. He said lots of us had to make sacrifices for our politics, and we did.

Tuesday, January 10

Radio and TV were leading on the MEPs' ad attacking us over Clause 4. On one level this was a pain, but on the other it could be the catalyst really to get us going on the debate. TB was due to go to Brussels, which is why the ad was there in the first place, and there was a case for making Clause 4 the story of the visit, and really laying into them. Peter M was around the whole day, and I asked Jonathan if he had met the new chief of staff. With TB motoring on Clause 4 and his Europe speech, he spent far less time working on PMQs, which was fine. On the plane out, TB was chatting to RC whilst I sat with Cherie and agreed it was going to be a long haul and it was far better that we were nice to each other. Dinner, nice chat with Neil who had been terrific on the media earlier. Had a nice chat with Sarah Macaulay. TB speech went well and the combination of that and the turning of the Clause 4 story gave us a strong press and set us up well for tomorrow. TB said he was impressed at the way we'd turned it around, and thanked us, said it had been a brilliant operation.

Wednesday, January 11

The papers were fine apart from a wanky editorial in the *Guardian*, which didn't even put TB on the front. TB surprised that the *FT* interpreted the speech as his most pro EU ever. I said name me the speech that isn't the most something yet. They can't cover a speech without it. Off with TB to meeting with [Sir] Leon Brittan [EU Commissioner, former Conservative MP, soon to be EU vice president], interesting on the euro, dismissive if moderately diplomatic re JM, and overall nice. I never quite understood why people disliked him so much. His looks probably, but he was clever and when he said to TB that if he became PM he would want to help him navigate the EU waters, it was well meant. Then [Jacques] Delors who was distant and seemed to feel himself possessed of some mystical ability to communicate beyond words. He said things which actually didn't make sense, but he said them with the panache of someone who could be in no doubt he was right. Meeting with Neil K, TB asked how far he should go with the MEPs. 'As far as you like.' The press were outside, and I'd given them some advance words, and they were amazed at how strong they were. Then when I went in, and got briefed on what he actually said, he'd gone further. Told one of them to grow up, another that the *Guardian* ad had been an act of infantile incompetence, another that if they had their way, the party would never be in power. I could see the smug smiles disappearing from the small bunch of tankies[1] who had had the idea for the scam in the first place. Alex Falconer [Labour MEP] who was the 'brains' behind it was marmalised. Wayne David [Labour MEP] weighed in behind Tony, then Glenys [Kinnock] who was brilliant and meanwhile I was ferrying in and out, giving the latest words to the press at the door, making sure none of the antis got there first, and lining up Glenys for the lunchtimes. We got the *Guardian* to take a piece from Clare Short, theme of TB showing real leadership.

TB off to see Jacques Santer [Luxembourg politician, President of the European Commission] while I dictated a rundown for the office so they could work the press gallery too. We led all the bulletins all day, then TB did a doorstep saying he believed in frank talking and repeating the importance of change. I knew we had shifted the dynamic when I heard ITN were doing a piece on 'what does this say about TB the man?' It was moving our way.

Back to London. Big Guns meeting was largely about Clause 4 and the merits and demerits of a ballot of members and how difficult it could be. Rail was also growing as a problem, RC saying we had to find a way of saying we would own the railways.

Thursday, January 12

TB worrying re devolution when I got to his place. Still in his pyjamas, CB reading the papers, talked to Euan about football while TB got ready. Left to record the Clause 4 video. No autocue but TB virtually memorised the script and did a terrific job which worked better because he was speaking straight to camera without a script. Off to Lord Snowdon's [photographer, former husband of Princess Margaret]

[1] Left-wing zealots. The Soviets sent tanks into communist Hungary in 1956 to crush dissent.

who wanted him in a denim shirt. Nice bloke, good pictures, really took his time. Hilary turned up a line from the Tories' 1974 manifesto which backed devolution and we had Heath, Howe, [Ian] Lang, Rifkind[1] all backing devolution in the past. So if it was the most dangerous proposal ever put before the British people, as JM now claimed, why had they backed it in the past? Office meeting re Clause 4. Jon Cruddas said Edmonds was already limbering up for a deal on the minimum wage. RMT could be turned but it would depend on how we resolved rail. Margaret McDonagh [Labour campaign organiser] went through the CLPs and said that without a ballot, it was unlikely we would win the CLPs, and the education issue was still hurting Tony. We were going to have to focus our efforts on core membership. It was obvious TB was going to have to do more than we bargained for.

Friday, January 13
Up at 6 to finish the Stanley Matthews [legendary English footballer] tribute dinner speech draft. Liz Lloyd horrified that we were going to Japan at the time of VJ Day – quite right too. I had to leave for Poole because I'd agreed ages ago to do *Any Questions?*, not sure if a good idea or not but hard to pull out. I felt it went really well, especially my exchanges with [[Jonathan] Dimbleby [presenter] on Camilla.

Saturday, January 14
TB clearly worried re my rail briefing. I said I'd got an agreement from Tony Bevins [*Observer*] that we would go through the story, and he'd make sure the headline wasn't bonkers.

Sunday, January 15
I'd promised *Frost* ages ago I'd review the papers and this was the day. The paper review went fine but I was asked about the rail stories and committed us to a publicly owned, publicly accountable railway system. TB was not happy with the way it was going, and didn't like my conspiracy line. He said are you sure we haven't committed ourselves to renationalisation, and I said no we haven't. But GB was winding him up in that direction. My line on *Frost* was playing on the bulletins, which was bad news. I didn't like being up in a way that the politicians ought to be so got on to JP who agreed words to go to PA and that he would do a doorstep in Edinburgh to get his voice rather than mine on the top of the story. The *Observer* story was

[1] Malcolm Rifkind, Defence Secretary 1992-95, Foreign Secretary 1995-97.

running out of control, and the whole day was taken up with trying to get back to a sensible position. Jonathan said we're exactly where we need to be: committed to defeating privatisation, options open if we don't. TB was worried re the appearance of a flip-flop. GB was furious that it was being said we'd committed to nationalisation. TB tense and angry as he drove to the Savoy for the football dinner. Gave him a few Harry Harris[1] jokes which went down well, and the speech went fine. Sat next to Pat Jennings [renowned goalkeeper] who was a lot brighter than your average football stereotype.

Monday, January 16

The *Mail* did a piece and a leader about me. I wish I hadn't done *Frost*. TB felt we had a real problem, flip-flop plus renationalisation was not a good place to be. I said the message coming through was that the Tories wanted privatisation and we didn't and that was the right place for the party and the public. It was just messy and difficult getting there. JP agreed with me it was not as bad as TB said but TB pretty down. I tried to cheer him up by pointing out that the *Telegraph* for God's sake had done supportive pieces on both rail and football. But he felt we looked ragged and incompetent. I began to feel I was the only one who had confidence we were moving to the right place on this. We had a bit of an up-and-downer, I said he had to keep his nerve and stop exaggerating problems because it had an effect on everyone else. I could tell he was being wound up by GB and Peter who had not been involved in the briefing in the way JP had.

At the office meeting, agreed we should set the Clause 4 tour in the context of a bigger national tour making speeches about the issues that really mattered to people. Strategy meeting even worse, JP and Peter at odds, and Peter saying that doing the Maples Report as a big number was one of the worst decisions we'd made and we did not have a clear strategy. JP said well why didn't you say so before? TB said he wanted me, PG, Peter and DH to come back with a written strategic plan by Thursday. PG gave a very intelligent assessment of our troubles, which were rooted in lack of clarity. I said there was too much defensiveness around, that the first sign of flak had people running in retreat, that on the issues highlighted by the Tories we were stronger than them but we didn't communicate confidence. TB looked really fed up. JM press conference was poor, no clear

---

[1] *Daily Mirror* football reporter, later *Daily Express*. AC often quoted Harris' copy in his own speeches, such as the description of Israel as 'birthplace of the legendary Jesus Christ'.

purpose or message, got TB reaction out by 4. Latest rail problem was JP on radio talking about the possibility of franchises being allowed to run their course. Meanwhile soccer story still going because Man Utd hit back at TB's attack on the price of soccer strips.

Tuesday, January 17

Had a decent sleep for the first time in ages. TB said he wanted a dedicated team working on Clause 4. He was not happy with the way it was going. It needed dedicated press work which Peter Hyman should probably do, and Anji should take over logistics of the campaign. PMQs, we agreed it should be rail because of tomorrow's debate. Bruce [Grocott] pointed out how hard it was to get TB to say the words 'public ownership'. He said all the party wanted to know was that he understood them, and what they believed in. He pointed out, very nicely, that MPs had found it a bit odd I popped up on TV talking about policy. I said don't worry, I've clocked that, I did those as favours but that was the end of it. PMQs was OK but JM had got a better press out of yesterday than he deserved, he was on form today and the Tories' tails were up. I said the only way to bring together the various egos and personalities was to give them a structure. I'd put together a campaign pyramid which had TB at the top, focused on Reaching out to Britain. Then three lines to JP (attack plus party), GB (fairness/campaigns) and RC (Clause 4), then strands out from them to the other big hitters, each taking a specific role in one of those areas. Peter M didn't think it would work because they'd all feel they should be involved in everything. I said they could, but each would have a lead role. Earlier TB said he thought RC's on-boardness was probably because he sensed GB was a bit off board.

Wednesday, January 18

Big Guns at 4 and we tried out the idea of TB doing overarching campaign, Reaching out to Britain, with the three strands out to the other three. I could sense JP's antennae twitching straight away, particularly re RC doing the Clause 4 campaign strand. RC, so on board at the moment that it was hard to fathom, said it was important TB's campaigning was not restricted to Clause 4 and that he was happy to 'provide cover'. GB said repeatedly that he felt there was a danger in wrapping all the campaigns together, that it would all be seen in the Clause 4 context and we would lose out on the anti-government front. He rightly identified the problem, as he often did, but I felt it was the wrong solution, maybe an attempt to distance himself and preserve his own campaigning position, and the smiles and raised eyebrows of JP and RC suggested they agreed with my analysis. RC gave total support, JP was a bit narky, whereas GB fought hard to maintain an independent campaigns function. TB said he would think on. I said we had to start making decisions because these structures were important for the rest of the campaigning machinery. We also needed to give people a sense of the concepts likely to dominate any new Clause 4, otherwise people would start to lose heart. RC said his speech would focus on social justice, opportunity, democracy, environment. As they went into Shadow Cabinet, RC took me aside and said had I noticed how GB was distancing himself from TB, and dropped not very subtle hints about his self-belief regarding the Shadow Chancellor's job.

Thursday, January 19

A bit sparky between JP and Peter M, which started with JP complaining about documents not being properly circulated and ended with him accusing Peter of being there virtually as GB's representative, which given Peter and GB were barely speaking, was a bit implausible. JP not happy the fairness campaign was being run as a separate entity, but it was clear GB wanted to keep it that way. Peter said there can be different tramways in a structured campaign and JP said 'Yes, and this is a different tram.' TB looked strained at the whole thing. Jonathan was looking on pretty aghast. I felt I'd tried pretty much everything to work out a structure that could bind people in, but it was going to be a hard slog. Peter M mentioned that the *Sunday Times* were doing some big piece on the battle of the spin doctors which was going to compare me doing badly with Howell James [Major's political secretary, friend of Mandelson] doing well. I said don't look so pleased about it, and we both laughed.

Big Guns mainly about Clause 4. RC had done a synopsis of his speech which was excellent. TB said he wasn't totally happy at all with the language but he agreed with the concepts. I said I would brief the Sundays on TB tour and RC conversion, and Rosie asked me later what about JP? I said this is ridiculous, do they all have to do something in every bloody statement we make? Another Clause 4 meeting, and Jon Cruddas and Margaret McD said the situation in the party had improved markedly. I asked why, and TB chipped in: 'He wants you to say it was his barmy rail story at the weekend.' 'It was,' they said.

Friday, January 20

Feeling knackered and pissed off. TB called me, Tim [Allan] and Peter Hyman into his office and said we were going through a difficult phase, but what was clear was that when we cut through to the public it was as New Labour, and there could be no going back on modernisation. He said he was going to have to bite the bullet with JP and make clear GB would be in charge of election strategy. I sensed real trouble but he said people had to play to their strengths and GB was the best person for it, and JP should concentrate on membership, political education, motivating the party. We told Tim/Peter H re Joy Johnson's appointment and said one of them may have to go to Walworth Road. TB was back on form, he said we had been knocked off course and off message for a while, but we had to learn from it, get back on the front foot, be tougher, stronger. He wanted daily meetings with GB, Peter M, Jonathan, JJ and me. We did a half-hour briefing with TB and JP for Sunday's programmes. It was crazy we'd got ourselves into this position and it was obvious from tone and body language that they'd be giving out different messages but JP was too proud to pull out Peter H pointed out that JP used 'anything' and 'everything' interchangeably, which could be a problem re, e.g., rail privatisation.

I worked up a briefing for the Sundays on RC role and TB tour, then told TB that Bevins was planning to lead on public ownership. He said if there is any sense of us caving in to union pressure, we are dead. He wanted a briefing that stoked up the modernising message. By the time he, Peter M and I had finished with it, it was virtually a threat to quit unless we got backing for modernisation from the CLPs and the unions. I put the emphasis on social justice and values, and said public ownership would have to take its place in the context of a mixed economy. Did the briefing, which the tabloids took as a TB threat to quit, and the broadsheets as raising the stakes. Then we heard Bill Morris was planning to make an unhelpful speech, wanting a strong commitment to public ownership – which was always going to be there up to a point – but calling for gas, water and electricity renationalisation. Got hold of Jack Dromey [TGWU official, married to Harriet Harman] who waffled on and accepted it would be unhelpful, but Bill wasn't returning calls, other than to the *Today* programme it seemed.

Saturday, January 21

Bill Morris prominent on the news. TB called and we agreed a reaction quote: public ownership was always going to be there, but emphasis on social justice and values, and Bill was causing trouble because of his own union difficulties. Delegated to Tim the job of getting someone up for the broadcasters, and he got Jack S, who was terrible, the worst possible line – the unions have seventy per cent of the votes so obviously they'll be consulted. I called all the heavies to get the emphasis on TB 'back me or sack me' social justice/values, and off public ownership/unions. Lance Price [BBC political journalist] had a really heavy line on Morris, a source saying he was puzzled, confused and pusillanimous. Christ knows where that came from, but everyone would assume Peter M or me. I knew it wasn't me. Bill M called and I said it would have been nice to know it was coming. He said there was nothing in the speech that would trouble us. I said what about the bit that you've heard nothing and seen nothing that could be seen as any kind of commitment to public ownership? He said he was trying to push his union towards acceptance of change and deal with the line that there is a conspiracy of silence between him and Edmonds. I read him the line I'd given to PA. Briefed TB on this who said 'Do these people really not see the damage they can do?' He had spoken to Ian Jack [editor, *Independent on Sunday*] re the CB story, saying it was a bad case of sexism. She did what cases she was asked to do. GB rang having seen the news saying it was awful and that Jack's sound bite was the worst imaginable – they've got seventy per cent of the votes so of course we'll listen! I got on to the BBC and ITN for the later bulletins and gave them a potted version of the Sunday briefing – on the tough end re modernisation, no deals, TB determined, and we turned it a bit. But the BBC kept going with pusillanimous and when I called Harriet re something else, Dromey said it was a pity because though it doesn't look like it, Bill was trying to help.

The *IoS* splashed on Cherie so I quickly organised Harriet and Tessa to respond so that it became a big row about press standards. Peter M came round for dinner and brought the papers. *S Times* piece re spin doctors not nearly as bad as it might have been, though their splash on the Lib Dems was unhelpful. The Clause 4 briefing went fine and set up tomorrow's interviews well. Peter on good form. Life would be so much easier if he was positive and helpful all the time, and not messing around. I had a sneaking feeling he was responsible for 'pusillanimous'. It was his kind of word and there aren't many people Lance would assume to be speaking for the leadership.

Sunday, January 22

TB still in his pyjamas. On good form though, and we all agreed had to push on social justice and upping the stakes re Clause 4/modernisation. Went through the tough questions, then passed on to Rosie, for JP, the line on tax story overnight, and the more emollient message re Bill M. JP was convinced Peter M was behind the attack on Bill. Bill went into overdrive on *Frost*, saying there was creeping intolerance in the party. Going through questions in the car on the way in I gave TB some more difficult questions. 'Are you by instinct a tax cutter?' Mmm, what's the best way to answer that? He called GB who said it's not a question of instincts. The Tories are by instincts tax cutters and they've raised them by 7p in the pound. Top answer. In the green room, I tapped him on the shoulder and said 'Are you really Labour?' And he said 'What are you asking me that for?' before realising I was back in prep mode. In fact both questions, or variants, came up. John Humphrys and the editor came in and JH made some crack about me being the real leader of the party. TB didn't seem too bothered, and did a brilliant interview. I was watching with some of the *On the Record* team. 'Vintage,' said John Rentoul [journalist, Blair biographer]. 'He's different class,' said one of the knob twiddlers. TB not that happy with his own performance but he was not always the best judge and was often too hard on himself when he was good, and not hard enough when he wasn't. The news was excellent, Lance running the line that TB saw winning on Clause 4 as essential for winning general election, comparing TB and JM re high-risk tactics and suggesting TB comes off better.

Monday, January 23

I raised the fact that Shadow Cabinet members were still going out and doing their own thing without regard to what others might be doing and we had to have better co-ordination. The atmosphere was a bit tense and nobody was terribly unhappy when TB had to wind up for another meeting. Afterwards Tom Sawyer said something a bit odd and worrying to me: that the main worry for a lot of people wasn't co-ordination in the Shadow Cabinet, it was Tony. I got home to a pissed-off Fiona and squabbling kids and felt pretty depressed: not much fun in the job at the moment and the family were beginning to hate everything about it. As I pictured weeks rolling into working weekends for months to come, I wondered if I'd done the wrong thing.

Tuesday, January 24

Up all night coughing and went to get antibiotics. Determined to take the kids to school after their fed-upness last night so got in late. Jim Callaghan called to say he'd heard Harold Wilson was close to dying and wanted to alert me because we would no doubt be involved in the press arrangements. PMQs went well, TB back on a populist track but he hated doing it and said afterwards he thought JM got the best of it. Nobody agreed.

Wednesday, January 25

In late again after taking the kids to school. *Times* poll showed Labour slip so I briefed Patrick [Wintour, *Guardian*] for his interview that we expected the polls to become more realistic. In fact the Clause 4 part of the poll was good, making clear people thought it would help Labour win the election, so they got the link. I told TB the press were after us re my boys' school [a bad OFSTED report] and he said, I think genuinely unhappy about it, 'I suppose all of you will get contaminated and targeted because you work for me.'

Thursday, January 26

RC was at the bottom of the stairs from my office and as I walked up, he said 'Can we stop the hectoring of party members?' I can't see any hectoring. 'The *Guardian* today is full of our hectoring tone. Why can't we persuade rather than hector?' He later told TB he was on board but . . . The but was never fully spelled out but I suspect it involved an understanding that if GB were ever to be moved, he was your man. JP came down and we headed off to Dean's Yard. JP was in rollicking form, laughing and joking and maybe feeling more at ease now he and TB had had their chat. As we arrived, he shouted over to me 'Have you got the key to wind us all up?' And inside he was loudly exhorting GB to cheer up. RC was reading cuttings, and drew attention to one which described him as the most articulate and intelligent member of the Shadow Cabinet. 'I think we should have a vote on that,' said JP. 'It would be more sensible than some of the votes we have,' replied Robin. Back to the House for a huge stack of interviews then straight off to King's Cross. TB read Sedgefield draft on the train. Did Peter Snow [*Newsnight* presenter] on the train, Andy McSmith [*Observer*, former Labour press officer, biographer of John Smith] who was pushing the line that TB was not of the party, and a chat with [Jon] Sopel [BBC journalist].

Got to Newcastle, drove to the venue which was excellent. TB did really strong opening remarks without a script, then Q&A. The audience was very positive and at one stage there were so many friendly questions I asked Phil Wilson [Sedgefield Labour Party] to organise a few hostile ones to get him going. Someone asked if the Clause 4 debate wasn't a distraction, and he gave his best answer of the night. Excellent. Shirtsleeved, relaxed, take on all comers, he was strong and confident. Then up to Trimdon Labour Club. Really good day for TB. There was a hilarious moment watching *Newsnight*. After TB had finished the interview, we went back to our seats and Peter Snow recorded the questions to pretend they had lots of cameras and it was done as live. When it went out, during one of Snow's questions, you could see TB's head in the seats behind him.

Friday, January 27

Headed north for Hartlepool where we were meeting Peter M for dinner. TB was on at me the whole time to find out what [*Sunday Times* journalist] Michael Jones' leader on Clause 4 would say and I'd say who cares, give me a break, we can read it on Sunday. He said this is all about winning. 'We're in opposition and when you're the Opposition leader, there is not much you can do. You can't make decisions that change people's lives. You only have words, and you take actions to get your words heard. Your policies are words because you're not in a position to put them into practice. And while that is so, and while the media are the vehicle by which our words are communicated and analysed, we have to influence them as much as we can.' He was preaching to the converted but every now and then I just got fed up being nagged to do it.

Saturday, January 28

Europe and the Tories again taking over as a story. Peter still winding up TB re *S Times*. I said if the speech is good, which it is, it will be reflected. We'd faxed it overnight to the Sundays and Bevins called me early and said 'I love it. It's brilliant. It's socialism.' I was with TB and passed him the phone, telling Bevins to say the same to him. He did so, adding for good measure that he thought the schools issue had damaged him. I briefed all the Sundays, pointing them to page 6, top two pars, and emphasising that public ownership was now in its rightful place. Arrived at the Labour Club in Trimdon to a fair-sized media crew. TB actually quite nervous about this one. He delivered it well and the core argument was pretty clear and would carry. Then we kicked out the media and he did a passionate off-the-cuff speech to his constituency general committee. Met up with Mum and Dad and headed to Burnley to meet the boys. Burnley 0, Liverpool 0. On the train back Fiona called to say Grace had had a convulsion and she was taking her to hospital. Got to the hospital, Grace not great and Fiona really fed up.

Sunday, January 29

In and out of the hospital all day. PG called relentlessly to ask re Grace and to say re JP that he was feeling down, and felt that apart from us two, people were gunning for him a bit. I said we should not forget JP's appeal to the party and parts of the public; nor the damage he could do if he so chose. Grace kept in again.

Monday, January 30

TB seeing JP to lay out how he wanted things to work. Anji called to say Peter was pushing for himself to be chair of one of these committees. JP making clear to Peter he would not be part of any committee he was creating. I said to Peter there were ways of doing this without driving JP off board. I was up at the hospital when TB met GB and others and out of that came word GB was asking for it to be made known he was in charge of election planning.

Tuesday, January 31

Took another day off, as did Rory. Lots of time on the phone re PMQs, TB deciding to do rail not Europe which was good news and by the end of the day both stories running fine for us. Anji called up for a general whinge about various things. Peter M on a few times claiming to be sensitive to the JP situation.

Wednesday, February 1

TB said his meeting with John Witherow [new editor of the *Sunday Times*] went OK. Witherow insisted there had not been an all-encompassing decision to turn vs Labour, it was just they had kicked JM so hard they felt they had to even up. He'd also had dinner with Stewart Steven [editor, *Evening Standard*], who both he and Cherie liked, and TB felt he could go the whole hog for us. He was very pro Europe and had had it with JM.

Big Four largely about Europe, RC saying we had to be careful not to get into too unpopular – i.e. pro European – a position. He said the media could only cope with Europhilia and Euroscepticism and we had to avoid being painted into a corner whilst at the same time maximising the government's troubles. Anji was finding it difficult to deal with Peter's shenanigans, in particular that he exaggerated our difficulties and problems, but TB was clear we all just had to work together and get on with it. Jonathan's arrival had also been difficult for her. Went for a briefing with John Chilcot [permanent secretary, Northern Ireland Office] on the current situation. We were talking about a joint all-Ireland body beneath a Northern Ireland Assembly and the Dáil. The Unionists won't like the substance – all Ireland – or the timing. TB asked what he could helpfully say, and Chilcot said to emphasise there was no deal or sell-out. He said it was like building a house and the walls were up but it was hard to get people to agree to put the roof on.

Clause 4 meeting, there was a worry we would lose the Young Labour vote on Saturday. TB would need to try to get Edmonds to change tack. Jon Cruddas regularly laughing out loud as TB fulminated against opposition on Clause 4. 'What are we saying? I'll fight, fight, fight and fight again to save the party that drives me mad.'

Thursday, February 2

In to finish work on the NI broadcast responding to Major. It seemed the only thing TB could usefully do was be supportive, look good and sound good and he did all that. He wrote in a section I didn't like about peace being a tender plant we had to cherish and the demons must not blight it. He also wanted a huge amount of detail about the document. It was taking away from PMQs preparation. He'd been planning on education cuts but then interest rates went up which made it easier – worse off under the Tories. Did well. His big worry on N Ireland was that JM hadn't really put the argument, and he thought he should, like he was Major's pressman or something. Clause 4 discussion, with Pat McF and Jon feeling we would probably just about win Young Labour, so I started to build the press up to it, with hopefully TB swinging some votes on Friday, and JP doing the same on Saturday. So I started to build it as the first electoral test on Clause 4. Rosie told me JP not happy with that so I went to see him. He said it was a strategic decision and he should be involved in that, not just asked to turn out as a fucking performing seal at the weekend. I didn't see this as that big a deal, but there was going to be a focus on it and so we may as well shape it on our terms. He seemed fed up with it, asked why he'd not been involved in that decision. I said it wasn't a big decision. I spoke to TB who was on a train to Nottingham. He couldn't see what the fuss was about. GB wanted 'equitable' in the new Clause 4.

Friday, February 3

I was pissed off at being in the papers over things that had nothing to do with me, like the 'pusillanimous' jibe about Morris. Later TB called, much more reflective. He said he reckoned that in our own very different ways, GB, Peter M and I were geniuses, the best in our fields at what we did, and the key to his strategy. But it drove him mad that we couldn't get on. I said I can get on with anyone but it has to be based on an understanding of what we're all doing. He accepted of the three of us, I was trying hardest to make it work. But he said when GB was motivated, he had a superb strategic mind and he would be brilliant come the election. Peter was brilliant at developing medium-term media strategy, and spotting trends and analysing how to react, and you are second to none at shaping message and driving it through the media. Fine, I said, but we are all flawed in our own way. He said when he was on the way up, the three of them could not have been closer. GB was strategy, he gave it intellectual context, Peter was delivery. They were brilliant together. I said it doesn't mean you can recapture it now.

I felt both of them unnerved him as a means of getting their view heard and accepted. On the train to Brighton he was meant to be working on his speech but spent most of the time leaning forward and looking out of the window. Did a visit to one of the worst blocks of flats imaginable, real poverty, then meeting some switchers. TB gave me another little lecture on how we were changing the face of the party, it was key to winning, and then changing the country for the better too.

Young Labour reception was terrific. Lively, bright, attractive people who were clearly on board. Then to the official consultation meeting which was a lot spikier than the earlier ones, including a full-on diatribe about the Oratory decision. But he did well, just took it and moved on. Anji arranged for us all to have dinner together but I got the feeling CB didn't want us around. Rosie kept on at me about yesterday and I said it just wasn't important enough to worry about. She said JP was determined to work well with GB and RC but he'd just about had it with Peter, who he felt was an Achilles heel.

Saturday, February 4

Spent most of the day locked in the Bedford on the seafront in Brighton working on the speech. GB came on and said he felt we should put something on Europe in it, and not say Major was facing both ways but that he was becoming more anti-European to appease that faction. TB agreed but wanted to repeat that the rebels were in charge of the policy over Europe. We were busy trying to build up the importance of the vote and present that and the conference itself as evidence of the changing face of Labour. Anji and Peter came to my room in the hotel while I was working on the speech. I hate noise when I'm trying to write but Peter was talking away, who is talking to the Sundays, have we got pictures sorted with the delegates? I was very short with him. He rightly said we should have cameras in for the Young Labour meeting and I said TB and JP decided yesterday not to and there was no point reopening it. He said we should not take decisions like that. I said well often we do, and sometimes it's because you've been bending Tony's ear. He waltzed out.

I carried on working on the speech, and was doing good stuff once everyone had left. I was interrupted by a call from Tom Watson, Young Labour organiser, who said the Clause 4 vote was 4-1 in our favour. Amazing. I went through to tell TB, who was pleased. We agreed he should do a doorstep with some Young Labour activists at 2.30 but he wanted to speak to Peter before we did it. We got him up and immediately had an argument about clothes. I was strongly of the view he should wear a shirt and tie, if not a suit. Peter thought he should wear cords and an open-necked shirt and TB and he were continuing this conversation as we were trying to finish the wretched speech. Even if TB had been the one wanting his advice, I felt it was another instance of Peter winding TB up over total trivia. The speech was a priority. His shirt wasn't. I could feel myself losing it, said he could not just swan in, upset what we were doing, then waltz out again. TB was like a dad trying to shush two squabbling brothers. 'Cut it out, you two, for heaven's sake.' Then we moved through to my room and Peter was on the edge and eventually tipped over. He said, I'm sick of being rubbished and undermined, I hate it and I want out. 'Get out then and we can finish the speech.' 'That's what you want, isn't it, me out of the whole operation.' I said I just wanted to be able to do a job. He started to leave then came back over, pushed at me, then threw a punch, then another. I grabbed his lapels to disable his arms and TB was by now moving in to separate us and Peter just lunged at him, then looked back at me and shouted: 'I hate this. I'm going back to London.' He went off and he was still shouting at me from the corridor, saying I was undermining him and Tony and I'm thinking who the hell might be out there hearing or watching all this. We sent Anji to go and reason with him. I looked out of the window at the group of photographers waiting for our doorstep, and mused on what they'd just missed. TB clearly felt I'd been too heavy and had provoked him, and perhaps he had a point. He said I had to get along with him. I said that was a tantrum and it could happen again. Anji said she felt she had been too hard on him recently. I said she shouldn't give an inch. This thing had to be put on a proper professional footing in which we all knew what everyone else was doing.

We did the doorstep, which was fine, then TB saw Peter and said they were going to go for a walk. It was like a classic family explosion, grim and upsetting at the time, but afterwards leaving the air clearer and people getting on better. Jonathan was irritating me with late comments on the speech, like should we use management consultants, and I said I thought he should have left that idea in the States. I talked to Anji after her session with Peter and she said the truth was we had to accommodate him because TB was clear he needed all the talents of all the people he rated and trusted. She'd told Jonathan about what happened, but then regretted it, fearing the more people talked about it, the more likely it was to get in the press. I said she should point out to Peter that I spent more time than anyone defending him but I felt, e.g. pusillanimous, that I could get more support in return. I said I felt my whole time was spent sorting egos. TB asked me to speak to him, because he was at the end of his tether. He said you are friends and you shouldn't fall out. I didn't want to fall out but I couldn't be doing with this. But I bleeped Peter and Anji to come up and we had a perfectly nice chat, calm after the storm. I think we both felt a little ashamed we let it get out of hand. Wrote this in the bath. What a bloody day.

Sunday, February 5

Speech went fine, especially good response on Clause 4/social justice. But the best bit was when he totally departed from script and did a big number on why people were in the Labour Party and how we'd only ever done anything worth doing by having the guts to get ourselves in order. What on paper was a good campaigning speech became in delivery a really powerful argument for change. Really good. Bit of an irritant at the end when the *Mail* tried to doorstep him on the *Mail on Sunday* splash saying the Oratory didn't recognise unions, but we brushed that off easily enough. We headed straight back and in the car TB spoke to Henry McLeish [Labour MP] whose wife was in Kirkcaldy hospital dying of cancer which, as TB said afterwards, puts it all in perspective. We listened to Hezza on the way back, really fighting back for the pro-Europeans. TB was chatting to Robin C and suggested getting a line running about the Tories' unfitness to govern. I then spoke to Robin, who said I trust you are impressed that I so readily obey the leader. TB also speaking to GB, then Paddy Ashdown about the Europe debate next week. The big story of the day was the Unionists talking about election footing and being nice re Labour. TB spoke to Mo to say we should be very statesmanlike about this, the line should be that peace in Northern Ireland was more important than any desire we might have for a snap election. The *Sunday Times* had a story that the luvvies were deserting us. It didn't strike me as all bad news. Indeed Alan Clark called to say he was going to write a pro-Blair piece on the basis that if he was getting up some of the luvvies' noses he must be good news – what the hell is Emily's List?[1] he said. 'I've come to the view that your boy is a VERY serious figure. I loved his speech.' He said the Tories were sort of getting their act together but Europe was death for them. Hezza was finished but the right wasn't, the Eurosceptics totally had the upper hand now.

Monday, February 6

Andy Murray [director of communications, TGWU] called to say Bill Morris knew I was not the source for 'pusillanimous'. Papers going heavily on 'Blair woos middle classes' including in *Guardian* good picture of Friday's visit. Also bits and pieces on Blair distancing from the luvvies, re the exchanges I had with the Folletts, when I let Ken know it was being said his PR people tipped off the press about TB/CB going there for dinner, and Ken sent me a very curt reply saying if that were the case he would sack them straight away. Clearly not happy. TB, Jonathan and I left for lunch with US Ambassador [Admiral William] Crowe and Jim Young [embassy official] at Wingfield House [official residence]. TB pushing a very pro-Europe, pro-EMU line, but [Mike] Habib [embassy official] saying he found RC as sceptic as the Tories, certainly no different to [Douglas] Hurd [Foreign Secretary] and Clarke. TB was theorising how Russia could one day be a member of NATO, and Habib was saying it was not possible. TB quizzed him why not, and said it was not necessarily his view that it should happen yet, but he wanted to challenge the assumption that it was impossible. If the pace of change in US-Russia relations continues to accelerate at its current trend, why would they not one day be full strategic partners? It was interesting but I could see Jonathan getting agitated and I suspect somewhere in the State Department there would soon be an analysis of the man tipped as next PM that contained the observation that he was either naive, or possessed of eccentric views, or possibly a real visionary. They would certainly have said he was pushy and unafraid to challenge conventional wisdom. Needless to say they asked him to visit the US and needless to say he said yes. In the car I said there was a case for his first big foreign trip not being the States. We'd ruled out Japan because of VJ celebrations, but it would be easy to put together a tour of European capitals. At one point we were just behind David Willetts [Conservative MP, nicknamed 'Two Brains'] who was heading to the Commons on a bike. 'Go on,' I said to Sylvie [TB's driver], 'knock

[1] A political network whose aim is the election of women members of the Labour Party to political office.

the next prime minister off his bike.' He's too brainy to be PM, said Jonathan. 'Thanks very much,' said TB. 'What does that make me?'

GB was not in a great mood, felt the campaign ideas I put forward were all too risky, or they had a downside you wouldn't be able to control. I started to count how many sentences he began with something like 'I agree but the trouble is . . .' One or two ideas emerged, like plans for GB's poverty speech the day after the Rowntree Report, but TB said afterwards he feared that gloom and sullenness may never change. But he is worth persevering with because when he engages properly there is none better. But it was clear TB, no matter how much he didn't want to accept it, HAD to accept his relationship with GB had changed, and was unlikely to get back to what it was before. I said he just had to accept that and adapt accordingly. The days when you, GB, Peter M worked effortlessly together were days when all three of you assumed GB was the leader. But you are now, and that has changed the dynamic. Peter was pretty quiet, probably a bit chastened after the weekend incident, which TB and I discussed on the train down to South Wales. TB said I must involve him. I know he's difficult but it is worth it. He will always give you an extra edge if you get his advice into the mix. I said how come he managed to fall out with everyone? He said it doesn't matter, he is still worth involving.

Tuesday, February 7

Tories were really in a mess on Europe right now. PMQs was fascinating. JM started to lose his rag. This was clearly the issue that really got to him. TB asked his third question and JM answered it with a direct question to TB. Betty stepped in, very helpfully, and said it was unusual for the PM to ask the Leader of the Opposition a question, so JM forced a wan little grin/grimace and TB, for the first time, got up to ask a fourth question. It hit home, and he delivered a word-perfect, unscripted clip that would carry on all the bulletins. Even though it raised questions on the single currency that we may not want to answer, it was a big hit and JM, with Norma [his wife] watching from the gallery, was really ratty and peeved. Then rushed off to Euston to get to Liverpool vs Burnley. Not a great game but we only lost 1-0. For the second night running, stayed in a dire hotel.

Wednesday, February 8

Serious opinion knew Major had had a hit. At the Clause 4 meeting at 11, Pat McFadden reported he thought we had 42 vs 28 per cent in the unions so far and we were moving in the CLPs. I suggested we target Scots opinion formers who might support us, and couldn't GB lead on that? Pat said that as with OMOV, GB was getting involved up to a point but wasn't putting his head too far above the parapet. He was assuming TB would do the bulk of the political heavy lifting on this. At the Big Four meeting, I asked RC if he could think of a Scot who could do for Scots opinion what he has done for UK opinion with his conversion and other speeches. Everyone looked at GB and JP said: Cometh the hour, cometh the man. Everyone laughed but Gordon, who said he had done lots of speeches. I said none that we had really built up to shift opinion.

I had another session with JP who said he knew TB wasn't happy with the way strategy was going. It was not an ego thing for him, but there were two points I had to understand: he had a legitimate input into all these decisions, and he would not be humiliated. He said he was working on his relations with GB and RC but he'd tried and failed with Peter. I undertook to make sure there was nothing major being discussed he was not aware of and involved in. Big Guns at 4 was largely about Europe, and how to respond to the Lib Dem referendum debate. RC felt we should have very little to do with it. We should field Joyce Quin [Labour MP] and not force a vote because: 1. we do not whip on Lib Dems' motions; 2. this would commit us to a referendum for the first time; and 3. it was all about Paddy and it was the wrong issue at the wrong time and we should keep open the option that an election decide this. Paddy was deeply pissed off we were not playing ball with him when he spoke to TB. TB had been given cover by the fact Paddy attacked us on Monday, so he might reflect it was his own tactical error.

Thursday, February 9

Jonathan said there was a problem re the luvvies' coverage because Ken Follett was saying it made it impossible for him to fund-raise if people were reading he was being distanced from Blair, and he believed we were responsible for all the briefing. TB said he would see him but did not want any political profile attached to it. Bruce said the distancing from the luvvies was going down extremely well in the PLP. TB said it was a question of balance.

GB was pressing for TB to do education at PMQs, which he rightly said was being discussed by the Cabinet today. I suspected the real motive was that he'd already told *Tribune* he was doing a major speech in response to the Rowntree report on Friday, in which he would set out Labour's anti-poverty agenda. TB did poverty and went well, getting JM to accept responsibility for reducing social inequality, then showing how he'd failed. To get them more on the back foot, half an hour later we put out the figures showing big rises for top civil servants, £3 a week for nurses. There was a new flank opening on social justice. Patrick Mayhew [Northern Ireland Secretary] came over to brief TB on Sinn Fein calling off talks because they'd found a bug in their HQ. The gallery was really busy with pay, Rowntree and Clarke's speech.[1] The TV news was terrific for us, seven minutes on poverty/inequality then a fair package on a Clause 4 meeting. Definitely turning.

Friday, February 10

Woken before 7 by TB re Clarke speech on Europe. He was firing on all cylinders, wanting to get hold of GB before he did the media to tell him to identify this as a defining moment. The press was disastrous for the Tories on a whole range of issues, but TB felt the Clarke speech put their divisions beyond repair. TB keen to do an interview. We went through the lines that the gulf was unbridgeable, they could not represent Britain's interests in Europe, and KC was closer to us than majority opinion in his own party. Spent most of the day working on Europe. TB was on to me several times from Scotland saying 'defining moment'. Yes, Tony, defining moment. The story was given another lift when Portillo attacked Clarke. By the time of the news it was just a rash of Tories saying different things and us in there with a clear and strong message. Started to get calls asking for a response that Rupert Allason was getting the go-ahead for the Court of Appeal re his malicious falsehood case against me.

Saturday, February 11

Papers OK, but a Peter M profile in the *Guardian* not helpful. TB not happy with it. Jon Craig [*Express*] had a piece saying the Tories were desperate to find an AC equivalent. I threw a few names around the Sundays. Burnley at Watford, crap match but Calum was mascot and had a great time. Only major story of the night was Charles Wardle resigning [as Home Office minister] over immigration.

Sunday, February 12

TB said he really did not like the Peter M profile. There were maybe only three people he had ever told the thing about wanting the Labour

[1] Kenneth Clarke's speech to the European Movement had been portrayed as a speech that would glue together the two wings of a divided Conservative Party. It set out new criteria – beyond those in the Maastricht Treaty – which would need to be met before Britain could consider joining a single currency, and consequently provoked outrage from Tory Eurosceptics.

Party to like and respect Peter, and Seumas Milne [*Guardian* journalist] wasn't one of them. The idea that you co-operate with a profile by Seumas Milne. TB asked me to speak to Jack S before he did *On the Record* to make sure re Wardle that he emphasises Labour would be firm but fair on immigration. TB busy quoting Churchill at me, Britain should be strong to stop other European nations being too strong, and wanted to do a speech on the subject.

Monday, February 13

Found TB in febrile bordering on foul mood, largely about devolution. The great Scottish debate between George Robertson and Alex Salmond had been last night and the big story was GR saying he would be proud to serve in a Scottish Parliament. It struck me as quite hard for him to say anything else, but to TB it was saying what you thought the audience wanted to hear. He would have been far better to be more challenging about the policy itself, and really go for the SNP. It was fair to say TB was not the number one fan of the policy in its current shape but I thought he was being a bit harsh on GR. I said we had to win the argument that devolution would strengthen not weaken the UK as a whole. Peter M's *Guardian* venture was still causing waves. TB not pleased, and losing patience. Peter's problem was that he felt he could only have authority and influence if people thought he already had it, and that meant they had to know about it through the media. TB said he accepted the briefing situation was intolerable and he would speak to him. He did so later in the day and by all accounts did not hold back.

At a rail meeting Michael Meacher put on his pained-vicar look. The vicar thing had come to me regularly with Michael ever since TB said he didn't know whether MM was religious or not but he always felt he'd make a better vicar than a politician. JP said in the end we had to make a POLITICAL judgement and we'd discuss it further. Later I bumped into Peter M and greeted him warmly. He said was that a greeting of friendship or hostility? I said neither, he should stop reading something into everything. He said he was right to read something into everything I did, that he knew he had to look after himself and he couldn't always rely on the people he thought he could rely on. He clearly had a lot of pent-up anger in there and now, very quietly, both of us anxious that the various people passing by shouldn't hear, it was coming out. He said that since I took the job, I had subjected him to 'unrelenting cruelty', undermining him, persecuting him. I said what on earth is the evidence for that? He said you underestimate the effect you have on people when you speak at meetings, when what you think is a humorous aside is taken by others as undermining. I said it's hardly unrelenting cruelty. He said it is if it happens again and again. I have pushed him over the top, he said. He said he had enough enemies without me joining them. I said do you sometimes think of yourself as your own enemy? He did one of his big 'Aaahs' – 'So that's where Tony gets it from, you're your own worst enemy.' I can hear him saying it. I said Peter, I have tried to involve you in a coherent structured way but I've made clear there cannot be two briefing operations. 'You have NOT tried,' he said, 'you have given me the cold shoulder.'

He said he always imagined I would not want him around for the first six months, but the truth was we needed each other and we might as well accept that. I said I was happy to work with anyone but it had to be on a firm basis. I couldn't have him just winding up Tony without me knowing the basis. We should just be open with each other. He said sometimes he wished he wasn't involved at all, and I said it's in your blood, you couldn't live without it. OK, he said, at least I accept I'm schizophrenic about it. This was one of several mental health references, earlier having said my unrelenting cruelty was psychotic. Later on we resumed the conversation. He'd earlier point blank denied briefing the *IoS* and *S Times* stories and I said I didn't believe him. He said he was phoned by the papers after they had been briefed by Jack S. I said that was palpable balls, if balls can be palpable, but he delivered it totally straight-faced. He kind of gave the game away though when he said he thought I shouldn't speak to Jack about this in case I 'undermined his confidence'. I said I already had, and I got the impression the first JS knew of these stories was when I called him. I saw TB later and said Peter had been a friend of mine for a long time. I liked him. I defended him when many others attacked him and I valued both his friendship and his advice and professionalism. I wanted to work with him but only if we agreed and knew the rules and all played by them.

Tuesday, February 14

PG gave his latest polling and strategy advice. Confirmed what we knew, Tories in deepening trouble but we had our own negatives and no real clarity about our positive identity yet. GB down on everything we proposed. Peter was also in negative mode. PG and I were pushing for something positive to be agreed and made to happen but this negativity kept coming back at us. GB had a point, usually, but there was a danger that in waiting for agreement on the perfect campaign, which everyone thought would be fantastic, we actually ended up doing nothing. He felt we should save what resources we have for post April 29 (Clause 4 vote), and maybe even wait for a few weeks beyond that. He flared up again when Jonathan said we had a policy team looking at the kind of modernising policies we might roll out after April 29 and GB said there would be trouble if we bypassed the policymaking structures. I said nobody is bypassing anything but if April 29 comes and goes without real follow-through we will be wasting a massive opportunity.

Anji called me later to say Jo Moore said Walworth Road was losing patience with the office and all the conflicting signals they were getting. PG called, equally fed up after the strategy meeting. He said if that is the group of people TB thinks will get him elected, God help him. It was AWFUL. GB was down on everything, Peter was wary of me and Jonathan and so over-questioned things he'd normally just agree with. I said it's reached the stage where if you said to Gordon 'I think we should have a VOTE LABOUR campaign,' they'd say we didn't have the right material for it. It was bloody paralysis. I called Jonathan and said unless we got this sorted we were heading for real trouble – we'd have two or even three rival campaign structures and we had to get one. I felt TB had to basically put JP and GB on probation and if they didn't get on and work together, someone else – probably RC – would have to be brought in. But it was difficult – politics and talent made it so. Jonathan said he was pleased I found the meeting as awful as he did. He was suffering major culture shock.

Wednesday, February 15

Meeting with the *Sun* team, Stuart Higgins, Trevor Kavanagh [political editor] and Chris Roycroft-Davis [leader writer]. I felt that Stuart, left to his own devices, would be up for going the whole hog and backing us, but TK and Roycroft-Davis were very right wing. I also think Trevor found it hard to adapt to me no longer being a journalistic rival but someone he would need if he was to do his job properly. They were obsessed with Europe and the single currency, which meant it was coming from on high. They said why can't we just rule it out, and TB said that would be absurd, dangerous and wrong. He was very firm on it. Stuart said we'd just have to disagree on Europe but they were keen for us to keep doing articles and having a proper dialogue. I spoke to Gus Fischer at the Newspaper Press Fund do and he said he wasn't happy with the tone of the anti-Europeanism. I suspected neither he nor Higgins were long for this world, and TK/Roycroft-Davis would be working like hell to persuade Murdoch we were bad news. Most of the main media players were at the lunch, and TB delivered a good speech well. Later, at the devolution meeting, there was lots of ribbing of GR over his debate with Salmond and his saying he'd serve in a Scottish rather than Westminster Parliament. TB asked GB if he felt the same and GB prevaricated.

Thursday, February 16
PMQs was a total triumph; direct hit for TB and Major was utterly useless, started badly and got worse. Ken Follett sent an extraordinary letter to TB re us dumping on luvvies, said it was clear the office was behind it and it bore the hallmarks of Peter's malice and my naivety. Charming.

Friday, February 17
Islwyn by-election. Papers superbly grim for JM. Sense of Europe divide widening. Up at 6 to head for TB's preparation for *Today* programme. TB in usual undressed state, still not convinced it was the right thing to do. But I felt the Number 10/11 fault line had never been more clearly exposed and we had to give it real definition. Humphrys tried to run the line we were just as split as the Tories but it carried very little punch. The only worry was whether we became defined by default as totally pro-European but long term that may be the right thing. JM's problem was blowing in the wind, so the more TB could give clear answers the better. Got home to find a garbled message that Robin Butler was hoping to speak to TB or Jonathan re a Gordievsky story. TB was on his feet, Jonathan was in the US so I called Butler. He said John Witherow had asked for a briefing from Stella Rimington about a 'spy story involving someone of historic political significance'. Robin Butler believed it to be Michael Foot. They were saying nothing. I told Robin I'd had dinner with his daughter Nell recently, where she was part of a team trying to persuade us to do a TB fly-on-the-wall documentary. I said I was planning to say no in the interests of 'closed government'. He said 'I'm glad you believe in that.' I briefed TB after his speech. He was worried both about the effect on Michael and the potential political fallout. I felt this was limited, that to most people the Cold War no longer defined their politics. It would be generational and would underline a break with the past. But I was worried about Michael. I contacted Meta Ramsay [former MI6 operative and foreign policy adviser to John Smith] and asked her to find out what she could. She came back and said it was bad news. The *S Times* had been in Moscow and confirmed just about everything. She thought they were planning

to confront Michael tomorrow. I asked Meta to brief DD and we should decide first thing what protection we needed to put in for Michael.

Most of the day taken up with the children, football and Michael Foot. Donald D called early to say MF had been approached by the *S Times* last night, which meant they were bound to run the story. MF called to say he had been approached by David Leppard [investigative journalist, *Sunday Times*], and he had said nothing, so Witherow had written to him asking him a number of questions about his relations with the Russians and some of the KGB claims. MF read me the letter and we agreed a statement he should read to them which made no apology for friendship with some Russians, but made the point he had such conversations and relations with people from many parts of the world. He seemed pretty relaxed but it must have been both a shock as well as a total pain in the arse. TB was anxious that I do not get too involved, and thought DH should deal with it but there were two reasons I wanted to help out: 1. the obvious personal reason that I like Michael and he would need some help; 2. that the *S Times* has really turned a bit nasty under Witherow now and I suspected this may be part of that and if the story was balls, we should make sure people knew about it. As word seeped out, I spoke to a number of people to ensure the story was rubbished when it appeared. I spoke to Neil in Brussels and agreed a statement from him that the story was offensive and absurd. I briefed RC who was to do *Frost*. I briefed Barney Jones [*Frost* editor] in a suitably pejorative way and found out who was reviewing the papers. When I spoke to Bevins such was his loathing of the *S Times* and of Gordievsky types, I felt it was possible to turn this to our advantage, or at least end with a neutral effect rather than the neutron bomb the *S Times* and the Tories might be hoping for. ITN later led on the story but BBC ignored it. The Foot story duly appeared. It was not worth the three pages they gave it.

The Foot operation worked well. TV news was ignoring it and the heat was turning towards the *Sunday Times*. Witherow did a pathetic interview on *The World This Weekend*, effectively running away from the story. [Andrew] Rawnsley [*Observer* political columnist] rubbished it on *Frost*, as did RC who was also terrific on Europe. Tessa came round for dinner to discuss with Fiona the idea Patricia and Tessa had had for an international women's day dinner. It all turned wonderfully bitchy as they went through who should and shouldn't be invited and I suggested we turn it into a play called *Should We Invite Benazir?*[1]

Monday, February 20

Jack McConnell [general secretary, Scottish Labour Party] called late last night to say the *Mail* were carrying a big blast at TB from Cardinal [Thomas] Winning [Roman Catholic Archbishop of Glasgow] about the party's refusal to have a pro-life stall at Conference. The attack was pretty heavy and TB was livid. He said he couldn't stand it when churchmen played politics like this, especially as TB had been trying to sort this out. His first reaction was to demand a right to reply but he agreed to take soundings – did he really want a Blair vs Catholic Church row raging throughout Scotland just as we were coming up to Scottish conference? Winning had been written up as a Labour supporter when he became cardinal and Pat [McFadden] felt from the fact it was the *Mail*, and so heavy and personal, that he was probably reaching out for some right-wing support. Also, Winning probably harboured hopes of becoming the next Pope. Both TB's and my instincts were really to go for him. I called Tom Clarke [Scottish Labour MP with strong links to the Catholic Church] and he said while he understood why we were angry, he thought a public response would make matters worse and he would 'have a wee word' with the cardinal. I was losing my temper at the way everyone had to pander and I said you could tell him he has actually made it harder to sort the issue. TB called after what he called a 'truly dreadful' TUC Contact Group meeting and said he was in no way going to pander to the guy and he wanted a robust response.

Tuesday, February 21

JM doing well on Ireland. As I was doing the gallery rounds, Jonathan called me to go back and see JP. JP had intercepted a letter from Tony Benn [Labour MP, left-wing Cabinet minister under Wilson and Callaghan] to all members of the Campaign Group, proposing they change their name to the Socialist Group and adopt the outgoing Clause 4 in their constitution. JP said it was a clear threat to wage guerrilla war AFTER the result. We called Patrick Wintour down to

[1] Benazir Bhutto, Prime Minister of Pakistan, 1988-90 and 1993-96. Dismissed and charged with corruption and money laundering. Hence, not an ideal guest at the time. Assassinated 2008.

JP's office and gave him the literature. The aim was to build it up in the *Guardian* so the less unreconstructed would go to tomorrow's usually low-turnout meeting and vote Benn down.

Wednesday, February 22

TB was at the NEC and someone said how well we'd managed the MF situation. Spent most of the day on JM's statement on Ireland. When finally we got it, it was clear he was planning to use the line that this form of devolution could only apply to N Ireland. Yet if it could apply here, why were our plans for Scotland and Wales such heresy and such a threat to the Union? He was going to milk Ireland for all it was worth – leadership, patience, attention to detail etc. – and hope nobody made an issue of the devolution read across. But TB felt best simply to support them on NI, show he was on top of the detail and indicate his own interest and commitment. TB was going to a dinner with Eddie George [Governor of the Bank of England], with JP, GB, RC, Alistair Darling [Labour MP and Shadow Treasury spokesman] and Andrew Smith. Bumped into Robin as I was leaving for home. Despite the rain, we stopped to chat. He said 'Do you remember that meeting where you suggested GB might make a speech on Clause 4 and he seemed reluctant?' I said I do. He said 'I'm bound to say GB does not put his head above the parapet. Dare I say it is what people dislike – a lack of courage in the party.' Then he did one of his little nodding 'Mmmmms' and wandered off for his dinner at the Bank.

Thursday, February 23

Called TB early on to be regaled with stories of last night's Eddie George dinner. EG had said to TB the City was not worried about a Labour government provided it was TB's government not Old Labour. JP then proceeded to play up to his Old Labour label, e.g. when house prices were being discussed, why do you people talk about housing in terms of house prices not homelessness? TB said Robin C was not far behind. He laughed and said 'I'm sure I heard Eddie say get me the BA emergency desk as we left.' Pat suggested TB call Winning later, which he did from the car, to say that he would be asking the Scottish Executive to look again at the decision for next year. We ended up discussing what we would do if we lost the election, and fell into one of our occasional near-hysterical fits when TB and I prophesied how we would tour the world becoming a political freak show as we explained how we turned a forty-point poll lead into a Tory landslide victory.

Friday, February 24

Major in Scotland, TB in Bournemouth starting to go into panic mode re Europe debate. He was worried that JM would somehow reassert authority and get the rebels on board. It was funny how TB allowed his nerves to show when he was building up for these big set-piece events. It was part of the process for him. It was partly about psyching himself up but was also to get the best out of us. When he was nervous, we pulled out the stops, even though he could be bloody irritating when he was in this mood. He called Derry and asked him to get his brain whirring on the subject and he called Jonathan to ask for more research work to be done. His mind was on nothing but Europe. Everyone else thought it was fairly straightforward but he was determined to make it complex and challenge himself to do it well. We were driven through some spectacular countryside to Bristol. I love getting out of London and always got a sense of relaxation and renewal from just looking at the scenery when it was like this. TB went off on his rounds as I headed back to Paddington. I read the papers and particularly enjoyed Ken Loach's attack on our 'Stalinist' approach to politics. His launch failure had obviously upset him. I despised these self-styled hard-left wankers who could self-indulge to their heart's content without it ever crossing their ill-disciplined minds that the sole net effect of their activities was a Tory government. Back in the gallery there was an excitable mood. There was none of the feeling we had feared that we were being opportunistic. The Unionists were adding to a sense of impending crisis. TB called in and sounded a lot calmer but Anji said he had been in mega panic mode all day. Helen Liddell [Labour MP, John Smith's successor in Monklands East] trying to sort the cardinal.

Sunday, February 26

[Fiona Millar's niece] Nora's christening. Got into a row with a couple of people who said the party would split after we won the election. I said if we had people like you in charge, there would be no chance of winning it in the first place, so fuck off. These people just have no idea how tough this is. They take winning for granted, imagine it just happens and then we can all go back to being unreconstructed Trot wankers.

Joy Johnson came round for dinner. She was hard-edged and full of good ideas but I sensed she and I, not to mention her and Peter M, would have our moments but she could certainly talk the talk. Fiona was impressed too. I said to her Peter can be a nightmare but he is on balance a good thing and she should just do her best to work with him. She was clearly close to GB, not too keen on JP and although not instinctively a Blair supporter, she was at pains to stress she would back him as hard as she could. Alan Clark called halfway through to say he was sure they would win the vote on Wednesday [on Europe] but it was another nail in JM's coffin, Clarke was finished and if 'your boy' did well, he'd be another big step down the road to the big black door.

Monday, February 27

TB happy enough with his main argument but struggling to find the words. He, Derry and I working on the speech on and off all day. Campaign Management Team meeting and JP steamed up because the goalposts were being moved again re the minimum wage campaign. We had envisaged it as a big national campaign but Harriet, clearly under pressure/orders from GB, was watering it down, because he didn't want us to make a major commitment.

Tuesday, February 28

News still dominated by Barings.[1] Re PMQs I said we should go for GB's National Grid pay scandal though I also prepared a possible line of attack on Europe to draw JM out and setting up the pro/sceptic dividing lines for tomorrow. I called GB from the cab and he was against doing pay, thinking JM would announce something as a way of shutting it down. I said that would allow us to present it as a great win for us but GB was, as ever, a bit cautious. TB thought about it, was fairly keen on Europe but opted for pay. Bruce and I worked up a line about monopoly bosses paying themselves monopoly money. Not a great success though, because TB wasn't thinking on his feet. TB did his first question, then JM did a U-turn, expressed his distaste for these pay rises and promised legislation to deal with it. GB had been right, and we'd discussed this possible outcome, but TB ploughed on with the questions he'd thought of before. As we left the chamber the press surrounded Chris Meyer [Major's press secretary, career diplomat] to get the low down on legislation while a little gaggle said to me TB had been very slow on his feet. I went downstairs to join TB, JP and RC who was telling everyone he was forty-nine today. TB asked me what I thought and I said I thought he fucked up big time. Major does a massive U-turn, and he just goes on with the prepared question, allowing JM rightly to say he hadn't listened to the answer. He said he just hadn't taken it in. I couldn't understand it because

[1] Barings Bank was bankrupted by rogue securities trader Nick Leeson.

we had discussed at length what to do if JM announced a change of tack – we would say about time too, and then put forward what we thought should be put in any legislation. He should have stuck to Europe because it was clearly all that was on his mind until the debate was out of the way. 'You've no idea how tough these big debates are,' he said. We carried on working on the Europe speech. Then RC came down in a state of high excitement. He had got hold of a confidential Number 10 document on plans to beef up the Western European Union, which JM would be announcing tomorrow, with [Malcolm] Rifkind doing a press conference. This was clearly their story for the debate. After PMQs TB was a bit low and I had probably wound him up too much. He went home early to work on the speech. I got GB, who was full of 'I told you so' to do a follow-up letter to JM, and some interviews, so that we could distract from TB's fuck-up, and the news was pretty good for us. GB did well and used the monopoly-money line really well. TB really beating himself up for being so slow on his feet.

Wednesday, March 1

JM got a mixed press. The sketch writers were pretty vicious re TB not thinking on his feet. To TB's house with him and Jonathan to work on speech. I worked on a small passage based on the WEU idea RC had stumbled upon. I was surprised how nervous TB was. He was really working himself up for this one. GB came round and we worked through the difficult interventions. At times GB and I were going at him so hard he said: Hold on, give me a break. He said you look like you're enjoying this too much. The toughest question to deal with was him supporting Labour's 1983 policy for withdrawal from the Common Market but between us we came up with a not bad line: I'd rather lead a party from being anti Europe to being pro Europe than the other way round. We were helped by having got hold of the Central Office briefing notes for the debate which indicated where they would be coming from. We worked hard on the section where TB was setting out five questions to which we knew Clarke and JM would give different answers, Clarke because he believed, JM because he was having to pander to the sceptics. I wrote a light-hearted section portraying the main sceptics as an alternative government. We had fish and chips and then left for the office. TB just wanted to be left alone to prepare mentally. Then in for the debate. He was brilliant, commanded the House from the beginning and never lost it, used the interventions well and really had Major squirming. Good jokes. His best Commons performance yet, I'd say. Major started badly, then got worse but recovered well and he was good when he went on the attack to interventions and he looked OK on the news later. The general feeling in the gallery was that TB did really well, and had moved up another notch today. TB was relieved it was over. I said it was a pain in the neck when he worked himself up for these big ones but it certainly paid off today. That was a pretty awesome performance. He was a bit worried we were being painted by default into a sort of Europe right or wrong position, which would be a problem. I stayed to watch the vote and we all looked on amazed as [Norman] Lamont went in with our lot. That would clearly be the story for the night. I bumped into [Douglas] Hurd later who said I had one of the most difficult jobs and was I enjoying it? I said I was, but it was made easier by having a leader who knew where he was on the big issues – unlike yours.

Thursday, March 2

Lamont the main story but TB got an excellent press for yesterday. We spent a lot of the day doing Scottish media which was always risky because when it came to the Scottish press, TB and I were both hopeless at hiding our irritation at them. There is a 'culture of grievance' element to all the media, but the Jocks have it with knobs on. I also think there is something in both me and TB they find irritating in that we are both Scottish in many ways, yet they view us as ultra English. He was born there and his dad is a Scot. My blood is one hundred per cent Scots, I play the bagpipes, follow the football team to World Cups, yet to the Scots I am English. Normally TB and I would calm each other down with media irritants but when it came to the Scots we were our own worst enemy, winding each other up by imitating them, often in their presence. When they came at him over Scotland being more Labour than England, and shouldn't that make him worried about Clause 4, he snapped back: Why can't they do better in elections then? Before he did the *Scotsman*, I said he should try to hide his antagonism a bit. GB called and TB said to him he'd had a day full of whingeing Jock journos saying they wanted devolution and they wanted no tax and they wanted Scotland to get more money and they wanted to win the World Cup and why was I stopping them? John Edmonds called to say he felt strongly full employment should be part of the new Clause 4. TB, rolling his eyes and shaking his head, was polite but firm, saying though the concept would be there, this was a statement of values not a policy list. Rodney Bickerstaffe [general secretary of UNISON] was in seeing TB, then he told me that three papers were doing stories that TB was refusing to back a figure or a formula for the minimum wage. Harriet was in a total flap about it, but this was the price for not doing a proper campaign on the principle. She said TB was obviously right but now we had a problem. I called the journalists to say we were planning a major campaign on the NMW [national minimum wage], that it would be introduced sensibly, pragmatically and at a level the economy could afford. Sally [Morgan, Blair's new head of party liaison] said Rodney was offside re Clause 4 and a lot else besides. TB was going through a downer on the party, as he always did when he was being exposed to the unions.

Earlier he had seen Major to discuss the Prevention of Terrorism Act. TB had written offering a bipartisan approach provided there was a review. JM refused and as they were meeting [Michael] Howard was releasing a parliamentary answer renewing the act for twelve months unchanged. JM said he would ask Howard to be restrained so we pulled back from putting out TB's letter to JM, which had the potential to embarrass Major. I felt it was a mistake to let JM draw him in like this. GB insisted on the two Eds (Balls and Miliband) coming to tomorrow's awayday strategy meeting. I joked that there were already too many Milibands, and Jonathan added on that maybe we should invite David's and Ed's dad too, not realising he had just died, so DM was a bit upset by all that.[1]

Friday, March 3

Down to Chris Powell's [advertising executive, brother of Jonathan] lovely house in the country. TB, GB (plus two Eds), Peter M, Jonathan, PG, DM, Joy J, Tom S and Chris Powell. Good morning session working on the core message and the best lines of attack. GB very cautious. Over lunch Europe, TB wanting us to build proper defences against the attack that we were federalists. I said we had to be as brutal about their policy as they were about ours. They said we were federalists. We should be saying they would take us out of Europe altogether and destroy our strength and prosperity. Peter M behaving a lot more constructively. Joy fairly quiet. The economic message in the end seemed to boil down to partnership and co-operation and competitiveness, which didn't strike me as being strong enough. We had to get a message that was rooted in living standards and people's aspirations. A poll showed us forty points ahead which was ludicrous. PG predicted us 41.5 and Tories 38 and TB, who was on good form, thought that about right. He said once Clause 4 was over, the drama would be replaced by a 'so what?' factor which was why

---

[1] Noted Marxist political theorist Ralph Miliband had died in May 1994, days after John Smith.

it was vital we then pushed on with a modernising policy agenda.

We then talked about election war room and campaign structures. Essentially TB wanted an executive team made up of me, GB, Peter M and PG with the rest as support. Peter M said there should be a separate cell doing the detail of election planning, and TB said that should be Peter/Joy with Anji doing TB's logistics. Ed Balls did a good presentation on Bank of England independence. GB pushing hard again for equality as the centrepiece of Clause 4. TB not happy with the current drafts and felt maybe we should start from scratch. GB said it should begin 'Labour believes . . .' and I said 'Blessed are the GMB for they shall vote it through; blessed are the T and G for they will threaten defeat but abstain in the end,' and for once there was a bit of universal laughter around the place, including Gordon. I remembered the laughs we used to have when I was a journalist helping him on his columns and campaigns. TB, probably primed by Peter, told GB his economic campaign must not become his NEC elections campaign, because the economic message must get through to the country, and GB looked genuinely hurt at the suggestion. He said he didn't even want to be on the NEC for the sake of it. He just wanted to do whatever it took to get a Labour government able to do the things we believe in.

Saturday, March 4

Rosie Winterton called and was on to yesterday's meeting and I had to obfuscate like hell. She said she'd heard there had been an awayday. Was GB there? Was Joy there? Was it a Blair meeting or a party meeting? I said I'd have to get TB to speak to JP about it. She said there would be trouble if he'd just handed GB election strategy like that. Walworth Road were complaining GB's team was hopeless for them to work with because they were so indecisive. I called TB to warn him JP knew about yesterday, which was inevitable. Tim paged me to call TB. He was on a train with JP and, according to Tim, it was absolutely grim. JP was really upset about the whole thing and TB feared he would just pull the plug.

TB called me after he got home, prior to leaving for a FCO do. He sounded pretty down about things. He said he honestly felt it was touch and go re JP. I said it was obvious he would find out and obvious it would have this effect. TB said he had given him a lift home from the station so they could talk things through a bit. TB had explained why everyone who was there was there but also said he was trying to refine our economic message with GB and trying to see how things on the economy would work in practice. I doubt JP would have bought that. I knew JP was not a master strategist of the kind TB saw in GB, Peter and me, but he had politics and he had soul, and he shouldn't be messed with. Also I was not as persuaded as TB of GB's skills heading up strategy. He could be indecisive, and also there was the obvious danger that he use the position to further his own agenda as well as the party's. So TB had to keep the other Big Guns on board, and he had to ensure his own people had the upper hand on any decision making strategy and tactical bodies. JP was already making the point that Joy was too close to GB. TB said we should maybe add Rosie to some of these groups so that JP feels more involved and represented. When I filled in Fiona about what had been going on she said people would be appalled that you could have a meeting like that without JP. The trouble with GB was that he ground down TB into accepting that there could be no in-between. Rosie called me later and said JP was really upset by this. She said it was more than a personality problem; it was a political problem that we had to resolve. She asked me how I would have felt. All I could do was say that TB was trying to bring about what he thought would deliver the best electoral campaigning outcome for the party, but JP's exclusion was more GB than TB. It wasn't a very good answer.

Sunday, March 5

JP on *Frost*, doing very well till Frost threw him a question about TB's interview in *Scotland on Sunday* in which he'd said we were NOT committed to regional assemblies. JP did his best but was clearly thrown and ended up contradicting TB. I spoke to Pat, who confirmed TB had said that in the interview, then JP called as soon as the interview was done, and we agreed the line should be that people can differentiate between regional government and regional assemblies. I spoke to TB at Ditchley and he spoke to JP to agree JP would make clear we were not absolutely committed to regional assemblies, but it was a bit of a problem, as confirmed when PA filed a 'shrouded in confusion' story. I called JP at the airport and after we'd dealt with the issue, I asked how things had been with TB yesterday. 'Bad,' he said. 'Very bad. I can't see how you can say this was anything other than a deception. That changes things for me. It changes my view of Tom and Joy who are party people, and it changes my view of everyone who was there and didn't think I should be.' He sounded as pissed off as I'd ever known him. It was turning into a nightmare day. JP called me again, said he had been badly deceived and would not forget it. He operated on the basis of trust with TB and that had been eroded on Friday. He would not cause trouble through the media but if he felt he was continually undermined, he would fight back and he would not use diplomatic language. Stephen Dorrell and [Lord] Jeffrey Archer [former Conservative Party deputy chairman] came to the rescue by warning the Tories faced trouble at the elections.

Miliband came round to work on the Europe speech before we left for Tony's for a Clause 4 drafting session. We met Peter Hyman on the doorstep at Richmond Crescent, and rang the doorbell to be met shortly afterwards by Cherie standing in the doorway saying it was Kathryn's birthday party and we could wait outside until it was finished, at which point she literally slammed the door in our faces. Gobsmacked is the word. We stared at each other, then shrugged, then laughed, then went to the pub round the corner. It was shut so we wandered back to find TB walking around the place trying to find us. I assumed he'd heard the fracas at the door, or maybe the slamming. But he made no reference to what happened with CB. Instead we crept in and, with the entertainer in full swing, we trooped up to TB/CB's bedroom to work. TB lay on the bed, the rest of us, including Jonathan and Pat who came later, perched on tables or sat on the floor. Derry had done a very good 'rights and responsibilities' passage and we sought to join that to our redistributive effort. But we just went round in circles and after a couple of hours of nonsense, we called it a day. I asked him if he thought Sidney Webb [Labour activist and author who in 1917-18 helped draft the party's new constitution] wrote the original lying on a bed with his acolytes on the floor and a racket from a children's party coming through the floor.

Monday, March 6

Up early, collected by Terry, picked up TB and off to Heathrow for Barcelona and the PES [Party of European Socialists]. On the plane TB worked on Clause 4. He was running out of time to get a text to all the people who would need to agree it. The news said the T&G would reject change. At the hotel we were met by RC. It was clear JP had told RC re Friday's events and RC was using it. He said TB should speak to JP because he was clearly not on board and maybe they should meet. RC said he should understand why JP felt as he did, that many people would think he was making a big mistake if he gave GB campaigns as well as Shadow Chancellor. It would be foolish and unfair, not least because unlike himself and JP, GB had been nowhere to be seen on Clause 4. There was more than a hint of menace in his voice and manner, and with TB not his usual bouncy self, RC pressed the point before leaving. He did not actually volunteer for the campaigns job but he came close. TB said he really wished JP had not confided in him. But he had, just as he really wished we'd never excluded JP but we did.

The T&G story was now running big back home so that was a blow too. Meetings with Gro Harlem Brundtland [Norwegian Prime Minister], [Lionel] Jospin [French presidential candidate], at which TB spoke excruciating French, and Felipe González [Spanish Prime Minister]. Then we went to the conference itself where JP was sitting wearing headphones even though it was Pauline Green [Labour MEP, leader of PES] who was speaking. We sat through a series of interminable and dull speeches before TB did his and tried to liven things up by dispensing with notes and just speaking.

I met Rosie in TB's room to review the full horror. She said JP was so hurt and angry he was thinking of telling us all to stuff it but he wouldn't. She was worried it would come out in the press and he would be undermined again. They thought GB was using Whelan to undermine him in the press, Peter was at it too, and if he then felt he couldn't trust TB either, it was hard. I tried as best I could to reassure JP that TB valued him but said he really had to be able to get in place the strategy team he wanted. It wasn't JP's forte. I didn't hide my preference for JP over GB on many levels but said if it came to a choice of strategist it would have to be GB. TB came back from the conference for a pre-planned 7pm meeting with JP, who didn't show. I called Rosie who said he'd already left. 'I'm not having this,' said TB.

We went for a drink in a tapas bar with Rosie in the docks and again he told her why he had to act as he did, that in the end he would have to lead an election campaign and he wanted to put the right people in the right places. Rosie was not sure how JP would proceed from here. TB said he would be the second most prominent player in the campaign and a big figure in the government. I went to see JP and Rosie later, said yes, there had been a deception but we had to find a way forward. He said he would never damage the party but felt it could never be the same again between himself and Tony. He said he had made a real effort with GB and Peter M and his reward was to be excluded from key meetings. He said if the idea was that he should just be an old-fashioned deputy who did nothing, he'd rather not have the job. I said he was vital to the whole operation and he knew it. But he was really fed up. 'I've gone through anger and I feel hurt because I thought we could trust each other.' We chatted till 3am. He showed me a two-page note TB had drawn up as a kind of job description which included attack but also working on key policy areas like the minimum wage and also preparing for government. He said in government he did not want a portfolio at first, but wanted to be deputy PM crossing departmental boundaries, ensuring ministers kept to a programme which would set the course for a second election win. He said GB was becoming more unpopular and he could see him off if he wanted to. On Peter, he said when he had dinner with TB that he told him all the things Peter said and did and Tony just said I know but what can I do? 'Sack him,' said JP. He was dismissive about GB's abilities on strategy. He said when he and GB had dinner, GB had been very blunt and honest about his feelings on TB being leader. He found it hard.

Tuesday, March 7

Up at 6.15 after three hours' sleep and in to see TB who was sitting in his room staring out at the sunrise. 'This JP business is grim,' he said. I said I'd been with him till 3. 'You deserve the order of Lenin.' He said that in the end you had to wonder whether we had enough really serious people to take this through. He said it was important he and JP spoke before we left at 7.45 so I fixed for that while TB had a bath. They only met for a few minutes but it sounded like a perfectly civil conversation in which JP emphasised he saw GB and Peter M as problems not just solutions. On the plane we worked flat out and by the time we landed, TB had his own draft of the new Clause 4, which was quite good. He put more emphasis on rights and responsibilities than we did, but the basic message was strong. Once we got to the office it was circulated to the usual suspects and lots of intense lobbying began.

PMQs went well despite TB being tired. He then saw a succession of union leaders on the draft words, including Jimmy Knapp [general secretary of the RMT union] who I always enjoy talking to. The meetings were going OK but we were meeting separately elsewhere and some of us, me, PG, Peter H, Bruce, felt it didn't yet do the business. It wasn't inspiring. Bruce said how it needed to be something that stirred the soul and warmed the blood, and he was right. These were important words we were working on and we had to do better than we'd done so far. Bruce felt unless it was 'Jerusalem' it was all waffle.

Wednesday, March 8

In early to write a new Clause 4 version based on TB's draft. Derry had sent him a new version, with the words 'FINAL DRAFT' rather grandly, and inaccurately, stamped on top. Bruce said he didn't like it, nor the other one. He said show me the words a soft Tory couldn't back. DM said it didn't set out what we stood for. Peter H hated it. I said to TB that he must not fall into the trap of thinking that because something pissed off the party, that would automatically mean it appealed to the public. We could end up where all the public heard was that he had a problem with the party. So we'd end up pissing off the party without appealing to the public. It had to be something that the party could support AND which appealed to the public by showing the party had changed. The debate about it was already doing that, so we had to build on that. Bruce said he couldn't support it as drafted. DM and Geoffrey [Norris, policy adviser] said pretty much the same. DM said he couldn't understand why I was so relaxed. I said it was because this was all part of the TB testing-to-the-limit process and I was sure we would get there in the end but it would be fraught and last-minute and he would probably write it in the end himself and we would force it through.

10.15pm both GB and Charlie [Whelan] called re the *Telegraph* splash about TB not wanting tax rates above 50p and even then only for very high earners. GB said this can only have come from the Blair office. I said nobody with TB's authority did this. He said Peter then. I said I doubted it. Then he was back to me, and I said I didn't like the accusatory tone.

Thursday, March 9

Mega busy. Took the boys to school, in to work on briefing note for the Scots press, based largely on the latest speech draft. I started to draw in thoughts from the Clause 4 draft but if anything the mood on it in the office was even more down than yesterday. JP was back and met TB to discuss the draft. He'd recovered himself, there was no mention of Barcelona, all very businesslike, but he felt the draft didn't hit the mark. We hadn't got the economic balance right, and there was not enough 'music' in it. He said Derry's draft was too lawyerish. He was also worried it would not get through conference even if it got through the NEC. He suggested we use two full days to get it agreed by the NEC. I said it would leak straight away and you'd have two days of turmoil. We should aim for Monday. JP was totally constructive which, given last week, was remarkable. TB spoke to Edmonds to try to get him to move his members on the Scottish Executive and thankfully he did so. We won 18-12, the news reaching us as we arrived at Heathrow. As we got on the plane, it crossed my mind it was at exactly this time nine years ago that I got on a plane to a Scottish conference and ended the day in a funny farm.[1] I felt a

---

[1] In 1986, on a reporting assignment for the *Today* newspaper, then owned by Eddy Shah, Campbell had been at the Scottish Labour Party conference while suffering the beginning of his nervous breakdown.

horrible mix of flashback, déjà vu and foreboding. I talked to Pat and Anji about it while TB worked on our draft and Anji asked if I ever worried there was a fundamental flaw in my personality that came out then and could come out again. I said who knows but I don't think so. I think the reason for my current strength and resilience is that whatever is thrown at me, it can't compare with what I felt then, and if I ever got near to it, I'd bugger off. Pat and I worked on the speech till gone 2. Jon Cruddas came in to brief us on where things were with the votes and as the noise levels grew, he looked out of the window, opened it, then in his thick cockney accent yelled out: 'These fucking Jocks – it's a fucking war zone out there.'

Friday, March 10

Bad start to the day. Barely slept and room service came charging in at 6.10 with a pot of tea, turning the lights on while I was still asleep. I said what the fuck's going on? He said it was my wake-up call. I said I don't need the lights on. He said he was worried if it was dark he would trip and spill the tea all over the bed. Then he plonked the tea down, opened the curtains and walked out. Last night's briefing went well and the thing was set up perfectly for today – assuming we won. TB said if we go down today, this is a very, very big blow.

We did a really nice photocall out by the river then TB and I followed Mari [Stewart, friend of TB] out to her house in gorgeous countryside maybe fifteen minutes outside Inverness. Lovely home, lovely surrounds, really calm and quiet, nobody knew we were there and it was just the place for TB to try to write his own version of Clause 4. We left for the conference. 'Ali, why do I do this job? It's bloody agony on days like this.' Even from backstage, without being able to see the audience, you could feel the tension in the hall. He got a fair enough welcome, got into his stride quickly. Brian Wilson's jokes went down a storm and he was away. But as before, the best bits came when he departed from the script, and he was strongest when he was making the link between winning the vote on Clause 4 and winning the trust of the people to win the election. The broadcasters loved it. I pointed the press to those parts of the speech that were quoting what was likely to be in Clause 4. I had a meeting with Joy Johnson and warned her JP was describing her as GB's poodle, and underlined the importance he attached to party staff working for the party, not individuals. I did the rounds to see what the media were doing with the speech, listened to some of the debate and then started to feel odd and my head was spinning, and I got that awful sense of people crowding in towards me. Déjà vu. A perfectly friendly reporter from Grampian

TV asked me a question and I froze, then asked him to go to the press office and I headed in search of fresh air. Thankfully I bumped into David Hill and I felt a sense of reassurance and the moment passed. I went into the hall for the rest of the debate. Helen Liddell, Brian Wilson and John Reid [Labour MP] were terrific. [George] Galloway was exactly what I expected – repulsive. After the debate I went and found a quiet spot in the dark backstage, still feeling anxious and trying to recover myself. Going bonkers at one Scottish conference, fair enough, but two! I was paged to go and see TB upstairs. I said to David Hill that I was feeling really tired and stressed out and could he take care of the briefing? I confided to TB later that I'd felt close to collapse at one point. 'What, psychologically?' he said. 'More physically but the head was playing tricks.' The pressure had been intense but as nothing to what we'd face in an election campaign.

There was still a problem with the computer and we finally got the result as we left for the airport. TB did a pooled doorstep then we headed off, with me still feeling weird, not helped by the fact that the countryside was so similar to the scenes I drove through to Perth on the day I cracked. TB was in his usual 'calm after the storm' mode. We listened to the chaotic results announcement on the radio where Kenny Macintyre [BBC Scotland reporter] said it had been a 'wee stooshie' [little bit of trouble]. We arrived at the airport, where they had been holding the plane for us, but by the time we got on to the tarmac the doors were closed, and we'd missed it. It meant diverting to Glasgow, which was another blow to the psyche as the airport there played a part in my breakdown. We had the *Guardian* with us to do an interview which was fine. The TV news was perfect.

Saturday, March 11

GB pulled out of *Frost* because he was worried he would be asked about tax. So what? Why shouldn't he be asked about tax? The answers were not exactly rocket science. It was not a problem. TB was delayed two hours at Manchester airport so he was able to work on it [Clause 4] a bit more. He was worried that because of the way the debate had developed, if he had the words themselves – 'public ownership' – in there, it would be seen as Old Labour whatever else we had there. When I saw Rosie at Tim's party she said JP would probably insist on public ownership. She also said JP intended to press his case tomorrow re GB.

Sunday, March 12

GB on early asking for a few Clause 4 draft phrases for him to put in his speech at Inverness. Bit of a nerve, as he had done less than others to promote change and had pulled out of *Frost*. I was pissed off that he could sit back and then come in at the last minute and try to use his speech to announce the new words. Blunkett did *Frost* and based on my briefing last night gave out what we would signal as the likely words – power etc. in the hands of the many – and the commitment to a more equal society. He overcooked the public ownership a bit. JP and Rosie came over for a cup of tea at 3.30 and we talked over general principles re Clause 4. JP said he would have to have a clear commitment to full employment and public ownership. I said TB did not want the phrases themselves though he was happy with the concepts. I showed him the latest draft. He was reasonably happy but said 'justice at work' should go back in. Fiona came back and JP was waxing lyrical about her fruit cake. Then a bizarre event, JP having just been raving on about 'the beautiful people', the doorbell rang and it was Tessa coming round with some apples from her garden in Warwickshire. She obviously thought JP was here socially, not realising she'd come in at quite a difficult point in quite an important meeting, when I was trying to persuade JP we didn't need the actual words 'full employment' in the final version, and she was telling us some long complicated story about a meeting with Diane Abbott. As she left he said 'Who brings the food parcels tomorrow – Harriet?'

To TB's, with JP playing me the Rolling Rose campaign theme. Cherie not very welcoming to any of us, particularly me, then she made an unconvincing fuss of JP before making some tea. I got cameras in to do TB/JP pictures then we got down to work. JP said the whole exercise had done Labour a lot of good. He said let's go through the areas we are likely to agree and leave the economic section to the end. I was pleased that we took out 'any other organisations' in the trade union section and that we injected 'public services essential to the public good' which was better than 'services on which the public depend'. They chatted away for four hours without much real disagreement. TB put the case line by line and was persuasive. We'd just about got everything agreed by 9pm. Once we had it agreed we sent it through to Jonathan and Sally in the office who were waiting to talk to key union and NEC people. I then discovered Jonathan was faxing it out to some of them, which was crazy. I called and said stop faxing as it will just get leaked. Talk them through it. TB spoke to Edmonds and Clare Short who both seemed OK. Only RC, TB felt, was continuing to be a tad tricky. TB said you can't believe how hard I've sweated on this, but I could tell he was happy with it at last. JP and Rosie came back for dinner and we analysed TB's relations with GB, Peter M etc., and JP made clear he just was not going to be undermined. He was going to see GB off on campaigns.

Monday, March 13

Papers were all fine from TB's point of view but GB had got the *FT*, *Mail* and *Telegraph* on the line that his speech was close to the new Clause 4 and got unions to back change. It was a classic piece of what we had been talking about last night, just not playing in a team. He was parachuting in at the last minute whilst those who had really done the job, JP and RC in particular, even Clare, were nowhere in the picture. GB was clearly building up support in the unions. TB was still making changes. He took out the line about achieving more together than we can alone, but between us JP and I persuaded him to put it back in. He was really in a state, fretting the words would get voted down at the NEC. In to see JP and Tom and go through last changes. One wanted 'the rigour of fair competition' which the other didn't like. As they headed to the meeting I gave the press some 'TB told the meeting' words, and drafted a TB/JP press release which they OK'd without change. TB/JP both did excellent opening statements in support of change and then they went round the table. During a break, I said I was becoming worried about the line about 'nurture the family', as apparently was RC. Also Dennis Skinner had said it would haunt him. I agreed with Dennis that it risked becoming our Back to Basics, because the press would think it gave them justification to go after anyone's private life. I was also worried about the overtones of nanny state, and leaving open questions about family definition, taking you into single parents, gay marriage and all that. GB's contribution was largely about repeating the draft that had been rejected. I got statements of endorsement from Neil and Michael Foot after the NEC vote, 21 for, 3 against, 5 abstentions, Beckett abstaining earlier. We went downstairs to go through the tough questions for the press conference, which went fine. Back to the House for a mass of interviews then I did the gallery, and made sure that people knew JP and RC had been heroic. I bumped into Ed Balls and had it out about the coverage of GB's speech. I said these things don't happen by accident. Ed insisted it was not Charlie's work and they were neither causing trouble nor taking credit.

Tuesday, March 14

The Tory response was woeful. JM was away so JP was doing PMQs. It was a lot tougher preparing because JP went over things in a very different, more chaotic way. But he had the very good idea of using a quote from the new Clause 4 in a question about executive pay greed. He was really nervous, terrified of failing, but he did fine. TB, as after every success, was at his most 'no complacency'. I had lunch with Bruce who was bending my ear re Peter. 4.30, meeting with TB, JP, Rosie, Jonathan and me. JP said TB had to know he would never let his ego get in the way of the best interests of the party. He would always argue privately and then get on with the job. But he would not have himself, or the position of deputy leader, under-mined. At the moment his authority WAS undermined because Walworth Road and others were conscious of different power bases. He said he had made clear he was willing to accommodate change but GB gave absolutely nothing, wanted it all his own way. TB suggested the rest of us leave. I said the trouble with that was that you talked, then you give us one impression of the meeting, JP gives Rosie another and we are no further forward in pinning this down. We need clarity and we need agreement, otherwise we will be strategically weakened. JP's temper rose and he really laid into GB – indecisive, not as clever as he thinks he is, not a team player, looking after himself. He said to TB 'You've got a real guilt complex about him because you've got the job, and he plays at making you feel guilty, and the other one [Peter] wheedles about and makes you think you need him and it's like you've got two fucking monkeys on your back. They get their authority from you and they abuse it. They damage you. If you make the judgement you need them fine, but my judgement is they damage you, and you'll regret it.' TB: 'Look, I am a politician not a psychoanalyst.' TB started to get that depressed and haunted look he gets when a meeting is going badly, but I said he had to face up to this and sort it. TB suggested Jonathan and Rosie try to write down a proper job description, get something agreed on paper and TB will get GB signed up to it. It sometimes felt like dealing with children.

Earlier I'd run into GB in the corridor and he cut me dead, which surprised me. I found out why from TB, who said GB had asked why I was briefing against him. I hadn't, but in his eyes me emphasising that JP's leadership role and RC's conversion had been pivotal to yesterday's vote was tantamount to briefing against him. Was it any wonder I didn't exactly glow at the idea of him being the campaigns supremo if this was how he carried on? I was really pissed off he'd gone to Tony like that and accused me of briefing against him. I called him and said 'I hear you think I've been briefing against you. That is completely untrue, and unfair.' 'OK, I accept your denial.' I said that's not enough. 'You have to believe it or we have a problem.' He said he would call me back. Charlie Whelan came over. I said this was a ridiculous situation. If GB had a problem, he should raise it with me himself. I did not brief against him. I wrote GB a note, asking him to accept my assurance and saying that if he ever thought I did that, he should raise it with me direct. He called later and suggested we meet tomorrow. Whelan said GB's trouble was that everyone attacked him and someone else had the job he wanted.

Wednesday, March 15

Meeting with Jonathan and Rosie to take forward from yesterday and try to get the two-headed monster of the campaign structure down on paper. TB leading a joint campaigns committee; JP a weekly campaign management team, GB chairing a daily strategy team. TB said to me and Jonathan there is no way they'll all end up liking each other but we have to get something down and force it through and make it work. GB's meeting idea from yesterday never materialised despite him later saying he had tried to find me. Another JP, Jonathan, Rosie meeting re JP's job description. He was adamant he didn't want a department even though history told you that was where power lay. But by the time we took our proposals to TB, JP had done well. Jonathan scratched his curly mop and said 'How did I manage to get us into this position? He ran rings round me.' TB then got a fit of the giggles, saying Jonathan had effectively handed his job to JP and JP was now the leader. We did not even get round to JP's agenda to be 'deputy prime minister'. He said he'd said a lot of harsh things about Gordon but he was sure he could work with him if we could just sort this stuff out. TB/GB had another discussion re JP/economics and TB said he was less hysterical.

Thursday, March 16

Meeting with GB/Peter M re Economics Commission which quickly degenerated into a spat between Peter and Joy when Peter, rightly, said that if GB did another 'feelbad factor' press conference on Monday it would just be seen as another dose of 'gloomy Gordon'. Joy tut-tutted and Peter asked her why she reacted like that and a minor row flared up. Then GB asked him if he planned to make any real contribution. Peter said he would contribute as he saw fit. Afterwards I went to GB's office for the meeting I'd been trying to have since he told TB I had been briefing against him. I asked him to accept I didn't brief against him. He said nobody in his office briefed his Inverness speech as wooing the unions, and that even if I didn't brief against him, I didn't brief *for* him and my job was to ensure there was nothing between him and TB. He said nobody ever briefed him up, and when I pointed to the briefings on his VAT or executive pay success, he said that was his own office's work. On the current difficulties, he said he had never asked for the campaigns job, he had enough to do trying to sort economic policy, and he had no desire to fight with JP. He was not in the business of divide and rule, as Robin was. He just wanted to get on with the job of winning. He said he was surrounded by enemies and I began to see an obsessive worry about his own position. I was clearly one of the enemies at the moment, and he started to remind me of things I'd written before. Again, it wasn't even attacks on him, but pieces I'd written about others. He said I know why you have to talk up JP, but it's unfair the way you write me out of the script. I had another meeting with JP to go over his role, and reiterated GB's fears about an alternative economic policy. He cracked a joke about being deputy leader from the back benches.

Friday, March 17

I had to see JP and Rosie about a briefing we were doing on his Rolling Rose campaign roadshow. He was very subdued and afterwards Rosie said she had never seen him so bad. He was suicidal and it was because with the 'two monkeys on his back' syndrome, he felt he would never really be deputy leader.

Sunday, March 19

Went over to TB's to start preparing for *Dimbleby*. The central message would be that we carry on modernising, and he wanted to focus on two areas: underclass/welfare reform, and a modern industrial policy. It wasn't brilliant. It was all too bitty and he was a bit cavalier in his answers on the minimum wage and Scottish legislation which would cause us difficulty afterwards. He knew he hadn't been great and that we'd missed an opportunity.

Monday, March 20

Office meeting, and TB still struggling to get a sense of strategy flowing. Everything came back to the unresolved GB/JP situation. 11.15, TB, JP, Jonathan, Rosie, myself. TB had a note from GB on what he might live with. He suggested he take responsibility for a Regional Development Commission. He said GB would never wear the unemployment angle but he would go for something on the regions. TB was due to meet GB and when he came he said he would meet him alone and asked me and Jonathan to leave. I knew what was coming: he would say GB had agreed to something and we'd all proceed on that basis and then GB would say that wasn't what they agreed. They were in there for an hour then he called JP down and we all piled in. He said JP could oversee regions with regard to public/private; quangos, regional regeneration and yes, jobs. I could see JP thought this was the business. As he left I said to TB I can't wait for the regional income tax and regional assemblies in every county! I could not believe GB had signed up to this but he assured us he had. Jonathan drew up a note and sent it to JP who said it was totally unacceptable. Any reference to jobs had gone. He said the economic guts of it were taken out. 'I've given, given, given half a dozen times and the other feller has given nothing.' He said it was ridiculous none of us had been in for their meeting – it's because he won't stand up to him. It's back to the monkeys on the back and it's not leading. Jonathan came up to join us and JP went over the same ground. He said he wanted a reference to social audit and unemployment. TB agreed to that. After he and JP left for the trade unions meeting I called GB to discuss the latest job description. I read it to him and he said they hadn't even discussed jobs and it bore no resemblance to what they agreed. I saw Rosie who said JP was worried because I appeared to be so glum and that usually meant things were worse than they seemed. I said who wouldn't be glum trying to sort this bollocks out? TB spoke to GB later and said he had to have a proper strategy team up and running and if need be he would have to chair it himself. GB came back and said he was OK re JP's commission provided it wasn't NATIONAL economic development. But his new thing was he didn't want the CMT [campaign management team] to keep so much of campaigns. It was a running sore. I said to TB we could not let this go on like this. But he was busy focusing on his *Spectator* piece on duty which everyone but him thought was utter balls. Jonathan was managing to stay cheerful, if confused, but Anji and I were reaching the end of our tether, and felt unless he faced up to this and sorted it, we had a real problem.

Tuesday, March 21

We were all getting frustrated and infuriated re TB's inability to sort things. He said he enjoyed confrontation and argument on policy and politics but he hated it when it was about personality clashes. TB said to GB we had to aim to sort and announce this today. GB, amazingly, was worried it would be seen as a blow to him. TB said he was more worried it would be seen as an anti-Prescott move and we had to guard against that. I started to work on a briefing note. I sent it around. JP wanted a reference to unemployment IN, and GB wanted the reference to economics taken OUT. TB did education at PMQs which went well. I briefed Don Macintyre [*Independent* political editor and later biographer of Mandelson] on the GB/JP scene and when I ran through the job descriptions, he said it's obviously a big boost for GB. I said it's a boost for all of them, and he laughed and said 'God, I would give anything to have been a fly on the wall when all this was being squared.' Phil Webster [*The Times*] loved it and said he thought they'd get a splash out of it. Ditto *Indy*. That was the position we were in now: any major development of policy or personality was big news and it was why it was right to hammer the details out before the press were on to it. TB getting worked up re his *Spectator* lecture tomorrow, which the great and the good would be crawling over. We decided to brief overnight and Joy wanted to do the briefing. TB said she was a lost soul at the moment and we should involve her more. I discussed it with Tom S who said she wanted to be involved in all the day-to-day dramas and she was not sorting Walworth Road.

Wednesday, March 22

We left for the QE2 [Queen Elizabeth II Conference Centre, Westminster] for the *Spectator* lecture. Huge interest, went well. Charles Moore though said it was 'very Blair – good atmospherics, little substance'. It was pitched as an appeal to One Nation Tories and it played well on the media. Home fairly early, then had a chat with Joy to advise her to root herself in Walworth Road, and understand the need to involve JP and never forget she works for the whole party. TB had dinner with GB/Peter M to try to get them back in harness. The *Spectator* lecture was the splash in several places. There had been all kinds of signs and signals in the past forty-eight hours that we were now seen as the government-in-waiting. It was almost as if we were being covered like we were already in power. That had risks as well as opportunities but for the moment we had to seize the opportunities it presented to us. Peter called after the dinner with TB/GB and said it was an absolute disaster. He felt he'd let TB down badly because he left early but he couldn't take it any more. He said GB was vile to him. GB's basic take is that he ought to be the leader and the only reason he's not is because we lined up the press behind Tony. It's incredible but he believes that is what happened. He asked GB what his role was going to be and GB said he didn't know. He said nothing. TB looked at him as though he were crazy. Peter said he wanted to take six months out and I said that wasn't realistic, and his role had to be formalised. He said it's OK for you because GB fears you, but he just despises me. We chatted like this for half an

March '95: TB's 'disaster' of a dinner with GB and Peter M

hour or so and as often with Peter, he said his main worry was TB and how he could best support him. But I have rarely heard him so down. 'I just don't know what to do.'

Thursday, March 23

JP saw Joy again and she left in a bit of a state. There were even rumours during the day that she would quit. Joy came to see TB to discuss her role. She was very unfocused and fidgety. TB said to her 'A lot of what is going on is a pain in the butt but it's politics. You probably want politics to be all about ideals and convictions and it is, but a lot of it is also stroking people and dealing with different personalities and making compromises between them. And it can be a pain. You have to be patient and stay focused on the things that need to be done to win.' TB was looking tired. Peter M repeated he wanted a break from it for a few months.

Friday, March 24

TB in the North-East and I got DB to do follow-up media on yesterday's speech which was still getting good coverage. I was hoping for a day off before heading for Wolves vs Burnley but TB called and asked me to write a passage for his speech on the theme of the Tories running out of steam, and show where we would provide the new energy through a change in policy direction. I went for a long walk with Grace over the heath and when she fell asleep sat down and scribbled something and dictated it over to the office.

Saturday, March 25

Alan Clark called and when Fiona answered, Alan said 'Fiona, hi, it's Tony, is Ali there?' and for a moment she fell for it. Alan said they were going to go for the 'Tory Tony' tag. I said fine, all your voters will hear out of that is that he must have changed the Labour Party if they're calling him a Tory. It's what we call a strategic conundrum, I said. Mmmm, he said, maybe we're fucked.

Sunday, March 26

Motoring most of the day on the BBC and on Tory troubles. David Hunt [Conservative MP, Chancellor of the Duchy of Lancaster] said on *Frost* there would be no challenge to Major. Rifkind said on *World This Weekend* there might be. Whatever co-ordination problems we had, these guys were all over the shop. Then Neil and Glenys popped round unexpectedly, having just been to see Sue Nye's baby. Neither of them liked the *Spectator* speech.

TB still very 'snappy'. He was angry that GB had disappeared for three days without anyone knowing where he was or how to get hold of him and that we were still not operating a proper strategy structure, so that strategy was still pretty much TB/AC hand to mouth. He said where do we go from here, and I said we cannot go anywhere without an economic message; and we cannot go anywhere without agreed and understood structures. Jonathan came to see me to say TB had bawled him out over the lack of good work being done on Europe. Jonathan said he was feeling suicidal about his inability to get TB to focus on one thing at a time and get it sorted. Today he was just raging against one thing after another. I said I think it's his way of getting us to raise our game. Pretty man management it ain't, but he'll be all nice again in a day or two. TB called Peter M from the car and whinged on at him as well. I took the phone and finally got TB to chill out a bit as Peter and I dreamed up the kind of news bulletins that TB might accept as a good job well done: 1. the Queen hails Blair as the best leader in history; 2. Thatcher urges Major to make way for Blair without an election; 3. United Nations pass a resolution saying Blair should be PM now; 4. The BBC can exclusively report another fantastic policy idea from Blair.

Arrived in Glasgow. Kenny Macintyre [BBC] said that Allan Stewart [Conservative MP and junior minister] had told him the canvas returns in Eastwood [preparing for local elections] were the worst he had ever seen for the Tories. The Clause 4 meeting was excellent. The whingeing had got out of TB's system and he really hit all the arguments. He dropped a little hint that he would quit if we lost the Clause 4 vote. He took a risk in saying of Thatcher that she was driven by a set of values, that they may have been wrong but they were deeply held, and that was the same for him. His peroration was the best of all the meetings so far and he got a huge standing ovation, which took the media by surprise. We drove over to Edinburgh and had dinner with his old school friend Nick Ryden. TB told the hilarious story of when he and GB met in Nick's house for one of the big discussions post John Smith's death. Nick left them to it and they went round and round in circles. TB was clear he should stand because he felt that was the best chance for the party, but GB was not convinced. At one point, GB went to the toilet. Minutes passed and TB was sitting twiddling his thumbs and even wondered if GB had done a runner. Eventually the phone went. TB left it, so then the answering machine kicked in and GB's disembodied voice came on: 'Tony. It's Gordon. I'm locked in the toilet.' They both ended up laughing about it. TB went upstairs and said 'You're staying in there till you agree.'

Tuesday, March 28

Just made PMQs after the plane was delayed. Margaret Hodge [Labour MP] asked about the BBC and JM had quite a dig at me which meant that as we came out of the gallery I was encircled and asked how many times I'd complained to the BBC. Oakley was there so I asked him to confirm I had never complained about any of his reports, which he did. Don Macintyre said the Tories had decided to make me an issue, as it played into their TB strategy, and I was a 'marked man'. TB said this was about trying to destabilise me, and portray him as my puppet. I wondered whether they thought they had something on me, possibly more stuff about my breakdown, and they were building me up so the papers could then tear me down. It was certainly odd hearing Major talk about me in the Commons on the ITN News. I remembered what Alan C said to me the last time we had lunch: the Tories are 'obsessed' with you, because they think their weakness is they haven't got someone like you. He said it was a way of them avoiding confronting their far deeper problems.

Wednesday, March 29

In my mail was a handwritten note on BBC paper, a memo from *Panorama*'s Nick Robinson to his bosses, Tim Gardam, Steve Hewlett and David Jordan, explaining the background to an interview with JM on Monday and raising problems with regard to the local elections. Of course it could be a forgery so I got Tim to call Robinson and just chat to him, get confirmation JM was on and get a sense that some of these issues were under discussion. Tim in no doubt. I got Don Macintyre and David Hughes [*Daily Mail*] to the Shadow Cabinet room and gave them a copy, explaining it was a breach of guidelines to make the kind of commitments they appeared to be making, and pointing out the local elections relevance. They liked it. DH said he'd already heard about it and had alerted *The Times*. I said to TB just watch this *Panorama* thing fly. I faxed the Robinson memo to Jo Phillips [adviser to Paddy Ashdown] who was with Paddy A in Scotland and to Olly Grender [Liberal Democrat director of communications] asking them to do nothing with it till the story broke. They got Robert Maclennan [Liberal Democrat MP] wound up to call for the programme to be pulled. I worked up a full briefing note for us to draw on when the papers dropped tonight. It was a beautiful story in so many ways. It was bad for Major because it would put him at the centre of a media storm. It made them look underhand because they were trying to gain an advantage re the local elections. It came with the BBC/Tory links in the spotlight. And it would have all the parties joining with us against them. Don Macintyre said there was a panic on at the Beeb. Beeb in a flap, Tories in a flap, Number 10 in a flap. Excellent.

Thursday, March 30

Papers excellent. *Times* splash, *Indy* second lead on *Panorama*, lots of follow-up and we were all geared up to go when the calls started. I called the *Today* programme to ask if they were running anything. Rod Liddle [editor, *Today* programme] said he thought it was extraordinary and dreadful for the Beeb but because it was so 'tricky' they were taking the 'coward's way out' and leaving it to the review of the papers. I called PA to say we were concerned the BBC were not covering this as a legitimate news story. Once in the office I wrote to Tony Hall suggesting the interview would breach their guidelines and suggesting a four-way debate with the party leaders. I knew it would be refused, as indeed it was by the afternoon, but we had to try to keep the pressure on. PMQs was OK. Odd moment halfway through when Teresa Gorman [Conservative MP] looked up at me from her seat and drew her finger across her throat and then pointed at me. It was all getting to them. Got a lift home with Tessa who said, worryingly, that JP had had dinner with a friend of hers and he had been pouring out his anger that he was being 'squeezed out'. Worrying if he was saying that semi-publicly.

Friday, March 31

Derry had got involved in the BBC row and agreed that Tony Hall's letter to me was totally unsatisfactory. He agreed they were in breach of their guidelines and should pull the *Panorama* interview. Hall refused to agree to anything we suggested and then Derry dug up an annexe to the TV licence under which we could threaten a judicial review. 'Old Melon-head', as we called him, was living up to it today, and enjoying himself immensely. The news was full of Tory fightback but with the Scottish elections days away, they were pretty stupid the way they went on and on about Middle England. I watched JM on *Anne and Nick* [daytime TV chat show], which was a total blowjob, about which we complained.

Saturday, April 1

TB on good form, but worried I may have gone too far on the BBC with the judicial review line, but was reassured Derry backed it too.

Jack McConnell called to say the SNP were interested in judicial review as well. Philip and Gail's party. CB made a straight beeline for Fiona and complained that I was running their lives, making TB do far too much, and preventing him from being a normal person living a normal life. She could see no good in what I did at all. Fiona, who was due to have lunch with her on Friday anyway, said she stood up for me as best she could but she was pretty heavy. She said TB bothered me far more than I bothered him. Today alone she had been there on five occasions when TB called me, and often it was to have the same conversation we had already had. I joined them and told her I was very sensitive to all this, that I tried hard not to intrude into their lives but if for example TB said he wanted a nationwide Clause 4 tour, she shouldn't blame me when we go away and organise what he asks for. That is the job. Then TB joined and we at last had a laugh about it. I said hello Tony, this is Fiona, she says you ruined her life and Cherie said, I'm Cherie, he's (i.e. me) ruined mine. Then Susie Orbach [psychotherapist and author] joined us and Tony introduced himself as my press secretary. Fiona said she'd told Cherie I was keeping a diary and a look of horror fell on her face.

Sunday, April 2

Jack McConnell called for advice re *Panorama*. *Scotland on Sunday* led on the possibility of a Labour/Lib Dem/SNP joint court action. Derry was against it but after speaking to the party's lawyer in Scotland, Jack and the Lib Dems, he agreed we should go for an 'interim interdict' through the Scottish courts to get the programme stopped, while the SNP were going for a judicial review. I finally got the news we were going ahead while playing golf with David Mills.

Monday, April 3

I was bleeped urgent on the way in by Jack McConnell who wanted all the *Panorama* papers. He and George Robertson were on and off all day as the court in Edinburgh heard the Lib-Lab appeal for an interim interdict and the Nats' call for a judicial review. TB called saying the Tory fightback was going better for them and he still felt we were not firing on all cylinders, that there was something missing from the operation. Bickerstaffe and other union leaders were complaining they felt they got nothing out of TB. TB said they have to get it in their heads that he does not believe in split-the-middle compromise for the sake of it. If they've got a point, we should listen to it. But HE is not going to indulge them, and the days they demand something and we agree to something just short of what they demand are gone. Issues and arguments should be settled on their merits. After a cup of tea with Tom and Sally, I went back to find Jim Cousins [Labour MP] storming out of the office because TB had just sacked him from his foreign affairs brief over last week's disappearance[1] with Ann Clwyd. Then TB saw her and sacked her too. I worked up a line with Derek Foster that they'd been sacked for going AWOL and failing to return when told to do so. Within minutes she was going round the broadcasters telling them how awfully she'd been treated but most of the press seemed to think good job well done, and Bruce reported the same reaction from the MPs. Then came the news Jack McC had told me to expect – we had won the case in Edinburgh and JM's interview was off air. That immediately became the main story and wiped JM's US visit out of sight. The BBC appealed and the appeal had to be heard immediately with the programme due out. The Nats were out on a limb. GR was thoroughly enjoying himself. 'O J Simpson[2] has nothing on this,' he said, 'high drama indeed.'

The BBC case fell to bits when a judge asked whether they would consider broadcasting such an interview three days before local elections in England. It was extraordinary either they or Number 10 thought they could do this. There was the obvious danger it would become a freedom of speech issue but I felt we were on a strong wicket. BBC news at 9 led on *Panorama*, a mess for the BBC and for JM, then Ann Clwyd which ran well for us. At 9.30 GR called to say the appeal had been kicked out. Tim, who had done a terrific research job from the start, was ecstatic. It had been his idea to get Derry involved and Derry had turned it. I tried to call Tony Hall to ask their next move but he was in a meeting with [John] Birt [BBC director general]. Later they said they were going to the House of Lords to get the interview shown. It had been a textbook guerrilla campaign. The hacks said JM was livid. He was being chased all over Washington on his 'great statesman' trip and being asked about an interview that would never be seen.

Tuesday, April 4
The BBC story was still leading, with Tony Hall doing the rounds looking agitated. The appeal was to be heard at 11.30 re granting leave to go to the Lords, and it was rejected. GB, for reasons no doubt to do with his own position there, raised objections (backed by Joy)

[1] The two had failed to return from a visit to Turkey and northern Iraq for three-line whipped Commons votes.
[2] Former US football star and actor accused of murdering ex-wife Nicole Brown Simpson and her friend Ronald Goldman in 1994. Later acquitted.

to TB going to Scotland the day after the local elections there. He said we needed to be doing more here on the privatisation campaign because Margaret Beckett wasn't pushing it. With JM away, JP was standing in for TB at PMQs. Decided on tax and then had the usual tortuous and fraught preparations. Rosie and I debriefed him on the TB/JP/GB meeting. He said GB had sat in the corner saying nothing. This echoed what TB said this morning, that GB had just refused to engage. JP said these three-way meetings should be regular but they only happened if he forced them and he couldn't understand why TB allowed GB to behave like that. PMQs was better than the last time he did it. Meeting with JP, Rosie and Joy. He said he wanted to wipe the slate clean with Joy but she had to realise her job was to serve the party as a whole. She was in danger of being caught in the crossfire which is why it was important all the lines were clear. He said he would take an active role in local election planning. He had tried to work with GB and would do so again, but he reserved the right to come to all of his meetings. If there were disagreements between the two committees it would be for him and GB to sort out, with TB to intervene if there were disputes. Joy's demeanour was still very closed and nervous. I saw TB re Europe and chat turned to GB. He said he was worried about him and just hated the fact there was all this suspicion around. TB saw him again later and according to Anji for once told him what was what: that he had to get it into his head that TB was the leader and he wasn't, that TB had all the support for that and he should stop brooding and get on with it. 'Do you think Robin was in here every five minutes whingeing when JP was moving in on his Europe job? He just got on with it.' Deborah Ross [*Independent* columnist] asked if I could introduce her to JP so she could tell him she thought he was sexy.

Wednesday, April 5

GB meeting. I'd paged Peter M to say I'd be late because I'd dropped my pager under a taxi wheel. I made it on time and sat down next to Peter. 'Alastair will be a bit late,' he told Gordon. 'I'm here,' I said, and he almost jumped out of his seat in shock. GB started to rush through the agenda and got to the third item before I pointed out he was going through yesterday's. GB was still pushing for TB not to go to Scotland. Peter slipped me a note saying if I give in to TB not going to Scotland, he's out of here. The meeting was a farce and Rosie and I went back laughing so hard that by the time we got back we had splitting headaches. TB was working on the Europe draft. Clause 4 meeting at which Margaret McD said we were doing well in the CLPs and Jon Cruddas said we were doing not so well in the unions. TB was worried that a good CLP result plus a bad union vote would aid the Tories' 'Trojan Horse' attack. Rory paged me at 6 to say come home, so riddled with guilt I went home to take him out to play football knowing I'd have to leave by 7.30 to go out for dinner.

Thursday, April 6

Finally got to take the boys to school after last night's scene with Rory. It was a beautiful warm day and TB wanted to go for a walk in the park. He said in addition to his bollocking of GB yesterday he had had a word with Peter M and told him to apologise to Tom Sawyer for the way he spoke to him yesterday. He said he was worried about the policy operation, and worried about Joy, and worried about Easter. He also thought Fiona didn't like him and he thought that would be a problem over time. He felt JM got more out of the fightback strategy than the press gave him credit for. He confided that Cherie was going to get silk, and we had a chat about whether she'd be able to carry on working if we won. We both thought yes but that her cases would be closely scrutinised and that might make it difficult. Back home to wait for the Scottish results. I was more convinced than ever we should go up for it, but GB and Joy were still arguing strongly against. People were phoning from Scotland all night as these amazing results came through. I called PA from the bath to put out TB's words.

Friday, April 7

Despite the results [the Conservative vote collapsed] the 8.45 meeting was particularly bad-tempered and unfocused. I tried to get GB's mind on how we deal with the Tory attack on Europe, on which TB felt we had to build defences, but he went off on one about the CBI [Confederation of British Industry]. It was hopeless. Then GB and Peter had a little spat over the question of the advertising agency. I told TB how awful the GB meeting had been. He said if GB did not get his act together he would have to take the thing over himself. I said it was a total joke, whatever the story was, he'd say we should put out some words from Andrew Smith! And why was there even a debate about whether TB should go to Scotland today? It was bloody obvious he should. We went through to the Shadow Cabinet room and the TB meeting was just as bad, for the same reasons. TB: 'Which senior people will be around during Easter?' JP: 'I've asked for a grid.' GB: 'It'll be sorted.' TB: 'What's happening on local council success stories?' Joy: 'It's in hand. Frank is in charge of it.' And so on. I said nobody doubts this work is going on but it would be nice to see some product and we can decide how to use it. TB asked to see GB and Joy afterwards and asked why they were so negative about everything. GB's body language was extraordinary. He and his team just sent out these doom-and-gloom vibes the whole time.

It was a relief to get out of the office and head for Heathrow at 11. We had Hunter Davies [journalist and Beatles biographer] with us all day doing a *Mail* mag profile. He did a good interview on the plane, and liked Hunter's style. He didn't take many notes, and he didn't tape it. He said he preferred to try to remember what his interviewees said then show them the quotes and if they didn't like them they could change them. TB loved hearing some of Hunter's Beatles stories. Hunter said he'd liked him but found him unconvincing on how he became a party member, and religion. I could sense he was going for the 'stands for nothing' angle, the machine politician, rootless, ruthless. We headed for the [Glasgow] City Hall where David Evans [party official] and Hilary had organised a hero's welcome and TB did a really good little off-the-cuff speech, then half a dozen interviews for telly and radio. There was a great moment when the Radio Clyde reporter came in. She had the most spectacular cleavage and TB, Hunter and I, plus every other man in the room, found it impossible to divert our eyes. Of course it was worst for TB because he was doing an interview with her, and she leant forward every time she put the microphone over towards him. It was an act of heroism that he managed to maintain eye contact, especially as I was by now trying to crack him up. Once she left, he did. Hunter had another session with TB on the little plane to Leeds, mainly about the family, Oratory, what he would do after politics. He said he noticed TB didn't mention Cherie without being asked about her. The Leeds meeting was in a beautiful hall, really nice pictures and atmosphere. Dad and Donald [AC's brother] came to the meeting which was nice. It was more like a rally compared with some of the earlier Clause 4 meetings which showed how the debate had changed. TB headed off to Trimdon. Hunter and I headed back to London, and he never stopped grilling me all the way back. I got the feeling he had taken to TB more as the day wore on.

Saturday, April 8

Tracked down RC at the Grand National and agreed words to put out on Europe, which was still worrying TB. RC, as ever, gave me carte blanche and I put out words based heavily on the note Philip [Gould] had done. Fiona and I went out for dinner with the boys.

She'd had lunch with CB yesterday which went fine. But Cherie said she'd seen a side to me in Blackpool that she had never seen before, that she thought I had been hard and cruel. She also thought I was running TB too hard. She did at least accept, said Fiona, that I did what I did because I had Tony's interests at heart but she felt there were real impositions on their family life and I wasn't sympathetic enough to that. They'd also talked about the fact that her work was beginning to be affected. She didn't know what she would do if they got to Downing Street. Fiona said she thought Cherie and I should just try to go back to year zero and forget everything that had gone on up to now. She felt Cherie was feeling exposed and vulnerable and without much help and support to call on.

Sunday, April 9
TB up in Sedgefield and we barely spoke which suggests he was relaxing for once. The main story was the resignation of Richard Spring [Conservative MP, parliamentary aide to the Northern Ireland Secretary] over a three-in-a-bed romp in the *News of the World* which quickly became a privacy story.

Monday, April 10
Meeting with Miliband re economic message which confirmed my fear we were nowhere nearer getting agreement on one, and we were unlikely to until GB became more inventive in his brief. Margaret Beckett finally did her big NHS speech which got next to no coverage at all.

Tuesday, April 11
TB was in a much better mood. He flew back to go to the Queen's dinner at Windsor. Lunch with George Jones who was complaining that we didn't take the *Telegraph* seriously. His political take was that tax could still do us in but that the Tories had probably had it. I went home early to play football with Rory then Hunter Davies came round to check his article. He said he liked TB.

Wednesday, April 12
Due to leave for Majorca at 5 so took the boys into the office and they stayed with Hilary and Kate whilst I prepared JP for his press conference. He was in a bit of a state but we agreed he just had to stay focused on rail and not get pushed off it. He wasn't happy after the event and said he was going to take a few days to rethink his role. The GB/Peter M thing was getting him down and he sensed a right-

ward drift. He said he was finding it harder and harder to work with GB and he wanted nothing to do with Peter. He cheered up when the kids came up and he was great with them. Calum christened him 'the Bear' and asked for his baseball cap, which JP gave him.

Thursday, April 13 to Monday, April 17

Had a terrific time in Majorca. TB had given me strict instructions to take a proper break and not call the office unless he called for me. But of course with Philip [Gould] there we spent an awful lot of time talking about our various problems and challenges and actually managed to get some good work done, honing messages and developing a sense of clarity about what the election campaign would look like. We also did some useful brainstorming on slogans, though in truth in 'New Labour, New Britain' we had the perfect strategic framework. PG made a very good observation re the 8.45 GB meetings. He said it 'felt like an away game for us', which it did. It felt like GB did not actually want us to be on the same team. He wanted things to be more difficult than they needed to be, which made everything incredibly draining. PG felt that I should take over all message work, Joy should do rebuttal and Peter be given a more hands-on and avowed role in campaigns. PG's other main theme for the time we were there was that the party didn't have a clear sense of what TB's mission or project was. They knew he was a moderniser, but they needed a sense of how that related beyond the party.

Tuesday, April 18

I finally cracked and called the office prior to TB doing PMQs. I also started to get a feel for what DH and HC called a nightmare of Peter M using my absence to try to take charge, and the GB problems getting worse when I wasn't there because there was nobody between him and JP, and him and Peter. Anji said the minute I was gone Peter was in like a shot. Pat McFadden sent me a draft of TB words for the local government launch which TB had decided to do himself. He said there was a piece in the *Sunday Mail* magazine which was pure GB propaganda, on the theme of TB being GB's dummy.

Wednesday, April 19

I called Anji on the way in from the airport, and then David Hill who said re Peter M it had been a definite case of 'while the cat's away'. He and Joy felt that he should have been briefing for Tony, but Peter was doing it, or using Tim and Peter H. Fiona and I went to a bizarre dinner party for Andrew Neil [journalist and broadcaster], a curious mix of weirdos and bright young things who were trying too hard. I took one look at the guests and made sure I was sitting with Fiona. The less of this socialising I could get away with the better.

Thursday, April 20

I called Peter M first thing to get his take on recent events. He was convinced Charlie was briefing against TB and that he was the source for the suggestions that the GMB were not certain re Clause 4. He said that in my absence everyone felt they could go out and brief and there had been too many voices, though of course the problem was that in most people's eyes, he was the most compulsive briefer of them all. He said he was also worried that GB was co-opting Joy to his own operation, not the party's, and he was alarmed that TB seemed to accept that.

The 8.45 meeting was the usual awful nonsense. Jonathan, Peter M, PG and I were actually sitting on one side of the room and the rest on the other so PG's 'away game' thought was borne out even more clearly. There was a rather nasty discussion about the PPB and whether we should carry on with the JM lying theme. Jonathan said TB wasn't happy with it, Peter said he didn't like it and Joy flared up. I felt having done it, we could not be seen to back away from it. TB admitted he had agreed to Joy to appease GB. I said GB's hidden agenda wasn't terribly hidden at the moment. 'Why does he never change despite all these heart to hearts you have?' and I answered my own question – because he can't accept you, not he, are leader of the party. He actually believes all that stuff his people tell him that he made an incredible sacrifice and the job should have been his.

Some of the hacks told me a freelance was trying to sell a story that I was having an affair with David Mellor's [Conservative MP, former Cabinet minister] secretary, which would be worth a few bob in a libel case.

Friday, April 21

I'd arranged for the CLP ballot results to come in as they were speaking so it would help the mood music. The CWU [Communication Workers Union] ballot result also came in, the only full union ballot with massive support and that leapt to the top of the news for the whole day. TB spoke to Anji who said she was worried that people felt Peter was too influential on him at the moment. Andy Marr made the same point to me yesterday, that Peter was poisoning TB and making him more hostile than he needed to be. Anji felt it in the context of GB, that Peter was winding him up to think GB was at it all the time,

April '95: GB's hidden agenda not very hidden

which simply unsettled Tony. I said I was partly responsible because I'd made similar noises based on the experience of the 8.45 meetings. Bruce was clear the problem was Peter and the solution was to push him out. I felt it was more complex than that. What the last few days did show, however, is that there can only be one voice speaking authoritatively for TB, and any others must come in behind that, not do their own thing. TB was cheered by the CLPs and CWU results and felt it must put pressure on UNISON and the T&G.

Saturday, April 22

The CLP results were remarkable and should have gone even bigger, but the morning was ruined by the *Telegraph* story on gays in the military. David Clark [now Shadow Defence Secretary] was on the *Today* programme and was abysmal. He belatedly pointed out it did not mean homosexual acts would be tolerated. After TB's third call on the subject – thankfully he hadn't heard the interview – I called Clark who disarmed me slightly by saying, all wide-eyed and innocent, 'I think we've fallen into a trap here.' You don't say. I put out TB words on the ballots to try to lift it on to later bulletins, without success.

Sunday, April 23

TB doing *World This Weekend* so over to Richmond Crescent to prepare for that. Called MMcD for the latest CLP figures which were excellent. For once I had a perfectly nice and civilised chat with Cherie, in which we both lamented how much of our time we spent having to talk to TB in his underwear.

Monday, April 24

JP said he wasn't happy that TB hadn't asked him when he was going to speak at the special conference. He was being written out of the script. I said this was nonsense. TB would open, and do a proper wind-up and JP would speak after the vote. 'So I'm Mr Fucking Punch.' Anji and I went to Joy's BBC farewell. I had a very heavy row with John Birt who said the *Panorama* court ruling was the biggest attack on the BBC's independence in its history. I said that was utter nonsense and they should just have admitted a mistake for once. He said he would never be able to look George Robertson in the eye again and I said don't be so bloody ridiculous.

Tuesday, April 25

TB came back from CB's QC ceremony. I had worked out a line of attack which TB improved by watching the news for once, and said why aren't the interviewers asking if the Tory rebels have given a guarantee that they will support the government in future votes on Europe? That became the question and then we rehearsed a line to use if Major came back at him with our own divisions – I lead my party, he follows his – which turned out to be the biggest blow TB had yet landed at PMQs, which produced a massive cheer on our side and a look of real pain on theirs. The PMQs hit [on JM restoring the whip to rebels] was gigantic, and with the GMB coming on board re Clause 4, it was a good day. Another mini drama when Iain Duncan Smith [Conservative rebel MP and future leader] raised a point of order about whether I was entitled to sit in the press gallery. These people are pathetic. I left with PG to go to a focus group in Harrow. The first group was very depressing. Only one person was aware of Clause 4 and the general view of TB was that he was too smooth and a bit oily, and they felt the economy was improving. The second group was better, with three women in particular who really liked TB, but the hatred of the Tories that was there a few months ago was beginning to fade. The need for a really positive agenda of our own, related to people rather than to the party, was clear.

Wednesday, April 26

TB came back from the NEC in a fairly typical post-NEC mood, and I briefed him on the focus groups. I said there were three main problems: 1. JM still had the potential to become popular again; 2. TB's appeal was not yet clear and too many people saw him as shallow; and 3. there was a sense of the economy improving and we did not have a clear economic message. TB said he was confident his own position would strengthen with exposure, but he was concerned re economic message. Jonathan told me that on the way back from the NEC TB said to RC that he'd be interested in his thoughts on economic message – a bit unfeeling with GB in bed with a bad back. We had a meeting on economic message – TB, AC, Jonathan, DM, Derek Scott, Geoff Norris, Ed Balls – at which Balls drivelled on endlessly about the competition speech planned for Monday. TB said afterwards to Jonathan that in future he only wanted grown-ups to attend his meetings.

Thursday, April 27

The Sundays were getting geared up for big pieces on Saturday's conference so I was briefing a lot of colour and background. CMT meeting at 4 was reasonably jolly for once. I think JP found it odd that Peter sat opposite TB. Joy at one point made an observation that nobody at Walworth Road was smiling on election night in 1987 which created a bad impression. 'We lost,' I said. I went for a haircut and came back to learn the *FT* had a Trade Unions for Labour document which allegedly showed the unions gave TB's office £180,000, and Hezza was lined up for a big Blair/sleaze attack. I called John Williams [*Mirror*] and Paul Wilenius [*Today*] and got them to do stories about JM putting Hezza in charge of a new 'Get Blair' hit squad.

Friday, April 28

A typical day of chaos and overactivity with the Clause 4 vote looming. I had over thirty pager messages while I was at TB's house. He was fairly happy with the speech but mid morning we agreed a new structure based on the need to make 'New Labour, New Britain' clearer. He rewrote it himself, section by section, and did it well, then Liz Lloyd and I put in his changes, and mine, and we had some decent lines. Philip liked it and sent over a one-page note, the analysis of which was so close to mine I think TB thought I probably told him what to say. We went through the usual black humour phase predicting TB's downfall within twenty-four hours and imagining all the various reshuffle plans of the various contenders. Tom S called to say there could be a messy start to the conference tomorrow because [Arthur] Scargill [president, National Union of Mineworkers] was calling for a court to review whether the conference was constitutional. Drama of the day when we heard that JP's pre-record for *Newsnight* on industrial legislation was a bit of a disaster area. Harriet had been due to do it but she had flu so JP stepped in. Though he kept strictly within policy, e.g. right to strike, getting rid of Compulsory Competitive Tendering, it just wasn't what we wanted up the night before the conference. TB threw a complete wobbly when he heard, throwing the phone on the floor at one point, going absolutely barmy, saying if this was up big we could wave bye-bye to the conference. It was an overreaction and I tried to get him to calm down. The words were just about OK, but the tone was wrong and JP agreed it was the sensible thing to pull out of the *Today* programme, so I tried to track down RC. Finally got hold of him after midnight and he was thrilled to be asked.

Saturday, April 29

Round to TB's at 8, with Liz [Lloyd] already there. We made relatively few changes, and no major ones. TB hyper again. Got to the office and Jonathan and David M both felt the speech ending didn't work, which had also been worrying TB and me. He asked me to have another go and I knocked something out which he quite liked, he rewrote it and we had a speech. We had the usual last minute 'Do we have enough jokes?' which we just about did. I said why don't you stand up and say 'Now, I'd like to turn to the party's name . . .'? I meant it as a joke but I could see he was tempted – as a joke. Pat called to say the TGWU were joining UNISON in opposing us. This produced the inevitable tirade. 'These people are criminally stupid. They simply do not care if we win or lose.' In the short car ride over to the conference [at Methodist Central Hall, Westminster], TB barely spoke. He had his speech on his lap. He was staring out of the window but taking nothing in, occasionally nodding forward to underline to himself a line from the speech running through his head. This was the moment I knew today would go well. He was withdrawing completely into himself, psyching up to deliver. The speech was good but if he could add twenty per cent in the delivery, we'd have a really good day.

We were taken to a little private room, where he was pacing up and down, and nodding to himself every few moments, then firing off questions to me which didn't really matter, and I'm not sure he even listened to the answers. This was all part of the psyching-up process, running down time, getting his mind in the zone he wanted it. We made a couple of last-minute changes before checking the script on the autocue. We marked up on his own script the lines that really needed to breathe, then Jackie Stacey [Labour Party staff] led him up to the entrance to the stage. 'Good luck,' I said. 'Go for it.' He smiled and nodded and walked on to the platform. Scargill was hissed as he tried out his legal challenge idea. I watched from the front, sitting next to [Tony] Bevins, and [Dennis] Skinner who had a new jacket for the day. It went well, and he got a good reception at the end. After Morris and Bickerstaffe spoke there was inevitably a lot of interest in the unions relationship side to the story. Brian Wilson made another excellent speech, really going for Diane Abbott who made some crack that members would vote for the healing powers of cabbages. JP got a standing ovation and the story was taking care of itself.

The plan after the result was for TB to make a short unscheduled speech and he and I went to the toilet at the back to get away from all the fussing and we went over a few lines. We agreed he could get away with the crack about the name of the party. He was quite emotional. He'd always believed that doing this would be an important precondition for winning over the kind of people whose support we needed, and the party had responded really well, despite all the dire warnings. He was pumped up and proud, he'd done really well and I said so, and it was bizarre, lots of noise outside, and the two of us hiding away in a grotty undecorated toilet and he says to me 'I think we're on our way.' MMcD got us out to give us the final result[1] and the relief oozed out of him. We'd worked out a line about him not being born in the party but being part of it. He started with 'Thank you.' It went fine, then we headed to the QE2 for the delegates' reception where some twat with a Trot poster came up to me on the way in and yelled 'Butcher! Traitor!' at me. I stopped and mustered as much visual contempt as I could, then assured him that if we win the general election then don't worry, thanks to wankers like him, there will always be another Tory government along afterwards. These people make me vomit. JP's speech was brilliant, saying how TB's courage and foresight made it possible and it was a great day for the party. Afterwards he took TB to one side, said well done, and now can we have a period of relative calm?

Sunday, April 30

Up at 6 to read the papers and over to TB's to prepare for *Frost*. The papers were excellent after yesterday but both of us were worried about the 'where now, what next?' questions. He wasn't happy about the quality of policy work and that was what we should have had in place for this moment. He'd impressed on everyone, including the Shadow Cabinet, that this should be the springboard to really strong policy work but it wasn't really happening yet. After the excitement of yesterday, he was back to his usual calm, dogged, think of all the things that can go wrong and work out how to avoid them mode. We were both tired and wishing we didn't have to be up at the crack of dawn but there we are. We had been so focused on yesterday that we hadn't given today the strategic thought we normally would have done. I went into the studio to listen to Jeremy Hanley who was quite good, for him, again attacking TB and saying Clause 4 was irrelevant. TB and I had a last run round the obvious questions then in he went. We stayed for a quick breakfast at which Hanley, having just slagged off TB, said to him what a remarkable achievement yesterday was. And as we left he came over to us, pointed at me and said to TB 'Look after him.' I didn't know whether he was being nice or warning they would be going for me. In briefing the press I started to point out the four areas where TB would now give licence to think the unthinkable and signal a sense of impatience at the policy development process. He still felt there was too much complacency around,

[1] A special conference at Central Hall, Westminster, voted to back Blair's Clause 4 reforms. The final margin was 65.23 per cent for, 35.77 per cent against.

that too many in the Shadow Cabinet felt we were so far ahead we could coast.

Back home for Grace's birthday party. Rory bit through his tongue and was in agony. Bickerstaffe called again for another whinge about life. Then the BBC ran stuff from the *Mirror* interview re what he said about the unions.[1] He'd said no more than what he thought and anything else would have been odd, if not a retreat. This was going to cause us trouble, though I could not work out how much.

Monday, May 1

The other papers picked up big on the unions comments and Blair's 'onslaught on the unions' was leading all the news. I was in early working on his press conference statement but clearly it would be dominated by this. JP was first on the phone, livid. 'There is a hidden agenda and I'm not going along with it. It's fucking crap and it's beyond my bottom line.' I tried to explain that all that happened was we did an interview without a clear top line and so they took out the strongest words. It was not a plan and there is not a hidden agenda. Then Rodney B called and said it felt like he was getting another kicking and I said for heaven's sake stop thinking everything is personal. He was about to do the *Today* programme and was angered by TB saying we could move towards 50-50, as was JP. The atmosphere in the press conference pre-meeting was tense. JP was in a real rage and barely speaking to anyone. GB was angry because he feared the unions stuff would overshadow his speech, and Clare Short was twittering on about not being too nasty to the unions. I lost my rag saying I can't believe how you just swallow whatever is in the papers and assume it to be gospel. TB, looking like he'd rather be at the dentist, said he would deal with all questions on the unions and he would shut it down. The press conference went fine, half on the economy, half on the unions. It was clear, though, the BBC had decided to go on the unions so I wrote to Oakley saying the TB/JP split was press driven and they should be covering GB's speech which had policy substance. JP behaved fine at the press conference but when Anji said why don't you travel back with TB he said he was walking back.

[1] Blair had stated that the block vote would be reduced from seventy per cent to fifty per cent. Commenting on the way the TGWU and UNISON had voted on Clause 4, he said: 'We need to reflect carefully on the lesson of all this and I'm sure the trade union people will do the same, because it is unhealthy if you get a massive disparity between party members and the way unions are going.'

Clare S called in her usual 'fount of all wisdom' way and said there was a 'malfunction' around TB and the PLP and the unions were up in arms. She was due to have dinner with TB so I suggested we had lunch and we met at Rodin's. She said she liked TB but trust was running out. People didn't believe he wasn't responsible for a lot of the briefing that went on, there were too many voices around him. She felt Peter M could be an adviser who did not brief the press, or he could appear on TV, but he couldn't do both. She said there was a feeling that nobody round TB really understood the party, that Jonathan was nice but ineffective. She thought GB was tortured and Robin was a clever egomaniac. I wondered if she ever applied to herself the kind of rigorous analysis she'd subjected the others to.

TB/JP and I met after TB got back from Southampton and JP said he didn't believe there wasn't a strategy to brief against the unions. TB said the blame for this whole thing lay with the unions because they had made themselves the issue with the way they had behaved during the Clause 4 debate. JP insisted there was a strategy. I could feel me losing my temper and I picked up the *Evening Standard* – Prescott threat to Blair – and I said was that a strategy or will you say these things happen? The truth is these things do happen and sometimes we make them happen and sometimes we don't. He calmed down a bit, but he said he had a bottom line. 'I'm of the unions and I'm for the unions and I think you kicked them too hard.' We weren't helped by Peter M on *World at One*, who was pretty provocative, especially as I'd told Bickerstaffe we were not putting anyone up on it. Rodney B came round for another general whinge. He said TB had to realise he would need the unions at a later stage. I reported back to TB who said they can just fuck off. We will never get elected if every little change produces this kind of nonsense. I said we just had to be careful that division and disarray did not become our main backdrop. He said JP has to understand it could get worse not better but we have set a course and we have to keep our nerve. I bumped into Nick Soames, who said that his lot had had it. Philip said however bad it felt on the inside, he had watched the news bulletins and from the outside it looked fine.

Tuesday, May 2

8.45 meeting, and Joy asked whether we should have a post-mortem on recent events. GB asked whether we could do more to kill the *Mirror* story on the unions, all hell broke loose. Peter said he was confident TB knew what he was doing and though it was a risk, the unions story was a good one, even if it meant detracting from GB's speech. That prompted a whole heap of tutting and headshaking. I made three points: 1. I accepted we should not be going into major interviews without a clear idea of what we wanted out of it in terms of a top line; but 2. when things like this happen, there should be greater co-ordination between the key players; and 3. there was too great a tendency for heads to drop and people to assume the worst when the slightest thing went not according to plan. I meant JP and Rosie in this particular instance but Joy took it to mean her, and of course it was GB's natural tendency too. GB rightly pointed out there were two very different views on the unions story. Peter was at his most provocative, really emphasising he thought it was a good place for us to be, and Joy stormed out. Charlie Whelan then muttered something under his breath about a Peter radio interview and Peter said 'It's no good you going around telling everyone we're trying to undermine Gordon, as you were yesterday. We're not.'

GB was handling it well and trying to calm it, but it was clear his people thought that TB's interviews, JP's, and our briefing, were all designed to detract from GB's speech. PG tried to inject a bit of humour, but it was all very bad-tempered, without doubt the worst meeting yet. I said I can't believe the way people flap the minute anything goes remotely wrong. Indeed, anyone looking in from the outside would wonder why on earth we were anything other than supremely confident. Rodney B came on to complain about the *Guardian* editorial likening him to Jean-Marie Le Pen [French far-right politician] and I said for crying out loud, I do not write *Guardian* editorials. He said no, but you influence them. I wish.

TB saw Bill Morris and said he was virtually palpitating. TB was defending Peter's line because it was forcing the unions to sue for peace. He felt he could see a way towards reduction of the share of the union vote, and probably, eventually, some sort of state funding. He said the public would tolerate the unions so long as there was no big rift with the elected political authority. I had a nice chat with TB who said he wanted me to get more rest but he was worried that every time I did, the operation seemed to fall apart. I said again that Peter had to be used properly according to an agreed strategy, not doing his own thing.

Wednesday, May 3

Told TB of Rodney's incessant phoning and he said he could see a way forward on the unions, move to a gradual reduction on union voting power after the election to 50–50 and over time an end to sponsorship. We left for the Hilton for TB's speech to the Newspaper

Society. It was OK but he fucked up the sound bite and tried to get back to it and it didn't work. The whole thing was very flat and in the car he said he didn't know why but he got nervous and couldn't understand why he had fucked up. Jonathan and I took the piss all the way back to try to make him see it didn't matter that much, but he wasn't happy with himself. It was one of his best and most professional traits: if he didn't do well, he liked to exaggerate how bad he had been, then work out how to improve. But it could be a pain for the rest of us, because we'd have to go over it again and again until he was satisfied he'd got something positive out of it for the future. He had a long and tense meeting with JP so he could take him through his thoughts on the unions, and it was easy to hear JP's reaction through the door. He then decided to see GB and RC separately rather than do a Big Guns – 'I'm not sure I can stand it today'. TB told GB that Whelan was a menace and he ought to think about getting rid of him.

I got a lift home with TB and RC who were meeting Paddy Ashdown for dinner. The plan had been to meet at TB's but I felt neutral territory was better so they were going to Derry's. RC said that if it got out that they were meeting, we should say it was to discuss how we maximise the government's difficulties. TB said that both in opposition and in government, it was important to us that the Libs abandoned equidistance [central positioning between Conservatives and Labour]. He wanted to be able to agree an approach on the Constitution because he felt it would help us politically, in opposition, and in the reality of making real change in government, if we could get the Lib Dems on board for some of the changes we planned. He said if we ended up with a smallish majority, it was important they did not feel they had to attack us the whole time and oppose as a matter of course. RC was probing and asked if it was true that 'Bobby' [Peter Mandelson] was out of favour. TB put on a big grin and said no. RC looked disappointed. 'I see the *Standard* called him the most hated man in the Labour Party,' said Robin. 'Not by the leader and his staff,' I said, and he smiled. On the unions, TB said if he didn't do anything that someone found difficult, he would end up doing nothing. 'I don't think anyone could accuse you of doing nothing, Tony,' said Robin. 'Though I think we might all benefit from a period of calm.' Despite myself, I couldn't help liking Robin. I liked his speaking style too, his little clipped comments and his perfectly formed sentences that were delivered as if he were in a play, and he was projecting his voice to the back of the theatre. And he was funny and, for the most part, good-humoured, if always with an eye on the main chance.

Local elections. TB was still having to see JP who had virtually threatened to resign yesterday. He said, I can't win. He says I don't involve
him or let him know what I'm thinking and when I do, he explodes.
He said he'd persuaded him to accept most of it. He said the Ashdown
dinner went fine but RC had been tricky, pushing hard on PR. Anji
said TB was close to the end of his tether with JP (intransigence) and
GB (just being deliberately difficult). CMT was better than usual but
TB still complaining he wasn't happy with policy development process.
JP was still in a major grump. Then TB, Anji and I had a set-to because
he said he didn't want to do the interview rounds in the morning. I
said he had to get personally associated with every advance and
breakthrough and we were clearly going to do well. I went home by
7.30 because I had to leave again at 9.30. Ended up having a big
argument with Fiona. CB had told her she was doing an article for
the *Telegraph* on the Chiswick women's refuge. I said something like
that had to be really carefully thought through, and she said I was
just trying to control Cherie. I said that was completely untrue. I'm
trying to avoid her doing damage to herself by setting herself up for
a fall.

Terry picked me up to go to collect TB/CB to go to Walworth
Road for the results coming in. They were at a dinner in Hyde Park
Gardens that had been organised for them to meet Princess Diana. I
rang the bell and said could you tell Mr Blair his car is here. I went
back to the car and the next thing TB is tapping at the car window
and he says 'Someone wants to meet you.' I get out and she's walking
towards me, and she says 'There he is, can I come over and say hello?'
and then she's standing there, absolutely, spellbindingly, drop-dead
gorgeous, in a way that the millions of photos didn't quite get it. She
said hello, held out her hand and said she was really pleased to meet
me, so I mumbled something back about me being more pleased and
how I didn't expect when I left the house tonight that I'd end up
standing in the middle of the road talking to her. 'It would make a
very funny picture if there were any paparazzi in those trees,' she
said. TB was standing back and Cherie was looking impatient and I
was just enjoying flirting with her. She said she'd told TB she'd wanted
to meet the man who protected him because she'd heard so much
about me. I asked if he had behaved well and she said yes, very well.
I said in that case I think you should come with us to Walworth Road
and create an almighty sensation. 'I just might,' she said. There was
something about her eyes that went beyond radiance. They locked
on to you and were utterly mesmeric. She had perfect skin and her

whole face lit up when she spoke and there were moments when I had to fight to hear the words because I'm just lost in the beauty. And I'm thinking how could I have written all those vile things about her? 'Anyway,' she said, 'I mustn't hold you back any longer,' and there's me thinking I would happily be held back for a long time to come. We shook hands again, she said goodbye to Tony and Cherie, we watched her walk back to the house, and off we went. TB groaned loudly and said he couldn't believe it. 'We'd barely started the conversation and she says "What's Alastair Campbell really like?" And she wants to know what you do for me, and how it all works and then she says she'd like to meet you, and how she'd feel a lot happier if she had a press officer as good as you, and all this.' Terry was laughing his head off, I was milking it for all it was worth, and telling TB he really shouldn't feel jealous, she probably quite liked him too, and CB was saying she was probably just being polite. I said I don't think politeness ever extended to feeling she had to walk out in the cold to say goodbye to her guest's staff. I was of course unbearable at Walworth Road, constantly winding up TB and saying to the rest of the office he was a bit bruised because Diana had just used him as a means of getting to me. Combined with the brilliant results that were coming in, it all made for a pretty extraordinary evening.

Friday, May 5

Up at 6 and round to TB's. Everyone was saying how extraordinary the results were but TB was straight away looking for the downside. Why was turnout so low? What if they dump JM and go for Hezza, would it give them a lift? In the car to the *Today* programme we were regaling each other re Diana. TB found her as mesmerising as I did. 'Have you ever seen a more beautiful woman?' He said he found her extraordinarily political, not in the party sense, but her awareness and her ability to communicate without always being totally clear. She had basically been trying to tease out his views about Charles and whether it would be possible to go straight from the Queen to William. I spent much of the day winding him up about her desire to meet me. He said her interest in me was because she was interested in media manipulation. No need to be jealous, I said. His interviews were strong. I bumped into Jeremy Hanley. 'Still spraying on the image, are you?' he said. 'I think you'll find there's more to him than that,' I said.

Saturday, May 6

I got the sense from my ring round of the Sundays that Ashdown was talking up dumping equidistance. I tried to talk them down from over doing Lib-Labbery. We were out for dinner when Tim called to say the *Sunday Times* and *IoS* were splashing on Ashdown. I was sure Peter M had been briefing up whilst I had been briefing down. I called TB and said we could not work like this. I was really fed up with it and said so.

Sunday, May 7

I called Peter and accused him of briefing the *S Times* and *IoS* stories. He said he had been talking to Andy Grice re JP and at the end of the conversation Grice asked whether the *New Statesman* interview was a sign of a softer line on the Libs and he said it was. He said his antennae didn't twitch and if they should have done he apologised but he didn't encourage the story. He said it was obvious Paddy was the source of the *IoS* story. TB called on his way to St Paul's and said I was being very harsh on Peter. He said the highlight of the VE dinner last night was when the Queen of Swaziland's dress fell apart and her breasts fell out and Cherie had to hold the dress up while they found safety pins.

Monday, May 8

Quiet day until calls started coming in on a briefing Harriet had done on the minimum wage. Various papers picked up from it that TB had ruled out a formula as well as a figure. She was probably reflecting what she'd heard TB say, but it was overdone and we had to talk it down. There was a tension in the approach to the minimum wage. On the one hand it was something everyone believed in and it was a central plank of any fairness campaign. We were going to have to do a lot more to win the argument on economic grounds as well as pure fairness, particularly when they started coming at us over job losses. We'd find ourselves being attacked on two other fronts: business and jobs.

Tuesday, May 9

TB, Peter M, PG, DM, Sally M, Jonathan, Anji, AC, meeting ostensibly to look forward six months, but we kept coming back to the short-term problems. The key, we agreed, was an economic message which just wasn't coming together. Also there was a sense in too many of the Shadow ministers almost that policy could wait till closer to the manifesto. But TB was pushing for the policy debate to be quickened. We were at one in saying that it was not enough to say the Tories were useless and that TB was an attractive new leader. There had to be an alternative policy agenda that the public understood and there had to be before anything else an understanding that we would be fine on the economy. TB called GB to say he wanted to take a meeting of the 8.45 people today. He told us he would say that all the unofficial briefing had to stop, everyone must stick to agreed lines and he would not tolerate nonsense from anyone. It sounded fine but then GB demanded to see him before the meeting – alone – and when they came through to the Shadow Cabinet room, TB was a lot weaker than before.

JP was doing PMQs so I went up to see him. He was in what I called his short-sleeves union rebel shirt, which he always wore when he was just in the office. He was doing health but said 'I can't believe politics is reduced to this, fucking words mumbo-jumbo.' He said he'd been right not to ask a question for twenty-five years. He went over it again and again, worrying about the emphasis, using his black felt pen to underline where he needed to stress a word. And on it went till he was reasonably happy, then he would go into the little room in the corner, get a long-sleeved shirt and tie and get changed. I'd noticed it was a habit he, TB and I all shared – never bothering who was around when changing clothes. I spoke to Harriet about her clumsy briefing and she said she'd been saying what Tony wanted to happen. I said it didn't mean he wanted it up on the day the Economic Commission was discussing the very issue. I always found it very hard to talk to Harriet. She clearly thought I was a bit heavy and I always thought she sounded like a lecturer reading from notes someone else had written, and she never paused for breath. She had one point – this was TB's view. I had one point – it wasn't politically clever to be motoring on it now, and we just ran round in circles.

Everyone was very down about the state of the campaigns machinery, and things got worse when I got home and Fiona burst into tears about the whole scene: I wasn't at home enough, I was distracted when I was, I'd been vile to her and to Cherie because I was totally focused on the job in hand and didn't have time for anything that got in the way of my perception of how it should be done.

Wednesday, May 10

I got a lift with Joy to BMP [advertising agency]. I said she had to involve more people in her operation because things would be fine when we were doing fairly well, but when things started to go wrong she would need friends and I felt she was making enemies by being seen to be too close to GB and not working for all of them. BMP had done some focus-group work, all fairly basic stuff, the economy being key and the public wanting reassurance about our basic competence. There was still no really clear Labour identity. It was like having one of our usual meetings in a different world. Nice tidy offices with gorgeous women on the reception. The meeting rooms were nicely laid out and there were endless supplies of real coffee, fruit juice and biscuits, pens and pads neatly laid out and people seemed to make an effort to be nice to each other. But I got a slight feeling they were a bit scared of us and they had to be encouraged to be really frank and say what they thought rather than what they thought we wanted to hear.

Back at the office Rosie came to tell me JP didn't want her to attend the 8.45 meetings because he thought they were basically just to promote GB and her presence gave his tacit backing to that. I said it was important she stay because we needed that extra bulwark against the GB machine. Clare S, Tom S and Sally all called to say there would be a real bust up if he moved against all women short-lists. TB said he would be a hero in most CLPs if he did. I said it wasn't as big a disaster as all that provided they were good candidates. Clare said the public love him but the party don't. I said having the public on side is quite a good position for a would-be prime minister to be in. She said it was a problem if he only ever wanted a fight with the party. I don't think anyone would doubt we had made a lot of progress in twelve months but it was mainly internal, and though Clause 4 had carried important external messages, and there had been huge and successful repositioning, we still did not have the broad policy appeal we would need.

A rare Big Guns meeting, mainly on the Economic Commission. GB hadn't brought all the papers again, but RC was at least up for the idea of a phased-in minimum wage and a low-pay review body to pave the way. I bumped into Michael Howard on the way out. 'You're doing very well I must say,' he said, but of course he had a wonderful way of making a piece of flattery sound faintly unpleasant and even dangerous. 'But whenever I think Campbell is doing well, I think of Burnley and that cheers me up, because they used to do well, and now look at them.'

Thursday, May 11

Cherie was over three pages of the *Express* re the women's refuge and she was planning a speech tonight that would be seen as very political, covering Europe, Clause 4, Hillary Clinton. Fiona was dealing with it but I mentioned it to TB and the fact she was doing articles and interviews and he went berserk, got her on the phone and said it had to be changed. He said she had a good press now but it would change the moment it looked like she was seeking a political profile. He was distracted on and off for the rest of the day, as he always was when he sensed the press moving in on Cherie, and her not necessarily understanding what their game was.

Pat and I were rushing to finish the speech for Perth and Kinross [by-election] before the flight. [*Daily*] *Record* poll had the Nats well ahead and us in second place, with thirty-three per cent don't knows. Ming Campbell [Liberal Democrat MP] was on the plane. His office had sent on to me a package with women's underwear in it from my stalker which had been sent to him by mistake. He said it caused much hilarity in the office. TB's speech for the by-election was at the Station Hotel, which had been a key venue in my crack-up so I was keen for the thing to be over as soon as possible. It was there I bumped into Julia Langdon [political journalist and author] and Geoffrey Parkhouse [political editor, *Herald*, partner of Julia Langdon], having walked up through the streets from where the cab had dropped me off, and I'd suddenly realised I had no cash and had to pay the cabbie by cheque and I could see first him, then Willie Woolf [*Daily Record*] and then Julia and Geoffrey all looking at me oddly, and of course I felt odd, but them looking at me that way made me feel more odd, off balance, confused, and even though I feel fine now, there is a nagging concern that something will set it off again and I'll only ever be one step from the edge. While TB was speaking I went to the gents, looked in the mirror, took deep breaths and told myself there was nothing to worry about. I was stronger than ever, then was then and now was now and I was in good shape. Most days I used my breakdown as a well of strength, but whenever I got too close to actual events, I felt vulnerable. I was chatting to John Reid who told me he hadn't had a drink for nine months. TB got a great reception and the mood was good but I was glad when we got back in the car and we headed for Aberdeen. He wanted more policy substance for the speech tomorrow and spoke to DM. Over dinner he was talking up the Tories again, saying he reckoned it was 50-50 they could come back and win, that he sensed beneath the surface they were getting their act together and we still had systemic problems. He was convinced that if he could get GB and Peter working together we would have a strategic operation second to none.

Friday, May 12

Alan Cochrane [*Telegraph*] was the latest to tell me the Mellor secretary rumour was doing the rounds again. It was unbelievable the way these things were put around and it just kept coming back. TB speech went fine and the Q&A even better. The audience was small-c conservative but I reckoned quite a few of them would swing our way. JM was having a go in Glasgow so it would play as a head-to-head, JM attacking us over the unions, TB making a pitch to business. Fine. We went with Bob Hughes [Labour MP] to the club where TB was a year ago on the day John Smith died. On the plane back we discussed the need for a proper plan and strategy re the Bank of England. He was sure independence was the answer. He was working on a stack of correspondence, and a few of them were requests he'd agreed to and then Anji or I had said no, and they were complaining. I said you can't on the one hand say we have to grip the diary and then on the other agree to every request that is made to you direct. He was laughing, said it was better that we were unpopular than him. 'Look,' he said, 'you should know by now that if I say "yes but speak to Ali", your job is to say no.' Even on the flight we had a couple of people approaching him to speak at functions and he did the 'yes but' routine. He also had a handwritten letter from Peter insisting he was really trying with GB but he was beginning to think it was impossible. He was for once in frivolous mood. In the car to the office he was due to speak to John Edmonds and he went into a parody of what life would be like in government. Breakfast with John, lunch with Rodney, dinner with Bill. I was supposed to be at the Keighley Clarets dinner but wasn't going to make it so I got TB to call Janet (the secretary) to apologise for me. She was gobsmacked. I got home to find Fiona tired and fed up having been wrestling with Cherie over the *Telegraph* article all day.

Saturday, May 13

Neil and Glenys, the Stotts and the Braggs[1] were due for dinner, but Neil and Glenys called off in the afternoon. I gave Alan Clark a call on the off chance because Richard [Scott] had always been fascinated both by him and by my friendship with him, and he said they could make it. The Braggs and the Stotts arrived first and we told them N and G weren't coming but Alan Clark was and Melvyn was absolutely horrified. He said he loathed Alan because of his objectionable views and also because he'd once written an absolutely vile review. Stott said he can't have been the only one, and I could see him winding up for a fun evening. Alan and Jane arrived in one of his Bentleys,

---

[1] Melvyn Bragg, TV writer and broadcaster, married to Cate Haste, also a writer and broadcaster.

May '95: Proper plan for Bank of England needed

which could barely squeeze through the two lines of parked cars outside. They came to the door, Alan leaving the car parked outside with the engine running and he says 'Where does a chap park his charabanc round these parts?' He was wearing tight beige trousers the likes of which I don't think the street had ever seen before and a toff's jacket. I said I wouldn't leave the keys in the car like that. He wandered off to find a parking space and came back for a rather embarrassed introduction to Melvyn but they both mellowed after a while. At one point Fiona mentioned there was a bit of crab in the starter and he went into major melodrama, rushing to the door shouting 'Crab, crab, I can't eat crab,' then throwing up very loudly in the front garden.

Sunday, May 14

The kids had enjoyed last night's spectacle of Alan's Bentley and his subsequent behaviour and had also discovered Melvyn had Sky, so we went round to watch the Premiership decider. Later saw Tessa who said the Blairs' dinner with the Rusbridgers had gone well, not much business done but very nice and chatty. TB had a rather different take. He said Rusbridger bordered on the Trappist.

· Monday, May 15

Meeting on the minimum wage. TB was determined to make the unions understand that he did not operate on the basis of them asking for something and us agreeing to something just short of it. He wanted to have the argument on the basis of it being a real argument about the rights and wrongs. The paper we were discussing was pathetic, the worst kind of old-style politics and he would rather we started from scratch. Anji, Jonathan and I met Michael Cockerell [BBC political documentary maker] to discuss his idea of a TV profile of TB. We were not sure but I felt something that brought out other sides to TB – his humour and his steel in particular – could be worthwhile.

The government pegged rail fares and Meacher's response was pathetic. He said it was a bribe (i.e. subtext popular) when we should have been saying it was a victory for our rail campaign. Gavyn[1] said we should be aiming our message at the FT leader writers and we should be challenging the Lawson view that you could have a real and a nominal economy. TB liked the idea of challenging the Lawson

[1] Gavyn Davies, former Downing Street policy adviser, 1974-79, Treasury panel of economic forecasting advisers, 1992-97. Married to Sue Nye, adviser to Gordon Brown.

theory that you could attack growth with one strategy and unemployment with another, and he was clearly feeling the need to set out a broader economic stall. My concern was that GB was making a speech on Wednesday in which he was putting forward new ideas likely to be seen as leading us to an independent Bank of England. It was full of newsworthy material likely to dwarf anything TB had to say. TB said there was an easy way to get him to drop the announcements, namely warn him there could be an outcry in the party. Gavyn felt it was important TB's speech be seen as seminal, whether it was newsworthy or not. I said I'm afraid in the world we're in you can't have seminal without newsworthy.

Philip G called after doing some focus groups with Stan Greenberg [American pollster]. He said they were excellent for TB and dreadful for JM.

Tuesday, May 16

The *Mail* did Cherie on the front and were gently developing the line that she was speaking up for powerful women against men. I went round to TB's where he was working out so I had a chat with CB. She said she was horrified the press had followed her to the Police Federation. I said she had to understand she was in a different league and if they thought they could go for her, they would. I waited till TB joined us before I said that she was very vulnerable to being built up so they could knock her down. TB said she shouldn't be doing speeches and articles that get covered in their own right because it plays into this. Jack C, who was speaking at the conference TB was due to open, had announced a cap on the profits of the privatised utilities. Neither TB nor GB had been aware so he went into a major spin, what the fuck is going on with major policy announcements just spilling out like this? As before, the media's basic assumption that we ran a Rolls-Royce operation came to our rescue, the *Standard* for example putting this, GB's speech and the briefing we had done on a legal paper as evidence of a major push on policy. TB was very ratty, called in Jonathan and DM to say he wasn't happy the way policy was spilling out.

Wednesday, May 17

Out at 7 to go to TB's with PG, Jonathan, Peter M and Stan Greenberg. PG was really sold on Stan but while I found him likeable and clever, I was never quite as sure as Philip that he had a real deep understanding of the difference between our politics and theirs. But he had been doing some groups with PG and what he was saying seemed to make sense, and accorded pretty much with how I felt about things. TB and New Labour were getting through and it was very much the two together. They liked TB but above all they liked him because he was offering change from the Labour Party they had rejected in the past. It wasn't just personality. Major was about as finished as it's possible to be. I was not as sure as that. It was probably right, but the public can be volatile and they like an underdog. If JM could get his act together and slowly give a sense of overcoming real difficulty and seemingly undefiable odds, he might just grope his way towards a turning point. Where we were all agreed was that the economy would be central to the battle, and if the Tories could generate a sense of things going better, and present us as a risk, that would be a major part of their overall package. The other factor Stan brought to TB's attention was fairly regular expressions of concern about his inexperience. Peter not very happy, said he hadn't got a real job and it meant he was just taking potshots the whole time. It was hard not to feel some sympathy. TB wanted him involved, trusted his judgement most of the time, but the neuralgic effect he had on some meant he had to operate mainly in private and he found that very frustrating. For all the rows and the skirmishes we had, I liked working with him because when it worked we were a good team. But there were downsides, not least the ear-bending of others who didn't want him near the place. We agreed that with the minimum wage at the TUC executive today, it was far better that I brief on it to get the debate on our terms, so I went in and drafted a note, got it agreed with JP, GB and TUC and did a ring round, and most of them seemed to buy it as a win for Blair.

Big Guns without GB, which transformed the mood. RC very chipper and JP not at all surly. There wasn't even a mini row re the minimum wage. If anyone was a bit off it was TB who was still angry at the way half-baked policy ideas kept spilling out without us knowing it was going to happen. I briefly did the rounds upstairs. During Shadow Cabinet I met Geoffrey Norris re GM schools. I feared we were sleepwalking to the worst of all worlds – enough in there for people to say we were dumping GM schools, but also enough to say we were changing the policy to suit TB's personal choice.

Cherie called me to say the *Star* wanted to rerun her *Telegraph* piece on Refuge. I said to her, and later to TB, and to Sandra Horley [Refuge], that I was worried they were in a classic build-up-to-knock-down mode and I felt we should play down. She said she'd maybe been a bit naïve but she felt it had been right to try to help a good cause. Geoffrey Dickens [Conservative MP] died, so the race for Littleborough and Saddleworth was on.

Thursday, May 18

In with Joy who was becoming a lot more human. Re PMQs, TB had decided on the way in that he would ask whether JM would accept the Nolan recommendations that MPs should declare cash received from consultancies. I checked it out with some of the journalists and they said they were sure Number 10 didn't have a line on it. TB was in a real state about it, in that there was an element of risk, in that JM may have a perfectly good answer and TB could look daft, but in fact it went really well. JM havered, as we expected him to, and TB hammered him and as he did so, the Tory back-bench opposition to Nolan became clear. I briefed this was the next area for a split that would become a fault line.

BMP did a presentation which I thought was very weak. Their idea was that 'quality' should be our central theme. TB and Peter M quite liked it. I thought it was weak and waffly. PG and DH both disliked it too. TB said more work had to be done on it. PG and I were concerned the agency wasn't really integrated into our thinking, which was not necessarily their fault, but it meant their ideas came slightly out of left field and that would only work if they were really original and strong. I said if you did that presentation to the Shadow Cabinet they wouldn't get it and they'd wonder why we had an agency when we had better stuff ourselves. I was very harsh but I feared that we'd end up trying to split the middle on ideas rather than go for something we really thought was good, and we knew could be made to work.

TB had to leave to see Bill Morris, who was storming about something Jack Dromey had said about him. As Peter M was the only politician left behind, TB asked him to chair the meeting, which had Joy seething, and it got worse when Peter started to speak to her in his most condescending manner. He was treating her like a child. PG said to TB later that it was a bad scene, that Peter treated her badly, and that she stormed out. TB asked me if it was as bad as PG was saying. I have to say if he had spoken to me like that I'd have taken his head off. 'Why can't they all just grow up?' he said.

Friday, May 19

On the flight up, TB was back to his usual question – did I think GB, Peter M and I would ever be able to work together properly? He said if you three were all motoring, at your best, and together, we'd be unstoppable. I said it ought to be possible, but I wouldn't hold your breath. We drove to Kinross with Jack McConnell, did a walkabout which felt OK without being great. Press were more interested in the first person he met when he got out of the car, a Nat who said she'd be sticking with the SNP. Off to Auchterarder, which didn't feel at all Labour to me, another doorstep then off to Glasgow airport. He wasn't sure the visit had been worth it and I felt maybe GB and Joy pushed too hard to get us to go. Got to Llandudno and speech went fine, TB as ever departing from the script. Within minutes of finishing, Peter Hain [Labour MP] and Ron Davies were both briefing their own versions of the speech. The Welsh press took the speech as an attack on gabby MPs which went down well. We headed straight back to Manchester, trying to decide where Ron would figure in a list of all-time most devious politicians. It had been a long day and not as fruitful as we had hoped when we set out. But it was always good to get out and about. I wound him up about losing his hair, and said maybe he should just go the whole hog and shave it off.

Saturday, May 20

TB called to say he thought the Tories were in real trouble re Nolan. He decided to write to JM to ask whether the new committee announced by Tony Newton [Conservative MP and Leader of the House of Commons] was to oversee WHETHER to implement Nolan, or HOW. It prompted JM, within a few hours, to put out a statement saying he supported Nolan and we were trying to make it a party political football. The letter came out as we were at the Cup Final and TB wondered if we had cranked it too far. GB had been keen to use his speech in Wales to say we were changing next week's Opposition debate to force a vote on Nolan. TB didn't want to commit and specifically asked him not to, but then GB did a BBC interview saying we would, which really annoyed TB.

TB got a good reception at the match. Afterwards I went home to collect Fiona before heading back to TBs because we were going briefly to Sue Nye's fortieth birthday party before heading to the Hollicks' party. CB was late and there was a tense atmosphere between her and me again after the Refuge business. Fiona said she should read the *Mail* and just notice the seeds they were sowing, and ask herself whether it didn't make more sense to avoid giving them the pleasure of watching her fall into a trap. In the car we talked about Diana, TB and I doing our best to wind them up by going on about how unbelievably gorgeous she was. TB said she was very manipulative and determined. CB said she clearly felt strongly and ambitiously for William and Harry. CB was in no mood for niceties at Sue's. The first thing I heard her say was something about the Shadow Chancellor wishing to pursue a different strategy to TB. Sue said to

Fiona she couldn't believe how rude Cherie was. Cherie said something like 'Sue will be working for Tony,' to which Sue said 'No, I'll be working for Gordon, but it's the same thing.' 'No, it's not,' said CB. Got the papers on the way home, lots of bad Nolan stuff for the Tories. I said to Fiona I hated going out. All that happens is I get my ear bent and can she stop accepting invitations. Another row.

Sunday, May 21

Bill Morris and Jack Dromey tore lumps off each other on *Frost*. I thought Bill won it. Gavyn Davies had done a good job explaining to me the big arguments in the Mais Lecture and I felt I'd got them into understandable English. Robert Peston [*FT* journalist] got and liked TB's arguments. The backdrop was strong, with Thatcher laying into Major leading the news most of the day. I set up the morning broadcasters then went off to football with the boys. Then TB called me and asked me to go back for a meeting with Gavyn and Derek Scott to have one last run through the speech, prompting another shouting match with Fiona.

Monday, May 22

TB had written a shorthand version of the speech as an aide-memoire for his *Today* programme interview, and I used it to do a shorter press release as a front cover to the speech. He'd put a lot of work into this one and it was an important moment. The John Smith prawn cocktail offensive had been about neutralising business and the City so that they didn't actively go out there the whole time and say Labour would wreck the economy. But TB actually wanted us to work towards a position where we supplanted the Tories as the party of economic competence. The Tories helped of course, but what today was about was laying out a series of economic messages which we could then distil into something for the broader public. Hezza was on [the *Today* programme] before TB and TB leapt on his attack on Thatcher as the architect of ERM entry at the wrong rate. We were honing the speech till 3pm. JM, Hezza and Clarke were at a competition conference and a gaggle of ministers was fielded to attack TB but all it did was increase the interest, and in any event we still got the lion's share of the coverage. There was also movement on Nolan, with JM writing to TB and appearing to give the sense the committee was there to see whether, not how, Nolan was implemented. But speech went really well. Jane Reed [director of corporate affairs, News International] called to say Murdoch was in town and we fixed a meeting for Thursday.

Tuesday, May 23

Excellent papers, very good leaders in the *FT* and the *Guardian*. 8.45 meeting, Peter M there for the first time in a while. Maybe he knew GB wouldn't be turning up. Derek Foster keen for us to keep pinning them down on Nolan. [Tony] Newton still obfuscating this morning. Also discussed all-women shortlists, with the NEC due to impose the first one for Slough tomorrow. Harriet came to discuss the minimum wage campaign. I had to go to Walworth Road for what was an uninspiring and badly chaired meeting on Littleborough and Saddleworth [by-election]. The general feeling was we had to mount the campaign very much as anti-Liberal but a lot of the campaign heavy lifting would fall to TB and I said he would want to make it much more a positive New Labour campaign. Alan Barnard [Labour Party organiser] said the Lib Dem candidate was not popular with the local party, but our local party was pretty grim. The meeting went on and on without reaching proper conclusions so I said I had to go back for a PMQs meeting and left. He was on for Nolan and 'whether or how' and it went fine, with JM having to climb down to where we wanted him. I noticed that virtually every Tory question was in some way about TB. TB noticed it and sat back with his neck hooked on to the top of the bench so that he was looking heaven-wards, eyes rolling and head rocking mildly every time they had another go.

TB was due to have dinner with JP tonight, and word came through Rosie and Joan [Hammell, Prescott aide] that he didn't want to have it at Richmond Crescent because last time Cherie had been rude, one of the kids had chucked fruit at him and just when they were getting down to real business, CB had come in and said it was time for Tony to go to bed. They agreed to go to Granita's.

Another bad poll in Perth. Catherine McLeod [*Herald*] told me the bloodletting and recriminations were beginning already, with people dumping on Douglas [Alexander, Labour candidate] Joy, TB, anyone. She said too many of the Labour campaign people were pseudo Nats.

I had a meeting with DM and Peter H re the health document. Margaret B was determined to put it through the policy forum in June but none of us really felt it was yet strong enough. I wrote a memo to MB asking if we couldn't do an interim report first, and warning that there was a danger of policy overload in June and we would not get the full political benefit of what ought to be a key policy document.

Harold Wilson died. I called TB to discuss what to say and who to put up. We agreed he and JP should do the bulk of interviews. I called Joe Haines who was clearly moved and had some good thoughts. He and Harold had never struck me as being close in the later years, obviously in part because of HW's illness, but even when Joe talked about the worse side of Harold, there was always a fondness and respect there. My last vivid memory was at a service for Sean Hughes [Labour MP, died 1990] when it was obvious to me that Wilson was moving in and out of coherence. One moment he was saying something nice about Sean, the next he was describing recent meetings with world leaders that you knew hadn't taken place. Physically too he was weakened and now he was dead. There is something about the media coverage of deaths now that is upsetting. There may be some sincerity in the attempts to sound upset and moved, but beneath the surface you know they're all just paddling to churn out as much as they can on the latest rolling news sponge. Then life goes on, as it did for us, with the day an odd mix of tributes and focusing on the by-election and women-only shortlists. Joe provided an excellent line re Chatham. He said Wilson was once making a speech in the docks there and paid a great tribute to the navy. 'Why do I say that?' he said, at which point someone shouted out 'Because you're in Chatham.' It didn't take long for the black humour to follow. We imagined the kind of obits TB would get if he ever made it to Number 10. Tim suggested we put out words from TB saying 'I saw Harold last week and he seemed fine but then as he knew better than anyone, a week is a long time in politics.' There were tributes in the House and TB did well.

JP was meeting Damon [Albarn] of Blur [pop group] to talk about the youth vote and TB and I popped in to see them. He was clever and articulate if a bit spaced out, and he seemed to get better than JP that his role should only be one of identification, that the minute celebs became too political in their statements they were a menace. So we talked over what he would and wouldn't do and JP clearly thought I was being heavy because he barked 'Stop yelling at him like he's a private and you're the sergeant major.' During the day TB was developing his argument re Wilson into one about the nature of the party – that Wilson had wanted to do more but had been restricted by the party. It was a way both of playing down the direct comparisons between them but also underlining the nature of change.

Thursday, May 25

A whole series of policy meetings which were taking far more of the diary post Clause 4. On health, Robin agreed that the document was not good enough and was persuaded we should try to get Margaret only to send the executive summary to the National Policy Forum. He said it was obsessed with structures, not patients, and the overall message wasn't clear. MB came in and was very dogged. She was adamant she wanted to present the whole document at Reading and nobody could shift her. She felt we gained nothing from delay. I said I feared it would be seen as Old Labour. TB was worried about the trusts not being allowed to own the properties on which they operated. 'At least we would be renationalising the NHS,' she said, referring back to a TB line. There was something very impressive about MB when she was digging in. She was often more than willing to be accommodating and had no hang-ups about 'the Leader's Office', like some of them. But when she was settled on something, she listened politely, fiddled with her little bunch of pens that she kept wrapped in a rubber band, and then said no. So she wore us down, which meant we risked presenting a dog's dinner to the NPF. Meacher came in to push for a transport policy document. At the end of the meeting I showed him *Taxi Trade Times* which had a front-page report slagging us off over his idea that black cabs be treated the same as minicabs. TB said he should review it and err on the side of the black cabs.

Friday, May 26

We just managed to come second in Perth and Kinross so that was OK. TB called from the train re all-women shortlists. I said I know you hate the policy but you're saddled with it so you're going to have to fight for it and try to turn the argument. Paddy was doing his end of equidistance press conference but still attacking, saying we couldn't be trusted and so on. 'Why can't these people break free?' said TB.

Saturday, May 27

Andy Grice called to say Thatcher had given an interview and said some very flattering things about TB and did I have anything to say? I gave a very anodyne response, which TB wanted me to revise after I spoke to him, and make it less critical of Thatcher. The *Sunday Telegraph* were doing a piece on TB/Murdoch, a subject which made all but the Murdoch papers totally neuralgic. The only scoop of the day was 'Thatcher praises Blair' which ran on the later broadcasts. Needless to say, TB didn't mind that at all.

Sunday, May 28

We were planning TB's visit to Germany and I called him in Sedgefield to say that the Bosnia story was now so big, with British soldiers taken hostage, that the visit would be about Bosnia as much as Europe policy. He said he wasn't sure what we should be saying on Bosnia and that he would talk to his 'new friend'. I thought he meant Paddy, but as he elaborated it was clear he was talking about Thatcher, and larding it on to wind me up. He said is it a good thing or a bad thing that she is on the news today saying good things about us? Good, I suppose. Exactly, and she will have a view on Bosnia that is worth listening to. He later spoke to Robin and they agreed to put out a tough line. Our minds were focused further when JM announced the recall of Parliament for Wednesday to debate Bosnia following the taking of the first UK troops by the Bosnian Serbs. TB decided to come down first thing to prepare for it. He was also worrying about all-women shortlists, saying it was a classic mistake, done for short-term reasons without thinking through how you'd actually put it into action.

Monday, May 29

Bank holiday and tried to work at home but the phones were going mental all day, not least Jack Dromey constantly calling for advice on his latest speech which he told me was going to make a 'big splash'. He was incapable of a short conversation and even when I tried to say I had a million other things on my plate, on he ploughed. TB called from the train. He was reading up on Bosnia and said should we cancel Germany. I said of course not. I was briefing TB's German speech in advance, mainly the line that he would tell Germany a Labour Britain would be no pushover. TB had a half-hour session with Robin on Bosnia. RC was loving it. As he left TB said he's very clever though not quite as clever as he thinks he is, and too pompous for his own good. TB went for a briefing with Rikfind at the MoD and came back convinced they were paving the way for increased bombing provided we could guarantee no harm to the hostages. Jonathan was in his element, running around commissioning work for the debate and typing out lines. I said to him no matter how important all this is, you realise there are no votes in it, don't you? He said but we have to deal with all these people in government. I said let's get there first. He said TB hadn't raised it with him. Pretty bad day all round, and Fiona and I had another row because she lost the Mont Blanc pen that I gave her and that was obviously my fault, presumably for giving it to her in the first place.

May '95: TB's new friend, Margaret Thatcher

TB was really troubled re Bosnia. 'This is the mother of all night-mares. I was reading all the stuff till late and I can't tell you what a nightmare it is.' He called Derry from the car who urged him not to think that he, as Leader of the Opposition, should have all the answers. All he could do was signal broad support for the government and display his understanding of the issues. Oddly, most of the papers appeared to support withdrawal of UK troops, and Derry agreed we should oppose that strongly. We discussed whether JM thought he would stand to gain politically out of this. We met RC and Jonathan on the plane and Jonathan and I worked on the Bosnia section for the speech while TB worried away on his argument note for the debate. I felt confident he would do well because he was well into his preferred mode of working now. He'd eaten all the facts. He'd analysed the big picture and the politics and now he would sit with a blank piece of paper and hone the argument. As Jonathan and I agreed, he could be a total pain when he was doing this, and we were there to have the same conversations with him, again and again until he was happy with the argument. Pain or not, it was the process and provided it led to a good end product, it was worth it. I said the best outcome for us tomorrow is people saying that Blair put the government case better than the government has.

We had lunch at the ambassador's residence, which had a stunning view on to the river. TB did the Beeb and then sat down to a lunch of seafood salad, pork chops and a fruit salad. These ambassadors really lived well, though this one had to work all through lunch, probably not realising he had become part of TB's circular conversation routine. Round and round we went, what would happen if we did withdraw, who would claim victory, could you do deals with them, all the questions he'd kind of settled in his own mind, but he wanted to assure himself he'd reached the right judgement. Off to the speech, more than 1,000 people there with a massive overspill and he was really witty in the Q&A. It was a shame that with Bosnia so big, and JM doing a press conference, it would not get much coverage.

Then with Rudolph Scharping – what a bore! – to the Bundestag where TB was to address the SDP faction on modernisation. He did it extremely well, and you could tell that everyone was making the comparison between him and Scharping. Back at the embassy we carried on working on the Bosnia recall speech. RC said it was right to be supportive, but we should hold the support at seventy-five per cent. JM was in part playing politics, he said, hoping to get some-thing out of the statesman card, and there may come a time where we feel we can't support him one hundred per cent, so we need to keep options open. Bosnia was the main focus of his meeting with [Helmut] Kohl [German Chancellor], which we had to keep short to be sure to get the plane. There was something very functional and impersonal about the Chancellor's office, and it was clear that everyone – the Germans, the embassy, the European media – were treating him as PM-in-waiting. But on the plane back TB and I had another discussion to go over all the things that could go wrong, and all the moves JM might make to get himself back in a winning position.

Wednesday, May 31

TB came in late and wanted to work on the speech for the Commons on his own. Eventually he tried it out on us at 2.30 but he wasn't really looking for changes and got irritated if anyone had anything other than major points to make. Yet again, he did really well. Derek Foster said afterwards that people were saying he was developing more and more 'gravitas'. He said 'I think we have a real Labour leader on our hands, and maybe a real prime minister – that's when your troubles will really start – and mine.' TB did particularly well on interventions which were mainly from hostile Tories using TB as a surrogate to have a go at the government without being open about it – [Peter] Tapsell, [Nick] Budgen, [Iain] Duncan Smith. During the debate the US announced they may send ground troops to Bosnia. Tony Bevins said that he watched Major during TB's speech and JM looked more and more nervous and that limp little smile kept coming on. Afterwards TB, having as usual forced himself to be over-nervous, was now on a high. TB wondered if Murdoch was doing some kind of deal with Hezza. TB had dinner with GB. Even with us, he still tried to maintain the position that he and GB worked well together, but now for the first time I think, he admitted GB was playing the positioning game, putting himself slightly to the left of TB for the NEC elections and also, should it arise, for any future leadership.

Thursday, June 1

Tried to take a couple of days off. Anji said to TB he should try not to bother me. It drove me mad the way he said I should have the odd day off but then phoned to ask me to do something, usually involving dozens of phone calls.

Friday, June 2

Peter came round to discuss L&S, Joy, GB. He said he'd really tried with GB but you know how hard it is. As for Joy, the problem was that he didn't really respect her judgement and she had the habit of taking everything personally. He said GB would take it as a personal setback if JP was closely involved in L&S. Liz [Lloyd] was already up there and said it was as if we had no campaign at all. You wouldn't really know there was a by-election on. She said there was a sense among the media that the Lib Dem candidate was, in the words of Jon Hibbs [*Telegraph*], a total prat. She felt we should be careful not to go too heavy yet because there was a chance the Libs might yet dump him.

Saturday, June 3

I called TB to warn him Jesse Jackson [American civil rights leader and Baptist minister] would be at the 'Churches Banquet' he was due to attend tonight. 'Oh God, how did I get into this in the first place?' Before he launched off on one of his diary diatribes, which consisted of him accusing me, Jonathan and Anji of filling his diary without ever discussing it. I said this was one he had insisted on doing as a favour to Adele Blakebrough, Ian Hargreaves' [*Independent* editor] missus[1]. I cheered him up even more by saying he'd be seated next to a drug addict.

Fiona and I went for dinner at [Ian and Andrea] Kennedys'. It was very jolly because Derry and Alison were there and Derry as ever was quizzing me on how the office was going. I said Jonathan was causing a bit of tension and he should get more involved in the things he's good at and less in the things he's not good at, particularly dealing with the party and the unions where he tended to put over an ultra-TB position. He said he shared my concerns about Cherie. He said he felt she was sometimes competing with Tony for attention, which was a terrible mistake. He felt there was a militant feminism brewing there. He had said to her that she could become the first ever 'first lady' who was a successful person in her own right and she would get enormous credit for that and she should concentrate on that side of her life. But if people felt she was exploiting her position to draw attention to what were really her interests, that reputation would be endangered. He was also worried about the prospect of Helena Kennedy heading to the Lords. He felt she would use it as a plateform but be of no real support. The problem was we were running out of time to put forward our list of working peers. I asked round the table who were the kind of people they'd like to see in the Lords. The most interesting suggestions came from Liz Elton, who

---

[1] Ian Hargreaves, editor, *Independent*, 1994-95, *New Statesman*, 1996-98. Married to Adele Blakebrough.

said Robert Winston [consultant obstetrician and gynaecologist, author and broadcaster] and [Sir John] Harvey-Jones [industrialist]. Derry said we should be going for people of real substance and depth, not anyone who could be dismissed as a luvvie or a crony. Every single person there said there was now no way that Labour could lose and I said that was a really dangerous mindset, that the Tories could come back, and I set out a plan as to how they could do it.

Sunday, June 4

Really quiet day. Anji called to say that Peter Stothard [*Times* editor] had called Jonathan to ask if TB would go to Australia to speak to all the Murdoch editors and hierarchy in mid July. TB was keen but she and Jonathan thought it might be better to organise around it so that he was visiting other countries too. My immediate reaction was that I liked the boldness of it which might be diluted if we tried to make out he just happened to be in the region and hey he was popping into the Murdoch annual bash. There would obviously be a lot of media interest in the Murdoch angle and there would be some rumbling in the party, but for all sorts of reasons it was quite an attractive proposition, and I'm not sure it isn't better just to say up-front – Murdoch has asked him to speak to all his editors and top executives and he's accepted, and then turn it into a major speech platform.

Monday, June 5

I was getting slightly alarmed by the rise in my profile. Nick Jones had another profile of me in the *Guardian*. Fiona said it was absurd that they thought they could mount a big attack on me based on something I once said about the *Sunday Times* in *Tribune*, but the point was the media and the Tories seemed more interested in me than most of the politicians. Needless to say some of our own people joined in. John Edmonds made a speech saying there were too many spin doctors. It was a ridiculous thing to say given how totally understaffed we were, and needless to say was taken as a whack at me. Presumably it meant he didn't want Phil Woolas, his own spin doctor, to get the L&S candidature.

I was on the way in when I got bleeped to divert to TB's. He wanted a meeting with me, Jonathan, Sally, Pat and DM. His friend Pete Thompson from Australia was there too, a lovely outgoing guy who had warmth and niceness written all over him. He was the guy TB had mentioned as having spent hours with him at university just talking and I think had helped give real shape to his religious and political beliefs. He sat in on our meeting, just listening, probably so

June '95: TB asked to address Rupert Murdoch's News Corp.

that TB could get his impressions of us all afterwards. He was obviously a real friend and someone of continuing importance to him. We went over the GMB speech structure. TB wasn't yet ready to announce the new relations with the unions but he still wanted this to be a big speech that made some waves on the theme of TB taking New Labour to the unions. The main purpose of the meeting was to try to clarify his mind on health and education policy. He agreed the current health document was weak and he wanted more input from outsiders who really understood the way the system worked, or more to the point didn't. He felt that as it stood, reasonable expert opinion would slam it. On education, we ran round the usual houses. He was clearly going to have difficulties with David [Blunkett]. And GM schools were nowhere near settled. TB had recovered his vigour. We went through the working peers list. Jonathan was enjoying his co-ordination role, though I could sense Sally getting irritated at his efforts to deal with the unions. Nobody was very impressed with Ivor Richard's [Labour leader in the Lords] list. I pushed Robert Winston quite hard and TB said he was exactly the kind of name we should be thinking of.

I set off to meet PG on the train from Euston. He regaled me with his holiday nightmare when the Kinnocks had lost his computer and he'd had to fly out to Brussels to retrieve it from lost baggage. Did some groups in a pub in Littleborough. The first group was ex-Tories thinking of switching, the second was ex-Libs thinking of voting for us. The first group was very dispiriting all round, not least the level of ignorance about anything to do with politics at all, and in both groups there was an undercurrent of racism coming through. The second group liked TB a lot more but the real progress came when we put the Lib Dem candidate's published views. He was seen as loony, extreme. JM also bombed all round. TB was stronger, but 'smarmy' was in the air again.

Tuesday, June 6

We bumped into Michael Meacher on the train back to London. Tim had briefed Andrew Marr yesterday on the black-cabs fiasco which Andy had used as part of a piece about how awful the Shadow Cabinet was. MM joined us and introduced us to his agent. One useful thing to come out of the journey was MM agreeing to brief the *Standard* on a rethink re the black-cabs policy. We really didn't want London's cabbies all totally offside. I spoke to TB as he headed for the Scillies for Wilson's funeral with Jim Callaghan and Barbara Castle [former Labour Cabinet minister]. He said they had a wonderful heated argument about devaluation. It was as if they were making the decision today. I met Chris Powell for another inconclusive discussion. I got a hilarious pager message sent through saying TB says can you tell JP not to grimace at PMQs. JP had his best PMQs yet so was in a good mood afterwards. Bruce [Grocott] came to see me to say he was aghast that TB was thinking of traipsing halfway round the world to speak to Murdoch's lot. He thought the party would absolutely hate it.

Fiona and I had dinner at TB's with Pete and Helen from Australia, Ian Hargreaves and Adele. TB was on really good form and CB back to her old pleasant and friendly self. A lot of the talk was of religion and it was clear it meant a lot to all of them. TB said he could sense that I found religion a lot more interesting than I let on. I said I'd never denied I was interested in it; but I didn't believe in God. I liked the fact that others did, and I was often jealous of the comfort and solidity that others took from religious faith, but I didn't have it, despite the upbringing I had, and I was suspicious of all funda- mentalist religious belief. Pete was clearly clever as well as nice. He struck me as being well to the left of TB but also pragmatic. I could see why he was the kind of friend TB would want to hang on to and keep in touch with. He was someone not afraid to speak his mind and yet was good at seeing another point of view and analysing where it came from. TB had a little tirade against woolly thinking in the so-called left so-called intellectual media.

Wednesday, June 7

I went in early to work on the GMB speech. TB and Pat were already there. He took out some of the more aggressive lines but it was still a strong speech which I was briefing as one of a series of 'more change' speeches on changing relations with the unions. TB was in angry mood because of a letter he had received from Jack Straw written on behalf of JS, RC, Frank Dobson and Chris Smith [Shadow Social Security minister] asking to meet him as a group on economic policy. 'This will be Robin's idea and he'll have put Jack up to it and I'm not interested in seeing them as a group.' He said it was like the Wilson era, the belief that all politics was plots and cabals, he just wasn't going to do it. He'd met Lord Tonypandy [George Thomas, former Labour MP and Speaker] at Harold's funeral and asked if they really were all plotting the whole time as the books suggested. 'All the time.' I worked on the speech on the train down but then got briefed on the 8.45 meeting, where Jonathan had apparently caved in to GB saying we should abandon Harriet doing a low-pay press conference tomorrow because it would stoke up everything before the National Policy Forum in Reading where Morris and Edmonds would both be. I thought GB was being too cautious and I was worried people would sense we were moving away from the minimum wage. We spent much of the day going over it before eventually I involved TB and he agreed with me and it was back on again. Speech went fine though he ran on too long at the end and we missed the train we were due to make to get back for lunch with [Lord] Rothermere [owner, *Daily Mail*] and the Mail Group editors. The atmospherics were interesting. Rothermere was charming but a bit detached and I sensed he was the referee in a battle for political control between David English[1] and Paul Dacre[2]. English was subtle and sinuous and had a light social touch. He also quite clearly loved Tony to bits and saw him as the best political leader to emerge since Thatcher. Dacre was the opposite of all those things – he couldn't hide his very right-wing politics even if he wanted to. He clearly had a sneaking admiration for TB but probably lay awake at night working out how best to do him in. He appeared to have two current obsessions – women's quotas and Europe. On the first, we were PC gone mad. On the second, he seemed to believe we were busy planting Germans under his bed so that they could come in and run the show once we got elected. There was something almost likeable about him, and he has a strong intelligence, but there is also something slightly barking about him. They were all quizzing away on cross-media ownership and TB was pretty non-committal. I thought it went reasonably well. These were not our kind of people but the reality was they'd had it with the Tories under Major and we might as well try to neutralise as best we could.

Big Guns was delayed because TB wanted a session with RC to make clear he wasn't impressed by the Jack Straw letter exercise. He had a different kind of RC/JS problem with a story in the *Standard* that TB had decided to put RC effectively in charge of the Scott Report [into arms sales to Iraq] which sent Jack ballistic. Big Guns was looking forward to the policy forum. Everyone agreed the health document was weak and news-wise we had to try to get the focus on GB and the economy document. GB was still trying to get us to cancel the low-pay press conference. I said surely we should be out there making the case for a minimum wage the whole time. It was potentially a hugely popular and successful policy but we had to make the case. Michael Meacher came in for another chat re cabs. He said he agreed

[1] Sir David English, former editor of the *Daily Mail*, chairman of Associated Newspapers from 1992.
[2] Paul Dacre, editor of the *Daily Mail* from 1992.

the only way to deal with it was a major climbdown story.

Meeting with Blunkett who didn't like TB's decision to go for one hundred per cent funding for Foundation schools. TB wanted us to be able to say there would be more independence for all schools. DB held his ground and we agreed we should have a last go at drafting a new introduction. DB said it was an argument between 'principle and presentation'.

We had to go to the dinner with *Mirror* editors at the Savoy. Montgomery came in for a drink and I tried to wind him up re L&S where we would need help. It was a really grim evening. Only Tessa Hilton [*Sunday Mirror*] seemed able to lighten it up at all. As Fiona said on the way home, time was when politicians would really look forward to a dinner with the *Mirror* but they had nothing to say.

Thursday, June 8

Went for a swim with Fiona at the lido for the first time in ages, lamenting how little time I seemed to find for things like that. Over to TB's and Cherie was still being nice. We left for the BBC where he was doing the first in a new John Humphrys series of longer interviews which were meant to be more reflective than the usual crap. TB told me he'd warned RC not to work in groups as he was trying to do with that letter. He had special access and that was that. He was also angry with RC for over-briefing the substance of the policy forum which would raise expectations too high. Anji and Sally had another go at me about Jonathan trying to get too involved in their areas without understanding all the subtleties, so everyone was a bit grumpy.

TB did a meeting on the health document which he finally thought was going in the right direction. TB said JoP wasn't immersed in the party and would take time to develop the right judgements and instincts but he was basically a good thing. I think that's right. In some ways it's quite helpful to have someone who sometimes questions things we take for granted simply because we always have, but I could see it was irritating for Sally and Anji if they thought he was trying to subsume their roles.

Peter came round for dinner to discuss his *Any Questions?* appearance tomorrow and while he was here a fantastic story broke about insider dealing at Powergen. Then bad news came through that the Oldham council seat we'd been hoping to get had gone to the Libs who had gone straight from third to first. It was very bad news for the by-election but as Peter left, I said 'Don't worry – at least we've got a scapegoat.' Ho ho, he said.

Friday, June 9

Today was the Shadow Cabinet awayday for which PG and I had both prepared notes. TB worked through several lines of argument which I briefed. The dividing lines between ourselves and the Tories were getting clearer. The meeting itself was pretty dire. TB did an OK introduction on the general scene and the dividing lines, and also warned them things could still go wrong, that there were still fears out there that we had to address – about our approach to tax; about the unions; about extremism. JP was excellent, and really got wound up about the need for them to get more active and engaged on the campaign front. But apart from GB, who did a good strategic overview but without much new to say on the economy, and Margaret, who was just solid and full of good sense, the contributions of the rest didn't add up to much. Partly it was the forum, and partly the fact that TB didn't steer the discussion. He just went round the table so people made a series of random points, and as the meeting wore on you could see people nervous they hadn't spoken, rather than working out whether they actually had anything useful to say. Jack S ignored crime and instead made a very Eurosceptic contribution. TB, however, did manage to get his way on everything and maybe this was in part how, just letting them say what they wanted. Jonathan said he found the level of debate and discussion appalling. The one thing that emerged during the discussion on the economy was that there was a fairly widespread concern we were being too conservative. But GB held his ground, saying that we were kidding ourselves if we thought we had slain all the negatives that people held against Labour and we had a lot more work to do on that.

At lunch JP told me he'd just heard his mum had cancer. Clare gave me a long whinge that she couldn't say NEW Labour. She thought it was right for Tony but it was wrong to try to force everyone to say it. I wasn't aware that we were, but it was what was going to get her a place in the Cabinet because if we stayed with her kind of politics we wouldn't win a bloody thing.

I had a good session with Margaret, who is a real pro, on the health document and we agreed we would brief nothing unless there genuinely was a leak. Robert Winston said yes to a peerage. Jonathan spoke to the secretary of the Honours Scrutiny Committee who said they might reject Swraj Paul [businessman]. TB said this was outrageous. If there was a genuine reason, there should be a genuine explanation or a genuine investigation.

The press conference went fine. Its purpose was really just to provide a contrast to JM's Welsh conference speech which was just an attack on us, by showing that we had a positive forward-looking agenda. TB/GB went for a little walk in the park nearby to discuss GB's and Peter M's respective roles which were still unresolved. They were in there for about twenty minutes or so, interrupted only by the occasional autograph hunter surprised to see them there. I could see GB's embarrassment or irritation, I couldn't tell which, that they were asking TB not him, but TB made a point of ensuring GB signed for them too. It was an odd scene. We managed to get a piece on the nine o'clock news after I complained that the six o'clock ignored it completely, and we led *Newsnight*. There was a very good moment watching Ben Pimlott [historian and political biographer] being interviewed and he said there are times when it looks like Labour only wanted to win elections, and Rory [now aged seven] barked at him 'Of course they want to win elections, you div.'

Saturday, June 10
TB, Sally, DM and Peter H went to the policy forum which went off fine. Amazingly, given it was sent to seventy or eighty people overnight, the health policy document didn't leak After the boys' football we left for Kevin's [Jones, university friend of AC] wedding in Suffolk and had a very nice time. I realised after a few hours that I hadn't had a single pager message since we arrived, and then learned we were in an area that didn't get messages. It was really nice seeing old friends, including some I hadn't seen since leaving university. I was amazed at how they – and their parents – seemed to view me in a different light because of what I was doing. It was clear that as far as every one of them was concerned, we were going to win and therefore I'd be doing something important in government. Tim's mum said she kept a scrapbook of cuttings about me and she thought I was doing a terrific job. She said she hoped I had a thick skin.

Sunday, June 11
GB's current complaint was the *Observer* story about JP and Peter M being in charge of L&S. If he could get into a state about that, was there anything he wouldn't get into a state about? TB said to me 'Do you think Major has to put up with this kind of thing?' Probably.

Monday, June 12
Thatcher was beginning to dominate, with a sense that she was going for Major, though the *Express* loyally, and ludicrously, reported it as her four-point plan for the Tories to win. TB was working on health and education again and worried that we were framing policy

according to what we thought the party would wear, rather than what we thought the national interest demanded, and he intended to press for more change. TB and I worked on his AEEU [Amalgamated Engineering and Electrical Union] speech putting in a section about JM being trapped in Thatcher's headlights. The Swraj Paul peerage episode was continuing with Jonathan having tracked down the details of what seemed the very minor episode said to be behind the honours rejection. TB and I both felt there was racism at play here and he was determined to press on.

We were driven to Saddleworth and shown to our hotel rooms by a very fetching young blonde woman with a see-through blouse so see-through she could easily have dispensed with it completely. He did a meeting with a group of switchers and as ever at these things, did it excellently. We left for Blackpool and the AEEU where he departed from the text but he delivered the sound bite on Thatcher which is what made the bulletins. On the train he redrafted the education document, wrote a new intro which was clearly pro GM schools. I said if he wanted to keep them he should say so. The problem was that keeping GM schools as they were was unacceptable. So was scrapping them outright. He was working towards a sense that he was stopping short of scrapping them but it wasn't easy and of course complicated by his own choice. He went through his union package with MMcD, ending union sponsorship of MPs, with money instead to go to CLPs. Also – a big one – National Policy Forum documents would take precedence over conference resolutions. And pay disputes would not be debated through the party machinery to prevent union pay disputes dominating conference. On the NEC, he wanted to come off it, let JP chair it and reconstitute it to represent CLPs, PLP, local government and unions in a different balance to now. He was adamant that there could only be two real sources of power in the party – the leadership in Parliament, and the membership in the country. He felt the unions would go along with him because they didn't believe membership would rise. He did. He also went through changes he wanted at Walworth Road and clearly trusted Margaret to deliver them.

Tuesday, June 13

TB called at 8 to say he was going to go on single currency at PMQs. My first reaction was it was mad because it would let JM paint him into the Euronutter camp. But with Thatcher causing him such trouble, and JM due to see the Fresh Start group of sceptics tonight, it was in fact the obvious thing to do. We also discussed GM schools, the NUT leadership having briefed they were reversing their opposition, apparently at the behest of Lowe Bell [PR company] who were advising them on their image.

I met Margaret [Beckett] and Joy re the health document launch. We agreed we had to start getting health stories more prominent in the media if we were to get the most out of a July 3 launch. I asked Morgaret if I could have another go at the executive summary and she agreed. She also agreed it was currently too producer-orientated and that it should be written more from the perspective of the patient. I said the press would want to present it as a compromise between Old and New Labour and it was better to be on the New Labour side of the divide. Vital to it was the response of doctors and we discussed the idea of some kind of charter of support for the reforms to which GPs could sign up. MB got the plot completely, said we could not turn the clock back, people were not interested in how their health care was delivered, they just wanted it delivered. Joy was in very mellow form, and made a couple of good suggestions.

Wednesday, June 14

Joe Haines called to say Gordon Greig [former political editor, *Daily Mail*] had died. I put out some TB words. Though he worked for the *Mail*, I'd always liked him and so did TB. TB got a bit of a mauling at the PLP, notably from [Andrew] MacKinlay and [David] Clelland [Labour MPs]. Mo called to say he'd handled it well but there was clearly a fair bit of steam rising. No doubt it would have risen still further if they knew we headed from there to Brooks', for lunch with the *Telegraph*. Max Hastings began by saying he'd been at a lunch at [chairman of Carlton Television] Michael Green's recently and there were lots of young people there, some of whom said they'd be voting Labour because it would make them better off, and Max assumed they were all mad. [Simon] Heffer [*Daily Telegraph* journalist] was now so rampantly anti Major he would probably even tolerate Hezza. They pressed on what they see as the weak spots – women's quotas, devolution, tax. TB was very good on the head and body argument, that contrary to the way they viewed it, the party was being willingly led towards change. I was always impressed by the way he managed to deal with people like this. Max isn't a bad man but the truth is neither of us would spend a moment in these people's company unless we had to, and yet whilst I can never wholly conceal my disregard, I guarantee that when we left they all felt TB had taken them seriously, been nice to them, and answered their questions well. You could sense that they really wanted not to like or respect him but ended up doing both, not least because of the contrast with JM.

Met David Bradshaw [*Mirror*] re the [Rupert] Allason case. Martin Kramer [solicitor] called yesterday and said he wanted to be sure I was happy they didn't settle. I said I'd be furious if they did.

After Shadow Cabinet a group of us met with BMP to go over the economic message. It was another unsatisfactory conversation. Chris Powell said he felt we had the right logic and now had to boil it down. But I wasn't sure about the logic. I kept pressing Ed Miliband to explain our economic message in a nutshell and what came out every time was an essay that went over my head and which also seemed to change every time I asked it. Joy and Peter M were still at odds every time they spoke. Another row with Fiona who said I was so consumed with the job I might as well not be there when I was. She accepted I made an effort with the kids but she said I just didn't have the time and my mind was always somewhere else.

Thursday, June 15

Today was the day TB and I both independently reached the settled view that Major was finished. The chatter was just incessant now. Jon Sopel [BBC] called to say the *PM* programme had a document from Tory MP Dudley Fishburn on how business should build links with a Labour government. Meeting with Jackie Stacey [Labour Party official] re the planning for the war room. She did a very good presentation on it. Meeting with John Bridcut [documentory-maker] and Andy Marr who were trying to persuade me of the merits of a documentary to record the early days of a Labour government. I could see the benefits to them, not least Andy making himself more famous, but I was unpersuaded of the benefits to us at a time when we'd have enough on our plate without having a camera crew and Andy Marr in tow the whole time. The rowing with Fiona was getting both of us down and I was trying to work out ways of cutting the workload. But it felt impossible. I had so much on today I couldn't even find time to get up to the gallery and talk to the press. Had a chat with Bruce, who was laying it on thick re TB and the PLP. He said a lot of them didn't like him, and they didn't like a lot that appeared in the papers about him. We had a bit of an up-and-downer. I said they had to be persuaded that one of the main reasons they were likely to keep their jobs, and some of them likely to be government ministers, was because of TB. He agreed but said good times in politics are always followed by bad and when you get the bad times you need friends and TB is not doing enough to make them. I said it was also important that they respected him and they would respect him less if they thought all he was doing was pandering to them. The reason he is where he is and the reason we are doing as well as we are is because he's different, he's not out of the mould, and I think we need to see that as an advantage. Usual endless PMQs preparation with JP, but he was in a good mood at the moment. He was struggling with 'xenophobes'. I wrote out ZEN-O-FOBES on a postcard and he got it. It went fine. After PMQs we had a team meeting. TB came through unannounced to thank everyone, which was pretty rare. Earlier he said we needed to think through how we would deal with Heseltine. He said Hezza would give them energy and purpose and he had 'clanking great balls' that would allow him to impress the public even if they thought he was a bit off the wall. He felt the media were giving us a fairly easy ride just now only because they loathed Major. He was in no doubt Hezza would be bad news for us and wanted me to stoke up the leadership row whilst at the same time giving the sense we wanted Major dumped. BLAIR HAZZA HEZZA SPAZZA, I said, and he laughed, but Heseltine was clearly on his mind more than he'd thus far let on.

Earlier, tax meeting with GB, Derek [Scott] and Gavyn [Davies]. TB said he was against putting up the top rate because of the signal it sent. I said, to laughter, 'Why don't we just join the Tory Party?' TB shot back, to more laughter, 'I could be leader.'

Friday, June 16

With the Old Labour tag being applied to health it was more important than ever that there was a sense of real change and modernisation in education policy, and TB felt we had to bite the bullet and get it done. PG and I met to work on a new strategy/message note. PG, while happier now his money was being sorted, felt Peter M's judgement was failing in a few areas he was supposed to be good at. I was coming back to the idea of three strands for national renewal and I worked till late on a new message map. It felt fine as I was doing it but when I read it late at night it felt weak.

Saturday, June 17

Tory turmoil still rampant in the press. I was really depressed, not just fed up, but the full-blown stomach empty but for a knot in the middle, and the mind feeling numb and unable to get out of first gear. I took the boys to football and got through that OK, but I was at a loss how to improve things with Fiona. The job had become a real problem. But I either did it well or not at all and to do it well I had to do it like I did it. We had another run round the block on all the arguments of last night which cleared the air a bit. She said the job had totally taken over our lives and she needed more help in adapting to that. I tried to say I did my best but in truth I'd just taken it for granted. She said I didn't listen to anyone now. I just did what I thought I had to do. I was worried about it all enough to talk to Peter, who said I should involve her more. The trouble was that whenever I got home I just didn't want to talk about the things that went on at work. I wanted her to think it was all fine whereas in fact most days were more or less a nightmare. Peter said I had to accept that TB relied on me for judgement and for delivery and that dependence would grow as the pressure mounted. It was important Fiona understood that, but for her to do so she had to feel more involved.

Sunday, June 18

I watched Margaret [Beckett] on *Frost*. She was fine on health, and even managed to say the party picked the right leader. Anji called to say TB and she had had a long chat re Jonathan on Friday, and she felt a lot better about things. DB called to say he thought things were going fine and he wanted to say thanks for helping him through what had been a difficult balancing act over the last few months. I didn't feel I'd been particularly helpful but it was nice of him to do that. Peter M called round pm to discuss ways of presenting Phil Woolas as a moderniser. He said that it would be hard to do because the press basically saw Phil as a union hack.

Monday, June 19

I was getting less and less enthusiastic about doing my *Tribune* column. On the one hand it was a useful platform and I didn't want to let them down. On the other I had so little time and I always knocked it off in a matter of minutes as the deadline neared and it was beginning to show. I had a session with TB to say that I really needed to try to spend less time in the office because things between me and Fiona weren't great at the moment. He said he and Cherie were in exactly the same state – she complained that he only ever came alive when he was talking to me, Peter or GB, that he used up all his emotional energy in the job and she needed support and he was too drained out to give it. He said though he always knew the job would be tough he had never really realised just how totally absorbing it would be, and just how much focus and effort it required the whole time. He said he didn't know what he would do if I wasn't there, and that I had exceeded his wildest imagination about what I would be able to do for him. He felt that Peter M, Anji and I were the three people he would regard as indispensable but his advice was to try to get home more and involve Fiona more. He wanted to be able to do something for her. But he accepted he was the person who put me under the most pressure – 'apart from yourself', he added. I also tackled him over something Anji had mentioned, namely that Carole [Caplin] was there when she'd been round to see him on Friday. I told TB I thought she was a time bomb and he should have nothing to do with her. He said he knew my views and there was no way she was going to be back like she'd been before but she was helping Cherie, and he did exercise with her on Friday. He made it sound like it was my fault because I'd said it would be mad for him to use a public gym. I said there was a real danger if people knew he was working out with her when CB was not around, that they'd start chattering about something going on between them, and it would be a grim rumour to deal with. He said, that is ridiculous, I've never laid a finger on her. I said I'm simply telling you what the rumour mill would do.

David Clark and Ed Balls came over. Ed had an extraordinary manner. He was always as nice as pie with me, but whenever TB was around he hovered between irritating and rude. TB noticed it too. He said Andy Marr had told him that GB's supporters were putting it round that the left shouldn't worry because taxes would go up. There was clear positioning to the left of TB going on. TB said it was the same in their private conversations, TB would say something, e.g. re the unions deal or the GM issue, and GB would then make it clear he would be parking himself just to the left. 'It is sad. He doesn't need to do it.' We discussed the Murdoch trip and agreed it was just about OK though I had slightly shifted to Bruce's view that the Party would hate the sight of him traipsing round the world to see Murdoch. Hezza not too great in the BMARC debate.[1] Alan Clark called after I got home and I couldn't work out if he was taking the mickey or not. He said he was calling as a mate. He said you know how once you said that if the Old Girl had any sense she'd make me party chairman and get me going round the country geeing them up? Well it could be on. I said are you joking, and he said it's serious, it's down to me or [Brian] Mawhinney [Conservative MP]. I treated it as a joke but he kept saying it was serious, and what did I think? I said it would be great news all round. What would Fleet Street think? he asked. I said they'd think it was bold, risky, a bit improbable but they would certainly not dismiss out of hand. He was a total bugger, I just couldn't

[1] Debate relating to the defence manufacturer BMARC and the export of naval guns and ammunition to Iran, via Singapore, during the late 1980s.

work out, even after we spoke, whether he was being serious or not, or whether he was just trying to plant a story on me and see whether I'd place it somewhere. The evening news was excellent – BMARC troubles for Hezza, JM's latest grief and Jack Straw's anti noisy neighbour plans. Then ITN broke yet another claimed leak from the Scott Report, this time saying [William] Waldegrave [Conservative Cabinet minister], Alan Clark and [Lord] Trefgarne [former Conservative minister] may have misled Parliament.[1]

Tuesday, June 20

I was all the more mystified by Alan C's call last night when he popped up on the *Today* programme defending himself over the ITN story. Troubles were mounting over education. Ron Davies wanted to call for an end to GM schools and Win Griffiths [Labour MP] was threatening to resign because we appeared to be accepting them. TB was now convinced the policy was right. The Tories were also confused about how to play it. At PMQs JM said we were determined to undo GM schools, which went down well with some of ours, but was the opposite of what Gillian Shephard said in the *Sunday Times*. So they had allowed themselves to be wrong-footed yet again and you wondered whether they actually talked about these things or just did their own thing. But TB got a rather menacing letter from Ken Purchase [Labour MP] saying it was a pity TB was prepared to divide the party over GM schools. As Tessa said later, the problem was TB was respected but not liked by a lot of the MPs. TB did the Joint Policy Committee on the education document which DM said was very tense and littered with long speeches from those not directly involved like Dobbo and Straw (who got very good coverage for his noisy neighbours plans today). There was also a big bust-up on grammar schools, which someone had briefed about, and after speaking to TB I said that a Labour government would improve standards for the many, not go to war on a few grammar schools.

PMQs was a choice between Scott, or Ken Clarke saying he was relaxed about calling a single currency a crown, a florin or a shilling.

[1] Lord Justice Scott's report on the inquiry into sales of arms to Iraq, published in February 1996, concluded that there had been a deliberate failure by ministers to tell Parliament the truth about arms-sales policy. While clearing former foreign office minister Waldegrave of lying to Parliament or in letters, the report described his evidence as 'unconvincing' and also criticised the fact that the conclusions of a meeting between junior ministers Waldegrave, Clark and Trefgarne, at which they agreed that guidelines regarding arms sales to Iraq should be relaxed, were never announced in Parliament or submitted to the prime minister.

We went for Scott, though both TB and I were of the view it was all a bit chattering classville stuff. TB said afterwards he felt Major's internal position was a bit stronger.

There was growing interest in education. Someone had given the document that went to the JPC [Joint Policy Committee] to Don Macintyre so I had a long session with him. I also briefed hard on the parent-power proposals. I felt the truth was that we were abolishing GM schools but didn't really want people to say so. TB disagreed, said we were keeping the best parts of the system and changing the worst so that all schools benefited from greater freedom. With the Tories confused about the line, we had a choice: present it as a U-turn basically accepting GM schools but modified; or stress the changes. TB was adamant it should be the former. This led to another late-night row at home, Fiona saying how could I have been massively opposed six months ago, and now I was prepared to accept presenting it as a pro-GM policy. I said I was perfectly happy with the policy, and that was more important than either the presentation or the perception. DB and I were both conscious of the fact that the briefing was important because TB's own circle had to be squared. DB wanted to press the 'GM schools should go' button. Bruce said there would be real trouble in the PLP but Kilfoyle was more relaxed.

In between finalising the education press release I was still trying to rewrite the health document executive summary where similar tensions were proving difficult to reconcile. It was a case of having to persuade Margaret B straight up that it needed to be more New Labour in tone.

Bill Morris came in for a meeting with TB. He clearly knew he was going to win the T&G leadership and was very aggressive, talking at one point about the need for parity between Labour and the unions in government. TB said afterwards, these people just aren't serious. It made him more not less determined to press on with the changes to the unions/party relationship. I spoke to Jane Reed [News International] re Murdoch trip. I said we were going to bite the bullet so we needed to work out a media strategy. I was knackered and about to go home when Fiona called to remind me we were going to [friends] Nigella Lawson and John Diamond's party. It was a bit of a grind. Is there any party Alan Yentob [controller of BBC1] isn't at? Simon Jenkins [former editor of *The Times*] was there with Caroline Waldegrave [wife of William], saying how much he liked TB. Interesting to see how long that lasts.

Thursday, June 22

The big excitement after PMQs was that JM was planning to do a press conference in the Number 10 garden. Nobody seemed to know for sure what it was about. He came down and announced he was planning to quit as party leader and call a leadership election. On one level, it was bold. But the fact that he was driven to it just underlined how pathetic he had become and how weakened he now was. It caused a bit of panic at our end. Joy went into panic mode, DH to a lesser extent, and TB was calm and measured and getting irritated at all the chatter. It was a classic time for calm heads. Anji and I managed to ease out everyone apart from JP and GB, who was terrific. He and I sat there rattling out lines at each other and then working out who was best to deploy them. It was basically a desperate move from a weak leader of a disintegrating government. GB agreed to do the immediate stuff then TB did a round of excellent interviews at Millbank. The media there were in full frenzy mode and we kept reminding ourselves we had to stay calm, measured and talk to the public not the press. There was a sense of real turmoil at Millbank and some of the Tories doing interviews looked close to hyperventilation. Teddy Taylor, Tony Marlow and Teresa Gorman [Conservative MPs] were all straight on the case. TB said as we went from one studio to another 'This is going to unravel for him.' He hammered the main lines of division, lack of direction, the sense of disintegration.

Back to the office and GB said we should be saying the challenge for Major is whether he had a radical manifesto for change. TB did that in the next batch of interviews. There was a real sense of excitement around the place but I'm glad to say I felt no sense of the mad adrenaline surge that seemed to be hitting some of the others. I'd been saying to myself for ages that it was important never to lose sight of the real audience, the public, who would not be sharing the sense of mania that was sweeping Westminster. To us, this was just another opportunity to get TB out there showing he was calm, reasonable, moderate and a real alternative to the weak and useless prime minister we currently had. I managed to knock off articles for the *Sun* and the *Mirror* based on what TB was saying as he went from one interview to the next. I got a lift home with TB so we could talk about the education speech tomorrow. 'These are interesting times,' he said. 'This next period will be crucial.' He felt JM might get a short-term lift but that long term he was finished and today was bad for him. He said the ideal for us would now be a contest with bruises which JM survives. He called me again later, said it was a good day for us. We had to keep cool, keep our nerve and press on. I could tell he felt it was bit-between-teeth time and I felt exactly the same.

TB was as ever trying to work out how JM could turn things to his advantage. One minute he was convinced JM was finished, the next that this could be the making of him and the route to recovery. I said I thought there was a real whiff of decay around Major now, and his party just wasn't serious enough. They hated each other more than they hated us, which was like Labour was in the past. We went over the main lines: that the divisions ran too deep now; that all Major's focus was now on party not country. We met a rather sheepish and worried-looking Michael Howard on the way into the *Today* studio. Even he was finding it hard to disguise how it felt today. News came through of the T&G result – a win for Bill Morris – which TB said was a disappointment. The truth was Jack D just wasn't a high-calibre candidate so another low-calibre candidate got back. Then news that Douglas Hurd was stepping down. TB was in total circular conversation mode, asking and re-asking what it meant for Major, could he gain from it, was he finished. I was briefing that our best outcome was JM victorious but bruised, second best was Hezza because the public didn't trust him and he was a divisive figure in the Tory Party, and always would be. On the way down it became obvious [John] Redwood [Conservative Welsh secretary] wasn't going to support him. He hasn't planned this, said TB. It is disintegration not strategy.

After getting back from Gordon Greig's funeral, Fiona and I went out for dinner and the second I walked through the door TB was on the phone saying he'd seen the nine o'clock news and it was a total blowjob for Major, who was coming out of all this far too well. Gerald K called to make the same point so I got Joy on the case with Tony Hall.

I watched the first half of the Rugby World Cup Final but then got a call to go to TB's. He was in a state of some agitation. He said he'd barely slept at all and it was the sense of uncertainty and the feeling for the first time since he became leader that someone else had the initiative. He was sure Hezza was on the march and that he would be a more difficult opponent. Equally if Major survived he could remake himself on the back of this, and that would make him a more difficult opponent. I said nobody said it was going to be easy. He said, I know, but I really want to think through how to deal with this. The picture is changing and we have to change it on our terms. On the way to the airport he got a call from Derry, who was really angry that TB was thinking of cancelling dinner with him, Roy Jenkins, the

Master of the Rolls [Sir Thomas Bingham] and the Lord Chancellor's private secretary to attend a conference chaired by 'Mister Rupert Murdoch'. In fact the Murdoch trip was looking iffy again because of the Tory scene. On the plane, RC joined us and TB was at it again, the same questions, what do you think, how should we react, who'll be Foreign Secretary, hoovering any mind he came across to help him settle his own. He gave Robin some guff about how he was largely responsible for Hurd going because he had been so effective. RC swelled visibly. Earlier he spoke to Bill Morris and said Bill's people were putting it round that he had a mandate to attack the party leadership. Bill said no, he intended to be constructive.

We arrived at Nice, and as we landed we flew right over the school where I taught. Out to the Pullman Hotel. Typical Eurononsense row at the start over whether RC could get into the dinner. TB wanted him there but JP said it might cause offence because not everyone had three big hitters there and blah, blah, blah. I think at these events people get too caught up in the process, they don't stop to think what the people out there might think if they saw it close up. I stole off for an hour while TB was at the dinner to see some of my old haunts [from AC's time there as a student], most of which had changed apart from the little bar near the school, and to my amazement they remembered who I was. Tim called to say the Sundays were looking grim for JM. The *News of the World* were moving to Portillo. TB wondered if Murdoch wasn't trying to go straight to Gingrich (Portillo) without stopping at Clinton (Blair). I thought Portillo would be brilliant for us. The Tories would split further and he would allow TB even more space in the One Nation ground.

Sunday, June 25

I went for a walk round the backstreets with TB. He was in constant fret mode as well as circular conversation at the moment. I suppose the two are linked. 'Can we really beat Hezza?' he asked. 'Of course we can.' 'It'll be difficult.' 'So what?' 'I suppose Major might survive but I think it's wishful thinking really.' 'It is the party that's fucked, and Major is not the great problem.' 'I suppose so.' Then he was back on to what a boost JM could get out of it. He was able to pull himself out of his gloom long enough to do an OK interview with Adam Boulton [Sky News political editor], then we went for another walk and he was back with the same bloody questions again, trying to get the measure of the three names in the frame. I said he was more than a match for any of them and there was a huge gulf between what Westminster thought of Hezza and Portillo, and what the public thought. He said he hated the uncertainty. TB did his usual spiel inside the summit meeting and I sensed Neil K wasn't very happy with it. JP spoke later, and was going hell for leather, causing real problems for the interpreters. At one point you could see half the people in the room staring into the interpreters' booths and watching them trying to make sense of it. One of them told us later that she just gave up, it was hopeless. She thought she'd made sense of the first half of a sentence and then he was off into another one.

TB was devoting every spare moment to thinking about the Tory situation. We had an hour to wait at the airport and he had a chat with RC, who said he thought it was unnecessary for JP to come to these events. Today had been embarrassing, he said, and there had been no need for him to be there. TB asked Robin if he wanted to be on the CMT. On the flight back, he said: Do you realise we could be a few weeks from a general election, and after that we could be in power? He said his brother Bill had said he reckoned JM would survive and stay to the election. He'd obviously called Bill over the weekend. He always did when he was worried. He was very lucky to have an older brother who was clever, nice, totally supportive and who had no interest whatever in a public profile and so gave him genuine solid advice and judgement. I was glad to get on the plane. No wonder JM talked about Eurocrap when he went to these summit-type events. As we got on, all the front pages were lined up in a rack, and they were absolutely dreadful for Major. 'He's had it, surely,' said TB. On landing the general view was that Redwood would stand and that JM was finished. He had said in terms that no Cabinet minister would stand. Alan Clark called and was in riotous mood. He said the whole thing was a total shower and meanwhile you boys are cleaning up all over the place like an unstoppable, unmatchable machine. He should have been with TB yesterday. It didn't feel like that.

Monday, June 26

TB was still wanting us to fight our way into the story, still worried JM was getting something out of it. The problem was they were only using our people as commentators not players. I bumped into Ken Baker. He had the look of a man who had gone beyond. He said 'Just sit back and enjoy it. It is a disaster for us. The party I love has gone mad.' I used the 'mad' line in a statement from JP after Redwood quit the Cabinet in advance of his 2pm press conference. TB was at the UN fifty-year celebrations with Major which meant he had time to think some more. Peter M thought we should cancel the health launch but on the contrary I felt it was exactly as they were imploding that we should be pressing on with our alternative agenda. I wrote to Tony Hall saying I was concerned about their coverage. Office meeting, TB really not happy. I said we should do as much as possible to keep his profile up. He agreed we go ahead with the health document. I agreed with Patrick Wintour that I would leak him our paper on strategy about the Tories. Peter thought we should be calling for the election, but TB and I felt when we did that, we had to make a real impact. I went with TB to Peter Stothard's party. Murdoch was at the do, and TB had a brief chat, RM repeating the Australia invite and TB saying we'd do it if we could. I chatted to Lamont re Redwood's launch. What he said wasn't bad, I said. I'd heard him on the radio and it sounded fine but when I'd got back from lunch I saw him on the TV and it was a huge mistake to have surrounded himself with all those multicoloured nutters like [Teresa] Gorman and [Tony] Marlow [Tory MPs]. Give Redwood his due though. He showed a bit of balls, and for the moment he's got momentum while JM swans round Cannes. Alan Yentob was there. Plus Salman Rushdie [author], who is just behind Yentob in the list of people who are always at the few dos I ever go to.

Tuesday, June 27

We barely figured in the press. Redwood did pretty well. TB was still veering between saying JM would win, then it was Hezza and then Portillo, and I said, what's that saying about worrying about the things you can influence and not the things you can't? He'd listened to GB on the radio and said he just wished we could set out an economic message that didn't sound so complicated. We've got a coherent message but we don't put it across properly, he said. I said I didn't think we had a coherent message yet. We finished TB's economics speech and drove to the Film Theatre. He was still very jittery. 'I just don't feel comfortable or confident about this. I'm worried.' He was wasting an awful lot of energy worrying about events he could only influence at the margins.

Redwood's press conference was the main event plus JM's response from Cannes. TB met union general secretaries to take them through the union package which we would need to push pretty sharpish to keep the agenda moving our way. Sally said he did well and stuck to his guns. On the six o'clock news, Jon Sopel was quoting 'friends of Portillo' saying he would definitely challenge in a second round if a further ballot, or force a contest later in the year with Hezza. I got JP words out saying Portillo was at it and it exposed the lying and cheating going on in a disintegrating party. I bumped into David

Mellor, who had the same look Ken Baker had. 'I assume you are orchestrating this farce?' he said.

Wednesday, June 28

Portillo's treachery was running quite big, with lots of interest in his getting new offices for a campaign HQ. Not much out of PMQs but I scripted a nice line about Redwood's prime ministerial spaceship which would whiz people to Planet Portillo. TB had accepted that JM was the least divisive of the various figures in the frame, that Portillo would split them badly, so would Hezza, but Hezza would cheer them up because he would attack us better than the rest put together. The Anji/Jonathan friction seemed to be getting worse, though it only got to Anji. Jonathan's strength and weakness seemed to be his ability to let things just bounce off him. More of a strength than a weakness for himself, but not necessarily for his relations with others. I find him perfectly easy to work with but sometimes I think Anji doesn't and it may lead to TB having to make a choice, which would be unfortunate. The TB/GB thing wasn't great either, and the press were beginning to pick up on it. Andy Marr said he felt GB was deliberately putting himself to the left of TB the whole time now. 'If I was a real journalist, I'd write about it!' he said. [Peter] Riddell told me *The Times* had a poll showing a boost for JM. 'Should we be worried, do you think?' TB asked. No. Andy told a very funny story about GB. He said to him, Gordon, do you ever relax at all? And GB said yes, I play golf at the weekends. He paused to let this sink in and then added 'That's not true by the way.'

Thursday, June 29

Complained to Tony Hall about the way the BBC were not challenging the false claims the Tories were making about us. My worry was that if this became a real contest, the airwaves would be filled with candidates and their supporters vying with each other to see who could attack us the best, because that is what their party was looking for. We had to fight to get our voice heard in the story, not least so we could make that point for the public. They were getting away with murder at the moment and all the BBC can say is why are you complaining, this story is a disaster for them. That is not the point, I told Hall. They cannot just tell lies about us and have nobody challenge it. The view of the opposition about the state of the government's leadership should be heard. I don't think they got it really, though possibly by complaining we got more coverage for health than we would otherwise have done. Meanwhile Redwood was

June '95: Run-in with BBC over Tory claims

dive-bombing and being exposed as a lightweight. DM and I had a row drafting TB's *Times* article on public services, which I felt had to have real cutting edge and DM kept defaulting to these policy wonk words that I found impenetrable.

Margaret B and her entourage came over to prepare for her press conference with TB. There was something wonderfully calm and calming about Margaret. TB was moving into his mildly hyper mode that he sometimes gets pre media events, while she just sat there, took out her compact mirror and touched up her make-up. When she took notes out came the bundle of pens and pencils bound in a rubber band, very schooly but something endearing about it, I don't know what. They ran over the tricky questions, which were all in the area of whether we saw it as Old/New, were we scrapping the market mechanisms, etc. It went fine and they both did well, though I could see TB, like me, could barely take his eyes off a foreign journalist we'd never seen before who parked herself in one of the front rows. 'Did you see that woman?' he said when he came back. 'I can't imagine which one you mean,' I said. As we raved on, he noticed Margaret nearby, listening. 'Oh sorry, Margaret,' he said, with his schoolboy-caught-by-teacher look. 'No, not at all,' she said. 'I quite understand.' I bumped into [Nicholas] Soames who said JM would win and if for any reason he didn't, he would back Hezza 'because he'd blast your boy apart'. TB did *World at One* on health, then we prepared for PMQs out on the terrace, which was searingly hot. TB had a capacity to endure any temperature, loves the sun, held his face up to it almost as if he was in conversation with it, while the rest of us were longing to go inside to cool down. TB was going on Europe/divisions but JM was at his best ever. Really strong. I expected TB would be in a bit of a state about it so escaped the gallery before the press could stop me and rushed back to the office. I bumped into Major as he was coming out of the office. There is always a chill. As Tories kept telling me, he loathed me, and could never understand how I had helped build him up when he was advancing through the Cabinet, and then tore into him once he made it to the top. For my part, I couldn't understand why he couldn't understand it, given I never hid my politics. He stopped for a moment, said hello, and I said 'Well done. I don't think there's much doubt about who got the better of today.' 'Thank you.' TB said 'I don't know what he had for breakfast but I'd like some of it next time.' I bumped into Portillo who had a face like thunder. 'I thought your boss was brilliant today, didn't you?' I said. 'Indeed,' he said and stomped off with that rather painted smile of his.

Home to get Fiona then we went for dinner at TB's, with Pete and Helen [Thompson, personal friends of TB], Charlie and Marianna

[Falconer], Ros [Mark, the Blair nanny] and her mum. Charlie is a total star. He is a total mess, with his clothes all over the shop, his shirt covered in ink, spilling and knocking things over, but he is hilariously funny and incredibly nice. He also has a fierce intelligence. He went one by one through the Shadow Cabinet and had us falling off chairs with his analysis. But he also gave TB a real grilling, and just didn't let go, forcing him to define New Labour, and at times I could see TB feeling pressured by it, thinking why am I having to defend all this in the one hour of the day I should be able to relax? But it was good. And then Charlie quizzed him on GB and TB tried to be diplomatic but again Charlie got to the point straight away. The only real criticism TB would make, even among friends, was that GB was sometimes too intellectual and overcomplicated things. Diplomatic, like I say.

Friday, June 30

TB filled me in on yesterday's meeting with GB. GB had said that I was briefing against him and TB told him that instead of being paranoid about me, he should use me, I could do a brilliant job for him. TB said he told him he had to grow up, and instead of being consumed with rage and jealousy, and thinking he should be leader, he should get on with the job that he's got. Re Peter, he said 'You're forcing me to choose one or the other of you which is ridiculous. You've both got talent and I need people of talent.' Anji had another session with Joy and told her she had to use us, stop seeing us as the enemy. I was beginning to worry about what it would be like in a campaign, with TB, Anji and I presumably on the road most of the time. I raised this when we had an internal general election planning meeting at 2.30 with Anji, DM, Jonathan. I said we should vary the pace of the press conferences, and not feel we had to do them all in London. I liked the idea of maybe video link-ups so that he could be doing it in Birmingham but the London media were also able to ask questions. Or he could do them from a factory floor or a schoolroom. And I said to DM we should start thinking now about making the spine of the campaign, from a policy perspective, serious lecture-type speeches rather than just big rallies. I liked the idea of launching the manifesto then rolling out a series of big, heavyweight speeches to big, heavyweight audiences and we should start thinking about them now – education, health, welfare, industry, Europe, building up to a big one on the economy, followed by one that brings it all together. We agreed that each day should have the one major TB event that really took our energies, and the rest should fall around it. TB was in the constituency and I think he felt reassured we were moving into proper planning mode re a campaign, but he was consumed re the Tory leadership. He reckoned we could be in motion of no-confidence territory by Thursday.

Monday, July 3

A group of us went to look at Millbank Tower which was now the clear preferred option for campaign HQ. The mood was good, and there was lots of black humour flying around – where would we put the boxing ring for JP/Joy and GB/Peter M bouts? Look how easy it will be for MI6 to track what's going on – they can see right in, etc. But it felt right. It was spacious and open and lent itself to any structure we wanted. The question I'd asked at all the sites we'd been shown was – could I imagine walking in here and seeing a full-blown campaign in action, and this was the first place where I could say yes.

Off to lunch at *The Economist* with TB to meet their top brass. A smugger group of people it would be hard to find. I could sense they didn't really know what to make of TB. He was good on welfare, and very pro EMU, and lamented the state of the debate on Europe. He probably came over as too calculating, even asking Bill Emmott [editor] at one point what did they want from a Labour government? He said they broadly backed us on macro, health, Europe, education, but they'd like more of a nod towards an independent Bank of England. We walked back past Carlton Gardens [Foreign Secretary's official London residence], wondering whether we could imagine Robin Cook living there. Not difficult – duck-to-water time. Got a lift home with Joy who was clearly feeling insecure. She asked if TB thought she was doing a good job. I said he thought she was capable of it, but had become a victim of the politics and didn't quite know how to surf the currents. I said she really should integrate herself more with us. She said she liked Anji and felt she could trust her. I said if she had me onside as well, that was enough, and she just had to watch herself.

Tuesday, July 4

Tory leadership contest. TB on edge all day. He'd convinced himself again that we were heading towards Hezza, and a real fight because Hezza would do a deal with the right and then just come at us all guns blazing. GB wanted to do a press conference tomorrow but I persuaded him we were better to stick just to TB's speech. TB was calling me down every few minutes to have the same conversation again and again. It was a real pain in the arse. 'I hate this,' he said, 'I hate the fact that we just have no control over any of this, that our fate is in the hands of 329 Tory MPs.' I said how do you think John bloody Major feels.

Because of all the fuss round the office when JM announced his 'resignation', TB told Anji he wanted nobody in his office but me, GB and Peter M when the result was announced so that we could focus properly on the response. I was in there for a while on my own with TB, just listening to him blather and rant about these wretched Tory MPs, and GB and Peter, letting it all out. I said for fuck's sake calm down. There is nothing we can do but wait for the result and then plan a strategic response. He was hopeful GB and Peter would speak to each other when the four of us met. Then he realised the absurdity that statement exposed. 'God it's unbelievable that we have to worry about whether they'll speak to each other.' Rumours started to circulate that JM had offered Hezza deputy PM and Tory chairman, then that it had all fallen apart. GB and Peter came over and joined us over orange juice and some very tired sandwiches. Even in their eating styles they were so different, GB a chomper with his jaws pounding back and forth, Peter looking with real disdain at the sandwich and then tearing off little pieces and popping them in his mouth as if they were aspirins. TB said the next period was really important. He wanted Peter to go to L&S [by-election]. He wanted the two of them to work together very closely. We agreed that whatever the result, we would go on the 'two parties' line, that they were divided beyond repair.

The result came through and TB leapt to his feet and said 'That's perfect, exactly the result we want.' Norman Fowler [former Conservative Party chairman] said it was a clear win for JM, and [Robin] Oakley started to run the Central Office line that it was similar to the scale of TB's leadership election. I paged him to say that was absurd and offensive. To compare a contest caused by the leader's death, and an open field, with a contest caused by the prime minister's hopeless leadership of a disintegrating party is ridiculous. GB and I bounced lines off each other and within a few minutes we had an agreed script doing the rounds. It was so frustrating that when GB was with you, and motoring, we had a very productive relationship. But it was all dependent on mood and all the time there was this lurking rage at us.

We agreed TB should do the Millbank rounds. We headed over there, driving past the circus on College Green. The 'two parties' line played strongly, and TB had recovered his confidence. The pain-in-the-arse nagging and endless re-asking of the same questions had been part of the process. But we had a problem, as I feared. JP was plunged into gloom having learned that TB had resorted to the old GB/Peter/AC axis earlier. Anji had been to see him to disabuse him of the notion this was another 'hunting lodge' incident. But he called me and I said it could have been handled better but he mustn't take this seriously. TB just didn't want a big twittering crowd and the only way he could keep it small was to handle it the way he did. It really isn't a big deal. Every time GB and PM were back in harness, JP felt sidelined by 'the two monkeys on his back'. Joy was just as pissed off but I said to her too she just had to understand that when it came to the big moments, TB had to be allowed to operate exactly as he wanted.

Wednesday, July 5

Reshuffle day. I had a nice chat with Stephen Dorrell who like other ministers had no idea what, if any, job he would be in at the end of the day. He was very friendly and I was struck again how politicians have to go about their business in an often cruel environment. TB appeared to be in some kind of mental agony about all this, just wanted to know what the lie of the land was going to be. I also expressed my fear that JM having stood up to the Tory papers, it would add to the sense of oddness for the Labour leader then traipsing across the world to see Murdoch. He said, 'Thatcher would have gone without a moment's thought.' And your point is . . . We were then bounced (probably, if inadvertently by Murdoch) on the Murdoch trip when we got a call from Andrew Whyte [News International] that Peterborough [*Daily Telegraph* gossip column] had called to say they were doing a story about it. He thought Murdoch had mentioned it to Conrad Black [*Telegraph* owner] who had told the paper. I really didn't want this dribbling out as a diary story and felt it should be done in a more orderly way, so after a chat with TB I briefed Robert Peston of the *FT*. He was amazed, as was I, that the *Telegraph* didn't see it as a big story. Maybe it was a stitch-up just to get it out there.

David Frost's summer party.[1] Huge mix of big political figures, media, business, lots of the Frost interviewees. I asked David English if the *Mail* had ever considered backing Labour. Loud enough for lots of people to hear, he said 'There's a first time.' Jill Dando there, looking fabulous. Carla Powell telling TB that it was because of me and my flirting with her on trips that Mrs T didn't trust her. Peter M working his way round. Imran Khan and Jemima Goldsmith. Conrad Black. Stewart Steven. Lord Stevens. Andrew Neil. Alan Yentob of course.

---

[1] Frost's guests, respectively, were: Jill Dando, BBC presenter; Carla Powell, wife of Charles Powell (private secretary to both Thatcher and Major, brother of Jonathan and Chris Powell); Imran Khan, Pakistani politician and former Test cricketer, and Jemima, his wife of six weeks; Stewart Steven, editor, *News on Sunday*; Lord Stevens, chairman, United News and Media; Andrew Neil, former editor, *Sunday Times*; Alan Yentob, controller, BBC1.

He was quite an operator old Frostie. TB had to leave for a Bank of England dinner so I got a cab back with Cherie. It started off OK, but then we turned to the GB/JP/Peter M scene and I made the observation that a part of all major politicians is deeply egotistical, otherwise they couldn't do the job. She said 'You can talk.' I said what's that supposed to mean? She said you are as complicated and egotistical as any of them. I said some might say I was allowing my ego and my whole life to be subsumed by her husband, so I didn't agree. She said we had to keep Tony calm. Then, as if none of what had gone before meant a thing, we talked about the kids. The big reshuffle story was Hezza's new role as deputy prime minister and we had JP up responding.

Thursday, July 6

Very little interest in the Murdoch story to my surprise, but Bruce Grocott went mad, threatening to resign and saying it would just stick in the party's gullet the sight of TB flying halfway round the world to see the man whose papers systematically savaged us under Neil [Kinnock]. Thankfully I missed the 8.45 meeting again, which was apparently even worse than usual. TB did well at PMQs, with a very good ad lib on Redwood and for once our backbenchers were properly organised and did a good job. The best news though was that JM was back to his old crap form.

Friday, July 7

TB had a really awful meeting with the union general secretaries. He was exasperated afterwards, said they just weren't serious people. Sally [Morgan] said that she always knew when he was losing it with them – he called them 'you guys', then it was 'listen, you guys', then it was 'for heaven's sake, you guys'. We were still fighting to get our voice heard. DH fought hard and won a slot for JP on the *Today* programme tomorrow. I had a slight problem with Peter M who was trying to persuade me Cherie should do a lot more at conference and that maybe Fiona should help her, though I half suspected he wanted Carole Caplin to go too. He put to me his proposal for a book, and said it would only work if I helped him and gave it my blessing. Later TB asked me, out of the blue, if I wanted to be an MP. I said why are you asking me now? He said if I did, and we won, he thought I could become a huge player in the government. I said what, you worried that GB and Peter won't last the course? He said think about it. I said he had to decide whether I could do more for the cause doing this, and helping him get there, or going into a different mode. I wasn't sure of the answer to that, but my initial instinct said stay with what I'm doing. He'd obviously said something to Peter because he said to me TB thinks you have a future as a key executive player in a top job independent of him.

Saturday, July 8

Paul Keating [Australian Prime Minister] called TB to invite him to stay at his official residence in Sydney when we went to Australia next week. He said he had a few things to teach him about how to deal with Rupert. He said Murdoch is a hard bastard and you need a strategy for dealing with him.

Sunday, July 9

TB called re the T&G speech, saying he was determined to push on the new unions agenda. Lunch at Derry's, which was really nice. We sat out at the back, enjoying the fantastic weather. Derry was on great form, funny as ever, but we also had a really good chat about the whole operation. He and I had very similar views, I think, of the main players and the main relationships. I told Derry what John Smith had once said to me about him – 'Derry is living proof that excessive alcohol consumption does not affect the brain.' 'I'll drink to that,' said Derry. He was worried that TB was 'too messianic', that he felt he could walk on water because he had risen so quickly and done so well since he rose. He also worried that TB did not read widely enough.

I started to get a whole succession of pager messages from industrial correspondents up for the T&G in Blackpool who had arrived to be given a six-page document on Labour/union relations which included some very explosive lines in it – there should be no further erosion of the link, a halt to constitutional change. Pain in the arse but I briefed on TB's speech. He'd say an arm's length relationship was better, and also employers would be properly consulted on minimum wage. I just managed to get hold of Mark Webster [ITN] before he did his report and it came out fine. We could use this to get some proper definition out of the speech. Most of the heavies thought it was front page lead stuff. *Today* programme wanted TB and I said no. I suggested RC who was in Edinburgh and not keen. I said it would be useful because of his credentials and he could say the document went over the top and that there IS a new relationship and quite right too. I could tell he wasn't keen but (probably wrongly) I talked him into it. He said one of the reasons this stuff flew was because people feared there WAS a hidden agenda because Mandelson was constantly briefing it and until Peter stopped, there would be problems.

I defended Peter, said there was no evidence at all that he was doing anything wrong on this, or pushing out messages Tony didn't want, and people just always wanted to assume he was involved. The truth is that if Bill Morris deliberately provokes this kind of situation, we can't just take it lying down. RC said 'I will do my loyal best to put the case,' but I sensed he was going to be tricky about it, and he said he had never wanted to weaken the union link. TB had been out all day so didn't really know the scale of it till he got back. He called after the ITN bulletin at 11. He was almost speechless with rage. 'I cannot tell you how much I fucking hate these people. They are stupid and they are malevolent. They beg me to go to their conference and then stitch me up, and then they will get all hurt and pathetic when I say what I think. They complain that we want to distance ourselves and then give us all the evidence why we should distance ourselves. I have no option but to go up there and blow them out of the water.' He called again later to say he was worried about Robin being too greasy and pro union. I said I'd get him to call. 'I'm finished with these people,' he said. 'Absolutely finished with them.'

Monday, July 10

Bill Morris all conciliatory on the *Today* programme, and then RC on at 8.20, making very pro-union noises, as he said he would, way too conciliatory, virtually congratulating Bill for saying he was prepared to allow an 'equal partnership'. By the time I got round to TB's he was pretty steamed up, but unsure how to deal with it in his speech. Peter M wanted us to go through Morris' statement line by line and take it apart, but I felt that would be too provocative and OTT. TB wrote a very strong section himself, the strongest I'd yet seen, saying we would listen to the unions, but making clear there would be no special relationship and certainly no favours. Very strong stuff in the current atmosphere. He was raging on the train. 'What really gets me is the way they beg me to go to their conference, otherwise nobody will take them seriously, then they go out of their way to embarrass me. It's pathetic. It's just not serious.' He said what he loathed most about it was the sense of it being a ritual – they get him to go, then set him up, then he has to hit back. PG called to say it was not possible to be too tough on the unions today. I called ahead to Bridget Sweeney [Labour events team] to get the speech off the fax before anyone there saw it, and also to organise some autograph hunters and well-wishers so there was a chance of avoiding too many pictures with Bill. Even TB would struggle to hide the contempt today, and it was better he was seen with people.

On arrival TB shook Bill briefly by the hand then went straight over to the little crowd that had gathered, signed a few autographs and chatted away for a little while. The atmospherics were very tense and I said to Bill, TB would want to go to a private room and work on the speech so they spent barely a minute together. We had the usual 'any jokes?' chat, and I said – partly as an excuse not to have to think of any – that the message would be even starker if he made no effort to soften them up at the beginning, and if he did the jokes we'd written re Hezza he should do them later in the speech. That is exactly what he did. He went out to polite applause and the first two pages were heard in stony silence as he delivered a very tough message. Then later he departed from the text and did a real tour de force on why he was so passionate about wanting a Labour government, with the subtext that these guys were in danger of stopping one happening. He really worked them over and by the end had most of them up for a standing ovation, which was impressive considering where the atmospherics were during the day. It was probably the toughest message a party leader had given to the unions, and they just about took it. Then we headed for Littleborough and Saddleworth. It was incredibly hot and the scenery awesome. ITN did a big number on the 'end of the special relationship', but the BBC barely covered it, fuelling my anger with them. TB and I had a little lapse into teenager mode as we looked forward to seeing the blonde barmaid again at the Saddleworth Hotel.

Tuesday, July 11

Bad start to the day because of the coverage on our Welsh MPs boycotting Welsh Questions yesterday because of William Hague's appointment.[1] TB was livid when I told him, saying people would think we just weren't serious. We had breakfast in TB's room, and he was a bit subdued. He said he hated the Welsh story. 'It is one of those things that defines you.' He wanted me to make it clear he wasn't happy with it. I said that looked like he didn't have a grip. He said 'I don't want anyone thinking I encourage student protest type politics.' He asked Jonathan to find out when Derek Foster knew and it turned out to be last week, so that got the rage going on again. He said it hardened his view that the chief whip had to be an appointed position, not necessarily out of the elected Shadow Cabinet pool. He

---

[1] Welsh MPs objected to Conservative MP Hague's appointment as Welsh Secretary on the grounds that he was English and had shown scant interest in the Principality through seventy-two Commons debates.

was planning to promise Derek a Cabinet position in return for agreeing and he wanted Nick Brown as number two. I was totally opposed to NB in that job because I thought he was basically untrustworthy. TB had a meeting with the trade union group of MPs which he said was truly awful, Eddie Loyden saying it was all about class war on the shop floor, others saying we would be even further ahead in the polls if we stopped distancing ourselves from the unions. I had a long chat with Trevor Kavanagh about the Murdoch visit. I said how long before you're having to write pro-Labour stuff, Trevor? I didn't get the sense he was totally on board for the RM operation.

Wednesday, July 12

Guardian poll showing the Tories only got a point gain on the back of the leadership contest, which was fine. Then Martin Kettle [*Guardian*] called to say there had been a terrible cock-up. ICM had given them the wrong figures and in fact our lead had fallen from 29 to 13. I didn't tell TB till later because I didn't want him to stop working on the Australia speech. When he heard he went into a total spin, doing a big 'told you so' number. I said it was obvious they'd get a lift but it wouldn't be sustained.

I got a lift in with Joy who said there hadn't been a single day in the job when she hadn't felt sad. I said she had to get more involved with us but she was difficult and we didn't have limitless time. Re the Murdoch speech he was clear what he wanted to say, but David M and Jonathan, who were having a go at a draft, didn't seem to get it. His basic message was that old left and new right had failed, the world had changed and we needed a values-based response around the themes of community to respond to the challenges and opportunities of globalisation. Our discussions got more and more heated, Jonathan saying the message wasn't radical enough, DM saying the arguments we were using were too simplistic, me saying we had to boil the arguments right down or nobody would listen. TB called after I went to bed, to chew the fat. I could tell the *Guardian* poll had unsettled him. 'You don't think they could win, do you?' he said. 'Only if we let them.'

Thursday, July 13 to Friday, July 14

TB was a bit worried re JP, feeling he was using the Hezza situation [Heseltine's appointment as deputy prime minister] to do a bit of shadow empire building. GB felt we needed more initiatives to show a forward agenda, e.g. on welfare. Aussie press briefing went fine. They were a friendly lot, interested mainly in nuclear testing, monarchy, links with Australian Labor Party, and of course Murdoch. TB said to me afterwards he was a bit taken aback by the level of interest in him abroad. I said do you think it might have something to do with the fact that people think you're going to be the next prime minister of the UK? He said yes but it takes some getting used to. We had Phil Stephens from the *FT* in for a chat and TB was very robust re Murdoch, saying it was an important opportunity for a major speech and the chance to show change. I volunteered to our press that the Aussie press had raised the monarchy and TB had said it was a matter for the Australian people. I was livid when Jon Hibbs [*Telegraph*] said this would be their main story – that Blair would not stand in the way of a republican Australia. It was a classic illustration of the difference between our media and overseas media. The Aussies were doing it straight, our lot always looking for an angle regardless of whether it really stood up or not.

We left for Heathrow at 8pm. TB suddenly in a real state re the speech draft, saying it wasn't up to the mark and we had to start all over again on the plane. There was a classic TB moment at the airport, when we were waiting in the Spelthorne Suite, and TB said what do you think about this, and read me a section of a draft. It was pretty good and I said so. 'Lee Kuan Yew [Prime Minister of Singapore] sent it to me. Great man. I think we should lift it direct then get the left press to welcome its sentiments, then tell them who wrote it.' We were taken to the plane and as TB and I settled down to start working, a rather unpleasant woman in leather trousers insisted we were in her seat. She was wrong but at least we had our mandatory hate figure for the long flight ahead. We spent the first two hours just talking over what we wanted the speech to do, and then started to write it from scratch. I was working on the New Labour and change passage while TB scribbled manically page after page. At one point, everyone else was asleep as we pressed on. TB was totally lost in concentration and producing good material, which I was honing before Anji typed it up. I was a bit fearful of the potential political downside of appearing to ignore the Murdoch/right-wing agenda so I persuaded him we had to challenge that agenda harder. We landed in Bangkok with something approaching a speech in shape. We were taken to the BA lounge and Tim had faxed through an excellent set of cuttings from yesterday. We managed to get a little sleep on the second leg though not much, but at least the length of the flight had allowed us to get a speech done. My main interest was in ensuring the speech was serious and strong so that we got as much for the message as for the fact that we were delivering it to a Murdoch audience. The party would instinctively not like it, but the response had not been neuralgic and any doubts I had were dispelled by the fact that the person who would be most pissed off that we were doing it was Major.

Saturday, July 15

We arrived 5am Sydney time, to be met by Frank Leverett from Keating's office, a lovely laid-back character who really took care of us while we were in Sydney. We were driven to Kirribilli, the PM's official residence, not over the top but nice, comfortable and in a beautiful setting looking out on to the harbour. TB was really pleased we had broken the back of the speech and also that Keating was going to the lengths he was to look after us. Overnight cuttings fine apart from an article in the *Guardian* that Peter M had been put in charge of a new group. It put TB in a real spin. I had to contact Tim to find out if Mike White [*Guardian*] had contacted him about it – he hadn't. I then called Peter who said it must have been briefed by Charlie Whelan. TB called GB and they had a real up-and-downer. GB was in whingey mode, saying that if TB wanted Peter in charge of policy, fine. TB exploded. 'He's not in charge of fucking policy. I've asked him to do something for me, end of story. It is not running policy. I'm trying to get a political show on the road and sometimes I think I'm leading a Toytown party.' GB went on and on. At one point TB just looked at me, shook his head, and rolled his eyes round and round. GB was now on to the subject of Nick Brown, saying he didn't believe TB would appoint him as deputy chief whip. TB said 'I can't believe this – I'm at the other side of the world about to meet the Australian PM and make a big speech and I'm having to deal with some nonsense about Peter in the *Guardian* and your worry that I won't give Nick bloody Brown a job!' TB was so angry after the call he went through to his own room to calm down but came back still steaming. It put him in a bad mood for ages until we just sat down and worked on the speech again, which got him out of it. The speech was in good shape now, definitely getting there, and I began to brief the papers on the central messages.

TB was on the cover of the *Australian* magazine. I really liked the 'nice kind of bastard' headline. It was very Australian but it caught the mix of charm and steel pretty well. Everyone had told us how friendly the Australian Labor Party people would be but these guys really were terrific, though some bad election results came in from Queensland which put a bit of a dampener on things. TB was enjoying himself and was convinced the speech was now a humdinger. That didn't mean we didn't keep working on it though, and it was hours before I got to bed.

Sunday, July 16

I went out for a swim at 6.45. Absolutely wonderful, literally swimming towards the harbour and the opera house. TB had woken up at 4 and worked on the speech some more, and was now happy with it. I'd arranged for Richard Stott to join us for breakfast and got him to go through the speech from a Murdoch angle. He liked it, thought it had a clear general message and there was enough in it for the News Corp lot, and enough for the anti-Murdoch neuralgics. He suggested we develop the family values section. TB asked what he reckoned Murdoch was thinking. Stott said the thing you have to understand about Murdoch is that he basically hates politicians. He sees them as obstacles to his commercial interests. So I wouldn't worry about his expectations, just say what you think because what you think strikes a chord with most people, whether they're billionaire media moguls or not. There was a bit of criticism of us going still kicking around but TB was confident enough in the speech now not to be bothered. Keating had sent a fourteen-seater Falcon jet to take TB, Anji, me and Greg [Turnbull] up to meet him at Port Douglas, his holiday resort. Keating was everything I expected – charming, tough, funny, totally at ease on the surface though probably a real furnace when he got going. His wife Annita also had a natural charm which put people at ease, and she was exceptionally good-looking too. On Murdoch he told TB 'He's a big bad bastard, and the only way you can deal with him is to make sure he thinks you can be a big bad bastard too. You can do deals with him, without ever saying a deal is done. But the only thing he cares about is his business and the only language he respects is strength.' It chimed with what I had been saying, but I suspected TB remained convinced the charm route was just as valid. Keating said Murdoch liked to be associated with winners. 'If he thinks you're a winner, he'd prefer to be with you than against you.' I asked Keating if he could coach Tony in how to hate Tories. He said TB was probably right because every time he went over the top he went down in the polls. He said one of his favourites was when some guy was laying into him and losing his rag, and he said 'Calm down before you have a heart attack – don't forget I knew you when you had grey hair.'

On the plane up to Hamilton Island, TB and Keating sat together at the front. Keating never seemed to slow down. He was a real bundle of energy, which was great when he was your host but I imagine could be wearing if you were around him the whole time. Greg, Annita and the bodyguards, Heggie and Hunter, all appeared to mix admiration, affection and occasional exasperation when they talked about him. He said to TB 'I've got some good advice for you about income tax – don't put it up. Ever. Tony, promise me you won't raise income tax. It's death. Labour parties round the world have enough to contend with without hanging that round their necks. It's not worth it.' He admitted he was in trouble re the election but he thought the country would be making a terrible mistake if it went for John Howard. 'A nobody, stands for nothing, nothing to say about the future.' He was a real buzz re policy, a one-man encyclopaedia of policy ideas round the world. 'You can never stay still. Always keep coming up with new ideas. In reality we should never have won the last election but we won because we stayed ahead on policy detail and people felt we had an agenda for the future.' We landed at Hamilton Island and just had a short walk across to the boat waiting to take us to Hayman Island [News Corp took over the island for the conference].

On arrival we stepped off the boat to be met by a Corporation photographer and cameraman and then Murdoch all smiles and leisure gear and nice to see you. It was an extraordinary place, not exactly my *tasse de thé* but fascinating nonetheless. The sea was the most exquisite blue, the climate near perfect even for me, and a mix of wild and exotic vegetation alongside very man-made luxury. We were taken first to TB's 'Japanese' suite while PK was taken to the 'Spanish' suite. The bathroom was the size of most rooms, all sunken bath and jacuzzi. A bit tacky but the view was fabulous. We had a valet called Glenn who was clearly thrilled to be looking after TB and would have done anything for us. I got the feeling if TB asked him to jump off the top of the building, he would have. As the barbecue was starting, Keating kept giving me little side-of-the-mouth commentaries. He'd said that Murdoch never really raised issues directly, and sure enough, the conversation kind of meandered around without the nub of issues being really tackled. The reality was the TB/PK world view was very different to the Murdoch view but that just went unsaid. There was an air of fencing to it all. I also got a fascinating glimpse into the way the editors work around him. I said to Murdoch that it was an important speech, that TB had put more of himself into it than any speech outside party conference and I reckoned it would go big, especially now we had fixed for News Corp pictures of the speech to be sent straight away to BBC, ITN, etc. A couple of minutes later, RM spoke across a few people to Stuart Higgins [*Sun*], and later to Peter Stothard [*Times*], and said that it was a big speech TB was delivering tomorrow. Of course, because of the time difference they would be getting it out of London and putting it straight into the paper. Both editors disappeared for a couple of minutes and told me proudly they had ordered London to give it a good show. *The Times* planned to run extracts. I was pleased, but the truth was they had been spun by their boss who had been spun by me. PK chatted up Murdoch for a while and at the end of the evening, Murdoch walking TB back to his suite, I straggled along with Paul. 'He was certainly making all the right noises; said he liked Blair, thought he had guts as well as brains, and he was going to win. The editors were picking up on that, which is why they were behaving the way they were. You have to remember with Rupert that it's all about Rupert. Rupert is number one, two, three and four as far as Rupert is concerned. Anna [his wife] and the kids come next and everything else is a long, long way behind.' I took to Keating big time. He told TB that RM was clearly warming to him, which was good up to a point. 'They overestimate the importance of their support for you, but if you can get it, have it. If you are Labour you need all the help you can get to win elections.'

Monday, July 17

Up early after next to no sleep. I went down to the business centre and bumped into Murdoch. I tried to prise him open a bit about what he was thinking but despite the twinkle in his eye, and the general warmth, he was very guarded. Any attempt at big talk was reduced to small talk pretty quickly. I went up to see TB who was sitting there in his underpants, having one last go on his speech. I filled him in on the coverage, which was brilliant. Greg was full of praise for the way we had managed to get the focus in the rest of the media on to the political and strategic contents of the speech, rather than the Murdoch issue. We met up with Keating and then off to hear Murdoch's speech. Fascinating, but a bit chilling, to watch all these grown men, and some women, hanging on every word, and knowing that an inflection here or there would influence them one way or the other. He could hardly have been warmer re TB, real praise, finest young leader in the world kind of thing. He also sent a chill down a few editors' spines when he went on about the failings of some editors, without naming names. TB did a brilliant job. The speech was strong, he delivered it well and as he left the stage you could see the heads nodding and these hard-nosed types all turning to each other and giving little grimaces of approval. PK was fantastic, going on and on in front of RM about what a brilliant speech it was, and how few political leaders there were who could give a speech like that. The Aussie and US people were really buzzing with it afterwards but I got the sense of real concern from the UK right-wingers. There was a nervousness about them, as though they were not quite sure how to react. TB knew he'd done well and was winding down. He had a long chat with Anna [Murdoch] while I talked to Higgins. He said the UK editors were going for a meeting with RM in Canberra on Friday and he was sure it was to get their orders to get in behind Labour for commercial reasons. TB was not a great one for saying thank you, but he said thanks – the media operation on the speech had a touch of genius about it, he said. The whole story could have been the party up in arms about me coming here. Instead we got a message that unites all parts of a new coalition, and coverage that will have made a real impact. Greg Turnbull said Paul could be a nightmare but he was a great guy to work with, and you couldn't do a job like this unless you felt that commitment. I felt exactly the same re TB. He could be a pain, and way over the top in his demands and expectations, but there was something about him that made you want to give 110 per cent, and of course there was the sense that I was playing a big part in seeing the Tories out of the door, hopefully for some time. Annita asked me to look up their son Patrick, who was in London. I asked what he did. She said he was at Saatchis [advertising agency]. 'Enemies of the working people,' I said. 'Like Rupert,' said Greg. Greg reckoned if PK won he would go after a year or so. PK said when he was out of office he planned to have an answering machine with the message 'You have reached the office of ex-prime minister Paul Keating. Now fuck off and leave me alone.'

We said goodbye, boarded the little jet that had been sent down to take us up to Sydney. Onboard was quite the sexiest, most pouting, provocative, overtly sexual air stewardess I have ever seen. I was sitting opposite TB and whenever she served him, she would swivel her near-perfect bum towards me, vice versa when she was serving me. Tony and I kept trying to avoid each other's gaze. I was quizzing her on her politics and she was pretty shtum, TB said please don't talk to her, it only makes it worse. His mind was already turning to things back home, and his desire to get Donald Dewar installed as chief whip. It was an odd choice at first but on reflection he might be made for it. I said it was important we didn't lose him as a media performer. Anji was sitting next to an Aussie brigadier, JB Wilson, and getting on really well and she brought him over for a long session with TB on Bosnia, which was helpful. TB and I then sat down to work on the ISH [Information Superhighway] speech. We were both on form at the moment and had it done in no time. Then TB did his usual thing of getting a new pad and a biro and setting out a few forward challenges on a single sheet of paper. Number 1, I saw, was 'building up GB'; 2. PLP relations; 3. Europe; 4. economic message. TB obviously felt he would have to do a lot of the economic message work himself. It remained a big problem that we didn't have an economic message easily understood by party and public. After dinner I took a sleeping pill and slept right through, waking up just in time for a quick breakfast before we landed at 6.50. The trip had been a huge success all round.

Tuesday, July 18
There was a story in the *Guardian* about the Mandelson/Roger Liddle book [*The Blair Revolution – Can New Labour Deliver?* published in 1996] which was another potential Peter PR disaster, following as it did the Mike White [*Guardian*] story about the Peter policy group. It clearly came from either Peter or Roger who, I now discovered, had a big piece in the *Guardian* yesterday setting out why he had rejoined Labour, with the usual SDP self-justifying line that the party had moved back to them. TB for once was genuinely angry with him, said he had no doubt Peter was responsible for the story, and it helped nobody at this time. Peter on the other end of the line was very defensive, as ever saying Whelan must have been involved somewhere along the line. 'If Peter did this, I'll kill him,' TB said, then called GB. That was just as joyless, and TB was very quickly deflated again, back to a stack of problems re Peter, still rumbles re Murdoch, the rail strike, Littleborough and Saddleworth strategy divisions, lots of people just thinking we were moving too far too fast. The Derek Foster story was really taking off and kept me busy all day. He knew he was being eased out [as Labour's chief whip] and was clearly depressed about it but he pressed on for all manner of concessions from TB, including a Cabinet job. I got a lift home with TB and told him what Mike had said. TB said he sensed the same thing, that there was a lot of grumbling about him. RC was off board. JP was off board. GB was on and off depending on his mood. We also agreed we had made a mistake re Joy. TB had said she either had to be integrated properly with us, or go. There could be no in between. He was convinced she had deliberately undersold his Information Superhighway speech. She was effectively GB's personal broadcasting officer.

Wednesday, July 19
The Foster situation came out not too bad, but Jonathan said we would regret going OTT in praise of him, and in particular the suggestion

he would definitely get a job. TB and I discussed Joy again. TB said it was not that she was without talent but that she was only really working for GB. JP had already decided to bypass her. I was beginning to work up a plan for TB's first anniversary as leader. There was a lot of angst and anger around. I was conscious of being like a bear with a sore head. It was probably because we'd had a major hit out of Australia, and we'd come back to all the same old nonsense, Peter, GB, the Derek thing, the press getting excited about a non-story re the unions. I drafted some TB words for his PLP meeting and briefed them. Blunkett called afterwards to say he had been absolutely brilliant. The chief-whip changes went through by a massive majority, 132–26, which was a real sign of maturity in the PLP. The big drama of the day centred on GB. TB met him at 4.15 and told him he wasn't happy with Joy. GB said she had not been allowed to do the job. TB said Don Dixon [deputy chief whip] would be staying in the job till October, and therefore Nick Brown could not go straight in. GB went ballistic, said it was 'another act of betrayal'. Ludicrous. GB said TB could not be trusted at all, and went absolutely berserk – over Nick Brown not being deputy chief whip. It is madness.

Thursday, July 20

Up early to go to TB's for his first anniversary interview with the *Today* programme, which was OK without being brilliant. The GB scenes of yesterday were clearly on his mind. The problem, he said, was that GB just wouldn't work with Peter and, in truth, GB didn't really want to work with me. Normally, when we drove from the studio to the office after an interview, he would call GB and/or Peter to get their view. This time, he didn't. There was a real danger of these central relationships just imploding and doing untold damage. At the 8.45 meeting I said I thought we should have a discussion about how effective we thought we were. I said I thought there were two big problems: 1. the Shadow Cabinet did not feel involved in what we were doing, and 2. there was little or no trust within this group. I was very calm, tried to be absolutely analytical, and could sense people feeling very uncomfortable. But though GB would obviously prefer us not to be having the discussion, he listened and did sort of engage. He said that this group was dealing with news management and it had never been envisaged as closely involving the Shadow Cabinet. I said, but they think it is important and it is. I said the real question, however, was the second one. If we were going to hold together during the pressures of an election campaign, we were going to have to get on better than we did, and get some trust and teamwork going between us all. I raised the Information Super-highway launch. It was very odd that I had been able to place four signed articles in four publications with four phone calls, yet we couldn't even persuade the broadcasters to cover it. GB took some of the blame for that, admitted he had never been enthusiastic about it, but Joy took offence, just threw down her papers and stormed out. It rather proved my point. DH weighed in behind me, saying he really felt there had to be some Shadow Cabinet ownership of the work we did. PG weighed in on trust. Joy eventually came back and sat there simmering. I said we had to be able to have open and frank discussions without people storming out. GB was very firm with Joy, but eventually asked everyone but me and her to leave. On Information Superhighway, Joy made the rather contradictory statement that she thought it was so boring she hadn't read it. GB said the problem was lack of clarity about what everyone was meant to be doing because TB said different things to different people. He wanted JP to run some campaigns but then put Peter M in charge of them so that he (TB) could bugger off around the world talking about economics. So he was in a rage now too, and he said this would be the last 8.45 meeting he did.

I left with Joy. She said 'Why was I brought here in the first place?' I said she clearly had talent but she wasn't letting anyone see it. I'd warned her of the relationship problems, Big Guns, Peter M, but she made them worse by being seen by all but GB as his poodle. I had tried with Joy but had reached the view there was no halfway house; it would be best all round if she went, though there was a real potential downside if she turned on us publicly. My sense of her was she wasn't like that at all but it had to be a worry. TB said he would tell her she had to work directly to me. I was more and more convinced that everything had to be centralised if it was going to work properly.

I bumped into Roger Liddle in the central lobby and warned him off doing too much on the theme of Labour becoming like the SDP. I think he got the point. There was an office drinks do which was pretty unsatisfactory because TB didn't really bother to say thanks to everyone. Then to [Labour MP] Geoffrey Robinson's little do at Grosvenor House. GB was relaxed for once, telling funny stories about his days in TV. Earlier TB met Bill Morris who asked why he snubbed him at the T&G conference. TB said he'd asked for it with that statement they had put out.

Friday, July 21

JP is very onside at the moment, full of advice for TB about how he could extend his reach in the party. At Newcastle, TB, John Burton and I headed off for a few meetings while JP and Rosie pretended to leave for Hull. In fact they were going to Beamish Fair and then coming back for TB's surprise one-year-on-party. TB did a Sky interview and was asked about the surprise party. 'You,' he said to me after, 'are what we call an arsehole.' He didn't like surprises. There was a lot of interest from the Sundays both in Murdoch and one year on, so in between the visits I was never off the phone. TB asked me really to build up GB in the briefings, so I did, though I sensed they thought I was protesting too much. It was all about TB being able to say to GB that if only he involved me more with his operation, he would get a better press and he didn't need Joy, let alone Whelan. First year over. Lots of progress. Totally knackered.

Saturday, July 22

The grumbling in the party was being picked up and exaggerated. Also lots of coverage on conference resolutions predicting trouble on minimum wage and education. The *New Statesman* and *Tribune* were stirring the party against us as much as they could. Later a spectacular row with Fiona. The boys had been fighting in the kitchen and she stormed out after yelling at me that I cared about nothing but the Blair operation, that she felt totally disconnected from it and I had no idea what it was like trying to raise three small kids while I was swanning round the world. Absolutely grim.

Sunday, July 23

Lots more left of centre whingeing in the *Observer*, Peter doing his best re Littleborough and Saddleworth on *Frost*. McIntosh [Oratory headmaster] attacking our education policy in the *Sunday Telegraph*. On the anti-TB grumbling, TB called a couple of times and said 'What is the charge sheet?' then ran through it. 1. Murdoch – 'We would have been mad not to go, and Hezza made a mistake in attacking me for it.' 2. Thatcher – 'Praising her in a limited way was a tiny part of the speech.' 3. SDP – 'Are we really saying we don't want them back in the fold?' 4. Unions – 'But the relationship has to change.' and 5. Littleborough and Saddleworth – 'The *Guardian*, *Indy*, *New Statesman* lot basically just want us to throw in the towel and say here you are Lib Dems, win.' He wanted me to organise pieces exposing what folly this all was. 'It's the history of our party in government, that the left will always believe the right's propaganda, and put it back out in different form.' He had seen Joy last night and asked me if I thought there was anything she could do. I said I thought probably not, though she had talent.

Monday, July 24

Joy came in for a chat and we went through to the Shadow Cabinet room. She said it had all been pretty grim with TB but she still felt she could work things out. She found it very hard to work within the structures we had, and had a particular problem with Peter. She knew she had not been delivering on campaigns but felt low and humiliated. I repeated that she had made a mistake getting too attached to GB and his office because it meant she had no support from the Shadow Cabinet when she needed it. 'But will I ever be inside the loop?' she said. I said TB didn't work like that. You had to be plugged in at the point at which he wanted you plugged in. Meeting with TB, Jonathan, Anji, to see whether we could find a role for Joy. TB really didn't want just to chuck her out. But he said he was terrified by the extent to which the whole media operation appeared to depend on me. He and I discussed our various domestic difficulties. He said they had a point – highly intelligent women who were interested yet felt uninvolved in what we did. They knew deep down we had to be obsessed with it to make it work, but it was so all-consuming they felt no space for themselves.

Tuesday, July 25

Fiona and I seemed to be getting on better but it was an effort to talk about work at home, if only because the minute I got home, I wanted to forget about it, and it was only the wretched fucking telephone that made it impossible. And the truth was you had to have your eye on the ball every minute of the day, because there were so many people around who were capable of dropping it. TB getting really fed up with the left whingeing, and at the fact we were on the road again, to Littleborough and Saddleworth. The mood felt OK without being brilliant. The line was that the Tories were out of it and it was a two-horse race and we were hitting all the New Labour messages as hard as we could and trying to sow real doubt re the Lib Dem candidate. Peter M was on top of things but already indicating a good second was the likeliest outcome.

Wednesday, July 26

Another ridiculously early start to go for the TB/GB/Bill Morris breakfast. It had been Bill's idea to try to build better relations and come to a deal on the minimum wage. It consisted of the usual whinges about 'sources' and why couldn't we be nicer to them? He suggested we set up the Low Pay Commission before we get into government so that people who felt we were trying to retreat from the policy could have their trust restored. Later, in Tom Sawyer's office, I saw a note showing that Bill said to Tom TB had 'behaved like a spoilt brat' at the T&G conference and deliberately snubbed him. I said Bill had thrown down a gauntlet and TB had picked it up, and would have been weak not to have done so. GB was very impressive at the meeting, tough but moderate, and constructive about how we might take it forward. It was fascinating how whenever outsiders were around, he managed to avoid the sulking and the juvenilia. The minute we were back in the car, he was back bending Tony's ear, this time over JP's Regional Policy Commission. He was worried JP was trying to extend his policy reach again. TB looked and sounded exhausted. NEC was quite fractious. Skinner attacked TB for going to the Murdoch conference, saying he got nothing out of it. TB was tired. Despite saying to the NEC that he had no plans for further reform, he gave a very clear impression that he wanted to go further than 50–50 in future. Sally was adamant that we could lose at conference if he kept pushing this line so hard. But TB did not want to give any sense that we were closing down the option of going further.

Jonathan had called an office meeting to go over the last six months. As the one usually hardest on TB, I found myself in the unusual position of defending him hardest and of saying, unlike it seemed everyone else, I had a very clear idea what it was that he was trying to do and say at the moment. But I accepted that if the majority in his own office could not properly understand what he was on about, what chance did the public have?

Thursday, July 27

I had lunch with Tom Sawyer, mainly talking about Joy. We agreed it would work better if I took over Joy's duties and we had DH on media, Fraser Kemp on elections and MMcD on campaigns working to us. Tom was very frank about the grumbling re TB. He said it had definitely picked up in recent weeks and he thought it was more than the usual July madness. We had a meeting on summer campaigns, but Joy hadn't really prepared what he expected. JP called in from his train – the track was on fire! – and said he was fed up chasing her up on it all. I think we had reached a conclusion about her and she was very down. I walked her to the Commons gates after the meeting and gave her a little kiss, feeling a total bastard in that it was probable that by the time we got back from the holidays, she'd be gone. Went to bed early then up just before midnight for the L&S result, lost by a couple of thousand votes, but enough for us to get a message going that we were winning new support in all parts of the country.

July '95: By-election loss but Labour winning new support

Holiday started with Fiona complaining that she was like a single parent, that three small kids was much harder than my job. We were hanging around on the Sunday when Neil and Glenys called and asked if they could come to stay for a bit. They were there the next evening, entering a bad atmosphere created by the fact Fiona and I had barely spoken on the way down, and rowed most of the time when we did. And I imagined N and G would be pretty offside too. I could sense that Neil was gearing up for one. He did the usual of messing around with the boys in the pool, lots of small talk, very long and not very important stories about Brussels, but then easing into UK politics. 'Who'll be chief whip then?' he'd ask, and I'd say probably Donald Dewar, and Neil would make a few disparaging remarks about him. Anything I said about anyone failed to meet with his approval. I'd heard whispers he was a bit disaffected with TB and the whole show, but it came bubbling out all over the place, boiling over on the second evening. All day there was a drip, drip of things – a joke or three about the Oratory, sideswipes about our policy on Europe – 'we don't have one' – endlessly on about JP not being up to it. On their own, there was nothing too serious about any of them but I could tell he was building up for a big old-fashioned NK rage. Indeed, when Glenys called Rachel [their daughter] to find out about her first day at work, I spoke to Rach and said he was really winding up for a big one.

It was while Fiona was putting Grace to bed that the next move up the gears came. Neil had done some vegetable kebabs on the barbecue and we were arguing about a French word and I said I wonder if there's a dictionary in the house, at which point he got up, his chair falling over, then he sprinted into the house, saying of course there'd be a fucking dictionary, and Glenys and I looking at each other and just shaking our heads and shrugging. He came back with his cheek muscles flexing like they do when he's close to totally losing it. We were nearing the full explosion, as first he tried to keep his voice under control, but failed every six or seven words; the hand movements getting wilder and wilder; then the heavy sarcasm – 'Oh Margaret Thatcher, not too bad you know, not such a bad person, quite a radical, and of course you had to admire her determination and her leadership – that's what the fucking leader says.' 'Now now,' I said, trying to calm things, but he was in that phase where anything you said just became a spur to further verbal violence. 'Don't "now now" me. I'll fucking tell him too – radical my arse. That woman fucking killed people.' Glenys weighed in now, saying that GB had refused to commit to 0.7 per cent of GDP on overseas aid. 'They haven't got a line on Africa,' she said. 'It's not just Africa,' Neil chipped in, 'they haven't got a line on Asia, Australasia, any continent you mention.' I said that was absurd. 'Prove the contrary then,' he said, and stalked off before I could answer. While he simmered elsewhere, Glenys said in more measured terms the problem was there were parts of the party that felt alienated by TB and the New bit of New Labour. The message was that everything that went before TB was hopeless. I said she and Neil were being too sensitive to that. Tony had been elected to modernise and be the agent of change. But he always stressed Neil's role as having begun all this, and they should not take it personally. She said down in South Wales they thought he only cared about Essex man. I said that was absurd – are you saying we shouldn't try to win back seats we had lost in places like Essex? We should never have lost contact with those people. By now Neil was back and said it was of course impossible for TB to address education policy now because he had chosen to send his own son to the SS Waffen Academy. I said his remark would be funny if it wasn't so ridiculously over the top but I'm afraid his humour had gone now. I said why don't you stop fucking about with the sarcasm and the jibes and say what you're actually thinking – what is the main complaint?

Glenys could see it was in danger of boiling over and said she didn't want a big row, but I said no, I want to know what he's saying because my job is to defend Tony and I want to know what the problem is, so he should spit it out. Eventually he spat it out – 'He's sold out before he's even got there.' 'Sold out on what?' 'Everything.' His face was inching ever closer to mine and at one point he picked up a kettle filled with newly boiled water which I feared was heading my way. 'What about a few specifics?' I said. 'Tax, health, education, unions, full employment, race, immigration, everything, he's totally sold out. And for what? What are we FOR? It won't matter if we win, the bankers and the stockbrokers have got us already, by the fucking balls, laughing their heads off. And all that before you go and take your thirty pieces of silver.' 'What's that supposed to mean?' By now his face was a wretched picture of hatred and rage. The word purple does not do it justice. It was on fire. And he spat it out – 'Murdoch.' 'Oh for Christ's sake, is that what this is all about, because we went to see Rupert fucking Murdoch?' 'You imagine what it's like having your head stuck inside a fucking light bulb,' he raged at me, 'then you tell me how I'm supposed to feel when I see you set off halfway round the world to grease him up.' 'We gave him absolutely nothing,' I said. 'You will. And he'll take it. You'll get his support and then you'll get the support of a few racist bastards, and then you'll lose it again the minute you're in trouble.' I pointed out again that if we were going to win, we had to get new support, and he went all patronising and sarcastic again 'Oh I never knew that, I didn't know you had to get new support. I wish I'd thought of that.' I said we can have a serious conversation if he wants but he shouldn't bother patronising me. More rage. 'Don't you patronise me,' he said. I said re Murdoch, what was the difference, other than in scale, between me working for a Murdoch paper, as I did, and going to his conference. 'The difference is you've got courage and bottle and you'd tell these fuckers what you think. Tony lacks the moral fibre to do that.' I said that was crap. Glenys said she understood why we went but I had to realise how much it hurt Neil, who felt Murdoch was actually evil. Neil calmed down a bit later and said his 'sell-out' analysis would have carried more conviction if he hadn't sold out once or twice himself.

When we were speaking again, a couple of days later, I said if he attacked Tony, I would defend him because that was my job, and not only did I support the New Labour strategy, in large part I devised it because we have to win new support and that is the key to it: change, compromise with the electorate, call it what you want. I said I believed in what we were doing and one of the greatest difficulties I felt was that people closest to me, including him but most important Fiona, who had basically taken his side in the row, didn't actually support what we were doing at all. I said at least you always had Glenys on side when you were doing the tough stuff. 'There was a lot she didn't believe in too,' he said. There was a chance our friendship would not recover from the venom. The row had taken place at the exact same place where a year ago he had tried to talk me out of working for Tony, which added to the uncomfortable dynamic at work. He said nobody wanted a Labour government more than he did but what was really important was the second term. We had to win at least two terms to make real lasting change. I said one will be a start and I have no doubt we will do things he will be proud of. He then started laying into the Shadow Cabinet, and complained we were woefully thin on talent. GB sometimes looked like he was 'afraid of his shadow'. RC 'gave Machiavelli and the Borgias a bad name'. JP would not stay loyal. Straw would roll over at whatever the Civil Service wanted. I asked if he thought Smith would have won. 'Just.' I said it will be more than just 'just' with TB as leader. I said can't you see he makes us much more electable? 'Why do you take NEW Labour so personally? If anything it is your creation, don't knock it.' Finally he started making some constructive suggestions –

TB should say in his conference speech that New Labour is Old Labour winning; that 1945 was New Labour, Labour renewing itself to renew Britain, 1964 ditto. After a while the rage subsided and we could have a civilised conversation again, but something had changed. And I was deeply annoyed at the way Fiona had sided against me pretty much through the whole argument. I barely slept the night of the big row, which was hardly a great way to spend a holiday.

The next day the whole thing kicked off again. I said to Fiona that even out of basic solidarity she could have sided with me when I was being assaulted like that, not just verbally but with a bloody kettle thrust into my face. She flew straight off the handle, said I'd totally changed, was completely obsessive, intolerant of any other point of view and she wasn't allowed to say what she thought about anything. I didn't allow any rational argument; everything had to be subsumed to the idea of winning, and it was not a life. I said I'd like to know if she'd be happier if I developed a strategy for losing. This set the scene for another awful day, the only enjoyable parts of which were when I disappeared with the kids. Later we admitted we were just getting on each other's nerves and it was hopeless. She said she was fed up saying the same things and me taking no notice. I said I was fed up hearing the same things. She said she understood why Cherie was so fed up. There was me, TB, Anji and the office inside a bubble and nobody was allowed in. I was on a gigantic ego trip being lauded to the skies for being brilliant and she was just an appendage. It was really grim. Earlier when Carolyn Fairbairn [adviser in Major's policy unit and an old friend] came round, we had to go through the pretence that we were having a lovely holiday, blah blah. Neil and I were barely speaking other than lobbing in a few sarcastic jibes, e.g. when I said I liked Keating and he'd go off on that, and I'd say at least he wins, and off we'd go again.

Wednesday, August 2

Neil said if ever I wanted his help or advice and support, I had it, and the things he'd said he would say to nobody else. He would be totally loyal and supportive in public but I had to understand if sometimes things boiled up, especially when he saw us consorting with people he despised. Glenys said friendship like ours was too important to let the job damage it. I said the only way I could do this was one hundred per cent to my own satisfaction. Yes, I enjoyed it most of the time, but it was all-consuming, as he knew, which is why he'd advised me against doing it. And I knew there was a price to pay, and it was paid by the family. Neil said he knew how hard it was but you had to work at finding time and space for the family. Beneath it all, Neil was working through real anger at his own position, and the fear that TB and New Labour were about using Neil as a foil, which was nonsense. It's just that TB would push change as hard as it would go, and he was able to do it because he was different. His lack of roots actually in some ways helped politically. He could do things Neil might have wanted to do but would have found more difficult. But it meant it was hard for Neil, and he couldn't yet give Tony credit. He said at one point the Tories are so useless a cheetah could win for us, and Tony is a lot better than a cheetah. I said the second part of the sentence is true; the first is not.

Thursday, August 3

Things were a bit less tense with Fiona. When the kids were in bed, we had another go at talking things through, which went on for hours, and many painful things were said. I said I felt I was carrying a huge load for others, and didn't feel supported. She said she'd tried to accommodate the job, and be positive about it, but there was no point denying she hated it and resented it. She said I'd changed, it was just drive and obsession on my side, anger and resentment on hers. I was unsure I could change doing the job the way I did it, and she was aware that if I stopped doing it as a result of this, I'd always resent it, and feel dreadful if things slipped back after I'd gone. We went round and round and things were better by the end but the reality was the job had become a massive barrier between us, and I couldn't see a way of improving things.

Sunday, August 6

We were half expecting the Blairs to come over. They had made their typically crazy and chaotic holiday arrangements, flying to Toulouse to pick up a car to drive to Tuscany, from where they would go back at the end of their holiday for a bit more time in Toulouse. We had a long chat about Neil. TB said he was worried Neil would be coming out with that stuff more widely. I said I felt it was a case of using a close friend to get a lot off his chest, and Neil was not one to give the press any comfort.

Friday, August 11

If ever proof were needed about the impossibility of escaping, it came in the last few days. Tim Allan called on Tuesday to say Frank Dobson had gone on *Today* to say we were suspending Walsall Labour Party because of allegations of intimidation or some such. JP had been against it, as he was to tell me repeatedly once the inquests were underway, not least because Brian Mawhinney was about to go on a tour of 'loony left' councils and this would look like – indeed was – a great propaganda coup for him to start with. The press, bored with Bosnia and in need of a bad Labour story, leapt on it, some saying it showed strong leadership, others that it was a panic measure to respond to Mawhinney. It seems the NEC had decided two weeks ago there were grounds for suspension, but even so the timing was awful. Meanwhile, as soon as the shit hit the fan, Dobbo started to distance himself from the decision. On Wednesday, Tim called to say that his time at the helm was turning into a disaster zone. 'What now?' I asked. He said Richard Burden [Labour MP] had written a piece for the *New Statesman*, which he'd given to *The Times*, which led on it under the headline 'Blair's Kremlin tactics'. This was some of the grumbling coming out. He also had a go at the 'kitchen Cabinet' so we would have another rash of profiles of me, Peter, Jonathan, Anji, DM, etc. My soft porn was up in lights again. Tim sounded really fed up and he and JP were never off the phone. The Blair-in-trouble mood was gathering pace. The worst thing about it for me was that Fiona and I had finally been getting on well and now I was back into work mode again.

Jeremy Corbyn and Max Madden [Labour MPs] had weighed in behind Burden so we got Dick Caborn [Labour MP] on *World at One*. Madden had said it was a huge crisis; Corbyn that there was widespread anger re Clause 4. The Sundays were getting very excited and gearing up for big 'Labour in crisis' write-throughs. Joy was desperate to do a Sunday briefing but Tim thought I should do it down the line on a conference call. There was so little substance to the criticisms but this was the kind of story that could just go whoosh in the middle of summer. I dictated a briefing note for Tim to give to the Sundays. By now the papers were full of civil war, honeymoon over and Blair's loathed kitchen Cabinet. John Edmonds fuelled things in a coded attack in *Tribune*, warning of the dangers of permanent revolution. If these guys were in charge, we'd have a permanent Tory government. JP said he'd learned a lot – that he should have backed his own judgement re Walsall; that we had to have greater control over political structures; and that there were too many centres of decision-making. 'Sounds like you're joining the control freak tendency,' I said. Of course all the kitchen Cabinet stuff meant more focus on Peter, which was one of the reasons for the grumbling anyway. I wonder if Burden had any idea it would have gone this big. His assistant's rather pathetic letter to TB suggested not. Some of the papers had run some of my porn stuff and JP was delighting in reading them out, and making me cringe and beg him to shut up.

Saturday, August 12

Took the boys out, got back and Fiona said Joy had been desperate to speak to me, not sure what about. Then JP called, said he hated bothering me on holiday but he needed advice. 'That silly cow' [Joy] had put Henry McLeish on the radio against Dennis Canavan and George Galloway. Worse, she'd told Henry JP wanted him to do it whereas in fact he'd said we should put nobody on because it would just make it run for another day. He ranted and raved, said she had no judgement. 'She said but John, I'm the director of communications. I said you couldn't direct a bus out of the depot.' Harsh.

Monday, August 14

Joy called to say it had been a nightmare and she couldn't believe how rude JP was to her. She said she bit her tongue but the truth was he was too slow to make decisions and his judgement was poor, and she was fed up of taking crap. I said I'm afraid taking crap is part of our job. She was pushing the line that GB was the only one capable of running a campaign, which had appeared in one or two papers.

Wednesday, August 16

Poor old Tim. He called up and said: Are you sitting down? He said the *Mail* was leading with an attack on the leadership by none other than Ronnie Campbell [Labour MP]. I said this had descended into farce. He said several of the papers now routinely had logos on 'Blair's mutiny' as more and more MPs mouthed off. I suggested to TB an interview when he got back but he felt that would be too defensive. He said there may be some good come of this. Clearly there was a need to let off steam, but the party won't like it and these guys will get a message from the PLP when they get back. He was also worried when I told him how much there was in the press re Peter M. He said they're trying to make it impossible to use him in the campaign, which would be very stupid. As for Burden, 'only in the Labour Party can you be attacked for being too efficient. There is only one thing that can stop the Labour Party winning the next election and that is the Labour Party. If we carry on like this, we can do it.'

Thursday, August 17

Drove back all day. I got home and remembered how last year there was a mass of envelopes on the mat, mainly cheques for my freelance broadcasting. This time we were greeted by a taxman's red letter.

Friday, August 18

There was too much interest in TB's return, as though he were flying back into a full-blown crisis. I was still strongly of the view he should not respond, and stick to the plan that he does nothing apart from the VJ Day stuff. I spoke to JP about the last few weeks. JP had said the number one rule was that I shouldn't leave the country. TB said that we could not allow a situation again where he, GB, Peter M and I were all out of the country.

Saturday, August 19

TB was wearing flip-flops, which looked absurd, and I said he should put shoes on as there would probably be press outside the house. GB had written a moderately conciliatory note re Peter saying he would have to have some kind of role in the election working alongside me and Joy. TB said the key now was showing that you could reconnect to the party by showing you could speak the same language as the public. Word had got back to Neil that I'd filled in Tony on a toned-down version of our arguments and Neil said the idea that he had lost faith 'defied a response'. That made me think Neil had just wanted to get a lot of stuff off his chest but he was basically there to help me and TB. TB seemed a bit down about things. He then told me, stressing it was in complete confidence and he had not told GB or Peter, that an intermediary had indicated to him that Alan Howarth [Conservative MP and former minister] was so fed up with the Tories he might consider defecting. It was the best thing I'd heard for weeks but TB said it was by no means in the bag. He wanted me to handle Howarth and make sure we had the conditions right for him if he came over.

RC was on *Frost* tomorrow so called for a chat and said to me there was nobody in the Shadow Cabinet who did not consider Peter to be an embarrassment, other than Gordon, 'and if I were Tony I would be very wary of Gordon's advice on anything.' Peter was complaining about how he always got the flak but I was Teflon man who everyone liked and trusted and I never copped it. He came round for dinner but left rather depressed. We agreed we had to mount better counter-attacks both against the Tories and against the kind of internal mania we'd witnessed. Without it, if the Tories got their act together and our lot carried on being daft, we could still lose. TB was on the rampage about them. 'These people would rather have a few columns in the *New Statesman* than a Labour government.' Later Fiona said Peter had

August '95: Tory former minister may defect

called whilst I went for the papers and TB had said to him that he was clear as things stood that GB would stop at nothing to destroy Peter. She thought that was why both TB and Peter seemed down.

Sunday, August 20

Spent much of the day briefing that we would turn the summer madness to our advantage and make conference a test not just of TB but of the maturity of the party. The story was dying down then just as TB, JP and Rosie W arrived for lunch, Alan Simpson [Labour MP] went on *The World This Weekend* and poured another barrel of vitriol into the system. TB said does anyone have a bullet? I pointed my finger at the radio and fired. The lunch was to go over the past few weeks and see what lessons could be learned. It got off to a very jolly start because Rory was on the street selling his toys to passers-by. 'Very New Labour,' said JP, who bought one of his daft badges. He said Joy was a disaster area, Charlie Whelan was a problem because he was such a gossip, and Peter was becoming a bigger problem for TB. He talked endlessly (and loudly, considering there were lots of neighbours out in their gardens too) about how he had handled the various mini dramas we'd had. He admitted he could have handled it better himself and he should have been firmer from the word go. TB said he was alarmed at how fragile things had seemed but he was worried about putting Joy out altogether. We also had to realise the Tories were bound to get their act together at some point. Rosie said we were also neglecting communications with the party. The media was all well and good and no doubt important, but the media fed on problems within the party which were often the result of poor communication. We agreed JP should do the media rounds and get out the message that the summer critics were playing into the Tories' hands.

Monday, August 21

Clare S gave us a problem on *World at One* where she seemed to contradict TB on women-only shortlists, saying we could go back to them after the next election. JP wanted us to stop placing articles hitting back at the critics because it was just keeping it all going. I met [Roy] Hattersley and asked when he was going to stop attacking TB. He said that TB had a policy problem and people in the party feared he wasn't Labour. He said Peter M, who he was about to interview, was a surrogate and had become a problem for him. I went to deal with the Clare S story which was taking off. I said why did you have to be unhelpful, and of course she went into her 'holier than thou' mode, saying what was unhelpful was people like me who didn't want anyone to tell the truth. She said the party wasn't happy. The hierarchy felt like it was TB 1, Peter M 2 and AC 3, and that was not good. She said TB had said the party is a crusade or it is nothing, and it doesn't feel like a crusade right now. She said we needed to hear more on poverty, more on the minimum wage, more on the traditional issues so we didn't think we were the *Daily Mail* Party. I said that is an absurd thing to say. The only person who had given the *Daily Mail* anything to cheer about today was her, just as her friends had been filling their pages over the holiday. It was the old story, the left inhale the right's propaganda and then exhale it in more toxic form. We were talking different languages.

Tuesday, August 22
The *Mail* splashed on Clare but we managed to keep it off the broadcasts. We heard from John Torode of the *Mail* that [former Labour MP and Shadow Cabinet minister] Bryan Gould's book had 'outed' Peter [as homosexual]. Later the *Express* called to say the *Sun* had done the 'Gould outs Mandelson' story. I called Peter to tell him. He was very upset about it. It was a nasty and unnecessary thing for Bryan to have done, presumably just to generate a bit of publicity.

Wednesday, August 23
Peter was feeling very low and vulnerable and obviously worried that this would create a climate for all sorts of stories to circulate. Lunch with Tony Hall [BBC] at Odin's. I tried to get him to understand why we get so frustrated re the inability to get complaints dealt with properly. And I served notice we were keeping tabs on the way they often took their news agenda from the right-wing papers. There were stories they had run recently that would never have had an ounce of BBC coverage if it had not first been ramped by the *Mail*. He was a perfectly nice bloke but dealing with him was like dealing with the Beeb generally, you got lots of 'I'm being very open and honest here, I probably shouldn't be saying this', the occasional slagging off of a colleague but in terms of substance you get nothing but the usual BBC right-or-wrong pitch.

Dinner at Neil's. The conversation was a bit stilted at first but eventually we had a decent chat about things. He felt Peter was now a real problem for TB. There was an impression of dependency, cultivated by Peter, which was very bad for TB. He talked a bit about the meetings he had with TB and GB after John Smith's death. 'I knew it had to be Tony but I also knew they had to come to that conclusion themselves and that's what I said to them on day one. On day three, I told TB it had to be him but they had to reach a proper agreement about it, or else they would be divided against each other for evermore.'

Thursday, August 24
DM and I sat down for the first real discussion about the conference speech. We had to reconnect with the party without in any way pandering. I was keen on patriotism as a central theme. Jill Sherman [*Times*] told me she was a good friend of Sam Hampson [a university friend] and he'd told her what a complete nutcase I was at university. 'Is it true you used to headbutt the cigarette machines until they broke?' 'I'm afraid so.'

Friday, August 25
GB back in action, and it showed. He was all over the news with a water story. I paged him to say I thought it was brilliant. GB was pretty relaxed for him, and seemed to have enjoyed his break. He was worried that conference was going to be very internal and felt we needed big policy launches every day to reach out beyond the party to the public. I said last year was about New Labour; this year should be about New Britain, so that means setting out what changes we want to make, and the purpose of them. GB agreed and suggested 'the real issues' as a driving theme. I suggested 'the people's agenda', which we could adapt to each main debate. GB said if we were up there setting out major policy direction, our critics would be marginalised and seen as obsessing over internal divisions rather than the challenges facing the country. He was confident we could win on the minimum wage both at the TUC and at conference. Peter M called later to say he was panicking about the Sundays. He felt really vulnerable. He said even if the tabloids didn't go for him, he was sure the columnists would. He had no doubt now that GB was determined to destroy him if he could. 'He has convinced himself that I destroyed his chances of becoming leader and he vowed that day to destroy his destroyer.' He said he felt people looking at him in a different way since the Gould outing.

Monday, August 28
I briefed one or two of the heavies on how conference would show the steps from New Labour to New Britain. Fiona Douglas [family friend, not in politics] came round for dinner and stunned me by saying she felt people were seeing Labour differently since the by-election and that Peter was a terrible, terrible negative for Tony. I said

I was amazed she'd picked up on that because I felt Peter was very much an 'inside the beltway' issue, but she was adamant. I discussed it with Bruce who said it was of course what he'd thought all along, and with Anji who felt I should tell TB. It was one thing for people in the Westminster village to be going on about him, but if it was getting out there more widely, it was a problem.

Wednesday, August 30

PG had prepared an excellent strategy paper re conference, the basis of which was Tory betrayal and New Labour's new approach. He felt Peter M was now too big a figure for a back-room position and had become a problem for TB if he stayed that way. Meeting with John Healey [TUC campaigns director] re TUC speech. He said John Monks was worried TB would want to use it to whack the unions and he hoped it would be more positive than that. JP was now on holiday in Antigua but clearly unable to relax. He called me to talk about Harriet and the NEC of all things. He was firing off on all kinds of tangents and eventually I said 'John, why don't you have a holiday and stop worrying about all this?'

Thursday, August 31

TB was in no doubt that the fall in his ratings was the result of the attacks over the summer. We have to start laying the law down a bit harder, he said. 'I'm not sure the party is serious enough to win yet,' he said. We went over all the problem areas for conference – minimum wage, Scotland, Northern Ireland, women-only shortlists – and he said he was confident we were in the right place on the arguments. I had a long chat with Chris Powell at BMP who said that they were getting no direction at all. PG was steering them on the Tory betrayal line, and I was urging them to think positive about us. I could sense he felt we were about the worst client it was possible to have. David Hill alarmed me by saying that we could lose the Scargill case which Arthur had brought to say our special Clause 4 conference had not been constitutional. He had offered a deal – I'll drop the case if I can debate my Clause 4 alternative at conference – which TB had rejected but which I thought was quite attractive.

Friday, September 1

It was TB's first full day back in the office and we had a session to go over recent weeks, during which we managed fairly quickly to get him into a depressive state. 'So what you're telling me is Gordon won't play, John fucked up, the party's lulus are at it and the press

268   *August '95: Poll ratings fall after summer chaos*

has turned against us?' Pat McFadden said TB underestimated the numbers in the party who didn't really understand what we were about, and we had to answer that. TB was having none of it, and said he needed to go big on the modernisation message. 'This is a classic piece of leftist nonsense – any leader who tries to broaden his party's appeal is then accused of abandoning traditional support. It would be a tremendous mistake for us to respond to that by trimming and cutting back, and I'm not prepared to do it. On the contrary, we have to push on even further and faster.' He was incredibly tanned, which underlined how long a holiday he'd had, and very feisty.

5pm meeting on conference. TB kicked off by saying he intended to use it to take on the kind of arguments that had been allowed to take hold in recent weeks. Tom S said he felt there was a real problem re Peter. It was not a head and body problem, but a neck problem – the party's opinion formers were not in very supportive mood. Jon Cruddas said there was a serious prospect of losing conference votes on the minimum wage, education, defence and PR and he would have to do some old-style dealing with the union leaders. Then Tom briefed on the Scargill situation and by the time he left for dinner with Neil, TB was feeling very fed up with life. He was clearly worried about GB and Peter.

Saturday, September 2

BBC ran a story saying the unions were moving towards us on the minimum wage. TB said the stumbling block for GB was Peter. 'It's crazy, but they basically want to destroy Peter. It is crazy because in my view this will be won or lost by the four of us and if the four of us work together we win.' Philip and Gail came round for lunch. Gail said the problem with Peter now was that he seemed incapable of playing any role quietly. At dinner with Neil, TB said at one point Neil said he couldn't understand why he thought he had a problem with him, to which Tony said 'Come on, Neil, you don't think Alastair wouldn't tell me, do you?' As TB assessed it, Neil's main concerns were education, foreign policy and any sense that New Labour was an attack on him.

Sunday, September 3

I was up at 6.30 and off to TB's to prepare for *Frost*. He was conscious that this was more important than most interviews. We didn't really want another Labour row story out of it, just a straight 'Blair blasts back' – and that is exactly what he delivered. The minute he finished I got a rash of pager messages, Fiona said the Tories would have watched it with a sense of horror because he was so good; PG that he had winner written all over him; Anji that it was his best for ages. Without being dismissive or rude, he had just put the critics in their place. I rang round the broadcasters who were fine and then the papers who universally described it as strong. TB was due to have lunch with Roy Jenkins before coming back to see GB. I wound up TB big time that all the papers were on to his Jenkins lunch and Woy had done a press conference to divulge what he'd said about all his colleagues. 'You're kidding me!' 'Afraid not.' And I made up a load of stuff, that he'd said you'd said JP was hopeless, GB driven by ambition, RC devious, Clare bonkers. I kept a straight face for at least two minutes, at one point saying, can you please tell me what I'm supposed to say? 'This is a disaster,' he said. 'What a bastard!' And then I fell apart. We both had a good laugh about it, which we probably both needed.

Monday, September 4

I had a brief chat with CB. She was pretty surly, and asked if she could count on my support to stop TB drinking caffeine. I told her I'd written to the editors asking them to leave Euan alone on his way to school [as a new pupil at the Oratory], for which she appeared grateful, though she couldn't resist pointing out the problem was people in the party – i.e. people like me – determined to make it an issue. The *Mail* had completely turned now. I wrote to Dacre saying how sad it was to see his paper becoming a poor man's *Daily Express* propaganda rag. 11.45 TB met Alan Howarth whilst I worked in the study. He stayed for around an hour and afterwards TB said he was hopeful. There seemed to be three options. 1. Resign his seat and fight a by-election as Labour. He didn't like that because they had elected him as a Tory. I didn't like it because we'd lose. 2. Just cross the floor of the House – he didn't feel that was honourable. 3. Resign and then find a seat to represent Labour.

On the way to Heathrow [bound for Dublin] I had a furious row with Paul Potts and Martin Cleaver at the Press Association because they decided to do a picture of Euan going to school. Then, Potts having said they would do no more about it, McIntosh [headmaster] called and said the PA reporter was approaching other kids and asking them re Euan. At Dublin, we were met by the ambassador and then off to Glencairn. I called Fiona and inadvertently set off a dreadful chain of events. I told her that Cherie had been very chilly again, that she'd been pleading with me not to take the piss re her efforts to get him off tea and coffee, and then said Anji had intimated that Cherie thought I was responsible for the Euan story in the first place (not the first time

I'd heard that). Fiona went off in a total rage, called Cherie, said she had no idea how awful our life was because of me working for TB, that I spent my whole life defending and looking after them, we got no thanks at all from her and it was an outrage that she could think I would tell the press about the Oratory. Cherie then called Anji and delivered what Anji called the worst tirade she'd ever received in her life, said she was trying to control Tony, and that if Carole didn't go to conference, she wasn't going to go either. Anji was in floods of tears, said she had never been on the receiving end of such venom in her life and was it really worth carrying on? I called Fiona again to tell her what had happened and she was really upset. By the end of the evening Cherie had phoned them both to apologise. But until TB sorted out clearly what was expected of her, what the role was meant to be, what the limits were, it was going to be a potential running sore.

Tuesday, September 5

Dublin. Extraordinary start to the day. My bedroom and Mo's were joined by a bathroom so I knocked on the bathroom door before going in. 'Come in,' she shouted cheerily. I pushed open the door and there she was in all her glory, lying in the bath with nothing but a big plastic hat on. I brushed my teeth, trying not to look in the mirror, where I could see Mo splashing around, and decided to shave later. She seemed totally unbothered by my seeing her naked in a bath without suds. I hadn't slept at all well. I was unsettled by all the Cherie, Fiona, Anji stuff. Anji was sure CB just wanted her out of the whole operation. None of the papers, apart from the *Herald*, carried the Euan pictures. This is what really pissed me off. I bust a gut to stop the papers and would get no thanks for it but if it had appeared she'd have been on the rampage. TB was speaking to Ken Cameron [general secretary of the Fire Brigades Union] and George Brumwell [general secretary of the Union of Construction, Allied Trades and Technicians] re the minimum wage, confident we could get a figure out but it meant a formula in. I was worried about it but he felt we could brief it as real co-operation, a new mood, actually give the unions a positive briefing for once. Pat [McFadden] and I disappeared for three hours to work on the TUC speech.

We met up with TB for the meeting with John Bruton [Taoiseach (prime minister) of the Republic of Ireland], who seemed in a really bad way. He was twitching, rubbing his eyes, then letting his head fall into his hands. He said the UK government had got themselves caught on the decommissioning hook, it was a mistake, the IRA would never do it and it meant logjam. He said the summit tomorrow was in some difficulty. It was later called off. He didn't doubt JM's good faith but he felt they had handled it badly. TB picked up on the depressive mood. 'God this is difficult politics,' he said. Bruton, to ease the mood a bit, suggested as a joke that we talk about EMU [European economic and monetary union] instead. He said he was absolutely convinced the IRA would not hand over weapons 'as a gesture', that Gerry Adams [President of Sinn Fein and MP for West Belfast] was coming under pressure because he was being told 'told you so' and that we were heading for deadlock. TB emphasised, rather to their disappointment, that our basic position was one of support for the peace process and that meant support for the government. It became clear the longer we were there that Sinn Fein resented this, that they felt we were doing it for electoral reasons, in that we felt there were 'no votes' in Ireland. Bruton agreed if TB were to split from the government it should be over something big. TB agreed privately the government had made a mistake in getting so firmly on to this hook. As Mark Durkan [chair and later leader of the nationalist SDLP] said later, it confirmed nationalist prejudice that all the Brits really thought about or understood was guns. It revealed intransigence and that made it very difficult for anyone else to change their positions. TB was clearly fascinated by the politics of it, and also the scale of the challenge. It was one of those issues where slight nuances could lead to huge progress or massive setback and crisis. Bruton had looked physically ill with it all. You could see the pressure he was under.

At the airport we met John Hume [SDLP leader] who gave TB a major monologue on how he saw things, how Sinn Fein were serious this time, and TB should use the visit to apply pressure on the government. TB was having none of it, but John got his revenge when we arrived at the Guildhall in Derry. I'd called ahead to TB's car to say there was a Sinn Fein demo and we should get as close as we could, then straight up the steps and in. But John H was in the car with TB and he got the driver to stop early, they got out and had to walk through two demos. TB seemed fine about it but Pat McF and I were furious, not least because Pat had asked for police help which wasn't there. TB and Mo had another chat re Peter in the car. He told me we had to get over the point that it was part of a Tory strategy to take out Peter because they knew he was good. 'He gives very good advice but he's a useless politician when it comes to advising himself,' he said. 'He's not like you; you can be devious and fly but you basically build alliances and make them work for you. He builds enmities.' Hillsborough [Castle] was nice. Lovely gardens. 'You can see why they'll fight hard to keep all of this,' said TB.

Wednesday, September 6

TB said he had been fascinated by yesterday but God, was it compli-cated and difficult. He was fizzing re JM. 'He's relaunching himself too soon. He's allowing this idea of a "new" Major to develop but there is nothing new in what he's saying or doing.' I called Fiona who said she'd arranged with CB for the four of us to have dinner on Friday to discuss her role. I could see where this would end up – CB and FM ganging up on me being a bastard and Carole rearing her head again. FM said she didn't like the AC/AH [Anji] axis and also the way we saw the downside of Cherie. I spoke to Anji later and she sounded crushed.

Thursday, September 7

Feeling really fed up, too much to do and not enough time to do it. Anji was still very depressed about the CB situation. I was not at all sure about Fiona working for Cherie. It would help in terms of her being more involved, and hopefully more understanding of how hard it was, but it would also mean our entire lives being taken over by the Blairs. I was very ratty all day. At the office meeting, Jon Cruddas laid it on pretty thick about the kind of problems we were facing – minimum wage, education, defence, PR. I joined Philip G in Watford for his focus groups. The first group was strong Tory/Lab switchers and they liked TB, hated the Tories, most would stay with us. The second group showed no enthusiasm at all and if the Tories had a decent strategy they could win them back. They liked the slogans focused on Britain, disliked those on people. I suspected they were Tory abstainers rather than switchers.

Friday, September 8

Slept badly, probably dreading the dinner tonight. I got to TB's early, JP and Rosie already there. TB and JP went downstairs for a short meeting during which TB was meant to raise the idea of JP taking on a portfolio. TB and JP emerged and had agreed GB would do election strategy, JP would do key seats, political education, organisation and have a policy role related to jobs and the regions. JP didn't seem too happy. TB said he felt it meant GB was de facto deputy leader, and there was no quid pro quo. JP wanted an announcement before the election that he would be deputy PM.

In the car on the way in, TB said the worst part of the job was the time it took to get people to work together. Rosie told me that JP felt he kept giving, and getting nothing in return. He was also furious I hadn't briefed him on the Scargill situation. But TB's view was currently less benign: 'He's basically saying if he doesn't get what he wants, he'll go offside.'

I went home to pick up Fiona then we set off for Richmond Crescent. I was dreading it. The worst-case scenarios were me walking out, or CB refusing to go to conference. Peter M, who was good with Cherie, was already there. TB was going on about the awfulness of his day, hours of JP, Bill Morris and others. Peter wanted to probe TB, almost seriously, on why he thought he had become a liability. Eventually Fiona said we should discuss Cherie, what role and image she was supposed to be developing, what was good for her and for TB, and how we managed conference. Cherie said we had reached the position where she felt unsupported, and she had a poor relationship with the office because she felt we saw her purely as a problem. She said she had a contribution to make beyond being a 'rich lawyer/wife'. I said I accepted there was fault on both sides. Things had got off to a terrible start because of Carole [Caplin] at conference last year. I felt Carole was a problem anyway and they had to understand if she became a story again, I would have nothing to do with it. I was entitled to views and judgements too. I added that I was coming very close to the same position re the Oratory as well. I said that both Anji and I had to take some responsibility for the deterioration in her relationship with the office. That being said, it was obvious she could add a lot. She was a working-class success story; she was a successful professional woman; she held a family together in what were clearly high-profile and therefore often difficult circumstances. If that was what the public knew and saw of her, she would be an asset. But I was convinced that the moment she developed a political profile of her own, somehow independent of Tony, it would be bad for both of them. She said she didn't disagree with that but we had never had a proper discussion about it. I said it's quite hard to have proper discussions with someone who slams the door in your face when their husband, who happens to be my boss, has asked me to come round on a Sunday afternoon when I'd rather be with my kids. Tony said what's that about? I told him. 'Cherie, that is disgraceful,' he said. 'You have to accept I am not a saint,' she said. Peter said he wanted to discuss what he called 'the simpering look', saying people didn't like it because it made her look like she was 'just' a wife. By now TB was getting irritated and ratty. 'This is really quite simple. You have two roles. One is as a supportive wife and mother. The second is as a compassionate intelligent person who does good things for good causes. There is one danger to avoid: that is the Hillary [Clinton]/Glenys [Kinnock] syndrome where you are built up in a way designed to undermine me.

September '95: Full and frank talk over Cherie's role

We agreed that Fiona would act as an adviser, paid, that she would work out with Cherie the causes and charities she should become involved with, and take charge of organising her profile. CB would do no interviews but she would do occasional speeches and articles. I asked Cherie what and who she meant by 'the office'. She said me, Anji, Jonathan, Sally. She felt we made decisions for TB without understanding they would have an impact on her and the family. I said I accepted that but they had an impact on our families too. We were all, always, motivated by what we thought he would want, based upon his belief that we should do everything possible to win. I said I'd be more than happy if I spent less time with her husband, and so would Fiona and the kids, but Tony and she had wanted me to do the job, and while I did it, I would do it properly.

We then discussed Carole. I said I felt whilst she was around I would always be worried about her. Cherie said she had felt very insecure about her hair and clothes and how she looked, and Carole had been a great help. Peter and I said we had to find someone CB was comfortable with. My worry was that CB would only be comfortable with someone we were not comfortable with, and that meant Carole. She was already talking about having her in a flat near the hotel at conference. I said if that happened we would just have another rerun of all the old stories, and people just would not understand. Given how badly it could have gone, the dinner went well. TB was very nice to Fiona, if not so nice to Cherie. Cherie and I were always able to have it out but then get back to being reasonably friendly. She said she often said things she regretted after saying them.

Saturday, September 9

PG had written a very downbeat account of the latest focus groups, identifying 'what do we really stand for?' as the central question they posed. It was not how I read it, but it was an OK way of getting people a bit more focused. Good news on the minimum wage front when John Healey called to say the FBU and UCATT had caved in to the pressure re a £4.15 figure, and it was now off the agenda. I wrote a briefing note for the Sundays, saying this could usher in a new era of more positive and constructive Labour/unions relations in which each recognised we had different but legitimate roles.

Sunday, September 10

Having said he didn't really want to build up the TUC speech, TB changed his mind and asked me to start to build it up. I was feeling tired all day. Anji had said I was the victim of my own success. The Shadow Cabinet were terrified of saying anything out of turn, but the downside was it meant they phoned me before saying anything, and there was something in that.

Monday, September 11

Hilary [Coffman] called with a bit of a bombshell. Patrick Wintour had called to say that Seumas Milne [both *Guardian* journalists] had got hold of Philip's 'Unfinished Revolution' memo.[1] It was one of those sinking moments when the words 'Oh fuck' flashed right across the mind. Immediately, I recalled his line about scrapping the union link. But there was more, like him saying we weren't ready for government; the need for a unitary command structure; there was plenty in there and it was all bad, which is of course why it had been given to the *Guardian* by whoever gave it. It was a massive problem. I didn't have a copy at home so I got Patrick to read it to me and I knew from the first two sentences that it was accurate. Jonathan sent me the memo at home and there were actually differences so I was able, honestly, to say to Patrick they'd been given a distorted summary, but what they had was bad enough and of course set up tomorrow's speech to the TUC really badly. I spoke to TB, PG and Peter and knocked out a statement for the *Guardian*, making the best of a very bad job. We would have to go on the offensive in the morning though and use it yet again to get over a change and modernisation message. I then sat back and waited for the barrage of calls. TB was plunged into real gloom. 'We are being sabotaged from within,' he said. Peter and PG were vitriolic about Charlie [Whelan]. Others thought it may have been Peter (as a way of doing in Charlie); one or two thought it might be JP (to do in Charlie/Peter and GB in one go) or RC (because he hated Philip, apparently). It had only been sent to four people – TB, Jonathan, Peter and me, but that didn't mean it might not have been copied more widely, or that it wasn't left lying around somewhere. *Newsnight* flashed up the front page which had three huge pictures of TB, Peter and me, which was a bit of a shock. TB called after his dinner with Murdoch. He said it had been fine, but they were playing both sides against the middle. He said the *Guardian* thing was a blow but 'if you can't stand the heat and all that'. I sensed he was now quite looking forward to tomorrow and using it to hammer

---

[1] Philip Gould's memo not only talked of ending the Labour Party's links with the unions, but also suggested Labour was not yet ready for government. Gould also recommended a command structure where all roads led directly to Blair.

a modernisation, no-going-back message. The phones were going mental at home. Every time I put it down, it rang. Needless to say the *Guardian* spun it as maliciously as possible. I just got hold of Jack S before *Newsnight* and he was terrific. I briefed Harriet for the morning and for once she was terrific too. Fiona said it was appalling to have this happening from within. 'This is the first time I've actually felt sorry for you.' 'Well, thanks.' I finally got to bed at 4 and just after 6 Tony called to say the bulletins had failed to point out the memo was seven months old. At least when the chips were down, I was always able to get up for it. I said to TB today could be quite a ride. He laughed.

Tuesday, September 12

The Philip Gould memo was leading most of the bulletins and all the other papers had followed it up too. TB was firing on all cylinders as we headed for the office. The speech wasn't that great, scripted for a different mood and a different atmosphere. We were going to have to redo it. He was firm in the view it had to be a very robust defence of change and modernisation. He didn't want any pandering to the unions and he wanted us very much on a people's agenda. I was setting the speech up as a big modernisation unapologetic blast, whatever the controversy caused by a leaked memo. Anji quizzed Charlie [Whelan] and came away convinced it wasn't him. Mo read the speech on the train and said she feared it would fall flat. Sally said there wasn't enough in it for the unions. TB said he didn't care. He said we would end the day stronger than we started it, but not by pandering.

Peter Hitchens [right-wing *Express* (and later *Mail*) journalist] was at Brighton station waiting for us and firing off a few barmy questions. We were driven to the hotel, where we had to walk through a small demo, met by Neil K and John Monks. JM said the *Guardian* story had changed the mood for the worse. The atmosphere around the place was very flat. TB, Brendan Barber [deputy general secretary of the TUC] and I left the hotel through another media scrum for the conference centre, the speech now done and dusted. TB got a cool reception as he walked on and he was struggling until he left the text and put some real passion into a defence of modernisation as the route to social justice and the delivery of what they believed in. JP was in a sulk re the GB election role and he sat in the audience wearing dark glasses and ostentatiously not clapping. Potential disaster had been turned into something approaching the seizing of an opportunity – namely the chance to set out the modernising agenda once more.

The atmosphere changed markedly after the speech. My pager was going endlessly with messages saying he'd done well. He had. Disaster turned to advantage.

TB had a meeting with Whelan who needless to say swore blind it [the leaked PG memo] had nothing to do with him and he wished we could all work together better. At the TUC dinner I had a really nice chat with Jack Jones. He said there was lots he felt he might have a go at us over but he said he felt energised by the scale of our ambition and the professionalism with which we sought to make it happen. TB did a terrific off-the-cuff speech about power for a purpose. It felt like an intimate occasion and Monks said that meant a lot to them.

Wednesday, September 13

Apart from the *Guardian* the speech came out not too bad but there was loads more about me, Peter M and PG in the papers which kind of drowned it out. TB was really fed up with the *Guardian* which was making life as difficult as it could within the party and fuelling as much dissent as it could. TB and I sneaked out for a walk on the beach. He was venomous about the *Guardian*. 'There is a left elite that deep down couldn't give a damn whether we have the Tories in power for ever,' he said. 'We have to break it and change it.' We got the train back to London, got early to the BBC and so went for a tea in the Langham [Hotel]. TB said to me that I was the pivot in his operation, that if anything happened to me he was not sure what he would do. We'd agreed to hit a low tax, better off with Labour message, and it went OK though Jimmy Young was fairly aggressive and it took a while for TB to get going. It wasn't brilliant, as we agreed in the car afterwards. He'd sounded testy and hurried.

RC was pretty offside at the moment. Anji said a letter had come in from a group of MPs which would be devastating if they released it to the press. 'You get the feeling of a near riot in the PLP and we're just keeping a lid on it,' she said. Jack C was solid as a rock. He said to TB ignore everything everyone tells you: you're on course, people out there like you, they think we've changed and all the stuff that people worry about in here is for the birds. He was terrific for morale. I got a bus home and a couple of people came up and said keep up the good work, which always made me feel better.

Thursday, September 14

TB was worried that the Tories would get something out of their Chequers meeting and he called to say we needed a big story up for the Sundays. His main concern at the moment was that for the first time the Big Three were all more or less offside at the same time. He was not in a good mood when he left for Bedford and the launch of the Rural Votes Project. He had a real go at Anji over the diary. Having asked for ten party meetings, he was now bollocking her for the fact that she'd put in two. We had a stroke of luck in the morning when Conor Ryan [Blunkett adviser] was leaked a copy of Gillian Shephard's note to the Cabinet on underfunding. It instantly put the heat back on them and totally kyboshed their Cabinet awayday. TB came back from the country in no better mood than he left, saying he didn't know how we were going to get back on the front foot. BMP finally came up with a good idea – John Major's Pork Pies. I liked it because it made the point about their lies but in a way that they couldn't really make a fuss without looking like they had lost any sense of humour.

We had a pretty vicious meeting with the *Guardian*, [Alan] Rusbridger, [Martin] Kettle and [Michael] White. Peter Hyman had dug up some examples of the more lurid and contentious coverage, and TB went through some of it. He said it added up to a picture that was biased, slanted, politically motivated journalism which did not report trouble in the party but sought to foment it. He went through some of Seumas Milne's stuff, T&G elections, the way they covered Peter. Rusbridger sat impassively, but Mike White was getting a bit agitated. Eventually Rusbridger spoke. He said he couldn't believe what he had heard. He said the paper had been very supportive of Labour. He said they had been incensed at TB's jibe that the *Sun* had more policy content. I said they had a unique position and they traded as being supportive; therefore they should show some support instead of swallowing all the right-wing propaganda against us about not standing for anything. TB said it was obviously entirely a matter for them how they ran the paper but if it reached the point where the paper was a problem for the party, we would have to get a message out to the party that the paper was essentially hostile and they should look elsewhere for honest coverage. Mike got very emotional at this point, whilst Rusbridger said we were paranoid. Mike said: 'I hear the ghosts of Harold Wilson and Joe Haines in the room.' It was not a happy meeting. TB said afterwards he was worried I was going to hit Rusbridger. Anji went off for a drink with Kettle who said that for once I had been calm and cogent, but TB went over the top. We were straight into another *crise*. Frank Millar of the *Irish Times* called to ask for my reaction to Kevin McNamara's resignation [the Labour MP and Shadow Northern Ireland Secretary resigned over Labour support for government policy there]. I said I didn't know he'd resigned. Nor, I quickly discovered, did TB. Jonathan got hold of him and he confirmed it, saying he'd faxed his letter down yesterday, saying it was about N Ireland policy and the approach to the trade unions. I quickly rang round everyone to try to break it on our terms.

Friday, September 15
The education leak was all over the papers and had taken pressure off us. I took the boys to school then worked at home on the conference speech. I couldn't get going so went out on the heath to try to get some creative juices flowing and eventually came up with a really good passage on patriotism and VJ Day. It was a great feeling when you finally got something that you knew would work. DM came round at lunchtime and in the next few hours we got pretty much a first draft together. Jonathan worked up an interesting list of potential policy announcements for conference. TB called a couple of times but he wasn't really focused on it yet, and in any event he was getting on our nerves. Anji said her lunch with Cherie went fine. Both on best behaviour.

Saturday, September 16
I tried my hardest to get Toby Helm [*Telegraph* journalist] to buy the line that the Southampton meeting [to which JP had not been invited] was no big deal but he was having none of it. I was playing in goal for the kids' football team whilst trying to deal with JP and Rosie. Rosie said JP didn't want to say anything about it at all. I said if we say nothing, it will be taken as true, set on their terms, and it will run away big. She tried him again but he wouldn't budge, so I called him on his car phone. He was perfectly friendly and I suggested he said that he was aware of the meeting, happy with the outcome and he and TB were working well. He said 'I'm not prepared to lie.' I said I'm not asking you to. He said we were in a new ball game. 'I've worked out that I am basically a managed entity and you are the one who manages me.' TB was in Sedgefield and when I finally got hold of him to say JP wanted to speak, and what it was about, he was furious. 'I'm fed up of all these egos,' he said. 'We have these people at the top of the party who just cannot get on. It is a fucking nightmare.' Anyway, he agreed to speak to him and a few minutes later JP called to say he was putting out a statement that this was a meeting about economic policy, there was no reason why it should not have taken place and any suggestion otherwise is mischievous. Progress then. He said 'We have turned the corner.' 'Good,' I said. 'No you don't understand, I've turned the corner in the other direction. There

will be distance and I will do my own thing with my own people. Tony has to realise this is about more than tomorrow's papers. It is about Brown and it is about the party. I have a responsibility to the party, and so does he, and until he sorts himself out with Brown, he's got problems.' He sounded angry and said TB had to get a grip of the relationships at the top. I said I couldn't agree more. He and TB called another three or four times during the day, but we were just going round in circles by now. Then, just to cap it all, Clare Short phoned for a whinge. She said we should drop the 'modernisation goes on' mantra because it is so-o-o-o boring. The old guard in the party feel that the Leader's Office feel contempt for them, she said. I said all that stuff about the office was overblown by a small number of MPs and journalists. The party were fine about it. She was due to do an interview with *On the Record* but she said she didn't want to do it because 'I'm not happy and I can't lie.' It must be terrible being the only person on the planet who tells the truth, but this is a cross poor Clare has to bear.

Sunday, September 17

TB called when I was still in bed, and said he was tired of the JP games. This was a power struggle between GB and JP and we were in the middle. TB said he would call JP and say he would not tolerate negotiation through the press. Anji came on to say Paddy Ashdown was in a flap because he'd heard *The Times* were going big on TB's comments about the Lib Dems. Indeed they were. TB had said he wanted greater co-operation with the Lib Dems, which was fairly innocuous but, as Paddy complained when I spoke to him, meant that TB, not he, would be dominating the media out of his conference in Glasgow this week. Eventually he and TB spoke and we agreed we would throw no more hand grenades into his conference. I thought it was a rather effective little operation.

Monday, September 18

TB's interview in *The Times* stole Ashdown's thunder and dominated their conference coverage. There was a special pre [Labour] conference Shadow Cabinet meeting. TB did a pretty good and sober opening. JP was looking very brooding and both he and GB were scribbling madly the whole time. When GB set out the outlines of our tax campaign, JP said 'That must not mean we are committed to supporting tax cuts.' TB was trying to be so conciliatory between them that it became almost comic. Though there was very little discussion of recent troubles, DD simply said it had all been very damaging.

Meanwhile there was nobody in that room who was left in any doubt that JP was really pissed off. TB took JP through to Miliband's office and said it just wasn't good enough for him to tell everyone he was pissed off, knowing as he did how it would all be seen. It was the story everyone wanted to write, and we shouldn't be helping them at all.

Tuesday, September 19

There were bits and bobs in the papers about JP, including a full-page *Mirror* editorial, saying TB must not freeze him out. This was a running sore, which in my view we could have avoided happening in the first place. TB met JP. They had thirty minutes together and then Rosie, Jonathan and I went in and TB said they had agreed GB to do strategy, JP key seats, RC policy. I said, we should brief it straight away with hints that there would be a role for Peter M. JP was clearly in much better form, probably because yesterday TB had told him that the reason why he did not yet want to announce JP as deputy prime minister was tactical, not that he didn't want him to get the job. After a good deal of toing and froing we agreed JP should do the *Today* programme. I had another long session with Bruce, who said the party, especially the PLP, was offside. He felt there was a head and body problem at all levels. I was really fed up most of the day, the JP situation was draining. TB left for Dudley [Labour event] in reasonable mood. There were 700 members, 100 turned away and he got a fantastic reception. It confirmed him in his view that our problem was with activists, not members. But Bruce was convinced the party desperately wanted to hear some of the old songs about building Jerusalem, and he felt TB had to stop kicking them.

Wednesday, September 20

David [Miliband] and I were finally beginning to make progress with the speech. TB came on after his *Money Programme* interview with Peter Jay [broadcaster, former ambassador to Washington]. He wasn't happy with the way that the BBC's coverage of our business tour was focusing so much on the minimum wage. Alan Rusbridger sent a nasty letter to TB, about the meeting with him and about the weekend briefing. Anji and I were worrying about tomorrow's funeral for Sam McCluskie [NEC member, former general secretary of the Seamen's Union]. GB wanted TB to go with him. I felt TB should go with JP, so there was endless faffing around on that. During the afternoon, I decided to go to see Burnley at Leicester, and I persuaded David M to come on the grounds that we would get quite a lot of work done on the train. There was a great turnout from the Burnley fans for a midweek league cup match, but we lost to two silly goals. The speech, meanwhile, was coming on fine, but it was 14,000 words long. TB said he would rather have too much than too little at this stage. The basic themes were fine but we were still short of the kind of big policy announcement that would connect with the public.

Thursday, September 21.

On the way to Sam McCluskie's funeral we discussed the big four problem with Tom Sawyer. Tom had a very wary view of all politicians, I would say. His big worry, particularly if we got into government, was that GB and RC would just be doing their own things, and most of the party work would fall to JP. He agreed that JP had deliberately been reasserting himself, and it was important that we didn't push him offside. He said that Robin was just waiting for Gordon to screw up, a view shared by TB. I said to Tom that he too had to help us manage these relationships. Tom and I agreed the best thing was that TB take control of the whole business. He said the feeling in the party was that Tony liked to kick them, whereas at least I understood where they were coming from. He felt I should have a bigger party role.

GB was waiting for us in the Arthur Conan Doyle suite at the Caledonian Hotel. GB was unhappy with the way my briefing had come out, feeling it hadn't focused sufficiently on the areas he was supposed to be in charge of, like posters, day-to-day, PPBs. The reality was that he would rather the others were written out of the script. GB, Tom and I shared a cab to the church in Leith and then waited for TB and JP to arrive. It was a fantastic service, terrific music, and you felt the whole event said something about Sam, and his personality. Tony, John and Pauline were in the front row with Jimmy Knapp. I stayed well back, partly not to look pushy, but also because I always cry at funerals. As soon as the music starts, I think about John [Merritt] and Bob [Fiona's father] and also I look ahead and imagine how life is going to be when Mum and Dad go. TB did a reading, JP made a fantastic speech, and 'The Red Flag' was playing as we left the church.

Friday, September 22

TB was on good form but of ten businessmen who were vox-popped, only one said he would definitely vote Labour. In his private conversations, and more gently in interviews, TB was starting to make clear we would not raise taxes, whatever the Tories did, and he was clearly getting the party ready for that. I had a meeting with Des Wilson [director of corporate and public affairs] of BAA. He said that not only, in his view, did business not mind a Labour government but they would positively welcome it provided we did not screw the economy up. TB was then taken on a tour of the airport, and a meeting with Richard Branson [chairman of Virgin]. As ever with Branson, they organised a huge media turnout, and although he was very good at looking like he was playing things cool, I got the sense Branson wanted the attention more than TB. I listened to Branson being cautiously welcoming of TB. He said that if there were ten TBs in the Cabinet, business would have no problem with Labour, though did express some concern about the minimum wage. But it was picked up by the media as a positive signal re backing TB.

Most of my conversations with TB at the moment were about getting a central theme for the party conference speech. Peter H, David and I were convinced it was in the patriotism area. TB was looking more towards the theme of community. He was also quite taken with the idea of projecting Britain as a young country.

Saturday, September 23

JP had done a terrific interview in the *Guardian*, and I phoned to say so, and also to say I thought his speech at Sam's funeral was terrific. He and I were now back on an even keel. We chatted on for ages, and after the recent difficulties, I was glad he was back on board. I always felt the operation was stronger if he was motoring. Andy McSmith [*Observer*] had done a story about a TB charm offensive in which he mentioned that Tony had phoned Rusbridger to apologise for our intemperate meeting. TB knew I wouldn't be happy about it, which is why, of course, he hadn't told me he was doing it. He felt the *Guardian* was in a position where it might come round towards us more, and he felt it was better that they had spoken and he'd apologised. Who knows? He may be right.

Sunday, September 24

TB was working all day at Michael Levy's [Labour fund-raiser and TB's tennis partner]. He called to say he wanted me to work on the start and on the anti-Tory section. We were now over twice the length and working on two separate drafts, but we felt we were making progress. TB called later on, to say he'd done some really good work. He also finally managed to track down Alan Howarth, who said he was on for it, and we could decide when he would do it. I said the eve of the Tory conference was the best time. TB had been worried that Howarth would be lost as a result of some of the madness that happened during the summer. Far from it. He said the Tories had shown themselves to be even more extreme and uncaring. But TB wanted me to think through how we handle it from Howarth's perspective.

Monday, September 25

TB called, just after 7, anxious that they were leading the news with what he called a bad story, business attacking our plans for a wind-fall tax on the utilities. I thought it was a good story. In any event, it followed from what he had said on the *Money Programme*, and what GB had been briefing over the weekend. Charlie had been in the pub on Friday, saying that TB had dropped a clanger on inflation. TB had done some good stuff on the speech and his main worry now was policy. We lacked the big policy announcement to give meaning to the general theme. I had the idea of announcing Alan Howarth's defection in the speech, but it could be seen as a gimmick and Fiona felt, having read the draft, that the speech was strong enough without it.

I went off for lunch with Rodney Bickerstaffe. He was way offside, claiming he could not move on the minimum wage, and on education he was in a rage, saying 'I sent my son to a local sink school because that's what you did, you supported your local school.' He felt TB wanted the unions right out of the party. He said that JP was vital to TB, and he tried hard to be loyal and we should appreciate that. He was very gloomy.

Tuesday, September 26

Fiona's dinner must have gone fairly well, because when I went over to TB's, Cherie was charming again for the first time in ages. TB and I left in the little car and headed for Totteridge where we were due to work on the speech at Michael's. TB was determined to break the back of it today. It took ages to get there because of the traffic, but it was during the drive that some of the best thinking on the speech came. TB was firing, and so was I, him rattling out ideas, me rattling out phrases and taking notes as he drove this tiny car with both of us scrunched up in the front. Britain falling apart, only a united Labour Party can unite it. Only a modernised Labour Party can modernise Britain. By the time we got there, we'd virtually rewritten the entire speech, and I had a mass of notes to decipher. He was still arguing with GB about whether Charlie leaked the Gould document, and on the drive up there he asked me 'Do you think GB and I will ever get back together properly? Whenever we speak now, there is a suppressed anger there.' Michael's place was a bit over the top for my taste, big security gates, white carpets, rolling lawns and all that. But it was a nice place to work, TB in the kitchen, me in the dining room. We left at 6 and on the drive back TB was on the phone to GB again, and it was clear from the side of the conversation I heard that GB was still angry about everything. TB was getting more and more fed up with it. He said you'd think being Chancellor of the Exchequer would be enough to be going on with.

He was due to see Alan Howarth again, and I said it was time we pinned him down to times and dates, and that you two stop talking about God and we ask him straight, does he want to help us finish Major off? TB called to say that Howarth is definitely on. He wanted a seat. Being honourable he felt that he should fight a by-election. TB promised to help with his seat, and made clear that if he failed, we'd help him out. TB had obviously been impressed by him, and reckoned he'd make a decent minister. He said to me, this is like getting a Soviet agent and you are the British agent who is going to bring him out in circumstances that benefit us and him the most. We kicked around the best possible dates to do this. The more I thought of it, the more I was convinced it should be the start of their conference. If the Tories really went for him, it would help us find him a seat. This is big stuff. If we had a successful conference, and then Howarth defined theirs, then the conference season would be a clear win for us.

Wednesday, September 27

Pre-conference team meeting, to give everyone their orders and make sure they understood that the press would be watching us like hawks. TB cancelled all his meetings, other than those related to the speech. He said the NEC had been pretty grim. Blunkett had voted against rejecting Liz Davies.[1] It was a classic piece of pre-conference Blunkettry. TB asked me to stay back to discuss GB. It is important in the run-up to conference, he said, that we emphasised the role of GB and RC, to show that there is a team at work. I said I was happy to build up any of them, and work with any of them, but it was such a pain that we kept having to get round the fact that the big players so wanted to be seen as such. There were times when you really felt they were working against us. TB said he simply did not believe GB would do anything to prevent a Labour government. But he did have

[1] A left-wing barrister and Islington councillor, Liz Davies had been selected by Labour Party members in Leeds North-East in 1995 as prospective parliamentary candidate. Labour's NEC vetoed the selection.

worries about Charlie. He said that if there was some kind of operation going on, it was being done without GB's authority. I was not so sure. TB said in politics, people think that things are black and white, but very rarely are they. There's nothing wrong in GB thinking that one day he gets the top job. The question is whether that stops him doing the job that he's got.

The highlight of my day, phoning Alan Howarth at home. As so few people knew, I found a very quiet spot at the back of the office, and called him. His first words were 'Do you think I'm mad?' I said far from it. We talked it over, him why he was doing it, his feeling that he was more in tune with us than he was with modern Conservatism, and me trying gently to persuade him that we should do it on that weekend between the conferences. He had a fear that this would be seen as cowardly, but I pointed out that his best hope of getting a Labour seat was for the Labour Party to see him as something of a hero, rather than a turncoat, and the key to that was the extent to which his former party reacted. So it was in his interests that we did this with real impact. Obviously he was worried about the reception he was going to get in his new party, but he just had to accept that his former colleagues will be very, very angry with him. But he also had to accept that the best way to the hearts of the Labour Party was to put the Tory Party into a rage. I also had to warn him against the idea of a by-election, because frankly he would not win it for us where he was. He wanted to know how JP would react, and again I said that provided JP felt you were doing this for the right reasons, and provided you accept that the politics of this demanded doing it with a real impact upon the Conservatives, then he would be broadly supportive. He was asking, I suppose, because he knew that deep down tribalists like John, and I felt a little of this myself, think there is something instinctively wrong about switching parties. However, TB had convinced himself, and talking to Alan, so did I, that he was doing it for the right reasons, and what's more, the more I talked to him, the more I felt that this could be one of the really big moments of this Parliament, which would help us reshape the landscape in the run-up to the election. He was clearly a decent man. He was worried that the press would get into his family, including his broken marriage. He wondered if him being a Lloyd's name was a problem. He wondered if it would be better to hear both leaders' speeches before finally announcing his move. I said again I felt strongly that this should be done before their conference. Part of me was worrying that if he got back into his own tribe, he might actually decide to stay there. Eventually he said that he'd made his mind up, and if I thought that was the right time to make the maximum impact, he would go with it. I said that I thought we should give the story as an exclusive to Tony Bevins to run in the *Observer* on the Sunday as the Tories gathered. Then as the paper dropped, he would put out the letter to his constituency explaining his decision. He should do *Frost* on Sunday morning, and get articles in the *Mail*, *The Times*, and possibly do an interview somewhere like the *Mirror*. I said I admired and appreciated what he was doing. He shouldn't underestimate how much was likely to get thrown at him, that was why it is important that the Labour Party took to him quickly, and I believed they would if it was presented as him, believing in social justice, leaving a party he thought did not believe in it and joining one that did. He was due to go to Scotland, and we agreed to stay in touch, and I said we would do all we could to support him. TB was straight, and we would protect him. He said the Tories would be absolutely vicious about it, but he was prepared for that. I said, you must have tortured yourself about this. Yes, he said, it isn't easy after twenty-odd years in the party. But it was definitely going to happen and what with the progress made on the speech today, it had been the best day for some time.

Thursday, September 28

Both Fiona and Rory had been up ill through the night, so I was pretty knackered as I headed off early to meet TB and head once more to Michael's. As so often, whenever we were getting going on the speech, he would get a message that GB wanted to speak again. This time, he was agitated about TB's interview on the *Today* programme, which had put the issue of taxation of child benefit on the map again, and GB was saying he was being boxed in. In truth, TB had said nothing new but there was such an appetite for TB stories that this kind of thing was inevitable. TB came off the phone at one point, and said that he felt GB simply would not come back onside again. As the day wore on, TB became more and more concerned about the central argument of the conference speech. He put it to one side, wrote the word 'argument' on a single page, then tried to sketch out the absolute core of the argument, time and again, scribble, scribble, scribble, then putting a line through it, then starting again. At one point, with this mass of paper lying around his feet, he thought he'd lost the one that got close to it, and the pair of us were on our hands and knees trying to find the one that he wanted.

Liz [Lloyd] was off sick, so Sue Jackson came up to start typing up everything we'd done. It was a bit of a nightmare for her, because the speech was now in bits of paper, so varied in shape and size that we called it the Origami speech. We had a good strong start to the speech now, and though the ending was not yet quite right, we had the making of it. As ever, making the policy section come alive was the hard bit. Alan Clark called and I described the scene of TB and myself scrambling around under the table, trying to find the right piece of paper, and he said it was always the same. If people could see politicians in those circumstances, they might think they were odd or hapless, but he's a great man, and you're doing a great job. He always cheered me up. TB and I had lunch and then found a football and went out for a kickabout in Michael's garden. Again, poor Sue was looking at us out of the window as if we were a pair of lost souls, but in fact, the little break did us good, because in the afternoon, we got going again. Michael arrived home, and they played tennis, while Sue and I left for the office. I could feel myself going down with Rory's cold, and also I'd lost my pager. By the time I got to the office, something had happened to TB's mood, because he phoned in a state of near despair. He said he read the draft again from start to finish, and it was hopeless. The argument wasn't clear, the policy sections were dull, and it just would not connect. He said he would have to start all over again. I said, don't be so ridiculous, it's a perfectly good draft and we have three days to work on it.

Friday, September 29

Another day of hell at Totteridge. David M, Peter Hyman and I headed up there through awful traffic and arrived to find TB in a dreadful state. He had a look of near panic in his eyes, which I think alarmed Peter. By now I knew it was essentially part of the creative process that drove him to get the best out of himself, and out of us. Part of him probably believed that the speech was terrible, but what he was doing was forcing himself and the rest of us into a state of worry that would produce better work. TB said we didn't have an argument, we didn't have good lines, we didn't really know what we wanted to say, and we were not properly defining what we meant by New Britain. I phoned Anji at one point, and told her it was a nightmare, and he was getting on our nerves, pacing around barking out contradictory orders, and we had to get him to calm down. Alan Clark called again and said it was so obvious that we were going to have a good conference, and they were going to have a bad one. He said what would freak out the Tories was if TB really made a pitch for the One Nation centre. It was uncanny. There was no way he could have known about Alan Howarth, but what he said confirmed that strategically we were bang on course, which is why Tony's fussing over the speech was so unnecessary. He kept taking out passages which everyone had agreed days ago were among the best in the speech, so then we would rerun arguments that we thought had been settled before. Then, to cap it all, the printer packed up, which threw both of us into a tirade, and eventually we left for the office to carry on working. Alan Howarth called, said he had thought long and hard overnight, and he agreed that it was best to do this at the end of our conference. He now sounded genuinely excited and ready for it. TB and the speech team went through it line by line, and all of us had the sense that we'd gone backwards again. He was literally pulling at his hair now, saying he was in despair about the speech, and he could not see his way out of it. Somehow, we had lost both the structure and any sense of the forward vision. It was now just a mishmash of different unconnecting passages, and long policy sections that would put the audience to sleep. The coherent theme that we had earlier in the week just wasn't there any more. I went home, pretty depressed about it all, though as Anji pointed out, it always was like this, it was the way he worked on really big speeches. He called in at 8pm and I told him about the conversation with Howarth. Even that didn't cheer him up. He said he was genuinely worried about the speech.

Saturday, September 30

I had a nice chat with Cherie on the drive down to Brighton, though TB was not in the mood for talking, and kept telling her to shush so that he could work on the speech. The news was focusing on rail, on which David Hill had been briefing, and Peter M wound up TB about it, taking his mind off the speech and going into one of his BBC rages. I was livid with Peter, because the truth is the Saturday night news didn't matter a damn, and what did matter was getting his speech sorted. There was a bit of a scene with Cherie and the police, when she asked why there were no women in the team, which did not please TB one bit. The police seemed fine about it, and even suggested it was a good way of breaking the ice, but I would be amazed if it didn't get out. David [Hill] was buzzing around, while Joy looked really miserable. The Sunday papers were not too bad, though I suspected Peter's diddling in the *Sunday Times*, which led on the notion of TB announcing a contract between government and people in the speech. It was deeply irritating. Major tried to get in on the act by saying he would challenge TB to a TV debate during the election. I put out a line saying we would welcome a TV debate next week. TB had to go back to some of the receptions, while DM, Liz and I carried on working on the speech. He got back, changed into his dressing room, and said he wanted to break the back of it tonight. Again, I said.

Sunday, October 1

Amazingly, we had GB, JP and RC all doing big broadcast interviews, and all driving on pretty much the same message. Neil came round, read the speech, and said he liked it, but it was way too long. Felt the argument was clear, which at this stage was more important. The speech team had a good session with TB, going through line by line, and it felt a lot better. But at one point, he went through to the bathroom, shouted for me to go and see him, and he simply said 'I cannot tell you how much I am panicking about this speech.' I said, I thought it was getting there, but he just wanted to go over the argument again and again and again. He and Cherie were staying in the main suite on the same floor as ours, and right into the early hours, I was being called in to have the same conversation.

Monday, October 2

When I went up to see TB, he was sitting in his dressing gown, staring into space, just shaking his head and saying it wasn't right. I left him for the office meeting, where I complained about the lack of security concerning the speech, having found two copies of the draft in the corridor outside the office last night. All that mattered in the next twenty-four hours was getting the speech in shape, though TB was due to do a visit with Kevin Keegan [former footballer and manager] and I said we must get an autograph book and a ball. We needed some decent pictures in advance of tomorrow. At a minimum, TB could get Keegan's autograph for the boys, but at best they would do a proper kickabout. He wasn't bad with a ball, and Keegan would in any event know how to make sure he did not end up looking daft. Everyone was horrified at the prospect of TB playing football and being made to look silly but I insisted we get a ball. TB went over to the conference centre for Gordon's speech. Charlie had mentioned to me yesterday that he was going to call for VAT on fuel to be cut but because I had been so focused on the speech, it had not really registered. I didn't think GB's speech worked, though the coverage he got was fine. Keegan was a nice, warm man, and I sensed he was basically onside. There was a huge media turnout. It was a fantastic success and provided the best pictures of the week. I asked Keegan to throw the ball at TB and get him to head it back. Then, they just kept going, I think for twenty-eight consecutive headers. TB said he had never been able to do that, in his entire life, though of course a professional like Keegan can head the ball towards a target in the same way most of us can throw it, so it wasn't that difficult. I asked TB whether it was worth considering detonating the Howarth time bomb in the speech. He said straight away, 'So you don't think the speech is good enough without it?' I said no, it's OK, but there is a case for really going for it.

I said I would tell Tony Bevins about Howarth today. I did so, as the NEC results were being announced, in a little corner by the press tables. I said to him, what is the biggest story that you have ever had literally fall into your lap? The story I did on the IRA, he said. This is bigger, I said. I told him what it was, and I saw tears welling up in his eyes. Are you serious? I said I was. I love you, he said, and I love him. I want to kiss you. We agreed he would not speak to Alan till Friday, nor to his office, but that he would quietly do some research on past defections. I loved giving a story like this to Bevins. He loathed the Tories, and he loved big stories, and I knew he would do this one properly. Meanwhile, I was faxing Alan all the main speeches and talking to him about some of the arguments we were trying to put together for tomorrow. TB was a lot more relaxed after we won the minimum wage vote, and also when he saw GB's speech, which he hadn't much liked, was playing OK. TB had felt the 'spend spend' feel to it had cut across the Iron Chancellor mode. He asked me to work on a new ending to the speech, and I went for a walk to try to get the creative juices flowing. It worked, and I banged out a passage, which I showed to Neil. He said it would make the whole thing go like a Beethoven symphony, which may have been over the top, but Neil was a good judge of what would or would not work in the speech. I gave it TB, and he loved it too. He had also done a good rewrite on policy, and we had a speech. Neil came up late and told TB it was a great speech, he needed to relax now, keep calm and be confident. He said he needed to put some real emotion into the delivery. 'They want to love you, let them.' After he'd gone, TB said thanks for all the work I'd done on the speech. He said the ending was the best thing I'd written for him. The one area where we were still weak was jokes. But then, just before we called it a day, a very good selection came in from Roy Hudd [comedian and comedy writer]. We were blessed.

Tuesday, October 3

I get maybe two or three sleepless nights a year, and it was pretty bad luck that last night should have been one of them. I finally gave up trying to sleep just before 6, had a bath, and then went through to see TB, who I knew would be up. I was feeling nervous and anxious and tried hard not to let it show, because I knew it would unsettle him, and I just about managed it. He was sitting in his pyjamas, looking worried, making fiddling little changes which neither added nor subtracted very much at all. As ever, he worked right up to the wire, still not totally happy with the policy sections, and constantly worrying that he would flop. There was a further major irritant, in that the verdict in the OJ Simpson trial, which had been obsessing the media, was to be announced at 6pm [Simpson was acquitted, watched live by a huge global audience]. The leader's speech is one of the few occasions in the political calendar where the media sit up and take notice, and obviously we were worried that the broadcasters would go with the OJ flow, and TB's speech would have to take a back seat. I wrote during the day, both to BBC and ITN, to ensure they clocked our concern and did not ignore the speech at the expense of a story, which, whilst clearly newsworthy, did not have that much to do with the lives of British people. Needless to say, once word of my letter leaked out from the BBC, the press stirred it up as best they could.

TB and I had a last run through the speech, and then went next door for autocue practice. The speech had a rhythm to it, and I could feel his growing confidence as he went through it. We were driven to the conference centre, up to the office for a final read through before he had to go on the platform. I got a note taken up to him, which simply said be strong and of good courage, and relax. He smiled and showed the note to JP. Brighton is one of the hardest halls going in terms of reaching an audience, as there is something about the acoustics that doesn't quite work, but it was clear from early on that he was going to go down well. He introduced Mary Wilson [widow of Harold], who was in the hall, and it was clear from the fantastic response she got that there was a warmth in the hall that he would tap into. They wanted him to do well. The BT section could not have had a better response. I was sitting next to Rosie Winterton, who was plying me with Liquorice Allsorts. All the sections that we had really struggled over, and those parts that he asked for me to deliver our best work, what he called the purple patches, really went well, which always made me feel a sense of satisfaction, a job well done. The reception at the end was tremendous, and TB looked great. It was clear that we were in for another good media response. The word being most commonly used was brilliant. TB was a lot calmer now, and knew he had done well. He had a meeting with Hattersley, who yesterday had attacked BMW drivers. Afterwards, as Roy left, TB was going on about how vain and pompous Hattersley had been. I phoned home to speak to the boys, who said the best bit on the news was me eating sweets. By the time we got back to the hotel, I was totally exhausted. TB, as ever, did not see any of the news, but I was able to tell him that it had been a real success. He said he could not have done it without me, and I said next time can we do it without so much emotional grief? We ended up having a huge laugh as we recalled the moment a few days earlier, when we had been leaning on a fence at the back of Michael Levy's garden, looking at sheep, TB saying that at this moment in time, without any speech worth the name, he would rather be that sheep than leader of the Labour Party.

Wednesday, October 4

We got great coverage for the speech, though the story about me and my letters to the broadcasters was starting to run too. TB had bumped into Blunkett earlier, who was doing the education debate, which was likely to get focused on the expected Hattersley attack. 'He is a fat, pompous bugger,' TB said. 'You are very wise,' said Blunkett. Geoffrey Norris called from the conference centre to say that Meacher was refusing to remove a passage in his speech about deterring investors. TB was really irritated and sent Jonathan down to the conference centre to sort it out. It was too late, as the speech had been given. Jonathan called and TB went ballistic. 'You have to understand, Jonathan, that you are not dealing with serious people all the time. These are not adults, as you and I would understand the term. You have to pin them down and get a real agreement.' He was livid and later, when Meacher did a dreadful interview on the live coverage, I was despatched to see him and tell him to do no more interviews. I told him that TB was genuinely angry, that it was utterly pointless trying to scare off investors and in any event, he should not have delivered a passage that TB's office had asked him to remove. Mo had warned TB that GB was building up a formidable power base in the PLP, and the party more generally.

Mirror lunch, which was awful. Montgomery made a dreadful little speech about the closeness of the *Mirror* and the party. Cherie was on good form, but I could tell TB could not wait to get out of there. It made me genuinely angry to think that as the prospect of a Labour government neared, the *Mirror* was in the hands of people who were about as Labour as the salt and pepper pots.

I was keeping in touch with Alan Howarth, and felt genuinely excited that within days of a speech that went down as well as yesterday, we would be springing a major surprise that would wreck the start of the Tory conference.

Ridiculously, the BBC story was still running, and John Birt was apparently really upset about it. I ran into [Norman] Tebbit and had a chat with him. He said he was appalled at the government's ineptitude and said he was glad to be able to help. TB said 'Are you sure you don't mind being seen with me?' 'Not if you don't mind being seen with me,' said Tebbit. He was really loving the attention. I bumped into Clare Short, who said that she was picking up a lot of complaints from journalists that I was too much of a bully boy. Diddums, I said.

I finally got round to talking to JP about Howarth. His initial reaction was not exactly brilliant. His concern was that it would be seen as a further sign that the Labour Party was moving to the right, not that people like Howarth felt the Conservative Party had become extreme, and now saw us as mainstream and moderate. I told them that on some issues, like tax cuts and arms sales, Howarth was way to the left of me. I said it was important that JP was on board for it, because in an ideal world, I would like him to do the media response on the day that Howarth defected. He asked me if TB had promised Alan anything and I said no, though he had said we would help him get a seat if we could. JP said we must work out a proper strategy, and at that point, I realised he was basically on board. Later he discussed it with TB, and by now, he was more seized of the potential value to us of what was about to happen, and we started to develop a line about One Nation Labour building a One Nation Britain. I explained the media strategy, i.e. Bevins, *Frost*, the articles, and it would be great if he could be up and about once the story broke. The only promise I had made Howarth was that we would try to create the circumstances in which the party made him welcome.

Friday, October 6

After last night's celebrations, this morning people were a bit tired and ratty. Even TB, who rarely drinks more than a couple of glasses, seemed a bit hungover. I had another long call with Alan Howarth to go through all the logistics. I told him that JP was on board, and that there would be the use of the phrase 'One Nation Labour' in his speech, which was very deliberate, and which we would point to after the event. The One Nation line was better coming from JP. The line went straight to the top of the news, and added to TB's end-of-week interviews, in which he made a direct appeal to former Tories to come over to us, we were in very good shape.

Before we left, TB saw RC to tell him he was worried that he was offside. He was really just putting down a marker that he had clocked what had been going on, though Robin continued to play dumb. TB asked me to go back with him and Cherie, only half in jest I think, said she was sure one day soon she was going to wake up and find me standing at the end of the bed. I said I'd been there this morning but she slept through it. On the drive back to London, I was paged to call Alan Howarth, urgent, and worried that he was getting cold feet. However, he wanted to run through the main lines for his interview with Tony Bevins. I put TB on to Howarth, who congratulated him on his speech, and the conference. TB was very solicitous. 'Now, are you OK? Are you sure you're OK? Is everything under control? Are we doing everything for you that you need?' We agreed to speak again after the interview. Bevins did the interview at 5, called me and said that the words were absolutely fantastic. He went back to the office and told [Andrew] Jaspan [*Observer* editor] even he could not screw up a story as good as this one. It was great to see the kids though I was barely through the door when the phone went, and it was TB, asking if I'd heard any more from Alan Howarth. I said to TB 'Let's see if we can get through a whole day tomorrow without speaking to each other.' Alan called again and said he was worried he hadn't done terribly well in the interview. I supposed he was just getting nervous, and I don't suppose I could blame him. Amazingly, not a word had leaked out anywhere.

Saturday, October 7

They don't invent days like this. I'd gone to bed after speaking one last time to Alan, talking through the final arrangements, and after weeks of indecision and doubt, he was clearly settled and sounded happy. I still had the feeling, even though I had tried to spell it out, that he didn't realise just how big it was going to be in the short term. I said we would need someone to be with him from the moment the story broke. Fiona and I both woke with a feeling of genuine excitement. I hadn't felt like this since the morning of TB's first conference speech. I could feel everything falling into place. I called Barney Jones at the *Frost* programme, and asked him to discuss this with nobody but Frost himself. I did not give him a name, but said that a Conservative MP would be defecting to us during the course of the day, and we would like his first interview to be on *Frost*. He was gobsmacked.

During the morning, I was keen to get JP to talk to Alan. I called John at 8 when he was still in bed. JP was a bit nervous. He was keen we make clear there was no deal, and that he would have to go through all the normal procedures. Even though he had concerns, I could tell he was excited by it. JP insisted I get Alan to call him, not the other way round. The call clearly went well. JP called me and said Alan began the call by saying hello, it's Alan Howarth and I'd like to join your party. I called Tim and said I wanted him to get together all the main press officers at 5pm. TB and Peter were both worried that the media would present the whole story as being about our office operation, rather than a man of principle coming over to Labour on grounds of principle. I thought they were over-fretting, but I called Bevins again, to get him to play down my role, and I sought and got a guarantee from Barney Jones that there would be no mention to anyone of my role in setting up an interview. Alan was home now, and sounded more relaxed than ever. He had told his daughter, who was planning to be with him after *Frost* to deal with the hordes. She was obviously a great support, she told him it was the best thing he'd ever done, and she was really proud of him. He said he was incredibly relieved by that. He said he wanted to be in his constituency to take whatever flak came from his local party. Good on him. The more I spoke to him, the more I realised what a basically decent bloke he was. I think the least we owed him was to do what we could to make sure that the reaction in the party worked to his advantage, which is why JP's response was so important.

Tim, Peter, Hilary and Joy arrived around 5. Tim and Peter, in particular, were incredibly inquisitive, and desperate to know. Eventually, I let Rory tell them, and they were totally bowled over. We went upstairs to the study, and I went through the background, explained what Alan would be saying, and the forward media strategy. I explained all the procedures that would have to be gone through in relation to the party, and also some of the difficult Q & As. There would be a huge demand for background colour, and I explained the background and how it had come about, but emphasised we had to make clear this was a story about the Tory Party becoming extreme and about New Labour becoming mainstream and moderate. It must not become a story about the great Stalinist Blair operation. Bevins was calling regularly to keep me up to date with how it was being done at the *Observer*. I tipped off some of the other Sundays, so that they could chase it in their second editions. I said to Bevins it would be better if he tipped off the broadcasters, so that they were ready for the later bulletins. Tim and Peter were playing snooker on the kids' snooker table, while we waited for the story to drop. Tim said this must be how terrorists feel before a bomb goes off.

Joy asked me to go downstairs for a chat with her. She said we had to talk about our relationship. I said there had not been a problem until recently, that she had said and done things at conference that hadn't helped her. She was overly concerned with how people saw her and had failed to work at the relationships that she ought to have worked at. I said, we tried to support her but she had not helped herself. We went round in circles for a while, and eventually she went. It was clear she was unhappy, and she wasn't doing well as a result. I went back upstairs, and the phones started to go crazy. Everything was working like clockwork.

Alan called just before the news came through. He'd had three meetings with his party officials. He said it was really quite moving, as they had in fact been very supportive of him. They have had very amicable conversations. He spoke also to Alastair Goodlad [Conservative chief whip] and he too had not been at all unpleasant. Alan said he was more convinced than ever that he was doing the right thing. The bulletins were absolutely word-perfect. They could have been scripted by us. Very quickly, we got out lines from JP, from the local regional party, and from the local constituency, and all very positive. Also, TB sent him a very nice letter. Peter Hyman went off to get the papers from King's Cross. They were full of more unpleasant rubbish about me and my role, but this was a real story that would blow the lot of it away. It had been a brilliant operation. The only slight glitch was when Peter M went on Radio 5 Live, contrary to our strategy of not putting up anyone until JP in the morning. Both JP and I were furious. Of course JP, because it was Peter, assumed the whole thing had been a Peter operation, when in fact Peter was complaining he had had nothing to do with it. I had to assure him this was just a cock-up.

Sunday, October 8

Papers superb. Last night had gone absolutely according to plan, virtually in every detail. It was clear from the interviews with Tory ministers that they were all under orders to mention my alleged bullying of the BBC, and of the press more generally, but it all sounded a bit silly in the context of such a huge story. TB said that the attacks on me were designed to increase my profile and make me less effective. The phone was going all day, journalists desperate for every last piece of detail, or just people phoning to say what a coup, and a masterstroke. Alan Clark had been on *Frost*, reviewing the papers, and of course he slagged off Howarth in the tribal sort of way you'd expect, but then called me at home and simply said 'Congratters, what a bloody coup, and your fingerprints all over it.' Howarth's interviews were word-perfect. He came over as clear, principled and honest and was being chased around the studios by John Redwood, looking shifty, and Brian Mawhinney, who looked in a real panic. Howarth called several times during the day, said he felt great, his daughter was with him and he was absolutely fine. Then the usual negativity kicked in. We started to get calls about his marriage break-up. The other line that was being run was it was all stitched up by me weeks ago, that Bevins had been part of it, and kept it tight for ages to wait to do maximum damage. As if. As Howarth came over as more and more calm, the Tories started to get nastier as the day wore on, for example Gillian Shephard saying she was worried about his state of mind, and then the word eccentric started to creep in. Alan must have called seven or eight times during the day, and each time he sounded more confident. He checked in before any interview, including a Radio 5 phone-in which went extremely well. He spoke to Major later on, and said that he would describe it as frosty but courteous. Then the line started to run that it was all about his disabled son, and this had affected his mind. That got him going. These people weren't just unpleasant, they were completely bonkers to think this was going to help them. If you add in the success of TB's speech, the way that he and JP had come together, the whole success of the conference week, we were now in a fantastic position. We'd also established a formidable reputation for competence, which would itself be important as we went forward. I knew Peter was hurt that we didn't involve him in the Howarth discussions, but it was more important that we planned the real thing in detail, and it had been seen through in full.

Monday, October 9

A sense of real damage to the Tories at the start of their conference. Mawhinney was looking more and more fraught. Alan and I stayed in touch all day, as he was being bombarded with television and radio bids, and must have done ten or more interviews during the day. The two main lines of attack were why no by-election, which was easy enough to deal with, and why this particular timing? This wasn't so easy, as they were all beginning to say it was vindictive, but Alan's tone was good, and he sounded fine. The Tories' shrill response, against his soft tone, did them no favours. Then we unleashed another story we had had up our sleeves to demoralise the Tories, namely that Tate & Lyle were giving money to us, as well as the Conservatives. Peter had had a word with Birt, who said there was no problem of principle to stop Joy going back to the BBC. TB said he felt some responsibility for Joy and was sad for her that it hadn't worked out. He said he wished he'd followed his own judgement. He did it to appease Gordon. He said I hope I'm not making the same mistake putting Nick Brown in with Donald D. I said I fear you are.

Tuesday, October 10

Tony Bevins called me as I was taking the boys to school to say that I would be very proud and pleased at the extent to which the Conservatives loathed me and talked about me the whole time. 'They're obsessed,' he said. He said they were behaving like headless chickens. Mawhinney made a silly little attack on me in his speech. Peter Hyman was working on a speech for tonight's Associated Press event, but we had fucked up big time. Nobody had really checked it out, and it turned out most of the media big wheels, plus lots of the legal establishment would be there, and we didn't really have a speech worth the name. I had a go at working something up but felt absolutely lousy. I had a lie down on the sofa in TB's office and fell fast asleep for several hours.

Wednesday, October 11

We met Howarth in the Members' Lobby at the House. As we came through we ran into Clare who was nice to him, and fussed over him. I took him through to the office, and we were very conscious of being stared at, and I could sense Alan was feeling uncomfortable but at least, for now, the Tory MPs were not around. TB had not been too keen on the photocall idea, feeling it would look like we were milking it, but my instinct was we had to keep the Howarth story going as long and hard as we could right through the Tory conference.

Thursday, October 12

TB had been on at me to take some time off and try to get some rest, so I stayed at home, and slept much of the day. The phone kept going, because there was a rumour sweeping Blackpool that we had another defection planned.

Friday, October 13

TB was seeing Joy first thing. I watched Major's speech at home. It was quite effective but without a big governing idea. TB called from the train north. He was insistent with me that he had been very clear with Joy. But later, she called me and said it had been a very positive meeting, he had been very nice, had told her she was not under pressure, which was all a bit odd. Major was getting a pretty good response to the speech, everyone saying it was his best yet. In truth, it was a good makeshift job in very difficult circumstances. I was in no doubt that in strategic terms we had won the battle of the conference season. The one thing I'll say for Major is that even when the going is tough, he's pretty good at showing he's got guts.

October '95: No big idea in Major's speech

Saturday, October 14

Press was OK for Major but not brilliant. TB, as he always did after a big speech by Major, was running his mind over the medium- and long-term significance. He thought Major had put down some pretty clear dividing lines, and now we had. I had a conversation with Gordon on tax and the Budget. My main worry was the potential inconsistency in our strategy, namely arguing strongly against tax cuts between now and the Budget, and then supporting them, or at least not opposing, when they came. GB wanted us to broaden the strategy to quality-of-life issues. We had to work towards a position where one could say that Britain would be better off with Labour.

Sunday, October 15

I had a long chat with Alan Howarth, who was thinking about how to handle himself when Parliament comes back tomorrow. We discussed where any nastiness might come from, the kind of Tory MPs best to avoid. Peter Snape [Labour MP] was going to be looking after him. Some of the Tories were briefing the press that Howarth would run a gauntlet of hate, which again underlined their pathetic response to the whole thing. We were at a dinner with the Foots and the Kinnocks and Jon Snow [journalist and *Channel 4 News* presenter] and Madeleine [Colvin, his partner]. Michael [Foot] was extraordinarily nice about TB, and also about the help I gave him in his Murdoch libel case.[1] Neil was in a very dark mood, really down on everything. Jill [Craigie, Foot's wife] was in great form, particularly when she got going about Barbara Castle, and how snide and vile she used to be to the wives of Cabinet ministers. Jon cheered me up with his stories from Blackpool, where he said we hung over the Tory conference the entire time. I don't think Neil or Glenys mentioned TB or CB once, and a sense of being offside was never far from the surface.

Monday, October 16

I was dealing with Alan Howarth through the day, choreographing his arrival at the House. Heseltine was due on his feet at 3.30, so that was the best time for him to go into the chamber. TB arrived and was very bouncy. He felt the Tories were fundamentally still in the same position, and Major had not really moved forward much at all. He had had a couple of good sessions with GB over the weekend and said he could see a way through our difficulties on the Budget strategy. It meant

[1] Having been named by KGB defector Oleg Gordievsky as a Russian spy, Foot successfully sued for libel.

concentrating on long-term economic message, and changing the nature of the tax debate. He also wanted to discuss the reshuffle. He wanted to put Harriet at health but was worried that Margaret would not move or accept Leader of the House. He thought about moving JP to the Home Office, but the likelihood was JP would not want it. He was concerned, as ever, that we did not have structures or strategy in place, and that too much was being driven by his and my force of personality, but that under the real pressure of a campaign, that would not be enough. I thoroughly enjoyed Alan Howarth's arrival, which I watched from the press gallery. Dennis Turner [Labour MP] brought him into the chamber just as Heseltine was speaking. It was a bit cheap, I suppose, but it still had the right effect. Alan looked nervous as he took his seat but he called me later and said he was absolutely convinced he had done the right thing.

We had another session with GB on the Budget strategy. We had to broaden the debate, make it about quality of life and standard of living, not just about tax cuts. GB was talking about a number of tax reforms that we could put forward. A new approach on tax, and burying the idea of Labour being simply a party of tax and spend, was perhaps the most important plank in the new Labour strategy. There was clearly an argument to be won inside before we took it outside. TB and GB had just about decided that we would not raise the top rate, again despite the inevitable pressures to do so. Again, it was about signalling the scale of change, the acceptance of competitive tax rates in an enterprise economy, and also because we knew that signalling tax rises at that level would simply be used by the Tories as 'evidence' of plans or intentions to raise taxes across the board. GB was still not totally decided but TB was pretty clear. He said the minute we signalled we were raising the top rate, as far as the public is concerned, that was us back to the old ways they rejected.

Tuesday, October 17

Philip sent through a note from the focus groups last night to say that the two conferences had barely impinged upon the public at all. He felt we had to do a lot more to reach people, especially women. I discovered that Cherie was going to be doing a press conference with Clare tonight on domestic violence. It had passed both me and Fiona by, and it seems it was Clare who persuaded CB to get TB's permission. He admitted it was a mistake. TB sacked about half a dozen junior frontbenchers including Martin O'Neill [Shadow energy spokesman], which I was worried about because if I was them I'd now just go straight out and vote in the Shadow Cabinet elections to cause as much trouble as possible.

October '95: No rise in top-rate tax

Wednesday, October 19

Another Budget meeting with Gordon. We were really just groping our way towards a strategy. We had plans for a press ad on the league table of economic decline, and a campaign focused on the real state of the economy. The Shadow Cabinet results came in, and they were pretty poor. Clare Short and Tom Clarke on, Jack Cunningham off, which was totally ridiculous. TB was appalled. These fucking people must be brain dead, he said. Margaret came top. It would mean though that maybe he could get her to DTI, which was a proper job that would appeal to her more than Leader of the House maybe, and so open up health. Jack came to see TB and was clearly upset. I went in to say that we needed a line. I assumed we would say that TB would keep Jack in a Shadow Cabinet job, which is what I had been intimating to journalists. But Jack told TB he wouldn't take one. He said his pride would not take it, he could not sit there with everyone thinking he's not been elected. Tony said I need the best people in there whatever these fuckers in the PLP do. Jack would not be budged. TB told him to think about it overnight. I went to join them and said he must not say to any journalist he would not take the job, as we had briefed the papers that TB hoped he would stay in a top job. Jack turned very nasty, saying his troubles all started when I was still a journalist and I wrote something about him being the Invisible Man, and I now have the nerve to question whether he would damage Tony. He can trust me but I know I can't trust you, he said. I was pleased when later he said it was all spur of the moment stuff, and I should forget it. TB called in Harriet, Andrew Smith and Margaret – health, DSS and DTI – and I briefed them as hard facts, to try to get something positive out of the reshuffle. It was pretty clear the press felt the vote was a bad outcome for us.

Friday, October 20

TB was at Richmond Crescent working on the reshuffle. [Michael] Meacher was in a dreadful state about the appalling press he'd got, and demanded to go to see TB at home. He did so and came back to the House with a ridiculous statement he said he had agreed with TB, to go out in TB's name, about how important he was and how he was going to have lots to do. I told Michael it was eccentric to think TB could put out a statement like that as his only comment following the reshuffle, but Michael said he had been uniquely humiliated. I assumed that TB had agreed the statement, knowing that when Michael came in to see me, I would know what to do. I said to Michael that I was refusing point-blank to put it out in this form. I did not mind briefing the press on the kind of sentiment it contained, and later did so, but TB would look foolish, putting out a statement like that.

At the office meeting, we discussed the forward speech plan, and *Richard and Judy* [daytime TV chat show]. TB was still not keen because he didn't like doing the personal stuff, but I felt we needed a few personal anecdotes out there to make him a bit more real for people not inside the village. As Peter Hyman said, sometimes he doesn't look like he's part of the real world, whereas the fact that he is is one of his strengths and something that should be more widely understood. We needed some kind of message story on the reshuffle, and the closest we got to it was a sense of JP putting a team together – Caborn as his deputy, Peter M doing key seats plus Shadow Civil Service minister. As ever Peter's situation aroused trouble. We'd squared JP but then, after I began to brief on it, we discovered that Derek Foster told TB he would resign if he got Peter. This was, as JP said, fucking absurd. He had no right to cause trouble about who was working where. JP said the problem was TB kept getting himself into trouble because he made different deals with different people on the same jobs. JP ended up laughing about it, and said 'I will say this for him, he always ends up getting his own way.' The briefing I did at 4pm was OK, though it was clear they were obsessed with Peter. I pushed the scale of change and the record number of women, and that was all fine and dandy, but Peter back from the cold was the only story they were really interested in. Meacher called several times to see how my briefing went vis-à-vis him. Foster called to be assured I was building him up. Spare me the bloody egos.

Anji called later on, to say that TB was very down on himself. He said he was no longer sure he had it in him to be prime minister. If he could not even stand up properly to people like Foster and Meacher, he worried. I called him and said what's all this self-doubt stuff? He said it was all right, but he hated these reshuffles and it sometimes left him wondering whether he really had it in him.

Saturday, October 21

Peter M called early to say he felt fine about the way things had come out for him, but we did have a problem in that Foster was still threatening to resign. Lewis Moonie [Labour MP] was refusing to work with Henry McLeish at health and TB, pathetically, gave in, moving Alan Milburn [Labour MP] back to health, to give Moonie lottery and broadcasting. The other big problem was the Whips Office. Donald [Dewar], doubtless being wound up by GB and Nick Brown, did not want [Peter] Kilfoyle as the pairing whip. So George Mudie [Labour MP] was to go there. This was another concession to GB, and there was a growing feeling, as I said to TB, that GB's operation was becoming very noticeable. He said, I know you are worried but don't forget that I go back with Nick even longer than GB, and if I can't trust GB I can't trust anyone. Pat McFadden put it pretty well. He said it was not open treachery, but the placing of side bets and building up support in the case of future eventualities. TB was still working through the ranks. We got a real Old Labour glimpse when we got the message that Joe Benton [Labour MP] could not phone him because he was on dock strike duty all day. Poor Milburn didn't know if he was coming or going, as TB's jigsaw pieces kept slipping. Frank Dobson called to say that Joan Ruddock [Labour MP] was furious that Hilary Armstrong [Labour MP] had been described as Dobson's deputy on the radio. Did it really matter, provided they all worked out what their jobs were?

I was pretty knackered and the last thing I wanted to do was go to a party, but I had promised Roger Liddle we would go to his surprise party for Peter. TB and Cherie came in with the Levys. Peter made a funny little speech saying he was now a real politician, because people had sung happy birthday to Peter, not happy birthday to Bobby. TB was not best pleased at the jokes that Peter was cracking about Jack Straw, who had been hopeless in the Commons this week, all trees, no wood. Michael [Levy] was in his element, but I found it odd that he had to talk up his own role in relation to everything. It is true that we had used his house to write part of the speech, and some of our best work was done there. But the way he talked about it, you would think that the kitchen table had actually written the speech, rather than just being the place where parts of it were written.

Sunday, October 22

I suggested to TB that he extend the Big Four to include Donald, because he did have the ability to make GB behave in a more grown-up way, and he might have the same effect on the others. I saw Gavin [Millar, Fiona's brother] and he agreed it was a mistake to ally ourselves too closely with [Derek] Lewis [head of Prisons Service]. We should have been more circumspect. I wish I'd followed my instincts more closely on this one. JM was on his way to New York for the UN fiftieth celebrations, and no doubt had another plank of his fightback strategy lined up. Kilfoyle called to say that if Nick Brown was deputy chief whip it would go down really badly in the PLP and make TB less secure. As I was half asleep, I didn't really take it in, though I agreed with the sentiment. It was only later that I picked up on the significance of him saying TB would be 'less secure'.

Monday, October 23

TB was in at 9 to finish the shuffle and first saw Derek Foster, who, after all the bluster about Peter, was fine. TB also had a long session with Nick Brown. I was strongly of the view he was a bad choice, that he was too much a GB man, but TB said he was the best person in terms of calibre, and he was going to follow his instincts. I told them of the call from Kilfoyle, and he said he was fed up of people whingeing about things without giving him a solution. I had a meeting with TB and Anji. TB said he was worried about his time management. I said there were too many people allowed just to wander in and out of his office, and Anji had to have the authority to stop them. He also probably needed to use us more in terms of softening people up for the difficult decisions. He admitted he had a real problem confronting people with the really difficult decisions. He said, I know I'll have to learn to do it but I really don't like getting rid of people, and sometimes I avoid confrontation. People sometimes see it as deviousness but actually it is a desire to avoid confrontation, unless it is absolutely necessary.

Tuesday, October 24

In the car on the way in, TB said he would see Joy again today, and sort things once and for all. Anji called Joy to fix the meeting and Joy said she didn't want to come in. Anji said she had to. She clearly knew what was going on, and shortly afterwards GB called TB and asked him for a ten-day reprieve to take stock. TB agreed, somewhat to our surprise. He said the important thing was that if she went, GB supported him over it, and this was the best way to do that. But I could not help feeling that this would weaken him with GB.

Wednesday, October 25

At the Big Four meeting, GB laid out the strategy for Robin C and JP, who agreed it made sense, though Robin was being tricky. He said it was a gripping narrative up to the point where we had to decide whether to support tax cuts or not. TB and GB were clear there was no logic in saying you would not support tax cuts, if you then abstained. You might as well vote for them. RC was clearly positioning himself to the left of GB. It was one of the more tense meetings of the Big Four. TB and GB did a pretty good job of being on the same page, JP had a rather knowing smile on his face most of the time, and Robin did his best to undermine GB's confidence in his own case. I went with Fiona to the *House Magazine* party in the Cabinet War Rooms and had a hilarious chat with Teresa Gorman, who said 'You are very clever, and making life difficult for us, but believe me, you are heading for a very big fall.'

Thursday, October 26

I saw Andrew Mackay, the Tory whip, who has the job of writing notes to the Queen on what's going on in the House, and he said he had put in his latest one that I appeared to enjoy the notoriety being created for me by ministers, which was the latest confirmation to me that this was a strategy. I went home feeling pretty grim. I had been crapping blood for days, and not mentioned it to anyone, just hoping it would go away.

Friday, October 27

I got a cab in, feeling wretched again, having been up several times in the night crapping blood. TB said in the coming weeks the centre ground was wide open for us. Ros [the Blair nanny] came to the team meeting and told us that Cherie was due to present prizes at a private school tomorrow, something which had been fixed up by her [legal] clerk. TB went to a party in Hull to celebrate JP's twentieth anniversary as an MP. TB said he enjoyed it fine, but Tim said it was one of the most unfunny events he had ever been to, full of party members doing sketches of JP's life, all very odd.

Saturday, October 28

I'd been up ill again much of the night, so called Tom Bostock [AC's GP] and arranged to see him at 10.30. He thought it might be inflammatory bowel disease, so I should take a sample to the Royal Free Hospital on Monday. He advised me to go private, and I said I couldn't do that. I was amazed that nobody had ever written that when I had my breakdown, I was committed to a private hospital. He said he was concerned about the potential impact of the workload on my general health and that he had no I doubt that the stomach problem was mind-related, stress, work, pressure, adrenaline, people attacking me the whole time. When I got back home, and finally told Fiona about what had been going on, the blood and everything, she was worried. I had not bothered to tell TB about the illness but Fiona mentioned it to him, and she said he sounded worried. Anji called me later to say that he had called her, and asked her if she knew anything about it, and she had said she thought I had been ill for a while, and that I should go to hospital for tests. 'But what will I do?' TB apparently said, and she said she called him a selfish bastard, and said he should phone and ask how I was feeling.

Sunday, October 29

Clare Short was on *Frost*, so needless to say, we had a pretty disastrous start to the day. She was loose on women-only shortlists, went off on one about Page 3 girls, and then about legalising cannabis. She said it was a personal view, but it was obviously going to run and took over the bulk of TV and radio coverage for the day, thereby blowing out plans to push home on the Tories and their lurch to the right. She was without doubt the most self-indulgent and attention-seeking of all the Shadow Cabinet, and I could not for the life of me understand why TB tolerated her. She went on and on about spin and media manipulation, but it is really all that she ever does herself; look at me, look at me, I say different things to everybody else. I didn't bother TB with it, but he called about 3pm, having heard from elsewhere what she'd been up to. 'I'm afraid she's just not serious or professional,' he said. 'Presumably, this has totally screwed up the lurch-to-the-right strategy? It is an entirely self-inflicted wound, born of self-indulgence.' He asked me to get hold of her to call him. He then asked me to put out a statement saying the position on the policy was clear, and he would remind all Shadow Cabinet members of the need to express party policy, not make personal statements that could and would be used against the party. I tried to find Clare, but she was nowhere to be found. Eventually, Anji got hold of her and she spoke to TB. She was very contrite. She then blathered on about her integrity and how important it was to her, to which TB said she was not the only one, but we are in a different league now and if you want to play in the big league, you play by the new rules. He was also furious that GB had refused to do weekend interviews, because he was holding himself back for Wednesday. It is absurd that our main strategy person will only do the things he picks and chooses. He has to learn how to play in a team. It reached the stage where TB was phoning every twenty minutes to say what a disaster it all was before eventually I said 'Tony, your calls are becoming very repetitive and doing neither of us any good. You and I agree about all of this. We have done all we can for today, let's leave it at that, but please, never tell me again that Clare Short has any redeeming features, because in my view, she has none.'

The best news of the day was that Derry put me in touch with Michael Farthing [eminent gastroenterologist], who could see me at

Bart's [St Bartholemew's Hospital] tomorrow. It turned out that he lives literally at the end of our garden, and was reckoned to be the best in this field.

Monday, October 30

I woke up to confirmation of the havoc Clare had wreaked. It was not just the issue, and this debate on drugs which was neither necessary nor helpful at this time. It was the fact that it prevented us from getting up what was becoming a potent attack on the Tories. TB's statement of yesterday had made our position clear, but he remained livid with her. He also had it out with GB, telling him it was no good him saying what needed to be done, and then not wanting to do it himself. GB claimed that he had been up for doing stuff at the weekend, but that wasn't true.

I took Calum to school, and then headed for Bart's. Michael Farthing was extraordinarily nice, great manner, very well informed, not just about health, but politics generally. He diagnosed ulcerative colitis. He said it was impossible to be absolutely sure what caused it, said it was not life-threatening at this stage, that it could be treated. He asked me if I was absolutely sure I could not go private and I said yes.

I arrived at the office and TB was seeing Clare. She was being very contrite. She put her hands in her face and said 'Don't worry about me being carpeted. I've carpeted myself.' We had what was for me and Clare a perfectly friendly chat, and she apologised for not returning calls yesterday. I was getting the stomach pains more and more regularly now. Even Cherie was reasonably nice and sympathetic about my health problems, although yesterday she did phone and said to me she just wanted to say she was thinking of Fiona, because I know how difficult it can be if people around you are ill. Fiona and I fell about laughing when I relayed the conversation to her.

Tuesday, October 31

Up for another day and misery on the health front. Really, really bad. Searing pain in the stomach. There was still far too much about Clare in the press, and much to my annoyance, given that yesterday I'd been ringing all over the place, urging the press to go easy on her, she called to say that I'd obviously been putting the boot in. I told her that was nonsense, but she didn't sound so sure. It is extraordinary the power over the media that people like her imagine me to have.

TB was keen to do rail in the House and we put together a

question which crafted a sound bite. Why, just this once, doesn't he stop pandering to the right wing in his party and listen to the people of Britain? It was clear from the reaction of Tory MPs, and from Major's long, rambling defensive reply, that this attack on the move into the right was making him feel very sensitive. The exchanges got the lurch to the right up again. The campaign was beginning to bite. I can always tell when that is happening, because the press start to ask about the process, when did we decide on this particular line, was any particular research done, blah blah.

TB displayed his continuing almost comic selfishness vis-à-vis my illness, both in the irritation in his voice when he asked whether I might have to take time off, but also when, as I was leaving early because of the pain in my stomach, he called me back to ask whether we had the right strategy to deal with the right-wing press. I didn't really object, as it happens, because I could see why, in his position, he would want to know he had around him the support he felt he needed, and in any event, he had already asked me how I was. But Anji said at one point to him 'You really are so incredibly fucking selfish. Your only thought in this is the effect on yourself.'

Wednesday, November 1

Coverage of Nolan was looking like it would dwarf out the launch of our Budget campaign. TB was a bit troubled that for the second time in not very long, he had made speeches to what turned out to be a pretty influential audience, without us really working properly on the speech. Apart from the conference speech, TB was too much a last-minute merchant, and that in part was why we ended up where we did. But we also had to get our act together better in terms of thinking and planning in advance. We worked up a strategy for Nolan, which stopped short of presenting it as a personal test for Major. But afterwards TB was adamant, to my surprise, that that was exactly how we should build it up. He said Major set up Nolan, it was his thing and now he was wriggling on it. We also had a discussion with Philip G and David Hill about the continuing lack of a big economic narrative. TB said 'I am going to have to do it myself,' and we agreed the CBI speech was the place. The problem was that GB just did not speak the same language as Tony on this, and while GB was fine when they were together, when he was out and about, he was ploughing his own furrow. GB also had the ability to make what we saw as fairly clear and straightforward messages sound incredibly complicated. TB and I left for Gordon Greig's memorial service, at the end of which Heseltine said to TB 'Here we are, gathering happily in a non-political way, and now I'm off to attack you on *World at One*.' TB replied 'I am sure it is a transition you will make effortlessly and with elegance.'

Thursday, November 2

Thanks either to the steroids, or to the fact that for the first time in their life my guts were now completely empty, I felt a lot better. I faxed over some suggestions for PMQs on Nolan. TB easily won against Major. It was a walkover. Sylvie picked me up at 2 to go to hospital, and I was seen pretty quickly. Michael [Farthing] said it was chronic, incurable, but treatable. He said it was likely that I would put on a fair amount of weight, because of the steroids, and possibly become hyperactive. As if.

Back at the office, there was a major scene at the campaign management team meeting, when Peter M stormed out, apparently when he saw Charlie [Whelan] sitting there. I got home, ate a huge fry-up, watched the news and then went to bed. Cherie called, and we had a proper nice chat for the first time in ages. She said she was genuinely concerned, and that I should think of myself sometimes, and maybe not work so hard for others.

Friday, November 3

Peter called to explain yesterday's histrionics. He said that Fraser and co had got the election structures agreed, with a proper role for Peter, and GB had been due to present them to yesterday's CMT. But he didn't. He merely passed over it and Peter said TB just did his glazed look. For a moment, he said, I'm afraid he went down in my estimation, because GB appeared more powerful. He said he was being manipulated in a game between TB and GB and until it was sorted, he was having nothing to do with the whole show. He did not storm out because Charlie was there, he said, but because the general situation was a nonsense. He was not having a situation where he had to go back to being Bobby, in the cupboard, not allowed out as a person in his own right. He said GB was playing a double game the whole time. He was fine with us when TB was there, but utterly hostile the rest of the time, and making life as difficult as possible. He said he had never been so fed up.

Saturday, November 4

Still not feeling brilliant. I went for a walk with Fiona and the kids, and then Michael Farthing came round to talk to me about the disease in general, and the side effects of the drugs. Rabin[1] was shot around 8, and then died about an hour later. I spoke to Robin Cook, and we agreed the statement to put out to PA. TB was genuinely shocked. 'So he's dead then?' He said that several times during a fairly short conversation. I could sense it had maybe brought home to him his own mortality, and that of anyone who puts their head above the parapet in public life. One minute you're the prime minister, the next some lulu comes along, and you're dead.

Sunday, November 5

Rabin's death, obviously, was dominating pretty much everything. TB was out in Norfolk with his sister but we were on the phone the whole time, first sorting out flights, then doing a piece for the *Mirror* which was a mix of obituary and consequences. TB called on his way to Northolt to meet Major's plane for the funeral. The CBI speech was just a week away and I suggested he use the time on the plane to work up a proper draft. He said it might be difficult as he was travelling out with Major, and was due to come back with Prince Charles and Ashdown.

Monday, November 6

I watched the live coverage of Rabin's funeral, which was quite an event. I got a brief glimpse of TB at one point but of course the cameras were focusing on the big players and also on Queen Noor of Jordan who was streets ahead in the beauty stakes. The Nolan rebellion was bigger than expected and I did the rounds to fan the flames and say it was now about Major and his leadership. Most saw it as a rout and real bloody nose for him. TB called shortly after landing at Northolt. He had found it odd being with Major on the plane. They weren't comfortable together, Major had been nervy and on edge all the time.

Tuesday, November 7

We went to the Hyde Park Hotel, where TB was making a speech at the Q magazine awards, largely as a favour to his old mate Mark Ellen [editor and Oxford contemporary]. His little speech was well received, and he posed for pictures with some of the musicians like Eric Clapton, Ronnie Wood and Bob Geldof. He clearly liked mixing with these types, partly because he liked their kind of music, but also

---

[1] Yitzhak Rabin, Israeli prime minister assassinated by a gunman in Tel Aviv because of his determination to broker a peace with Arab nations.

in the car back he kept going on about what an extraordinary, fantastic life these people must have, their wealth, adulation from women, and not only are they allowed to be irresponsible, they are meant to be. Of course, if we win, he'll be one of the biggest names in the world, but not with the freedom these guys have.

Wednesday, November 8

Excitement in the gallery with the news that Hugh Colver[1] had resigned from [Conservative] Central Office. Mike Brunson said he was not a political street fighter like AC for Labour. TB had Conrad Black in for a chat. TB felt that although the *Telegraph* would always be Tory, we could neutralise their attacks. He also had it in his head that we could get a Labour supporter to get hold of the *Express*. We had an internal meeting on the Queen's Speech debate, TB again talking about the need for the economic narrative to be strong. If we can kill them on the economy, they have had it.

Thursday, November 9

GB did a brilliant job getting up his welfare-to-work proposals, which by lunchtime were leading the news, but at some internal cost. On the way in I bumped into Rosie who said JP was really angry and had already been speaking to Robin. They were pissed off, both at the policy and the flavour of workfare [plan for young unemployed], but more than that because they had not been properly consulted. I got TB to speak to Robin and both of us spoke to JP through the day. I called Charlie to say GB must speak to them, otherwise it will spill over. This was a classic GB problem. The policy direction was clearly right, but he worked in secret and didn't want to bring people along. So he didn't worry about getting agreement from anyone apart from TB. It wasn't so much bad politics as bad management by both of them.

TB was working at home on the CBI speech, but kept phoning up. David M and I were working on the speech for the Queen's Speech debate, which last year had not been brilliant, and we went back over some of the Neil and Thatcher debates to see what kind of Opposition speech worked best. I wrote some very strong negative lines about Major, like six out of ten young black people in London

[1] Colver resigned as director of communications saying 'What they wanted was a political propagandist; someone who would argue that everything the other side say is rubbish, their people are rubbish, and everything we say is wonderful, and our people are wonderful. I believe that the level of debate should be higher than that.'

are out of work, and what does the boy from Brixton say to that? TB was a bit squeamish about it.

Robin later complained to Tom Sawyer that he must protest about Gordon officially. I called Charlie again to say GB must speak to some of these people. It was stupid getting them offside when a few phone calls would have meant we had no problem at all. He was doing the right thing in the wrong way.

Friday, November 10

GB's failure to keep people onside had landed us with a real problem. RC in particular was on the rampage, writing a memo to TB suggesting ways of 'getting GB off the hook he has impaled us upon'. Anji and Sally were being inundated – Chris Smith, Dobson, Mo, Kilfoyle, Blunkett – all saying he never consulted. TB was letting it just bounce off him. I said to GB he must speak to some of these people and win them round, which he didn't.

Saturday, November 11

JP called from Hull re GB, he said 'It cannot go on like this.' He doesn't consult. He insists on being consulted about anything anyone else is doing but applies different rules to himself. If it doesn't change, I will move against him because everyone is sick of it.

Sunday, November 12

Awful day, felt I was achieving nothing though the phones never stopped ringing. The drugs were taking their toll, my face starting to puff out. Sally said the anger at GB was not subsiding. Tim did a very good job briefing the Beeb and the later bulletins said the CBI speech would be his most daring raid yet into Tory territory, presenting Labour as the party of enterprise.

Monday, November 13

There was huge interest in the CBI speech. TB did a good interview with Jim Naughtie [*Today* programme], said we would treat business and unions no differently, pushed our line on education as key to a modern economy. Fiona Gordon [West Midlands regional director of the Labour Party] was terrific as ever, with a group of West Midlands businessmen lined up for reaction to his speech. TB had done *GMTV* and *BBC Breakfast* and said he didn't want to do them ever again, because he hated doing TV in the morning and the questions were so superficial. We cheered ourselves up on the train journey by imagining different sorts of introduction to the speech. My favourite was 'Comrades, Comrade Chairman, Comrade Chief Execs, Comrade Rich Fat Gits.' We got back to another row with the BBC. We had agreed to do *Newsnight* but Tim discovered the whole film was being set up only to do tax. We had agreed to do a general wide-ranging interview so I phoned and said it was off. It was sharp practice and they could fuck off. Eventually, they agreed they would broaden the agenda to all the issues in the speech and apologise. I asked for a written guarantee it would be as live, no cuts.

Tuesday, November 14

Excellent coverage of the CBI speech. At the morning meeting, I suggested that given last week's trouble over the lack of discussion, it would have been wise and politic to have ensured Robin was at least aware of what was going on. GB, who was otherwise on form, went into his arms-folded, head-into-neck shell and said people who briefed against their colleagues in the *Guardian* had themselves to account for, and this was a Treasury issue. I simply repeated I thought it would be sensible to talk to him, but clearly he didn't intend to discuss it with Robin. I discussed the fallout from last week with Donald Dewar. He is a great admirer of GB, but said Gordon was incapable of simple diplomacy. 'He is basically a caveman, and can get very melancholy in his cave.' Donald felt we were heading for a big rebellion on the Budget. I said I was convinced that if the Tories could combine tax cuts and a big Labour split over the response, they were back in business. I was not at all convinced that we were all yet clear about the strategy, and before long we had to get into a position where we were advocating tax cuts at the bottom end, with some changes at the top, though TB was adamant we would not be raising the top rate.

TB was locked away in his room most of the day, working on the Queen's Speech. At the Shadow Cabinet meeting, TB started with a real stern warning about people briefing these discussions. He said whoever it was was not a serious politician, and that if people wanted to discuss these things, and make complaints about their colleagues, or general strategy, this was the place to do it. GB then gave a long, rambling and rather unconvincing account of last week's events, trying to pretend there was nothing much new in what he said, and that it had all been properly discussed through the right channels. RC sat there with a face like thunder at the end of the table. JP just glowered at GB. GB went on and on for ages and was not convincing. He then got on to his Budget strategy and said that he was going to move the agenda at the weekend on to the concept of a lower starting point tax. Those already involved in the discussions knew what he meant but it was perfectly clear that most of the people in the room didn't have a clue what he was talking about. He was simply saying enough to be able to say, if the shit hits the fan next week, that he had discussed it with the Shadow Cabinet.

I left to work on the speech, and later discovered there has been a big row between Gordon and Robin. Robin said he had not been consulted, it had not been handled well, and GB, instead of taking it on board, fired straight back at him. Then JP apparently had a pop at Harriet, which I was sorry to miss. TB said it was the worst Shadow Cabinet he'd ever attended, and he was worried that maybe he was too young, that John Smith would have held the ring. TB told Gordon he had not handled it well, to which GB did his usual 'Maybe it would be easier if I just went away.' We also had trouble with Peter M refusing to go to meetings on Thursday on long-term planning, as he had not been properly consulted. TB was generally a bit down about the Shadow Cabinet, about GB's inability to deal with people, and about what he feared was general complacency. He had told the Shadow Cabinet he would throttle the next person who said we had already got it in the bag. He was sure, as I was, that the Tories could put together a fightback from the Budget if they could get tax cuts plus Labour division running together. It was their last throw of the dice, but it was a throw and there are eighteen months to go.

Wednesday, November 15

The build-up to Diana's *Panorama* interview dominated the papers.[1] There was also a front-page story in the *Guardian* about Joy, which everyone assumed was put there by her, or certainly someone trying to help her. TB saw Joy at 5.30 on their own. Afterwards he said nobody was to say anything. He told Joy it was not working, trust had broken down. She said she was sure we could work it out. But if we disagreed she would go after the Budget. He did feel a moral responsibility to Joy and said to me later he thought maybe there are ways we could use her.

I stayed back to chat with TB. I'd worried him by telling him the *Sun* was doing something on his bald patch. Sometimes these little things got to him more than the big things. He said he wasn't sure the public would want a bald leader, and I fell about. He and I both felt the Queen's Speech debate hadn't been that great, but the

---

[1] Interviewed for BBC's *Panorama* programme by Martin Bashir, Diana, Princess of Wales revealed there were three people in her marriage.

general view was different. With the CBI and the Queen's Speech out of the way, TB said he would talk to GB and establish where we were.

Thursday, November 16

News came in that *Today*[1] was closing at 5pm and tomorrow will be the last issue. Stuart Higgins was first to tell me the news and he wanted TB to write a piece of support for the *Sun*, basically saying that *Today* readers should read the *Sun*. I said it wasn't possible, because he couldn't be seen endorsing products so directly, but we would write something. Then David Seymour [*Mirror*] called to say the *Mirror* wanted something, backing the *Mirror*. This was very tricky. I felt we had to do both without offending either, though I was in no doubt TB was more interested in the *Sun* than the *Mirror*. I got him to call Montgomery to explain why we had to do the *Sun*, as well as them. I called Les Hinton [executive chairman, News International], and said that before we committed ourselves in print to something that would clearly provoke and anger the *Mirror*, I had to have at least some assurance that there would be no return to the really bad old days at the *Sun*, because if and when that happened we would have a real problem in the party. He said he could guarantee that, though there would be no final decision about what they would do politically till closer to the election. Later, I discovered that the TB article was not going in the *Sun*, but as part of a *Sun* insert in the final issue of *Today*. I told Higgins I thought that was sharp practice and he insisted he'd always made it clear that would happen, which he hadn't.

Friday, November 17

I was worried that a mix of tax cuts, Labour division and a newly resurgent Tory press would have us in a very different position by Christmas. I told this to TB and he was alarmed. He said 'Normally if I am worried, you say don't worry. So when you're worried and I'm not, I get really worried.' He was confident we can work around the Labour division issue, provided we handle the Budget properly, but he was worried about the media. Major was having lunch at the *Mirror* today. He was consumed with what Murdoch was up to. When

[1] Newspaper founded by Eddy Shah in 1986. First national newspaper in colour, produced without crafty trade unions. Appalling colour which became known as Shahvision. Bought by Murdoch and eventually became a left-of-centre paper. AC was assistant editor (politics) 1993–94.

Higgins called asking for another piece, we agreed to do it, which meant pissing off the *Mirror* even more.

I went to the [advertising] agency to see the new PPB, which was fine. GB was getting up a weekend blitz on tax. Then out of the blue, as is so often the case, came the 'news' that Meacher had briefed journalists that Labour would be happy with four per cent inflation. It went straight round the City. TB spoke to Meacher who denied saying exactly that, though he did speak to some journalists on that subject, he said. I spoke to Meacher just after going home and his defence was that he had put the point in a question not a statement, and I said I cannot believe he could fall for that.

Saturday, November 18

Tony and I were taking our boys to the Tottenham vs Arsenal game, and we went round to pick them up. But his boys were late, so had to go without them. On the way up, he told me he felt nervous and depressed, and didn't know why. After the game, I was speaking to Bevins, and was told the *Observer* had a full account of Tuesday's Shadow Cabinet meeting. As it was read to me, TB could sense my mood. He said afterwards 'What am I going to do with these people? These are not serious people at all. I'll have to tell them that if they cannot be trusted to have serious discussions in the Shadow Cabinet, we won't have them.' Bevins said that he was picking up underlying claims that GB was out of control. I called Charlie Whelan to say I would put out a pre-emptive statement saying there had been a detailed lengthy discussion of our Budget strategy, and there was the widest possible support for GB's approach. TB's immediate suspicion was that it came from Mo. Peter M felt that since she got on to the NEC, she'd got too big for her boots and now saw herself as the next Edith Summerskill [1901-80, doctor, feminist and Labour Cabinet minister]. TB was also concerned that maybe JP was involved, as a few days earlier JP had said to him 'Sometimes I feel you only notice me if I threaten to go public.' TB called GB in the car and said we could turn it to our advantage by hitting the line that it showed that TB and GB were back in harness together, and this may annoy some in the Shadow Cabinet, and it scared the shit out of the Tories. He came off the phone in deep gloom. 'The trouble is that we have very few really serious people. You, Gordon, Peter are better than anything they have, but we don't have strength in depth.' I said, I sometimes stay awake at night worrying that I would be part responsible for getting Michael Meacher into Cabinet. 'There is absolutely no chance of that I can assure you,' he said.

Sunday, November 19

First call was from Robin Cook. 'It wasn't me,' he said of the *Observer*, adding with his customary wit, 'I think if it was me, I'd have hesitated in describing my own speech to the meeting as brilliant.' No, I said, but you have plenty of people who would do it for you. He got the point. The next call came from TB. He said GB was in a real state, absolutely furious and convinced that it was all the work of Prescott. He said it was a disaster. He was in a real gloom, even by his standards. This is just a character assassination, he said – they had clearly spoken to more than one person, and been briefed pretty fully. Both Fiona and I felt, however, that maybe some good could come out of all this, namely that GB would start to behave in a more collegiate way, and realise that a little bit of work with his colleagues would prevent a lot of the antagonism. There was little sign of it, though, and amazingly GB blamed TB for the *Observer*. TB also spoke to JP, who denied having anything to do with the *Observer*, but who also said that GB was indeed out of control, and he had to get a grip of him and wake up to what was going on.

Monday, November 20

TB was consumed by his feelings about the Shadow Cabinet. He said he would have to speak to GB to get him to get his act together with his colleagues. He would have to speak to JP to get him to behave. And he was so alarmed about Robin that he felt that the only way to deal with him was by sending a shock through the media, as we had done over Clause 4 at Blackpool when RC had been similarly messing around. TB believed that Mo, Dobson and possibly even JP were sources for the *Observer* story. TB was very down about the whole thing. He had a very frosty meeting with JP later. Basically, JP said, the briefing against Gordon would only stop if he was brought under proper control. TB took that as a tacit admission that he had been involved in the briefing. JP told him GB was a real problem for him 'because he won't accept that you are the leader and he's not'. Around 5pm, I went into TB's room as he was on the phone to Gordon and it was the same old stuff, him telling Gordon that he had to change the way he operated, otherwise it was a lasting problem.

I had lunch at the DSS with Andrew Mitchell [Conservative junior minister], who was a good gossip. He told me had been with Heseltine when they heard news of John Smith's death, and both had been rendered speechless. They knew instantly that it probably meant TB would be leader, and he would win. He still clearly felt there was a small chance of them getting things back.

I got back to the office to a problem. Dick Caborn [Labour MP, spokesman on competitiveness and regulation] had put out a press release calling for a Monopolies and Mergers Commission inquiry into BSkyB, this on the day that TB was seeing Les Hinton and Bill O'Neill [senior executive, News Corporation]. It was a pretty extraordinary thing to do and had been done without any reference to us, JP, Margaret or Jack Cunningham. It set TB off yet again, 'Sometimes I feel we have to win this election on our own, with everyone else doing their level best to stop us.' JP spoke to Dick and said to him that it was the ABC of politics – you get clearance before you say anything. I got JP to agree that I should brief that he had told Caborn he had not been reflecting party policy. I agreed the line with TB who now had a different concern, namely that it would look like toadying to Murdoch. Earlier, he'd seen Michael Meacher, who wanted to complain to him about my briefings against him, and TB was supposed to tell him he'd fucked up too often, and ended up saying he'd write to John Monks, making clear TB's total support for Meacher's enhanced status. He said he had given Mo a warning shot, but I wonder. He said he'd given GB a going-over, but GB did not give me that impression afterwards. I went home to watch the Diana interview, which was quite extraordinary, and would wipe everything out for days.

Tuesday, November 21

The papers were totally wiped out by Diana, who got a fairly good press. Nick Soames had attacked Diana, suggesting she was mentally ill, and we put up [Andrew] McKinlay [Labour MP] to attack him. TB said he was going to have more words with Robin before tomorrow, and with GB, which he did. TB's relative youth was preying on him, and he was saying again that he wondered if they were losing respect, the sense of fear that has to be there from time to time. Upstairs, there was far too much talk of Cook's people, Brown's people, Prescott's people, as if everyone was working against each other. If it went unchecked, eventually it would amount to a challenge to his authority.

We left for the Association of British Editors [editors' lobbying group] dinner. It was clear the high-profile media audience was hoping for a media speech, so they could talk about themselves, and there was a lot of muttering afterwards that he gave a bog standard party political effort. I had a very good chat with David English, who said he really believed in Blair, but he'd be very surprised if the *Mail* would do anything other than back the Tories, if holding their nose. He said Paul Dacre hated Major, but could not bring himself to be nice about Labour.

Wednesday, November 22

The papers were still wiped out by Di, Bosnia and the [Rosemary] West trial. At the morning meeting, GB was in a terrible mood, really down, so down that later I raised it with Donald. I couldn't really understand why Gordon was so low, because I was beginning to get more and more confident we were finally getting the message right in the run-up to the Budget.

TB went to the PLP where he did very well, and where he was pleased to see that even people not normally totally supportive felt real anger that Shadow Cabinet members had been briefing against each other in the *Observer*. The big task of the day was to lock JP and RC into a strategy of not opposing tax cuts. JP, however, went AWOL, presumed pissed after the *Spectator* lunch. It was the one day in the year when JP, traditionally, had too much to drink. I was strongly of the view that TB should send him a note saying this was unacceptable, and he could not miss big meetings on subjects as important as the Budget strategy. However, TB was relaxed, saying we should go ahead with the meeting, and agree the Budget strategy. TB later got JP to agree to the tax strategy, and by then I had already briefed, at TB's behest, that the PLP had backed GB and that TB intended to tell the Shadow Cabinet that he backed GB one hundred per cent and people had to understand that. TB did not mind if this was seen as bad for RC, but by the time I came back, he'd squared Robin and was now worried that it would backfire. So I did a ring round to make sure nobody was writing up my briefing as a rebuke of Robin. It was quite a delicate task to perform.

At the Shadow Cabinet, TB pretty much read the riot act. He said that when he read the *Observer* story, his reaction was not just anger, but fear and frustration that they could not discuss anything serious in this forum. He said if we found out who the sources were, he would have no hesitation in sacking them, and they would never serve in the Shadow Cabinet or a Cabinet. 'Hear, hear' went round the room.

TB and I had a meeting with Tony Hall [BBC], who was full of his usual 'I hear what you say'. TB explained to him that he felt we had legitimate complaints that were not listened to. He also said that on economic issues, it was very much the Tory agenda that dominated. He said the BBC was biased against the Tories on social issues, and against us on tax or the economy. Hall suggested GB and I go to see the senior editors 'to tell them what you are all about'.

Thursday, November 23

Another day totally dominated by GB/ RC/ JP crap. Check-up at Bart's, which was very, very good. I was very cheered up by Michael

Farthing telling me health food was bad for you, and I should stick with chocolate. We agreed that TB should do tax again at PMQs, which was fine, and the big story was Major gagging Soames, and with McKinlay having asked the question, we were into the royal story, whether we liked it or not, and it was very much Labour on the side of Di, who was now in Argentina. JM was poor again, and TB fine, but the Brown and Cook personal stuff was getting in the way of a pre-Budget strategy.

At the CMT meeting, we agreed we should raise expectations about tax cuts in the Budget, and I briefed the *Mail* and others that we were expecting and planning for a 5p tax cut. We discussed the royal situation, with Donald and Gordon adamant we must not become involved.

TB saw JP for what he said was a very frank discussion. TB said he had to decide whether he was on board or not. JP said there remained a problem with GB and he had to rein him in. TB said GB was there and he was staying there, and we had to decide whether egos were going to get in the way of what had to be done by all of us. He said afterwards that what JP lacked in cleverness he made up for in shrewdness, but he really needed to become more on board than he had been. JP looked pretty subdued as he left, and I said I would see him tomorrow with Ed Balls to brief him before his interview. Who is Ed Balls? he said, and stormed off.

Friday, November 24

I was desperate for a day off but, as ever, things got in the way. There was more crap in the papers re GB and RC. I had lunch with David English, who was great fun as ever. He said the *Mail* would almost certainly back the Tories, but it would be sotto voce. He would not be surprised if Rothermere recommended that they backed Labour. But if they did, he thought Dacre would probably resign.

I had to go back for a meeting with JP to brief him for the *Frost* programme on Sunday. I explained that the personality stuff between him and Robin and Gordon was what *Frost* would be into and he had to knock it on the head. Even though Balls was in the room, JP could not conceal his contempt for GB. I asked him what he would say if Frost asked him if he liked GB. 'I'll say we have a lot in common, like we both wear shoes.' He wanted to be able to say that the logical conclusion of a 10p starting rate is a new top rate, and I told him TB would be furious if he did. Ed said surely the message is that people should just unite in support around the leader. This sparked JP off. He said the truth was that he and Robin were excluded and their supporters felt that. He said that if people felt there should just be blind loyalty to the leader, because he did things well, we were talking Hitler. He said TB was a leader in every way, and had done things no other person in the party could have done, but it was enormous change and the party had worn it. But they had to be taken with him. At the moment there was a feeling that it was all TB and GB and the people around them and the Shadow Cabinet briefings are a response to that. It was the rest of the party saying you have to listen to us too. He said he deplored leaks, but it was a direct result of people feeling they were not properly involved. Robin was getting all the blame, but there were other people involved who were just as angry. He said he would answer questions on this in his own way. 'I'm reaching the point where I have to think about my own credibility in the party.' At least Ed would take back to Gordon the reality of what JP was saying. I told TB about JP's general mood and he said we had to get together a strategy for dealing with it all. 'I just do not know what I'm going to do with these people. They are absolutely impossible. If they can't get on God knows what we do. This could lose us an election unless we stop it.'

Anji was organising a visit to a family in Enfield on Monday, as part of our tax campaign. As ever, because of Jennifer's Ear,[1] we were checking out every last detail. Then, just as I was leaving, we got calls from GB's office, wondering why we were doing a visit which would blow out GB's press conference on Monday. I said has it ever crossed your one-track GB minds that we might be doing this as a concerted effort, a co-ordinated strategy, to show that all the key players would be singing the same tune? TB was getting more and more exasperated, and I was feeling more and more that if only the Tories could get their act together on this, we could be in real trouble.

Fiona and I went out for dinner with Charles and Carole Clarke. Charles said he thought TB was performing well, but the impression was that I was holding the show together. The rest of the discussion was largely about Gordon. Charles went further than others had done, saying that he felt GB could actually lose us the election. He said that if TB and GB had stood for a leadership election, GB would have been humiliated. TB owed him no obligation at all. TB feels he

[1] During the 1992 general election campaign, Labour featured, in an election broadcast, a five-year-old girl who had waited a year for a simple operation. The Conservatives revealed she was the granddaughter of a Conservative supporter, and the resulting storm over the ethics of using a child in national politics was widely thought to have damaged Labour.

has to concede to him the whole time, because GB pulled out, but he shouldn't. The real problem, as Fiona said, was that TB would not stand up to GB, because he did feel that he owed him something for having stood down.

Saturday, November 25

There was a big piece by Patrick Wintour in the *Guardian*, re GB/RC. Not good. Also, Peter Riddell and Andy Marr did a *Today* programme discussion, Riddell in particular pushing my line that it was about personality not policy. I called TB ten minutes later about something else, and he said he'd already had GB on complaining about Peter Riddell pushing my line. 'Everything I do at the moment just seems to make things worse with him,' he said. We discussed whether to put out words on the Budget. GB had made it clear to TB that he preferred TB to be the first to hint publicly that we might not oppose tax cuts, because there may be flak in the party about it. I was getting very bad vibes about the way things were going at the moment. I warned TB repeatedly that I felt we were getting into very dangerous territory. The public could understand personality clashes but they knew they represented something else. Just before I took the boys to football, Gordon called for a full-scale blast, filled with real anger. He clearly believed that I had deliberately briefed PA to give the impression that there would be greater consultation with the Shadow Cabinet, thereby communicating the sense that he had not consulted before. You can always say there should be greater consultation, he said. But look at it, you now have Mo in the *Telegraph* saying that she should be consulted, because she is the spokesman on youth. Who the fuck is she? He said 'these people', by which I think he meant JP and RC. You cannot give them anything because if you do, they take more. You're giving them concessions, and so rewarding them for cheating and deceiving and leaking. He said he knew for a fact that JP had briefed the *Observer*. I said that was not remotely proven. But he was adamant. He was on for ages; it was a long dirge of discontent and dire warnings that things would get worse and worse. I called TB from football, and said I really believed we were into dangerous waters, that we were about to take a dive in the polls and he had to get these people in on Monday, and tell them that they were all as bad as each other, and that he did not intend to put up with it any longer. The trouble is, he said, that they basically know I cannot really do without them, so I don't have any real sanction over them. GB has to be Shadow Chancellor, and Robin has to be in the Big Four. I said they had to be shocked into fearing that they were responsible for the damage that has been done. GB was treated like a mullah, surrounded by his disciples, who could see nothing other than through their own perspective.

I called round the Sundays trying to push a modernisation-goes-on line, but it was difficult. Then Rosie called to say the Sundays were asking why JP was not going to see Clinton. I said this is fucking Toytown. I called TB again, who was now playing his guitar and there was something surreal about the conversation: me exasperated, at the end of my tether, emphasising to him how bad I felt things were, and him gently strumming his guitar, occasionally humming, occasionally replying to me if I raised my voice loud enough. Robin called to say he was taking legal advice about the suggestion that he had briefed the *Guardian*. Peter M said he was sure that Charlie Whelan had briefed [Andy] Grice on TB telling the Shadow Cabinet that they will be sacked if they briefed against colleagues. We were going through a period of absolute mania. I was getting really exasperated by the Big Four and by TB's inability to sort things out, and to stand up to the other three in a way that made them behave.

It was so bad, the only thing to do was laugh about it. I rechristened the children John, Robin and Gordon, and when Rory and Calum misbehaved, I threatened them with the sack. Then, just as things were calming down a little, I ate a piece of toffee and a bloody crown came out, and I had to go to the London hospital to try to get it put back in. I got the papers later, and there were quotes from what TB had said to the Shadow Cabinet. It tended to underline his own fear that his authority been weakened and that there was a lack of respect in certain quarters. I said to TB I felt he should call the Big Four together on Monday and really thrash it out.

Sunday, November 26

Robin called at 8.45 to say he'd seen some of the papers and wondered what the rest were like. Much the same, I said. He said he felt very hard done by, as he'd not done anything at all outside the Shadow Cabinet room. He felt he had done what he'd had to do, to challenge GB and get him to water down a proposal he strongly disagreed with, and make the point that there should be more consultation. Since then he found himself continually briefed against by 'Brown aides' and he failed to see how he could be expected just to take it as he was now getting the blame. I told him that GB had insisted to me that his people were under orders not to brief and he just laughed. I had to cut him off because I said I wanted to see JP on *Frost* and I said I was very worried about John. He said you're right to be worried.

He is under great stress and very emotional. As it turned out, JP was fine, very good about GB, constantly saying how strong his proposals were, though he got a bit stuck when Frost kept on about whether the tax plans were for a year or for a Parliament. It created a problem, and also gave GB and his people something to moan about. The direction of the party was clear and RC was driven if anything by his negative view of GB, as was JP. It sometimes felt as if they were looking for issues to fall out over. My big worry was that it would all feed into one of our big weaknesses, namely that this was all about Blair but the rest were a disaster, who did not believe in this New Labour thing at all.

Monday, November 27

Breakfast with David Frost at the Carlton Tower Hotel. He was convinced we were on course for a big win. He was desperate for us to agree to a TV debate when the election came, and to back him as anchor. I had very mixed views on a debate. On the one hand, TB was good on TV and should win easily enough. On the other, if we stayed ahead then bizarrely, it would be the prime minister, not TB, who had the underdog advantage. But my main concern was that with our media as it was, there would be enormous focus on the process and the packaging, and there was a danger it would add to the reasons why people were turning off politics and political presentation. But David had no such doubts. He thought politics needed it. Though he was a messy eater, I always found David funny, interesting and charming. With most people, I would find it unacceptable to have them lighting up a cigar, and billowing out smoke all over the place while I was eating, but with him it was somehow OK.

Back at the House, it was all fairly quiet. Paddy Ashdown had survived a knife attack, so there was plenty of interest in that. We spent most of the day working on the Budget speech. Donald came in, and we said he should start to sound out support for not opposing tax cuts. TB said people may not want tax cuts if asked about them in opinion polls, but they will happily take them if they are offered them in a Budget. GB agreed on all the main lines and how we should pursue them. I felt we really had to go for this. It is the last throw of the dice for them and if it fails, they've had it.

Chris Powell from the agency had a very good idea of booking the electronic billboard in Piccadilly Circus so that we could put up our main Budget messages and get some coverage tomorrow before, during and after the main speeches.

At the House TB was in fine form. He'd done a new intro and a new ending to his speech. He was dreading it, and was nervous, pacing up and down, asking me to throw difficult interventions at him as he went through the more important passages of his draft. GB was being helpful, and kept popping in with ideas. At one point, Gordon and I were throwing interventions at TB, so quickly that he put his hands up and said hold on, hold on, it won't be as bad as that. The only big row of the day came when Ed Balls and David Hill, who had been briefing JP, Margaret Beckett and Chris Smith, came down looking worried. They'd been briefing them on the main lines to take in post-Budget interviews, and when Ed said we would be abstaining on any income tax cut, JP claimed not to know and was clearly steamed up. David was sufficiently anxious to say to TB he should speak to JP, but TB was by now fully focused on the debate. I called Rosie, and I said, what was the problem? He was aware of our overall strategy, and whilst it is true this was specifically discussed at the meeting he missed last Wednesday when he didn't come back from the *Spectator* lunch, he knew this was the basic position. He must not roll around the place causing difficulty on this. Then, perhaps going over the top, I said if he hadn't been pissed last week, he wouldn't have missed the meeting.

Precisely one minute later, JP appeared at TB's door and said to me 'If you've got something to say to me, say it. In the Shadow Cabinet room, right now.' He was furious both with Ed for what he called snitching and with me for responding in the way that I did. He said 'When I explode, you'll know it. I just asked if that was the strategy and if he was including it in his speech, because it had not been specifically discussed.' I said it had been discussed, and I thought the two of them discussed it too. He said TB often left a meeting with one impression, which is not always the impression others have. He said this was a case of the party being bounced again, and the party would not take it much longer. People were fed up being bounced. He said, I can see the political arguments for it and I can see there are some circumstances when you have to bounce the party, but let's at least admit it is being done. He said that he was excluded from the discussions on that, and he'd grown used to it, and this had all been sorted by TB and GB with Donald helping on the side. 'I've accepted that, but I'm going to do things my way.' I believed that TB had squared this two weeks ago, and he said this was typical Tony. He thinks he's agreed something when he hasn't, and he tells everyone that he has.

We got the press releases from the government at 2.30 and GB quickly identified some good lines – a massive hike in CAP [Common Agricultural Policy] spending, cuts in training and education, PFI [Private Finance Initiative] the focus for extra health spending. As to the specific tax cut, we would have to wait for Ken Clarke to be on his feet. When he announced that it was 1p, I felt we were home and dry. TB was terrific at the start, poor in the middle, absolutely brilliant at the end. That was what people remembered, so when we came out of the chamber, the general view seemed to be he'd done well. The economic team in the Shadow Cabinet room did some excellent fast number crunching, so we were able to build proper analysis on top of the instant reaction that TB had delivered. TB came back from the chamber pretty relaxed, and said later that maybe for the first time he had felt a sense of real control in there, that he had nothing to fear from them or their arguments, and that the Tories were close to being broken.

Wednesday, November 29

Up at 6, ready for the post-Budget interview blitz. I was at TB's by 7 and he wasn't there, because he was taking Euan to the tube. At 7! Poor kid. His first interview, with Jim Naughtie, was dreadful, one of the worst he had done, and he knew it. The moment he came out, he said why did I do that? That was dreadful. I didn't get over any of the messages, not even 7p up, 1p down. He got better as we went on and by the time he finished with Sky, he was on good form. GB had done well on the Budget strategy, but Philip said he had been with GB and his crew till gone midnight working on the ministerial broadcast. He said it wasn't like a team, but a court, chaotic and full of paranoia. Murray Elder, Ed [Miliband], Joy, Charlie Whelan, Michael Wills [TV producer and prospective parliamentary candidate], Douglas Alexander [former GB researcher, later an MP]. He said it wasn't pleasant. I suppose that as it had been Budget time, it was inevitable that GB would be seeing things through the Treasury perspective even more than usual. We worked on Gordon's broadcast script, and Peter Hyman came up with a very good paragraph saying 'you must be as disappointed as I am with this Budget', but the rest of it was all a bit downbeat.

President Clinton was in town and unfortunately was going into overdrive in his praise of Major, first at the press conference in Downing Street, then in the address to both Houses, and later at the dinner. He was really pushing out the boat, so much so that only half in jest, I asked his press secretary, Mike McCurry, if he couldn't rein him in a bit. We got the police escort to Wingfield House [US ambassador's residence]. A minute or two after we arrived, Clinton and Hillary appeared and they had a brief chat in the hall before the two of them went out to do a doorstep. It went OK, but it was not going to penetrate the wall-to-wall Major/Clinton coverage, though whether it mattered much at this stage, I wasn't sure. The meeting itself began with a bit of an embarrassment when TB introduced me to BC as a 'legend in his own lifetime', which must have baffled him a bit. The chairs were laid out as for a formal bilateral meeting, TB and BC facing out to the rest as the two sides lined up opposite each other. He was much bigger than I imagined him to be, both taller and fatter. He had enormous strong hands and size 13 feet that looked even bigger. He said that once he and Boris Yeltsin swapped shoes to see who had the biggest feet, and Clinton did.

They went over Ireland, pretty perfunctorily, with Clinton asking TB where it would end, when surely at this stage he was likelier to know the answers. Then Bosnia, again TB saying why we were supporting the government, and how it was vital that Congress backed him on it. They only really got into their stride when they talked politics. TB went through New Labour, explaining what he was trying to do in general terms, and in all the different policy areas, which Clinton said sounded a lot like what he was trying to do. McCurry said TB's conference speech had been closely studied in the White House. Clinton had an interesting line about how achievement was less important than definition in the information age. He said there is no point saying what you've done, keep saying what you're going to do, have a clear direction. Reagan and Thatcher did it and didn't have to achieve that much. Like TB, he talked a fair bit about the polls and media, and like TB, he was at his best when talking about how to win support and manage change. He said the Congress having gone against him, and with the press more in conflict mode, he was always striving to get his message over to people direct. He was hugely impressive on strategy, especially considering he had just forty-five minutes' sleep on the plane last night. He said it was important to any progressive party of change to have mainstream values, and mainstream economic policies. They got on pretty well, though I thought Jonathan overdid it when he said he could feel a very special chemistry. Clinton did appear very solicitous, and wished us good luck as we left. McCurry asked me what would be helpful for him to brief. I said to stop him greasing Major so much. McCurry was one of those people I liked instantly. He was laid-back, very funny, but clearly on top of his job. We talked about campaign methods, and developed some of the themes TB and Clinton had been discussing. He thought they had hit it off pretty well, and Clinton had said afterwards he appreciated TB's political observations. TB called after the Downing Street dinner, which he said was fine. He said he hated being photographed arriving at the door, because it looked so presumptuous.

Thursday, November 30

JM got a great press for the Clinton visit. There was nothing much we could do about it, and we barely scored on TB's meeting with Clinton, other than pictures of him and CB going to Number 10. CB told me she hadn't much liked Downing Street. In particular, Major had been all over her with false bonhomie, making jokes about tape measures and whether she would want to change the curtains. She also didn't like the feeling of being his guest. But more important, I think it hit her for the first time that it really wasn't a home so much as a stately home, that there would be no real privacy, no escape or freedom from the people who work there round the clock, and it would be very difficult to bring up children there. TB said that although it was perfectly jolly, he didn't really like being there as JM's guest. Also, by the evening we had been getting pretty sick of Bill shoving the boat out for Major.

Friday, December 1

The papers were already getting bored with the post-Budget exchanges, but we had to keep going at it. The attention span of the media was now so short. It used to be that the Budget would be the main story for days afterwards. And people were bored with New Labour already, too familiar with it, and we had to start making a fresh impact. It also meant TB had to start meeting more people and being seen around the place more. There was a danger of him being seen as too Westminster-based.

Saturday, December 2

TB called in the morning, and said he was going to check out through Derry, who knew Michael Farthing, whether I was really fit again. He said 'This is entirely selfish. If you disappear, the whole show stops.' I assured him I was fit. Yesterday, Charlie Whelan mentioned Andy Grice might be doing a 'Labour to dump 50p rate – no top rate'. He said that TB and GB had discussed this, and asked Peter to try to get Grice not to write it. I called Andy and got the distinct impression he was going to splash on it, ahead of their Budget poll showing that it had bombed, and indeed we had gone up since Tuesday. I said it was premature, no decisions taken, blah blah blah, and I would dump on it heavily. I didn't care who had told them, he was jumping the gun, and I would make that clear. Amazingly, they didn't run the story. Peter M, who had also weighed in, said he had never known a case of the *Sunday Times* backing down on a story. He said they'll hate us when we do it.

Sunday, December 3
Peter called round for dinner to go through his book chapter on TB [in *The Blair Revolution*]. I felt it was too slavish in some parts and too critical in others. He gave the impression he lacked self-confidence, was not a good politician, glazed over when listening to colleagues, and paid no attention to detail. Peter M said he'd been discussing with TB whether we could get a system in place to allow me more time off, possibly an understudy.

Monday, December 4
Went to a meeting with Jonathan, Philip, Peter M and David. We agreed we had to get TB reconnecting in a way that he currently was not, that he had to be out with real people, had to be seen to be tough, as he had been over Clause 4 vis-à-vis the party, and now set out tough messages to the public. I suggested, for example, that he should take our education policy document out to teachers, particularly opponents, and try to win them over, and be seen to do so. PG felt he needed some kind of national tour/crusade, connecting, winning people over in argument. DM put it well when he said that people really took to TB because they felt he was different, and there was a danger that the more time he spent in Westminster, the more he became like just another politician. I discussed this with TB later. He had to be more human, less like Prince Charles, more like a human being. By now, I said, he should have an image founded on acceptance that he is tough, decisive, clear-sighted, in touch, someone who understands what people's lives are like and what politics can do for them. We agreed that the central message of tomorrow was rights and responsibilities built around a new contract between citizen and society.

Tuesday, December 5
TB and I had a long chat about GB. He's brilliant but flawed, he said, again. 'He is like Peter in that he sees things very clearly for other people, but is less clear about himself. I can remember the moment

when in the back of my mind I felt he would not be leader. It was after the general election when Neil had stepped down, and GB would not even contemplate challenging John Smith. I felt he could have won, that the party might have wanted to jump a generation. But he would not run, no way, and he didn't want me to run for the deputy leadership. And something in me began to wonder if he really had it in him; whether maybe it was something he preferred to want, rather than to be. Yet if only he'd handled himself differently, he would be leader. 'I never actively wanted to be leader and I never expected to be leader. I was always sure, like most other people, that it would be GB. It's because of his personality and his way of working that he's not married. He is brilliant in many ways but not complete yet. He could still be leader. I would be perfectly happy to be under him. I always felt he would be leader and I would be a reforming Chancellor and then go on to do something in Europe. But when John died, it was not as clear. In fact it was clear to me that I would stand and not Gordon.' I told him of the time Fiona was interviewing Gordon in Edinburgh, and the two of us went up to spend the weekend with him and Marion Caldwell [QC, Brown's girlfriend until 1994], who was lovely. But you wondered how she managed to stay with him. Her flat was nice and homely. His was a tip. First, there was the moment when the photographer asked him to put on more casual clothes, and he came back having changed the colour of his tie. He also, or so he said, had gone out and bought some pastries, and kept asking whether we would like these pastries, which we never saw. And then when the photographer produced his own packed lunch, Gordon helped himself to a sandwich. We also noticed a mug keeping the window open in the kitchen, like it was a student flat.

Wednesday, December 6

We discussed TB's 'image problem'. I identified it as an odd mix of being both too aloof and too familiar. We were falling between two stools. People were not sure what he was about. I said we seemed to be too focused on the Tory agenda, and we had to open up a clearer and more definitive left-of-centre agenda that was still New Labour. TB had the excellent idea of publishing a pre-manifesto next year, and then going out on a huge nationwide tour in which he consulted and debated and at the end of the process we publish his contract with the people. I liked it. I could easily see this as being the means by which he could reconnect. He said it would provide focus, get attention and allow him to visit every key seat. Anji later told TB that the feeling in Walworth Road was that his authority was damaged,

December '95: TB's 'image problem' discussed

that people felt his best friend was deceiving him and he would not face up to the reality.

Thursday, December 7

A meeting with TB, GB and Peter, at which GB and Peter had a row about the way we had handled JP and RC. GB's line was basically that the recent row was badly handled and instead of appeasing them we should have 'defeated' them. He said we were presenting it as a personality clash when we should have said it was resistance to modernisation and it would be swept aside. He was adamant he had done nothing to start the row, or fuel it, and Peter said he didn't need to because 'you have a press officer who was doing it for you'. GB said 'I could sort JP if you wanted me to, but I would do it differently to the way you guys do.' He said it would come back to haunt us because we had not resolved the basic policy issues at all. He went on and on, and I felt it was unrealistic. I said it was daft to think we could just ignore them or wish them away. GB said he felt we did too much to keep them on board, and at heart we were talking policy differences not a personality clash. I said JP just wanted to be properly involved, that was all, and if we kept him informed and involved, there was no problem. RC may be a different case but it was less important. If we had JP on board, and engaged, RC's influence and ability to cause trouble was restrained. It all got terribly heated. TB, who had watched first GB and Peter, then me and GB, have it out in a pretty open and sometimes brutal way, said later it had been therapeutic that Peter and Gordon had had a big row. TB was beginning to worry about who was around at Christmas. He said he was not confident about leaving JP in charge of strategy and media if we were off. Later, another bad scene with Fiona, who said she was having to hold all the minutiae of family life together, while I was off on this exciting glamorous life. I said it didn't feel like that, and it was going to get worse not better as we got nearer an election.

Friday, December 8

I was barely awake when the phone rang and it was TB complaining about the BBC report on his [Glasgow] *Herald* interview, saying that we had ruled out tax-raising plans for the first term of a Scottish Parliament. He said it was an outrage, that all he said was that there were no plans currently. So even before I was out of bed, I was having to make a round of calls to journalists and politicians in London and Scotland. It rather perfectly proved Fiona's point that it just never stopped.

I was working on a speech for tonight on the Tory Lie Machine, which was very strong and detailed all the recent activities at Central Office. TB read it on the plane and was a bit worried that it went too far, that it was too strong for him and was best delivered by JP. I felt sure we had to go for the Tories at their own game, and get our retaliation in first. Yes, it was a tough speech, but it was about time they felt some heat, and time that our people saw TB putting it on them. TB phoned his aunt in Glasgow, as he always did whenever we were in Scotland, leading me always to ask why he only ever phoned her when he came up here, as if a phone line from England was somehow different. He said it was one of his little ways. We got to the Hilton in Glasgow, and I watched the local TV news, which was dreadful, ultra negative, and I called to complain.

Tim called to say both BBC and ITN were keen on the speech, and in particular the line we had briefed on the Tory Lie Machine, which prompted TB to worry once more whether it was the right thing for him to do. I called Peter to get him to call TB at the hotel and put his mind at rest. Peter thought it was fine, but TB also wanted to speak to GB. He thought it fine too, as long as he didn't mount personal attacks himself. The speech went fine, but TB was still worrying about it afterwards. He never liked doing the rough stuff, because it reduced him to the level of other politicians, but there were times when an anti-Tory message would only fly if he did it. He did one of his 'I've got a great team' numbers later on, and said he sometimes wondered how we got through the work we did. So did I.

Saturday, December 9

The Lie Machine line really worked. *Scotsman* splash, big in most of the papers. Chris Leake of the *Mail on Sunday* came on, and knew about the [recent] TB/Prince Charles dinner, and understood it was all about education. I said he understood nothing and we would not even confirm it had happened. He would obviously write whatever he wanted so there wasn't much point helping him either way. At Stirling University, the students' Q&A was excellent, TB at his best, engaging, funny, motivating. The more he did these things, the more convinced I was they should form the basis of our election events. The students came out buzzing.

Once home, I spoke to Charles Anson [Buckingham Palace press secretary] re the *Mail on Sunday*. During the conversation, he dropped in that JM was seeing Charles next week to pave the way for 'the divorce'. He just dropped it in, so gently that it was a few moments later before it registered. I said did you say what I thought you said, and he said yes. I said it's good job I'm no longer a journalist, and said it was very kind of him to feel he could trust me with that kind of information. On the dinner, we agreed we would simply confirm it had taken place but not brief in any detail at all.

Fiona was in a real state again, saying life was unbearable because of the job. She said I had to see it from her perspective, that it was as if my relationship with TB and the office had replaced my relationship at home, which I said was ridiculous. She said she was beginning to resent TB because he put me under so much pressure, and he was basically selfish. I said he was in a pressured job and he shared the pressure round the people he felt he could trust and rely on, and I was one of them. She said he didn't deal with problems properly – e.g. Joy, e.g. Peter, e.g. his relationship with GB – and I ended up picking up the pieces by working round the clock to hold it together.

Sunday, December 10

Things were still bad with Fiona and she was in tears when I left. I was going to have to be much firmer with TB about putting limits on the work I did. I spoke to Peter M later and went through all Fiona's arguments, and he said the real 'indictable charges' against TB were his failure to deal with Joy, and his failure to stand up to GB, both of which had serious knock-on effects for me. Anji said it was also crazy that I had to spend so much time with JP. But then again, she said, you are the only one in our operation that he trusts, so it is inevitable. By the time Jonathan and I got to TB's, I was in a pretty foul mood. After going through the briefing on Austria [Blair was to visit Vienna for the Austrian elections], he said to me 'How do we conquer the cynicism that is growing up?' I said surely by going back to basic promises, on issues that really matter, in language rooted in values, that we are confident of meeting. And we need to articulate a new politics. The plane was delayed by fog, so the conversation went on, and he said he was worried that people were getting bored with him. He felt he had lost the edge, and he was also worried at his seeming inability to get the others to work as a team, which underlined the sense that we were a one-man band. He was clearly going through one of his more vulnerable phases. He was showering me with flattery. He said he had very nearly not asked me to be his press secretary, because he feared I would not do it. I could never work out whether his flattery, which was in marked contrast to my regular piss-taking of him, was totally genuine. But he regularly said that he felt GB, Peter and I were touched by genius, which explained our flaws too.

It was interesting the Austrians were so desperate for him to go out and take part in their elections. We worked on the speech and the script for tomorrow's press conference with [Franz] Vranitzky [Chancellor of Austria]. Before dinner with ten or so rather earnest Austrian journalists, Vranitzky's team briefed us on the very careful line they wanted us to tread on the euro. Though they were pro, they didn't want that to be the story out of tomorrow. TB was on terrific form during the dinner but like me, he couldn't understand how the Austrians looked so fit and healthy considering they were in the middle of a campaign. He said 'Campaigning is the one activity sure to make you look like your passport photo.' After the dinner there was a private chat just with the politicians. Vranitzky said that Major regularly peddled the line at summits that he was pro-European and there was really no difference between him and TB. He said we should also be wary of the Tories' closeness to the French. TB said left-of-centre parties had to find better ways of communicating together. Right-wing parties still had a lot of the best tunes, and they were still better at communicating together.

Monday, December 11

We were staying at the [Vienna] Hilton where TB, Jonathan and I had breakfast to go over the words for the press conference. It was one of the most bizarre campaigning events of our time. There was an enormous long slogan running along a fold-up backdrop, which meant that even if the cameras filmed the whole backdrop, you wouldn't be able to see the words. The press were sitting around at coffee tables, seemingly mingling with people who had just walked in off the street. The sound quality was poor, and yet nobody seemed to mind. Vranitzky spoke, and gave a long and turgid preamble about social democracy, with nothing about the campaign at all. TB looked on and I could tell he was wondering when the guy was going to say something which might actually connect with the voters. TB was much briefer, and sharper, and a lot of the questions were to him, about New Labour. On the plane back, we worked on TB's speech to the British Board of Deputies, which he wanted to make about social morality. We wrote in a muted passage on Philip Lawrence's death.[1] TB wanted to make the link between wider social breakdown and the lack of moral purpose, whilst being sensitive to the charge of

---

[1] Headmaster of St George's Roman Catholic School, Maida Vale, London, who was stabbed to death outside the school gates in December 1995 when going to the aid of a pupil who was being attacked.

ambulance chasing. But sometimes single events like this acted as symbols. TB's speech was delayed because of a bomb scare, but it went fine. He liked the Jewish community, and it was the right place to give that kind of message. He also felt the Jewish community had a significant influence on the way others thought about things. He felt, for example, that if there was a general sense that the Jewish community were supportive of us, it helped our reputation on the economy.

Tuesday, December 12

At 10 we had the first meeting of the general election planning group, the official one to be chaired by Peter M, but with JP in attendance. There was the kind of jollity you get in the first of a meeting like this, and also a certain excitement to it. Although there had been a considerable amount of planning already, you had the sense that this was now planning in earnest. Peter chaired the meeting exceptionally well, drawing JP in, soliciting the views of others as he laid out some general ideas on what he thought we should do. We went over the lessons to learn from previous campaigns. Peter went straight on to what he saw as the things we needed to achieve out of this group – clear message, consistency and good communications between all the various parts of the campaign. I went through some of the weaknesses I sensed from the media side of the fence. There had to be political ownership of the manifesto by everyone, otherwise there would be different voices on the same issues. People had to rally round when anyone fucked up. There would inevitably be mistakes made and the press would want us to play the blame game. We had to avoid that. I started to get calls from the gallery to say that David Lightbown [Conservative MP for South-East Staffordshire] had died. The press were terribly excited, because his majority was just 7,000, which would clearly be under pressure.

Wednesday, December 13

Peter Hyman confirmed to me that Harriet was thinking of sending her second son to a grammar school. I exploded and wrote a letter advising her strongly against. I said it would result in political damage to herself; it would be awful for her son, because he would be thrust into the media spotlight; and it would damage the party at a time when the post-Oratory wounds were healing. I expressed myself very forcefully. I showed TB my letter and he said I couldn't send it. I should talk to her instead and say what I thought, but don't send her that letter. Even he was baffled, saying she had just about got over all the fuss about her first one going to the Oratory, and now she decided to go even further. TB and I went over all the old arguments we had been over so many times at the time of the Oratory row. I said this was the issue that most worried our own people. He said whatever you do, make sure Rory and Calum get a good senior school, because if bright kids are not stretched they go off the rails.

At the meeting of the Big Guns, Robin Cook circulated a paper on the euro referendum, saying he was worried our holding line of 'popular consent' was wearing thin, that the Tories were going to do it, it was inconceivable we would not have to follow in offering a referendum, so we should do it first. He put the case pretty well but, as I expected, GB put a very forceful case against it, and I found myself in broad agreement.

I went to the press gallery, largely to find out how much interest there would be in going with him on a trip to the Far East. This was building up as the next big office vs home row. I'd promised Fiona I wouldn't go, but the media interest was clearly going to be huge, and TB was starting to make it clear he would want me with him if he went ahead.

Thursday, December 14

Central Office announced that Charles Lewington [political editor, *Sunday Express*] had been appointed to [former Conservative director of communications] Hugh Colver's job. I toyed with the idea of going in to rough him up a bit, but decided Tim should put out a line that I had taken the day off to celebrate.

Friday, December 15

Fiona and I had dinner with Philip and Gail at the River Cafe. PG said there was a pattern emerging at CMT meetings, where GB effectively overruled anything that was not his idea, and TB went along with him. He said TB should not be in meetings that he does not chair. It undermined his authority. The problem was if TB had agreed GB should chair these meetings, but if he wasn't there, GB and Peter just contradicted each other the whole time, and nothing ever got decided. PG said we couldn't let anything get in the way of a strong campaign. He said I would be key to it because I was the only one who was liked and trusted by TB and JP, and at least respected and feared by GB and RC. He said he was worried that GB could destroy our campaign unless we kept very close to him. Both Gail and Fiona said how time-consuming and wasteful it all was, dealing with these relationships endlessly. PG recalled his time at GB's flat to go over

December '95: Cook worrying about euro referendum

the recent broadcast. He was sure they spent the whole time slagging us all off as well.

Saturday, December 16

I took the boys to Swansea vs Burnley, reading the papers on the way, and rather alarmed at just how much about me there was in them. I had to rush back because we were going out for dinner with the Blackburns [family friends]. Hugo Young [*Guardian* political commentator] was there, said he thought the general election was won. Tom Bower said he had been at a dinner last night with Nick Lloyd [former editor, *Daily Express*] and other Tory journalists and 'they were actually terrified of you'.

Sunday, December 17

I called TB as he was preparing for tomorrow's statement on the Madrid [EU] summit. He said he intended to say it was time for a great national debate on the biggest issue facing the country. We simply cannot go on pretending this isn't going to happen. I said fine, good idea, but it was important he was not seen to be totally on one side of the argument. He said fine, but we cannot leave the argument as one between JM and the sceptics. We had to lead the debate now. People may not like the single currency but they do not want to be left behind. His instincts were clearly pro Europe, and that risked being portrayed as pro the single currency whatever, but he said that was a risk we would have to take. It is better to have clarity, he said. Without clarity we lose everything. His view was that it was ultimately in our interest to join, but I was worried this was the issue that would lose us a lot of the new support we had built up.

Monday, December 18

The main focus of the day was the Commons statement on Madrid. TB was confident we could really pin Major down on it, make him look weak, but the reality was all too apparent in the chamber, where TB looked like a man on his own and JM was able to exploit our divisions. JM, as Bruce [Grocott] pointed out immediately afterwards, was clearly very happy with the position he had and looked comfortable with it. TB looked personally comfortable, but the party behind him did not. TB was far more confident about Europe than I feared he should be and the statement was far from being a success. He came over better on the news than in the chamber, but I felt this was one of those situations where maybe TB's approach was intellectually sound, but politically vulnerable.

Tuesday, December 19

JP chaired a pretty awful meeting on the South-East Staffordshire by-election. He started by saying he wanted to know why we didn't get working-class people in focus groups. I said we did. He also baulked at using Alan Howarth in the campaign. I said he was a very good asset in a by-election in that area. TB had just had a meeting with JP, supposedly to bollock him for being offside, but it appeared to have had very little effect and he was back at his petulant worst. It was going to be an important by-election and we agreed a sizeable pre-campaign budget. Preparation for PMQs was a nightmare because TB just kept complaining he didn't know what was the best thing to do. In the end it went OK. TB was really tired, felt questions had not gone well. I felt we were all a bit jaded. He was also worried the rail privatisation was becoming a possible winner for the government, much more than we thought. He felt that we did not have the intellectual case against them. Peter M was desperate for me not to go to the Far East, because he was worried that if both TB and I were away, he would not have the authority and there would be nobody to hold the ring.

Wednesday, December 20

TB was locked in with GB, and it was one of those where the raised voices could be heard. Afterwards, TB said to me 'I don't believe this, but he was actually complaining that he was not consulted enough. And he was still talking about some column Andy Grice wrote weeks and weeks ago, which he claimed did him over, and it was my fault somehow.' The reality was nobody was consulted more than GB. Indeed he had a virtual veto on most things. TB claimed that he said to him: Sometimes I wonder whether you aren't a little bit crazy.

JP's radio interview was fine until he got on to the single currency, when he was all over the place, and virtually promised a referendum. I listened to a tape and it was not quite the disaster we feared, though that was only because the whole thing had been so incoherent you couldn't actually use the quotes to do a bad story of substance. So we might get a few JP gobbledegook headlines, but so what? JP knew he had fucked up though because he asked to see TB. He wanted to assure Tony that it had been a cock-up, not a deliberate move to push forward on the referendum. He was worried, given what Robin was up to.

Big Four, with RC back on to the referendum. Now he was saying he thought Major might do it in his New Year's message. Robin was of the view that we should do it first, though he had accepted there was no great long-term advantage. It was just that he felt that if the government did it, it would be impossible for us not to follow suit. JP and TB said it would be very difficult not to have one, while GB and I both put the view that it really didn't matter who did it first and that whenever the Tories did it, we had to be able to hammer home the point they were doing it out of weakness. After a lot of discussion, it was agreed if they did it, we must stick to a line that we have always said there may be a case for a referendum – hence popular consent – but JM was doing it out of weakness, not for the national interest. TB was clear he didn't want to commit to a referendum at this stage. We could be talking about the election after next, he said. The *Sun* had a big story on the Queen telling Charles and Di to divorce which would keep everything else quiet for a day or two.

Thursday, December 21

I knew TB had been tempting fate yesterday when he said to RC and Clare that the one thing we can be sure of was that there will be trouble over the holiday. It came in spades today. The day started fine, all OK at home, the papers filled with Charles, Di and the Queen, so not much pressure on us at all. JP came rushing into our office with the Christmas card which had been done by the agency and had been given out at the party's Christmas carol event. It had the words that Peter Hyman and I had done on the twelve-days theme, but the illustration for seven sleazy scandals was a picture of a condom, a whip and a topless woman. It was absolutely awful and JP was furious. I said don't bother TB with it yet. I paged Joy. She was up in the gallery and had already given cards to ITN, the *Sun*, the *Standard* and the *Mirror*, in whose office she was. I said no more were to be given out. I asked how on earth it happened and she said if anyone was to blame it was her. She had seen it, but it had not registered when they showed her a copy in rough. I went downstairs and TB was on the phone to GB. Both of them were absolutely livid. They had not been that keen on the card idea in the first place and the blame game started. GB continued to defend Joy and put TB on the defensive about it. Later GB was putting it around I had cleared the card, which was balls. I had written the script but there is no way I would have OK'd a picture like that. It was stupid. I told him so and he denied saying I had cleared it. JP was on the phone to Joy demanding to know who was responsible. Chris Powell called, and apologised. He said that Joy was not really to blame, she had not seen the final material. I did point out, however, that she'd seen it this morning when she took it round the gallery.

Dealing with the royal story was difficult. Some felt TB sailed too close to Diana, stressing that she should have a role. JM didn't say much at all and we looked a bit opportunistic. We agreed if the Christmas card became an issue, we had to say that TB was livid and it had been withdrawn. As the day wore on, it became clear that the *Sun* and others were going big on it, so we deployed the line we had agreed earlier. We finally got an itinerary for Singapore and Japan and put out a calling notice, plus an appeal for privacy when the family was in Australia. We had our [Leader's Office] Christmas dinner at the Athenaeum. There was one heart-stopping moment when Hilary paged me with a fake message from David H, saying the Christmas card story was leading *News at Ten*.

Friday, December 22

The *Sun* coverage of the card was, in Tim's words, 'perfect spinola', as they presented it as TB acting to deal with a bad situation, with a sideswipe at Joy on the way. I took Calum to Euston to buy tickets for Burnley tomorrow, and went past Joy looking very forlorn.

Saturday, December 23

Very quiet, apart from a story about Peter's bloody book [*The Blair Revolution*]. The *Observer* had been sent an old synopsis which Bevins said was hilarious. Blunkett called me re the same. It appeared to propose all manner of new policy ideas which would cause mayhem in the party. I told Peter we had to kill it off. I was paged by Rosie, who said JP was very exercised. I said it was important we did not get a big row story from it because it would run right through the holiday if we were not careful. She agreed but said John wanted to say something. I called JP and he was in a very boorish mood. What people want to know is whether there is one rule for Mandelson and another for everyone else.

Sunday, December 24

David Hill called and said Prescott, Cook, Dobson and others were all winding each other up about the *Observer* story. I called Rosie to say she should calm him down. All JP needed to do was say that he had been assured this was an old synopsis and the book would not contradict party policy. GB called later and said Peter could say nothing that deviated from party policy, even if it meant changing the book at this late stage. GB wanted me to speak to TB in Australia about it and I said that was not necessary, we would deal with it and that would do. He said he was worried that in a day or two we would be into 'Mandelson runs Blair' territory. When TB is back, we should all sit down and agree how we deal with Peter because this is not on. GB wanted to get Peter effectively to rewrite the book and take out anything difficult for the party. After a lot of toing and froing, we agreed a statement for JP saying that he had been assured the synopsis in the *Observer* did not reflect the book contents, the book does not contradict party policy and is consistent with his position as a front-bencher. The various conversations reflected the personalities of the different players. Peter was all innocent and hurt. RC was all injured pride. GB imagining all the worst-case scenarios, sensing potential disadvantage for Peter, and even thinking that TB should be called in Australia to deal with it. JP wanted to wind things up while pretending to calm them, and he was also worried that the party would think he, JP, had given his blessing to the book. I lost count of the number of calls from Robin. The whole lot of them were a complete pain in the arse today.

Monday, December 25

Peter M came round with presents for the kids. I told him, following my conversation with GB yesterday, that he had to sanitise the book to make sure people could not say there was one rule for him and another for the rest. Peter was determined that in the coming year he should establish himself as a politician, not a spin doctor, and the book was the key to that. I could not work out whether, as both Fiona and Anji believed, all these stories were being actively encouraged by Peter. He appeared pretty relaxed about things, though I got the impression his constant complaint about headaches was serious. He had spoken to Robin and apologised for any embarrassment from the *Observer* story, to which RC had apparently replied 'I think the embarrassment is all yours.' Peter's view was that the whole New Labour project needed a bit of an intellectual push and that the book, and this kind of controversy, was actually not a bad thing.

Tuesday, December 26

Another day, another pain in the arse. As well as having JP, RC and GB still on the rampage against Peter's book, the *Independent* splashed on the review of our devolution plans. The truth is that TB had mentioned this to Don Macintyre [*Independent* political editor] in Austria and I had said Derry might be the chair of a review, and it was now the splash, the first meeting having taken place. Needless to say, the Scots went into a total tizz. They wanted an absolute denial of any such review. Tim rightly said that the trouble with an outright denial was it may be that TB wants to end up with a reduced majority of MPs in Scotland. Don had called the group a 'commission' and I said the best we could do was deny there was a commission, but we could not deny outright that the policy was under examination. I said we should say the policy outlines were set but there was a team looking at detailed implementation. George Robertson came on and said the *Independent* story must be killed. Donald and Gordon both felt that the new committee should not meet and we should say so. They said it would cause havoc in Scotland. The Nationalists were out straight away saying it was all about us backtracking on our commitment. Gordon kept asking me to deny the existence of the committee. I said it was very hard to claim that nothing was happening. The press knew that Macintyre would not make up something like this. The rest of the press would assume the story was accurate. What's more, they would assume it came deliberately from us. The trouble here was the two-audience problem – the English would feel it was perfectly sensible to think through whether, with its own Parliament, Scotland might end up with fewer seats at Westminster; and the Scots, who felt that any word of change of existing policy was seen as a retreat from the policy as a whole, and who didn't much like anyone other than the Scots having a say over the policy. GB painted the worst picture possible.

Neil and Glenys came round in the afternoon. Glenys said Neil really wanted to have a proper relationship with TB but did not always feel his views were valued. Glenys said they had watched all the *Wilderness Years* programmes [four-part BBC series surveying Labour's misfortunes after defeat in 1979, aired in November and December 1995]. It was like rerunning all the worst parts of our lives, she said, and it had been awful to see all those people attacking him. Peter arrived and I recalled how Neil had said the next time he saw him he would kill him. The murder did not take place.

Wednesday, December 27 – Sunday, December 31

TB was calling more regularly, not least to gloat about what a marvellous place it was and to say how pleased he was that I was here, keeping on top of things. His kind words didn't go down too well – Grace was ill, I had an abscess on my tooth, the cellar was flooded, and Fiona was not best pleased that I was about to head for Japan. GB was constantly on complaining he didn't have a clear message or strategy. All of this, unbeknown to us, was about to be overshadowed. I was out at the theatre with the boys watching *Oliver!* I got a few pager messages but because it was so dark in the theatre I couldn't read them. I went outside. They were from Anji, urgent, had I heard about Emma Nicholson [Conservative MP]? I hadn't. I called and she said Nicholson had defected to the Lib Dems. I said get TB on the other line now. Talking through Anji, we put together a statement. There had been rumours about a defection for some time but we thought it was Robert Hicks. We said this was a disintegrating government unable to govern. I was keen to get Alan Howarth pitched in but couldn't find him. TB was keen to play the One Nation line which of course Nicholson was playing for all it was worth. It was a huge boost for the Lib Dems which didn't seem to bother TB, because he felt the lasting impact was damage to the Tories, not success for the Lib Dems. It also kyboshed yet another relaunch, Major having pre-recorded interviews to get off on a better footing for the New Year. Heseltine got very personal about Nicholson being overambitious and talked about her having had requests for jobs turned down. We got JP on to just about everything. Swindon vs Burnley was off, which meant a day out to talk things over with Neil was off.

I spent much of Saturday in absolute agony and eventually agreed I had to see a dentist. On Saturday night we had dinner at Neil and Glenys', and ended up having a big row, which started about EU policy on quotas, but ended up with Neil raging about 'Tony's friend Rupert'. Neil seemed to be saying that Europe was a pain and full of wankers, but whenever we said anything anti Brussels, he went into a rage, and said we were falling for myths peddled by the right-wing press, the Tories and the Labour leadership. When I groaned at that one, he said OK, not the leadership, just Robin Cook. The argument was in full flow when TB came on to speak about the speech for Japan, and about Nicholson. I told them that Paddy was clearly encouraging a bit of Labour bashing from Emma in her interviews. He said he was getting a bit fed up with Paddy who had to realise there was always the other strategy, which was going full frontal for the Libs. I got him to have a chat with Neil, but that didn't help things either. Neil really wanted to be part of things, yet found it hard to deal with. As we left, he said to me we still haven't had that long philosophical conversation; I suppose we know what each other would say and we would both agree. I wasn't so sure. I didn't have the difficulties he had. What I think he found hard was the fact that TB had to emphasise the theme of change, and sometimes that felt as if part of it was defined against him. I said take care, and he said no, it's you who needs to take care.

TB faxed through an argument outline for the Japan speech so that I could start to brief and we could work it up. He said he didn't feel Neil had been very comfortable when they spoke on the phone. I said he doesn't feel part of things. The second I put the phone down, Neil called and said Glenys had said he had been very tense last night and if he had been a bit off with everyone, he apologised. It was just that he felt there were all kinds of ways he could help. If TB wanted his advice on dealing with these difficult relationships at the top, for example, he was there and he had a lot of experience.

Monday, January 1, 1996

RC was the first call of the day and after the pleasantries, he was back on at me about Peter. I later had a bit of a row with Peter when he called to see how I was, and I said I thought he was very selfish if he thought TB should go to his book launch. It would give the whole thing a different dimension which it just didn't need. He got very hoity-toity, said he had given no thought to a book launch, when I knew he had. The *Daily Star* did a page lead on some old article I'd written for *Forum* magazine on sex and smoking, and JP called Fiona to wind her up about it. At least it showed he was back on humorous form. He was joking about how often he was speaking to GB while TB was away. GB was keen that we get up the response to the Conservative Party ad on the economy quite quickly and we agreed we should go back to the economic league table in which we had gone from thirteenth to eighteenth and ask the question 'Which country?'

Tuesday, January 2

I worked on a briefing note on the Japan speech, based on TB's note. I was worried that the event rather than the speech itself was the story as things stood. I spent much of the day on the phone to GB in Scotland, and between us we wrote the response to the new Tory ad on the economy. Geoffrey Robinson had been asked by GB to see whether he would put together a bid for the *New Statesman*. Geoffrey came on to say he had told GB he would buy it if it was helpful. He said he thought it was important to have serious intellectual debate on the left. He was worried not so much about what it could do to help up to the election, but whether it would do us any good in government. It seemed to me that all GB was interested in was a pro-GB *New Statesman*. GR sounded very urgent, said it was going into receivership soon, and it would cost a lot to get out of it. He was never off the phone about the ad and eventually we groped our way towards a line that Labour was launching new attacks on the government over rail, water and the real economic issues. The Japanese meanwhile were going crazy re TB's speech, wanting a copy now so that they could translate it. Fat chance.

Wednesday, January 3

TB called very early to say he was faxing through a draft right now, and that he was happy with the argument. He had tried it out on Paul Keating who liked it. I knocked up a briefing note and got the press together at 2. It didn't really fly, though I sensed they wanted the visit to go well, because that fitted the current 'government falling apart' dominant scenario. The questions were not too difficult, other than when I was asked for a classic definition of macroeconomic stability. TB was rightly exercised that we had still not properly dealt with the Tory ad. He said there was a risk their facts would take hold. I said the problem was that maybe thirteen out of the fourteen facts they had deployed were correct, so we needed a different set of arguments. I said there was an added bonus, in that GB and I were working together for the first time in a while. I didn't feel TB's draft cut the mustard. I felt it would be very odd to a Japanese audience to hear a British Opposition leader talk about school homework and home/school contracts.

TB's speech wasn't right, and it was lacking something. It was not yet worthy of the billing or the event. I called Peter M to get him to write a note to TB to say as much. I'd been conscious of the weakness of the speech when briefing on it. I was also trying to put together a piece for Alan Howarth for the *Sunday Express*, that appealed to One Nation Tories to come over to Labour. I tried to put more politics into the speech, and added sections on the single currency and the social chapter. Anji said she'd spoken to TB yesterday, and he'd said he was determined to change the way he worked; he was fed up having to spend all this time dealing with GB and JP; he had to build new alliances. He agreed that he'd been drifting. She'd also spoken to Peter, who had said, with some justification, that I had always been against the book. 'He is not really New Labour, you know,' he said. I made a mental note to remind him that it had been I who had invented the phrase New Labour, and he with others had resisted using it at conference last year. I worked for much of the flight to Japan then took a sleeping pill, which worked OK but I woke up feeling pretty grumpy.

January '96: 'AC isn't really New Labour' – Mandelson

Thursday, January 4

We were staying in the Tokyo embassy compound, an extraordinary set of very British homes in what must be one of the most valuable pieces of real estate in the world. TB called me after landing as he was being driven in in the ambassador's car. He was worried that he'd been filmed by the BBC on arrival and he was dressed very scruffily, with no tie. I got Jon Sopel to agree we would organise better pictures if he could get them not to use the arrival shots. TB, of course, had also worked on the speech and we had the usual problem of trying to marry two drafts, without losing the central line. Once we got all the main changes in, TB went for his main briefing dinner with the ambassador [Sir John Boyd] whilst I tried to make sense of the speech. It was all too right wing to me. Liz Lloyd felt the same. She called to say she felt there was nothing new, and was very little John Major would not support. TB looked terribly hurt when I told him that. But it was true.

Friday, January 5

We had been advised before coming over to get lots of calling cards, and the embassy explained it really was important, not just for us but for TB himself. The Japanese set huge store by calling cards, and the ambassador really felt that we should get some good ones for TB. They went off to get some printed for all of us. The basic drift seemed to be that the more senior the person giving out their card, the longer you looked at it before bowing a little and then putting it away in your wallet. This made it much easier for TB, who as the star attraction and most senior political figure there could always be the first to put it away. But even then, he had to be careful not to put it away too quickly. As the day wore on, and he began to run out of his own cards, and get them mixed up with the cards he had been given, he ended up giving the German ambassador's card to a businessman from Sony. They gave him a very warm reception for the speech to the Keidanren [Japanese business organisation]. Afterwards, I went into reporter mode and collected comments from some of the top businessmen. They were extremely flattering, including one or two who said he was the kind of leader Japan needed.

We left for a meeting with Ichiro Ozawa, the Leader of the Opposition [New Frontier Party], and during the meeting it emerged that the prime minister [Tomiichi Murayama, Japan Socialist Party] had resigned. To our astonishment, Ozawa acknowledged the news and then carried on as if nothing had happened. TB said he would fully understand if he wanted to cancel the meeting to go to attend to what would no doubt be a very busy day for him. But the guy was adamant that they should see out their allotted time. It lent a rather surreal atmosphere to the meeting. It did give TB his one good joke of the day, when he said he was very favourably disposed to removing prime ministers, but the one he had been hoping to remove was British not Japanese. There was one tricky moment, when TB was introduced to someone and asked who he was, and the ambassador said 'You know, the former prime minister,' and TB said 'Ah yes, I know the face.' There was the odd schoolboy comic moment too, as when a Japanese businessman said 'Ra whole of Japan is rookin fowad to your erection.' I said we are hoping for a big one and TB spluttered while the Jap put his thumbs up and said 'Big one, big one.'

Tim called to say Heseltine had really piled into TB on the *Today* programme, saying the visit was a confidence trick and the Japanese were only being polite in saying nice things about him. I thought it was a big mistake. There we were, beginning to worry that the story of TB's visit would not fly, and Heseltine piled in, gave it legs and suddenly we were leading the news. TB was due to do a press conference at the press club. I wondered how many British journalists would go to a press conference in London for the Japanese Opposition leader on the day JM resigned. Yet there were over eighty at it, which underlined the extraordinary interest there was in him at the moment. Tim was worried that Sopel's reports were so positive he would get into trouble. The reality was that TB was making a big impact though, and the Japanese saw in TB a very new and attractive kind of leader. I wondered if they would have felt the same if they had seen him later, sitting in his bedroom at the residence, wearing nothing but his underpants and an earthquake emergency helmet which we all had in our rooms, pretending to speak Japanese.

Saturday, January 6

I was finding the time difference particularly difficult, and didn't sleep at all well. We had a lunch at the British Chamber of Commerce, probably the most dismal part of the visit. A dull collection of people, and the vast bulk probably Tories. On the *Today* programme, TB was very slow to warm up but did well on the general political scene. He talked of the need to pass the baton to a new generation. [John] Humphrys didn't ask about tax, which must have been a first.

On the flight to Singapore we felt knackered but at least we felt we'd done well enough. TB said he felt the Nicholson defection was a bigger blow to the Tories than we may have imagined. He felt they had to get their act together by Christmas, and they hadn't, and she had torpedoed their New Year strategy. We had our first real chat about the difficulties while he had been away. I said it had been pretty non-stop and it required a lot of effort, particularly from me and David Hill, to keep up the least semblance of calm. He showed me a letter that Major sent him complaining about comments JP and RC had made. He got the sense that Major was trying to engineer a break-down in relations, so the really dirty stuff could begin. He asked me what I thought I would do in government, if we won. I said I hadn't thought about it much. He said I suppose you should take over the press operation. I said given that I knew absolutely nothing about economics, he could make me Governor of the Bank of England. We then started giving out fantasy jobs to people in the office; Jonathan to run the TUC; Sue Jackson ambassador to Washington, Peter Hyman to be governor of the BBC. He asked if I thought most political leaders and their staff had as many laughs as we did. I said I doubted it. We then settled down to work on the speech for Monday. We were met on arrival by the high commissioner, [Sir] Gordon Duggan. Singapore was even cleaner and more regimented than Japan. The residence [Eden House] was set in fabulous grounds with a wonderful collection of birds. I made a few calls to build up post-publication coverage of TB's piece in the *Sunday Express*, which was a One Nation appeal to Tories to come over. I called home as the football results were coming through and Burnley had lost 5-0, which added to my growing sense of tiredness-induced fed-upness.

Sunday, January 7

I had slept for about two hours when I was woken by a very alert cockerel. At breakfast, TB said I had to take more care of myself. 'You'd be useless to me dead,' he said. He said he played tennis, and kept in shape, and he was worried that I worked too hard without doing exercise. We had the makings of a very good speech on the theme of stakeholder economy, and the more I briefed it as our core economic argument, the more confident I became that it was a good description of our economic pitch. TB and Anji went to church and Anji called to say there were a lot of press there and they would like a briefing. Locals from the *Telegraph*, *Guardian* and *FT* were there and I could tell when I started to brief the substance of the speech that they were really up for it. I think it was the *Guardian* guy who first said 'Is this stakeholder economy the big idea?' We were running late, and I went into the church to ask TB if he could leave the service early and he looked at me shocked, and said certainly not. TB felt he was on to something with the stakeholder economy idea. It was a way of conveying the economy is about more than money and jobs, it was also about what sort of country we wanted to be. It worked perfectly in tandem with One Nation. It was also a washing line from which to hang all the different parts of economic policy. David M was ecstatic about the speech, felt finally TB had found a left-of-centre message on the economy. TB said we now needed two things, the sense of the team and main players working in harmony, and the public feeling the Tories were no longer making the economy improve.

Monday, January 8

'Stakeholder economy' was really taking off. A meeting with the prime minister [Goh Chok Tong], tall, handsome, highly intelligent, well-informed about the UK and with interesting views on the economy, housing and social services. Later TB went off to see the deputy PM [Lee Hsien Loong, son of former prime minister Lee Kuan Yew], and then Lee Kuan Yew for what was a fascinating discussion. The authoritarian streak in him [Yew] was never far away, and there was a certainty in which he expressed his views that went beyond anything I had seen before, and which made him come across as a bit arrogant. But it was impossible not to be impressed by his depth of knowledge and his intellect. He had a detailed and acute insight into UK politics. As he went through the Tories' problems, in particular their failure to resolve the post-Thatcher questions, I wondered whether any of the top Tories had actually heard this. It was priceless strategic advice. He was convinced we would win and that we would need at least two terms to do the job. He was pretty acute on our own weaknesses too, which he felt were a lack of strength in depth and he was concerned our baggage would hold us down, and TB had to be very clear and strong about change. Then news came through that Mitterrand had died. We were due to have dinner at Raffles [Hotel], where journalists filled me in on Lee Kuan Yew's interviews. They said he virtually came out for Blair, was very warm about him, and said it would take two terms to do what he wanted. Also, he was a bit down on Thatcher. Journalists were thrilled and that was their top line.

I took a call saying Jack Cunningham had been told by Virginia Bottomley [Conservative National Heritage Secretary] that Sir Christopher Bland was going to be chairman of the BBC and what was our line? I spoke to TB whose instinct was that we should not get too involved, though he was in no doubt there would be attacks because he was a Conservative and, he thought, a donor. Jonathan got hold of me with a message from John Birt, who said that Bland was OK, and we shouldn't attack him. On the plane home, we went over some of the longer-term problems. He kept coming back to his Big Four relations. He pointed out how well the operation went on a trip like this when he was not caught up in the incessant personality stuff, gossip and nonsense. I took a sleeping pill and slept for about six hours.

Tuesday, January 9

The plane landed around 5.30 so everyone was feeling pretty grumpy. Also, most of the papers were leading with the legal row over women-only shortlists, which put a real dampener on things. The real danger was less the substance than the fact that it stopped the roll we were currently on. Singapore was still getting good coverage, with Lee Kuan Yew's words playing well, but the other story kicked it off most front pages. On the women-only shortlists, TB said Derry had a concern they may not be legal and there may be good reason not to appeal. TB said he could recall telling John Smith it might be illegal, and John said he was being old-fashioned. TB said he had had a rather worrying conversation with Donald [Dewar], who had admitted 'I basically see things through the eyes of Gordon.'

Wednesday, January 10

A story saying Thatcher would make a speech tomorrow, and attack Labour, but also saying the Conservatives had to stay on the right. I called TB, and we agreed this was an opportunity, that we should really build it up, and say Major could either be a Thatcherite or a One Nation Conservative but he couldn't be both. I suggested TB do an article for one of the Tory papers which both analysed the Tory Party and put forward the core ideas from the stakeholder economy speech. Charles Moore [*Telegraph*] agreed to take it but said he had to get Thatcher to agree to it, because she was also doing a piece for them on Friday about us, and she may not want to look like a response to Blair. We got RC in for a briefing so that he could do the media on it all. He was glad to be asked and of course one of the fascinating aspects of the recent episode was that GB was barely involved. The Tories were briefing hard that the stakeholder speech was a huge blunder by Blair, and I said to him the most important thing was that we had to be positive and confident. I could tell he was nervous, as he often was whenever Tories really came at us, but I was sure the public would not buy the Tory line on this. Robin could not have been more co-operative. He was in and out of the office in between his interviews, and bang on message. He also seemed pleased when

I told them that TB had been pretty sceptico on the single currency in his private sessions on the trip. Later, at the Shadow Cabinet meeting, he paid a grovelling little tribute to TB, saying that the abiding images of the start of the year are Nicholson's defection and TB in the Far East looking more prime ministerial than the PM. Everyone agreed it was a good start to the year, but there was still an extraordinary complacency around the Shadow Cabinet table.

Thursday, January 11

TB thought the *Telegraph* article itself was fine, but the front-page report saying he was claiming Thatcher's mantle was a problem. I felt let down by Charles Moore who hadn't told me he was running it like that and he later apologised and admitted it didn't represent the article's contents accurately. It had got him into trouble with someone far more fierce than me, namely Maggie, who had pulled out of her agreement to write for them because of the way he had presented our piece.

Thatcher's speech came through, brilliant for us, a full-frontal assault on Major and his leadership. The Tories were lamely saying it was really quite helpful. The *Today* programme wanted TB. He said no and suggested GB do it. GB said no, he was waiting till Monday when he had a big speech. No doubt there would be another reason why he couldn't do Monday when Monday came. It can be a nightmare getting him on as part of a team offensive. I said RC was up and doing really well and we should just keep going with him. GB glowered.

The mood in the morning meeting was awful. Here we were, TB just back from a successful trip abroad, his speech setting the agenda, the Tories going through one of their internecine phases, we are way ahead in the polls, but a Martian landing in that meeting would have thought we were on the skids. GB was already moving against the stakeholder economy, suggesting we should broaden it to the stakeholder society. Philip and I argued strongly for sticking with it, saying stakeholder economy had more edge and was less easily dismissed as just warm words. That much was shown by the controversy since he made the speech. I said we finally had a sense of an economic message that set us apart. GB was hating every minute, which was ridiculous. He clearly didn't like the idea of TB giving the key economic speech that had made an impact. The atmosphere was awful, not helped by Peter making a pretty full-frontal assault on Joy by saying he felt there was no campaign on rail privatisation and that the party political broadcasts had been poor. But more seriously, I got the sense GB was set to undermine the stakeholder economy idea. TB came out of the meeting, pretty fed up. He told GB he had to get a proper relationship with me and Peter, or it would be impossible to put him in charge of a general election campaign. He was back in deep gloom. The trouble was a lack of any real team spirit. A few of us, mainly PG and I, and Donald, tried to rub along with everyone, but it was getting more difficult. It was amazing, the way the press thought we ran this well-oiled machine, but inside the machine on days like this, it felt very rickety. The relationships at the top were a disaster area at the moment. Robin was on board because it caused trouble for Gordon. JP was not on board. GB was offside. TB was exasperated. And Blunkett called later to ask why he was being sidelined. Aaargh!

Friday, January 12

I got a lift in with Tessa [Jowell] who was a bit wobbly at the moment because of the sisters putting pressure on re [all-women] shortlists. TB said he had spent a very stressful hour on the phone to GB who was not happy about Peter. I said he really had to stop letting them pressure him the whole time. The other drama of the day was TB driving into a dog, and agonising about whether to report it to the police. He did, so it was bound to get out.

Saturday, January 13

Because TB was on *Frost*, I got the Sunday papers sent round and there was stacks on the stakeholder economy fallout and they were all asking me what it meant. I also sensed that they felt we were a bit of a one-man band which was fine in Opposition but would become a real problem in government. I started to get calls that Scargill had announced he was definitely setting up a breakaway party. I put out a line to PA that it was a powerful signal how much we had changed. Arthur was locked in the politics of half a century ago. It also dented the Tory line that the stakeholder economy speech signalled a return to union power.

Sunday, January 14

Up at 6 to go through the papers and then to TB's. The main aim of the *Frost* interview was to define stakeholder economy on our terms, not the Tories, or those of the left. We spent the next hour going through the difficult questions on unions, company law, or trying to focus minds on what we wanted to achieve. He said, I think people underestimate how radical I want to be on education and welfare.

We are at a turning point and we have to make this work. He said he planned to be sceptical on the single currency.

Monday, January 15

Into Millbank Tower, and a meeting of the general election planning group, at which the task force leaders went through what they were all doing. Peter M was in the chair, very clear and in command, and with one or two exceptions, people responded to him well. We both felt we needed to strengthen up on rebuttal. Ed Balls suddenly told us that GB would have a strategy paper to present tomorrow, thus annoying Peter once more, who later complained to TB about the chaotic way of working. Then to the House, where TB was in one of his worrying moods and going through all sorts of problem areas that we had to address, shortlists, party reform, plus the usual. He feared the Tories would get benefit from economic recovery and that the party would start to cause more trouble for us. It was pretty clear that GB did not believe in the basic stakeholder economy message at all, or if he did, he was determined not to say so. TB was clearly anxious and very twitchy about all manner of things. What is missing most is a strategy that is agreed and understood by everyone. At one point, discussing GB, he said 'I'll have to take over strategy myself and run the whole show.'

Tuesday, January 16

At 11.30 we had another by-election meeting when JP complained again that we did not get working-class people in focus groups. Philip did a good presentation from recent groups, which concluded by saying that the messages that were beginning to connect were One Nation, stakeholder economy and partnership with the people. Peter was worried that we lacked hard edge when it came to tough decisions. I was worried we didn't have our defence and attack lines sufficiently integrated and said it was important that we all felt confident in the lines that we were deploying. It was no good if TB was saying one thing and then when the other Big Guns were being interviewed or doing speeches they spoke a different language. GB gave me one of his injured looks.

Earlier TB had another row with GB saying he couldn't understand why Gordon could not get on with Peter, Philip and me and we should just get on with the job of preparing and implementing a strategy. In fact GB had been a lot better recently, but only by comparison with what he had been like. Then, out of the blue, another problem. John Monks had done an article for *The Times*, which basically said that stakeholder was indeed about union power. After some negotiation with John Healey, Monks' right-hand man, we got them to agree some changes, and lines to put out. John Healey called me later when he realised *The Times* was splashing on Monks' piece. He said I had to understand John M should put his case for strong trade unions, and they are part of the stakeholder model. I said it was obvious that they would have played this the way they were playing it, and it played right into the Tory analysis of the speech. It's really depressing when this kind of thing happens, because John M is one of the sensible ones.

Wednesday, January 17

Amazingly the Monks article wasn't running on the news. Nonetheless TB was in a rage about it. How did this happen? Why did he do it? Also the changes that I had agreed with John Healey had not happened. When I called him he said he had been stitched up. I then went a bit over the top, and said if you're talking to John Monks tell him not to visit Richmond Crescent, because TB could cheerfully kill him. The morning meeting was the real grumpy Gordon works, first of all economy and then Monks. Of course, as he had been against the stakeholder economy speech throughout, he was quite pleased with the Monks attack because it played into his view that the speech as a whole was a disaster area. He grumbled about it all day. At the Big Four meeting, we had a presentation on general election finances. GB was incredibly gloomy about the stakeholder economy situation, and said if we were not careful, everything will be defined on someone else's terms and not ours. He was on a real downer at the moment, and it was a total pain in the arse.

I went back upstairs to work on tomorrow night's speech, then home. The *Mail* was splashing on Cherie at Derry's book launch, saying she was doing a Hillary Clinton, and promoting laws on gays. What a ridiculous paper it is.

Thursday, January 18

GB was on the *Today* programme and did OK, but anyone who knew him could tell that he was deliberately emphasising opportunity economy rather than stakeholder economy. Later TB and GB had a private session, GB complaining again that he was never consulted and that we had not thought through the consequences of the speech. He successfully troubled TB, who began to wonder whether we had the right definition of the stakeholder economy. I said we would have done if Gordon had got involved rather than tried to undermine it from the word go. TB was incredibly nervous, considering this was a fairly straightforward visit [to Derby]. But GB was getting to him. GB called him on the train a couple of times and managed further to unsettle him. I said can't you see he is trying to undermine confidence in your own speech? He said how do you know he doesn't have a point? I said because it's always a different point. At the CMT meeting Sally told Joy that TB wanted to see her tomorrow. She got on to GB who complained that this is not what he and Tony had agreed. TB said it had gone on too long and it had to be sorted. Later, TB said it is tragic. The guy devoted his whole life to becoming leader of the Labour Party and he feels he had it taken away at the last minute by friends who betrayed him. He really believes that. Anji said he still thinks he can win. TB said he wasn't so sure. At Derby, he did a stack of local media and the meeting went fine, but without the sense of drama or energy that we generated over Clause 4.

Philip called and said the focus groups in Edgware were the best he had yet done. He said 'I wish Gordon had been there.' Two people said after the stakeholder economy they felt they finally knew what TB stood for. The party liked it too, he said. Over dinner at the hotel, TB chilled out a bit and went through the Shadow Cabinet, doing a few impersonations. His Jack C was his best. He said we didn't use Jack enough. 'I know people say he can be a bit lazy but he's got clanking great balls and I like him.'

Friday, January 19

The hotel was pretty grim, and I slept badly and by 6 was working with Peter Hyman on the speech draft for the business breakfast. It was fine, but in showing it to TB, he was in a bit of the state. He sat there in his underpants and dressing gown, at a time we should have been in the car, and just muttered that we did not have a real message, and we are underestimating the strength of the Tory fightback. Major was speaking to a big conference in Birmingham and his speech was being trailed as a riposte to TB, which was absolutely fine, and exactly what we wanted. But TB was worried. He said the trouble was that in saying we should be the enterprise capital of Europe, Major does have a message, which binds in inflation and tax and everything economic they want to talk about. It is allowing them to get their version of the economy established. I said I cannot believe that Major gets you like this. Even his friends say he is a loser. He said we didn't have a strong enough line for the speech. That may be true, but the advantage of Major having a big speech today was that the media would put the two of them head to head and focus

January '96: Philip Gould reports 'best yet' focus groups

on central arguments. It is exactly what we needed. We arrived, pretty late, but the breakfast meeting went absolutely fine. TB was not on his best form but the mix of humour and straight talk worked well.

We did a visit to a British Aerospace lab, where I had a really bad anxiety attack, the first in ages. Heart racing, feeling disorientated, very anxious and not sure why it started. The great thing is being able to know it is happening, and what to do, just peel away, find a quiet corner, think things through, stay calm. It was essential I didn't get too tired. It was the one thing that worried me about the campaign itself, exhaustion leading to loss of marbles and judgement.

Harriet paged me to say the *Mail on Sunday* had been on to the grammar school that her son was going to. David Hill had advised her to brief the *Independent* and the *Mirror* in the hope the coverage would not be so grisly, and some of the sting taken out, and I said I agreed with that. I told her however she handled it, I thought she was mad to be doing it, and she should fasten her seat belt. TB then claimed we had never had a proper discussion about it and I said that was balls. We had discussed it ad nauseam and I had written her a letter advising against the move which he had refused to allow me to send. 'Do you ever think you would be a better leader than me?' he asked and I said no, because for a start I lacked his patience. He said the MPs wouldn't mind, because I was more in tune with them. Ho ho.

Tom Sawyer arrived with a note on how to handle Joy. She said she knew for some time it had been slipping away. She was worried there would be a briefing operation against her. I promised that we wouldn't and I said I would make sure Peter and others didn't either. I liked Joy. It just hadn't worked out and it was very sad for her, but it was pointless going on like this. I said I would do all the briefing on it and talk her up as best I could. She and I left together and went back to my house to work up some statements. I asked her how she felt. 'Sad, just sad,' she said. I got the strong sense of someone who was basically a nice person who found herself in the wrong place at the wrong time. Jonathan called. He had had lunch with Chris Meyer [JM's press secretary] who advised that we have a press secretary who can do government and party, and scrap the Government Information Service.

Saturday, January 20

The *Mirror* and *Independent* did Harriet reasonably nicely, as we expected, but she was going to get a rough ride and she deserved it. 'Harriet's hypocrisy' was the *Mail* splash. Of course she seems so thick-skinned, at least on the surface, you could never be sure what she was thinking. What really pissed me off was that we worked round the clock and things like this could set us back so quickly. Only TB seemed to feel any support or justification for what she was doing. JP said he intended to raise it at Shadow Cabinet, and that people in our position had to accept there were broader political considerations concerning personal choices like this. The Sundays were full of Harriet, and there was still reams about stakeholding. Fiona made the point how extraordinary it was that news seemed to be all about the Labour Party. The Tories might as well not exist, and they were the government.

Sunday, January 21

I was playing golf with David Mills when Tim A paged me to say Clare had attacked Harriet on *GMTV* and it was running big. TB hit the roof when he heard about Clare. 'Anyone would think Harriet had murdered the bloody child,' he said. 'The ability of the party to lose perspective is unbelievable.' I said that on the contrary I felt she got off fairly lightly. But he was absolutely livid about Clare, said he was sick of her self-indulgence. I tried to put personal feelings about both of them to one side. In truth, they were both in the wrong. Harriet should have more regard for JP's point about political consequences from personal actions, while Clare can never resist presenting herself as the conscience of a certain view of the party. There was something repulsive about her when she did her commentator-not-politician bit. But I pointed out to TB that he was in danger of getting damaged himself because he had one rule for some, e.g. Clare being slapped down over drugs when she stepped out of line a tiny bit, and another rule for the Harriets and Peters of this world. He said I know Harriet is foolish and selfish, but we should keep it in perspective. 'It's a personal decision' is all we need to say. Clare, he said, was simply being unprofessional in doing what she'd done. If you're in a hole, the job of a politician is to think how we get out of it, and help others out of it, not make things worse. I said surely you could see the damage – here we are in the middle of people vs privilege, trying to get up equality of opportunity, and she comes and totally fucks it over. It is selfish and stupid, and she needs to understand how we feel. Blunkett called to say he'd decided that tomorrow, he will say something about it at the start of the education debate and then move on, and say the policy was not changing and will not be changed. He said he was under real pressure to denounce Harriet and he wished he could because he thought she was behaving like a silly selfish cow. If we didn't contain it, I said to Fiona, it was one of those things that could take five points off the polls overnight. There are all kinds of reasons why people don't like politicians, but hypocrisy probably comes top of the list.

Monday, January 22

Clare did her best to say she had been misquoted, but she was the splash in several papers, and it was clear the Harriet story was going to run. Gerry Steinberg [Labour MP] resigned from the education committee in protest. But I felt the most significant piece in the papers was Peter Riddell's [*Times*] column where, in a piece on the Tories, he said that the reason the stakeholder speech was being attacked so vigorously was because TB did not check it through with GB who was out of the country. It was a classic piece of Gordonology. I said to TB he should not underestimate the anger and if he was alone in defending Harriet, this would become his next big problem in the party. There was a piece on Joy in the *Guardian*, clearly briefed, presumably by Charlie W, as me and Peter forcing her out. On Harriet, we decided it was best to put up Tessa, speaking as a friend, rather than have it as a policy issue. TB, Anji, Jonathan, myself and Bruce Grocott met when we got back. TB was irritated by Bruce who was telling him what he didn't want to hear, namely that the party would like to see Harriet go. TB said he would not wear that and the public would think we had gone mad if we forced her out over this. I repeated what I said to Harriet, that we would all be run ragged on this for weeks to come. He was adamant she should not go. Jonathan suggested that she should offer to resign and he refuse. I said that was the worst of all worlds. It was not going to happen. He said the only answer was to fight this through. I said that meant at some point HH was going to have to defend herself in public and if that is where it was heading to, we might as well get there quickly. If she was doing an interview she should do Channel 4 because Jon Snow would be tough, she'd have to survive it and it would play straight into the papers. Then we would organise others to come out in support, much as it stuck in their throats. I called her at home, told her about the discussion and said it was a case of sooner the better. I said it was high risk, high gain. She said she had flu. I said she'd have to put it out of her mind. We had to do this today. OK, she said. She came in and we sat down in my office to go through all the tough questions. She said thank you for doing this, I know you hate it, and I appreciate it. We ran over some of the arguments then did a mock interview with me playing Snow. She veered from nervous to arrogant. Before she left to do the interview, I took her to see TB. GB was also there and we went over the answers again, the hardest of which was how would she vote in a ballot. GB said again she had to say she was against selection. TB said all she could do was to be a parent first and a politician second and come over very human. Then we heard the *Mirror* was planning a front-page piece urging her to resign. I got them to take a piece from Harriet. I said to TB the worst thing was that it reminded people of the Oratory and in the party created the sense of one rule for friends and another for others. The general feeling was that Harriet had done very well in difficult circumstances, and I made clear that TB backing was there, and he felt she'd shown courage.

Tuesday, January 23

DD asked me to go into the Shadow Cabinet room. He said 'I hate to say this, but there is absolutely no support for Harriet at all and it is damaging Tony.' PMQs was probably Major's best fifteen minutes since TB became leader. He absolutely savaged him over Harriet. TB looked desperate. JP, alongside, was grim-faced, fuelling the accurate speculation that he was deeply pissed off, both with Harriet and the support we were giving her. TB saw JP twice after questions. JP said he could never say he supported what she did, but he would always back TB. I told them that the press really smelled blood now. I had been mobbed after PMQs and the tone of the questions showed they were all convinced she would have to quit. I said she would not be quitting, end of story. That life was likely to get a lot tougher and we had to hold our nerve and not buckle under the pressure. I said the easy thing to do would be to sack her but TB, unlike JM, did not buckle. There was a real intensity to questioning, and an aggression, but I think I did fine. Even though I disliked what she had done, I knew it was now a battle of a different order and we had to win, so it was time to pull out the stops. We were still struggling to get anyone to defend her on TV, but eventually I persuaded Mo to do it, only half jokingly saying that if she didn't I'd reveal her stepchildren were at a public school. Jack Cunningham, who is always a team player, also agreed he would go out. Mike Brunson called to say the government whips were saying Harriet had private health insurance, which as she didn't gave us the opportunity to say this was now becoming a Tory dirty tricks operation and we could start to turn it. I emphasised that TB would be toughing it out and urging the party to close ranks. It was all a bit depressing though. It's one thing to work round the clock and work your balls off for things and people you believe in. I didn't feel like that about Harriet or her decision. I shared a cab home with Blunkett who let rip at Harriet and he said he was pretty close to the end of his tether. He had done a series of interviews but refused to say yes when asked if he supported her. He ended up witnessing a dreadful row between me and Fiona, who wanted to write a piece for the *Express* about how parents can make their local schools better. The way she had done it would be taken as a full-frontal attack on Harriet and would draw us, including I feared the kids, into the story. David said virtually the entire Shadow Cabinet thought Harriet should go and she would do TB a lot of damage if she didn't. I said true, but as he has decided she's not going, whether we like it or not, we have to work within that. TB told Anji he felt so strongly about it that if she was forced out, he would quit. I doubted it, but he felt it showed the party at its worst. I felt that as self-inflicted wounds go, it was one of the worst we had had to deal with.

Wednesday, January 24

With TB speaking to the PLP, and Harriet in the House for the debate, today was the day this thing would come to boiling point. I hardly slept at all and when I did, I woke up sweating. For the first and I hope last time, I had both Harriet Harman and Donald Dewar in a dream. Philip sent over a note from last night's groups in Watford, which were absolutely dreadful. Harriet's hypocrisy had turned things against us overnight. GB was due over for a meeting with TB, me and others at 8.30 but first he asked to see me in the Shadow Cabinet room. He started aggressively. 'Who briefed Sopel?' I said I had no idea. He said he hadn't been distancing himself from TB; he had been trying to avoid giving a clip for the news. He said you don't know how many Shadow Cabinet members are opposed to Harriet and to Tony for supporting her. I said I know very well. The question is what we do about it, and how we help resolve the situation with minimum damage. We went to see TB who was very pumped up about the whole thing by now. He said he wanted all hands to the pump. By the end of the day, I do not want anyone to be in any doubt that she is staying, and I want people to be saying we did the right thing in keeping her. There is no alternative to this whatever, he said. If she goes, I honestly believe we become unelectable in the eyes of the public. Not because the issue is so important, but because they would think we were stark staring mad to allow something like this to become a full-blown crisis. This has got to be seen as a test of our mettle and it is a test that we have to pass. We put together a plan of action for MPs who would go up on the media, and others who would speak to the PLP. TB then saw JP and said he had to stop making it so obvious he was opposed to Harriet, and he had come on board. TB and Harriet were both due to go to the PLP. I said to her you have to say sorry. Not regret, not dismay, just say sorry. Otherwise you are dead. These people are out to kill you and saying you understand their anger might stop them. She seemed, actually for the first time, a bit down and I said you should also say you were warned it would lead to problems but you never imagined it would have been like this. That's true, she said, nobody thought it would be like this.

TB went to the PLP and put up a passionate defence of her, and also spelled out the broader political consequences if she went. Peter M and David Hill came back raving, said he had been absolutely brilliant, and turned it. He said she'd done what she'd done, and whatever anyone thought about it, the only people who benefit from continuing division over it are our enemies and it is time to draw a line. He said what matters was the education of all kids, not a row about the education of one. David said you could see them responding and respecting the fact he had balls. The feedback going from MPs to the press was that TB had basically saved Harriet. I was briefing as hard as I could for her but I found it hard not to let my feelings about Harriet show. The *Standard* showed things turning though, early headlines about Harman pleading with MPs changing to 'Blair crushes revolt'. TB said he was sure we had done the right thing as he came back to prepare for his Northern Ireland statement. You could feel the press warming to a new story, namely that we had hung in and turned things. TB called me in later as he was meeting with Robin. He said I should brief how brave he thought Harriet had been. 'Aw, fuck off Tony, I think I've gone beyond the call of duty already.' Blunkett called later to say he thought we had done a brilliant job considering how difficult it had been. 'You and Tony are a pretty formidable team. I hope I never cross you – either of you.' TB had turned potential disaster into a modest near-triumph.

Thursday, January 25

We had survived at some considerable cost though the papers remained grim. Worse, we had been opened up on several fronts, trust/hypocrisy, TB/JP, Old/New, spin, policy inconsistency. Harriet called to say there was a lot of press outside her house and she was staying in because Joe didn't want to go to school. Well there's a surprise. She was trying to do the victim thing, but though I felt sorry for him, I could feel very little sympathy for her or Jack [Dromey]. The national curriculum test results came in which were a bit of a disaster area for the government, and which gave us the chance to get back on the offensive on education. This was broadly agreed at the 9am meeting, which was a bit happier than yesterday. Then another piece of unexpected good news with a speech from Adair Turner [CBI] more or less backing us on stakeholding. TB was due to open the new media centre at Millbank. We went with JP who was still pretty fed up. GB looking as grim as ever and the body-language was really intense all day. I dread to think what a passing behavioural psychologist might have made of looking at us all. TB was all smiles for the staff, full of talk about working as a team, pulling together for the fight ahead.

TB wanted a post-mortem on the Harriet situation, and I admitted that in the first day or two I didn't do enough, because it was Harriet. The anger I felt then I still felt now, especially as though she had sort of thanked me, she had not said thank you to a single one of the politicians we had persuaded to go out and defend her. PMQs did not really go according to plan. Major was very strong again. The press felt we shouldn't have done education. I explained afterwards that if we had not done education, on the day of such bad news for the government, it would have shown that we had allowed ourselves to be knocked off course by Harriet. We agreed we had to get back on the front foot quickly.

Friday, January 26

The papers were not as bad as I thought they would be, though there was lots about it being Major's best PMQs. Harriet was talking about doing a round of interviews and I said bad idea. Anji had a row with her when Harriet later failed to call TB at the allotted time, and Anji asked if she had any idea how much damage she had done. By the time TB spoke to her, she was in tears, and therefore TB was very soft. 'I'm afraid I'm a sucker for a crying woman,' he said. At the office meeting we tried to go over lessons learned. We felt we had done OK once we hit the crisis management buttons, but we would still take a big hit in the polls because all we'd had was wall-to-wall division mixed in with hypocrisy. I said we had to have better systems of communication between TB and JP that went beyond Tony and me speaking to John on an ad hoc basis.

Cyril [Parry, Glenys Kinnock's father] died so I called Neil to commiserate. He was appalled by Harriet. He added that TB, who was not the most loved person in the Labour Party, was even less loved now, having stood up for her, though he understood why he felt he had to do it. Like me, Neil could not understand how Harriet and Jack had put their son in that position. It will make his life impossible, he said. I just cannot understand that. He said if he had learned one thing as party leader, it is that the real troublemakers are often on your own side, and often unexpected.

Saturday, January 27
Weekend from hell. Again. To stop all the press being wall-to-wall Harriet, we had to get a story to trail from Monday's speech. After speaking to TB and Blunkett we went for accelerated learning, fast-track schooling, and offered it as an exclusive to Andy Grice. He came back after a while saying the *Sunday Times* would not lead on it, so I put it around more generally. The *Independent on Sunday* said they would splash on it. TB went over to see Peter M in Hartlepool and discussed the election structures. We were working towards a situation in which TB was head of the campaign, with GB in overall charge, Peter running the week-to-week strategy group, with me in charge of daily news management. Amazingly, we had ages ago invited Harriet and Jack to come over for dinner and this was the night. She called in the morning and said she would understand if we didn't want them to come. I said no, they should come. She said yes, she agreed it was important she carried on as normal. They arrived and HH was back in non-apologetic, non-contrite mode. Fiona asked her how she had felt through the whole episode – not what the line was, but how she felt – and HH came up with a lot of guff about how there was a real gender issue here, how important it was that she hadn't been crushed, as if men had wanted to crush her and women had been cheering her on.

Sunday, January 28
GB called in a state of, for him, high excitement, after listening to Heseltine on *The World This Weekend* say that Labour was 'on the side of the villain'. We managed to scramble GB on to the end of the programme, demanding withdrawal, and getting up a row about the nature of their politics. This was the current pattern, someone goes over the top against us, tries to get us on the defensive, and we have to keep fighting back. We had to keep showing confidence on education. Mike White [*Guardian*] said he thought TB was showing balls of steel. 'It looks like it will be Major-Balls[1] vs balls of steel at the election,' he said. GB went to see TB in Sedgefield during which they agreed the following set-up: 1. twice-weekly meetings of TB,

[1]A reference to the double-barrelled surname of John Major's father and elder brother.

GB, Peter M, AC and PG, to decide strategy; 2. daily meetings to be chaired by AC on news strategy; 3. Peter M to move to the media centre to run it, Peter H in support; 4. Tim to do rebuttal under a senior politician, possibly Steve Byers; 5. RC, JP and Donald etc. as front-line communicators. JP was seemingly pissed off that GB did the response to Heseltine. GB said it was because he was the duty person. In reality, it was because he reacted quickly and well.

Monday, January 29

TB was up in Hemsworth[1] for the by-election and was meant to be doing a broadcast at lunchtime. But the BBC link failed. I called JP who said he wouldn't do it. He was totally off board. 'Look,' he said, 'I understand you have a job to do, and you have to get someone on the telly because TB can't do it. But the game has changed. I'm not just going to drop everything every time you ask. I'm the deputy and that means deputising but I've had enough of this kind of nonsense.' TB was in the doldrums now, said he could see real trouble and could not see the best way out of it. We got his education speech finished by 4 and the accelerated learning was going big and the Tory attack was playing into our hands. I did a briefing on the speech at 4.15 and there was the usual 'What's new?' and where is the money coming from, but it was well set up. He was speaking in Southwark Cathedral, and although I was slightly worried about us using a church as a backdrop, he was in good form. I watched the new coverage in the ITN links van, and it was excellent.

Tuesday, January 30

Compared with TV coverage, the papers were grim. It wasn't just the *Mail* and *Express* slanted against us, but the left-of-centre papers too. There had been a change of mood. At the morning meeting, I wanted to do a series of questions to expose Tory hypocrisy and show we were happy to fight them on that ground too. Donald wasn't keen. I felt down, probably because I was tired. TB said I looked tired and asked if I was 'wobbling'. He said, 'I wobbled yesterday. Did it show?' I said no. 'I don't want you wobbling the day after I wobbled.'

At 11 TB chaired a meeting with me, GB, Peter M, PG and Jonathan to finalise the structures on strategy. These were to be presented to Friday's Shadow Cabinet away day as a done deal. TB said we were

---

[1] By-election caused by the death on October 31, 1995 of Derek Enright, Labour MP for Hemsworth, West Yorkshire.

not even at the races at the moment, whereas the Tories were beginning to motor. TB later said he had his worst ever meeting with JP, who was more offside than ever. Letter from Harriet, saying sorry and thank you. I went briefly to Joy's farewell. Jeremy Vine [BBC journalist] was lobbying me for TB to do an interview on God. I didn't realise Jeremy was a big God man. He said there are a lot more of us than you think 'and I reckon there are votes in it for you'.

Wednesday, January 31

GB turned up for the morning meeting, which was a relief of sorts. He wasn't terribly focused today but, maddening though he could be, it was far better that he was there than not. He was going mad at the [increase in MPs'] pay story, saying we must make it clear this would not be a spending priority of a Labour government. He said this is a Tory trap and Labour MPs are falling into it. I totally agreed with him, but when I suggested he go up on the news and say so, he was against it, and said it should be left to Ann Taylor [Shadow Commons Leader]. It meant, as ever, that Paddy Ashdown was coming out squeaky clean, saying he was happy with his pay, and we looked a bit grubby. Rosie called from the NEC and said things with JP and TB were awful. Diane Abbott said it was because TB had no advisers around him who understood the party that he had been lulled into thinking Harriet would not be a big story. TB said his recent meetings with JP were the worst yet. JP was complaining he was carved out of things, and TB said yes he was, because he was not doing things he was supposed to be doing and was wanting to do things he should not be doing. He said sometimes he felt like JP would have to go. But that was impossible. First, constitutionally it was not possible. Second, politically, it could destroy us. The reality is that this is just TB blowing hot and cold on JP who has been blowing hot and cold on TB. But when the dust settles, they usually warm to each other and it is the relationship I am least worried about of those at the top at the moment.

Thursday, February 1

I got a lift in with Joy to what would be her last morning meeting, and she was taking pictures of us all. Neither DD nor Gordon were there, but we all agreed TB should do health. Philip called earlier to say we should get up a real attack against them, and I went off with Peter Hyman to draft some tough lines both for PMQs and TB's speech tonight. We were keen to get going on the idea of a fifth-term nightmare. It was good knocking copy but TB was nervous, and we had to tone it down, because he wanted always to be able to say we had the moral high ground. We had a long-term strategy meeting – TB, GB, PG, Peter M, AC. The theme of security was strong, and we had to get up the message that 'You're not safe with the Tories'. TB's speech tonight was a good vehicle. At PMQs, the Tories were better organised again, and gave Major a massive cheer as he sat down. TB did fine, but they were doing better and it was infecting the media mood. I briefed Brunson who liked the speech, and got it running second on *News at Ten*. Robin Oakley said the BBC would not be doing it so I had a row with him, then with his producer, then the editor of the nine o'clock bulletin, who said I never replied to his letters. TB was anxious about the speech, feeling it was just knocking copy, and not him. Peter Hyman and I persuaded him it was OK and he did it well. TB hardly ever watched the news but by a happy coincidence, he watched *News at Ten*, which was brilliant for us.

Friday, February 2

I woke up to the good news of a fairly good win in the Hemsworth by-election.[1] Coverage of TB speech was fine, despite some sense of it being over the top. The *Mail* had another piece on Cherie so I briefed Bevins on how the Tory press was getting back on board with CCO [Conservative Central Office], and targeting Cherie. But TB was in a great mood as we drove to Bloomsbury for the Shadow Cabinet awayday. TB and JP had a private session beforehand, and afterwards came out and both said it was 'all sorted'. The problem with JP, probably to his credit, was that he was incapable of hiding what he really thought. And he clearly wasn't happy, and at times looked a little crushed. Other than when he spoke or intervened in a pretty hostile way, he tended to sulk. TB told them the election was a battle between hope and fear. People wanted rid of the Tories, and were warming to us, and we did give them a sense of optimism. But the Conservatives would seek to scare them about change, make them worried that they couldn't take the risk. We had to turn that around, make it clear it was the risk of another Tory term that was the real threat. 'You're not safe with the Tories' was a strong and clear message and we had to put it over vigorously. TB announced that Peter M was going to Millbank and there were one or two raised eyebrows but key people had been squared. GB did a good spiel on overall strategy. Ditto RC on policy. He was puke-makingly onside at the moment.

[1] Labour's Jon Trickett won with an increased percentage of the vote.

There was a moment of farce at the end when the photographers wanted a snap of TB and some of his colleagues on the steps. We couldn't really do it without JP, particularly in his present mood. But he had disappeared. Eventually I found him in the toilet with Tom Sawyer who was telling him it was time to stand up for the party against the leadership and stop being rolled over.

Then it got worse. The broadcasters wanted someone to do short clips for bulletin pieces on 'Not safe with the Tories'. TB didn't want to, probably rightly. He wanted GB to do it. Rosie said we should discuss that with JP. I completely blew my top, saying we would never get anything done if every time we had to put someone out to do a clip for TV, we had to get agreement by committee. But GB picked up on the tension and said JP should do it. It was a simple message and I briefed JP but he was dreadful. All that was needed was a 'Good meeting, positive policies, and make sure people understand not safe with the Tories', but he didn't deliver it. Back at the House, I went up to see him because he was so offside and we ended having a furious row. He said he was excluded from anything and he was just going to walk away from it all. He thought TB was making a mistake with Peter because of the book coming out soon. He repeated he would walk away and I said who is going to be helped by that? He was by the door by now, and he walked back towards me, looking very hurt and angry, and for a second I thought he was going to get violent. But he stopped short, looked at me, and there was just a sadness across his eyes and his face. 'I'm tired,' he said. 'I'm just tired. I wanted it all to work, but I feel excluded and squeezed out. He's got Gordon in one ear and Mandelson in the other and he's not got time to listen. There is no trust.' I said he exaggerated all this stuff. He had as much say in the big things as anyone, and TB knew his worth. We had it out for half an hour or so, and I think afterwards he was a lot happier, but Christ it was wearing.

Saturday, February 3

We got a surprisingly good press out of the awayday briefing and it was one of the quietest days I could remember. We went to Brentford vs Burnley and I was interrupted just once during the entire game.

Sunday, February 4

I could feel myself going down with something. I watched GB on *Frost* and he was excellent. I missed Clare on *Dimbleby*. By all accounts she was absolutely dreadful.

Monday, February 5

TB seemed to have had a bad weekend. He normally came in very bouncy and focused with a list of things for us all to do. But he was very unfocused, distracted, and convinced the press were turning badly. He said he could not see how we could get back on track. Everything we did was seen through the prism of difficulty and fightback, and though he knew that the Tories were posing more of a threat, he felt sure the public did not really want to see him going for the jugular. He felt, however, that they had a story to tell, and we didn't. They were using all their intellectual arguments on rail, economy, health, education. They had simple stories, access to media that would tell them, and it was hurting us. He was in one of his total mithering moods, which was driving me mad, so I left him and said please don't call me back if it is to have the same conversation again.

TB was desperate to get the strategy paper agreed and signed up to by all. GB agreed in theory but then when it came to agreeing content, he kept finding a reason not to reach a conclusion. It was also clear that TB was giving up the fight on making the stakeholder economy message the core of our economic argument. It was striking today how TB was almost deferential to GB. He so much didn't want to upset him or push him offside that he let him make the running. I could sense others noticing it, and TB's authority weakening as a result. I said to him afterwards this was exactly the time when he should be laying down the law, telling not asking, making clear that the speech in Singapore was the core economic message and we all had to push it.

Tuesday, February 6

I felt awful and stayed in bed with a chest infection all morning trying to bang out sections for the speech for the local government conference, building on the hope against fear theme that TB had raised last week. DM came round to work on it. I spoke several times to TB before he did PMQs and noted that not once did he ask how I was. A *Guardian* poll was not that bad, us down one, the Tories up five mainly at the expense of the Lib Dems. Philip called after the campaign strategy meeting. He said there had been an extraordinary moment when Chris Powell said to GB they had a script for the next broadcast and GB said 'Show it to Alastair. It's got stakeholding in it.' PG said he made it sound like a disease.

Wednesday, February 7

I was still feeling dire. TB called, going through his usual press speech panicola. Later Mawhinney played into our hands. Instead of focusing his attack on our policies on devolution, he defended the hereditary principle, which got the news and the dividing lines exactly where we wanted them. People vs privilege. Betty Boothroyd came out on the side of the Scott report being given to the Opposition before the statement on it in the House. Tessa Blackstone [Labour peer] was terrific against the Tories once they started making the defence of hereditaries [hereditary peers] their big point, though Ivor Richard [Shadow Lords Leader] was incredibly pissed off we had put up Tessa not him. TB called from the car after the speech to say he felt it had gone well and he liked the argument. He said his real worry at the moment was the press. The *Mail* and the *Express* were gone, he said. It's not impossible to see the Murdoch lot going the same way. It will be hard to get our message over with the little press support we have. We agreed he should see Murdoch soon.

Thursday, February 8

I shouldn't have worked yesterday, felt dreadful today and spent all day in bed. It didn't stop TB calling, first to say he was a bit alarmed about the *Sun* two-page spread on his days at Fettes, based on an interview with an old Fettesian. This put him into decline on two fronts: first he said it showed the Murdoch press was turning, and second he said with the whole press ranged against us, it will be impossible to get our message across. He and GB had a spat about rebuttal, because GB wanted Nigel Griffiths [Labour MP and whip] involved in a senior position, and Peter said he lacked judgement. The lack of trust between them was a real problem, which affected the operation at all levels, and meant too much was falling on TB. To nobody's surprise, the Gallup poll showed our lead cut from 39 to 26. We put together the line that the previous lead was a distortion, but the Harriet effect was working through. There was a big sense of build-up to [the] Scott [Report], but I doubted it would do the damage being predicted. The government would see it first and spin it better, and they were clearly not going to accept all the findings. It would be one of those huge Westminster things which largely passed the public by.

Friday, February 9

Another day off sick and at 11, at Fiona's instigation, I went to see an acupuncturist, despite my fears of needles. I almost fainted when the needles went in, and again when they came out. TB was working on the speech for Sunday. He sent the text through and DM and I both thought it was really poor. We spent hours trying to turn it into a real speech. TB wanted to make trust the central theme but we could not make it work as a speech. Also, hope vs fear was not going to excite anyone in the current atmosphere. My gripe with TB in these times was that when he was down, he let it show, rather than roll up his sleeves and get going again. He insisted he was like this in front of a very small number of people. We ended up having another row over Harriet, because he was now convincing himself she was not the problem, the party was. They were not his friends. They would kill us if they could. The *Mirror* called early evening, said a bomb had gone off at Canary Wharf and would TB do a piece. We had to sort out a TB doorstep and statement while DM and I tried to make sense of the speech. Anji was fed up with him at the moment too, feeling he was just not getting his act together, and his head was dropping.

Saturday, February 10

I didn't feel well enough to go off with them to Birmingham so stayed home to work on the speech. I managed to draft a terrific ending, and Roy Hudd sent through some great jokes and one-liners. Anji called for another whinge about TB, his lack of grip and the speed with which he was descending into despond these days. She said TB had received a letter from Blunkett complaining that we had successfully calmed down all the egos but people still didn't really know who was in charge, or how the campaign structures would work.

Sunday, February 11

We went to dinner at the Foots', with Salman Rushdie. Salman and Elizabeth [West, his future wife] were clearly fed up with having to have protection [Salman was still under the threat of murder]. He was very polite about the bodyguards, but felt there was no reason why he should keep having them. He was also angry with the party, said he had had plenty of promises of help from [Roy] Hattersley, [Gerald] Kaufman, TB and Chris Smith. But he didn't really feel they had delivered much for him. Both Michael [Foot] and Jill [Craigie] were convinced we were going to win. Jill was terrific company, very funny, and full of terribly bitchy stories about Michael's old colleagues. Michael said TB was a massive asset. He was young, exciting and clever. 'He is a film star,' said Jill, 'a film star.'

Monday, February 12

I was still not one hundred per cent but determined to go in. The real talking point was a bad *Sun* story. As I feared, it pushed TB into a 'what do we do if the whole press is against us?' phase. I said he had to raise it with Murdoch and get his cards on the table. The only language these people understood was strength. At the general election planning meeting, we discussed key seats and Margaret McDonagh said there had been a shift away from us in canvassing. A long session on economic policy. GB's office had prepared a four-page note. Needless to say there was no room for stakeholder – the word or the argument – and then the reasons came in. Ed [Balls] said that the problem was that it lent itself to other people's definitions. I said you could say that about anything. GB said our main economic message was investment and opportunity. This was being different for the sake of being different. It would have been easy to marry these arguments but GB was determined not to be in the same place. They were really arguing about substance whilst claiming to be arguing about presentation. TB was clear the government needed to prepare the country for a future based upon an economy in which everyone had a stake. He saw stakeholder economy, One Nation and new politics as core messages which came together. GB was on a narrower point, and basically arguing for intervention and investment. They could end up at the same place, but they were arguing about different ways of getting there.

Tuesday, February 13

GB's lot were going through a real pain in the arse phase. He suddenly announced he was getting some research done on the issues we had discussed yesterday. In other words he was going to do his own thing and would ignore everyone else. He was impossible. The truth was we had gone for too long without a strong economic message and now we had one, because it was not his work, he was going to sabotage it. On Scott, the government said RC would get a copy at 12 with the statement at 2.30. The first spin on this would be vital and the government would be able to apply it. Jonathan had had lunch with his brother Charles who said the Tories had promised Conrad Black a peerage. These people are corrupt, said TB. But he was generally anxious about the press and wary of tomorrow's meeting with Murdoch.

Wednesday, February 14

GB did not come to the morning meeting. It was pretty clear he was going to have less to do with these meetings. It was a mixed blessing. On the one hand, he could be a total pain. On the other, when he was motoring, he was good. But it was incredibly wearing. Jonathan came along with the reply from [Trade and Industry Secretary] Ian Lang's

February '96: 'Tories have promised peerage to Conrad Black'

office about the ridiculous arrangements for us seeing the Scott Report, which were hilarious.[1]. Spent most of the rest of the morning working on TB's speech to the British Retail Consortium tonight. We had a crap draft. Following TB's visit to John Lewis, I tried to inject a re-statement on stakeholding. By lunchtime we were number two on the news and this sent GB into apoplexy, and later he complained to TB. It was clear he did not want TB to get any coverage for anything to do with the economy.

TB saw Murdoch and Les Hinton at Murdoch's flat in St James's. Harriet and the school had changed the mood, and they were clearly wondering if he was still in charge. They hadn't much liked the party response, he said. He felt that Murdoch personally liked him but Hinton was not so sure. He said there was nothing we can do to change their minds on Europe and they think basically that I'm OK but the party is not. TB wanted me and Peter M to see Les again soon. In between working on the speech, I was in constant communication with Robin who was loving the theatre and the farce of the Government's conditions on the Scott Report. The attempt to get greater prior access was defeated in the Lords by the hereditaries. Then came a letter from Alty there would only be one copy made available to us, which RC would have to read in conditions of secrecy. I drafted words for RC and we led the 5.40 news with the whole nonsense. Robin said I don't think it would be wise for our wives to know just how much time we spent together on Valentine's Day.

Thursday, February 15

Morning meeting was all about Scott and it was nice to have Robin there, clear, confident and in charge. His manner at these meetings was very proper, officious, never far away from pompous, but he was always in command. He went off for what he called his solitary confinement in the DTI where he would be allowed to read the report. Preparation for PMQs was a bit odd, as we were basically just waiting till Robin returned. Neither TB nor I thought the government would be terribly damaged. RC came back at 2.30 and quickly, succinctly and with a very stern demeanour, took us through the main points. He said the government would have a lot a difficult questions to

[1] John Alty, principal private secretary to Ian Lang at the DTI, had written offering Opposition spokesmen sight of the report three and a half hours before its general release, and only under supervision by DTI officials. Jonathan Powell's riposte ran thus: 'Dear Alty . . . Mr Blair has no intention of coming to the DTI to read the Scott Report under the extraordinary and insulting conditions you propose.'

answer, and he would call for resignations. He said, however, that there was a 'bastard of a paragraph' which explicitly cleared them of any conspiracy. Lang was very robust in the House which cheered the Tories up. Robin and Ming Campbell turned it around pretty well. The general view was RC was brilliant in the House and very deftly dealt with the concerted efforts to turn it on him. The office was working really well, particularly Tim. The general sense was it was damaging without being fatal.

Earlier, we had an awful strategy meeting. TB, AC, Peter M, PG and Jonathan, and finally, twenty minutes after the start, GB arrived. It was like a wrestling match. Everything was a problem. It meant we had everything pretty much on hold. Later, he phoned up and said we were losing the argument on Scott, but had no positive proposals. TB was pretty weak with him again. TB complained that we lacked a governing theme at the moment. I said our best theme was the many not the few, people vs privilege. GB said it was the condition of Britain. He said we were doing too many themes and not sticking to them long enough. Like stakeholder economy, I said, and he glowered. It was truly awful. GB was at his sulkiest and Peter at his snootiest and TB at his most withdrawn. Eventually, TB snapped and said we absolutely must get this sorted out. You people have the authority to agree it. Just do it. Robin was getting rave reviews, which was no doubt another reason GB was so low. I had to leave to go to the Royal Free [Hospital] where Calum had an infected cut and they were keeping him in, and I stayed the night, sleeping on a not very comfortable chair.

Friday, February 16

The broadsheets were bad for the government, the tabloids less so, saying basically that ministers had been cleared. Robin had the very good idea of a press conference with Ming Campbell. At the pre-meeting, Robin was at his most elevated and pompous, saying how much time he wanted for discussion, and how much to gather his thoughts alone. He felt that the Tories were getting away with it but we could pile on the pressure. I went to the Savoy for the *What the Papers Say* awards. Chatted to Les Hinton and we agreed Peter M and I would see him soon. I chatted to [Paul] Dacre, who didn't like me pointing out his paper was now truly back in the Central Office locker. Virginia Bottomley did the main speech which was incredibly boring.

Saturday, February 17

The Scott coverage was going against the government, particularly in the heavies and the columnists. The tabloids were pretty much losing

February '96: 'We are losing argument on Scott' – GB

interest. The best news was that Peter Thurnham [Conservative MP] had confirmed he may quit the Tory whip and gave Scott as one of the final straw reasons. It took the story on in a much more favourable direction and led the news all day. Robin was getting pretty good press, though Boris Johnson [assistant editor, *Telegraph*] had a profile which concentrated almost entirely on his rivalry with GB, and how good GB was. RC said though the rivalry thing is totally overblown, 'It is extraordinary that even when it is so clearly my job to attack for the Labour Party and do well for the Labour Party, there are people in it who are willing to attack me instead of the government.'

Philip's groups were showing yes, there was a problem for the government over Scott, but also a growing problem with TB and trust. That sense that he was more than just another politician was diminishing. Harriet really hadn't helped in that regard. Robin was terribly pleased with Macintyre's piece in the *Independent*, and asked me if I was the source who said RC was a joy to work with. I said I was. The feeling is entirely mutual, he said. He said he thoroughly enjoyed it when he was working with the inner team like this. I had a major whinge about GB to TB and emphasised how different it had been working with Robin, who was so co-operative, and TB said yes, but of course it is in part so you think that Robin is behaving like that, and when the chips are down, when we really are up against it, I suspect I can still count on GB but not necessarily count on Robin.

Sunday, February 18

Peter M phoned to say he'd had lunch with Michael Wills on Friday, who had told him, so nonchalantly it was clearly again in the GB camp, that Gordon would never reconcile himself to doing things the way we did because he believed that we – and Peter in particular – were out to destroy his career. It was complete balls but revealing that Michael could say that so openly. It was also extraordinary that despite nominally being in charge of overall strategy, GB had had so little input into planning on Scott.

Monday, February 19

I stopped by to see JP on the way in, partly to discuss his poster launch at 11.30 and to decide whether last night's IRA bomb at the Aldwych, which he narrowly missed on his way back from a meeting with TB at Richmond Crescent, meant we should postpone the poster, and also to discuss his discussion with TB. As ever, he said it took to the end of the meeting before TB really came to the point when he said there had to be a coming together and a strategy to put over to the public that they had indeed come back together. TB also felt JP should do a departmental job. JP was still not sure. I have to work out whether that cuts across everything else I do, he said. What I do accept is that we cannot afford any more bad press about the relationship. It's bad in its own right, but it also has a debilitating effect on the party. But he emphasised that he wouldn't tolerate being frozen out. But I sensed the discussion had gone well, because he was in a far better mood than in recent weeks, and joking that he still couldn't bring himself to say 'New' before Labour. I said I'd get him there. We agreed to sit down and work up a plan. He said he had told TB that although Peter had a lot of talent, it would be a disaster if he allowed him to become a front man. He's got the same sneer as Mawhinney. JP said he had spent half his political life on the outside, and could do that again, but he was now deputy leader, and it would not do any good. I said there were enough bad relationships at the top without TB/JP being one of them. He seemed up for it. But we had to understand that he was deputy leader, he had to be in the loop, e.g. he said I have no doubt at all that Tony would want nearer an election to parachute a few people into key seats at the last minute. It always happens, it always will. The reality is I can help but I can only help if I know what is going on.

Bumped into Heseltine. 'Ah,' he said, 'the gloss is coming off. You've had a good run, but now we have the measure of you.' I said that was not how it felt to us, and I would rather be in our shoes than theirs. I said we were both hopeful that [William] Waldegrave would stay. He said 'He'll stay because he's got integrity, something you people wouldn't understand.'

TB, JP and RC went to a meeting with key seats candidates and TB came back saying they were pretty poor quality. He said he only spotted a handful with the potential to be exceptional. At the 6.30 strategy meeting, GB was not there again. Peter confirmed that he and GB had not spoken since their roles were agreed. GB was organising an economic campaign, Peter was working on the local elections campaign, and it was as if these were separate entities. GB had pretty much given up coming to the morning meetings. TB was downcast and Peter laid it on, saying Millbank staff didn't know who to take orders from. Philip said it was only when I went over there and just laid things out that they felt some sense of clarity. And there was still always a risk that GB would try to get something different done.

The Brit [music industry] Awards should have provided some light relief but I hated the whole thing. TB was tense, so was I, Cherie and Fiona were twittering and saying I was being boring and Northern and shouldn't worry so much about things going wrong. TB was at John Preston's [music industry executive and husband of Roz Preston, assistant to Cherie Blair] table and kept looking round to share looks of 'Is this wise?' There was a little flurry of excitement earlier when Central Office complained that Virginia Bottomley should have been given an award to present. They must be mad. If we were concerned that TB might get booed, I think it could be guaranteed that she would. Anji came to get us at 9.20 and then we had a long wait hanging around backstage, while TB paced up and down and, when outsiders left us alone, endlessly rehearsing the little speech we'd done about the importance of the music industry. I've rarely seen him so nervous. I suppose it was partly because this was not his usual environment, but also it was such a huge audience, live and on TV, and if something did go wrong, it would be high impact. David Bowie [musician] came in for a chat. They did a lot of small talk, and he gave his views on the various people who had been winning. He said he'd be happy to come out for Labour, but he was worried he would open himself to attacks because he was a tax exile. He didn't exactly help TB's nerves when he said this audience could be hellish and given that some of the musicians from Oasis and Pulp [bands] had already misbehaved, anything could happen. After he left, I said 'Oh dearie dearie me,' and we went into a little black humour phase, imagining the worst-case scenarios, TB walking on to the stage, and doing a Neil at Sheffield,[1] then getting stormed by some of the druggies and the drunks at the front. After an hour or so, somebody came to take him up to the stage. Even in the time we had been away from the main action, the atmosphere had got a lot worse. I didn't like it one bit. As he went on, there were a few cheers, a few boos but generally, it was just a very pissed, very druggy atmosphere in which he neither looked nor sounded comfortable. Apparently it looked a lot better on TV than in the flesh. Even though it was one of the shortest speeches he had made, it was still fairly long for this kind of event, and maybe a bit too serious. I suppose we just about got away with it but as he came off he said thank God that's done. I had a chat with Mick Hucknall [singer] who said there were going to be a lot of disappointed people if we lost.

[1] The Labour Party (which was ahead in opinion polls) had held a 'US-style' political rally at the Sheffield Arena on April 1, 1992, a week before the general election. Neil Kinnock's enthusiastic reaction to the crowd was widely criticised as 'triumphalist'.

GB did at least turn up for the morning meeting, but it wasn't great. He and TB had different views about how to use the policy papers that would be part of the pre-manifesto process. GB complained endlessly we lacked substance but when pushed on how to fill the gap, he gave the last answer but one again and we went round in circles. We agreed the policy papers should form the basis of the Partnership with the People process but couldn't get agreement on how to do them, or what subject. Even when we agreed the economy first, we split hairs. It was absurd, arguments being invented for the sake of having an argument. Peter had a wobbly because TB had seemingly told him he was too imperious, and he hung up. I said to TB he had to be tougher with all of them. He said the problem with Peter and GB was that both of them knew they were better than the rest at the things needed to win an election. He said yes, GB could be a pain, but even when he was a pain he would still add value. Philip called late and said the first-time-voter groups he'd done were the most depressing of his life, not necessarily because they hated us, but because they knew absolutely nothing about politics or the world around them.

Wednesday, February 21

Peter was at the morning meeting doing his usual flicking through papers and not really taking part. GB was not engaged on Scott, but on better form on other stuff. On the way back to the House I told DD that I was getting very dispirited about the relationships at the top of the party. He said yes, JP is like a bear with a sore head. I said I meant GB. He said it was difficult, and GB was disengaged. Donald laid the blame at Peter's door. He said look at the way he behaved in these meetings, sitting there, saying nothing, ostentatiously writing notes and hoping everyone thinks he's writing to Tony and that basically this meeting is not important, and 'I can get what I want done in different ways'. Later, we had an internal meeting, at which I said to TB he had to threaten them, make them all realise they were not indispensable. Tim was dealing with the latest exchanges between TB and JM, including a private letter in which JM was very petulant and threatened to release their private correspondence. He was clearly getting more rattled. TB took a meeting on the Broadcasting Bill. He was concerned that we would make the line too anti Murdoch to please the party, rather than through a real assessment of the issues we were dealing with.

Anji paged me to call urgent, and said Mo had been told that the

News of the World were doing a big kiss-and-tell exposing Robin. Fiona had been at Cherie's with Roz [Preston] and Scarlett Maguire [media adviser] and Carole [Caplin] turned up. Fiona said she was worried Carole was clearly back in there again and the press would be on to it pretty quickly. TB had to speak to her. On the Robin front, I got Anna Healy to approach him, warn him re the *NoW*, and he said there was nothing new they could do.

Thursday, February 22

I read Peter's book on the way in, and even though it was in the main fairly anodyne, I could see how it could cause us problems. After GB turned up late again, TB said to him that if things got any worse he would have to take the strategy job from him because it wasn't being done. GB apparently said fine then shrugged his shoulders. 'I'll give it all up if you want, including Shadow Chancellor, and campaigns.' His arriving late at meetings appeared to me to be calculated, a way of him saying that he refused to accept he was not the number one here. I was not yet happy that we knew how we intended to launch [pre-manifesto] *Partnership with the People*. Again, there was a GB problem. The pre-manifesto had not been his idea, and he therefore constantly raised problems about it. A real breakthrough came with a letter from the Scott inquiry complaining that ministers were selectively quoting him and so distorting what he said. So the story was up in lights again and later Peter Thurnham saw Major to resign the whip, so Tory turmoil was back.

Later I got a call from Robin asking me to go and see him. He said what do you know? I said we had heard that one of the Sundays was planning some major exposé of his private life. He did one of his big sighs, nodded and said 'Could I ask for the secrecy of the confessional on this one?' He said obviously TB should know but he didn't want it to go beyond that and in particular he did not want Peter or GB to know. He said that between 1983 and 1987 he had an affair. She was a wonderful woman, it was a marvellous time and he often wished she had been the first love of his life because he felt they were made for each other. His wife eventually got to know and he ended the affair. Their marriage went through a very rocky period indeed but they just about survived. Then today, he said, the woman called to say she was being pestered by journalists. She had said nothing to them, other than go away. Mo had been led to believe the woman had done a deal with the paper but Robin said he was ninety-nine per cent sure that was not the case. I said fine, but nonetheless, do not rule out the prospect that your conversations with her are being taped. I could tell RC was worried though, and I said you have been so high profile over Scott they will be desperate to get the story and will offer a lot of money to friends and relatives, etc. I asked if there was a former husband. He said yes. We agreed that if it became clear they were going to do so something, Robin should do what Paddy [Ashdown] did, pre-empt with a press conference, get the facts out and make clear that was that and he would never talk about it again. If we were pushed late into Saturday, we would simply give the papers a statement, draw on that later, and then say and do nothing. There was a mixture of sadness and worry in his eyes and as I left I said I'm sure it'll be fine, and I just hope you can concentrate on the speech. He called me back as I was heading down the corridor. 'Give me your honest opinion – what is the prognosis?' I said I reckoned there was a 60–40 chance it would not appear this weekend. He said would it really be such a big thing, something that happened ten years ago, and I said I'm afraid with our press it probably would, and we would have to manage and contain the damage. But he should not for one second think it would cost him his career. We will deal with it, and I do not believe TB will be censorious or judgemental. TB was remarkably relaxed about the whole thing. He said that even if it did come out, though it was horrible for Robin and his family, there would be a lot of people saying so what?

Friday, February 23

Collected Peter and we headed to Wapping to see Les Hinton and Jane Reed [at News International]. They were clearly worried that party pressure would lead us to adopt positions on the Broadcasting Bill, and legislation if we got in, that would hit their business interests. Les said they felt a bit under siege, because all the other media groups were against them. He said Murdoch was hated and feared by the rest of the media, yet as a group they did a lot of good. He was hated in the 1970s because of all the Dirty Digger antics, in the 1980s because of Wapping and now the charge was that he wanted to run the world through television. I said feelings ran pretty deep, not so much because of Wapping but because of the way the papers treated Labour historically. Les said Murdoch was losing interest in Britain, because he didn't feel wanted. We ended up discussing Murdoch's own media image problem and they asked for advice. I said I never understood why he didn't do more media himself. Peter said they came across rather like the Labour Party of old, under siege, defensive, feeling they had no friends. They needed a clear vision, a leader to articulate it, and the media strategy to deliver it. People think you're monopolistic, not pro competition, not pro quality. Fear and hatred often go together, and some people are scared of Murdoch, because they think his mix of commerce and politics is too powerful and they have to understand that. It was an interesting encounter. From the outside, you get the impression of a company clear about its purpose, driven, focused. They felt completely misunderstood. It was not dissimilar to the way the outside world saw us as driven and focused and together, when beneath the surface there were all these tensions bubbling the whole time. I emphasised that they had to understand that there would be a big price to pay in the party if we restricted and curbed the natural desires of people to do something about Murdoch, and ultimately the *Sun* and *News of the World* really went for us.

Nick Raynsford [Labour MP] called with an excellent story that Portillo had stepped in to stop TB being invited to speak at Greenwich Naval College. It was the kind of personality/political story that went down well on a Friday. We decided we should give it to Bevins, and then brief the other papers on it for follow-ups. I had a good meeting with Melvyn Bragg who felt we should be doing more on the role of the arts in school and with poorer kids in particular. I like Melvyn. For all his image as one of the luvvies, he had a good political mind and he struck me as a giver not a taker. I saw Peter Riddell and then briefed him, as I had others, that Peter's book was not as exciting as people might imagine, that TB had not read it and that the main ideas were Peter's and should not be seen as a ramp for TB. Peter was of course pissed off that I was talking it down, but I felt we had to.

Saturday, February 24

It was time for a bit more mischief, so when Bevins asked me if there were any more Tory MPs who had contact with senior Labour sources, I did not disabuse him of the notion. I played down the idea of defection, but said that there were others who wanted it known they were keeping in touch with us as a means of trying to get Major to hold back on the lurch to the right. He wanted names, but I did not tell him about TB's meeting with [Peter] Temple-Morris [Conservative MP, later to defect], and in any case TB did not believe he would defect. I was more confident. I briefed the heavies on our basic line on Peter's book, and later briefed the Greenwich story more generally to get the broadcasters interested. Peter was preparing all day for *On the Record* and also trying to drum up interest for the book.

The papers were excellent, thought there was too much about Peter, rather than about the substance of the book. Robin called, relieved there had been nothing in the *News of the World*, and we discussed how to keep Scott going. He was more confident again, without being cocky, so altogether more likeable. JP said he and Pauline had bumped into Major. JM said 'I'll keep the seat warm until you get rid of Blair.' Pauline was seemingly bowled over by how witty and charming he was and said 'He really is as tough as old boots.' Fiona and I went to TB's for dinner. The idea was to discuss Cherie. Peter M, who'd done a good interview on *On the Record* today, was there. TB said JP had called in to complain about Peter's interview and said he could not stay in his team after the *On the Record* interview, because he broke with policy. On Cherie, we agreed that the next time the *Mail* did a piece doing her over on the cases she did, we would get a round robin to *The Times* signed by barristers. We also needed to encourage more positive profiles. TB felt there was an image problem because she was being defined by enemies not friends. Essentially it was the *Mail* running the line that she was rich, to the left of Tony, didn't care about her kids, etc. We also discussed what she would do if we win. She said she wanted to carry on working, though she might have to do fewer cases. Fiona was worried about the profile *Vogue* were doing, and also that Carole Caplin was around and capable of doing damage. We agreed on balance that it was better that she did not go to the US. All we would get was Hillary comparisons. She was keen to emphasise that she only wanted her career, the kids, and to be supportive to TB. She wanted to be with him all the time during the election, she said.

Needless to say, eventually the discussion turned to the real bane of his life, GB's and Peter's inability to get on. Peter played mock hurt that we were lumping the two of them together but I said they were as bad as each other and frankly I cannot remember a time when all of them were working more or less in unison. Peter said he was NOT as bad as GB but he had to respond when GB was so intent on destroying him. I said – and CB chipped in her agreement – that TB still failed to behave like the boss with GB. He was too deferential, too keen to say that he was right even when he got things wrong. Cherie said he only understands toughness – you can't be soft with him. Fiona said 'You have to be tough on Gordon and tough on the causes of Gordon.' Peter laughed, and said 'I'm afraid I am the causes of Gordon.' TB insisted that he worked like hell to make the partnership work, but GB wouldn't work with him properly. He said it was like dealing with a girlfriend who every time you looked at another woman thought you were having an affair with them. I said he had to show more leadership and make both of them feel more vulnerable. None of us were indispensable.

Monday, February 26

It was all building up for the Scott vote in the Commons tonight. Although nobody felt we would win, it was going to be a big day. In the debate, Robin was absolutely brilliant. He had done most of the work himself, using our research material, and did a really fantastic forensic, and witty, job. Andrew Marr said it was perhaps the best performance he had ever seen. Lang was pathetic against him, and Robin totally skewered Heseltine. It allowed us to say that if the Ulster Unionists were genuine in saying they would listen to the debate before deciding, there could be no question as to which way they should vote.

At the 5.30 strategy meeting, GB again tried to get everything back to his agenda, saying the focus should all be on opportunity. Peter and I argued that to focus everything on the word opportunity was old, tired and failed. It made people think of opportunism the second they heard the word. GB was in a foul mood, particularly as everyone was saying how brilliant Robin had been. GB had not been in for the debate. Rumours started that Major and Mayhew were seeing the Ulster Unionists and the feeling grew that he would buy them off. In the end, they came with us, but we lost by one vote. Robin was absolutely basking in glory, everywhere he went being told he was fantastic. I have to say it was pretty impressive the way he held it together, given he probably spent the entire weekend fretting about being done over.

Tuesday, February 27

RC got a brilliant press, and deservedly. I got to TB's where he was meeting Stan Greenberg [American pollster] who did a presentation that would bother him on and off all day. Stan felt things were pretty much the same, but there was a problem with TB and trust and we should be worried about it. It had been happening before Harriet and of course that had made it worse. He felt that when we were doing Clause 4 there was conflict and real change and drama but people had quickly forgotten that and now it was as if he were just another politician. We needed further party reforms to remind people he was the agent of change, new, modernising. In the car on the way in, TB said he felt his confidence had been jolted because of troubles with

Gordon, and the public picked up on this sense that he no longer felt completely in charge. There was probably some truth in this. Certainly they were going through their worst phase yet. I didn't make the 9am meeting. DD was apparently in the chair in Gordon's absence and said he thought we had dropped stakeholding because it failed to make an impact.

Earlier, I went to see JP to get him to do a stakeholder statement to go with the PPB tomorrow. He was fine but said the trouble was that TB and I worked up the whole thing together on an aeroplane, and then expected everyone just to row in behind it.

Wednesday, February 28

Peter and Gordon were barely speaking again. I got a message that TB wanted me at the NEC. It was a horrific scene. Clare went OTT in the debate on the selection process for [North] Swindon. She said it was a dreadful establishment fix to parachute in Michael Wills and spoke in lurid terms but neither TB nor GB went for her as I felt they should. She stormed out saying the party had become disgusting. Margaret Beckett came back with us in the car and said Clare was silly and overemotional but there was a lot of bad feeling around. Everything news-wise was then pretty much blown out by Diana's announcement that she would divorce. Later, I went to Peter's book launch party. He was angry that TB was not going. It was all small talk and lots of people butterflying around. I hate these kind of events, one inconsequential conversation after another. I left feeling depressed and tired. I was also worried by what Tom Sawyer said earlier, that he was worried that the NEC and Shadow Cabinet were not really scared of Tony. The unions do not really respect him either. He said JP was a real problem too, and TB had to be tougher.

Thursday, February 29

I went to see JP and said did you know that Hattersley never voted against Neil at the NEC? He said, with real anger, that the Swindon situation was despicable, there was far too much fixing going on, and it wasn't even being done well. When this kind of thing was done by the left, we deplored it and we should deplore it when done on the right too. He said I will have to back TB in hard times too and it's important I have some credit in the party, that I'm not seen as a patsy. He really ranted then about Peter's book, saying I had handled it brilliantly and prevented it becoming a real problem in the party by distancing TB, but he said it would still cause difficulties for us. Told TB I was worried and he said exactly what do you mean? I said I felt the relationships at the top were so poor that we were incapable of producing a real strategy. GB was disengaged, Peter was obsessed with his book and offside because he thought I hadn't been supportive of the project. I said my other worry, fuelled by Tom Sawyer, and also JP's and Clare's behaviour yesterday, was there was no real fear of his leadership, because people sensed he was not clear what he wanted to do. A lot of this, in truth, was Harriet but it went deeper.

Friday, March 1

The *Mail* finally did the story of Donald, Derry and Alison.[1] It wasn't very nice for any of them, though in truth, given it was the *Mail*, it could have been worse. Derry was in a state about it, said is it any wonder people are put off going into politics and public life when you get this shit thrown at you, everything in your past dragged up? GB's office suddenly decided they wanted to do a press conference at the same time as TB was speaking to the women's conference. Ridiculous. Simon Walters [*Mail on Sunday*] said he was doing a story that Tory MPs were worried Diana would become a Labour MP if she became a commoner. I said his ability to make up stories and pretend they were soundly based knew no bounds. Ron Davies' office called to say that in an interview with BBC Wales he had attacked Prince Charles as immoral, raved on about him talking to trees, and basically said he wasn't fit to be king. Extraordinary stuff. I immediately drew up a statement from Ron apologising and withdrawing the remarks, as I knew TB would be absolutely livid.

I spoke to TB, who was by then on the train coming back from Wales. I read him the statement I had drafted. I said all we could get out of this was hands up and deal with it quickly. I suppose because it was Friday, and I was keen to get home, we were rushing a bit. I said to Ron TB was not at all happy, he would insist on an immediate statement, and here is my draft. 'Oh shit,' he said, 'this is sphincter-twitching time. I don't really have a choice, do I?' I said no, you don't, and the sooner we do it the better. I said he should write to Charles to apologise personally. OK, whatever you like. I called TB again and suggested that on arrival at Paddington, he do a doorstep saying the matter is now closed. TB agreed but as the day wore on, TB felt he should have taken the opportunity to sack him. The story led all the bulletins. TB called when he got home and said, I wish I'd sacked him. I said the mistake was saying the matter is now closed, which was my fault.

[1] Donald Dewar's wife, Alison, had left him for Irvine. The Dewars had divorced, and Alison and Derry Irvine married.

He said 'How are we going to get this party elected when we are surrounded by fucking imbeciles? We were just about getting back on our feet, and along comes Ron to shoot us in them.' Anji called and said Ron's wife had called her to say this was the end, she was going to leave him and Anji told her that would make matters a lot worse. Although it was a total pain, and gave the sense of chaos and disorder, I had a sneaking feeling it was less damaging then Harriet, because of course quite a few people will agree with Ron. We had to hope it was a one-day wonder.

Saturday, March 2

Peter woke me to say we must do something about Major piling into the Ron Davies story from Bangkok, which was now leading Radio 4. I called RC who was in the studio in Edinburgh about to do an interview. 'What on earth was Ron thinking of?' he said. We agreed he should attack Major for demeaning himself, attack Ron for stepping out of line and attack [William] Hague who, having said Ron should apologise, now that he had done so, was saying he should resign. The most helpful moment of the day came when Charles Anson called from the Palace to say that he was telling people as far as Charles was concerned, Ron apologised and that was the end of it.

Meanwhile, Anji told me that last night TB called her literally RANTING about the fact that Tim and I put out the statement from him saying the matter was closed. I said we did fuck up, but that was because TB didn't focus enough and because I was doing too much and was too tired. Also, I would rather he ranted at me, rather than about me to you or anyone else. I said the same to TB and pointed out that at various points yesterday, I had been working directly for JP, Robin, Frank, Andrew Smith, Donald, Mo, and dealing with him and Ron, so it was no wonder I occasionally got tired.

Sunday, March 3

I woke up very depressed, the worst it had been for years. I felt totally dead inside and knew it was going to be a struggle to get through the day. I don't think most people, who say they're depressed when they mean they are a bit fed up, really get how bad it can be. TB, who is never down for long, doesn't. I don't think Fiona does and of course for her, like me, there is the nagging fear that it leads on to what it led to before, a cycle of depression and hyper-ness that ends in mental meltdown. On days like today, dead days, every single thing, getting into bed, getting dressed, putting on a sock, brushing teeth, starting the car, answering a phone, saying hello, becomes a huge challenge. You have to summon the energy and strength to do it and when it's done you wonder if it was worth it. Then I see Fiona and the kids being normal, having normal conversations, and you know you should take part, or at least be civil, but you're dead inside and you can't do it.

Only the kids can get me out of this, so I took them to Regent's Park and we played football, and Rory got into a match with some kids and won 4–3. I listened to *The World This Weekend* on the way back and even though there had been a massive bomb in Jerusalem, they still led on Ron D and the Royals, and a succession of MPs were on saying it's right to have a debate about the future of the monarchy. TB called again – 'What sort of party is this? Do these fuckers want to get elected or not?' On reflection he felt we had handled it OK if not perfect, and it might have made matters worse to sack Ron. TB called again and I said I was exhausted and depressed, the worst I'd felt for years.

Fiona and I had agreed to go with some friends to an Eric Clapton concert. I said to her I shouldn't go, I'll be unbearable, but she did the 'They'll be disappointed' number, and she felt I was agonising inside because when pressure came on, I was filled with doubt about whether I was doing the right thing and whether all the pain and the sacrifice was worth it for these people who made our lives so difficult. So I went, but I hated every minute of the concert. Halfway through I said I was going for a pee, and went out just to be on my own. I stood there and there was this awful racket going on inside, loud music, people clapping and yelling and pretending they were young, and I felt totally disengaged from all of it. Not scared, not that I was close to the edge, or that I was heading for a Scotland '86 Mark Two, just disengaged, dead inside, and desperate to get home. It was a real 'life is a bitch and then you die' moment.

Monday, March 4

I had a real struggle to get out of bed. The Royals and Ron show was still rolling on, and he was getting plenty of support from MPs and public and there was a danger that he was becoming a bit of a hero for having launched a debate when in truth he had behaved like an idiot. TB was doorstepped aggressively on the Royals and whether there should be a Commons debate on the monarchy – which was of more lasting importance, a media-driven non-story on the Royals, or what GB was saying today about job insecurity? I know which is more important to us and the people of the country. End of story.

The office meeting went over recent problems very honestly.

Millbank wasn't functioning properly. GB relations were getting worse not better. TB, to my amazement, said his big worry was I was over-worked, that it was unsustainable for me to keep going, seven days a week, in the way I was and we had to work out a system that allowed me time off. Peter said he would like to do more but he was inhibited in briefing the press. TB said there must be no such inhibitions. I said the problem was that the press would always think that in part Peter had an agenda, because he is a politician as well as an official. The real problem was the dysfunctionality of the relationships at the top, which made it so hard to pin down strategy.

TB said we had to create some sense of excitement and interest in the policy debate. The press did not feel we were telling them an adequate enough story about what a Labour government would be like. He said he was confident in the policy positions but we had to get that debate going in the country. He then moved on to saying he wanted more party reform. 'Why not go to thirty per cent on the block vote?' Sally [Morgan] rolled her eyes and sighed very loudly. 'Please Tony, let's get through this year's conference on 50-50 first.' Sally, who had been a teacher, could sound and look very teacherish, and that was the manner on this – like a teacher telling a naughty boy not to push his luck. She also had this habit, when she'd made a point, of then looking very closely at her fingernails and stroking them with her other hand, which added to the sense that she had made the only point that mattered, now can we move on. It was all the more effec-tive for being understated. 'Oh all right then,' he said, grumpily, and Sally looked at me and allowed herself a triumphal little wink. I pointed out that it was on January 16 that TB first produced his forward strategy paper, and asked us all for comments and amendments. GB had still not responded. We had a discussion about how to respond to gays in the military. A government survey had found, surprise, surprise, that there was massive opposition to it. TB felt it was one of those areas where we had simply to say we would review the policy in government.

Tuesday, March 5

I got in early and TB was already there finishing the housing speech, which was running fine. He saw this as an important middle-range speech on a policy area too often overlooked. As we left, JP was in the car park downstairs and shouted across 'Never mind the home-owner, what about the homeless?' The speech went absolutely fine, in front of a 500-strong paying audience, mainly experts, and then we went to a visit in Camberwell, a young couple whose flat had halved in value in five years. Went up to see JP who was doing Questions. We ended up having an argument, because he said we never mentioned the homeless, which was not true, and I said so. I thought he had been joking earlier, but clearly not.

Wednesday, March 6

TB went through what he wanted from *Partnership with the People*. Tom Sawyer had produced a fascinating diagram analysing our problem areas. He had written inside a circle 'Winning the general election and staying in office'. Orbiting the circle were six boxes: 1. Shadow Cabinet pulling in different directions; 2. PLP not fully on board; 3. Unions preparing to make unreasonable demands; 4. Isolation of party activists. 5. NEC not focused on future; 6. Campaign and media – politicians not in harmony with party machine. It was a good summary. He said 'You don't realise how isolated you are.' And he said JP was a common theme in the six problem areas. We had to address the weakness of the links between the Leader's Office and the party.

The Big Guns meeting was turned into a meeting on rail, joined by Clare. Clare went off on one, saying the Big Four process was appalling. There should not be a big four. JP's face was great – he screwed it up into a look of wondrous, withering contempt. GB slumped into himself. TB looked at me and rolled his eyes. There is something truly awful about her when she is on her high horse, which is most of the time. TB got fed up with it fairly quickly and said he would write a form of words on rail in the next twenty-four hours, which would be agreed by the four of them and he would use it in a speech.

The Shadow Cabinet was ill-tempered too. Harriet of all people wanted to vote against the Private Finance Initiative Bill, and everyone else, apart from Margaret Beckett, who was using it to argue against private money in health, wanted a reasoned amendment. Harriet was beaten, so went bleating to TB afterwards.

Thursday, March 7

Pat McFadden and I went through the speech for Scotland tomorrow with TB and he suddenly piped up that he had plans for major change to our devolution policy. He wanted to limit the tax-raising powers. He wanted to promise a referendum before the Parliament is established. And he wanted to be explicit that power devolved is power retained at Westminster. That, he said, is the answer to the West Lothian Question. He said it in that way he has of making clear he has thought it through and it will be very hard to dissuade him. I had no problem with any of it, and thought it was both sensible and right. But Scottish politics is a nightmare and Pat rightly said there would be hell to pay in the party, not least from GB, but TB said they'll just have to live with it. He said he had been reading Roy Jenkins' book on Gladstone, and the reason he didn't do home rule was because these same kinds of arguments were being put to him, and they were nonsense. He said he was absolutely clear about this. He intended at some point in the not too distant future to make a big speech on it, then stay for a few days and take all the shit that was flying, and win the argument. 'We would fall ten points in the polls because of all the noise and then do you know what will happen? The party will breathe a sigh of relief and the public will think we have seen sense and we will finally have a defensible position.' He was terrific when he was like this. I could forgive him all the circular conversations and the weakness with some of his key relationships when he was like this: clear, principled, determined and set to lead from the front. The Scottish media would go into one of their frenzies but he was right – it was the sensible thing to do and only he really had the balls to say and then do it. David Hill had complained about the number of Tories on the *Today* programme so they said they would take GB for the 8.10 slot tomorrow. He refused, saying there was the chance of an interest rate cut. TB spoke to him, then I did and between us it took forty minutes to persuade him it was a good thing to do.

Friday, March 8

TB did a new Tory attack section for the speech and I redid the bit on TB telling the Shadow Cabinet to spell out legislative priorities. It was a perfectly good speech and its New Labour tone all the stronger for the fact he was doing it in Scotland. On the plane to Edinburgh we had the usual last-minute scramble for jokes, which was always a pain because basically he expected me to do them. 'I am not a fucking comedian,' I said. I stopped the air steward and asked if he would ask the pilot to tannoy an appeal for jokes for TB's speech. 'Don't worry,' said TB. 'He's mad.' I came up with a line on Dennis Canavan who had said TB was autocratic. 'I'm surprised you said I am autocratic, as I expressly told you not to.' I watched GB during the speech and he looked awful, scowling, rolling his tongue round his mouth, slouched, his hands locked together really tightly. Whenever the audience responded well, he looked even worse, like he was sucking lemons. TB's speech went down fine and the press all went for the right line – warning on priorities, hard choices, no tax and spend. The Scots media were intrigued by him saying there were 'no plans' to change the number of Scottish Westminster MPs. They were right to be. It wasn't as exciting as last year's Scottish conference, but he did well. On the plane down, we discussed Israel. I said he should be careful about Michael Levy. He may be a great fund-raiser and a good bloke, but the press were determined to get their teeth into him big time and even if he has done nothing wrong his whole life, you can see how they'll try to portray him and it could be damaging. TB was sure Michael was straight, and a good thing. On GB, he said 'Can you see any way I can put him in charge of an election campaign if it goes on like this?' I said no. He said, GB thinks you are against him and you must try to rebuild that. I said I do, but he makes it impossible. 'I know, but he is fundamentally a good thing and we have to work at it. I suppose in the end it boils down to him feeling that I had always accepted he would lead the party, and I would help him, but when it came to it, I let him down. It may be he will never get over that, I don't know.'

Sunday, March 10

Geoffrey Norris [industrial policy adviser] paged me re trouble on the rail front. Clare S had called him to say Brian Wilson was clearly briefing on rail for JP and she was being asked to respond. 'Obviously,' said Geoffrey in that splendidly sarcastic way he has, 'Clare doesn't want to generate stories about division so could we stop Brian doing this?'

Monday, March 11

Went to Millbank and started the day with a row with Peter. I said I didn't think he should have said on *Crosstalk* that TB was reading his book. He came back, very angry, and said 'What should I have said? That the leader's press secretary sabotaged the whole project, that he filleted it of decent ideas, made sure there was nothing controversial or interesting in it? That's the truth of it – there, you have been found out and you don't like it.' He later wrote to TB that he understood he was angry that Peter had said what he did. In fact, TB didn't even know what Peter had said, and nor had I suggested he did. But this was the kind of playground rubbish we had to deal with all the time. It also worked, as TB later told me he was worried about Peter and I had to do more to keep him involved. I said 'I am charged by you with helping you to win the general election. I cannot also be a psychiatrist to all the other people who are supposed to be helping us bring that about.'

The main purpose of the general election planning group was to watch Philip's video on highlights of the '87 and '92 campaigns. There were a lot of good lessons. Tax, tax, tax. The Tory onslaughts were impressive and the Labour defences of the attacks were woeful. We said we would not tax and spend yet all the main headline commitments were about spending. The discussion afterwards was sober and subdued, not least because a lot of people in the room were those who had been there then. Everyone started telling their 'how awful it felt' stories. I said I remembered when Fiona and I went round to Neil's when he and Glenys got back to Ealing from Wales on the Friday night, and it was just incredibly sad. Glenys had gone to bed exhausted, and Neil was just sitting watching a film on telly. If it had gone according to plan, he would have been prime minister. And he was just another bloke in slippers and a cardigan watching a film he'd have forgotten he saw by the morning. Sad. Really sad. I used all this to say it could happen again, all that we were doing up to now was the skirmishing, but in the campaign the real arguments would get tested in real heat, and we had to have the policies and the arguments honed and the politicians firing on all fronts. David [Hill] said we needed our politicians to be more aggressive. He said the Tories in 1992 were incredibly aggressive, very skilled at getting a message over. I went back to the House for a meeting on *Partnership with the People*, and more signs that GB was trying to delay. Margaret McD said there was no sense of direction at the moment. TB was sure that *Partnership with the People* in the pre-manifesto process was the way to get that direction. But people were still not clear what exactly we were launching.

Tuesday, March 12

Europe White Paper day. The morning meeting was the usual dispiriting affair. GB was not coming up with new ideas while blocking those of other people. Peter was there but contributed virtually nothing. Even on Europe and the White Paper, Gordon seemed to have nothing to say. Back in the office, Anji said JP was refusing to have anything to do with the fund-raising dinner at the Savoy. We had to push up the profile on fund-raising, both to show a more professional approach, but also make the people who gave money feel more comfortable about being identified as business supporters. Straight to meeting with the [advertising] agency, plus GB, Peter M, PG, working on poster ideas for a tax campaign at the end of April. The line was that the Tories hit you where it hurts and the main poster showed a man, hands in his pockets, tax and more taxes written on him, and another one of a poor man being squeezed by a rich man. I didn't like them but the others did.

Wednesday, March 13

Clare Short was on the *Today* programme at 7.10 on transport, and sounded totally incoherent. She was barely comprehensible at points, constantly wittering about the policy being one of 'breathe and move'. Later I played the tape to TB and he sat there, groaning. At the Big Four, JP came bounding in in a great mood for once and boomed out 'Hello Gordon, how are you?' and GB just stared at his papers and said nothing. JP tried again. How are you, Gordon? And he ignored him. JP looked at me, shook his head. They discussed rail, Robin pushing to know the final position, GB silent, JP rambling. Clare had produced a ten-page paper which was incoherent. During the meeting, Kate Garvey came in and said there had been a dreadful shooting in Dunblane[1] and a large number of children had been killed. George Robertson was up there, and TB spoke to him. It was one of those events that made everything else stop.

Thursday, March 14

The media was totally overwhelmed by Dunblane and a real sense of national grief. TB said George had told him there was a strong feeling he ought to go to Dunblane. Major was due to go tomorrow, because he had a fund-raising dinner in Glasgow, and obviously could not go to Scotland without going to Dunblane. TB said if Major asked him to go as an all-party visit he would, but George was very insistent. The meeting itself was awful with GB rewriting everything to do with tax, and Peter M insisting that tax had to be the main focus, otherwise nothing would be done, and all the advertising would be a waste of money. God knows what the agency people thought of the indecisive shambles that we presented. Peter was petulant. Gordon said everything was a problem. Philip was adamant that we had to go on tax, as was I, but Gordon kept trying to take everything round to job insecurity. He then chipped in that in any case he was going to go to the States and would only be back the day before the campaign was launched. Peter then threw up his hands and said we might as well scrap it, but TB said no. Afterwards TB gave Peter another bollocking. Anji and I both went to see him and said he had to threaten them that they would be replaced if they carried on like this. He said

[1] Thomas Hamilton, a rejected and unbalanced youth worker, massacred sixteen children and a teacher in the gym at Dunblane primary school near Stirling.

he had tried that but both of them knew that they were better than any of the others in what they did, and the only threats worth making were realistic ones. Give me a realistic alternative and I will take it. Someone said Robin, and he said what, the person who thought we should have stayed unilateral, the person who told me doing Clause 4 would destroy the party and I would live to regret it? But we were paralysed and the whole party was being affected.

Back at the House, George came to see TB and said it was his and Michael Forsyth's [Conservative Scottish Secretary] view that both TB and Major should go to Dunblane together. TB said he really did not want to push his way into this, and only wanted to do what was right. George spoke to Forsyth, and they agreed Forsyth should speak to Major and suggest they go together. As we heard nothing, and time was marching on, Anji called Alex Allan [principal private secretary] at Number 10 about 2pm. She said he sounded very nervous and said that the prime minister felt it would be tasteless for them to go together. On the contrary, she said, if it was true, as George and Forsyth were saying, that the community wanted TB to go there, the most tasteful thing would be for them to go together. It would be very odd if Major wanted somehow to veto this. TB did not want to be pushy. On the other hand, we did not want to end up in a situation where he was criticised for not going. And Major would surely not want to be criticised for stopping him. I could sense a big row story coming on, which would help nobody. PMQs was, of course, very subdued and very moving, and during George's statement, which I felt captured our mood best, I found myself with tears rolling down my face. Major said he would be going there tomorrow for the whole House. TB saw him afterwards, just the two of them for part of it, and came back saying 'He really doesn't want me to go, that much is clear.' He said he didn't want to push this, but if GR and Forsyth felt as strongly as they did, they should see Major, which they did. TB said Major had said Thatcher always wanted to do these tragedy visits but he hated it and he felt it would be wrong if there was a big circus there. TB said that was not Forsyth's view, that the community wanted political support. If the community felt they should go together, that will be the best thing to do. Forsyth and George discussed it with Major, and then, with Rachel Reynolds from Number 10, they came through to see TB.

Forsyth and I had a perfectly good relationship and as we went in, to lighten the mood, I said 'One day this will all be yours.' It was his view that rather than have two VIP visits, they should do it together. They told Major that the entire community would appreciate it if they both went. He said he had said to Major 'If my judgement is proved wrong, you can sack me,' to which Major had pointed at George and said 'Yes, but I can't sack him.' He finally agreed they should go together. TB said later he feared JM was trying to score points. Forsyth said it was very important there was nothing in the press about the discussions about this, and we agreed that he should tell people at his briefing later that TB was also going with JM. JM, having first been over the top against, now appeared to be over the top for and he asked TB to have dinner with him at the Hilton in Glasgow. TB felt not, not least because we were going to stay at George's. There was an enormous amount of pissing around, before finally getting away in the Number 10 convoy to the airport. On the flight, I had a chat with Jonathan Haslam [Major's press secretary], but all pretty inconsequential. TB was fretting that they would brief the press that he had barged his way in when in fact he just wanted to do what everyone else thought was right. Major and Norma were chilly with TB, and as for me, I might as well not have existed. It was odd considering we used to be quite friendly but JM, and I suppose she, had never understood that once he became PM, it was a different game. I had built him up in print in part to help undermine Thatcher. At Glasgow, we split off and headed to Dunblane and George's place. Forsyth was very solicitous and kind. George introduced me to Forsyth's wife, who said she hadn't realised that I was tall and handsome as well as famous! She was very friendly, and I saw a very different side to Forsyth. Later TB started to tell George about his plans on devolution, and I could see George was getting more and more nervous. I watched the Scottish news and it was perfectly obvious that it had been the right thing to do to go together.

Friday, March 15

I called Jonathan Haslam to check whether Major would be wearing a black tie. We had a few hours to spare, and TB used it for a discussion with George about devolution. TB was insistent that our policy was flawed, that the Tories could use the issue for both their tax campaign and their campaign on the break-up of the UK. He was absolutely sure we would have to pledge a referendum, and make clear that power devolved would be power retained. George was horrified, not least because he feared it would mean tearing up a deal with the Lib Dems, which had given him thus far political cover. Then when George had to go out for a call, TB said I know I am absolutely right on this. This is the reason why every home-rule bid has failed, because they have not had the guts to answer the real questions. He said to George, they would have to make changes in government anyway, to which George said yes, but then we will be in government. What if this stops us getting there, because of the outcry in Scotland? TB said there would be no reason for an outcry. Why shouldn't there be a referendum? If people want it, they should make it clear. Why shouldn't we make clear that power devolved is power retained, because that is the reality? Westminster will always be a superior body.

The chief constable and his assistant were both very shaken up. A lot of cigarettes were being smoked. The prime minister arrived shortly afterwards, and the chief constable gave a presentation of what happened, which was absolutely chilling. He took them through events very factually, very quietly, Hamilton killed them systematically, one by one. It was not clear why he stopped. I felt a bit sorry for Major, who clearly felt he had to respond in some way, but couldn't really find anything to match the enormity of what they'd just heard, and so made an odd-sounding enquiry about whether Hamilton watched videos. 'I know a lot of my colleagues are worried about videos,' he said. The chief constable said there was no evidence. TB said very little, simply that the police and the community had the support of everyone. John and Norma totally cut me dead again, which I thought was incredibly petty. She had also had a chat with Sandra Robertson [George's wife] who said she found her very cold. The reality was they didn't want us there. We left for the hospital, where there was a huge media scrum. TB first saw a child, then two teachers who were recovering. The hospital was so quiet, very little of the usual hustle and bustle, just very, very quiet. TB was as upset as I've seen him.

He and Major were then taken into a room filled with groups of doctors, nurses, paramedics, ambulance people, all the different people who had been involved. Again, you were struck by the quiet, the cold sadness that everyone felt, and the trauma those who saw it all were going through. JM was better at this private event than he was speaking publicly. TB and he did a short doorstep, no questions. When I was briefing the press, they were talking about who did we think did best out of the doorstep, and it was awful even to think in those terms, but I suppose these are important occasions, moments when the public do make judgements. We headed to the school. This was grim beyond belief. We drove up past an enormous media presence to the school gates. 'Welcome to our school.' Little bags hanging from pegs through the windows. Major, Norma and TB were taken to see a parent who had lost a child. George and Forsyth and their wives were taken through to a room with seven round tables around which parents were being comforted by friends and experts and volunteers. Some were grieving openly, weeping uncontrollably, beyond comfort. There was some trying to raise spirits, but it was impossible. TB came in, and then started to go round table by table. I chatted to the head-master, Ron Taylor, who told me what it was like going to the gym on Wednesday. There was so little I could do, he said, get the children out, then just plugging wounds with paper towels, anything we could find. TB was taken to see the gym, and there was a large pool of blood where they thought the teacher was trying to shield one of the children. Ron said the man chased them around the room system-atically, apparently even following one of them into a cupboard. Ron could not stop talking. His compassion was very powerful and he was clearly a strong character. He said the images just kept coming into his head, he doubted they would ever go away. He said the most chilling moment was when he was stuffing paper towels into a little girl's back wound, and as she rolled over there were two bullet holes in the front too. TB said the woman they had been to see had lost her husband last year and was pregnant.

I asked him later what his God thought of all this. How could he see something like this and still believe in some great divine being who offers nothing but good? He said just because the killer is bad, does not mean that God is not good. He and Major then laid a wreath, and did another short doorstep. Though TB was as moved as I have ever seen him, part of him was always the professional politician, and he wanted assurance that nobody could say he barged in and that he had handled himself well. Finally, Major spoke to me. 'There are no words for this, are there?' he said. 'Grim,' was all I could mutter. All day, I found it very hard not to cry. You looked at the class pictures and they could have been kids at our school, any school, anywhere. There was a little crowd of local people who TB spoke to, others were watching silently from their homes across the way. It was hard to imagine that this town could ever get back to normal.

In the car to the airport, we were silent. Ron Taylor said he couldn't get the image out of his mind and no wonder. Both George and Forsyth said how plausible many people had found Hamilton. George said that when he took his sons out of Hamilton's boys club he was attacked by middle-class parents, who defended Hamilton. The whole day was incredibly harrowing and it was wonderful to get home and see the kids. I felt guilty when I watched the news and found myself thinking as the pressmen had done, seeing who came across better, TB or Major. It was TB. Both he and George had handled themselves well. The man who had made the deepest impression was Ron Taylor though. He had a huge task ahead of him and I wanted somehow to help, but knew it was unlikely that I would, or could.

Saturday, March 16
Peter's interview on *A Week in Politics* was flammed up in the *Mail* as him saying that we might regulate the press if they didn't behave. The Tories ran with it. TB bollocked him later, saying we needed more results and less swanning around.

Monday, March 18
Dunblane was still enormous, and the sense of grief around the place, even in London, was palpable. The Queen had gone yesterday and pictures that looked like she had been crying were big everywhere. The community was now making calls to scale down the coverage and let them grieve in peace. TB was getting worried about the SE Staffs by-election. He said he got the feeling that the Tory candidate was strong and ours was not and he felt we needed another strategic mind up there. He gave JP a mild bullet, saying it was vital that we won it. GB was in Washington, so the regular strategy meeting was calmer than usual but not very productive. Peter went through where we were on next week's economic campaign. The trouble was that TB did not come to conclusions and knew he couldn't on this, because GB was not there. [David] Miliband complained we had effectively given him a veto on policy and it was now the same on campaigns. I said that I did not like the title *Partnership with the People*. It was weak. We agreed instead on *Contract for a New Britain*, and it transpired that GB didn't like that either, surprise, surprise. The meeting was incredibly frustrating given how much we were having to put into it. I was in a way playing devil's advocate to Peter, both re the title and over the policy content of the documents we were beginning to assemble for launch. Nick Pecorelli [party official] used the phrase 'downwardly mobile' in relation to Tory policy, and I felt we could make that stick. David Mellor was doing a big number on gun law. I thought we were terribly weak. I felt we should be calling for a ban on guns. It was the right thing to do anyway but after Dunblane even more so. I was pointing people to George Robertson's remarks at the weekend that it should be necessary to prove the need to own a gun, rather than the police prove unfitness to hold one. Otherwise Mellor was making the running on this.

March '96: Tories make running on gun law

Tuesday, March 19

There were more bad stories about the by-election in *The Times* and on the *Today* programme, and TB was pressing the panic-stations button. We agreed we would launch our offensive campaign on the economy on Monday, and got working on figures for it. We were going on guns at PMQs. Mellor had been running away with things yesterday. TB did fine, lined us up against the gun lobby. Meanwhile I was working on a briefing on small businesses for Mike Brunson, not least to try to take away from the big-licks briefing the government were doing on Major's speech tomorrow. I briefed Brunson that we would legislate to deal with late payment and he loved it. Then we had to get the speech on it in shape for tomorrow. The draft was poor. TB, who was due to have dinner at the Levys', said he would come in early tomorrow, and I felt we should finish it now. It was quite an important speech, establishing Labour not just as the party of opportunity but aiming at that key small business sector. We worked on it for a while and finally got it done in the back of the car on the way to Michael's. It was a ridiculous way to work.

Wednesday, March 20

TB and I had a row about the way we worked, and the last-minute-itis that really affected our competence and our ability to get the most out of these speeches. TB had agreed with Matthew d'Ancona to do a piece on his religious beliefs for the Easter edition of the *Sunday Telegraph*. People knew he believed in God, if not perhaps how important it all was to him, but I could see nothing but trouble in talking about it. British people are not like Americans, who seem to want their politicians banging the Bible the whole time. They hated it, I was sure of that. The ones who didn't believe didn't want to hear it; and the ones who did felt the politicians who went on about it were doing it for the wrong reasons. We had lunch at the *Sun*, which was pretty tough because by and large this was a group of very right-wing people. In the end, they would do what they were told but TB left in no doubt that if it was up to the people in that room, they would not want the paper to back us. Where they were basically coming from was that the party deep down hadn't changed. [Stuart] Higgins assured us there would be no Glenys-style rough stuff on Cherie. Afterwards TB said that was not a good meeting and they are not very nice people, with one or two exceptions. I said did you notice the portrait of Murdoch in the room where we had lunch? It was one of those in which the eyes followed you round the room. Hilarious. But they were all a bit Moonie-fied. As I said to Higgins afterwards, are you telling me all those people independently came to identical views on Europe?

On the train to Tamworth [for the South-East Staffordshire by-election], I flared up by saying that all our problems were caused by inability to get GB and Peter M working together and ill discipline of others, and until that was sorted we were nowhere. TB was in one of those agonising and demanding moods, complaining that he had to do so much himself to get anything done at all. I said it was no good just moaning. Take Gordon. What chairman of what company would allow his chief executive to go abroad for a week 'to think' before the launch of a major new campaign? Or Peter. Why did he tolerate the way he behaved in meetings? We had a spat and he just stared out of the window. The journey was one of the worst, because he was fretful, indecisive, and Anji and I were both in foul humour too. The journalists told us that the by-election campaign was not as well organised as the Tories', whose vote they felt was holding up in their traditional areas. The local media appeared more confident of our position than the national guys who were buying the Tory bullshit.

Peter came to see TB to complain that GB had vetoed yet another poster without seeing it. He was also still resisting the 'Contract' idea. In the car with CB and TB on the way to the airport we talked over how egocentric TB could sometimes appear and it was important he was nicer to Cherie in public. At Manchester, I'm afraid my rudeness got the better of me again. During the [Chamber of Commerce] dinner, a woman came out and said that they bought their tickets a long time before they knew it was going to be hijacked by a politician. I said if you have a problem speak to the organisers. What sort of speech do you expect from a politician but a political one? She said you are just as rude as everyone says you are. I said ruder, because I couldn't stand fools and there were lots of them around. TB said I had to watch my rudeness. He said I know you're in a bad mood but don't take it out on these people. He said I don't mind Anji clearing up afterwards for you but I don't want to have to do it myself as well.

Things were looking bad for the government on the BSE front. Good by-election coverage. There was a bad story in the *Express* where the head of the wretched Oratory was quoted as saying he hated the word comprehensive. There was the usual pandemonium in the Blair bedroom, Cherie getting her make-up done; she had lost the boots she wanted for her rather over-the-top turquoise suit. I told them re McIntosh and they both insisted yet again that it really was a comprehensive school. I was winding TB up all day re the Oratory and the fact that he was getting a bit thinner at the front – 'Chapter 27 – I'm not going bald and it really is a comprehensive.' We had agreed GB would do the Sunday lobby to try to get up an economic campaign. But all he did was bang out a few facts and figures, reheat some old stuff, and they didn't really bite on it at all. DH and I tried to get up the feel-good story from earlier in the week, and push on with BSE. GB had been sullen before the briefing, saying nobody would be interested, and then he ensured that they weren't.

Saturday, March 23
GB's briefing went pretty much nowhere, which led him to have another go at TB, saying there was little point having an economic campaign at the moment. He was impossible when he was like this. Some of the Sundays felt that BSE could kill the government, because of the cover-up angle and because of the cost. There was a karaoke at the school do, and we made prats of ourselves by doing Abba.

Sunday, March 24
TB was having dinner with GB and phoned to say that Gordon had been bounced off the *Today* programme, because there were so many Labour people on already: Harriet, Jack [Straw] on sentencing and Paul Boateng [Shadow minister for the Lord Chancellor's Department] on family law. I called *Today*, and said I was going to start pulling people to get GB on, but they said they didn't want Gordon at all, and wouldn't take him even if we pulled the others.

Monday, March 25
TB said his dinner with Gordon had gone fine, but I guessed from the body language that it hadn't. Mad cow disease was still dominating the news. TB, Jonathan and I were due to have lunch at the US Embassy with the ambassador [Admiral William Crowe], Mike Habib and Jim Young [embassy officials]. TB emphasised how hopeful he was about Northern Ireland, and how important it was the US stayed engaged in Bosnia. It was clear they wanted to pull out but it would be very difficult. They were very keen to stress that we would get a good reception in the States. The second we stepped into the car on the way back, Peter Hyman called to say Harriet was all over

the place on BSE in the Commons and he was really worried about her. We got back just in time to watch and she was awful. It should have been so easy to put the hard questions without making it party political but she completely blew it. For once TB watched the news and even he felt she had disabled us by giving them something to counter-attack. 'What a silly arse,' he said. I always told you she was lightweight, I said. We called a BSE strategy meeting. Harriet was as ever completely unabashed, spouting away about what we should do, totally oblivious to the fact that everyone in that room thought she had been absolutely hopeless today. Gavin [Strang, Shadow agriculture spokesman] came over as well informed and confident, and he agreed that we should now concentrate on the history, mistakes had been made, and on the breakdown of trust. Harriet's woeful performance gave the Tories something to attack and when TB called me later, he said 'She has disabled us, hasn't she?' Not unreasonably, she was being reported as having called for beef to be banned in schools. We had warned her to put this very clearly as a question, but she had virtually issued it as a statement. One of the drivers gave me a story about Waldegrave's car number plate, which was CJD, and said it was being dumped, because of the BSE crisis. I gave it to the *Sun* who put it on the front page.

Tuesday, March 26

GB was in Scunthorpe and the only people at the morning meeting were me, Philip, Jonathan and Nick [Pecorelli]. It was ridiculous. We had a massive launch on tomorrow without any agreement on the title and we were still in bust-up mode on rail. I was speaking to Robin. He said that he had huge reservations about TB's man-management style, and felt that the rail issue had been handled dreadfully. He could not believe that they had negotiated a statement – that is, he, Clare and JP – and then TB had just rewritten it in front of them. The election planning meeting was largely about the leader's tour. I made a presentation about the feel of it, how we had to communicate a sense of energy and direction, and how it needs to be the driver of the main message, totally locked in to what was being communicated at Millbank and around the country. I said I wanted the buses to carry a clear consistent message that could be understood whatever order they were filmed in.

I briefed TB on what RC said about his man management. He was obviously doing BSE for PMQs, and did most of the work himself, with long, careful, scientific questions to which, when he delivered them, Major went on 'Labour scaremongering' which, following

Harriet, he would have done whatever TB said. It allowed TB to go back hard, on 'mind-boggling incompetence and always blaming others'. I had a bit of an up-and-downer with Harriet, saying she had opened a flank we need not have opened.

Peter, Jonathan, Anji and I told TB he was handling things badly. TB said to Peter that he was putting him in a position of effectively saying that he could only have one out of Gordon and Peter working for him. I disagreed and said he'd simply given GB too much clout, he was too deferential and GB abused the position. He would not go with anything that was not his own idea, and he would not work with other key people. TB said he did not want him offside. I said he was both offside and unproductive at the moment. It was extraordinary that on the eve of an important pre-election launch, we had no title and no clear agreement on the general strategy. It was useless. I went away to work on a new title and eventually we came up with *Road to the Manifesto*. I put it to TB who was now upstairs having a curry with JP. They were fine with it and I said what a crazy way to work. The press, who continued to think we ran a smooth operation, would be amazed if they knew how a decision like this was reached, and how haphazard and last-minute it was. It was no way to run a railroad, I said.

Wednesday, March 27

Big day, off to the NEC to agree *Road to the Manifesto* plus Big Four press conference. TB got good press for PMQs on beef, government a bad press for dithering, delay and incompetence. I went in early to a meeting with TB, GB and Peter. TB was at first more interested in talking about BSE, with the government in such trouble. At one point GB said that if there was any more briefing by Brian Wilson he would have to retaliate, at which Peter and I snorted and said 'Come on.' What does retaliate mean? asked Peter. You'll find out, said GB who was being very Gordonic. I was more confident that we would get a good press out of today and make them feel something big was going on. I then headed to Walworth Road for the NEC. There was a lot of concern expressed about whether there should be a party ballot on *Road to the Manifesto*. Robin was supportive, making clear he backed it provided there was no usurping of conference. Dennis Skinner said we would have problems over it. I spent the morning doing TB's and JP's press releases. TB was constantly worrying whether it would fly or not, and was very jumpy. TB was keen to get out of Walworth Road and over to Millbank. We drove over and did a tough Q&A session with Peter and I playing the press, before Gordon and Robin arrived. TB had to assure GB that we were not overpushing the 'Contract', that we were not briefing it big.

The media liked it. Mike Brunson said to me 'Nothing better than hitting them while they're down.' They were interested that while the government was trying to go quiet, we were pressing ahead with a new policy process. There was also interest in what it all said about relations with the unions and the union link, and what policies would change as a result of the process. Tough questioning on tax, but TB did fine. Robin chipped in well, and JP pushed hard on political education and party involvement. It felt right, it felt it was going big and would worry the Tories, who had published their own consultation on what the party believed. TB was on very good form. It was impressive the way he just pushed to one side the downs and difficulties that had been driving us mad, and presented a strong, coherent and confident case.

Thursday, March 28

We got massive and pretty positive coverage. My briefing on the 'Learn as you Earn' smart cards got good coverage in the middle market. Sally M was worried though, as the unions were furious at the focus in the papers on cutting them out. We hadn't pushed in that direction, but you could never persuade the unions otherwise. We headed off to Tamworth. TB was worried we'd have problems with the party and unions re the emphasis on a ballot. Sally said Rodney Bickerstaffe was threatening to take Maggie Jones [UNISON official] off the NEC because of her voting with TB against his instructions. TB's other main concern was beef. Jonathan was working full-time on getting together a package of proposals for us to put out with the backing of people like Sainsbury's and McDonald's. Jonathan had done an extremely good job on it. The National Consumer Council backed us too, making Major at PMQs look very petulant indeed. We'd managed to sort out the technology to deliver a live link from a shop floor in Tamworth, linked up to Blunkett, Meacher and Byers in London. It worked brilliantly and everyone at the media centre said it was a huge success. TB did brilliantly considering he had bad feedback in his earpiece. Fiona Gordon and Bruce both said there was no need to panic now. Indeed, there was a better feeling around the place, lots of posters, a huge flag outside the pub, the local media good. The visit was definitely a success.

Clare was refusing to sign a letter to Warburgs [UBS Warburg, investment bank] because I said 'achieve greater public ownership and control of Railtrack'. She told Jonathan that she had a conscience and would not sign it with the word 'greater' in it. She was due to do the *Today* programme and a big speech in Swindon tomorrow. I got TB to call her, and we agreed she would not do *Today*, and we would say 'extend' not 'achieve greater'. Then another problem. Last night we lost a Commons vote on VAT by one vote and Harriet was missing, because she said she had a terrible migraine. Jon Sopel was on to it and Peter wanted us to move heaven and earth to stop it. Peter said Don Dixon [deputy chief whip] should say he'd given her permission. Don said he hadn't, but was happy for us to say he was content with Harriet's explanation. Sally was anxious. She said the NEC was in meltdown because the papers were saying the unions were on the way out. She urged me to tell TB it was a real problem and he would have to be very, very careful about it. True, but at least we were back on track, back on song, with a strategy being driven forward.

Friday, March 29

I was up at 4.30 to write TB's speech to the Federation of Small Businesses. The theme was that the government were behaving more and more like an Opposition and we were preparing for government. TB did the speech and Q&A and got a very good reception, two standing ovations. He had always identified the small-business sector as an important one, and this couldn't really have gone better. But again it was pretty clear what their concerns were. One person asked 'We may like you, but what about the rest of them?' and there was even a round of applause at that. It was a growing problem. And as if to remind us, Clare did her speech in Swindon and defied our instructions not to do clips and interviews. We pulled her from *Today*, *World at One*, and the *PM* programme, and then when I heard she was doing *Channel 4 News* and *Newsnight* I paged her to say that TB was adamant she do no more interviews. TB said again that she was out of her depth. Then another problem. Mo was giving the Sundays a statement saying the government had made an error of judgement in part of the handling of the [Northern Ireland] peace talks. She had told Anna Healy she had cleared it with TB, but I doubted that very much and said I'm sure TB will be furious. Indeed he was and said we should pull it. I called Mo and said it couldn't go out. She sounded angry then said if that was an order, fine, but I wish you people would make up your minds. I told her she had misread signals. I had told her that I thought TB thought it was OK to be a bit more distant from the government. That didn't mean distancing herself from TB. Earlier TB told me that I must not be so anti Harriet in the office as this was influencing everyone else.

Saturday, March 30

The Tories were in Harrogate for yet another comeback, relaunch, fightback, call it what you will. The problem for them was that BSE was pretty much wiping out everything for them, but they had done a good job trailing Major's speech on community care. They claimed they were new ideas, which they weren't. Nonetheless, the BBC were going pretty big on it. The BBC were a real problem at the moment. They were falling for all sorts of crap, anything the government put their way whilst we were finding it very hard to get coverage of positive initiatives. This angered TB who was in one of his 'the broadcasters are against us' moods. Calum and I went to Wycombe for the Burnley game, another disaster, we were crap, lost 4-1. TB was on several times later worried we were getting the line wrong on beef, still felt that we should be more consensual and Harriet had really fucked up.

Sunday, March 31

Up at 6, had a quick bath and then to TB's to prepare for *Frost*. In the back of the car, we were doing the usual me playing the interviewer, him giving the answers, and being occasionally thrown and doing his startled rabbit look – 'What is the answer to that? What do I say to that?' It was interesting how these things worked. He would always start slowly but by the time we got to the studio, he was almost in full interview mode, and that would continue when we peeled off from the BBC hangers-on and locked ourselves away in the dressing room. Usually, by the time he was on the sofa, he was fired up. Peter Sissons [BBC broadcaster] was doing the interview, and was pretty soft. Beef, NEC/ballot, future policies, TV debate. But later BBC ran with Bill Morris, who on *GMTV* warned they would resist a ballot because conference was sovereign. I had a bad weekend with Rory who was constantly, and justifiably, complaining that I wasn't there enough and when I was, I was on the phone.

Monday, April 1

There was an excellent April Fool in *The Times*, an ad urging people to call [Conservative] Central Office for a tax refund. We got in for a meeting with Donald, Mo and Jack Straw re [Michael] Howard's new anti-terrorist measures. Jack had wanted to vote in favour but had now moved to abstention. TB still wanted to vote for, and said it would only cause a big rebellion if we went round saying it was a problem. It was obvious the Tories were simply trying to flush us into a difficult position for the party. TB was pretty appalled they could behave like this but it was of a piece with the charge that the government was now behaving like the Opposition. Both of us had very mixed views about a TV debate. In theory, it was an obvious thing to do, but I always felt with our media as it was, it would all be about the process, who was wearing what, who did the make-up, how did the presenter do, so I was not sure you'd get the big debate it was meant to generate. We were beginning to worry that they would announce a referendum on the euro after Wednesday's Cabinet meeting. TB was beginning to worry about the referendum issue and I stoked up the press to write about rifts in government.

Tuesday, April 2

The referendum issue was on the boil and was an obvious contender for Questions. I went to TB's first thing and we agreed to dig out all Major's quotes on referendum where whatever we got him to say would cause him problems with one side of his party. We had to get into a position where if he did move on referendum, it was a sign of weakness, rather than the prime minister acting in the national interest. We definitely did the right thing for PMQs. Major looked discomfited, his party looked troubled and the broadcasters got the message that the aim is to position him as weak. I spoke to GB again and then to Robin. RC wanted to use it to move on a referendum now, but I said that would detract from all we were actually trying to achieve on this, which is to keep options open and to portray JM as weak. I felt totally comfortable with our position, Robin continued to say it was not tenable. Then it emerged their plan was not to promise a referendum as government policy, but say that it would go in the manifesto at the next election. I spoke to Robin and he said he would do the media. I said TB would not be at all happy if he tried to move our position on this. He agreed not to. Sue Douglas [editor, *Sunday Express*] came in for a chat and said she would try to get the paper to back Labour, if she could. She was very flirtatious, big on eye contact, always leaning forward when she spoke, flicking her hair, flashing her thighs. TB called later, and we agreed it was potentially disastrous to the Tories, that if we played it right they could end up in the worst possible position on this. He said I should keep very close tabs on Robin who was doing interviews. Robin told me 'If I'd had my way we would have moved on this first,' but I didn't think it mattered at all that we would end up following them. Major was looking weaker all the time.

Wednesday, April 3

I was up at 6 to do my *Tribune* column. I wish I could bring myself to tell them I didn't want to do it. It was a real hassle and I wasn't putting enough into it. The referendum was the splash in most of the heavies and big on the broadcasts. GB felt it important that we presented Clarke as weakened at this stage; also, on beef, that we should be seen to be trying to get the EU to lift the ban after last night's meeting of EU ministers, and present it as Douglas Hogg [agriculture minister] coming back in defeat. We had a potential problem in that the Tories would try to portray this as a Europe row with all the anti-EU tones. So the situation brought problems for us as well as for them. On the euro referendum, the press were asking when we were going to announce one and of course there were fresh moves notably from Robin to move. The mood was getting better at these meetings, but GB still tended to see everything through his own telescope, about his own position, angling to do anything on the referendum, for example, when even Donald was saying it should be Robin. I spoke to Robin several times during the day, and he kept banging on that we would not be able to sustain our 'referendum or election will decide' position for long. I felt that the longer we were able to present this as a story of Tory splits and Major's weakness, the longer we should hold out.

We had a good turnout for my briefing on TB's US trip, and it was clear from the questioning the tabloids were trying to build up to present it as a snub situation. Jonathan had been warned by Peter Westmacott, the number two in our embassy in Washington, that there was concern that the hype was being overdone. But I went ahead and continued to hype. Mo came to see me to say next Tuesday she wanted to put out a statement, laying down what the government should do with the Northern Ireland election planning. She said they would then not do it and we could say we disagreed with the bill. I couldn't readily see the logic. Jonathan joined us and we agreed she should be cautious. She was beginning to feel the heat of TB's desire to be too close to the US government on this.

Thursday, April 4

I tried to have the day off but the phone and bleep never stopped. The American news magazines were starting to press for TB's time. Both the *New York Times* and the *Wall Street Journal* went on the line that he would not undo Thatcherism. I went to John's [Merritt] grave on the way home and had one of my imaginary conversations and asked him what he thought about me going to the Oval Office, the

White House, not as a journalist, as part of a political team on the run into the election. I imagined him laughing, shaking his head and asking when I'd get a decent job.

Peter M came round for dinner. He said GB had taken hold of TB. 'He can faze him, and so get him to do things he shouldn't do, and not do things he should. I can always tell when Tony has been speaking to Gordon, because his whole attitude is different, slanted against me. Gordon discusses nothing of substance with anyone other than Tony. He maintains OK relations with you because he cannot be seen to be off with everyone but he doesn't really talk to you and he doesn't talk to me at all. He disables us and cuts our effectiveness by between twenty-five and fifty per cent.' I said I was also worried that in deferring to GB, TB lowered his authority in the eyes of others. Peter got very upset when I said I thought he and GB were as bad as each other. He denied it, said he had been driven to behave like this because GB was so vile to him.

Saturday, April 6

As we were leaving for Tessa's for the weekend Fiona and I had a dreadful row when I made a crack about how much luggage we were taking for one night, and it spiralled out from that. The tensions of being constantly on call were dire at the moment. Jonathan called to put me in touch with the guy from Jewish Care who was due to be going to the States to make contacts re fund-raising. Jonathan felt we should be up-front about it and show it was a sign of our professionalism. I was anxious and felt he should be more discreet than that. We didn't want a fund-raising story to cloud the American visit. Sarah Womack [Press Association] called to say the *Sunday Express* had a piece on a Central Office document that was being sent to US journalists on Blair's un-American activities. These people were unbelievably useless. I could hardly believe it that they had done this, as it was another own goal. None of the Yanks saw him as anti-American, and all it would do would heighten interest in the visit, which was what we wanted. When I got the thing sent over, it was a pathetic piece of work, cobbled-together rubbish about old party policy positions. David [Hill] had given suitably dismissive quotes and I added to them – pathetic, good for us as would increase interest in the visit. The *Sunday Telegraph* were splashing on the row engendered by TB's piece on God. I felt fully vindicated. As I said to TB: 1. never believe journalists when they say they are doing you a favour or giving you a free hit; 2. never do an interview without someone else in the room, and

3. never talk about God. Hilary and David H felt it wouldn't play too badly but I sensed a mini disaster, as it was Easter, and they were trying to spin this as Blair allying Labour to God. When you looked at the words, he didn't say that, but he said enough to let them do the story and get Tories piling in saying he was using his faith for politics, and saying you couldn't be a Tory and a Christian. This was the permanent risk with UK politicians talking about God.

Sunday, April 7

It was interesting that every paper's lead political story was to do with us. I was frankly more worried about God than anything and I got Hilary to call every political reporter and leader writer to make sure they realised he was explicitly not saying what the paper said he was, namely that Christianity and conservatism were incompatible. It was always going to be an uphill struggle because they took the lead from the spin the *Telegraph* put on it. Fiona and David H were of the view that it was not so bad for us, that many people probably thought there was a contradiction between right-wing conservatism and Christianity, and it was another dimension to Tony's character, which would make him more appealing to certain people. It was clear from the calls I was getting it was destined for the splash in most papers; of course the *Mail* were winding themselves into a frenzy.

Monday, April 8

GB called and we agreed God was a disaster area. TB had called him from Spain because he had not been able to get hold of me. We joked about TB going to Tamworth tomorrow to say he had been resurrected. The papers were pretty mega on TB and God, the splash almost everywhere with several bad editorials saying he was playing politics with God. Fiona and David Hill were still of the view that it was basically OK. When I spoke to TB he admitted it was an own goal, totally unnecessary. 'I should never have agreed to do it and I won't do it again.' He said he wanted the American speech to be a definitive economic statement, and the assurance that Labour would be a good bet for inward investment.

Tuesday, April 9

The US build-up was going well, *People* mag was out, *US News & World Report*. Jonathan called to ask what we wanted Mike McCurry [Clinton's press secretary] to say. I said our media would judge things on the length of the meeting,[1] and the way he was treated, not least the media arrangements. He suggested a joint press call which might be too optimistic but that was what we should aim for. I said they should also say that TB's stance had been helpful on Ireland. Jonathan called again later to say he had seen Mike [McCurry] and Tony Lake [Clinton's national security adviser], that they said the Tories were pissed off at all the advance hype but they were perfectly happy and would help us all they could. The meeting would certainly overrun, they would do a walk through the garden, and would certainly allow the media in. Also Mike was up for doing a joint briefing with me just for the UK press. They were certainly pulling out a few stops. I had a bet with Bruce that I could get Clinton to say 'Brian Jenkins' [Labour candidate in the Tamworth by-election] in the White House, without just asking him to say it. More good news from Washington, that Colin Powell [former chairman of the Joint Chiefs of Staff] wanted to come to the dinner at the residence. On the drive back, we got into mildly hysterical mode. We were looking ahead to the US and tomorrow's meeting with Boutros Boutros-Ghali [UN Secretary General] and I started to imagine what the world would be like if everyone had to have three names, à la Boutros Boutros-Ghali. I said to Fiona Gordon that if she married GB, she could call herself Fiona Gordon Brown which for some reason TB found ludicrously funny, and kept repeating it and laughing.

Wednesday, April 10

The pre-US coverage was OK, but what most of them had taken out of the PA interview was his line that Cherie didn't want his job. Clearly there were two things it was impossible to discuss rationally with our press – Cherie and God. There were thirteen journalists on the plane and thankfully we had been upgraded to first class so we could avoid them. TB was working on the speech, writing furiously, page after page, big writing, hair awry, head down and clearly totally focused. I took him up the plane to talk to some of the press and later it was clear we had a problem out of it. Jeremy Vine told me that Robert Peston was getting terribly excited and telling the others TB had ruled out tax rises for people on £40,000. In fact the figure had been used as a figure of speech for a band that people on average earnings might think was a lot, but it's not really, but he did not go beyond the line

[1]The trip had to be closely choreographed because of the visit made by Neil Kinnock, when he was snubbed by Mrs Thatcher's great friend, Ronald Reagan. Kinnock was given less than half an hour for his meeting with the president. The snub was rubbed in by a dismissive White House briefing.

– no plans. But Peston was clearly winding it up, and I had a very public argument with him, saying that if he wrote it, based upon what TB just said, it was akin to making it up. TB was back at the speech and asked me to write sections on tax, and what we meant by the radical centre. He had done a pretty good job on the main draft. The tax fandango was worrying TB, because the message it would give was that we DID intend to tax people higher on incomes over £40,000. So what they may have first interpreted as a low-tax story would quickly become a high-tax story. I was furious with Peston. He had single-handedly inspired headless-chickens syndrome in the media.

They had put us into the presidential suite at the [New York] Hyatt and we did a few calls before Liz [Lloyd] arrived and went off to type up the speech in my room before we headed to the UN, to get briefed by the ambassador [to the UN] John Weston, and his team. Weston and his number two both came over as very traditional Establishment FCO people, Garrick club tie, light suit, public school features and Weston stuck to TB like glue. Boutros Boutros-Ghali came over to me as a manic-depressive, and we had got him in a depressive mood. I was struck by how much he talked about the problems facing the UN, administrative, bureaucratic, rather than problems facing countries of the world. Walked to Plaza Hotel for the business meetings on the twenty-seventh floor, including George Soros [financial speculator and philanthropist]. It was fine, and though TB faced one or two hostile questions, he disarmed them pretty well. The UK press were hanging around outside and I briefed them as the meetings went on. I asked Soros if he would speak to them. I said one of our key aims of the visit was to give messages of reassurance to investors in the UK and if he were to say something positive, that would have a major impact in the UK. He was fine about it, and he basically said that the idea that Labour would deter investors was a scare story. He said that TB had made a good impression. It was an important endorsement. The tax situation was causing problems at home, at the by-election, GB saying we could not rule out a 60p rate. This is the problem of ever talking about figures, even in background friendly chats with the press.

Back at the hotel, TB rewrote the middle part of the speech and I rewrote the beginning and the end and we tried to drive home the radical-centre theme. The speech finally came together, as per usual, at the last moment, when TB was flagging and wanted to go to bed and I said he would feel a lot better in the morning if we cracked it now. He said all we need is a better final passage on Labour as the party of the centre and could I write it? At this point, TB went over to the corner of the room, ostentatiously sat down at the piano, flicking back the bottom of his dressing gown like it was a pianist's coat, and started to play 'Frère Jacques'. I wrote a new last page which distilled the argument he had been making in the various drafts. As he continued to play badly on the piano, his open dressing gown now exposing his private parts to the world, I said what would a fly-on-the-wall documentary make of this particular scene, and we fell about. The speech was fine now. I slept very lightly. At one point I was dreaming I was in the back of a car being driven through a vast open space. I looked out of the window and the kids were standing there looking lost. I got out of the car, walked back to them and we played in what was like a desert. I woke up and called home.

Thursday, April 11

I spoke to JP first thing about the by-election to make sure we had everything in place after the result. He made a joke about TB always going abroad to announce policies. He was confident it was going well. He said GB was fuming about all the tax stuff. TB and GB later had a heated discussion in which TB repeatedly denied having briefed on the lines the papers said he did. He said 'Look, it has happened and I put my hands up to it. It was a very small mistake which they turned into a big thing.' We had not planned the story, but he wouldn't have it. TB was having to make the same point again and again. First stop of the day was *Good Morning America*, and on the way TB kept saying that it was so sad that he and GB had been so close, had a great laugh together, and now it was just very hard work. Tim called to say *World at One* were doing tax, surprise surprise, so I called them and gave them the best lines from the speech. I started to prepare a written briefing, which also incorporated an attack on Major for getting involved in the tax story, saying it was a mistake to remind people of him and tax on a by-election day.

The press conference afterwards was mainly for American press and TB did a few questions, BSE, New Labour, general election timing. There was a marvellous moment when he was asked where our policy on Taiwan differed from the Conservatives' and he clearly didn't know. 'Obviously our position is close to that of the government,' he said. 'Whatever that may be,' I said to Jonathan. On the drive to the airport, TB, who felt that the day had gone well so far, was expressing concern about Peter. 'I don't know what has happened to him. He has become so lordly and difficult in his manner.' He was also trying to assure Jonathan he really was interested in foreign policy. On the plane to

Washington, TB worked on the series of speeches he had to make on arrival. I was working on the series of different by-election responses according to the size of the result. During the day, I had been keeping in touch with Fiona Gordon and she was getting more and more upbeat as the day wore on.

On arrival, TB disappeared off with the ambassador in the Rolls-Royce to see Alan Greenspan [chairman of the US Federal Reserve], while I left to find the bar where Mike McCurry was coming to meet me and our press. It was a really nice thing for him to do and an excellent meeting. He talked up TB while lowering expectations. He said it had been very odd in the November meeting, because someone in the room had said it was almost as if TB was the senior figure at times. He said Clinton wanted to carry on basically where it left off last time. Mike and I had a chat about how to handle things. He said Clinton wanted to do a walk through the garden, but they were coming under pressure from the embassy not to do anything that would wind up the story that Major was being punished. Mike and I agreed he would give a very positive readout. They would talk up TB on Northern Ireland, and TB's role in left-of-centre politics. He was clever and funny and had a light touch. He was obviously going to help us make it a success. TB said earlier that we should underline after the by-election that the Tories had no friends at home and no friends abroad. Some of our press assumed the White House was pushing the boat out because of Major's lot helping Bush.

TB was really motoring, winning everyone over. I was meanwhile getting the cuttings and speaking to Tamworth. The reception was fine, they had put together a good list of people. I was surprised that Colin Powell remembered me from the last meeting in London. I was seated between Tina Brown [editor of the *New Yorker*] and [former *Washington Post* editor] Ben Bradlee's wife but I was like a cat on a hot tin roof waiting for the by-election result. I had an interesting chat with Tina and Harry Evans [former editor of *The Times*] about how awful the modern press was. I gave them my usual scenario on how we could lose. It was almost 3am when I finally got the result from Fiona Gordon. 13,700 majority. I felt like bursting into tears. In fact I almost did and later, in the privacy of my room, I did. Fiona G was as cool as a cucumber. I went through to tell TB straight away, and though he knew he shouldn't overreact in public, I could tell he was ecstatic, especially as in the last couple of hours, I'd been winding him up by saying it could be as low as 1,500. I wanted him to be the first on and we had got things lined up so that he could go straight into the [David] Dimbleby [election results] programme. We went down to do it and I could only hear TB, not the questions, and I could tell Dimbleby was straight on to tax as his second question. I could see TB was going strong, staying cool and dismissive. The lines on the by-election were easy, fantastic victory for us, humiliation for them, contrast between us with a positive programme for government, them drifting and directionless. I got him to speak to Fiona G and thank her and the team. 'This is unbelievable,' he said. 'They are in real trouble now. I can even see them moving to Heseltine.' No problem, I said.

Friday, April 12

We had breakfast at the *Washington Post* with a very right-wing editorial board who gave him a bit of a kicking but he handled it well. Kay Graham [*Washington Post* publisher] was impressive. She showed inordinate interest in his article on God, and wanted a copy faxed to her. We fixed up pictures of TB calling JP and Brian Jenkins, with cameras both ends. TB had spoken earlier to John to say well done. I'd spoken to him and he said to tell people 'I'm not a class warrior, but a class act.' JP was getting huge coverage by saying he was middle class and prompting lots of coverage about class divides. Then we left for the White House. TB was more nervous than I'd seen in a long time. Several times he took me to the corner of the waiting room to ask about minor details, some not so minor. 'Do I call him Bill or Mr President?' Clinton was waiting just inside the door and greeted everyone individually, then introduced TB to the rest of the US side. There was a fair bit of small talk, Clinton explaining some of the paintings and artefacts, asking about New York, putting people at ease. I was surprised at the level of turnout on their side. Clinton, Warren Christopher [Secretary of State], [Robert] Rubin [Treasury Secretary], [Tony] Lake, [Leon] Panatta [chief of staff], Nancy Soderberg [US policy official on Ireland], McCurry.

The American pool came in and threw one or two domestic questions, and then the next pool, with lots of eager Brits. Peter Riddell from *The Times* broke the silence. 'Do you think you're sitting next to the next prime minister?' There was a pause, both smiled and you could feel Clinton's mind whirring, thinking carefully what to say. 'I just hope he's sitting next to the next president,' he said. TB looked nervous, though he got into it. Clinton praised our statesmanlike stance on Ireland, as Mike said he would. The last time I was in this room was as part of the press pool and I can remember thinking how little time you had to ask questions or absorb the atmosphere, and how quickly they bundled you out. It was strange to see them being parcelled out, much the same people I used to be with, and I stayed behind, and then listened to and took part in discussions about the big issues of the day. Clinton surprised me in several regards. His enormous feet were all the more noticeable because his shoes were even shinier than TB's. His suit and tie were immaculate, as was his hair. He had huge hands, long thin fingers, nails clearly manicured and he used his hands a great deal as he spoke, usually to emphasise the point just before he made it. I was also struck at the amount of detail he carried in his head. Like TB, he was good on the big picture, but he backed it up with phenomenal detail. He was a people person, terrific at illustrating policy points by talking about real people, real places. He was also tremendous at working a room. He was more relaxed than at the meeting in London, presumably because this was his territory and he was less tired, but if he made a long intervention, he found a way of addressing part of it to all the different people in the room. It's a great talent in a politician, and in his manner and his speaking style, he engages you, makes you feel warmly disposed towards him. I guess that wasn't a surprise, and it shouldn't have been a surprise that he was so big on detail, but it was. Also like TB, he came alive talking about strategy, campaigns, message. He got it instinctively, more than probably any political leader in the world. There was one revealing moment when Clinton said of our stance on Northern Ireland, 'It's smart,' then a pause, then he added, 'and morally right.' You felt he saw it in that order. I won my bet with Bruce. The deal was I had to get Clinton to say the words Brian Jenkins, and I couldn't just say 'Say Brian Jenkins.' Knowing as I did how big he was on campaigns and campaign methods, I put a few 'Vote Brian Jenkins' stickers on my notebook and whenever I spoke held it tight against my chest, stickers showing. I could see he was looking at the stickers and after a while he said 'Who's Brian Jenkins?' Our side fell about, and I explained the bet, and he said he was glad to help.

TB said straight out: how do you win support for more equity and justice without it meaning more tax? Clinton said the private sector was the key, that we must not be defined simply as a public-sector government, but bind in the private sector, emphasise their role in wealth creation. There was a clock just to Clinton's left by the door and after twenty-five minutes a tall young blonde woman, beautifully dressed all in black, came in, gave him a nod, smiled at the room and then closed the door behind her. It was time to go, but Clinton kept talking, more talking and eventually got up and he carried on talking. Mike and I disappeared into the corner to agree we would say they met for thirty-five minutes, more than scheduled, very friendly, useful, productive, go over the issues they ranged over. Mike then took us through to the Cabinet room, TB included, and he said he would say it was a forty-minute meeting which covered Bosnia, Ireland, world economy, Europe, mad cow, etc. He had been a terrific help. We then collected our thoughts and went through what TB should say at the stakeout spot. Again, I found myself thinking of previous visits here, on the other side of the fence. In particular when Neil [Kinnock] was stitched up by a combination of the White House, Number 10 and our disgusting right-wing press. I got a certain satisfaction from seeing them straining to hear TB's every word, and knowing that this time, because the White House had been so helpful, there was no way they could write this as anything but a success. Before the press conference TB said he wanted a chat with me alone, and I worried he was going to bollock me for the Jenkins scam. In fact he just wanted my reassurance. 'Am I doing OK?' I said yes, but you are letting your nerves show, just be yourself.

To CNN where Anji and I watched from the control room, where a huge guy was barking orders and laughing at the fact that there had been an Easter Bunny Party in the by-election. Towards the end we could see TB was getting a nosebleed. The big guy started shouting 'Cut the talk, cut the talk, the guest has a nosebleed situation.' I said to him if he had been in Britain, they'd have carried on so they could have a TB nosebleed live on TV. We then went for a meeting with Al Gore [Vice President], which was fine. I was surprised how heavy he was and how much he relied on cue cards to speak. I was sitting next to someone who was literally ticking off the lines as Gore delivered them. It was interesting that whenever TB was away from GB, JP, Peter, all the nonsense, things went a lot smoother.

Sunday, April 14

Charlie Whelan woke me up to say that Clare Short had fucked up on *GMTV* by saying that she thought people like her should pay more tax. At first I felt we should completely ignore it and hope it would go away, but eventually we got Clare, through Jo Moore, to put out words which retracted what she said. Though it would probably not be a huge problem, she gave the Tories a chink to attack. The press was a total disaster area for them at the moment and this would give them a bit of relief. Michael Levy called. He was gushing, saying that TB had been raving about my performance in the States, how I hadn't slept for days and had been absolutely sensational on the trip. I got the feeling that he wanted similar recognition. He was desperate for me to know, which I did, that he'd hosted the dinner at which TB met [George] Soros for the first time. He spoke rather in the manner of a chief of staff. We have to do this, and we have to do this, we have to do that, TB said this, TB said that. I suspect a lot of it was bullshit but TB does rate him. The terrible thing is he has to be told it all the time, there is a nervousness, a need constantly to be recognised for what he was doing. I left Tim to do most of the briefing, and Jon Sopel quoted senior sources saying it was about Clare's competence, not tax. It was clearly going to be fairly grim in the papers, though we just about managed to contain it. The work of last week, while not undone, was seriously undermined. She cannot be trusted to behave in a professional or competent way. TB was at Michael [Levy]'s and called several times purely to say how exasperated he was about people like her. It would be so much easier if I did not have the party around my ankles the whole time, he said.

We took the boys to Liz Symonds' [general secretary, First Division Association – the senior civil servants' union] party. I chatted mostly to Robin Mountfield, Heseltine's permanent secretary. He said the Civil Service is not hostile to the idea of a Labour government. They're actually gasping for change, he said. He said [Sir Robin] Butler [Cabinet Secretary and head of the Civil Service] will be as loyal to TB as he was to Thatcher and Major. But there would be difficulties about me and Jonathan in particular. The trouble with me was that I would have to be a political appointment but with the Civil Service working for me, and that could make for difficulties, though a lot would depend on the personal relationships that developed. TB could change the rules but it was important that TB worked through what he wanted to do, and built support, because he would require goodwill to make real change. He felt I probably should be press secretary, and Jonathan should perhaps be head of policy rather than a wide-ranging executive. I also chatted to a rather attractive doctor, who confided that she had dreamt about TB and that whenever she met him in these dreams, she was wearing no underwear. What she wanted me to do with this information was not made clear.

Monday, April 15
I woke to Clare Short all over the papers, being lauded by the Tory press for 'letting the cat out of the bag' on tax, and as if that wasn't bad enough, then she came on the *Today* programme. None of us knew she was going to be on, ostensibly about the Railtrack prospectus being published today. Of course she was asked about tax, and not only defended what she said yesterday, but then launched into an attack on the anonymous sources attacking her. Her language was

loose and intellectually lazy as ever, and she made it sound like a principled position when in truth she had simply fucked up. TB and JP both called straight away. TB said the problem was that she was out of her depth. JP said simply 'That woman is fucking mad.' TB asked me to get her to call him which she did. He said afterwards she was contrite but later, she was telling people, for example Charlie Whelan, that the real issue was me, and the way I constantly briefed against people. There had been a fair bit of pickup for Andy Grice's story about defections and lots of the papers were beginning to do pieces on who the defectors may be. This is something we can fan for some time before naming names. The usual suspects were all denying it, and the Tories were beginning to say it was a destabilising ploy by me. Whatever, it was going well.

I was due to go to TB's for a meeting on *Road to the Manifesto* but we agreed I should go to the JP/DD press conference instead. JP said he was annoyed that he was forced to defend another mad cow from the Shadow Cabinet. He was also irritated a line had gone into his press release about the pre-manifesto ballots. But he was fine at the press conference, and he and Donald had them all laughing afterwards.

I did my best to alleviate the Clare situation. I said there was no need for TB to bollock her because she had done some self-bollocking. I said there would be no impact on the political landscape because everyone knew only TB and GB would speak on tax. Charlie W said afterwards 'That was a very professional performance. Talking her up while knowing they would portray it as talking her down.' Back at the office I wrote to Clare, and after TB made one or two changes, he agreed I could send it. It was pretty strong stuff, about how she had single-handedly undermined our campaign strategy.

Tuesday, April 16

The papers were pretty grim. As my letter to Clare said, the roll we were on had stopped, and needless to say she was being feted in the Tory press, while the *Guardian* and *Independent* were doing it as a 'gagging' story by the big bad bullies. TB did not think the press was that great for her, but I felt it was better than it should be because they preferred a story about trouble for us to one about incompetence and unprofessionalism by her. At the morning meeting, I suggested that Donald say something on collective responsibility to counter her 'soul and conscience of the party' bollocks. Donald was hesitant, but later agreed to an article. Donald and I went to talk it over with TB. He said even though we were all angry, it was important to stay objective about Clare. He said I should remember what Machiavelli said, if you are not going to kill, don't wound. We are not going to kill her, so leave it, he said. I said she was going to continue to build herself up as the great heroine of the left, and it was unacceptable. But TB said there was no real support for her in the party, it was a media thing, which is what made it different from the Harriet situation. There, the party felt I was in the wrong. Here, they think I'm in the right. Then I saw a letter from Max Hastings about the airbrushing of a picture in the *Standard* in which a bottle of beer was removed to make it look like JP was drinking champagne. JP was very exercised about it, partly because he didn't like the image of himself drinking champagne, partly because it was so dishonest. I saw it as a great story to show how the media behave. I put together a JP statement, I wound up ITN and got ready to push it after Questions. Given all the stuff in the press that was picking up about me and spin, I was keen to make an issue of the press early on, and the *Standard* story was a perfect example, especially as Hastings had already apologised, though only privately, to JP. TB was fine at Questions, after which I pushed the JP story.

Wednesday, April 17

Clare had a piece in the *Guardian* in which she was interviewed by Mary Riddell putting the 'honest woman' crap, saying that TB had said she was principled and fair and honest and she made the mistake of thinking that others were too. What in fact he had said was whether there was any chance of her ever doing an interview without creating a problem. Now we had the answer. I suddenly realised I had forgotten Mum's and Dad's birthdays [a day apart], and felt dreadful. Even though we were not great birthday people, it showed how little space I had in my mind for anything but work, and I phoned up to grovel. TB didn't like the *Sun* piece about Peter and me [alleging Stalinist tactics] and asked me to call Higgins. Stuart said he was fed up with me complaining every time something wasn't right. I said fine, I will get a right to reply elsewhere, and I spent much of the day writing a piece about the trip, press standards, etc. TB also issued instructions that if there was any briefing going on against Clare, it had to stop. Lunch re the Allason case, which would be the next thing to get me up in lights whether I liked it or not. They emphasised how important it was to keep calm and be respectful to the judge. They were clearly worried I would lose my rag, and I promised I would not. They said there were some small discrepancies between events as I remembered them and events as David Bradshaw remembered them re the day the [parliamentary] Early Day Motion went down. They

April '96: Standard apologises to JP for 'fake' picture

were confident though and said it would be a good idea if I heard as much of the evidence as possible. [Martin] Kramer [legal team] said Allason would be nervous because he could not really believe that this was going to happen. It was a very odd feeling heading towards a court case when the only witness for the other side was a Labour MP [George Galloway] who seemed to hate me more than he hated the Tories.

TB, Pat and Liz were having a meeting on gays in the military. TB felt that the only solution was the American way, don't ask, don't tell. TB said it was a difficult issue, because no other country had put forward gays in the military without support from the military. He felt a free vote was the only way to get through.

At Shadow Cabinet, TB issued a warning that in future they must be accompanied and briefed by media minders for any interview. He confessed he too had got into a problem on tax, and all of them had to be careful. The press were desperate to twist things against us. He also warned that the Tories were monitoring all anonymous quotes. Clare wasn't there so it was a bit pointless.

Thursday, April 18

GB was at the 9am morning meeting, and on good form. He was worried because we had nothing positive coming up. We needed to combine our anti-Tory attack with something positive and forward-looking. TB said he felt we were still lagging behind on economic message, and Philip agreed with him. GB had a big speech tomorrow and we had to prise it out of him before we got to what it was that he intended to say – he wanted to take child benefit from 16 to 18-year-olds and move the money elsewhere in education and training. It was part of a broader review of 16 to 18 funding. As ever, nothing had been squared with his colleagues and it meant a hastily arranged meeting with Chris Smith [Shadow Social Security Secretary], who TB said to me yesterday he considers to be something of a disappointment, and Blunkett, who had been anything but. Apparently they were fine about it and so, later, was JP. Again, though, there were legitimate questions about process. GB's main worry was that what the Clare row had done was get everything back on to tax and spend, and we had to go back to basics. I agreed, but TB and Peter were not so sure. TB was looking at me to get GB to get up the broader economic message on opportunity and security in a world of change. GB was saying we must use it to get up equality of opportunity. He was angry that Robin was putting himself forward as the defender of the poor. GB was also alarmed that we had so many policy papers coming up.

One such was all over the *Guardian* this morning saying we would tax company cars. It was a classic easy hit, briefed by somebody, but lacking context or intellectual underpinning. GB was right in saying that if I were making spending promises, we had to say where the money was coming from. It was a much better meeting. I felt GB was beginning to engage more.

I then had another meeting with the lawyers and went to Gray's Inn to meet Charles Gray [QC for AC in the Allason case]. They went through some of the tricky stuff, Bradshaw saying that he didn't tell me about his direct involvement in the motion, though I recalled that he did. I quite liked Charles Gray but I was alarmed that he appeared to know so little about Galloway. He seemed confident though. He said the most important thing was that I stay calm and under control.

David Hill called to say that the *Today* programme would be doing something on the Cook vision vs the Blair vision. I called Robin and it was not the friendliest of conversations. I said we had a problem in that the media now assumed that he had a deliberate strategy to put himself off centre from TB and cast doubt on TB's politics and that was now potentially very damaging. He said that if Tony would make one or two speeches about poverty it would not seem so news-worthy when someone else in the party did so. That's a matter for you and him, I said. I have to deal with the fallout and there is a genuine danger you are laying down a fault line between the two of you, with TB in the centre and you deliberately positioned on the left. He said he could not complain at the way the stories were written, but he didn't like the headlines. I said that he was in danger of being unprofessional and incompetent, because the headlines flowed from the speech. He was being very tricky at the moment. Later TB spoke to him to say he was not best pleased. I was briefing up the notion there would be more defections if Major kept pushing to the right. I went home early to get the children to bed and read all the Allason documents.

Friday, April 19

Chris Smith called to say he had not agreed with GB and TB that child benefit for 16 to 18-year-olds should be scrapped. I said I would soften the line for TB's speech. This was being a bit disingenuous as I had been closely involved in drawing up the line, and had briefed *The Times* on it myself. Chris said they had told him there would be a review of the effectiveness of child benefit but he said what was being briefed now went well beyond that. Later JP paged me and he said TB had not been totally frank with him yesterday. He said we had to really watch Robin who was making the kind of speeches JP made all the time but spinning them to be the standard-bearer of the left and we were heading for two camps. JP said I know it's not your job but TB is dreadful at this kind of thing, he doesn't manage them well. Child benefit got a mixed review in the office, but I felt it was far better we were getting problems on policy and not the usual nonsense. The trouble was that it had not been thought or worked through all the relevant people and it was not clear who would benefit. During the day we tried to get it shifted to the question of a broader welfare review and I wrote a briefing note for Ed Miliband to brief on GB's speech, setting a more general context. David M and I did a briefing for the Sundays. They were so bovine. They had no real interest in politics; their only interest was finding a cheap thrill story or getting us to say something daft. Ewen MacAskill [*Guardian*] called to say he had asked Charlie W for GB's speech yesterday and Charlie had said I had insisted it was briefed selectively.

Saturday, April 20

GB's child benefit plan got a fair enough press though some, including TB, were worried we had said we were taking something away from people without making clear they would be getting anything in return. PG was more broadly worried that TB and GB were not singing the same tune. Tim did the ring round and it was all quiet though there was a problem with the *Sunday Times* who had done a so-called survey of our MPs on tax, and a majority surveyed said more tax, and they were splashing on it. 'Why do these brain-dead people answer their brainless questions?' TB asked later. It can only be because they're brain-dead.

Dinner at [lawyer] Maggie Rae's and [PLP secretary] Alan Howarth's. Donald was there, in very good form. Alan and I had a row about Clare. I said it was nonsense that she spoke out on grounds of principle. She'd fucked up and then made matters worse by casting around to blame other people. Donald was on my side, said she was not a team player and thought only of herself and how she was perceived. Fiona had been at a conference on women and the law with Cherie. Maggie said she felt Cherie was trying to have her cake and eat it, by being both a private citizen and lawyer but also have the benefits of being a public figure. I had the papers sent round and they were pretty grim for us. Donald felt the party was going through a mad phase. Clare had done us real damage. Donald said she was a liability, addicted to being the news. She had another go at me on *A Week in Politics*.

Sunday, April 21

JP called at 7.30 on his way to the *Frost* programme. He shared my concern there was so much about me in the papers, and agreed it was because of Clare. He put her in her place with a very strong line on collective responsibility. On the whole it was an excellent interview. The only loose word the Tories might go for came when he agreed with Frost that some people pay less and some people pay more. It was a statement of the obvious, but with our media even statements of the obvious could get twisted. TB called later and said he was more convinced than ever that we had to come out with specifics on tax. It was the obvious thing to do, he said. He was livid with Clare, who was due to be seeing him and Cherie tonight. I doubted he would go for her. He said he was in the mood to nuke her but I laid him a bet she would be telling everyone in the morning that he had been nice as pie. I chatted to Michael and Alison Farthing [neighbours] over the fence and Alison said she was with Clare on this. For some reason even intelligent people bought her line that it was about free speech.

Monday, April 22

Our fears about JP's interview were borne out. He was really annoyed with himself. Everyone felt yesterday he had done a really good interview but a couple of stray words had allowed our opponents to hurts us. Trevor Kavanagh did a really hostile piece saying we were clearly intending to hammer the rich on tax. 'Prescott attack on Short' was the *Times* splash which was ridiculous. JP said he didn't attack her at all, simply reminded people of collective responsibility.

TB claimed that last night he had been really hard on Clare, and that GB was too, and made it clear to her as far as he was concerned the blame on this was all one-way. I doubted it, but then he was shown the press release of her remarks on *A Week in Politics* and was livid and asked Anji to draft a letter to her, saying she must stay off TV and radio for some considerable time. He was pretty fed up.

We had a long-term strategy meeting but inevitably the discussions came down to what to do about tax. TB felt that the question of principle we had not addressed was whether the rich should pay more. GB believed this was not a question of principle, but solely dependent upon the economic conditions of the day. TB was of the view that we would have to make clear whether we felt the rich should pay more, and what we believed the top-rate limit should be, but GB wanted to hold off for a long while yet. GB felt we should just keep the line that we had certain tax principles but rates depended upon circumstances and time. We also discussed whether to go on the attack against companies who were advising on tax avoidance. TB said to me that whether we liked it or not, tax would be the issue, and we must neutralise it. I went to Geoffrey Robinson's party for Ian Hargreaves [former *Independent* editor, now *New Statesman* editor]. I stayed a few minutes and bumped into Clare, and told her she had done immense damage. She said 'I didn't start it, you did.' Utter nonsense, I said, and off she went. I went home to study the papers for the Allason case.

Tuesday, April 23

On Clare, TB said I had to cool things, and stop making my feelings about her so evident. He quoted the Bible at me for once. 'Vengeance is mine, saith the Lord.' Allason had done his statement and his basic tack was that I was lying, that I was behind the Early Day Motion against him, and I had got others to lie for me. I walked to court, fortified by a chat with TB who said he did not believe Sir Maurice Drake [the judge] would much take to Allason. I was met outside by Charles Collier-Wright [Mirror Group legal manager], then Katherine Rimmell [legal team] inside. She told me that he said I was lying. She said he would not be happy that his big case was being heard in a very small, poky court, number 29. On the way in, I saw Allason talking to Christopher Sylvester [journalist, friend of Allason] and I said it must be nice to have your own press officer here. He said were you here this morning? I said no. Oh, he said, you missed all of the fun. He claims to have four sources for my involvement, but could only name two, Galloway and George Parker [*Western Daily Press* journalist], who denied it. To me, he was so clearly not credible and I asked why the judge wasn't just kicking the thing out, but Katherine said the judge would have to hear it all the way through. I was a bit worried when Charles Gray said even if he won, we would win in the Court of Appeal. Allason at least seemed to drop the line that the EDM was written in my handwriting. It was quite something to watch him at work, sitting there as the cheeky boy, enjoying teasing the lawyers. Charles went for him a bit over his 'litigation is my hobby', and his briefing to the press on the case, but didn't really go for him. I asked him afterwards when he would go for him, and he said he would do it when he thought the judge thought the same. There were some perfectly ludicrous moments, as when Allason claimed that George Parker said, re the source for the EDM, 'You've got me there, yes, it was Alastair,' or when he explained a wrong date by saying his computer always put on the date of retrieval. The judge seemed to be bending over backwards to help him. He didn't look impressed at Allason describing litigation as his hobby. I felt pretty confident and more so later when I went over the highlights with TB. His basic line was that I lied and had bullied all the others into lying for me. Charles Gray said we did not have him yet. 'He is a very slippery customer.'

Wednesday, April 24

Although *The Times* did a big piece, and the *Guardian* and *Express* smaller pieces, the court case was largely ignored, which would have pissed off Allason who doubtless wanted lots of coverage for himself in what he was presenting as his David and Goliath case.

TB did well out of yesterday. I went to the morning meeting where DD took me aside and gave me some sound advice that I must be polite at all times, and avoid personal attacks even on Galloway. He said Galloway was one of the most dangerous people he'd ever known and would be a real menace in government. He was an oddly charismatic character, he thought, and had a fair number of Scottish MPs under his wing. The NEC was due to discuss Swindon [North], and whether Alan Howarth should be allowed to be a candidate. I chatted to TB on tax and also suggested to him that we should do a day trip to Italy to make him the first foreign leader to see the new Italian prime minister [Romano Prodi]. I then left for court.

Charles Gray twisted Allason in knots and he suddenly came up with a fifth source, prompting Gray to ask him if he was making it up as he went along. There was a long pause before Allason said no. Otherwise it was all pretty tedious, though I felt Gray was coming good. He returned to the theme of Allason spreading lies about me. By the time I got to the office, I felt confident that there was no way this could go against us. The afternoon was not so good. Charlie Wilson [Mirror Group director] could not remember detail, for example that he had interviewed me with Arthur Davidson [QC, former Mirror Group legal director]. Gray fucked up with Galloway. I had given him a note of an exchange in the House of Commons when Allason was attacking me, and Galloway shouted 'He's up there,' and Allason said something along the lines of 'You're going to get it, Alastair.' Gray got mixed up and wasted a few minutes. Galloway was absolutely disgusting, alleging seeing me getting signatures for the EDM, about the War on Want stories I'd done on him, about all manner of things. I just listened impassively, and then as the day wore on I felt the anger rising in me. Galloway called me every name under the sun and had the press clearly lapping it up. Hugh Corrie [former *Mirror* lawyer] came in and we had a good natter about when he came to lecture us [for the *Mirror* trainee scheme] in Plymouth. Allason was poor on his feet and Gray was good. Though he said Galloway had been very difficult to get hold of, he did get him to contradict Allason. Allason had said that he could not have been sure that he would be able to rely on Galloway to give evidence for him. Galloway said he was always willing to help Allason nail me. Earlier, a row with Wilson about whether he or Davidson should have carried out any investigation into the complaint about the motion and my alleged role. I left court less confident than at lunchtime and feeling taunted by the bile from Galloway.

Thursday, April 25

I slept very patchily, partly out of worry, partly because Grace was not well. I was going over some of the questions and answers in my mind, and getting more and more angry. I had a bath at 5.30 and Grace was there, throwing her little penguins into the water. The lawyers had advised me to have a sharp object to spike into the palm of my hand if I felt my temper rising and I asked Grace if I could take her baby penguin. The papers, predictably, concentrated on Galloway's attack and the *Guardian* as ever used a picture that made me look as unpleasant as possible. Thankfully, the tabloids were pretty disinterested. TB said he felt that it was coming over as a spat and not damaging. Went round to TB's at 8.30. We discussed PMQs and I suggested he do a line that they had lost the moral authority to govern. I missed PMQs because I was giving evidence. TB was full of good advice and confident from what he had read that Allason's case did not stack up, and I would be fine. We discussed Peter. TB felt he was very detached. I said he was too interested in promoting himself and building up his relationships with these ridiculous glitterati people. We drank endless cups of tea and then I left for court with his 'calm, polite' mantra firmly in mind.

I arrived early and went for a coffee in a little cafe round the corner. I was looking for omens. First, a woman came up to me and said she hoped I stuffed that Tory. Then Gloria Gaynor came on the radio in the cafe with 'I Will Survive'. Both things made me feel strong and confident. I felt clear and focused as I walked to the court. Bradshaw was excellent. Charles Gray said to me afterwards there is not a judge in the country who would not believe he was telling the truth. He was asked by Allason if he was falling on his sword because I was in a difficult spot. On the contrary, he said he had dragged me into a difficult spot because of his misjudgement. He said he was not prepared to see an innocent man hang but nor did he want to put his own head in the noose. The judge clearly liked him. The judge also, I think, thought Peter Kilfoyle was an excellent witness. Charles Gray said he still could not read the judge but felt he was coming round. He didn't enjoy Allason making a minor point that held up the start of morning proceedings.

I was up straight after lunch. I felt very nervous. I decided I would look at Allason as infrequently as possible. The lawyers said his tactic would be to rile me and I must not let him do that. I took the oath, then Gray began by asking me to read my statement, stopping me as I went. I felt confident in what I was saying, and confident I would not lose it with RA. The judge picked me up on several things. I sensed he didn't like me too much. The press were now there in such numbers some were standing, others sitting on the floor. Allason failed to get me going and came over as pathetic when he focused e.g. on my porn or my fight with Michael White [*Guardian*, following White joking about the death of *Mirror* owner Robert Maxwell]. I was in there from 2.30 to 4.30 and thought I was going to be released. Bradshaw, Arthur Davidson, Martin Cruddace and the rest of the *Mirror* legal team – all made positive signals that I was doing fine. I had been calm, even-tempered. He had been all over the shop and as I was about to leave the box, Gray said to the judge that he no longer knew what the case was because allegations made on day one were not being made now. Allason looked very hurt as Gray issued a pretty withering assessment of the way he had pursued the case today.

The judge said Allason should reflect overnight on what his case was and come back in the morning to say what it was. I assumed, rightly, that meant I would be back in the morning so he could put direct allegations to me, and I would be re-examined by Gray. I couldn't really talk to the lawyers so headed back to the House. Andy McSmith [*Mirror* political journalist] was there. He had literally had nothing to do with it and was really angry at being caught up in it all. The [Leader's] office was terrific, very kind and supportive. At the strategy meeting, I was not really with it and I knew it was going to be hours before I unwound. I was exhausted. At home, the kids were brilliant. I told them I had squeezed Grace's penguin and thought of them whenever I thought I was losing my temper, and Rory looked really proud and happy.

April '96: AC in the witness box

Friday, April 26

The press from the court case was as expected, mainly going on what Allason said re my old 'pornographic' articles for *Forum* and the fight with Mike White. I wasn't sure it would impress the judge much. I took the boys to school, and then headed to court. The case was becoming bigger in the eyes of the media. Paul Foot [investigative journalist] and Richard Ingrams [of *Private Eye*, satirical magazine] sent good luck messages to the office. I was in the box for an hour, going over some of the stuff from yesterday as Allason directly put the allegations of lying, cover-up, disinformation, half-truths, sophistry. Maybe because I was more confident about the outcome, I was more antagonistic towards him and the penguin in my pocket was getting the treatment. By the time I'd finished, I had a huge red welt in the palm of my hand. Gray raised the press coverage, particularly the pornography, and asked if I thought it was relevant. It was odd how when you are in there, you weigh up every word really carefully and the moment you leave the box, you forget the whole thing. The lawyers felt I could not have done better. Heather Rogers [legal team] said Allason was one of those people you wanted to hit. They all felt the case was turning our way.

I went for lunch with Arthur Davidson who was anxious to get it on record that Allason's claim that he [AD] had said he did not trust me was balls. It was a beautiful sunny day, and I was just desperate for the case to end. The judge said he would have to wait until Wednesday for summing-up, and judgment possibly on Thursday. I read Charles' summing-up notes which were given to the judge to study over the weekend. Allason said he could not give his because they were incomplete. The latest twist was that the Treasury Solicitor wanted the papers, because as the case concerned parliamentary proceedings, there may have been a Bill of Rights implication. I assumed this was another Allason wheeze. I walked back from court exhausted, confident and longing for the judge to condemn Allason and Galloway.

Saturday, April 27

The press coverage from the case was largely slanted against me again. I had barely followed the news this week and was conscious of how much time and energy this had taken up. Gray's submissions were excellent, and I could not see how we could lose. I'd also enjoyed seeing how skilfully he had got Allason and Galloway to contradict each other. The general view was that we would win. I was getting a steady flow of phone calls wishing me luck – Geoffrey Goodman [former *Mirror* colleague, editor of *British Journalism Review*] called to say get the bastards. Ditto Eve Pollard [formerly AC's editor at the *Sunday Mirror*]. I went to get the papers and there were a few big background pieces on the case, again missing the real point.

Sunday, April 28

I was so consumed with the case that I was not really thinking about politics at all. TB was due to do election visits for the locals and we had not really planned for it. Mum and Dad were down for Grace's birthday party. It is amazing how much comfort and strength I get from the children in times of stress and difficulty. The Tory splits were serious again, and there was a lot of talk about the party actually splitting over Europe.

Monday, April 29

I was up at 6 to work on some argument for Charles Gray's summing-up. Although all that mattered really was the result, I also felt he had to get the press coverage to turn against Allason and that meant going for him a bit harder.

We were doing a visit to Basildon, so I left for TB's and then Fenchurch Street. He had had dinner with Peter last night and told him there was too much swanning around and big-wigging and not enough hard work. He told him success depended not on his loyalty but on delivery. We arrived at Basildon to be taken straight to the home of a Labour family and a couple of switchers. They were set up in the front room with tea and cakes. We did pictures, small talk and the Sky live link. TB did fine. There was a good atmosphere, and then he did a mini press conference for the locals in the kitchen. Then to a shopping centre walkabout where one or two Tories tried and failed to disrupt. TB didn't really look like he was into this. I felt he had to get more engaged in situations where frankly, you can't always control what happens, and at least try to look like he enjoys just being out and about with people.

On the train back he wanted to discuss Peter Hyman, Tim Allan, and whether we try to bring in David Bradshaw. He said that for eighteen months he had been asking for the job of taking on the press in argument rather than just at the headline level, but it hadn't really happened. It happened occasionally if he or I did it, but he said we didn't have the time to do it systematically. He was adamant that he had torn a strip off Peter, but I doubted it. TB was worried about *Road to the Manifesto*, worried that we didn't really have a strong economic message. The usual stuff. He didn't feel we had a grip of the policy process throughout the party. He didn't feel confident in good ideas going forward. He also felt we were slowing on party reform.

Tuesday, April 30

TB had seen some of our MPs last night. If the Tories had been there, they would think they were in with a chance. It was awful, he said. They simply inhale Tory propaganda about us and then exhale it in a different form. Diane Abbott going on about spin was a classic example, he said. He asked her whether it was spin the way she went out of the NEC to give her version of what had gone on. He said Ken Purchase [Labour MP] had constantly interrupted him on child benefit. Amazingly, Galloway was due to see him tonight. Had also had dinner with David English and Paul Dacre [*Mail*] and said it went well. He felt English was desperate to help, but Dacre was prejudiced and difficult. Dacre confirmed Tim's tip that the *Mail* would back Michael Howard [for Conservative leader], and it was clear the question of the leadership was up again. Heseltine's speech tonight was being seen as a leadership bid.

After PMQs, TB came in and said he was sure Major would go. He was also preoccupied with gays in the military. He was worried, but slowly moving towards voting for the Brown/Currie amendment.[1] He was of the view that it would lose votes among the troops but the amendment was probably right and would be difficult not to support. He spoke to Derry several times, and Peter, though by the end of the day we were no nearer knowing what to do. The gay lobby would start soon enough. He was worried both that the top brass would think he was a wanker, and the troops would change votes on the back of it. But nonetheless, he said on the principle it was the right thing to do, and he was moving towards supporting the amendment.

I had a meeting with PG. He said we just had to get back on to big arguments again. GB had effectively killed stakeholding. His speech last week was a different take to TB's. We had to get back with strong language on our own terms. He said there was no point thinking GB would support what we were going to do. He was on a different agenda. We were then supposed to have a strategy meeting but GB didn't turn up. Hilary said Fiona had had a call from a *Mail* journalist, asking if Cherie used a homoeopath called Jack Temple, who was featured in last week's *Sunday Express* having done something called

[1] Conservative MPs Michael Brown and Edwina Currie tabled an amendment to the Armed Forces Bill, seeking to end the ban on gays serving in the military. Ultimately Labour did not support the amendment.

dowsing, which involves swinging a pendulum over the body, for Diana and Fergie. Fiona spoke to Carole Caplin who said yes, she used him. Hilary spoke to Cherie who said yes, she did. I got her to come into a meeting with TB, Jonathan and Peter M and raised it. Peter and Tony said we know about this, it is nonsense. We talked about it on Sunday because it was in the papers and Cherie said she had only had some homoeopathic pills from him. I repeated my view that Carole was a total menace and TB had his head in the sand about it. Peter seemed particularly keen, peculiarly so, to defend these fucking people and it later emerged, I think from Anji, that he had also been to see this character. TB, as ever, wanted to believe the best of Carole which was nice on one level, but unprofessional on the other. Fiona thought it was inevitable that someone would try to piece together a story of how Carole had some kind of weird control over Cherie. She was so rational on everything else but not on this. As it was Grace's birthday, I left early. Anji told me later that TB and Cherie had a furious row about it. Cherie blamed it all on the office, saying we exaggerated the problem to make it feel like a crisis.

Wednesday, May 1

Tory turmoil was big news and the leadership issue was live. If I was the Tories I'd be complaining about the media hysteria that was now starting. Pretty quiet on our front. I dropped Mum and Dad at King's Cross and then went into the office to see TB and discuss the speech and gays in the military. TB was still agonising on this. We also discussed CB. He said they'd had a terrible row last night, and he still could not bring himself to admit that Carole had any kind of hold on CB. I said I feared that with her around, we were always inches away from a disaster. Jack Temple was one thing but a paper could easily piece together a picture of Carole as some kind of weird guru, and it would be very damaging. Hilary had spoken direct to Temple who said she saw him regularly and she was there last month. Fiona and Hilary agreed not to tell TB but when Fiona had lunch with CB, she raised it. Cherie obfuscated and said yes, she had been there recently. I also warned TB that I feared Carole's story could come out through someone else, for example the boyfriend she'd just split up with. Roz Preston was at the end of her tether and so was Fiona.

I had a message overnight that we were going to be in Court 24. I walked from the Commons, hoping it would soon be over. I ignored Allason on the way in. Charles Gray did pretty well though the judge interrupted him a fair bit and seemed to think maybe there was malice

May '96: AC's concern re Carole Caplin's boyfriend

in the way Bradshaw and the *Mirror* behaved. He was also angry that McSmith had been dragged into it. I felt OK about my own role but it was not plain sailing. I left for a lunch organised for media executives from around the media at ITN. Peter Preston [former *Guardian* editor] was chairing it. I took five minutes to put our case fairly aggressively and then Q&A. I said it was impossible to complain to the BBC, it was like wrestling with a snake. I said they were obsessed with spin and spin doctors but we had a job to do the same as they did and our jobs were different. I blasted *Panorama* and its continuing drive downmarket. It was all combative and they clearly didn't like us much. I said they had to understand we were not going to let them be judge and jury on how the political debate unfolded. TB was in endless meetings on gays in military. Shadow Cabinet discussed gays in the military. John Reid had worked out a position for TB who wanted to vote pro gay but was worried about political fallout, particularly in the troops.

Thursday, May 2

It was judgement day, both in terms of the local elections, and for me in court. The *Telegraph* were the only ones to do much on yesterday's evidence, a further example of them only really being interested in anything that might damage me, rather than the truth about the case. I left TB in Trafalgar Square and walked to court, via a quick coffee in the same cafe I went to on day one. There were more journalists than ever and I waited until the latest possible time before going in. Martin Cruddace had been a huge support and I filed into court with him. Drake came in and very matter-of-factly went through the case. Then he started to spray things around a bit. What a bastard. Although he threw out the case, because there wasn't one, he said Bradshaw was indeed motivated by malice and that the story was false, but no damage was proven. The most direct criticism was made against me, probably because I was bolshie, to the effect he hadn't found me convincing. When he made the criticism directly, I felt I think for the first time in my life an instant pounding of the heart, and I was shaking with rage inside. For a moment, I felt like shouting out, but had to sit and listen as he went on. We won the case but he was determined that we shouldn't feel like we had won. I got more and more angry as the day wore on. Everyone said all that mattered was that I won but it left a really nasty taste. Worse, he did not even criticise Allason directly, and he said Galloway had been credible and coherent. It was all deeply offensive and upsetting. Bradshaw wrote me a very nice note and kept saying sorry.

Meanwhile, we heard that the thug who Eric Cantona had attacked was jumping out of the box and attacking counsel.[1] I know how he felt. Allason got up and made a little speech. The costs were awarded against him, though not for one part of the case. As I looked at the judge, I felt total contempt for him. My pager was going off with an endless series of messages saying well done, congratulations, but I didn't share in the feeling at all. The judge gave Allason comfort which in my view he didn't deserve. Gray, Kramer and Cruddace were all appalled, though stressing I should go out and say that we won on all counts and that was the end. There was a general acceptance that the judge was politically motivated.

I did a brief doorstep with about fifteen photographers crowding around. The story would be Allason lost and it would cost him dear. Drake's comments, however, would doubtless be used again and again by the Tories and enemies in the press. It was all over, and we had won, but I felt shitty about it, which is of course what Drake intended. I went into a growing rage about his remarks and I was also feeling they would become a problem. I get called in a case about a story that has nothing to do with me, and end up having my character assassinated over a period of days and then a judge makes a statement that will be used against me for years. I was really depressed about it, and preoccupied. Fiona was great, said he had lost and I had won. I talked to TB about it several times and he was adamant it wasn't a problem. I collected him at 11pm and we went to Millbank Tower as the [local election] results came in. Basildon [council] falling to Labour was a great moment. There were now huge areas that were Tory-free zones. But the turnout was low. The papers arrived and several of them went hard on the judge's attack on me. *The Times'* later editions had [Ken] Livingstone [Labour MP] and others calling for me to be sacked. TB did not want to leave till the Tories lost 600 seats, so we didn't get away till gone 2.

Friday, May 3

I was up at 6, worrying, and said to Fiona I thought it would be hard to go on if the Tories managed to make Drake's words stick. The *Guardian* profile mentioned accurately that I had thought about resigning if I'd lost. Bevins called and said everyone knew I was

[1] In a match at Crystal Palace in January 1995, the Manchester United player Eric Cantona had launched a 'kung fu' style kick towards a spectator, Matthew Simmons. Simmons was later tried for threatening language and attacked the prosecution counsel after being found guilty.

straight and I shouldn't worry. TB and Peter both felt all that anyone would remember was that I won, he lost, and the sense being communicated was that I was as hard as nails. TB was on great anti-complacency form. Major was doing the rounds, so we decided to do everything too. TB did an interview with Bevins, and pushed the line that the Tories were splitting in two and there were Tories who had more in common with us than the Tory right. Alan Clark called to say 'Congratters' as did David Davis. He said whatever the Tories said in public, they preferred me to that shit. The local elections fallout was going badly for the Tories. Cherie had spoken to Fiona and they were barely on speaking terms. This was because TB had ordered CB not to go to Carole's gym and not to see her at home. So today she went to see her at her sister Lindsey's house. Cherie and Lindsay both felt I was to blame for the whole thing. The *Mail* was running the story about Jack Temple. I was exhausted, in bed before 10, feeling grim. Some of the Sundays were doing big profiles of me, which again was completely as a result of the judge. Maybe I was overstating it, but I sensed it laid the ground for real trouble. As ever, the kids were fantastic. I had a huge laugh with them, and it didn't seem to matter much any more.

Saturday, May 4

I was totally fed up and destabilised, which is of course what the Tories would be hoping for. TB called and tried to assure me again that there wasn't a problem. He said sometimes people are very good at assessing problems for other people but aren't so good when it comes to themselves. Believe me, he said: this is not as bad as you think. Fiona was brilliant too, very supportive, but I was beginning to get worried. I suppose what was worrying me was that I was now considered to be fair game in exactly the same way a politician was. Cherie called and was very nice about the case. She said ignore it, leave it be. The Jack Temple piece had appeared in the *Mail* today, and I later discovered from Michael Levy that she was feeling that I had it in for her, which I didn't, but it wasn't easy. I went for the Sundays and again it seemed so unjust that I had been to court over a story I didn't write in a case that I had won, and anyone reading the papers would think I had been the loser. Both Mum and Dad said just ignore it. Dad said as long as your conscience is clear there is no problem, but I said it's always complicated when it is political like this. Audrey [Millar, Fiona's mother] said this was the Establishment at work and they are still very powerful. They know you are a very important figure in terms of getting a Labour government, and they would like to destabilise you, so don't let them.

I spoke to Michael Levy, who said TB had been there on Friday and had said I was worried. I should not let a few remarks by a judge change anything. He said it was obvious the press and our opponents would try to dig as much dirt as possible on the people close to TB. We had to be strong. These people were not going to hand over the keys without a fight, and they were desperate. He said that Cherie had been really low on Friday, and she was convinced I was against her. I said to Michael that I was very sympathetic to her position, but that because she and TB didn't always discuss these things in detail, sometimes we didn't know what line to project and develop. I felt that she believed that when we pointed out what the press might do or say, we were expressing OUR view. For example, when I said she could be portrayed as Glenys [Kinnock] or Hillary Clinton, or as a crap mother, or as Islington woman with all the homoeopathy stuff, she felt that was me expressing my view. In truth, that was me trying to explain where I felt our enemies were trying to take her profile. The public saw her as a mother, wife and career woman and because she avoided the overtly political profile, she had a strong image, which could easily be threatened. She said to Michael that she thought I would prefer her to be Norma [Major] Mark Two. I said that was absurd. I just need to know how she and Tony want her to be, in terms of the public image, and we could help get her there. Michael clearly saw himself as a main man. He emphasised again and again how close they were. We are family, he said. He said he could be a conduit with Cherie. I said it was not necessary to complicate things further. Cherie knew what the real problem was between us: I thought Carole was a problem and she didn't.

The political problem of the day was child benefit. Joe Murphy [*Sunday Telegraph*] had called yesterday interested in a story that Shadow Cabinet members were not happy with the 16 to 18-year-old child benefit review. We gave him the standard line on tough choices, part of the education funding review, etc., but by the time his paper came out, it had been mangled into Blair overruled Brown, humiliation for Brown, etc. I got Tim to rubbish it both to Murphy and to those who called, but it was clearly going to run. I quickly got hold of the main political editors, and tried to kill it. GB said we had to keep a very tough line on child benefit and we would look ridiculous if we backed down. The best thing he could do would be to set a target for reduced welfare bills and, if not, to set a defence of the proposals so far, he said. I said we had been very tough in briefing on it and I could not understand why the left was against it.

May '96: Michael Levy re the Blairs, 'We are family'

Monday, May 6

I was woken by GB in a flap because of the papers, which I hadn't seen. 'Child benefit rift' in various forms was leading most of the broadsheets. He clearly felt we hadn't been tough enough in backing him up even though the *Express*, for example, reported that TB had stepped in to back GB. The *Guardian* has another complicating story, namely that we were going to reverse decisions on jobseekers' allowance and unemployment benefit in a victory for the soft left. GB said there had to be tougher briefing on this today, and that we had to get back on track with it. He said he would go on *World at One*, and we needed a blitz of articles. TB was getting very concerned about Chris Smith's speech. David M and Peter Hyman both reported that Smith was very offside, particularly over GB's way of managing things, and they said he was not in the mood for being pushed around. I spoke to him several times during the day. He denied absolutely having anything to do with stories in the papers. Clearly then, I said, someone was briefing on his behalf, and he said if so, it was without his permission. GB suspected Robin Cook was behind the whole thing.

I got Peter Hyman to go to Chris' office to help finish the speech and the article for the *Guardian*. GB meanwhile was doing one for the *Independent*, building on the tough-choice theme. GB was excellent on *World at One*, clearly not backing down on child benefit. He said to me earlier that it would look weak and pathetic if we keeled over at the first sign of trouble. The top line from the briefing note was that Labour wanted lower welfare spending and Chris Smith was saying that. TB spoke to him, and got him to argue in some of the GB toughness, but it was not, when it came, a very good speech. The truth was Smith had been given a big job, and didn't appear to be up to it. He was constantly looking over his left shoulder at the MPs who elected him to the Shadow Cabinet, and he was also captured by the poverty pressure groups. Virtually the whole day was taken over trying to deal with the story.

Tuesday, May 7

Chris Smith was on the *Today* programme at 8.10, and his remarks were far less gung-ho than GB's. It was a big story and a problem. The external effect, what the public were hearing, was that we were taking away child benefit from one million people. There was no sense of anything being put in its place. The internal problem was that it was TB and GB against everyone else. And the truth was, though TB would not say this to anyone, that he was worried about the proposal.

It was hanging over everything at the moment. TB complained about lack of grip, things just popping up from nowhere. The Tories, with better press support, were now coalescing around an anti-Europe, pro-enterprise, right-wing social policy agenda. It added up to a fairly clear message. All we had was that we were not the Tories. We had no real economic message. TB was quite down. He was still angry with Clare and though we all had to accept that child benefit was a problem, retreat was not now an option. Already editorials were saying to fudge it now would be to show weakness. That is exactly how TB and GB felt.

I went to Millbank, and a meeting chaired by Peter M on the under-25s – 'The Lost Generation', a campaign planned by GB next week. Again, I felt we were going into something without being clear what we really wanted out of it. They had four days planned on this, first a press conference at which all we would get was questions about child benefit. GB would get coverage, but nobody else would. It was all being driven by GB, who was in Germany for the next couple of days. Then on to Cherie, where Fiona and Roz reported to me, Hilary, Jonathan, Anji and Kate that they were at the end of their tethers because she wanted a public role for herself and because of the difficulties of Carole's involvement, particularly in all the mad stuff. We decided that the next discussion must involve her and Tony and that they must confront our concerns about what was going on. We agreed, and even I did, that there could be a problem casting out Carole. Fiona/Roz said they felt Cherie was dependent on her, because TB was so busy elsewhere. TB came into the room and we asked him, for example, whether they had thought about where they would live if we won, and whether Cherie would work. It was fairly clear from the look that they hadn't thought about it much at all. Re work, he said probably, but she wouldn't do cases to do with the government. I asked whether Carole would still be around, and he said no. He insisted Carole was not going to the house at all, but Fiona knew that not to be the case.

Wednesday, May 8

Worked on the briefing line on gays in military. TB had seen Ian McKellen and Michael Cashman [actors and gay rights activists] last night and been supportive of the principle but said that there were military as well as civil liberties issues and change would have to be done in consultation with the chiefs of staff. TB briefed me on the speech. He had decided on One Nation radicalism. Pat and I tried to fathom out what it meant. We ended up discussing child benefit. It really had developed into a bit of a disaster. TB said letters were pouring in. It's the old thing about Labour taking money out of your pocket, he said. I said if we backed down it would damage GB and therefore damage him. He said if we were throwing one million votes down the drain, it was worth taking some damage to prevent that happening. Jonathan reported a hilarious moment from Shadow Cabinet when Ron Davies asked Jack Cunningham if we would protect the Five Nations rugby from satellite TV. Jack said it was also events like the Coronation that would have to be protected. 'I'm not sure I'd want to watch that,' said Ron. We were having a load of people round for dinner and David Blunkett came early and had a massive whinge about GB. He said GB had this extraordinary ability of doing the right thing in the wrong way and alienating people who, handled properly, would support what he was saying. He then said, can I say something that I will only say to you two and don't want to repeat when the others arrive – I think Gordon is bonkers, then he roared with laughter. I got a message to call Piers Morgan. He said the *Mirror* was leading on Allason running off to France with some woman. He clearly thought I should be pleased but I only sensed more trouble out of it, especially as a Tory motion was going down about me.

Thursday, May 9

The *Mirror* did six bloody pages on Allason, which was ludicrous, and I felt sure it would backfire on them in some way. There were also some bad polls today. We were five points down in the *Guardian*, and support for devolution was down in the *Telegraph*. Donald was worried about TB being isolated on gays in the military. He had fully intended to vote for the Currie amendment but said he would abstain if that helped TB. DD was a team player.

There was a great hoo-ha about the fact that we wanted to move the morning meetings to 9.30 at Millbank. Donald was squared on Tuesday and mentioned it to GB, who didn't know. 'I guess the thinking is that if it is there, Peter might actually attend the meetings,' said Donald. TB was seeing GB re child benefit, and was now of the view that we had a real problem, and there was actually a case for considering a total reversal. He said that the splits were damaging, but acknowledged that there was some strength to be gained from facing up to tough choices, but he felt we had to have the discussion. GB was very keen that TB defend him in his speech tomorrow. I said fine, but we didn't want child benefit to be the only news out of it. We wanted something that transcended that and got our basic core position out there again. The strategy meeting was not just about the speech, but also the campaign on the Lost Generation for next week. A huge amount of work and planning had gone on, at GB's instigation, involving Blunkett, and Jack Straw's people. Peter M therefore got very irritated when Gordon said he didn't think we were ready for it on Monday. Peter and I both sighed volubly, given neither of us had been keen in the first place, but we had actually tried hard to make it happen. Peter got terribly defensive and very hoity-toity and I could sense he was losing it. He said Gordon, this was entirely your idea, we have all been trying to make it work without proper direction from you or your office, and now you are rowing back. They started talking very loudly at each other, just a few decibels short of shouting. TB, who for once was sitting in the chair by the TV, rather than at his desk or in his usual place on the sofa, said for heaven's sake keep this under control. Peter then stood up, said no, I won't, I'm not taking any of this crap any longer, and he stormed out, slamming the door. TB just shook his head, while GB stared at his papers and then started scribbling. Then the meeting resumed as if nothing had happened. I said, looking at Charlie Whelan, that I didn't think it would be helpful if that exchange was in any way communicated to the public.

Peter came back later to collect his coat and TB said 'You cannot talk to Gordon like that in a room full of people,' and Peter said in that case he was happy to quit doing the job that TB had given him. 'I have had enough. I am not going to put up with it any longer, being undermined by GB and getting no support from here.' He picked up his jacket, walked out again and slammed the door even louder than before. I looked at TB and he looked at me, and we both stood there shaking heads. TB sat down and said 'What am I supposed to do with these fucking people? It is impossible.' It was so absurd that we ended up laughing, probably because we couldn't think what else to do. To be fair to Peter, he'd endured a fair bit of provocation. I went through to the Shadow Cabinet room on the way for a pee and Peter and Anji were in there talking. Anji was trying to calm him down but he was still in a terrible state. He launched into a tirade against me, saying I was playing all sides against the middle and didn't I understand GB was determined to stop anything that he was behind, and he got no support from TB or me, even in relation to something as ridiculous as having our meetings at Millbank. I said it wasn't a case of playing all sides against the middle, it was a case of trying to get you people to work together, our failure in which was driving TB to a state of total exasperation.

Friday, May 10

An absolute pig of a day. I got to TB's house to find him in a flap about welfare and we were trying to get the facts together. Neither of us were yet happy with the speech, either. We got into the [BBC] radio car and Roger Mosey [*Today* programme editor] came on to say it would be about the Tories not being trusted and did anyone trust politicians? It started that way but got into gays in the military, on which Peter Tatchell [gay rights activist] had attacked TB for abstaining. This was despite producers saying gays in the military would not arise. These people were impossible to deal with. We were also having to deal with JP, who, wound up by Rosie from yesterday, was going off on one about not being involved in the Lost Generation campaign. Why he should be so agitated was beyond me, but he was. Margaret McD called to say that the Lost Generation campaign just was not coming together. She said the trouble was they hated each other and their hatreds were affecting how we operate. I said to TB if the Tories could have a run of luck, and the press really got into how bad things were between key people, we'd have problems.

To Swansea and straight to the conference centre for a round of Welsh interviews. Ron Davies had stitched us up again, getting us to say the assembly would be 'inclusive' and then briefing that this was TB signalling support for proportional representation for the elections. He was incapable of doing anything undevious. I saw Neil and Glenys briefly and Neil said we were going to walk it. We left straight after the speech and just made the 15.32 train, with TB still mithering. It was a crap speech, a crap visit, a crap journey home where at one point I hid my head in the curtain and said please, please stop mithering. I gave TB my worst-case scenario for the Tory fightback. I said he was not giving us direction or leadership, particularly to the people at the top, who were falling to bits. Jonathan said the whole thing at the moment was pathetic and amateurville. TB kept saying what do I do, give me solutions not problems. Jonathan and I both felt he had to threaten them, and mean it.

Saturday, May 11

I was woken up several times in the night over *The Times*, who were splashing on Phil Webster's story about Peter and GB not getting on and Donald was supposed to be facilitating a reconciliation. My line that this was news as comment, and not a story based on fact, and that they were two key members of a highly effective team, was not very strong. People knew that Phil did not dream stories up out of nowhere, and it might have the effect of forcing Peter/GB to grow up a bit. Indeed it was amazing it hadn't come out already. It was bound now to become part of the body politic, something to cheer the Tories up, something that would put our people on the defensive. Philip said that Maurice Saatchi [of the influential advertising agency Saatchi and Saatchi] had told Ruth Rogers [restaurateur] they were planning to sit back and watch Labour implode, and then build out a strategy that TB was a wimp. TB was fed up with it all. He went to the FA Cup Final and had a fantastic seat in the front row of the royal box but pulled right back when Cantona went up to get the Cup. I had suggested to Jack Straw to get his evidence to the Cullen inquiry [into Dunblane], calling for a ban on handguns, out to the Sundays, not least because they would be filled with GB/Peter and child benefit nonsense. Jack briefed the *Mail on Sunday* who splashed on it and by the end of the day it was number two on the news. Andy Grice [*Sunday Times*] was doing a big piece on who hates who in New Labour, and some of the other Sundays were pretty much the same. This was the effect of the Peter/Gordon situation, and it was laying down real problems ahead. I felt we were in worse shape than for some time.

Sunday, May 12

Neil and Glenys came round in the morning. Neil felt we weren't doing enough, setting up relationships in Europe. He feared there was no real alliance building going on. He had been trying to get some of our people to meet in Europe, for example to see what actually happens at European Council meetings, but there had been very few takers. He also knew that Andy Grice had if anything understated the extent of some of the dreadful personality clashes and mutual hatreds. TB called in a pretty bad state re the press. I said, as I had many times, that he had made two people feel they were indispensable, and they took liberties. Jeffrey Archer was on *Frost*, reviewing the papers and went straight to the Grice story.

I called JP later. He was totally offside. I said TB was moving towards telling Peter to get lost, and JP said I'm afraid I don't believe it. He'd spoken to TB several times over the weekend and told him he could live with the decisions TB took but he was not having the party being run by Brown and Mandelson. He was planning to tell Peter tomorrow that he had to clear everything on the Civil Service issues with Derek Foster, and he was going to kick him off his campaign team. JP told TB that he could either go on as a patsy or fight back and put the party view. The party view was that Peter/GB were now damaging the party, and they were treating Tony with contempt. I was listening to *World This Weekend* when TB called and said he was desperate and really didn't know what do. He was sure that Peter had briefed the *Times* stories and it was unforgivable. He said GB was on to him moaning the whole time, and I said he too had to feel they could be replaced. I was getting fed up, and pretty disrespectful of all of them.

Anji called, really worried, saying it was worse than it had ever been. She told TB she felt he came over as very weak. He'd asked her to get Peter in at 9.30 tomorrow, but Peter said he was going to be busy seeing a businessman from Hong Kong. Ben Wegg-Prosser [Mandelson aide] called her to say it could not be cancelled. This is what JP meant by treating with contempt. Both of us were telling TB that he had to make clear to both that they could go. Peter had apparently written a resignation letter to TB and TB had dropped a reply round at his flat. They were all behaving like children.

Monday, May 13

The papers were pretty grim. Anji had told TB last night that we felt he should threaten them with the sack. He said 'I can only do that if I am prepared to see it through.' I called him from the car on the way in and and he said it was grim. I repeated, as I had done many times before, that he had made the mistake of making them both feel indispensable. He saw Peter at 9, first on his own and later with Donald. TB said if he didn't improve and work with GB he would have to go and leave the operation. Donald confirmed he had indeed read the riot act and Peter could be in no doubt how seriously he took it. After he left, TB said he was worried about how all this affected his authority. The continuing coverage of Peter and Gordon, Simon Walters' account of the meetings of MPs, plus the row on child benefit, it all added up to a political problem. TB said if I had three or four other people who could do what they could I would replace them, but I don't. Gordon is driven, Peter is driven and they can behave rationally. But they can also behave irrationally. TB and I discussed what I should say to Andrew Marr [*Independent*] who was writing about it. I briefed him and he was clearly very anti Peter and I stressed that the party would be unforgiving on both, but also that anyone who took on the Shadow Chancellor, so close to the leader, could not win. I probably went over the top. I see, I get the message, said Andrew. I stressed that there was no ideological difference, and it was all about personality. I said that they had to get their act together. The fact was the press were on to it and we had to try and shape the coverage.

I had a nice lunch with Don Macintyre [*Independent*]. I played down the GB/Peter situation as best as I could, but Don knew what was going on. He felt Peter was too grand, and Gordon was too paranoid, but equally felt that the Tories were nowhere and we were going to win. The two met with Donald and agreed they had to work together, Peter working to GB, etc. TB told me he had told GB they could not go on like this, that they were both at fault. He said that if they couldn't work together, and Peter was forced out, then GB would have to give up the strategy job and Charlie would have to go too. He said he felt he'd given Peter a real fright, probably for the first time. He said I should veer towards boosting GB in briefings. I wrote a briefing note on the fact of their meeting, and their determination to bring damaging publicity to a halt, and pointing out that they would continue to work together, and the party wanted everyone to focus on the task ahead. It was ridiculous I had to do it at all. GB then tried to persuade TB there should be no briefing, no doubt because he had his own briefing operation lined up. At the weekly strategy meeting, it was comical, the way that Peter was trying too hard being nice to and about GB. Gordon was still turned in on himself and only pushing his own ideas. There were doubts about the Lost Generation campaign but GB had briefed it to the *Guardian* so there was no going back on it now. Peter was blaming Anji and me for stirring things against him again.

Tuesday, May 14

There was tons in the papers re GB/Peter and all very grim. I was pissed off enough for TB to say later he was worried I was becoming disaffected and disengaged. I said I couldn't stand watching all these egos operating like this and then be expected to spend my life defending and promoting them. Peter had got too grand, Gordon was obsessive and self-obsessed and TB had allowed them to become indispensable. At the morning meeting, Gordon was late, Peter was silent, both pretending to be nice to each other. JP was doing a speech to civil servants on the role of the Treasury and he or someone on his behalf was briefing that it was a different line to GB. TB called me and said to tell JP that if there was a big JP/GB split story he could say goodbye to everything. I had the feeling that apart from me and TB, nobody was really seized of how potentially disastrous all this was. Bruce came to me and said Eureka, then wrote me a diagram of the relationships that were causing us trouble. GB/PM. AC/PM. RC/PM. JP/PM. PLP/PM [PM being Peter Mandelson]. 'Do you get the point? What would Sherlock Holmes make of that do you think? Maybe that PM was the problem.' We then had a problem with JP's speech which was clearly a deliberate pop at Gordon. These spats were becoming a real problem, and I was finding it harder and harder to rebut some of the stuff being put to us. It just wasn't tenable to do the usual line about them working together when the whole time the press were getting briefings from the various camps against the others.

Wednesday, May 15

GB was on *Today* and did pretty well, considering all the crap surrounding it, and managed to get up the Lost Generation. He did a very professional job, though God knows how he felt when he said Peter is brilliant. I arrived at TB's full of anger that this is still going on, but TB said GB did a very good job, and showed why he still has faith in him. But he said he felt his relationship with both of them would never be the same again. I repeated endlessly that I felt there had to be some evidence of them being put in their place to draw a line under this, but he said you could not do that with the Shadow Chancellor. He was livid with JP over his speech yesterday, and called him in once we got to the office, told him it was criminal and immature. JP said he only ever got listened to when he rocked the boat, and there had to be a real change in procedures and the way things were done.

Before the pre-meeting, I said to TB that he must not defer to any of us, because that always made him look vulnerable in front of some of the bigger beasts. But the mood was not good. GB was a little more humble than usual. Blunkett and Smith were trying to help. Jack Straw took me to one side and said that TB really had to stand up to Gordon and stop being bullied. Donald Dewar was doing the [Commons] press gallery lunch and I went as [*Independent* journalist] John Rentoul's guest. Donald was hilarious. 'The last time someone proposed a toast to me was at our wedding and a fat lot of good that did me.' The gallery was hard work. There was a lot of gossip going around, and the story of a split had moved from them to us. TB was pretty apoplectic about it all.

At the Big Four, TB said it had been a dreadful week. Robin said it was important we present whatever way forward we agree not as being about discipline but direction/policy. GB emphasised the need to get back on to the *Road to the Manifesto*. He said there must be more consultation and there would be. He said he would get Andrew Smith to involve more people more deeply in spending discussions. TB said it was important all members of the Shadow Cabinet felt involved. JP said yes, the media would inflame divisions, but what is wrong is our procedures and they have to be got right. He said there had to be more collective decision-making. TB said there could always be improved consultation but it should never excuse indiscipline. This is about professionalism. JP returned to his theme. This forum doesn't work, we don't meet enough, we don't discuss things. This was meant to be a check on policymaking and it hasn't worked. We exist because we do represent different views, and ours are not taken into account. There is no real forum for discussion. TB said if people think it is tough now, they should wait for government. JP asked if the *Road to the Manifesto* process was going to lead to policy changes and TB said straight out – yes.

We went through to the Shadow Cabinet meeting in a really bad atmosphere. Again TB said it had been a dreadful week. There was anger in the party. The obligation on the leadership was to ensure proper consultation and that also meant those consulted had obligations too. He said there would be more involvement of the Shadow Cabinet but nothing justified the lack of discipline. People talking to the media feeding these stories is unprofessional. The irony is that there is no great ideological split between us. Far from it. He quoted Heseltine who had said the Tories may not be capable of winning but we were still capable of losing. He said we're in a different framework now. Hostile things make news. Comments about colleagues make news. I promise the broadest possible consultation but there must be reciprocal responsibility and history will pass a very cruel judgement if we fail now. Doug Hoyle [Labour MP, PLP Chairman] said MPs were frustrated and angry as they were being reasonably disciplined and people at the top were not. Jack Cunningham was terrific. He said, I've been here twenty-six years and thirteen of them at this table in opposition, and that is more than enough. If we cannot have proper discussions in here, then the Shadow Cabinet becomes dysfunctional. He said he had also learned that parties that squabble about power before they get it, do not get it in the end. MPs are angry and are saying for God's sake get your act together. The public will not vote for divided parties and the Tories must be delighted at the ammunition we had given them. Also, he added, if the Shadow Chancellor is ever isolated we all pay a price in that too. Jack Straw came in, said a lot of this is about political maturity. People are always willing to believe the worst of colleagues and it's bad. We're paying the price of complacency. Ann Taylor said the party was in a state of anxiety, anger and horror. We're beginning to think that we could lose. Dobson said the off-the-cuff remarks about tax and the row about the launch of the child benefit plan did more harm to the party than the nutters. GB then made a very conciliatory statement, insisting he would involve people more and he was determined to learn from recent events. TB said he wanted everyone to understand there could be no excuse for indiscipline at all, at any time. It was a less bad-tempered meeting than the Big Four. GB had at least shown a bit of humility, and accepted he had not handled his colleagues well. Earlier TB had said to me I really had to try harder to deal with Gordon. Your trouble is that you're like me, you cannot understand why people behave like this, but you have to understand we are the exceptions. Most people in politics are prone to madness, they are not rational at all. But even so, Gordon and Peter are brilliant and we have to work with them. He felt the Shadow Cabinet had been cathartic and would help us draw a line. The press sensed that TB's leadership could be damaged by this and were going to push it as hard as they could. The inability to keep them in order looked pathetic and unprofessional.

Thursday, May 16

More crap in the papers. The general impression was that TB had read the riot act, and tried to draw a line. The Lost Generation campaign was largely lost. The morning meeting was moribund. Charlie Whelan was really beginning to come across as a deeply unpleasant character. I was in a foul mood at the strategy meeting, said very little, and felt slightly sick that the two people who had largely landed us in this mess, Peter and Gordon, were happily continuing to dispense advice to the rest of us about how to get out of it. We all agreed we had to get back on to the *Road to the Manifesto*. TB seemed better than yesterday, felt the situation stabilising and that it was not as bad as people thought. I felt this was ridiculous, and said so. I said the party was pissed off, and that we had not learned from mistakes. Insiders and outsiders felt that there was an elite and no real involvement for the party. We had to improve how we operated and we had to give clear direction. TB was far more sanguine and I felt there was a danger that cloud cuckoo land was moving in. We failed to agree on a plan for the weekend, other than to worry about different ways of getting out a story about the Big Four leading a fightback. Left early with Philip to sit in on some focus groups. They were not as bad as they might have been but the sense of division was beginning to get through.

Friday, May 17

Another dreadful day. A week of disaster areas. The *Mail* and *Times* splashed on Clare's transport document, presented as a tax on cars. TB's first call was at 7.30. 'Now, I'm worried.' Why? 'Did you hear

Robin [on the *Today* programme]? He was dreadful.' The transport story was consuming him and he was asking me and Jonathan to get it dealt with by 10. He wanted a line-by-line rebuttal, but the more we looked at the document the clearer it was the story was pretty soundly based and though we could legitimately say it was a travesty and from an old draft, the document was total crap. This was a document we had recommended be dropped but TB had seen Clare and given in to her. It was also the document that unbelievably went through the Joint Policy Committee. Peter called several times but frankly I couldn't be bothered. 'How are we going to get out of all this, my friend?' he said. 'Why are we in it?' GB also called twice in the morning to try to get the Clare business sorted and agreed we should rebut it without doing a massive rebuttal. The problem with this is it will become about tax very quickly, he said, as ever thinking about his own perspective. I had several up-and-down calls with TB during the day, because I felt so much of this nonsense could have been avoided. He said, I am still very confident, because I know we are going in the right direction. The *Road to the Manifesto* will take care of this. Peter called again and said what could he do to help? I said nothing. I also said he should not do a joint briefing with GB because the press would make too much of it. I was very grumpy at the team meeting. I was fixing up tomorrow's visit to Moss Side and Liz and I were working up a briefing on firearms. I was tired, fed up, not feeling we were going anywhere. For the first time in ages, I felt there was a real possibility of losing. Thankfully, again, the Tories came to our rescue, Howard and Clarke making very different speeches on Europe.

Saturday, May 18

TB was in Sedgefield. I called and said I thought we could get coverage on the call to ban replica guns. I wrote a briefing note which I gave to PA and by 11, according to Anji, it was leading Severn Sound radio. So presumably it was going big elsewhere. It was frankly a good diversion from the National Policy Forum, and all the rows. They were dying down a bit in the papers. I travelled up to Manchester with Jack Straw, Janet Anderson [Labour MP] and Ed Owen [Straw's adviser]. The guns plan was second on the lunchtimes, showing it was possible to turn the agenda with something fairly innocuous. The train was late and TB got to the policy forum before us. He gave them a very tough message to the effect that if a council behaved like the PLP recently, they would be out. We headed for Moss Side and TB did a very good Q&A with about fifteen young people, with the cameras only in for the first bit. He was on form and was better when the cameras left, genuinely asking for their views, and listening. I sensed they liked him. They said they wanted a better image for the area, that it was not all drugs and crime. TB was asked by one reporter whether the visit was designed as a distraction from the splits at the policy forum. If it was, it worked. Overall a definite success. Afterwards TB said he'd really got something out of meeting the young people. We went to the town hall where a number of workshops were going on. I said to Sally it was like the Pope blessing the faithful. We went to Old Trafford to get some videos at the Man United shop for Nicky and Rory then left for the plane. He was livid with JP at the moment, and going through one of his 'GB was right, we should have gone for Margaret [Beckett]' phases. I don't think he ever really meant it but said it whenever JP had annoyed him, as with the speech this week. I felt MB was great but said she wouldn't have pushed the boat out for change which, when the chips were down, JP had always done so far. TB said yet again I had to make more effort with Gordon. I said it would help if Gordon made it easier. He felt Peter was less effective than before, because he was in a different world now, leading a ridiculous social life, not doing what he was meant to be doing. He still felt Peter gave added value, but it had been hard not to lose a bit of respect in recent weeks.

Sunday, May 19

The *Sunday Times* had a headline poll saying that we were now seen as being as divided as the Tories, though in fact the figures did not say that. There was lots of the usual bollocks about it being TB's worst week yet. Peter Kilfoyle called to say that he had just been fronted up by the *Sun* about his daughter doing a kiss-and-tell on a three-in-a bed romp with Robbie Fowler [Liverpool FC striker]. He was clearly in a flap, and I couldn't say I blamed him. I said he should simply have a short statement ready for use when he got calls about it, saying he was sad she had spoken to a paper reviled on Merseyside, and that she could always rely on the family for love and financial support. The other drama of the day concerned Michael Meacher. Tim called to say that Meacher had said to *Red Pepper* [left-wing magazine] that we would abolish the jobseekers' allowance. In fact we were reviewing it. I said to Tim to check whether he said it. He spoke to Ian Wilmore, Meacher's press guy, who said that he had written it and not cleared it with Meacher. We just about killed the story but the *Telegraph* splashed on it as a way of saying the splits and the rows were still causing us problems.

Clare was on the *Today* programme talking about the Railtrack share offer, and she sounded all over the place again. She was votes down the drain every time she opened her mouth. At the team meeting TB went through some of the problem areas. He was very down on JP still. Margaret McD said the problem was that JP went round the place being difficult, making comments about TB. I defended JP and said that all he was asking was to be properly involved, and that was not too much to ask. Margaret said Clare was also constantly attacking the Blairites. As for Meacher, I said to TB he should see him and tell him that this was an embarrassment and if the latest fiasco was down to Wilmore, Meacher should sack him. It was unbelievably unprofessional. TB was writing to GB to say he must be contactable at all times and he must get more involved in Millbank. He'd obviously had a decent rest yesterday and was firing on all cylinders again and on much better form. Peter was full of *ex cathedra* pontification. TB had said to Anji last night that I had done a brilliant job organising things for Saturday, and I should know that if it came to him settling on me or Peter, I was the one he felt he couldn't lose. I spent most of the day trying to think of stories for the trip to Italy on Thursday, and the *Standard* interview. The thing we had to be emphasising at the moment was strong leadership. After the meeting TB asked me to stay behind and we discussed JP. We agreed that if there was to be a bust-up it was better it came sooner not later. I said my experience of John was that he was fine, if everyone said what they thought and was open and honest about it. He just couldn't stand being kept in the dark. Jonathan sat in on their meeting later and said that TB had been very tough with him. JP said he would think over a few things. TB also saw Meacher and said unless he changed his outlook, and his ways of operating, he could not really expect a serious job in government. Meacher left close to tears.

Tuesday, May 21

During the day we heard Major was going to do a statement on beef. The word was there would be no great retaliatory measures, but as the text of the statement came through it was clear Major was going to go hard on it, and suspend co-operation with the EU until the beef derivatives ban was lifted and there was a clear framework in place for the broader ban to be lifted. It sent TB into a bit of a spin. Peter felt TB should support Major's statement. TB did a couple of TV interviews, which I thought were pretty poor, and said so. The story was not about us but for some reason TB was in a total state about it, worried it was going to play really well for JM on the patriotic, anti-European front, and that we would end up on the wrong side of the argument. He said he did not want to attack what he was doing but he did not want to support it either. I said we had to reserve judgement until it became clear what it all meant, and that is the position we should take to Rome. He said this was classic Major, very tactical, all about trying to put us in the wrong position, rather than deal with the issue.

The key question was how the farmers would react. Liz [Lloyd] established that they would give it a cautious welcome. There's no doubt this is all about trying to create a problem for us, said TB. Bruce came to take him away and he looked awful, when in fact it was a big problem for the government. He pulled himself together and did OK but it was a points win for Major.

Wednesday, May 22

TB's concerns about Major getting big licks were borne out. There was lots of 'war' talk and the front page of the *Express* had him wrapped in a Union Jack. The *Guardian* and *Independent* were scathing but the overall impression was good for him and TB was widely panned for his performance yesterday. The morning meeting was a gloomy affair, considering the beef situation. TB had told Jonathan we should be cautious but work up a more effective line of questioning. What did the threat to withdraw co-operation actually mean in practice? I was writing a briefing note based on TB's views and the top line was that he will be asking the Italians to lift the ban when we went there tomorrow. TB came back to say that he accepted people would say our line was opportunistic but he could not possibly support what JM did, yet nor could we oppose it hard for obvious political reasons. It was classic Major. So we had to say that we found the negotiations useless, but they had now embarked on a strategy, and we were not going to undermine it while abroad tomorrow.

The Big Four meeting, with Robin absent, was very unproductive and bad tempered. JP barely spoke and was clearly brooding. At Shadow Cabinet, Jack Cunningham, Margaret Beckett and George Robertson all said this was a dangerous moment and we had to be careful. If Major pulled it off, we would have to be very alert and skilful in our response. Robin called from Hungary to ask if he should do the *Today* programme. I said no, because it was hard to read these situations from abroad. He said I cannot believe I am hearing all this nonsense, talk of war cabinets and the like. I said we would try to stay out of it until tomorrow, when TB would have to get involved in a very high-profile way in

Rome. This had really made him anxious, more than I expected it to. TB was right, that this is largely politically driven, but we had to deal with it. TB felt that if the public finances prevented tax cuts, they would have to look to other areas for enemies and Europe was the obvious one. He was worried that the Europeans would just cave in.

Thursday, May 23

Labour giving the Tories 'wary backing' was becoming the watchword. Terry picked me up at 6.45 and we went for TB who was very worried about the way it could all play and the potential damage. He called GB and said to him that we had actually to decide if we supported the government's non-cooperation policy or not. GB was keen to move it to another question, but TB said in the end the question had to be answered. The real question was getting the ban lifted, and we had to put forward positive measures, and we were not sure the government way was the way to do that. TB had reached the view that we had to have a stronger line. His main worry, as ever, was that Major would get big licks. He believed this was less about the ban than Major getting the Tory tabloids back on board and thus far, it was working. Major's hope was that we would paint ourselves as being anti-British while the Tories were anti-European.

As we drove into Rome, TB spoke to GB. In the end there were just three positions – support, opposition, or sitting on the fence. We were helped by the fact that we were abroad and we could get breathing space by saying we did not attack the government abroad. There were only four journalists on the plane, all delighted to discover the spin doctor was translated as 'curator of the image' in Italian. I briefed them but it was tricky. I wanted them to say Blair backs Major, but without us being totally tied into him. We had the usual bollocks from the Foreign Office, the ambassador [Sir Patrick Fairweather] saying they could not have cameras in for the lunch at the residence. I got agreement from [Romano] Prodi's people, so it was clearly FCO.

TB's meeting underlined how much they looked to TB abroad now, both for leadership of the left and inspiration. There were posters of him on the walls, which was weird unless just put there for the day. It was clear they were 'waiting for Blair'. While it again underlined how seriously we were taken, it was potentially also a problem in the current atmosphere, the sense that 'they' wanted Blair, rather than Major. We walked to the PM's office, which was splendid without being over the top. Prodi, who somehow failed to strike you as being a prime minister, and who spoke too quietly to be heard, told TB that the Major government was being incompetent. TB said he wanted to be sure that Prodi could say it was still his intention to support lifting the ban on beef derivatives and that he would not attack the government. Prodi was clearly unimpressed by Major's threats. It was clear the ambassador didn't want TB doing media with Prodi, but I set John Sergeant up to doorstep them as they walked by. Afterwards, six or seven questions because of the time taken for interpretation and TB was very supportive of the government, without saying he was backing non-cooperation.

In the car to the airport, he was worried he had gone too far in support. I felt fine with the line we had now, but he was fretting. He wanted me to make it clear that in part he was being so supportive because we were abroad but if they failed to sort it out by the Florence summit, we would start to go for them. The ambassador told TB he felt the whole thing would end in tears, which made TB more sceptical about our line. The FCO clearly felt it was crazy, and that we would not necessarily get our way and then what? Prodi furthermore told TB that Major may have made it harder to lift the ban because they could not be seen to be giving in to blackmail. We landed to a great row going on because [Foreign Secretary Malcolm] Rifkind had launched into TB, saying that he was pathetic, sitting on the fence. TB wanted us to fight back by saying it made clear they wanted to make it a political issue whilst pretending the national interest was engaged. GB and I wanted to go further and really blow it up against them. TB and Peter felt we should let the Tories get more and more political about it before piling in. TB felt that they were making a mistake. Then we heard Mawhinney had really gone for TB too. I put out a fresh statement from GB. I did a ring round and the feeling was it was beginning to unravel for the government.

Friday, May 24

Terry collected me early and I headed for TB's before we left for the awayday at Philip's. PG was on great form but a bit nervy at having this thing at home. The morning session was meant to be TB, GB, Peter, me. But as it was at Philip's TB felt he had to have him there too, and he asked Jonathan to take a note. He started rather bizarrely, said that he thought we ought to begin by him and GB talking about message, so that we could all listen and then give our views. 'Samuel Beckett would love it,' I said. TB was probably trying to tease out from GB a more advanced economic message. If so, it didn't really work. The reality is that both of them were saying the same thing but refusing to acknowledge it. I felt – and later said – that if we had all stuck to stakeholding we could have made a real impact because when you boiled down what they were saying, that was what it was. TB talked about social inclusion being a precondition of economic strength and success. GB talked about opportunity being extended and that forming the base of a work-led opportunity economy. There was nothing between them yet you'd not think it from hearing them. It was reasonably good-humoured but not terribly productive. There was also a near-physical mutual irritation between GB and Peter. They didn't even go through the motions any more. If Peter spoke, GB looked away or wrote. If GB spoke, Peter either stared at him intently or he flicked through his papers. But they hardly ever followed each other in conversation and when they did, there was a hint of venom. I didn't feel we made much progress but TB said at lunchtime he felt we had. He told me he felt clearer about the decisions that had to be made.

In the afternoon session, on attack, I was taking part whilst trying to write a piece for the *News of the World* on the BSE (Blame Someone Else) government. We got back to tax and the economy. TB said he wanted to kill off some of the taxes – tartan tax, teenage tax, savings tax. We were getting a reputation we had been trying to shelve. He was exaggerating to make a point. GB did the same on stakeholding. He said it led to too many promises we would not be able to keep. He said we cannot offer everyone a job or a home but we can offer opportunity. I said opportunity was too weak. Stakeholding had worked because it was new, exciting, it acted as a peg and crucially it was being attacked by the Tories which allowed us to get definition from it. They don't attack the idea of opportunity. TB said the *Road to the Manifesto* must be led by an economic message. He said can the party get to know and love Gordonomics? Peter said the problem was people were confused and people at the top were not signed up to the same message. At lunch GB was very quiet, Peter did a rather half-hearted and lacklustre pitch on election planning, saying it was advanced without really going into detail. There was some discussion of postponing the *Road to the Manifesto*. I said this was ridiculous. We had made a decision and we had to stick to it. I was getting exasperated. I said six weeks on we still didn't have agreement on the time of a regular morning meeting, and we couldn't agree on a venue. Peter threw one of his tantrums as the argument degenerated into who was to blame for the fact that we couldn't find a time to suit everyone. TB said to me later that maybe he had to accept Peter and GB would never be able to work together again properly. He said Peter should be under no illusion the onus was on him to make it work. He felt GB was indispensable in a way Peter

May '96: Peter M's 'lacklustre' election pitch

was not. TB and Anji both felt the day had achieved something. I felt we had gone over all the same ground again, without making real progress.

Saturday, May 25 to Saturday, June 1 (holiday in Majorca)
I tried very hard to switch off while we were away. Not easy of course, because Philip [Gould] yaks constantly about the party, and never tires of discussing the main themes and the main players. Through the week, beef remained the main story. PG was worried that TB's qualified support line, whilst evidently clever politics in the way it thwarted what JM wanted out of it, might lose him points with the commentariat and the chatterati. The office said the *Sun/Times* were being very supportive of Major on beef, and clearly the whole strategy was about getting us into a bad place and trying to move Murdoch papers towards him on Europe. As ever, we spent a lot of the time talking about GB and Peter. I said that if we were a private sector organisation, one or both would have been sacked by now. They were behaving appallingly. Peter felt that I had not given him the support he needed. I felt, however, that he was the author of his own problems. I had been warning for some time that a new kind of high profile focused on lifestyle would turn him into a liability if he was not careful, and that is what was happening.

PG was nagging at me to come up with a fresh slogan for the next stage and into the *Road to the Manifesto*. We had a couple of brainstorming sessions at one of the little bars on the beach and eventually I came up with 'New Labour, New Life for Britain'. I liked it. It took the basic slogan but gave it a sense of process and energy which would be illustrated by policy rather than strategy. I also came up with the idea of a poster campaign targeted at ten hot spots where aspirational Brits went on holiday in the summer. Going Places with New Labour. I think that boiling down our discussions, we felt that TB had to follow his instincts more. When he was being himself and following his own instincts, he was providing both leadership and excitement in politics. But the internal dynamics were tending to make him a bit defensive, take fewer risks, settle for the centre of gravity. He was at his best abroad because he didn't have everyone bending his ear and trying to inject little bits of their own agenda. It was really nice by the end of the week, felt relaxed for the first time in ages.

Sunday, June 2
Nicola Pagett [actress] had a long interview in the *Observer*, clearly talking about me. She didn't refer to me by name but it was all about

a stranger she wrote to and was obsessed with, and it was clear from some of the specific remarks that it was me. I talked to PG about how to react if she or her publicist, assuming they knew, told a journalist it was me. I told TB, who thought it was hysterical. Anji didn't really take it seriously, but I showed her some of the letters and she said 'Oh my God, this will be public in twenty-four hours.' Sue Jackson, who had kept all the letters and who had never discussed them with anyone, was really angry and upset, and convinced that the whole thing was just a publicity stunt. But I sensed from the letters I had read that there was something very genuine about her madness, and I didn't feel threatened by it, just a bit anxious if it became a great media blah. Clearly there would be some media interest now she had done this interview. Apparently it had all come out first in the *Mail* saying she had gone mad, and then she did this interview in the *Observer*. I spent some of the morning reading the letters I had never bothered to read. Some of them were fascinating, not just for her observations about herself – she moved in and out of rational thinking – but also about me and some of the situations we found ourselves in.

Monday, June 3

Finally, after all the messing around over the last few weeks, we had the first of the morning meetings at Millbank Tower. GB and Donald were not there. TB was determined that the *Road to the Manifesto* was going to go ahead and we had various discussions during the day about whether to delay the June 27 launch because it was so close to the Euro '96 semi-finals. TB was happier in our position on beef, and in the meeting with Robin later, RC said that though he had been sceptical, he now felt we had probably done the right thing. Peter M had devised some new structures which he tried to bounce off me. He was worried about us not being disciplined enough, but these structures all appeared to have him at the centre of them. We were heading for a hectic period. I went back to Millbank with Tom Sawyer, who seemed to have replaced me as the person who listened to all JP's grumbles. He felt it was all about his ego and his position. About 3.30, Tom called Anji to warn her that JP had gone berserk because he had heard that TB had had a meeting about *Road to the Manifesto*, that it was going to be war, and that he was going to set his people to oppose. It sent TB into a spiral. 'What am I supposed to do with these fucking people?' For the first time he said we may have to go all the way with him and say there will have to be a leadership election. If he can't hack it when it's like this, what on earth will he be like in government? TB had said to JP just before the recess that he would not tolerate this kind of nonsense any more, yet here we were back to it over the fact that TB dared to have a meeting about *Road to the Manifesto*.

TB then saw Derry and GB to try to persuade GB to agree to his plans on devolution, particularly our answer to the West Lothian Question, namely that power devolved is power retained. I drove home with TB. He was not convinced that GB had signed up to it but he said he was definitely going to do this. It is the only way we will get support in the end, he said. He was still confident that the *Road to the Manifesto* process would get us back on track. I was back on steroids because of a recurrence of the stomach problem [ulcerative colitis].

Tuesday, June 4

The beef derivatives ban was lifted last night, and most of the press presented it as a success for the government's beef-ban fight, though most included the line that it was already expected. Philip's focus groups had made clear the qualified support strategy was absolutely right. I was late because Rory had his sports day in which he won the 200m, the long jump and the relay. He was really proud of himself, but trying to hide it. I was in by lunchtime for a meeting on Questions. TB and I also discussed GB and Peter. I said that I was in the basic position of qualified support/non-cooperation, and he laughed, but I was serious in saying that they had to show they were able to behave better if I was going to co-operate fully. TB said it was deeply depressing, that so much of what would decide whether we succeeded or failed was dependent on the psychological makeup of a small number of people.

I worked last night and today on a TB vision statement to put to focus groups tonight to go with 'New Labour, New Life for Britain'. Philip showed me Saatchis' suggested ads for us, which were quite good. 'Better for everyone' was the positive theme, 'Enough is enough' was the negative theme, and they somehow triggered the New Life line. Everyone I tried it on liked it, and the focus groups really liked it. They said it suggested hope, verve and opportunity, getting things moving. PG said it was way ahead of all other lines tested, positive and negative. Also, the statement I'd done for TB was seen as visionary and convincing, and they liked the idea of small but basic pledges, rather than grand overblown stuff.

I went to the four o'clock Millbank long-term strategy meeting. As usual, GB and entourage were late, and I said I was fed up wasting time waiting for meetings to start. Once the meeting got underway, we discussed the two campaigns, *Road to the Manifesto* and Lost Generation. I argued strongly that the New Deal/Lost Generation should be a subsidiary part of *Road to the Manifesto* and that if they were seen as separate, our main communications effort would fail. Philip had come up with the idea of a youth manifesto to show it was all part of the same thinking. GB was clearly hoping to run the Lost Generation campaign as a separate thing as a way of bolstering his NEC campaign. Peter, PG and I went along with that but I was adamant that it should be subordinate. I had decided that both with Gordon and with Peter I was going to argue more vigorously at meetings like this, unnerve them a bit, make them understand that I knew what the game was for both of them. PG later sent a note from [focus groups in] Watford, really positive on New Life for Britain, much stronger than Better off with Labour, which GB wanted. He said that only three out of eight knew who GB was, which was ridiculous but showed what we were up against. PG said the New Life for Britain statement shifted votes. I called TB and said I was really cheered up because I was beginning to think we're getting a message through. The Tories were in real trouble, but I never felt that would be enough. We had to have our own strategy, and push it through.

Wednesday, June 5

I was very cheered by Philip's groups last night, as was TB. I got into the morning meeting, and even though only Donald, me and one or two others were there, I said we should start on time regardless. JP was on the rampage about Peter's *On the Record* interview, he having pulled out, then to see Peter on instead. TB's interview in *Parents* magazine, in which he said he had sometimes spanked his children, was out. It was probably an OK story but it could get out of control so we had to organise a quite positive response. There was a problem in that Cherie was on a NSPCC committee. I felt OK about it but with *Newsnight* calling all Shadow Cabinet members we sent out a line to them saying ignore any surveys. We had a brief discussion on Friday's education speech. We then went for a meeting with Harriet, her staff, Peter M and PH to go over her document on getting rid of waiting lists. It didn't strike me as credible unless it was clear that there were tough choices – in other words, e.g., you would have to sack administrators to pay for nurses. We went through it with Harriet who was not very clear. We agreed we should redo it. Page one should be the ten-point plan, then tell the story of what happens to patients in the Tory system, and then what would happen under the New Labour system and then put the central argument. I got back to the Big Four meeting. GB did not engage much and just did his paperwork. Robin gave us a very pompous run around the block on beef, saying how good our strategy had turned out to be, as though he, rather than we, had been the author of it, a speech he later repeated to the Shadow Cabinet.

Thursday, June 6

TB came out of the smacking row fine, though CB was not happy about it. The *Sun* and *Guardian* both had leaders that were supportive, which must have been a first. I was feeling a bit on the edge. Peter M was still behaving far too grandly. GB was on much better form at the moment. I went back to write a briefing note on tomorrow's comprehensive school speech. TB was keen to get up the notion of modernising the comprehensive principle. TB had promised David English he would offer a piece on the speech to the *Mail*. I did a note and then called Dacre to offer them a big briefing. It became clear to me that the *Mail* were going to do it as a 'dumping' story, rather than a positive pro-comprehensive speech, and so I briefed the *Guardian* and *Independent* too. I wasn't at all happy that the *Mail* would set the tone and so I talked up various angles elsewhere. There was a danger that we were going to get the tough New Labour headline, as TB wanted, but that we would unnecessarily anger the party and so diminish the value of what was in fact a good speech. At the weekly strategy meeting, I was pushing for 'New Labour, New Life for Britain' as the next-steps slogan. TB clearly liked it. We also went over worries about the health waiting lists document. Nobody felt confident Harriet would be able to handle the tough questions, for which we didn't really have the answers. GB agreed we needed tough choices written into it. I had to leave early for a hospital appointment re my stomach.

Friday, June 7

I called Alex Ferguson [Manchester United manager] to fix an interview for the party magazine. He was dead keen. I did a lobby briefing on the speech. I admitted I was surprised at the level of interest, given that setting was already happening, and TB had said much of this before. Several of them were pissed off that we had gone to the *Mail*. The *Telegraph* overdid it with the streaming headline. We were really piling it on for [Conservative Education Secretary Gillian] Shephard, saying we had won the argument re selection vs standards. I called Max Hastings to complain about the *Standard* splash which said there was massive opposition from our MPs when in truth there was not.

Everyone in the office was saying it was a great spin operation. TB was calling so often, and usually about the same thing, that I ended up pretending to be an answering machine – if your call is for Alastair Campbell, and you are his boss, please leave a message after the tone, explaining whether you are saying something you have not already said ten times. At least it was possible to have a laugh with him, and he had no trouble being told when he was being irritating, as now. The speech was playing fine. It wasn't until *Newsnight* that anyone accurately pointed out that there wasn't actually anything new in it.

Saturday, June 8

Terrific coverage on the speech, and four or five good editorials. With the Tories looking more and more ragged, it had been a good week. I could also sense the beginnings of a climbdown on beef. Alan Clark called and was in despair. 'I think we're probably fucked,' he said. 'It's like the patient got ill, and the doctor prescribed antibiotics, but the patient didn't improve, and if anything got worse, so we whacked in a few tons of cortisone but nothing, absolutely nothing, has happened to make things better. So that says to me the patient is enduring a slow and lingering death.' I said you've quite cheered me up, Alan, and he said 'Congratters, I have to say you guys have been playing a blinder, and our people just don't know what to do.' He was in excited, excitable form, emphasising every single word as he spoke – 'AND OUR PEOPLE JUST DON'T KNOW WHAT TO DOOOOO.'

I took the kids' football class at school and then to TB's for lunch before heading for Wembley [Euro '96, England vs Switzerland]. I had an unusually pleasant conversation with Cherie. When she wanted to be charming and friendly, that was exactly what she was and it reminded me of the impression she made when we first met. I could never quite fathom why she couldn't maintain that most of the time. The truth was that on most of the occasions we met now, there was usually politeness but not the friendliness there used to be, but today she was full of warmth and good humour, asking after the kids and saying how grateful TB was for everything I did for him, etc. The two of them were due to see [Sir] Robin Butler [Cabinet Secretary] tonight and hopefully go over some of the questions that I don't think they had really turned their minds to, like where and how they intended to live, and what she intended to do by way of balancing family, career and consort roles. I don't think either of them had really got the measure of the scale of change that was coming if we won. I only found out about the Butler meeting by accident, and TB had not even told Jonathan about it, who had got a bit jumpy of late because I think he was unsure of his own position. I assumed this was Butler making early moves to carve out a relationship with TB independent of me, Jonathan, Anji or anyone else.

The buzz from the hacks was that the Whitehall machine was on the one hand quite excited about change, and the knowledge that there would be a number of outsiders coming in with TB, but also anxious about it. TB said he and CB had been talking about the election campaign itself and Cherie would travel with him but when we got to places would have her own itinerary. We talked about JP, who was due to see him tomorrow to discuss what job he would do in government. This was in part politics, but there were also a lot of ego and status issues to address, and it was the kind of stuff TB couldn't stand dealing with but he would have to. TB thought JP was moving to the idea of being Home Secretary, but that would lead to an inevitable clash with Jack. TB was thinking about splitting crime and the constitution, but JP wasn't right for the constitution job.

We got to Wembley and met Kevin Keegan and Alex F. Alex told us that they had had some useful work done on stress management in the final days of the Premiership and that he would pass it on to us, as it might be useful during the campaign. It was a poor game and when Switzerland equalised, Jack Cunningham had to hold me down to stop me jumping up and cheering. Partly it was the Scotland supporter in me, but also there was part of me that did not want a great nationalist football fervour creating a feel-good sense that could let the Tories win back a bit of a lift. I have no idea whether sport can do that, but there has to be a chance that it can, and it's the last thing they deserve. At half-time, Denis Howell [Lord Howell, former Labour sports minister] said to me 'If England win, expect a September election.' I left the match pretty confident England were not going to win the tournament. In the car afterwards, we discussed GB's idea that he move to Millbank. I said I could see the benefits but the big downside was the potential loss of control, and the extra mayhem Whelan could cause there. TB said it was very hard to say no when we had been saying that GB should get more involved. He was telling me about his last dinner with Roy Jenkins at Derry's. He does a good impersonation of Woy. 'I see you, Tony, as someone carrying an exquisite, beautiful, hand-painted vase over a slippery floor and as you proceed across the floor, vase in hand, you can see your destination, and you can see the likes of Harriet Harman and Clare Short lunging towards you, and you don't know whether to run or to tiptoe.'

Sunday, June 9

TB was seeing JP later who told me his line of argument would be that he wanted to be one hundred per cent supportive but in return he had to be one hundred per cent on the inside track. TB remained nervous about making him a de facto deputy PM because he would be wanting to charge into every area. He thought – though I tried to disabuse him – that JP would be content with Home Office plus regional development. What was true was that JP was trying harder to be co-operative but he wanted a major job in government and deputy prime minister was still what he felt most suited to. They also agreed he would have a major public role in the *Road to the Manifesto* process.

Monday, June 10

GB had a grumpy start to the week. I had put my bag on the chair next to me, then suddenly he appeared, made to the chair, unceremoniously threw the bag to the floor, and sat down. 'Hello, Gordon,' I said, picking up the bag. 'Oh, sorry, was that your bag?' Everyone laughed, apart from him. It was a ragged kind of meeting, lacking focus as we bounced around from issue to issue: how to tackle Heseltine's – or Heselteen as GB called him – Competitiveness White Paper [on improving the UK's global market performance], continued worries about Harriet and her paper. I went back and did a phone interview with Alex [Ferguson] for the party magazine, which was strong and which we would be able to get placed elsewhere without any trouble. At the office meeting, TB said he wanted me to put together an operation to boost JP in the press. He was also going to tell GB that he would have to work more closely with JP. He had clearly got the status message last night. We discussed GB's offer to move to Millbank. I was still very wary, because it would give licence to Whelan to brief on anything and everything and there was a danger the press office would be destabilised.

In the car on the way to lunch at the *Mail*, TB said he was confident JP really did want to come on board. He said I had to keep in constant contact with him, because I was the only one in the office he really trusted and respected. He wanted me to have a word with Pauline too and explain that if JP became Home Sec, he would get a flat in London and a house in the country. I said I didn't think Pauline would be that fussed. He said he felt RC was basically on board too just now. He had seen him last night, and found him far less difficult than he thought he might be on devolution. We arrived at the *Mail* and were taken upstairs to drinks and then lunch. [Lord] Rothermere

June '96: TB nervous at making JP his deputy

and [David] English did most of the talking, Rothermere friendly and warm, English reminding me of someone who felt he had to keep spirits up the whole time, even though they weren't terribly low. [Paul] Dacre was pretty mellow for him, but he must be hating the softening of the *Mail* line. TB was on terrific form. Of course the speech had helped set the scene, but you could see them wanting to disagree violently with everything he said, but they couldn't, not because he was pandering or being right wing, but because he was talking moderate common sense, and above all he was saying what we would do, not just that the other lot were fucking it up. They pressed hard on whether the party had actually changed, but he pushed back just as hard. Dacre said there was no way we would be able to control the left, and we would be forced to let public spending rip, but again he was having none of it, and he pushed back hard. There was an almost visible impact on Rothermere and English. There was no way we were going to get these people to back us, but if we kept those two vaguely on board, we would stop Dacre's maddest excesses. As we left, English said 'You should keep coming; you get more and more persuasive every time.'

Tuesday, June 11

There was a lot of excitement around the place at the build-up to [Eurosceptic Conservative MP] Bill Cash's referendum bill [private members' bill] which was coming up today. We had more to go on later when, on *House to House* [lunchtime TV programme], Quentin Davies [Europhile Conservative MP] forced Cash to admit that his European foundation had taken money from [Sir James] Goldsmith [billionaire businessman and founder of the short-lived Eurosceptic Referendum Party]. We got RC words straight out and successfully cranked it up. GB was more relaxed than of late and asked me to stay on at the end of the meeting. He said he was very keen for me to get behind his Lost Generation campaign, and he would like to do it with me. I said I was always happy to help run good campaigns, and we lacked a bit of bite at the moment, because we were too diffuse in what we were trying to do.

JP said he realised that he had wandered offside and with the election nearing, he knew he had to be onside. He'd said to TB on Sunday 'It's time to tell each other what we hate about each other. I hate being frozen out when major decisions are being made, or at least major issues being addressed.' He said he didn't like the way TB danced to GB and Peter M if they were being difficult. TB said to him he would not be able to offer him anything really major in government if he thought he was going to operate as he did when he was offside, constantly obstructing, etc. JP said he knew he had to change his outlook and his ways of working. He said he had to be more relaxed about things. He had to work harder at getting on with GB. I said he had to accept that TB drove hard from the centre, and there were times when we had to do things quickly, be flexible, and it wasn't always possible to share every thought in every thought process. I said sometimes he saw exclusion where none existed. Sometimes he complained about not being involved in things which if we had involved him he'd have thought why are you bothering me with this? He said he wanted to be on board, and be seen to be, and I said we would have to get over a briefing operation as we did with Clause 4, making clear he was heavily involved in the *Road to the Manifesto* process, and playing a key role.

TB felt we had to show to business that on education, welfare, competitiveness and Europe, the Tories just could not be trusted to deliver. TB was desperate to get coverage for the speech, not least for a business audience, but it was like flogging a dead horse. It showed once more that the media only really wanted to cover policy if there was an internal conflict story, whereas the government could make news by announcing any old crap, and often did. TB was going on again about getting rid of [Alan] Simpson [Labour MP] somehow, to show that we would not put up with permanent rebels.

We flew back by helicopter, and London looked absolutely stunning. If the weather was nice, it could compete with anywhere in the world. In the car, he showed me a letter from Lord Mackay [Lord Chancellor] who was offering to accept five of our six amendments in exchange for not killing the Family Law Bill. The letter had a tone of desperation but TB said he was still torn. He said he was probably 52–48 in favour of keeping the bill, amended as we wanted it, but he said there was a problem because most Labour people wanted to kill it. JM would be livid beyond belief if we killed it, but my instincts were that we should go for it. We had a bit of a problem later with the *Star* chasing a story that Jack Cunningham's and [Shadow sports minister] Tom Pendry's Euro '96 tickets went to someone else, possibly via the black market. I thought it was probably balls but said to TB that if it was true, it would be hard not to sack them. TB felt there was nothing wrong with them giving tickets away but if someone had profited, it was a bit different.

The vote on the [Bill] Cash [referendum] bill was dreadful for the Tories, and we successfully got up the Goldsmith/Cash funding story.

Wednesday, June 12

I was late in because Calum had said he wanted me to take him to school, which reminded me how I used to take Rory virtually every day but since working for TB it was an exception when I did. The morning meeting agreed we should make a complaint to Sir Gordon Downey [parliamentary commissioner for standards] re Cash/ Goldsmith. I wrote a briefing note to start the process of building up to *Road to the Manifesto* properly. This was a really important step in the communication of policy development, and it just wasn't there at the moment. We were having lunch with *The Times* at the Reform Club. Anatole Kaletsky [columnist] asked if TB would keep the Treasury as it was, or reform it somehow. TB said he was not persuaded by the argument for a Department of Economic Affairs. 'I'm not a great fan of creative tension,' he said. TB gave nothing much away but was not on form as he had been at the *Mail*. More and more at these lunches, they were talking to him as if it were already in the bag. That notion was underlined by the issue of the Family Law Bill, TB having decided he wanted to save the bill but make it clear we had won a stack of concessions. I had written a line making it clear we would judge on merits, not act purely out of the desire to defeat the government. They took that as tacit support and quite liked it.

Thursday, June 13

Fiona and I had had another row about how much I was working, and how distracted I was the whole time at home, and we didn't speak all day. TB was going crazy at our failure to put over a clear economic alternative that actually meant something to people, and we were missing tricks on the economy all over the place. GB felt the same but then didn't want to do too much of the public stuff himself. JP told me how determined he was to get on with GB. They were even going to go to the football together. TB was very effective at PMQs when he talked of government policy bearing the imprint of the last person who sat on Major. The press felt it was Major's worst for some time. GB was very off form at the CMT meeting, just not engaged and looking exhausted. There was a growing sense of government crisis and JM looked furious on the news. I said we had to get a grip of the GB situation, because he was not really driving what he was meant to be. TB said he would come good and we had to be patient. Later he was furious when he heard GB, who had refused all our efforts to do the *Today* programme on the economy, was planning to go on to preview the England vs Scotland match.

Friday, June 14

TB was still going on about how the *Today* programme kept running major political packages without a Labour voice. He was up in Sedgefield but must have called three or four times to make the same point. I left with Jonathan and Margaret McD for [publisher, philanthropist and Labour donor] Paul Hamlyn's, where we were going to be trying to persuade him to pay for a four-page tabloid pull-out on the *Road to the Manifesto*. He looked very frail and tired but was solicitous of everyone and clearly a nice man. But the presentation wasn't so good and I could sense Hamlyn had doubts. The mock-up consisted of a TB quote on the front, the key pledges inside in standard Latin text, a few TB quotes and a phone number on the back. It looked like it had been cobbled together overnight and probably had been. Hamlyn looked unimpressed. For some reason I felt really down, as low as I've been for a while.

Saturday, June 15

Manchester bomb.[1] We had to organise TB's reaction on TV. I took the kids' football class and then we set off for Wembley [for England vs Scotland]. We had good seats, but apart from [England midfielder Paul Gascoigne] Gazza's goal and [Scotland midfielder Gary] McAllister's missed penalty, it was all a bit flat and anticlimactic. However, on the way out, you got a sense of just how much of a feel-good factor you could get going on the back of all this [England beat Scotland 2-0]. 'Football's coming home'[2] was being sung everywhere you went, plus the less melodious 'Eng-er-lund'. JP had gone with GB and the two of them were sitting together, and seemed to be getting on, which was progress. I bumped into Nigel Clarke [ex-*Mirror* colleague/football reporter] who said that for the first time he would not be voting Tory. The Manchester bomb was massive across all the media and yet there was no sense of fear in London, which was odd, and again presumably an effect of the football.

Sunday, June 16

JP called and said he wanted to speak to TB about the labour market paper that was going to the contact group tomorrow. A few weeks ago, that would have spelled disaster but he said he was determined to

[1] An IRA bomb had devastated the shopping centre of Manchester, injuring 200 people.
[2] The refrain from the record 'Three Lions' by David Baddiel, Frank Skinner and The Lightning Seeds.

be onside and he just wanted to know how TB wanted to play it. He said he and GB had a good chat and they had made their peace. He said he had got a bit pissed at Geoffrey Robinson's party but the upside was he bet GB a tenner England would win, and he paid up – 'I must be the only one who's ever got money out of him.' We had dinner with Tessa [Jowell] and David [Mills], who was being chased by the *Sunday Times* re work he had done for Silvio Berlusconi [Italian businessman and politician],[1] probably wound up by CCO. He tried to explain exactly what he did for him, which was hard to follow, but appeared to be helping him set up companies to accommodate changes to the ownership laws, or indeed sell them. I couldn't really fathom it. He insisted it was all above board, but the press were likely to try to fling around a load of mud and I could see Tessa was a bit worried about it.

Monday, June 17

TB was anxious about the speech and our general positioning on Europe. We had a decent enough draft which we worked on during the flight [to Germany], making it snappier and he seemed to me to tone down the single-currency section. He was clearly determined we should not be painted into the single-currency-come-what-may corner. I worked on a briefing note on beef based on what he would be saying to [Helmut] Kohl. He was working flat out on the plane. I felt the story today should be TB putting the case for UK beef and raising pressure on Major whilst tomorrow it should be pro-Europe, but no pushover. We landed and were driven to Bonn. In the ambassador's residence he went over the speech again then off to the meeting with President [Roman] Herzog. There was a large media turnout and they were interested in every little detail, which again underlined they were basically treating him as if he were already PM.

One of the president's advisers said they'd been at a dinner with Ken Clarke recently who said the UK would be with Germany and France in the single currency in 1999. TB later told me his plan was to rule out the UK being in the first wave of the single currency and fight the election on that basis, win and then hope to be in a position to recommend entry at the next election. It would have the added bonus of splitting the Tory Party right down the middle. The president and later Kohl were adamant the single currency would go ahead and be successful. TB seemed to me to be more sceptical

[1] Mills was found guilty of accepting a bribe from Silvio Berlusconi, but he always denied the charge and on February 25, 2010 his conviction was quashed because the case ran out of time.

about us going in the first phase, constantly stressing the difficulties economically. I found Herzog impressive, bright, interested, clearly well informed beyond the usual brief. We travelled over to Kohl's office which was remarkable for the huge number of elephant ornaments around the place. Kohl was even bigger in the flesh than I had imagined him to be, huge great jowls flapping when he spoke, and large slabs of flesh pouring down his frame. It was not pleasant and yet he radiated a strength and a confidence that was no doubt helped by the size of the frame. I briefed that we would reverse our position on beef after Florence [EU summit] if the government failed to get a timescale on compensation. This was totally unfair as we pretty much knew they would not get it, and it led to the press saying we were moving away from a bipartisan approach. When I later told TB how the briefing had gone, and that the press were saying we were preparing to cut loose from Major, he didn't much like it, but I assured him it was fine. We then got a message that [Malcolm] Rifkind was saying we were unlikely to get a deal at Florence. I discussed with TB and we put together a line about the need to redouble effort to put the scientific case. We wanted to be more positive about Europe but we did not want ourselves in a position where we could be caricatured as saying Europe regardless, come what may, right or wrong. The problem was the speech now had the feel of a fence-sitting job.

We worked on the speech before dinner. I was put at the end of table up with an editor, a diplomat and a former diplomat. The diplomats both felt our stance was not pro Europe or pro Germany enough. They all fell very hurt by continuing anti-German sentiment, as with our tabloids. I think TB won most of them over. The ambassador, Nigel Bloomfield, struck me as a total Tory, pushing the government's position rather more than was perhaps necessary but then again, I guess that is his job. TB struck a rather cautious note on the euro and the commitment was more mood music than substance. Later, he and I went for a walk down by the river, and worked out which sections still needed working on. I went off to work on tightening it with TB doing a bit warning Europe could fall behind Asia. There were some marvellous Cook and Brownisms in the suggested changes that were being faxed through. For example, Gordon wanted to talk about being 'concerned' about the single currency, rather than talk about 'hesitation', and RC said he would rather say 'prudent' on public spending, not fierce, as TB wanted to.

TB felt he had got on well with Kohl. The talks had over run by a long way and TB felt Kohl had a good understanding of our position on beef, and the difficulties we had. TB said he was finding it very hard to deal with the beef issue. 'Opposition is a shit job.' He was clearly wanting still to be broadly supportive, even though he felt the government were ballsing it up. The speech briefing underlined just how hard the Europe issue was to communicate. On a quick read, the broadsheets had decided this was TB adopting a sceptical tone, whilst the tabloids basically felt it was TB signing up to the euro. Someone said 'You're basically saying you won't be in the first wave but you want it to work so you can be in it in future and so you won't be trying to derail.' That was about the size of it, but it was more complicated than our hacks liked things to be. On the way to the airport, TB was fretting about whether we had pushed the pro button too hard. I said they had taken out of it what they wanted to take, so the sceptics were sceptic and the pros were pro and nobody had died and what a lot of effort for not much. The main thing was that as a visit it had gone well, and he had shown once more he could impress any company. We landed and heard Hezza had launched a huge attack on the speech, which was terrific, and likely to ventilate coverage well. Went down for a meeting with TB, GB, Peter M, Tom S and finally we were near to agreeing campaign structures. Even the GB/Peter mood seemed a lot better than before. TB said he wanted GB to be more active in economic rebuttal. He felt the Tories were beginning to get up a positive economic message and we were not in that argument as strongly as we should be. GB was insistent that now was not the right time to go full motor. He said we had the basics in place and there would come a time when we went out all guns blazing and it wasn't now. Just the odd missile would do, I said, and to be fair GB laughed.

GB was also sceptical about the idea of the five specific pledges. He felt they were too small and we would be accused of lacking ambition. I said the whole point was for them to be achievable. The public are tired of grand promises and want to be able to believe the promises that are made. There were clearly a few difficulties ahead on the policy front, though. Trade union reform was obviously a bit sensitive and it was not clear where e.g. JP, GB or RC were on it. GB was making clear again he was not overwhelmed by the devolution ideas. RC called me after and I said we had missed him in Germany and how was Llandudno? He replied in his most RC-ish tart way possible 'I have to do these trade union conferences because Tony seemingly will do none of them.' We had to go for dinner at Michael Green's. We had quite an interesting discussion about the sound-bite culture and I said media and politicians were equally to blame for the way it had developed.

Wednesday, June 19

I'd missed the morning meeting because I was taking the boys to school but seemingly it all turned ugly with DD and GB making clear they were opposed to the position and angry about our briefing on labour market reform. David Blunkett called and said 'We need to speak before I do something silly.' I went to see him and as he made coffee, a process which always amazed me, because he did so with absolute confidence, knowing where everything was, not spilling anything, knowing how much to pour, etc. When you sat back and kept in your mind the fact that he was totally blind, he became even more impressive. But even so, it was clear he was angry. He reeled off a list of the occasions when he had toughed things out on our behalf – the Oratory, Harriet and the grammar school, opt-out policy – and he said he may not have been happy doing it but he did it because of the greater interest of TB and the party. But the briefings on the labour market document were the last straw. He said, I've taken a lot of shit before, but I am not prepared to play the fall guy again. I let him go on a bit and then, I'm afraid, I exploded too. I said I was constantly having to deal with difficult situations, usually created by politicians, and in this case principally the single currency, and I may have gone a bit far on the regulation briefing but I was operating under pressure and I didn't have time to call and go over every word. But let me say this: the reason I get like I do, and maybe sometimes go over the top, is because I am sick of politicians diving for cover as soon as there is the slightest, mildest flak flying their way. Are you telling me you couldn't face down a few hacks or a few union activists on the back of this? I said I always tried to understand what pressures the top guys in the party operated under, but you get a handle on the pressures we operate under. I said he and some of the other politicians, they dipped in and out of these high-profile, high-octane very difficult situations. We were living with them all the time, every single day. He just had to accept that was the way our life was at the moment, and if it was shit for him, it was even more shitty for me, and I'd thought he might understand that better than maybe GB or some of the others do. He was clearly taken aback, so much so that he was literally speechless. I knew straight away I had gone over the top, and I would have to apologise to him, so I did so

June '96: Blunkett 'not prepared to play fall guy again'

straight away. I said Christ, David, things must be bad if you and I are shouting at each other. I took his hand, said let's shake hands, accept an apology from me for talking to you like that, and let's try to put it behind us. He said sometimes it's good to clear the air, but he found that a bit upsetting, but he knew it wasn't personal, and he valued the way we worked together. I said let's try to forget it. I later wrote to his Braille secretary to give him a written apology too.

Beef was the main story of the day, with the government clearly moving towards climbdown. We had a BMP [advertising agency] meeting, me, Peter M and Margaret and they did a long presentation about a poster idea, a fat man being propped up by lots of little people and the headline 'Still a Conservative supporter?' I didn't like it. Peter didn't get it, and Margaret thought it was sneering towards people who voted Tory. Their creative guy said the key to communication was simplify then exaggerate. I said it did neither. Anji was in Blackpool, going over preparations for Conference, and said Joan [Hammell, Prescott aide] was trying to organise Special Branch protection for JP. TB said if it is just about status, I'm not too bothered. It's only if he thinks he can run the show that I'm worried. On the train to York we talked about the football and whether in fact there would be some great feel-good factor out of England winning. I said in the end people are not daft, and if Major looks like he's trying to milk it, it will backfire. Added to which, I still couldn't see England winning it. We got picked up at York and driven to Harrogate by a driver who would not stop talking. TB asked me why I was so grumpy at the moment. I said it's because I was not giving enough attention to my own children, because I was having to deal with rows created by big kids at the office.

Thursday, June 20

TB was sure the government was in real trouble now. He believed the deal the government struck [in Florence] over beef was worse than they would have got without the policy of non-cooperation. I came up with a line that 'It was not a deal but a rout' which ran on all the bulletins. Hilary [Coffman] came on to say that without reference to anyone, Clare was today publishing her transport document. Even by her utterly self-indulgent standards, to do so on the day TB was speaking to a major health conference, and the government was in turmoil, was pretty unbelievable. We got back to London to find the *Evening Standard* splashing on her half-baked transport drivel. Philip and I agreed we had to do a big in-your-face campaign on 'New Labour, New Life for Britain'. On football, the press were pressing us desperately to get caught up in euphoria, and I felt we had to be careful not to either look like we were exploiting it or make the mistake of trying to fuel it.

Friday, June 21

We agreed at the morning meeting Blunkett should release the labour market paper, and [Stephen] Byers should brief on it. TB was worried about it all day, but I felt the steam had pretty much gone from it, it would be reasonably low-key. His concern was yet another load of union blah, as they were pissed off with it, but some were being fairly supportive, as was the CBI. I was thinking of stories to give to Patrick Wintour as it was his first week at the *Observer*. I didn't want him particularly focusing on us so I steered some of the Tory stuff we had picked up his way, re David Davis [Foreign Office minister] threatening to resign and David Maclean [Home Office minister] who, according to one of Tim's Tories, was thinking about quitting too.

I went to a meeting at Millbank to talk over the design of the New Life document. We agreed it should have Tony all over it, but there should also be pictures spread through it of JP, RC and GB. I called Paul Hamlyn to thank him for the money he had donated to help us promote the whole *Road to the Manifesto* process. He had said he was doing so on the basis that we did the specific pledges, as discussed, so that was a bonus as it would help us win the argument to go for the pledges. He was really taken with the idea of fairly minimal pledges rather than grandiose promises.

TB was to move on devolution soon, as early as next Friday, and he was clearly enjoying setting out the absolute limits of where he hoped to go. He said to Pat McFadden – how would they feel if we dropped tax powers? And then laughed, really mischievous, and Pat said you know exactly what the effect would be – they would go berserk. TB said well, we definitely need to commit to a referendum and I also want to make it explicitly clear that power devolved is power retained, because in the end that is the intellectual logic of the whole thing, and it is also the nearest you'll get to an answer to the West Lothian Question. Pat said he thought we could win them over on two out of three but there was no way they would swallow no tax-raising powers. If we pushed for it, there would be resignations. TB launched into a great diatribe, saying they wanted too much and they wanted it too easy. He was not convinced on tax, and he was not convinced the Scottish Parliament should have primary lawmaking powers. Glasgow City Council doesn't. It didn't go down well with Pat, but it was obvious now TB was just pushing the argument as far as it could go without actually intending to go that far. Pat said you don't like this policy, do you, and TB said he could be made to like it if he could be persuaded it would work, but he did not feel the Scots Party had really thought it through. There was a danger they would just ride a tide of emotionalism on it, and fail to think through the policy consequences, and he was determined to make sure they did that. Philip called with what he called a bad poll from the *Sunday Times*; we were down two to fifty, they were up four on thirty-one. It sent TB into a bit of a spin, which was ridiculous. I said if you had been told one year ago that we would be almost twenty points ahead this close to an election, would you have taken that? I think so. We had to be careful we didn't get into a habit of thinking we were just going to move further and further ahead. We were defying the laws of political gravity as it was.

Saturday, June 22

TB was working at his place, and me at mine, on the *Road to the Manifesto* document, and after the third or fourth call it was clear we were heading for the usual two-drafts problem. He said just carry on doing your bits and then let me marry them to mine. When I read his stuff, it was a lot better than the first draft, and he was by far the best person to put the New Labour case, though some of the language was a bit too high falutin'. However, we had definitely made progress. We agreed that though it needed policy specifics, what we had to get right most of all was an argument, and a narrative that set out clearly where we were, how we got there, where we were intending to go, and how. I broke off for a couple of hours to take Rory to a five-a-side tournament. He played well enough but when they were knocked out, he threw an absolute monster tantrum and we had a dreadful row. I realised as I was arguing with him that he was behaving just like I used to when I lost.

I watched the football in the afternoon. Spain should have won [England won 4–2 in a penalty shoot-out] but I was beginning to think that it was written in the stars England were going to win the whole bloody tournament. There was a real sense of nationalism out there. Every other car seemed to have a St George flag or sticker, and 'Football's coming home'[1] was on wherever you went. Harriet called, anxious that she was going to be able to go ahead with her waiting-lists paper. It was a lot better, and was likely to be one of the areas for the pledges, but there were still problem areas and we put it on hold again.

We left for Will Hutton's party at Woodstock. Anna Ford [BBC broadcaster] was with Bob Marshall-Andrews [QC, Labour candidate for Medway], who was one of those people who managed to deliver absolute drivel with total authority and have half his audience thinking he had actually said something. If people like him stood on what they actually said they believed, rather than what we were saying nationally, they would lose their fucking deposits. Gavyn Davies and Ed Balls were close to euphoric about the football. Jackie Ashley [ITN political correspondent] thought the Tory press were gearing up to revert to type. I congratulated Andy Marr on the *Indy* front page, which was a picture of Shearer's boot, but he seemed to think I was taking the piss. RC seemed to be the only member of the Shadow Cabinet there and was quite rude to David Goodhart [founding editor of *Prospect*, centre-left essay-based magazine] who wanted to have a conversation about something Timothy Garton-Ash [modern historian and columnist] had written [on EU expansion in Eastern Europe and defence co-operation]. RC said 'I'm a bit Old Labour about this, but in general I don't like the idea of killing people.' Margaret Cook [his wife] was there, face a picture of misery. She said 'You should not apologise for being Old Labour.' Wet-fish time. I didn't take to her at all, a mix of sourness and misery. Even this crowd, most of whom would prefer ballet to football I would reckon, were caught up in the football thing, and with another poll coming tonight showing things moving back to them a bit, I was beginning to get quite worried about the whole thing.

Monday, June 24

Tony had had dinner with GB last night and tried to get him more focused on economic rebuttal and *Road to the Manifesto*, apparently without much success. There was lots of education in the news with the White Paper due tomorrow, and amazingly Chris Smith's welfare-to-work paper was leading the bulletins for most of the day. TB had done some more work on our reworked *Road to the Manifesto* draft and it was excellent. It was clearly written and for once we had a policy-heavy document that was fairly readable. There were still problems ahead, though. We didn't have long to go and we still had issues to sort on health, pensions, GB's tax-and-spend argument, and we also had TB's speech on devolution. The morning meeting was fairly straightforward but GB was worrying about the tax-and-spend implications of the welfare paper, and pensions. We were working hard on him re the pledges but as ever with something that wasn't his idea, he was taking a long time to come over. But I think he was moving now.

TB had been working on the devolution argument and he said he was adamant he was going to make clear his view there should be no tax rise, there should certainly be a referendum and it should be made clear that Westminster was the ultimate constitutional authority – power devolved is power retained. I was concerned we had not done the political groundwork, e.g. with GR, RC and DD. TB said they were more onside than we thought. He said he had pretty much squared DD. I spoke to Donald who said if TB thought that, he must be mad. He thought he was embarking on a dangerous course without thinking through the consequences. Yet I found when you made the argument, they all felt compelled to agree with the logic; they just didn't like the internal politics. I said to Donald that with TB, the logic is likely to prevail so I think we should get planning for the storm, if storm you think there will be. Donald said it was all totally unnecessary. I said the idea of ruling out a tax rise in the first term of the new Parliament was already in the air; the referendum had its own compelling logic, and the third part of this – power devolved is power retained – is just a statement of the constitutional position.

GB was not keen. I was trying to get a sense of how not keen so I raised it at a couple of meetings, and his body language was bad, and he said we would have political problems, but he didn't mount an argument of substance, which was interesting. At the office meeting, TB was on great form, firing all over the place, on health and the economy in particular, saying he would go on calling for a proper economic narrative till he was blue in the face. I met Charles Clarke who said the main lesson of past campaigns was that we needed clear command structures of politicians and staff covering policy, organisation and communications. He was not sure we had that remotely in place yet, outside possibly communications. He felt on policy that we lacked clarity because some of the big beasts were still playing games and flexing muscle.

The tabloids were gearing up for the football [Euro '96 semi-final between England and Germany] and there was lots of coverage of all the anti-German stuff in the papers, 'Achtung, Surrender' in the *Mirror*, 'Let's blitz Fritz' in the *Sun*. The beef statement went fine, with TB on form and right on top of the detail. Major wanted to give the impression the ban would be lifted by November without actually committing himself, and TB pinned him down well. At the strategy meeting, we were trying again to get GB going on economic rebuttal. I never understood why he was so reluctant on this. The Tories were running an ad in the *Express* that people would be £450 better off next year, and we had to demolish it, but he was always looking for arguments not to engage. There was another meeting on something else later and TB and I had another go, but without saying he wouldn't, it was clear that he wouldn't up the game on it. TB later told me the dinner last night had been pretty awful. GB had arrived late and had been very offhand with TB's friend Paco Pena [Spanish guitarist] and his wife. He said that others had been moaning about GB for some time, but this was maybe the first time he felt that the very special relationship they had on the way up was just not the same, and never likely to be.

When we had a *Road to the Manifesto* meeting with GB, Peter M, Margaret McD, Jonathan, Matthew [Taylor, head of Labour's policy unit], DH, I noticed TB coming back very strong on some of GB's arguments, which normally he might let go. He was signalling I think that he intended to change tack in how he dealt with him. GB was still arguing against the specific pledges but the argument was getting weaker. TB then had a difficult meeting with George Robertson. He said he wanted to make the announcements on change [devolution] this Friday. He said there was never a good time to do this kind of thing but *Road to the Manifesto* gave us the space to do it. It would be devious not to and he was confident once we got these arguments out in the open, we would win them more easily than people thought. GR's reaction was not dissimilar to Donald's, that yet again TB was provoking unnecessary fights, though when you got on to the substance of the arguments, they were not far apart. TB said he could only promise what he intended to deliver, and this was the best way to do it. Referendum; make clear where our instincts on tax lay; and make the big constitutional point. He said every home-rule effort up to now had failed because of overambition or overemotionalism. We had to be hard-headed. GR said for some, it would be a political nuclear explosion. TB said, I know I am right on this, and I know it has to be done sooner rather than later, as part of *Road to the Manifesto*. GR could see TB was not moving and he said he would have more trouble with the executive, the press, the MPs, and his team. He was sure John McAllion [Labour MP and Scottish spokesman] would resign. He felt you could do the tax and referendum bit, but not the third element. TB said it was a statement of the obvious, power devolved, but power retained.

Tuesday, June 25

I went for a swim first thing to try to draft in my head a note on the coming days. I had been worrying for some time that we had not got the basic ground work done on the changes to devolution policy. He had not even spoken to Ron Davies about Wales. There was a big build-up to the White Paper on selection in schools, and [Gillian] Shephard was very poor on the morning media, not at all confident. We had decided to try to get up the line about the return of the eleven-plus. TB was worried we were being forced into a position of total opposition to all selection. There was a huge turnout for the 9am meeting for once and we went over education, Europe, health. Donald said he, GB and GR had been discussing TB's proposals and felt it was better if George did it all on Thursday and TB went up on Friday. He said it was very important it was not seen as the leader coming up on the big bird and telling us all what to do. He said he agreed with the idea of the referendum, but was very resistant to the idea of making clear Westminster retain power over it all. TB, in truth, was also very anxious to lose the tax-raising powers as well, but was going along with it for now. We asked Jack McConnell to come down for the day and start to get things in motion. TB had got hold of RC and squared him. Both GR and DD were on terrific form. They realised TB was adamant on this, and they had come round, or at least appeared to have done, to the intellectual strength of the position, and they now seemed up for it. GB had not turned up for the meeting which may have been his way of signalling that he had not shifted his position at all. Pat felt GB/RC would see how it went, then distance themselves if it went down badly. GR and DD had clearly decided just to get on with it. We went endlessly over the detail. TB said to them, I know there are suspicions about me on this one, but I am telling you this is the way to deliver it. It's like the minimum wage. Because of the methods and arguments adopted in the past, we have failed historically to make it happen. Emotionalism has had the upper hand. You have to root this in the pragmatic realities. The referendum is the key, and the only answer to the West Lothian Question is to spell out the constitutional reality.

At the backbenchers' meeting I gave John McFall [Scottish Labour MP] the idea of wishing England well vs Germany and condemning tabloid xenophobia, which he did, sufficient to lead *News at Ten*. I got back and told TB, GB and GR that Tony Bevins was on to the referendum story. Bevins had read me his intro, something like Blair considering extending referendums, so still not hard, and hopefully would lay the ground without causing an explosion. TB saw Ron Davies who thought the referendum idea made sense. He was also pleased that TB was backing proportional representation for Wales, but he said he would have to square a lot of people. He said virtually all the Welsh MPs were against it. When TB said to him he should mention his support for the idea of a referendum at Shadow Cabinet, but not say we were talking about PR, Ron said 'I like your style, Tony.' There was then another meeting with TB, DD, GR and Pat, and the atmosphere was now a lot more relaxed. Jack McC was also there. 'Sorry for landing all this on you,' said TB. 'No problem,' said Jack, 'we can manage it fine.' It had been an interesting exercise in leadership. TB had been pretty determined, and without that it is unlikely we would have reached the position we did. The others were basically opposed at first, but came round in time. He had certainly won the argument on the referendum and was now looking for a convincing way of making clear the tax-raising power would not be used in a first Labour term. I said to DD 'Don't worry, we are good at this kind of thing, and it's going to be fine.' 'Too bloody good,' he muttered, but he was in good humour. They were happy TB had not gone for the ultimate 'power devolved, power retained' position, namely that Westminster would have to agree every bill. It was clearly going to be a big deal up there, and probably fasten seat belts time.

Wednesday, June 26

Bevins splashed on the referendum and this, allied to Andy Marr's column [both *Independent*], led to a rash of calls from the Scottish media and an assumption that we had planned the whole thing, and it had been deliberate. That was not quite right. I had wanted to begin to get some of the arguments out there but avoid an all-out frenzy. That was going to be hard now that it was written hard, and lots of people were being brought into the loop. There was a danger it would get out of control. The pledges were beginning to take shape – jobs, health, education. We needed one on crime and we were coming to the view that youth justice may be the right area. There were several meetings on this through the day at which we finally agreed we should not do 10p tax rate as one of the pledges. PG and Peter M were keenest but I felt it was something to do later in the campaign. To make it one of the pledges risked having it out there that we were cutting tax to 10p. I was now of the view we should have four very specific pledges and maybe a general economic aim. TB saw Paddy to square him re plans on Scotland, and at Paddy's press conference, he was asked if he had discussed the ideas with TB and said no! Not sure how he works that one out. He could easily have danced around it.

There was huge interest in the Scotland stuff now, even with the tabloids, and I spent a lot of time saying it was a mini version of Clause 4 – there was a big argument to be had and we were absolutely confident of winning it. I could tell GR and DD were still suspicious. But they were doing well. It was going so big we agreed GR should go up and do interviews, which he did fine. He was getting flak from the PLP but managing well, as was DD. There was to be a meeting of Scots MPs at 6. Brian Wilson said you had to hand it to TB, he liked doing things the ballsy way. But we were not going to get through this without GR and DD. Anji said the news was strong, lots of comparisons with Clause 4, leading from the front, risk, etc. Michael Forsyth [Conservative Scottish Secretary] looked uncomfortable in the bits I saw. Major's speech on the constitution was getting a fair bit of play but there was now more interest in us than them on this issue.

We got to Wembley for the semi-final with Germany and the atmosphere all the way up towards the ground was extraordinary. I had never really supported England, and for political reasons I found myself rooting privately for Germany, though as I was sitting next to one of JM's bodyguards, even though he was a Scot, I pretended to be backing England. It was one of the most incredible matches I've ever seen and to be fair to England, they could and should have won and there was a part of me willing them on. But by the end [England lost 5–6 in the penalty shootout] I felt relief. 'There goes the feel-good factor,' said Denis Howell. I then felt a total heel when I called home and the boys were crying their eyes out. JM looked a bit ashen. Just as we had been worrying, however irrationally, about the political benefits to him of England winning, so a part of him must have been banking on this. He looked pretty sick and the atmosphere at the back of the royal box was not great. At the end ITN came up and asked TB if he would do a live interview and he made the mistake of asking JM if he planned to do anything. JM said no so TB said he wouldn't. I tried not to let my happiness show as we walked to the car. Once we got in, I said 'Yesss,' and shook my fist. TB said could you save any celebrations until you get home? I said don't pretend you feel any different. When we dropped him off, I said *Gute Nacht, mein Kapitän. Jetzt sind die Tories gefuckt.*

Thursday, June 27

The Scottish press was a disaster area. U-turn, betrayal, etc. Very big and very difficult. Obviously the England defeat was massive down south but there was lots of play for the referendum stuff here too. Major had totally stitched us up, when TB stupidly asked him to agree not to do media after the match. I can just imagine the laugh he and Michael Howard had in deciding to do it after we left. Apparently there had been a security alert, and Major had to stay at the reception. TB said he now regretted not doing media, and saying something supportive, and he wished he had backed my judgement. That gave us our running joke for the day, and we would need one. Scotland calls started early. George called Anji to say it was imperative that I stopped saying there were more bombshells to come. I called him to say I had said no such things. He also said John McAllion was thinking of resigning as Scottish spokesman. TB said I'm not having any of that nonsense, and it should be sorted out, but nobody could find him and we didn't get it sorted until later. TB was worried that the whole thing was coming over as an issue purely about Scotland.

I was on my usual anti-Scottish media kick, saying they were out of touch with their readers, that what people want is the Scottish Parliament and this is the way to get one. TB was convinced that though the public did not like split and turmoil, they would get the message that the policy had changed and it had taken balls to change it. The Tories could not quite get their lines straight on it, and we were just about containing things at the moment. TB was beginning to wonder if we were doing the right thing, but not for long. He said whatever the position and how it feels in the eye of the storm, at the end of it we will at least have a position that can be defended. George said at the press conference that they had first discussed the referendum idea in Dunblane which was true, but I thought it was daft to say so, as it could be thought to be in bad taste.

Pat McFadden was clearly getting fed up that TB and I were moaning about the Jocks so much. They were quite aggressive back. Eventually George got hold of McAllion who said he was resigning and that was that. We put out a short TB statement saying he regretted the resignation. Malcolm Chisholm [Labour MP] replaced him and we got it sorted for the late bulletins. The hope was all the bad news was now out and tomorrow we could start to turn it. It was all building up to a big day tomorrow. We had to get on to the issue of leadership, we had to get it clear that TB would deliver the Parliament. The problem was that the Scots felt every time he moved on this, it was a ploy to stop the Parliament. Mum called to say that Dad had had prostate cancer diagnosed. I felt bad that I got to see them so much less than before.

Friday, June 28

The papers were grim, even worse in Scotland where it was all a betrayal and sell-out. Here too the headlines were all crisis, backlash, usual stuff. I was still confident it would be OK though George [Robertson] and Jack [McConnell] said it could be very tricky, and it was very important TB did not fly up and lecture them all. Pat was working on the speech for Scotland when I arrived at TB's. I had inserted three new passages overnight. One, he will lead the yes campaign and he does not fight campaigns to lose them. Two, nice words about McAllion and George. Three, I do not intend to lead Britain like Major. The Tories' line was to present strength as weakness, saying we were backing down under pressure from [Michael] Forsyth. 'Are we in a mess on this?' TB asked when I got there. There really was no argument against it. Why shouldn't people have a say in their future? The real problem was that they didn't like the way it was done, they didn't like his style.

All the way to the airport, Pat and I were changing the speech and TB was trying to get the Scottish Executive on board for the decision this afternoon. TB was in combative form. What do they want these people, another Tory government? Jack was playing a blinder and was clearly confident. Every time I spoke to him, I felt more confident. We finished the speech on the plane and there was an awful moment when the screen went blank and I feared we had lost the whole thing. TB was now looking forward to this. He was always confident when he felt the argument was right. We were met by George and Jack, who gave me the unbelievably grim Scottish papers. We were organising union leaders and JP to make statements backing him. George said the executive was being very difficult. The real problem was lack of consultation. George was getting hammered in the press and it was largely about the fact they didn't know in advance. I said to Jack McConnell it was amazing how Scottish I felt until I came up to Scotland and heard the Scottish media whingeing. The guy from the *Sun* was a total wanker.

Then to see the chair of the Scottish Labour Party [Davie Stark]. TB was appealing for his help and it was clear he would not get it. He said the party felt they were being pushed too far, and this was one step too many. TB said he was happy to apologise for how it all came out, but it was not going to be enough. He felt he was facing a purely emotional response. Also, as TB kept saying, the main objection appeared to be that if you gave people the option, they would not want it. That went for the Parliament, and for the tax powers.

We left for the speech venue. The library where it was taking place was absolutely beautiful. TB was OK but at his best when he left the script and got passionate about winning. Bob Thomson of UNISON was telling everyone TB was in real trouble, and could be finished on this. TB then did a series of excellent interviews, he was really pumped up and going for it. He wanted me to brief that was all part of the wider pre-*Road to the Manifesto* change. We were late for the Labour executive, which made what was always going to be a hostile atmosphere worse. There was lots of talk of betrayal. One of them said they had been lied to. TB stuck to his guns, made the argument as he had done before and it turned our way when he said you also need the referendum to make sure you have the clear consent of the people which will be needed to get it through the Lords. Bob Thomson said why not just create a thousand new peers? That was what did it for some who came to our side. TB was firm without being rude and gave them a few facts of life. We left for the airport, moderately confident, then Pat called to say we had won 20–4 on the new policy, and 16–12 on defeating the old one. TB said he never thought we would do as well as that. It was quite a triumph in its own way. On the plane, TB was going through his mail, including a letter from Basil Hume [Cardinal Archbishop of Westminster], saying that he would have to stop taking Communion in a Catholic church.[1] TB wrote back 'I wonder what Our Lord will make of this.'

Saturday, June 29

Considering the scale of the turnaround, the press was very grudging. DD called to say that though we won, the damage was serious and lasting. George said that the Scottish press, though not perfect, was a great improvement. He thought the *Herald* was beginning to turn our way. Peter had briefed some of the Sundays on *Road to the Manifesto* but it was all a bit vague and waffly so I spent much of the day trying to harden it up. We had the lead in all the broadsheets. But what was clear was that the *Road to the Manifesto* process was really building. We also had the pledges more or less right.

Sunday, June 30

Tony Banks [Labour MP] was up saying we were Tories Mark Two, and TB was too autocratic. I briefed DD who was doing Sky and BBC and he said there was real and growing anger at TB and the office at the way he pushed the party. The BBC coverage was terrific, though. Most of the papers were going down the road of 'new powers to get MPs to toe the line in government'. There was a lot of 'ruthless Blair' around. We were responsible for every single splash in the broadsheets and they kept coming to us for more.

[1] Although an Anglican, Blair often took Communion at a Catholic church in Islington. Hume later conceded that it was permissible for him to attend a Catholic church while on holiday in Tuscany.

Monday, July 1

The *Observer* story was turning into a bit of a disaster. The *Indy* splashed on a story about crushing dissent. They carried a picture of TB in a Nicole Farhi sweater, the kind of thing I would not be seen dead in, which must have been one of CB's brainwaves. TB realised we had made a mistake in getting up the party reform stuff at this time. I hated these situations where I had to defend something we did, when I knew it had been daft and even worse, lots of the MPs would have thought it was my bloody idea. Bruce said they were up in arms about this stuff. JP had been trying to reach me and TB yesterday. He wrote a note to TB saying he was dismayed about some of the reports re the *Road to the Manifesto*, and the publicity surrounding the idea of MPs being subject to a new review. I hit the roof with Rosie, because what JP was doing was swallowing crap in the papers, or fed him by journalists, and putting it straight back at us. Rosie said they had been led to believe that I was steering them in that direction, which was bollocks. I'd been trying to play the damn thing down.

GB was in a bit of a strop, I assume over the Peter M briefing to the Sundays that we would spend the same as the Tories. He came in and threw the *FT* down in front of me, but without any comment. The meeting was very bad-tempered and we achieved very little. DD and I later saw TB who said that though it was a mess, the leadership message was out there and provided we actually won the argument, which we will, the fuss would be forgotten. DD laughed. I couldn't quite work out whether he viewed TB in this mode with affection, concern or disdain. Maybe a mix of all of that, but I think he liked his frankness.

TB went quickly from his strong leadership mode to head down, non-communicative, fed up. The Tories were having a political cabinet and [Conservative director of communications Charles] Lewington did a ridiculous briefing saying all their strategies for TB had basically failed so they were going now to do 'New Labour, New Danger'. We were close to finalising the *Road to the Manifesto* document and the style of it, but we were still arguing about the pledges. TB was unhappy that RC had neutered the section on the family. Peter M felt it was not New Labour enough. JP complained he had not seen the latest draft. Liz said she thought it had too much Tony in it. It was all a bit bonkers. At one point, I was trying to rewrite the intro to TB's new brief, editing the document as a whole, working on a briefing note, working on ads, trying to get sign-off on the pledges, I had Ron Davies wanting to go out and do some mad new departure, JP still banging on about loyalty pledges and who said what to whom; it sometimes felt like a madhouse. He said he accepted what I said about not pushing the loyalty pledge stuff but I was not convinced he believed me. He said he had seen it too often – something is run through the press, then it's denied and then it's policy. I said like what? I had a couple of effing and blinding sessions with him, we both let off a bit of steam and that was that. I got home and was going to bed when there was a rash of late calls about a story that TB had taken Catholic Communion which was likely to cause a bit of upset here and there.

Tuesday, July 2

NEC. Clare [Short] was making endless minor points. She said she objected to us describing ourselves as a party of the centre. [Dennis] Skinner, his timing excellent as ever, said 'I'm just relieved it doesn't say we're a party of the right.' Everyone laughed, but she was incapable of recalibrating to circumstances. Though he voted against, Dennis was supportive in what he said, supporting TB's argument that we should not be putting in all policy now, and that we should be rolling out policy through the summer as part of the overall campaign. By and large the argument was won. TB was on form at the moment, and so was GB who was inclusive and consultative and who even gave a good impression of not having written the economic section himself by making some suggested changes. The party was definitely changing. I was still working on the *Road to the Manifesto* twelve-pager and we were still not sorted on the pledges. We also had to get going on the economic speech for tomorrow. I felt that despite the recent troubles we were in better shape than the headline coverage suggested.

PMQs was fine, with Major not on form, despite all the back-benchers going on 'New Labour, New Danger' stuff. We were also having to deal with the communion story. We said TB was happy to give up taking Communion in a Catholic church if it was a problem. As with all these personal kind of things he was worried it would harm us, but I felt most people would be sympathetic and a lot of people would not understand or care. The Tories didn't move in. I went to the TUC party and as ever had a nice chat with Jimmy Knapp about Ayrshire [birthplace of AC's mother], then met Fiona and we went to David Frost's party at Carlyle Square. There were very few Labour people there, Leo and Margaret Beckett the only obvious ones. Loads of Tories. Cecil [Parkinson] was very nice and full of good advice – don't totally cut off your enemies and don't forget your friends. [Norman] Tebbit was full of beans. He said he had been with

Austin Mitchell [Labour MP] today who said New Labour was autocratic. 'I said no, it's aristocratic and the main aristos are TB and AC,' he said. I had a nice chat with Chris Meyer [diplomat, former press secretary to JM] who was totally contemptuous of the way JM operated. He said JM was far too bothered about the papers, spent too much time looking at them, thinking about them, worrying about what they would say and what effect it would have. It was interesting to go from the TUC party, where the mood towards us was sullen, to this one where it was wall-to-wall media and Tories and they treated us like we were masters of the universe. Fiona and I went out for a quick dinner before I had to go back to the House to meet TB, who was now beginning to fret about the economy speech tomorrow and the launch of the document. He felt there was a danger the pledges would lack impact. I felt they would be fine and, more important, that we would be able to use them again and again in campaigning and speeches and interviews.

Wednesday, July 3

TB was worried about the Catholic Mass story, fearing it was doing us damage, but I honestly felt people would by and large not get the fuss. He was sitting there, in his dressing gown and underpants, his hair all over the place, with a slight look of the mad professor, and I knew it was going to be a long day. We had to have a top line for tomorrow. A lot of the policy stuff was already out there, and there was a danger that MPs' pay would become the story. The review body had recommended massive rises, especially for the PM, which of course TB would get if we won. He was not keen to take a position on it, and worried the whole issue would overshadow the launch. Once we got the usual last-minute speech panic out of the way, we were on our way. It wasn't a great speech but it had enough to keep us going through the day, and the Q&A went fine.

Amazingly, JM was doing a statement on the Stone of Scone![1] Unbelievable. It struck me as a Forsyth ploy to get up a great symbolic gesture and keep up the Scotland issue on their terms. But a statement by the PM. Please. We got back and Jonathan was in with DD

[1] The stone, said to have been used as a pillow by Jacob (Genesis 28:10), is also known as the Stone of Destiny and has for centuries been used in the coronations of Scottish and, after its capture by Edward I in 1296, British monarchs. The announcement of its return to Scotland by Major's Conservative government was intended to be a symbolic act of goodwill to undercut Labour's devolution plans.

who said we must not underestimate the potential impact this would have in Scotland. I didn't. I just felt the politics of it were so obvious but, classic Majorism, quite difficult to attack. It meant that time we should be spending preparing for the launch tomorrow had to be spent on TB getting ready for this. TB said we had to use tomorrow's 'New Labour, New Life for Britain' launch for another general repositioning of New Labour, the radical centre, all that. I felt there was sufficient build-up. It was about a confident TB marking out the next bold steps. TB asked me to do a brief presentation to the Shadow Cabinet. I said to them I know there are people who think the pledges are not dramatic enough but the polling shows that people are fed up of big promises. I also told them that we now required absolute discipline in making sure the message of the *Road to the Manifesto* was communicated. I said they would be amazed how little was known about us or our policies. I had seen some recognition polling recently and TB was alone in being broadly recognised. He told me off afterwards for being so direct about that. 'I'm not sure the best way to deal with them is to say nobody has ever heard of them.' I could have been more diplomatic but there are times when their discussions appear to be founded on the thought that everyone out there is following every twist and turn. If we can get through a few very simple messages to the majority of people, we will be doing well, and TB is the key to that. The statement on the Stone of Scone was like a journey back into a different age, and one in which JM felt more comfortable. TB said afterwards 'I felt like I was under the influence of a hallucinatory drug.'

Thursday, July 4

We got huge and largely positive coverage overnight. Terry [driver] collected me and I was met at TB's by CB saying that the press said TB didn't take his full salary two years ago and she didn't want any more of that populist nonsense this time. TB said he agreed with me that the suggested rises were so big that we could wave goodbye to 'many not the few' if we went for it. He was still in his pyjamas, and looked half asleep but he was already honing down the speech I had drafted, and nodding along as he imagined himself saying bits of it. The more aggressively he nodded, the more it meant he could hear himself saying it, and making an impact, and there were more nods than usual at this stage, so we were on the right track. He made a few scribbles, asked for the changes to be put in and then went upstairs to get dressed. It was a good strong statement and we had it done by the time we left. I'd arranged for a camera in the car from his place to the House. He was bounding up the stairs when we arrived and was obviously up for it. 'God, nobody can say we have not done a lot in two years,' he said to nobody in particular. He'd agreed GB should chair it with JP away nursing his injured foot. That meant Robin Cook should say something too, so I culled something on the *Road to the Manifesto* process and called him to say TB would like him to do that part at the launch. For some reason, RC, whose normal complaint would be that he was NOT being used at events like this, went off on one. 'Can we ever plan something and just stick to it? I'm tired of all this last-minute stuff.' I said I'm sure he could handle it and he did one of his long sighs and said 'Well yes, like a loyal soldier I will but I really must say blah, blah, blah.' In the car to Millbank, TB was getting psyched up, nodding to himself and going over the points he wanted to emphasise. The *Guardian* ran a line that GB had overruled 'TB aides' who wanted to use headline-grabbing gimmicks, which I raised with him and he denied all knowledge or involvement. TB did well during the questions though he commented later that GB was trying too hard to look like he was leading rather than chairing the event. *Panorama* were there constantly filming me and Peter M as part of the new obsession they had. TB was pumped up afterwards and we stayed back for a cup of tea with RC, who felt the whole thing went well. Back at the office, TB said re MPs' pay that he was sure JM would reject the review body's recommendations. The written answer came out at 4, rejecting some of the recommendations, and TB was keen we say we would support Major. The launch was deemed to have gone well upstairs and was still leading the news later on. *Channel 4 News* was awful. They vox-popped people who had no idea what we had announced. Maybe if the fuckers told them rather than playing their silly games. The royal divorce [Prince Charles and Princess Diana] news came out at 8.30, led the later bulletins and the feeling around the place was JM's people had got the news out to fuck us up.

Friday, July 5

Diana/Charles was getting massive play but we still did pretty well out of the New Life launch. On the way to Heathrow, TB was complaining again about the workload. JP and Rosie were waiting for us and so began twenty-four hours of exhausting and circular chatter about whether JP should do *On the Record*. There was no overriding need but he obviously felt sensitive at not having been at the launch and his ego probably made him want to be out there showing he had been part of the whole thing. The plane was an eight-seater, and on the flight down TB and I were trying diplomatically to steer him away from *On the Record*. I feared they would zone in quite easily on the areas they knew JP didn't feel comfortable on and we would end up with a negative start to the week. There were times when JP was the right man for the weekend media but this didn't feel like one of them. TB felt these Sunday programmes were a waste of time unless you had a clear story to promote and take on the news agenda, and in this case we didn't. Finally, at 7pm, as I was driving into town with JP, he said 'Fine, give it to Blunkett.' He was a curious mix of strength and insecurity. He knew he had a powerful position within the party, but he also felt insecure about his own position vis-à-vis TB, and he over-worried about what other people thought about his intellect. If only he could be more confident, and show more confidence, he would have a greater role. But because he started from an assumption that he was being excluded, he started from a bad position and then read too much into things. And he was still obsessed with GB and Peter M and their relative influence and access. The meeting in Gloucester went fine, TB and JP both on good form. We flew back to Heathrow and TB headed off to the North-East. Earlier, as we had spent ages discussing with JP the rights and wrongs of doing one wretched interview, he said sometimes he thought Margaret Beckett would have been less trouble and he said he blamed me because even though I was only a journalist at the time, he had been taken with how forcefully I had set out the case for JP to him. But he accepted that JP supported him on Clause 4 and on other difficult issues in a way that Margaret might have sat out.

Saturday, July 6

I had failed to see off the cold that had been coming on and now had a chest infection. I had to take the kids' football and later go to the school barn dance and felt crap. The *Sunday Telegraph* splashed on McIntosh [headmaster] saying the Oratory would have to go private if Labour policies were implemented. He was a total menace, and a wanker to boot. TB insisted he was just naive and didn't realise what the press would do with what he said to them.

Sunday, July 7

I was in bed most of the day, and was on penicillin. The main focus of the day was the Shadow Cabinet elections story and whether they would proceed. We were keeping to a strictly neutral position but nobody really believed us because they knew what TB's instincts would be. The vast bulk of MPs thought they should go ahead. DD called to say it would be very difficult and if we were going to win a vote, it would require the whole whips' machine to get involved behind TB. He said it would be seen as one more loyalty test and the troops were getting a bit tired of loyalty tests.

Monday, July 8

I was up half the night coughing, felt ghastly and took the day off. I went to see the doctor who said he had been following the press closely and he reckoned both my chest and stomach complaints were work-related. TB called early on. 'I hear you are not well. Sorry about that. Now ... what are we going to do about McIntosh?' In other words, even though you are ill, I assume you are still working flat out for me? I'd spoken to McIntosh yesterday and made clear what TB thought of what he said, and said that the only effect was to damage Euan by getting him into the papers again. TB was supposed to be seeing McIntosh anyway and agreed he should cancel it because it was likely to get into the press and just keep the thing going. It would look odd and whatever they discussed the press would say it was TB trying to silence him. PG called with bad news from the private polling, which had us down on 48–32 from 56–27. He was also worried, as was I, that we didn't have enough follow-through planned on *Road to the Manifesto*. We never got this right. We would put so much energy into the big moments, which was right, but then we always had a lull before then planning what should have been built in to the original launch plans. Ted Heath [Sir Edward Heath, Conservative Prime Minister, 1970–74] attacked 'New Labour, New Danger', which was a bonus. But I imagined the sense of economic upturn was responsible for the shift in the polls which, if added to any continuing sense of disunity, could still get them a bit of a lift in the run-up to summer.

Tuesday, July 9

TB's main preoccupation was still the Shadow Cabinet elections and whether or not to hold on. He had clearly moved to the view that they would have to happen, but that we should do them quickly and afterwards they should be linked to greater disciplinary checks on the PLP. He said some of these people he absolutely hated. They bring nothing whatever to a Labour victory. He spoke to JP who was canvassing opinion, and later JP and I had to deal with a story given by Dennis Skinner to David Bradshaw [*Mirror*] that JP was going to intervene by making sure that they went ahead and Harriet would survive as part of a deal. Most people seemed to think there was no chance at all of Harriet surviving. The situation was made worse by the fact that the vote on MPs' pay was coming tomorrow and most MPs wanted to vote for it. TB wanted to vote against it and was only stopped from imposing a whip by Donald, Ann Taylor [Shadow Commons leader], Doug [Hoyle, PLP chairman] and others saying they would not be able to deliver it.

PMQs was excellent, with TB really going for JM on the state of the economy, using some of the facts and figures we'd been trying to get GB to do for ages. GB was still arguing that we had to wait for the right time to go on the attack, and maybe this was it. I was sure that if we had been on the offensive a bit longer, we could have halted what seemed to be a bit of a turnaround for the Tories. TB and everyone else was pissed off that the New Life for Britain launch had just died, because of lack of follow-through strategy.

TB left after PMQs to go to the Oratory for Euan's school report. We had to get a decision about the Shadow Cabinet elections so when he came back, Anji, Sally and I, with Peter M, ambushed him. Peter suggested Harriet should say she was not standing. TB's worst scenario was Harriet off and Ann Clwyd on. The best scenario was Harriet off and Jack Cunningham or Joyce Quin on. Earlier, when getting ready for PMQs, TB said I've always feared the scenario that the public sense there is something wrong with our MPs, that too many of them haven't really changed. You have to realise that thirty to forty of our MPs are there only because they were selected at a time the party was mad. Some of them are useless. They offer nothing at all but they can damage us badly.

Wednesday, July 10

I woke up to headlines that William Hague was in Korea having completed the biggest ever inward investment to the UK, so they were going to be up again on economic good news. Ken Clarke also got away with his economic forecasts. It showed what you could do with a bit of verve and nerve. Mike White [Guardian] did the story I persuaded Bradshaw not to do, that JP would save Harriet if we held the Shadow Cabinet elections quickly. Our current problem was clear at the morning meeting, that after all the build-up to the launch, there was no clear strategic follow-through. DD told TB that there was a serious slippage in those who said they would vote with him for pay restraint. We were in a bit of a mess on this, and not firing on half let alone all our cylinders. PG's focus group last night showed that only two people had been aware of the New Life launch, and we had now just disappeared from view. It was dreadful – all that work and then we just disappear when the aim was to break through. It was back to the old syndrome – if it was in the papers and on telly for a day then everyone thought the world would have heard about it, and it was bollocks.

GB was alarmed about MPs' pay, convinced that we would end up with the story being Labour MPs voting it through, despite Major saying he would stick at three per cent. I had a long chat with TB, who was now of the view that it was probably not possible to go without the Shadow Cabinet elections, and it was therefore all the more important we coupled them with new disciplinary powers to deal with the real bastards in the PLP. TB was really down today, especially after the whips' meeting. Bruce [Grocott] said there was no real problem that they didn't feel they knew him, and they had no idea what his bottom line was, and he wasn't seen around the place enough. They felt that he didn't really have much time for them. But he felt that was no reason for the hostility currently being directed towards him. He felt some were simply a menace, who wanted him to do everything on his own and do nothing to help and as much as they could to hinder.

Major was on the news four times at lunchtime: pay, the meeting with [Nelson] Mandela, Wales, and Northern Ireland. He was looking good and motoring. We could not really go on as we were. We were not at the races in the last few days.

TB was really down about the PLP. Bruce said Tony must take a lot of the blame himself. He had been warning they were going offside because we didn't pay them enough attention. Just before Shadow Cabinet, TB called me down to see him and DD. TB came up with the idea of asking them to abstain on pay. DD said it would not work, and so it turned out when TB raised it at Shadow Cabinet and one by one they spoke in a way that made clear where they were on it.

Thursday, July 11

A truly dreadful day. TB was useless, I was tired and useless and fed up. I was worried it was all about my health, I could not get going. I was also feeling the Tories were beginning to get their act together. TB called early to say he couldn't see how we could avoid elections and he was moving back to hold them in the autumn, not in July. I had no idea whether that was right or wrong, but felt that we were going to take a hammering, because there was an assumption that TB did not want these elections at all. At 9.45, with JP on the phone, he met the others and agreed they would go ahead. He was plunged into gloom. In the afternoon he was reduced to having a little nap. I was having one of my fed-up-with-TB days. He could not even make a decision whether to take his pay rise. We were being asked about it all day. I also had a fairly friendly but heavy-edged chat with CB, who of course was concerned that I was trying to persuade him not to take it, which is what he would be telling her. JP called from the train and said he had an idea for helping Harriet survive in the Shadow Cabinet poll. He said we would just get everyone who loathed her to vote for her.

TB was in a real gloom by the time he came back from the Mandela lunch. He said sometimes I think this party doesn't want to be led. What on earth is the point of these elections that will do nothing but provide a target for our opponents, and nobody believes that if we win this will be the team we have for long? We got nowhere. At one point he was asleep on the sofa. Earlier he just sat there with his hand on his face, groaning. My blandishments to get a grip were met by silence. We left for the Savoy and the gala dinner. He managed to lift himself for the evening and did fine. The Cantona shirt Alex [Ferguson] gave us raised £17,500 in the auction.

Friday, July 12

Pay was still rumbling away in the press and TB was still anxious about taking the full rise. Peter M was worried about last night's Tory broadcast which although full of lies and distortions he felt was highly effective. There could hardly have been a worse day to try to make news from a press conference – Charles/Diana divorce being announced, Mandela in Brixton. TB was on form though. On pay he said he would simply say he would take three per cent. He got DD and Nick Brown [deputy chief whip] in for a meeting re the Shadow Cabinet elections. Nick felt it was just about possible to get HH back on. TB said if she went off, and Jack C came on, fine. If she went off and Ann C came on, not so fine. We wanted the five women to be Margaret, Mo, Ann Taylor, Clare and Harriet. There was a possibility Joan Lestor would not stand [due to ill health] in which case he felt there was a case for getting Hilary Armstrong or Joyce Quin to stand. TB was also worried at stories that we were asking middle-ranking good people not to stand and it was vital there was no suggestion we were behind that. He wondered if it would be possible to keep HH, get Jack C back on, and Clare and Meacher off, but he conceded that may be too ambitious. The fact this was going to take up so much time and attention underlined that we had probably been right not to want them, but Nick was convinced if we had not had them we would have had trouble running right through the summer.

Had lunch with Sue Douglas [editor, *Sunday Express*] at the Howard [hotel]. She is very sexy and knows it, but I felt she was trying too hard to come over as one of us, possibly thinking I would talk to Clive Hollick about her. She didn't feel the Tories were getting their act together. I sometimes found myself in the bizarre position of talking up their prospects to journalists who were too keen to write them off. The last thing we needed was a sense that it was all over before battle had been truly joined.

I got back for an excellent meeting on conference with Jonathan, DM and PG. We were tossing around a few ideas. Because *Road to the Manifesto* had been a major policy event, it would not be so easy just to announce new policy as the spine to the main speeches, and we needed to think about events which could carry the news and political agenda too, e.g. outsiders who were going to be there and using the platform to say interesting things about them and about us. Like, for example, [Steven] Spielberg was bringing a studio to the UK if we backed the film industry with real policy change. Though we were disappointed that the New Life launch did not carry through, it was the right message base for conference and we could get a lot of work done between now and then. PG had done an excellent note on how we could build momentum out of it. He said Kennedy had said 'In ten years we will put a man on the moon' – he said what is our 'In ten years?'

Saturday, July 13

Really quiet day for once. The Sundays had a field day of invented drivel and rubbish on the Shadow Cabinet elections. the *Mail on Sunday* had some crap about TB being fed up with RC, which claimed to have a quote, which TB wanted dealt with. RC was agitated no end as well. The problem with these elections was that it laid the ground for endless personality clash stories and the press basically felt they had free rein to say whatever they wanted.

Sunday, July 14

I suddenly realised that I hadn't spoken to TB at all yesterday, which must be the first time since God knows when. We talked a bit today and I said I still felt we were under-estimating the extent to which the Tories were getting their act together, and we were still wrestling with old problems. I took the kids to the Sobell Centre [North London leisure centre] for Calum's birthday party. PG was there and we had a mutual whinge and moan, particularly on the failure of the main politicians to get up proper lines of attack.

Monday, July 15

Ireland was massive in the press. Mo was trying to move from the government a bit, presumably with the Shadow Cabinet elections in mind. I'd tried to kill the *Mail on Sunday* story about TB being fed up with RC by saying it was a malicious invention. We also got news of a tracking poll showing we were slipping on economic optimism, which again must be a reflection of the Tories getting up a positive economic message. TB was seeing David Owen [Lord Owen, former Labour Foreign Secretary and co-founder of the SDP] at home. Owen seemingly said that he would not endorse him but his support for him would emerge 'by osmosis'. That would be fascinating to witness, I said. I felt that the strength of Owen's support, though it might do more good than harm, was probably being overrated in the office.

TB had been to the Grand Prix yesterday and had really enjoyed it. He was stunned by the technology and impressed by Bernie Ecclestone [president and chief executive of Formula One] who he reckoned was a supporter. He'd also been playing tennis with Alan Sugar [businessman, chairman of Tottenham Hotspur FC] who had said he would happily do a party political broadcast supporting us on business. Nick Brown told TB that Joan Lestor was standing down [from the Shadow Cabinet]. In an ideal world, he would like to see Clare and Meacher off, but he was warned that the minute we tried any fancy stuff, the first victim would be Harriet. JP was pushing for Hilary A and Joyce Quin to stand to stop Ann Clwyd but that didn't work either. JP and Nick both thought Harriet could be saved. TB was worried about what RC was doing and the thirty-odd left votes would leave GB, DD, etc. down the list. JP said you can't have everything.

There was a TB, GB, Peter M, AC meeting, a bit of a disaster. Peter M sought to be calm and helpful but GB was brimming with anger. He either sat and scribbled, and gave a good impression of ignoring anything anyone else said, or he raged at us all. TB had written them both a note saying he was alarmed at the state of our operations, and it had seemed to have had the effect of making Peter more co-operative and GB less. Doubtless it could have worked the other way. GB said he had been the one arguing most forcefully that we needed a clearer strategy post *Road to the Manifesto* but we had insisted all the energies went into the launch. There was a grain of truth in that, upon which he now built a mountain, almost as if we had conspired to stop ourselves having a proper strategy because we were obsessed with the launch. I said it was never one or the other; it should have been both, but he kept going on and on, saying we hadn't wanted a follow-through strategy, which was absurd. He was in the worst strop for ages, and wrapped it up in big-sounding arguments which didn't stack up. TB said, politely, several times, that if he didn't think we had a problem with our basic strategy operation, then we had a fundamental disagreement. We went round and round and eventually I lost it, and said why do we have these endless arguments about things we could agree in five minutes if we wanted? I said the other problem was we never put anything in writing from these meetings, so what was communicated down the lines depended on who was doing the communicating and we kept taking out of the meetings different views according to what we all wanted at the start. GB said 'Your main problem is disunity,' and now moved the goalposts to RC and others. He said none of the politicians were on-message. I said they don't know what the message is. He said they don't want to know. He was being absolutely impossible, to such an extent it was almost comic and at one point TB did indeed just laugh out loud. He said Gordon, the Tories are upping their firepower, and we are not matching it. We had another go re the economy but he said it was a slow-burn issue and we should get the timing right. When will that be? Don't know. It all depends. On what? Lots of things. He said we had to be careful it didn't all blow up in our faces, house prices and what have you. I said in London, people were seeing good economic news in the *Standard* every day, but there was no 'on the other hand' from Gordon Brown, to which he said 'I'm already gloomy Gordon to them.'

Tuesday, July 16

TB and I had another circular conversation on where we were. He still felt the mood had not changed but certainly traditional Tory support was going back and also there was still an air of doubt about us. He said to me and Bruce G, it's really quite simple. If it's New Labour, they'll go for us. If it's not, they won't. Later I ran into Francis Maude [former Conservative MP, candidate for Horsham]. He usually looked more downcast than probably he was, and he said that the Tory vote was coming back to them, and it was going to be close. I got home to yet another row about not being there enough and not really being there when I was. Philip called from Watford, and said the groups were excellent. He said that if we did things right, every single one of the people they saw (all former Tory voters) could come over. PG said he had seen Ed Balls earlier who had been full of bile re TB and our determination to go on the economy now. I just did not get these guys sometimes.

Got a call from Patrick Hennessy of the *Standard* who said he had heard TB was hardening the line on the tube strike following pressure from colleagues. I said this was balls. The line had not changed; we were pushing for arbitration which was binding and the case for strike action fell. But on speaking to TB at home, he immediately worried about a story saying we were weak, so he didn't mind one bit if they said we were hardening the position. I knew he would say that. I called Hennessy back and said to him we are hardening the stance but it is not a U-turn, make of that what you will. It went from page 2 to the splash.

TB was at the PLP and came back pissed off because Alan Howarth [Tory defector] had been rejected by Manchester Wythenshawe without a single nomination. At Shadow Cabinet, TB gave them a lecture on unity as we went into the elections, and he made clear there should be no daft business going on, though the fact he said it underlined an understanding it probably would be. He also emphasised that the Tories were beginning to get their act together and just because they were getting no credit from the press was no excuse for us to get complacent. RC took me to one side afterwards and said he had decided that because relations between us were so good, he did not feel the need to appoint his own press officer. 'Gordon has Whelan and look at the damage he does to him.' Wink.

We did pretty well with the tube strike switch. JP offside again. At 11.30 he came to see TB, and as he came through the door said 'What are the deadly duo up to today then? I wake up every dawn not sure what to expect.' He was not his usual self and said that now he just accepted these things happen. TB said he was consulted. JP said being told once you've decided to make a shift is not the same as being consulted. He was not prepared to put out a statement saying he supported what we were doing unless he had the full picture, and he was not sure he did. He was not as steamed up as he sometimes gets, but steely. TB said after he left 'He wants to have it all ways. He wants to be with us on the inside track, but he wants elements in the party to think he's outside.' I went to see JP afterwards and said he was wrong if he thought there had been some great strategy to force a shift in position. I explained how it had evolved, largely as a result of the *Standard*, and it was a problem if he didn't believe that. I said he tended to see conspiracy where it might well have been a cock-up, though admittedly one that got us to the position TB wanted. Eventually we agreed a written line, JP saying the reports of a great rift were a nonsense and me ruling out compulsory arbitration.

Jackie Ashley tipped me off that ITN were leading on an interview with JM in which he was getting six minutes, on the election, economy, run round the block. I primed David Hill to make a fuss so that hopefully we would get more air time next time for TB. The ITN interview was soft as hell and we complained.

Anji called to say she had had a dreadful row with Cherie. She was really upset, felt it was very hard to stay at times. Fiona took CB's side, said that she felt excluded from the way the office worked, yet it had a massive impact on her and the children's lives.

Friday, July 19

The papers were awful. A two-page spread in the *Sun* on Phoney Blair, a repeat of [columnist Richard] Littlejohn's 'All things to all men' piece from the *Mail*, leader, cartoon, Kavanagh analysis. The papers full of TB/JP split, details of meetings, plenty of evidence of JP's anger, and his success in having got TB not to go for compulsory arbitration. I called Rosie from the car and said this was disastrous. Partly by way of distraction, I successfully wound up Patrick Hennessy about the ITN interview with Major. Apparently there had been stacks of genuine complaints. I called the office and said we must get it up big time. TB was in a bit of a gloom. He felt the *Sun* had decided to go for him personally because it is not enough just to go for the party. He said there were times when he despaired of his colleagues. The journey to the airport was spent mainly with him just staring out of the window. The plane journey [to Manchester] was equally grim, except for TB's hilarious account of dinner at Michael Levy's, and Matthew Harding [Chelsea FC vice chairman] pissed, constantly going on about Tony's dad being deaf and at one point asking the woman next to him if she fancied a lift home with him. I would rather walk, she said.

I called Jeff Postlethwaite [Prescott's press officer] and told him he could not brief on TB/JP meetings without my express say-so, and he had better move fast to deal with the dreadful stories he had created. I said if the Sundays were full of TB/JP splittery, we were in trouble. The Manchester bombsite visit was fascinating and I was really impressed by the cops and the council people and they were determined they were going to build something special out of what had happened.

Saturday, July 20

I played golf for the first time in ages and was just five over for thirteen holes, which was bloody amazing considering how long it was since I played. The *Mail on Sunday* interview was not great. The only news story they did was Nicky to go to the Oratory too, which pissed off TB. It was pretty much a waste of time all round. He said it was very hard to have any sense of direction or control at the moment, and it was all because of these wretched Shadow Cabinet elections. I wish I had not allowed myself to defy my own instincts, he said. I caved in to the weakness of others.

Sunday, July 21

In between trying to have some time off with the kids, a few things out of the Sundays had to be dealt with. TB phoned several times and was fretful, having the same conversation again and again about whether the country had actually changed mood. He said the Tories had strong lines of attack, far better than ours, and they were disciplined in communicating them. Told JP we should deal with the story about him not backing Harriet. It was absurd. He obviously felt he owed TB one, however, because he said he would get out a line that he was backing her.

Monday, July 22

TB was off to the contact group and Sally said that he was in a foul mood, and doing his usual 'you guys' every time he argued with them and then saying they were going to lose us the election. He called me from the TUC to say they were going to get the big stick by the end of the week. 'I've had it with these people.' When he came back he said he was thinking of taking everyone by surprise with a big reshuffle, switch JP to home affairs, Straw to do competitiveness, Meacher overseas development, Short jobs and youth, [Chris] Smith transport and green, Frank Field [Labour MP] social security, and his first act would be to dump GB's child benefit proposal. I said it was certainly very bold. My worry was that Frank was unreliable, a bit up himself and basically a prima donna better at talking ideas than making them happen. But TB was clearly keen for something bold to get back on the front foot. He held a meeting to review strategy and the Shadow Cabinet, during which JP said Donald should do something about Diane Abbott. Suggested JP do something in his speech tomorrow night, for which I drafted a section on the group who permanently cause trouble.

Our main media event of the day was a meeting with ten *Sun* readers. I had the idea on the back of Liz spotting Major doing women's magazines. Margaret McDonagh put her network into operation re readers putting in questions and clearly some of them got through. TB was good with them, lively, and though he said nothing new in the answers, they seemed to like him. At 5pm we had the so-called strategy meeting. It was now absolutely preposterous. We had no sense of strategy at all, and no direction. TB was not engaged, just constantly going on about Shadow Cabinet elections and how he had been right not to want them and GB saying we had a problem because of the publication of the anti-single currency document by Labour MPs tomorrow which meant there was no point doing anything. GB had nothing positive to say, simply identifying problems.

Tuesday, July 23

TB and GB were both exercised by the Alan Simpson/Denzil Davies [Labour MPs] launch of their document opposing the single currency. TB was also turning his mind to a reshuffle. He said even our bone-heads ought to realise that it would be madness to kick off Harriet now. He was also moving to the idea of deselecting one of the perma-nent rebels *pour encourager les autres*. DD was not sure the PLP would back it. TB was confident they would and it would go down well. On and off through the day, he was canvassing opinion re Frank Field. Donald was opposed on the grounds that Frank was unreliable, the same concern I had, though I was attracted by the boldness and the signal it sent on welfare reform, and his determination to appoint his own team. GB suggested putting Frank Field in as [social security] number two and making him part of a welfare review committee, controlled by a Treasury person. Alistair Darling was emerging as the probable moderniser from the outside.

I was sorting reaction to the euro row. We were successfully getting people to take off their names and calm it as a story and then Denis MacShane [Labour MP] idiotically gets involved in a televised slanging match with Alan Simpson, thereby giving the broadcasters the story they wanted, namely Labour just as badly split. We agreed he had to do Europe at PMQs but didn't know quite how. In the end it all came together well and he had one of our big successes, just timed right for the Shadow Cabinet elections and end of term. It was a real hit. Major tried taunting over the Simpson, etc. document asking whether he agreed with it. TB just said no and then splattered him.

Then back to reshuffle discussions. Jack [Straw] asked TB if the stories about a swap with JP were true and TB did not outright deny. He was worried what JP would or would not accept. Gordon's argument was to put Alistair Darling or Andrew Smith at social security and Frank as number two.

On the train north, TB had a long session with Jim Naughtie doing a piece for *Reader's Digest* and he asked what TB's biggest mistake was. An honest answer would probably have been the child benefit fiasco, but he said it was reacting too slowly to the Harriet story. He and JP chatted re Harriet and for different reasons agreed it would be a disaster if she went off – TB because it was a blow to him; JP because it would show he couldn't deliver. The Sheffield meeting was fine. JP chaired it well and was probably more popular with the largely Old Labour audience than TB. We left with fish and chips for Doncaster. On the train, TB spent the whole time chatting to JP, trying to suggest a departmental brief in the Shadow Cabinet reshuffle but he was having none of it.

Wednesday, July 24

A quiet day, waiting for the Shadow Cabinet election results. I wrote a briefing note on the expected outcome, a vote for unity, etc., with quotes from JP and a line on the PLP 'rights and responsibilities' review committee, and a new deal with the PLP. DD was even more opposed to Frank, having mulled it over. He said he was sure it would end in tears. He just wasn't a team player and he was not sure about his abilities either. He was clearly worried we would overdo the briefing on Harriet. I assured him we would not. I bumped into Gwyneth Dunwoody [Labour MP] 'How is your party?' she said. 'Our party, you mean,' I said. 'No, I mean your party.' GB was pressing hard to get Chris Smith out of social security. He had a go at TB and JP and also asked me to go and see him in the Shadow Cabinet room, away from everyone else, and that was the only thing he wanted to discuss. He said he didn't have the drive or inventiveness. I agreed with that. But I was not convinced his ideas for replacements would have much of that stuff either. However, I basically bought the argument and, to my amazement, found myself arguing for Harriet to be given a fresh start at social security. It was also important to get Clare where she could do less damage. GB felt it was important to put safe people into difficult areas and the best people into the jobs where we would be campaigning most. TB was worried Clare would simply refuse a move. JP asked for environment and transport in addition to shadow DPM, which hit the deck. Frank Field came in to see TB at 4.30 and he offered him number two at DSS. He said there were reservations about him coming in, because people felt he was not a team player and he had a good deal on record that the Tories would be able to attack, but TB was keen to have him in. FF, having first said he was worried about us losing the bottom end of the working-class vote, and that he felt he could help on that, then said he felt maybe it was in the party's best interests if he stayed where he was. TB said he would nonetheless like to have him in government. FF came to see me and I said TB had toyed with the idea of making him number one but it was difficult and there were a lot of objectors. I didn't make it explicit that I was one of them, but I went through some of the reasons. He said he would certainly be interested if that were to arise and I said I would go back to TB with that. GB had been to see Clare to sound her out on youth unemployment, but all I could see in that was her causing mayhem – strike law, industrial relations, social chapter, minimum wage. She would be a fucking nightmare. Never was so much effort required to deal with someone so useless. She had another ridiculous tantrum tonight, storming out of a live BBC interview because she was asked about the tube strike.

When the results came through, TB felt it was bad news, and that the story would be his enemies at the top, his friends at the bottom. But we got words out very quickly, before the full results were out there, and I felt we could be fine out of this. I called a briefing in the lower gallery, away from the PLP where they were getting the results, and gave them plenty of meat and quotes, etc. There was total agreement Clare had to be moved but no agreement as to where. After the results, Anji paged her seven times saying TB wanted to speak to her, and she just ignored it. JP came to see TB and said the TV walkout ought to be the final straw. The woman's a liability, he said, and she doesn't have a leg to stand on. Eventually, well after 10, Sue Jackson found her in a bar and she reluctantly saw TB. He saw her alone and after she left Anji and I went in and he said she had gone completely ballistic, couldn't understand it and she was refusing to move anywhere. I said to TB if she fucked him around too much, he should just kick her out and see if anyone really cared. But even as I said it, I felt it was not sensible politics. That being said, a lot of people were saying to him, politicians and staff alike, that we worried about her far too much. She was not very good and not as popular as she or the press thought. TB said she's crap as a friend but I think she could be even worse as an enemy. These reshuffles were always difficult and he was clearly talking himself into minimal change. I said he would just have to swallow hard, prepare himself for a dreadful day tomorrow and get on with it. It would all be forgotten in days.

The Shadow Cabinet elections went OK in the press though there was quite a lot of 'rebuff for modernisers'. TB saw Chris Smith at 8. Clare was due to call, as agreed last night, at 8.30. She didn't. Anji paged her or her assistant, Victoria, seven times. We heard nothing. Her office said they didn't know where she was. At one point we were told she was in the bath. Anji told TB who said 'What a bloody show this is – I am sitting around waiting to conduct a reshuffle while one of the least competent members of the team that's being reshuffled finishes her bath.' So it would seem. The image of Clare in the bath was enough for me to want to change the subject. He eventually spoke to her at 11.30, and she said she was adamant she wouldn't move. TB said, after another conversation, that she would have to move. In all he spoke to her three or four times. GB spoke to her probably just as often. She was offered ODA, Chancellor of the Duchy, youth unemployment, green, issues for women. It was ridiculous. She had said so hard she wasn't moving that I imagined she would resign and I went away to draft a statement, some warm words from TB plus an account of all the gaffes she had made down the years. It was probably more therapy than something I intended to use, but I couldn't really see how she could stay when she was refusing move after move. Word got out fairly quickly she was refusing jobs. It could have been her but JP's theory was it was Meacher because he was angling for ODA and assumed if it was out there she had turned it down it would be hard for her to go back on that. ITN and BBC were both planning big Clare stories so I got out the Harriet/Chris Smith straight swap for the lunchtimes. But Clare was the real interest, which of course she would be loving. Eventually she agreed to the move (to ODA) but also wanted to be on the welfare-to-work committee, under GB, with Frank Field on it. I wrote up a briefing note to present her in the best light I could, much as I loathed her, but there was no way it would be seen as anything but a demotion.

TB had not been impressed by my account of Frank's conversation with me. He could not see how Frank felt it was wrong in principle for him to come on to the front bench, but it suddenly became right if it involved the top DSS job. TB now had to get Meacher to do green issues. MM was worried it would be seen as a demotion, which it wouldn't, but he had to be persuaded. He wittered on for fully half an hour, purely on that, with those intense eyes and his head bobbing around from side to side, and an ability to start one sentence before the last one had finished and so ensure a near-total monologue. What good he thought it did him was beyond me. Smith's and Darling's appointments were confirmed and I got those out. Chris Smith's move [to health] was being presented as demotion with, he and we assumed, some help from Whelan. I did the briefing at 4.30, very laid-back, criticising nobody, and they all seemed to think it was a strong story for TB. They had all been hoping for a 'Short sees off TB' story but it didn't come. Meacher had really fucked it for them both. I had been a bit worried about the press going for a great 'wonderful Clare – too honest and pure for New Labour'. But when push came to shove, she took the job he wanted her to.

Friday, July 26

There was a mixed press for Clare's demotion. Both the *Sun* and the *Mirror* were supportive, but there was a ridiculous John Rentoul piece in the *Indy* headlined 'Save this national treasure'. I called JP and said I wondered if it wouldn't be helpful to get it out there that he was every bit as determined as TB to get her out of transport, but he was not so sure. He was worried the reshuffle was seen as a step to the right. It was clear parts of the press were going on a 'sanctify Clare' kick so I got Tim and Margaret McD to organise letters to the *Indy* and *Guardian* pointing out the other side to the story. As ever, we had the right and the left in unholy alliance; the right egging her on to be ever more self-indulgent by building up this rubbish that she alone spoke her mind; the left just too naive to see that if they and the Clares of this world were ever allowed to hold sway, we would become a one party, Tory party nation state. Some of the pro-Clare stuff was utterly puke-making.

Saturday, July 27

TB called from Sedgefield. He said even he could not quite believe the extent to which the left press was falling for the left-right alliance trap on Clare. It is the history of Labour down the years, he said. Inhale the right's propaganda and spew it out in more noxious form. The right say we have ditched our principles, then the left say it with more venom because they talk of hurt and betrayal. He said the key to it all was keeping JP on board.

Sunday, July 28

TB was worried about the discipline stuff. I hated the way he got me to start these things and then when I did, he would want to rein back. [Ken] Livingstone rather proved the point about the unholy alliance in that he chose to write about the current situation in the *Mail on Sunday*, a right-wing platform for a left-wing anti-Labour leadership perspective. With TB up north I'd been hoping for a quiet day but he called the whole time, and of course the press was really up for it as a Sunday for Monday scene. He must have called six to eight times, usually to say the same thing. He was worried we were building the rebels up and setting them up as the big political story of the summer. As well as being fed up with them, he said he was getting exasperated with GB and RC. He said he was thinking of doing an interview with *Tribune*. I pointed out GB and RC had done it recently and hit all the usual left buttons. He was scathing about it. He said you do not get anywhere with different messages for different audiences. He was in a real rage, saying some of our people went round business audiences being pro business, and unions being pro left and in fact both would respect them more if they said the same thing to each. He said if he did *Tribune*, it would be to deliver a very New Labour message. He said there was a significant minority of our MPs who didn't really mind if we won or lost. It was like an academic game in which the only way they could get to play was by being permanent rebels and critics. He said it would take at least a decade to change the culture of the party. 'I just hope we get the odd election victory along the way, so they finally get it into their thick skulls that without power, you achieve nothing, which is precisely what we have achieved the whole time I have been here.'

Monday, July 29

There was far too much discipline stuff in the papers. I had made a mistake in briefing [Andy] Grice as I did, and allowing it to gather momentum. As TB had said, he and I had been responsible for two internal party matters, this and the party reform paper, and on both we had cocked up in spades. Brian Wilson did a good job on Livingstone on the *Today* programme, but it was appalling the way [John] Humphrys treated Ken with kid gloves, and did the usual sneer job on Brian. I was later on the phone to TB in Sedgefield when Tim passed me a note to say *Today* had told him Clare was coming on tomorrow. It was the first any of us knew about it, and typical. TB said 'If she messes about in any shape or form, I will have to sack her. It is ridiculous the way she behaves.' Peter M was of the view we should have gone the whole hog and lost her when we had the chance, as we were only storing up trouble for later. TB was in surprisingly jovial mood, though I noticed the black humour creeping in, which it often did when we were either under pressure or off form. He said between us we had cocked up and we were losing our touch on the party stuff. We knocked around a few ways of cocking up even more. He was far less hyper than yesterday when he couldn't stop talking. TB was seeing JP up in Sedgefield and JP was not happy with the way it had gone. As ever, he assumed there had been some big clever strategy and he had not been asked his view. TB tried to assure him there had been no big strategy and he accepted it had not turned out very clever. JP was, however, very much on for being hard on these guys. 'I think he wants to be executioner,' TB said.

Tuesday, July 30

I caught most of Clare on the radio; it wasn't long before the self-indulgent stuff kicked in: how lots of people were writing to her (she made it sound like a death in the family) and how she was hurt, a well-chosen word which would be the story. But the PLP was pretty much on our side. TB called just once as he finished the junior ranks in the reshuffle. I sensed his two and a half hours with JP had not been totally productive. I took the boys up north. Dad was a lot thinner.

Wednesday, July 31

Someone had leaked the home affairs select committee report on guns, which showed six Tories against a ban. It led the news and so again took the immediate pressure off us. At the morning meeting, Peter M was in the chair and we went over guns, plus how to get TB more plugged into the [Atlanta, USA] Olympics, as he was due to do a live link-up with some of the British athletes. When TB came back from the NEC he said Skinner had been terrific. He had couched his criticisms on the discipline issue in terms of basic support. He said TB did not have to prove he was a strong leader, people knew it instinctively. Dennis also said that for the first time he was picking up signals that the Tories were making more inroads and we had to be careful. Sally and DH both said the atmosphere at the NEC was very brittle. I said it was a good job I wasn't there. I might have been compelled to admit we had fucked up big style. I said to Sally that to fuck up, as TB and I had done, twice in a few days, was the strongest sign yet that we needed a holiday. GB called me to say JP was on the rampage and I went to see him upstairs.

He launched into a huge great tirade against the campaign, GB, Peter, Margaret McD, anyone really. He said first he wanted a bigger role, then he didn't want a role at all. His main beef was that he was just being presented with campaign ideas and expected to front or present them, but he was not properly consulted in the planning. He said he wanted to get one member of each front-bench team and get them working as a unit under him. He said he was continuing to press TB to get rid of Peter from his team. He wanted to see TB but I knew TB was leaving early, and said he had gone. I did my best 'Calm down, calm down' but he was very steamed up. I spoke to TB later and he said simply 'Oh God, what now?' Earlier he saw Clare, who cancelled an interview with Fiona today, and she assured him that her aim was not to cause trouble. She said she was taking a hit for not standing for anything. Fiona interviewed GB for *House Magazine* today. She said he didn't once look her in the eye, and it was as if he was reading from a script. She said after ten minutes she pretty much gave up trying to get anything out of him.

Thursday, August 1

Joy Johnson had a piece in the *New Statesman* saying TB didn't speak the people's language and spoke of too many high-falutin' concepts. It's funny how the press can view people as being hopeless when they are doing a job but, when they're gone, and they slag off the people they used to work with, they are suddenly seen as unimpeachably wise.

TB had lunch with Neil [Kinnock] and they were joking about swapping jobs. Neil was more relaxed than of late and seemed more sympathetic to some of TB's problems. He was angry that ODA had been seen as a demotion. I said that was entirely because of the way Clare and Meacher had behaved in the run-up to the decision.

Joy Johnson was on *World at One* and I called GB and said what on earth is she up to? He said what does it have to do with me? I said it's fair to say his office is rather closer to her than we are, and he said are you saying we put her up to it? I said no, but you might have a word and suggest she is not doing any good. He was unbelievably defensive about her. Charlie W had earlier claimed to me he tried to stop her writing the piece, which I doubted. The problem at the moment was GB, with CW's help, building a separate media and political network. Mo called TB to say that John Kampfner [journalist] was doing a very bad profile of Chris Smith and she said she knew for a fact GB's people had been doing him in, saying he was moved because he was hopeless, and TB and GB had both shredded him at the Joint Policy Committee. I called Kampfner and said it was balls, hugely exaggerated, etc., etc., and he said I hear what you say but it's hard to ignore where it is coming from. He virtually said Ed Balls and CW.

JP was feeling doubly snubbed – first because of an *FT* diary piece saying TB/GB had discussed Shadow Cabinet over a breakfast at Simpson's. Second because TB had not seen him last night when he wanted to see him. He was up in Hull getting the Freedom of the City which you'd have thought might have cheered him up. But he told TB point blank he was not having Peter M in his team. He said he'd asked TB to sort this months ago and he had had enough. TB ended up just saying I've had enough of this and slamming the phone down. He said some days he felt JP was a problem, other days GB, other days RC. They were never on song together. I worry that if we get in power, these traits will become real problems. He told JP he had to think about whether he was really suited to the kind of job he thought he wanted. It was a very difficult conversation which ended badly both ends. I suggested an 'election planning portfolio' that would indicate stepping up a gear on election planning. TB wanted that to be under JP but when I spoke to JP, it was clear it was a non-starter. He said he was happy for it to be a separate special unit, but not part of his team. This was getting silly. He said TB had promised he would deal with Peter, get him properly integrated like anyone else, and he hadn't done it. He still acted like he was in a league of his own. Then he had a go at me, saying all the briefings about discipline had been unhelpful and counterproductive and caused us real problems. But Peter was his big beef. Then Peter came on, aggrieved that in the official list of appointments he appeared to be linked with Brian W. He sent TB a note saying the media would not know what to make of this. I felt sorry for TB at these reshuffles, because so much of his time and energy was spent massaging egos and dealing with conflicting views of people's strengths and weaknesses. We had not even managed to track down Brian and go through all this. When we did, he was very grown up about it. He called me at 6.30 and his first reaction was just to laugh, because he could easily work out why it was happening. He had a good conversation with TB who said he was grateful. There was no way some of this nonsense would not get into the press in the coming days and TB was pretty close to despair about the whole thing.

Saatchis did an OK 'Enough is enough' presentation. It was OK without being brilliant, though PG was raving about it. The main attraction for me was the idea of Saatchis coming over to us, as a company. TB and I talked about how much we needed a holiday, but we were not leaving in good shape. The Tories were beginning to pick up on the economy. JP was mega offside again. Peter was out of control. GB was being a pain. RC was onside only because the other two were offside. Charlie W was causing trouble. The Shadow Cabinet middle order were not adding much, and some of them did absolutely fuck all unless asked. TB said the last few days have been kindergarten politics. TB was having dinner with Peter M and just before I went to bed, he called and said he felt JP was the biggest problem at the moment. I said don't let Peter wind you up. TB said did I think he was moveable? I said to be replaced by who? Maybe Mo, he said. Oh don't be ridiculous.

Friday, August 2 to Monday, August 26
We set off early and caught JP on the radio just before we reached the coast. He was off-message without being disastrous. We took a couple of days to get down to Provence, just outside Malaucene, but the house was nothing like as good as the one at Flassan, and we all sensed we were in for a crap holiday. The house was in the middle of nowhere but joined to another one, where there were two massive, disgusting dogs who barked all night. The pool was not finished. Fiona got ill and only when we got back did we learn it was actually quite serious, and it meant she had a pretty miserable time all round. The boys didn't like the house, hated the dogs and spent a lot of time fighting.

Nor was it quiet on the work front. Clare Short did one of her unplanned, stream-of-consciousness self-indulgent interviews with the *New Statesman*, in which she talked about TB's reliance on 'the people who live in the dark' and so sparked another great round of blah about me and Peter M, etc. It was a classic summer rubbish story, all self-inflicted and which led to a steady stream of calls and press trying to find out where we were. The right-wing press did their usual revolting bilge about Clare being so honest, etc. Later in the holiday JP did a similar, though more restrained interview on the whole spin thing, and the need for us to be more substance not style and it all kicked off again. Peter M was holding the fort and we spoke a few times but he always sounded a bit down. He did well to fight back when the Tories used Clare's words as part of their negative campaign, and he worked up a huge row about their 'devil's eyes' poster.[1] Peter Hyman apparently managed to get the Bishop of Oxford out on it and they turned the whole thing into a bit of a disaster for the Tories. It was still running when we got back.

We had cut short the Malaucene part of the holiday and went to stay for a couple of days at the place where Philip and Gail had rented a much nicer house, though in an area not quite as pretty as ours. But the kids finally had a decent time, and PG and I were able to talk a bit about what we would need to do when we got back. Fiona was

[1] Conservative posters showing Blair with demon eyes and carrying the message 'New Labour. New Danger' attracted widespread criticism.

feeling wretched pretty much the whole time, and by the end we were all calling it the holiday from hell, and we were all keen to get home. I said to PG I had been getting more and more alarmed about 1. economy; 2. JP, GB and RC and their inability to work together and with TB; 3. unity/discipline, which I feared would kick in big time if there was the feeling of a close election; 4. the press, and particularly the *Mail*, were now reverting to type; 5. BBC, obsessed with the issue of spin, allied to a growing interest in me personally. TB felt the biggest of these was the economy. We spoke a couple of times and at least he was having a proper holiday. But he was low. He was worried about the party, and he felt our big players were not yet really ready, psychologically, for the fight ahead. Amazingly, our position in the polls had held up but TB's ratings had taken a dent, which was less surprising. The charge that he would do anything to get votes was beginning to stick. JP or his people did a couple of silly briefings, including one saying he had been forced to stand up to TB on the discipline package, which kicked it all off again. TB felt the public would be getting fed up with the party. JP felt it was more that TB kept pushing the party to the brink, leaving him no option but to take a stand, and make sure the party knew he had. That was what made TB angry, though, because he felt it was more JP worrying about his position in the party than the party's position in the country.

Tuesday, August 27

I didn't feel very refreshed after the holiday and had mixed feelings about going back to work. I had a meeting with Peter M, PG and Margaret McD to go over where we were. We agreed that the main difficulty was a lack of clear direction that everyone understood and bought into. They all felt too that the left was becoming a problem again, and that JP/RC were giving them credence in a way that could undermine New Labour. All four of us felt strongly that it was the 'new' part of that equation that was going to help us win, but there was still a lot of tension and some suspicion aroused by it. Peter, having worked more over the holiday than we did, was more down than any of us. PG was more optimistic. I was still worried re the JP situation. I was worried that TB would allow his personal anger at some of the nonsense to lead him to make a political miscalculation. I still felt that despite it all, JP was basically OK, and potentially a great campaign strength. Added to which, whether TB liked it or not, he had a place in the party's heart that we should use not challenge.

TB called from the car the moment he landed. He was met by lots of photographers following up the story that the Italian press had fallen for him. Peter M and I went out to see him at 4.30 at Richmond Crescent. He was wearing shorts and a T-shirt with a big letter Q on it. He was tanned and seemed very chirpy, and moderately sympathetic when I told him we had had something of a holiday from hell. We went through all the various problem areas and he concluded that he needed to get out there more. He realised that he was being seen as all things to all men, a bit managerial even, and it had to be much clearer that he was a conviction politician. The problem was that New Labour was defined by our opponents as an electoral or political device. We had to show that he was New Labour out of conviction. I said the most important challenge of the coming months was for TB to connect with people, and for the party to see that happening, based upon his convictions as a left-of-centre political leader. 'You'll have to find me the convictions,' he said, half in jest. He was not yet properly focused and in back-to-work mode. He kept coming back in with reminiscences about his holiday. I was a bit alarmed at the extent to which he seemed excited at having met Bryan Ferry [musician]. He had played tennis with him, Dave Stewart [musician] and Rory Bremner [impersonator]. He had come back with far better feelings towards JP than when he left. It was GB he saw as the most difficult at the moment. Then Peter and he started a little squabble because he referred to Peter's position being 'unclear' and Peter did one of his little 'I wonder whose fault that is' flounces, and off they went. Peter said afterwards he sometimes felt TB was embarrassed about him. Peter and I left at 7, having enjoyed a running private joke between us to see how long we would be there before we were offered a cup of tea. We got one just before we left. Peter M came round for dinner. He said TB had this unerring capacity to demoralise him. He didn't feel it was deliberate, but a consequence of his failure to give him a proper acknowledged role.

Wednesday, August 28

We had a meeting on conference and agreed there had to be a sense of TB coming out fighting. Deborah Mattinson [pollster] had done some research showing TB on a down and JM on a bit of an up. TB felt it was because latterly he had only been seen sorting the party, not addressing issues that mattered to people, and we had to get back on that. He was on good form, and revved up on the idea that we had to find better ways of him promoting himself and engaging better with people. Charlie came and told me that JP had written to all members of the Shadow Cabinet saying that all policy documents had to be sent to his office as well as the Leader's Office. He had also reversed a decision to scrap the campaigns and election committee. So he was still pretty much on the rampage. He was doing very little to attack the Tories at the moment, which was meant to be one of his big things. I was beginning to feel it would need him to come a bit of a cropper to show that he couldn't do this kind of stuff unaided. He felt he was invincible within the party.

Neil and Glenys came round for a drink and we went out for dinner at the Camden Brasserie. To our and their amazement, Robin and Gaynor [Regan, his secretary] were two tables away. Robin went a weird pink colour when he saw us, a big false smile and a wave, while Gaynor looked sick. RC came over. There was something I needed to fax to him, and could I fax it to his office. It was probably a big charade to pretend he was not going back to her place. Neil said it was odd that he and RC used to be so close that Robin once came to see him for advice on whether to leave his wife or not. Now they were not that close at all. Neil still confident we would win, but felt we had real problems. JP a loose cannon who could hole the ship. Short a disaster but bizarrely popular in parts. He felt we should get someone to speak to Barbara Castle to stop her causing mayhem at conference. 'She has been playing the sentimental choir of the Labour Party for fifty years and will do it again.' *The Times* had a poll with us down two, and TB down a bit. TB said maybe it was best we took a dip now and came back later. I took a decision not to help JP when preparing for Questions, or with his speeches until he stopped all the current nonsense. Austin Mitchell had a big whack at TB in a piece in the *New Statesman*. Diana/Charles divorce came through. Peter M saw her at an English Ballet do and he called me afterwards to say she had been asking for me, going on about how strong I was and wanting to see us again.

Thursday, August 29

Austin Mitchell's piece was running quite big. *Today* did no fewer than five pieces related to it. RC called at 7 for a briefing on various things for the 8.10 slot and was absolutely brilliant. The line re froth/trivia vs substance was working well and we were going to get decent coverage today. At the morning meeting we agreed we had to get Jo Moore [press officer] to call Mitchell and ask him to stop doing interviews, and that TB should do a doorstep early on to swat the story for the lunchtimes. He was on good form and did it well. I felt we were having to fight the old fights again. But Mitchell was an opportunity to get up the idea of TB's tour going out to the people, and also the sense that TB was back with a bang. On the way out to the car, I ran into JP and pretty much ignored him. There was little point as things stood getting into an argument about anything.

Plane to North Wales, then helicopter to Rochdale. There was a really nice atmosphere and people were very warm towards TB. It was always good to get out of the bubble and get a different perspective. We then went on by helicopter to Granada and a tour of the *Coronation Street* set. Again, the atmosphere was really warm and there was a buzz among the cast the moment he arrived. Liz Dawn (Vera Duckworth) was excellent, as was Sarah Lancashire (Raquel). Good pictures and a nice feel to the whole thing. The Street itself was packed with real people who gave him a terrific welcome, and although it was a bit surreal to be doing a walkabout in Coronation Street, it was a good thing to do. His body language was better than usual too, plunging in and really engaging, rather than the Prince Charles-ish approach he could sometimes take. TB had a meeting with the Granada bigwigs, Charles Allen, etc.

We headed for the hotel and JP and Rosie were there. The atmosphere was dreadful again and I thought it was time for Rosie and me to try to clear the air. I said it was appalling that the man who was supposed to be spending the summer attacking the Tories got more coverage for attacking us, and therefore effectively sanctioned others to do so. I said I was really pissed off at some of the briefing against me and also how details of TB/JP conversations were briefed out. I said I always tried to keep JP and his interests on my radar but in the end I worked for TB and if this didn't stop, they could fuck themselves. She insisted JP had nothing to do with the briefing against me, and I said I found that hard to believe. Also, sometimes the media picked up stories from body language rather than briefing and JP had to be more careful about the signals he sent out. JP had another go at having a chat at the *Road to the Manifesto* meeting but I again put up the barriers. We had to leave for the fund-raising dinner which was on the Baker Street set [built for the Sherlock Holmes series] at Granada. Again, the mood was warm and positive. As a first day of a mini campaign, it had gone well, and the atmospherics had been good, and TB on form. But there was no doubt we were facing a different mood. The Clare stuff about 'people in the dark' was now coming up on the doorstep and doing real damage.

Friday, August 30

We got huge coverage in the heavies, fantastic pictures from *Coronation Street*. The *Sun*, however, carried nothing, and had an article by

Major. It set TB off muttering all day. TB met JP over breakfast. TB said to me later he told JP that he feared if things went on as they were, we risked losing the election and that he could not even promise him a big job, let alone deputy prime minister, unless there was change. There was a constant balance to be struck between appealing to the party, in very traditional ways, and appealing to the public more broadly. TB thanked Blunkett for his help over the summer and said later he felt he was one of the few really bright people we had. Meanwhile George Robertson was phoning us regularly saying he had to speak to TB re tomorrow's executive, where there was a fair chance we were going to get hammered on devolution. TB felt GR was panicking and it would be fine.

On the train back we tried to have a long-term strategy discussion. He said it was difficult to get beyond the fact that the people at the top were not cohering. He said we are paying for the calibre of people who came into the party when it was mad. I said he was part of the problem too, because of the way he worked, the way he didn't address problems until it was too late, and the fact he played insufficient attention to keeping the party together. I also said he had to settle Peter's position as he fell between two stools – he was neither politician nor spin doctor. In theory, TB saw him as a politician, but he didn't really treat him as such. Also, I said both Peter and I were expected to do too much. He kept saying he wanted us to do long-term thinking, but we were never able to escape, and particularly me, the day-to-day detail, not least because he kept bothering us with it the whole time. He asked me to think up a plan for him, to get a broader personality fleshed out in the public mind, and to make sure people did not buy the idea that he was less attractive than Major. He said our problem was he couldn't sufficiently delegate party management to his deputy. He ought to be able to delegate strategy to GB but GB wasn't engaging. GB was no better after the holiday. Yesterday he told us he did not believe the economy was the reason for the Tories' rise in the polls. TB was beginning to wonder whether RC wasn't the only person capable of doing the campaign job.

I got home and worked out I had had more than fifty pager messages during the day. I had forgotten how awful it could be out on the road, when the phone and pager just never stopped. The tour had started OK but Fiona said there was definitely a new tone in the way we were reported. She said Mike Brunson was very snotty and everything was presented as a struggle. It was also beginning to bite that TB didn't believe in much.

Saturday, August 31

Thatcher was saying TB handled crises well. I was on the phone pretty much all morning, dealing with Scotland. TB said if we lost the vote, we should have a members' ballot. I spoke to Clive Hollick about the changes at the *Express*. Clive said he had spent some time with Murdoch in the US and he was clearly impressed by TB personally but thought we were a bit too craven. He reckoned Murdoch would have more respect if TB looked a bit tougher towards him. He did not fear governments, he feared regulation. Clive said he could not believe how the Big Four were failing to act effectively. He said it was beginning to look like a one-man band, and GB was barely visible. I went to Millwall vs Burnley and during the match got the message that we had won on the Scottish Executive.

Sunday, September 1

Arrived at TB's at 7.45, and I put to him the point Hollick had made, that he was too much of a one-man band. TB felt that was OK at the moment, because he had to fight back. TB spoke to GB in the car, worried that Frost might come at him on the windfall tax. GB was still saying the economy was not a problem for us, which was breathtaking. TB and I went off to a quiet room and we ran through some of the difficult questions, and then he went to the studio. We got there to discover there was a *Panorama* crew filming me the whole time for their silly fucking programme on spin doctors, and a news crew doing likewise. I complained both then and later and Tim Orchard [BBC] called later to apologise. TB was on very good form, though didn't answer well on discipline or the NEC. We managed to get the story where we wanted it, TB challenging the Tories over funding and saying he could only lead in this way. Most of the papers felt he did pretty well. TB was off for lunch with Roy Jenkins, which was the last thing I wanted to come out today. I spoke to Michael Levy, who said he shut the office fund at £1.3m, and had raised £5.5m for the new Labour election fund, a lot of it from Matthew Harding, Paul Hamlyn, Bob Gavron and Swraj Paul [all Labour donors]. JP paged me, asking for Richard Stott's number, no doubt assuming I had put Stott [now a *News of the World* columnist] up to writing that JP was a cross between a menopausal agony aunt and a limp-wristed hairdresser.

Monday, September 2

Coverage of *Frost* was rather dominated by JP's refusal to say he was a social democrat, which fucked things up yet again. When, in the morning meeting, Jeff Postlethwaite said that JP was speaking at a meeting with Austin Mitchell, there was a sense of disbelief. Later, when Daisy Sampson from the *House Magazine* called to say that JP's office had promised a piece for conference and now said they could not do it, I said to Jeff it was unprofessional and added, don't worry, I'll pick up the pieces for John as usual. Then came a bleep message from JP. 'I'd like to see you in my office tomorrow. Until then, please stop making personal remarks.' I called Postlethwaite to bawl him out and asked was there anything we could discuss without JP going off and making trouble. I could not see how there could be any trust and openness, if TB/JP meetings appeared in print, if I was briefed against, as had happened in the summer. He denied again having done any of it and said it would not be in their interest to do it. I said I didn't understand what their interest was.

We had to get back on to the main themes before conference and get up a positive campaign. I spent much of the day speaking to business people saying that we needed their support at the business conference tomorrow, either speaking in our favour or at least saying we were not mad. I worked on the TB personal strategy paper and did a note re business.

I spoke to Tessa who said the feeling was that JP, RC and GB were getting ready for defeat and where they would be if we lost. It was one of those days when even though TB wasn't around, far too much was going on and the phone never stopped. I had a meeting with Matthew Harding to discuss how we might get out that he was our biggest single donor. I felt we could do it with a Sunday paper, then an article in the *Sun*. He said he wanted it showed it was possible to be rich and Labour. He was, like a lot of people who are that rich, a bit fond of himself but he was likeable and funny. *Telegraph* asked for a response to the fact that Major was going to take Norma campaigning with him as their secret weapon. It was the splash, and I didn't react quickly enough. We should have been saying Norma is clearly a nice and intelligent woman, but if the Tories think the election will be swung on that, it shows how desperate and out of touch they are.

Tuesday, September 3

Norma was pretty big in the right-wing papers and we decided not to get involved. I had thought there was a point to be made but it was no win territory, which of course was why they had done it. Of course if we had done likewise they would have been very different, lots of the new Glenys, the new Hillary [Clinton], who wears the trousers? etc. I suspect the whole thing was actually an effort to smoke out Cherie and make her feel she had to have a bigger profile.

I went upstairs for my meeting with JP. After the recent stand-off he was very emollient. He started by saying 'You and I are heading down a collision course and I really don't want that. I value what you do for Tony but I also value what you do for me. I see you as a colleague and a friend and I don't want to lose that. Everyone knows you are not just an adviser, you are a player and we are usually on the same side. But I cannot have you sniping at me or undermining my staff.' Clearly everything I had said had been relayed back verbatim. We went through his various gripes one by one – he assumed I was responsible for Stott's column, which I wasn't. He felt I should have discussed the discipline briefing with him, because it got out of hand. He felt I was too quick to want to crack the whip. Then it became a long thing about the nature of 'this fucking job, which is neither one thing nor the other'.

I pointed out it was the job he had always wanted. He said he felt less and less consulted, more and more marginalised, less and less happy with the political direction. He was barely speaking to Peter M and he found GB very hard to stomach at the moment. He denied having authorised the briefing of the private conversations and he would clearly have to find out who that was, and deal with it. He said the stuff about not wanting Peter may have come out via Roy Hattersley as the two of them had a conversation about the difficulties of being deputy leader. On we went, maybe an hour or more, and at the end of it he said some days he just felt sick inside because he wasn't sure what direction we were going in, wasn't sure where he fitted. He said TB should realise that of all of them, he was the one he could trust the most, because he had no leadership agenda, whereas e.g. GB and RC did. I said he had to get himself into a different mindset, and a different modus operandi. I said both of us underestimated how we could communicate what we thought without saying a word. He accepted he put out bad vibes too easily to MPs and the press. I said he should be motivating people at Millbank more, attacking the Tories more. He said he did not think GB and RC were the great strategists they reckoned themselves to be. Nor were they good at nuts and bolts. Give him a proper strategy, he said, and he would help do the nuts and bolts better than anyone. It was a good conversation and even though we had both raised voices at times, we had cleared the air and knew we had to get on to a better footing from now on. He later told Anji it had been a rapprochement. 'He knows I won't be bullied by him, and I know he won't be bullied by me.' I then spent much of the day setting up the business conference for tomorrow. I was getting out more businessmen but I said to Tim why the fuck do we have to do all this stuff? What do all these other people do who see these businessmen all the time?

Wednesday, September 4

We got some decent coverage of the business event, some of the people coming out for us but something very odd happened overnight. The *Mail*, *Telegraph* and others had stories saying we were going for 10p/15p starting rate of tax. Tax inevitably became the story. TB called GB to ask what was going on and GB said he knew nothing about it and assumed it came from me. He even claimed he was not aware it was in there at all. So he was asking us to believe that the Shadow Chancellor, and not just any Shadow Chancellor but one who paid attention to detail, had not acquainted himself with the contents of the business prospectus we were publishing. Hardly. Jonathan told me GB was planning some deal with Spielberg who was going to back our film policy and put up the idea of a big studio here but GB was refusing to let anyone see the paper on it. TB was terrific on the *Today* programme, though talking too fast and it got bogged down on tax. Beforehand he was fretting about the Cherie/Norma business, probably too much though I agreed it was all a ploy to smoke her out more into the political arena, and then try to make her an issue. The *Sun* had done a Cherie vs Norma scorecard, and Norma came off best. It was all silly, but we needed to be alert to it.

Thursday, September 5

TB had done a good outline note for the conference speech, focused on the new challenges of the millennium. DM came round and I worked at home all day trying to work up a first draft. I told the office not to bother us unless really urgent. TB called a couple of times, first so we could have another moan about GB who was seemingly still blaming me for the 10p tax story, and also to go over the drafting. I'd done some fairly good knocking copy, but I had not really come up with any great lines. The business conference coverage was overshadowed by tax and there was still a lot of 'Labour not credible' stuff. Jonathan called to say Robert Peston [*Financial Times*] had called and knew about the Harding donation, so I spoke to Harding and we agreed to bring forward the plan we had agreed. The main thing was to get it big on the broadcasts. Harding was a bit nervous about doing interviews but Fiona reckoned he was the source of the *FT* story. I doubted it. PG said tax had gone straight into the groups as a problem.

Friday, September 6

We got great coverage out of the Matthew Harding donation story. I could tell he was a bit nervous now. TB said we had to be careful not to overdo it. I agreed with Matthew that he would do an organised doorstep simply saying why he was backing New Labour. I filled in TB on my chat with JP. TB felt there was a case for keeping things in the deep freeze for a while yet. He said he had a real problem at the moment because he wanted Peter M centrally involved in the election but both GB and JP were making clear they would have nothing to do with him.

Saturday, September 7

Devolution, which had led the news all day yesterday, was a dreadful mess. It was of course massive in Scotland and George R was taking a real hammering. The whole thing had been very badly handled and the real reason for the disaster was the behaviour of the Scottish Executive. The Tories were making hay. First thing, TB and I finished today's speech over the phone. Neil came round, his basic line at the moment was that the Tories were coming at us big time and we were not really giving people any inspiration. We moaned about the Shadow Cabinet. TB's devolution speech ran OK on the news, later alongside Heseltine attacking our devolution fiasco. Fiona called CB and discovered that Carole Caplin was there. Later, CB told me she wanted to be chairman of the Bar Council, which was surely impossible. Neil stayed for dinner and when I told him how GB would not go for the Tories on the economy, he said he always had the same problem with John Smith. He said he really appreciated GB and TB when he was leader, because they would always weigh in for him if he asked. Neil was still finding it difficult, I think, and he spoke the language of support but when his real self came through, he was not terribly keen about a few things.

Sunday, September 8

TB was reasonably relaxed, but one of his constant refrains was that bad stories for the government just did not run on the BBC. I took the kids swimming them round to TB's where he was due to do a *Scotsman* interview with Peter MacMahon. MacMahon had the Scottish papers with him, filled with tales of woe and disaster. Robertson for the chop mainly, and TB defended him. He said the main question was whether we want a Scottish Parliament and how you get it, and that was what he was interested in. He also kept saying there were other issues that were being lost. Several Scots MPs called during the day with various tales of woe, ending with Tam Dalyell, who said his local party had met and agreed that the only way to deal with it was a post-legislative referendum, i.e. 'Do you agree with the Scotland Act as passed by Parliament?' He had a point, and it was not far from TB's thinking, but Tam's idea of discussion was to say something and then say it again and again with mounting incredulity unless you agreed with him. It was a long conversation. TB was scathing about David Steel [former Liberal leader], who had done an interview attacking TB's competence. Where the fuck was GB? We had Major writing 26 million letters and getting up tax and he was nowhere to be found. I had got a few words out of him for last night but this required sustained engagement and leadership from him, not a few snappy lines from me. TB had started to say 'Onwards and upwards,' I noticed, when things were getting a bit rocky. He said it to GR and Donald today. He was on good form at the moment and refusing to allow events to get him down.

Monday, September 9

The day was really just a blitz of Scotland. Glasgow then to a school in Hamilton, then the walkabout in Kirkcaldy, which went well, then to do the poster in Dundee, a good party meeting before heading to Aberdeen to do a *Road to the Manifesto* meeting. 700 people there, and TB was in really good form. His main line on the recent troubles was 'So what? We now have the policy that we want, and can defend.' He was very tough on Steel, and very tough on the Tories. TB still felt that we had real trouble with the BBC at the moment, that they were not interested in anti-Tory stories but the slightest problem for us was big news. At the party meeting, we had to fight our way through an SNP demo which was pretty nasty. Some of them were behaving like hooligans. 'Tony is a Tory' they were singing. TB handled it fine and the meeting itself was good. TB was incredibly nice to George. He knew he'd been through a bad time and TB was telling him he was a great man and if there were more like him, we would have no problem. Ann Begg [Labour candidate for Aberdeen South] in her wheelchair chaired the meeting, and TB did a terrific off-the-cuff wind-up, which went down really well and produced a standing ovation. He was really motoring and it was just a question of how long he could keep going like this. On the way out, there were lots of people pushing forward just wanting to shake his hand. He'd got back that effect he was able to engender when he became leader. He was always good when he took a debate head on after it flared up.

Fiona went to a focus group with Philip. She reckoned the public had seen through the Norma stunt. She also said there was a real loathing of Major at the moment. We had to get back with a proper attacking strategy. But today showed we could still get up a message. The *FT* splashed on Blair ruling out a higher rate tax rise, which made me think Peston was seeing too much of Jonathan. We talked about Murdoch and TB said if the *Sun* really went for him personally, he would have no option but to go for him in government. He felt JP was the reason the *Sun* was turning back against us, plus the stuff on strikes. The Tory move on strikes was utterly political. He was confident the public did not want them back after this election, and it was all there for us to win. The media were trying to balance it up, he said, because they think we may lose. He said Robin called him yesterday to say he really wanted to be more involved in planning and TB agreed. TB was wondering whether he could be in charge of attack. He accepted that GB just wasn't working with us at the moment and it was no good just hoping he would come back into the fold.

Tuesday, September 10

Things were hotting up at the TUC in Blackpool. Jon Cruddas called several times to say things were getting a bit hairy. The problem was that Blunkett seemed to be suggesting first compulsory arbitration and then new ballots if a new offer was made to workers. This was taken to mean new legislation on the issue and the unions were up in arms. As ever, the real problem was they didn't know it was coming and felt bounced. John Monks was livid. He later spoke to TB and was only slightly more emollient. Then he spoke to me and said that only TB can kill this. 'You'd better decide if you want it to be razor-hot down here, because that's the way you're going on this.' None of us could recall him ever losing his rag like this before and it bode ill. TB spoke to DB and said the worst thing now would be to back down. We got to Blackpool, and on the flight I could tell TB was getting his dander up about the unions and the way they thought they could gang up and dictate policy. We were met by Cruddas and Brendan Barber who wanted TB to rule out legislation, as DB was doing. TB refused and gave every impression that we might do it. There was a very intense and difficult conversation at the airport where TB said the worst outcome for us was a flip-flop. He made clear he thought if they hadn't overreacted, we could have managed it, but there was no way we could be seen to back down because they had got themselves up in arms. Cruddas and Barber looked really fed up. Brendan just shook his head and said I don't think we're in for a very nice evening. When we got to the hotel, Monks' body language was awful, and the mood was sour. TB did a doorstep where he did not say what they wanted him to, and the mood got even worse. I had these wankers from *Panorama* following me around, and they said TB was resiling from stories planted by spin doctors. I engaged a bit but I'd decided the best approach was to get heavy if they talked real bollocks, but basically take the mick out of their sad little obsession. The line I pushed with the industrial hacks was that there were no plans for legislation but it had not been ruled out. TB was locked away with Monks for twenty minutes before the dinner. Monks looked crestfallen. He had one of those faces that tended to show sadness and vulnerability anyway, accentuated by his walk, which was slow and a bit unconfident, but tonight he looked really fed up. Pat's view was that they all wound each other up, egged on by the labour correspondents, and they were prone to headless-chickenry. John Healey said he felt betrayed and there was a real lack of trust. I tried to explain this was cock-up not conspiracy. I warned TB the media would be full of chaos, confusion, etc., and he said that is better than backdown. I don't want any sense of backdown. *'Nil panicandum,'* he said.

Brendan and others clearly thought TB was behind all this. They were going on strike again and he said it gave us the chance to say there should be a ballot and these people were showing why there needed to be new ways of looking at this. TB said to me and Jon C 'We have to look in control even when we clearly aren't. What matters here is people realise we are serious about New Labour.' He was politely received at the dinner, but I was in and out most of the time trying to get the press in a better place. *Panorama* around again, and I accused them of lying in front of other journalists. TB had a drink late on with Monks, Barber, Healey and Jon C and the mood was a bit better but not much.

Wednesday, September 11

TB said he felt more comfortable with the arguments and I organised some media. TB's main message that we would govern for the whole country was coming through. Tim called to say it was all running well provided there was no sense of backdown. We ran into the *Panorama* team and TB gently told them they were out of order in harassing me and making it hard to do my job which was actually a lot of the time helping their colleagues. They then chased me up the stairs waving some pathetic cutting about Peter, now saying we were bullies and a threat to free speech or some such nonsense. The whole concept of the programme was ridiculous but it showed their obsession with process not policy, which was becoming a real problem. I said I simply did not believe them when they said they were looking at the Tories too. They were obsessed with me and Peter because we were doing the job professionally and they obviously preferred dealing with amateurs.

The mood with the brothers was a bit better as we left. I was briefing that one of TB's skills was the ability to turn problems into opportunities. TB was again talking about his exasperation with GB and he said the MPs were getting exasperated with the Big Three. We had pre-empted the TUC vote on a £4.26 minimum wage. The debate and the vote were predictable. Although it had been a messy couple of days, he said it was important that we had been able to show there was no question of us being in the unions' pockets, or having policy dictated and decided by them. We got back to a meeting on party conference. I was not happy that it was planned sufficiently well to make a real impact. This had to be really good, better than the last one, with more fireworks and more impact. TB wanted Shadow Cabinet members making speeches pre-conference on the challenges we faced, and then use conference to flesh out the answers.

Thursday, September 12

The main issue was Iraq and RC wanted us to distance ourselves from the US action. Peter M was back from holiday and I briefed him on the events of recent weeks and said TB was totally exasperated re GB and felt he was doing next to nothing to help. *The Times* wanted TB pictures done today and it turned out it was because some of the press were doing a story that we were planning to sever all links with the unions. TB and I agreed we would say the story was without foundation, but again he did not want the denials to be so angry and emphatic that it looked like we were in any way intimidated by the unions. It looked like a lunch or a dinner up in Blackpool. I got Sally and Jonathan to carve up a Shadow Cabinet ring round. TB said on one level this was not a problem but it would become one if there was a huge great row. I said there is bound to be. Obviously someone has said something to a selective group and it will become a huge thing. Cruddas established that Steve Byers was being named as the source. Tim tracked him down, I spoke to him and he said he had a meal with four papers but said nothing to substantiate the stories. We put out a line to that effect. Steve was in a bit of a state, very penitent, but I knew that on one level, TB would not be too fussed. But though we had just about ridden the roller coaster through the week, this had the potential to take it to a much more dangerous place. Pat and Cruddas felt there was a chance the unions would really try to screw us at conference now.

Friday, September 13

Bedlam in Blackpool. In part this was about the industrial correspondents wanting to be doing the stories that normally get nicked by the political reporters, so they were cranking it all up for all it was worth. Edmonds called for Byers to be sacked, which was easily dealt with. Monks was very critical in his closing speech, and he was entitled to be cross that the most modernising TUC for years had been effectively wiped out by us and I was worried it would store up trouble later on. The morning meeting was very unproductive and Peter M and I ended up having a huge row, which started with him thinking I was going over the top attacking the BBC, then me asking why TB and JP were having to do a party seminar and degenerated into an argument about who should be doing what, with me saying I was taking on too much of the load that should be handled at Millbank. He said it was inevitable because in the end people wanted the leader's view. We calmed down and he said the problem was he was unable to get any kind of working relationship with GB. He had sent him a memo setting out how he thought the whole thing could work, and he got back a short and snotty reply which might as well have said 'Frankly I couldn't care less what your plans are.'

I spoke to Alex Ferguson about whether he could come to conference and even maybe speak at it. He said he was happy to do a visit but if he spoke at the thing itself, the club would not be happy. He said Martin Edwards [Manchester United chairman] had expressed a bit of disquiet about him having a political profile. He said the thing is in football if you fall out too badly with your chairman, you're finished, so I don't want to push it too far. We have different politics but we get on fine, he said.

TB/JP did the party staff thing and got a fantastic reception. The whole thing was very good for morale and was definitely worth doing, as I said to Peter. TB left for [film-maker and Labour supporter] David Puttnam's place in Wiltshire where he was going to work on the conference speech. I felt there was too much Lib-Lab diddling and we just didn't need it right now so he agreed to tone it down.

On Byers, the thing was raging away but again the message was coming through that we would govern for the whole country, not vested interests. There were three schools of thought: 1. that it showed again we were not in control of events; 2. that we were divided and divisions were always harmful; 3. that it was all part of some grand master plan to show TB was not in the pocket of the unions.

Alan Clark called to say he was going for Tunbridge Wells and had commissioned a poll in which the Tories were 43, we were 32 and the Libs 18. He said he was amazed, thinking we would have been a poor third and his confidence in his own judgement had gone.

He said TB was doing well but the party was the problem. He said Central Office were 'totally fucking spasticated from top to bottom'. He said there were three different camps, all split on how they should be campaigning and they were wasting millions.

Saturday, September 14

Byers was big, and we were only just getting away with the notion that this may have been part of some calculated strategy. It was actually a bit of a mess but the underlying message did come through. We just didn't need it to run on and on. Bill Morris was excellent, clearly not wanting to get it up as a big divisive thing. TB's concern was the shambles element, people thinking if this was what they're like in opposition, what would they be like in government? I briefed the Sundays that we had not gone to Blackpool looking for a row but once it happened it became an opportunity to show we would govern for the whole country. We were not going to get a good press though, and I brought forward announcing Bob Gavron's half-million donation. I agreed a statement with Bob. However, we had another self-made problem on the way. Tim had drafted an article for Kim Howells [Labour MP] in which he said the word socialism should be 'humanely phased out'. I had seen the draft, made some changes but not all of them went through and it was sent to the *Sunday Times* with that line in it. It was just what we didn't need as we were going into the weekend trying to calm things a bit. Also Blunkett had briefed Tom Baldwin on the *Sunday Telegraph* that he had rapped Byers' knuckles, which wasn't very helpful. Every Sunday broadsheet was intending to lead on a basically negative Labour story. Fiona and I went out for dinner but ended up having a big row because the phone never stopped and I spent most of the evening on the fucking pavement outside.

Sunday, September 15

Another day of damage limitation. The BBC, needless to say, was going wild with the Kim Howells stuff, which was getting totally OTT coverage and Kim appeared on *Frost* to give it legs, despite us suggesting he now shuts up. He's such a laugh though that I find it very hard to give him a hard time. Glenys was on reviewing the papers with Bernard Ingham who said we were a total shambles and if he was Blair's press secretary, he would shoot himself. Glenys said Alastair is not going to shoot himself, to which Frost said he might if Burnley were relegated. I was getting mentioned far too much on these programmes and of course *Panorama* was not going to help. I got

Gerald Kaufman on to *The World This Weekend* to try to do a calming job re Howells/Byers, and he did it brilliantly. Gerald is a grown-up, and someone who can make a point with real force and wit. I told TB he should drop Gerald, Michael Foot and Bill Morris a line because all three had been voices of calm amid the headless-chickenry. GB was meant to do the *Today* programme tomorrow but said he had flu suddenly. We agreed TB would do it. Had a heavy session with TB later, told him I was fed up having every day taken over with clearing up other people's mess.

Monday, September 16

TB was still at Puttnam's place, really charged up again, but the BBC were for the moment obsessed with this debate about the word socialism and we were still unable to get things on to policy. GB was worrying that we were putting the emphasis too much on consumption not investment. TB said again he was worried I was doing too much, not working properly with GB/Peter and needed to delegate more. I said I would be able to delegate more if GB and Peter were properly engaged, because then they would be sharing out the delegation. It was a bloody nightmare at the moment. But then came something that illustrates the problem. There he is, telling me I'm doing too much. Then he takes a call from RC who wants to talk about his speech on Thursday and TB says 'I'll ask Alastair to help you write it.' Unbelievable. Then he comes off the phone and I say oh thanks, just add to the bloody workload, and he says it won't take you much time, just knock him out a speech and make him feel involved. Then he starts telling me to delegate again. I know, I said, I'll get Rory and Calum to do Robin's speech for him. TB said en route to the LIFFE [London International Financial Futures and Options Exchange] speech that he felt relaxed and strong and he thought it was really important he didn't let the others drag his mood down. The LIFFE top brass appeared to be the usual mix of working-class boys made good and upper-class wankers who would have been driving buses if they had gone to different schools.

Tuesday, September 17

I knocked out a few pages for RC's speech on Thursday. A big pro-TB, pro-New Labour message and I was interested to see how much of it he took. In the end he made just a couple of small changes. No doubt he had picked up on TB's irritation with GB and was going into an onside phase. I spent the rest of the day working on the conference speech, but I was still struggling to get killer lines. I called

TB at one point for a chat to see if I could get something off him to get me going, and he said he was writing an article in response to a cartoon in the *Guardian*. I said you're doing what? Have you gone mad? He said that a lot of the critiques against us started in this way and we had to challenge them. Tony, I said, please don't write an article in response to a cartoon. People will think you are bonkers. Fiona and I had dinner with Tessa [Jowell] and David [Mills] and I sensed they were worried at where this Berlusconi thing was going. David was adamant he had done nothing wrong but Italian courts were very different to ours and God knows where it would lead.

Wednesday, September 18

Major was on *Today* and I thought was particularly poor. His new buzzword was the 'morality' of a low tax, small state. As Andy Marr said, it was a bog standard economic speech with the word morality in it. It was clearly a response to the idea of TB being a Christian Socialist, but it was not at all clear to me what he was talking about. Peter M persuaded TB to do the *World at One* to respond and engage in the debate. I was reluctant at first, but was won over and TB was really on form again. Everyone upstairs was commenting on how good he was at the moment. I called him and asked to be put through to the New Labour Cartoon Rebuttal Unit. He laughed but said we did have to tackle the underlying arguments because they were bollocks. The left was always a whisker away from making the charge of betrayal, which would then be used against us by the right. Just after lunch Nick Hewer arrived in his red Merc to drive me out to Brentwood where I was going to see Alan Sugar. Nick had his own PR company and did stuff for [Alan] Sugar. He said he was worried, and so was Alan, that he would be open to ridicule if he suddenly came out for Labour. It was impossible to know whether these business guys were doing this out of conviction, or because they had a genuine conversion, or whether they thought there was something in it for them, like an honour, and of course all you could go on was judgement because these things never got said. But I was in no doubt Sugar was one of the few businessmen reasonably well known by a fair number of real people, and was a greater political catch than most of them. Nick said Sugar was not comfortable with being well known.

I met Sugar and we went through to the boardroom. It was less luxurious than I had imagined, comfortable and convenient. He was more nervous than I thought he would be. He was also not naturally articulate but one of those people who did not communicate by words alone. He said he liked Tony and he bought the idea of New Labour.

He thought the Tories had lost the plot and the country needed a change. He liked Thatcher, supported privatisation, but they had wasted the money. They should be spending it on health and education and tackling crime. I get the feeling about Blair that he understands ordinary people, he said, but he understands business too. I've met him, I like him and I think he is worth a shot. He said he was not worried about the unions because they had no rights now anyway. I said that was the kind of statement that I might prefer he didn't make. He said his main worry was that he would be labelled a hypocrite. I said I was confident we could avoid that. The most important thing was how the story first entered the public domain. If it did so on our terms, properly planned, and with impact, we would be in control from the start, and we would stay in control. He said he didn't want to be seen jumping on a bandwagon. I said we would do everything we could to minimise the flak, and worry the Tories that if they really went for him, it would lead to others coming our way. I said we should have a proper discussion of his views and his reasons for switching. On the basis of that I would draw up a core script which we could use for briefings and articles, and then maybe he would do *Frost*. He looked a bit panicked at that and said he was not great on telly. He said he wanted to wait until the election. I said that WOULD look like bandwagon jumping and my idea was to do it before conference this year. We then had a more immediate thing to sort – TB opening Spurs' new training ground on Saturday. Kilfoyle called to say GB and DB had had a shouting match because DB believed, probably rightly, that Whelan was the cause of stuff against him in the *Independent*.

Thursday, September 19

RC briefing went well and he called to say 'We' (!!) must be very pleased with OUR coverage, like we were some kind of double act. I left early for TB's but he was running late, even though Monks was waiting to see him. I listened to JP on the radio and although he seemed to raise the decibel level every time he said 'socialism', he was fine, very pro TB and by and large on-message. TB and I were both beginning to panic a bit that though we had lots of good material for the conference speech, we didn't yet have the purple patches that really connect, and he was looking to me to work on that. I missed the morning meeting but Peter said GB was rude to him and he might as well not have turned up.

TB was doing an interview with Mary Riddell [journalist] and we discussed beforehand how he should try to open up a bit more on the personal front. People wanted to know more about what he was, where he came from as a person, who and what shaped him. He said, I hate doing all that stuff, people hanging their lives out for others to stare at. I said it was important because some people out there would only connect with us through him and his personality, and until they had got that they would not even get near the whole policy area. He did his usual policy stuff with Mary, and was on good form and when she started to push him on the personal front, he started hesitantly on the kids. Then she asked him if he ever felt stalked by tragedy – dad's stroke, mother's death, John Smith's death, and he went through each of them and how he felt and when he talked about his mum he really opened up, and I found it quite moving. I had never really heard him talk about his mother in such detail before and there was a real naturalness and warmth in his words, and a look in his eyes that was half fond, half sad and when he had finished talking about her, he just did a little nod and a sigh and then looked out of the window. I said to him afterwards I'd never realised he was so close to his mum because he had never really opened up like that before, even in private. He said she was a wonderful woman and he still felt guided by her. What would she make of where you are now? I asked. Heaven knows, he said. I think she would be anxious for me, but proud. Dad is always saying I wish she was here to see this, she would be so proud. He said he hated talking about this kind of thing in interviews, because there were things he felt should stay personal. He said the thing that his mother's death had given him above all was a sense of urgency, the feeling that life is short, it can be cut even shorter, and you should pack in as much as you can while you're here, and try to make a difference.

Friday, September 20

TB was working at home, and so was I, ringing each other every hour or so to bounce ideas and lines and passages. We were nowhere near yet. He said how did the stuff you did last year on the flag come? I said I wrote it on holiday after watching a military ceremony. He said well take another holiday if that's what it takes. I spoke to Anji about the GB/JP/Peter M situation. I think one of the reasons TB is quite chipper at the moment is that he has just kind of reconciled that they are not going to work together very well and he'll just have to work around the situation as best he can. He seems to have decided mentally that there is only so much he can do about it so there is no point losing sleep. JP is there, has huge strengths but can be really hard to work with, so let's look to the strengths and manage the rest. GB is brilliant but difficult so let's allow him to decide when he wants to be brilliant and work around him when he's difficult. Peter M wants to be more engaged but feels rebuffed so let's make him feel more involved and get him to take the same attitude to GB.

GB was launching the result of the child benefit review. I had said yesterday I didn't think it should be called an interim report, because it just flares it all up without resolution but apart from that I had had very little to do with it. We had decided to let GB get on and do it. After the press conference TB asked me how it was, and I said I don't know. On the speech, I finally got going and did a good passage on morality and on 'Labour's coming home'.

Saturday, September 21

I took the boys up to TB's because they wanted to come to the opening of the new Tottenham Hotspur training ground. Sugar was his usual gruff self. He took us through for a cup of tea, did some fairly half-hearted introductions but was not very comfortable. I wondered if in fact he was very shy. He and TB did little speeches, TB did the opening, then Pat Jennings [Tottenham goalkeeping coach] got TB to do a little kickabout with Ian Walker [goalkeeper], who for some reason he called Tim. I said to Walker that if he let in a few goals there was an OBE in it for him.

We got back to TB's and DM and Peter H joined us for lunch. We went through all the various bits [of the conference speech] we had all been working on. My worry now was policy, or lack of really driving policy ideas. Jonathan and Geoffrey Norris had met George Walden [Conservative MP] to discuss his ideas of getting grammar and private schools more integrated into the state system. I said I didn't see how we could go down that road without a huge conflagration in the party. The charge of backdoor selection was too easy. TB said 'I'm with George Walden on selection.' DM looked aghast. So was I, and we launched into a furious argument. I couldn't work out if he was just being devil's advocate, really trying to find how far he could go, or whether he meant it. He said when it came to education, DM and I were just a couple of old tankies [communists].

Sunday, September 22

I went for a long walk with Calum and got a few more lines. My favourite was 'The first wonder of the world is the mind of a child.' I was getting some good stuff on the concept of the team/community as well. And I was trying to play around with the 'Give me the child at seven and I'll give you the man at seventy,' with something like

'Give me the education system that's thirty-fifth in the world today, and I'll give you the economy that's thirty-fifth in the world tomorrow.'

Monday, September 23

I was out on the heath at 6, desperate for a bit of inspiration to get the creative juices going. I'd read all the drafts so far and we had lots of good stuff, and a good argument. But TB was right, we needed the real purple stuff. Anji called to say that JP was causing trouble over the idea of TB being alone on stage when he spoke. He was saying it was daft, if we were meant to be showing TB had the party with him. But televisually it was far better to have TB up there on his own, but JP was already calling round the NEC to stir. The phone kept going, I wasn't motoring so I went for another walk, then came back for a bath. TB called me and said he'd just gone back over last year's and he said the ending was so good it will be very hard to better it. We had all these notions – modernisation, team, potential, One Nation – all kicking around and it was just a question of getting them into a driving theme and then having the lines and the moments that really brought it alive. We had the argument sorted, which was good, but we still didn't have a speech.

Tuesday, September 24

I left early for Paddington and worked all the way to Devon on the speech. I was met by Frank (Sue Nye and Gavyn Davies' driver), a nice man who talked all the way to Baggy Point. TB had done some good work and I spent the first couple of hours basically knitting the two drafts. After lunch, TB and I went for a long walk along the top of the hill, looking down on the sea. He had said that he wanted to badge the coming years as an era, and we knocked around a few ideas, the age of this, the age of that, but nothing really worked. On the drive to the train, we went past some of the places we'd been to with Neil after the '92 election when we met up in what was one of the gloomiest holidays we'd ever had. We went past the skittle alley at Braunton where someone came up to Neil and said 'I voted Tory and now I wished I hadn't.' I said Neil was very nice to him. 'I'd have killed him,' said TB. On the train back, for reasons which were not entirely clear, we both got a terrible fit of the giggles when we were pretending to interview each other about our assessments of the Shadow Cabinet, and going OTT in saying what we really thought. There was a woman further down the restaurant car who looked at us as though we were completely bonkers. 'We're allowed to laugh,' I said when she walked by.

Wednesday, September 25

Liz [Lloyd] came round and we worked at home all day. TB said the NEC was pretty grim, though at least JP was being supportive and helpful. But the issue of whether TB was on the stage alone or not was reopened. Tom Sawyer had caved in to JP, Diana Jeuda [Union of Shop, Distributive and Allied Workers] was all worked up apparently and TB said he wasn't fussed, so the whole thing got reopened again. Margaret Wall [Manufacturing, Science and Finance Union] said we should have the whole NEC behind him on the stage. At first nobody would second the idea, but seemingly Clare came in, silly cow. TB said the Shadow Cabinet was more friendly and productive, but he was a bit alarmed there appeared to be so little support for doing anything to Jeremy Corbyn for inviting Gerry Adams to launch his book at the Commons.

Thursday, September 26

The splash in *The Times*, and a smaller story in the *Sun*, said that GB had told the Shadow Cabinet he was considering a 50p tax rate. He had said no such thing and as far as TB was concerned, it was a non-starter. But we were pretty confident GB himself had given the story to Phil Webster [*The Times*]. It was his way of cuddling up to the party before conference.

I was due to work at home, but TB called and said he thought I should go up with him to Totteridge. He was going to be working on the speech at Michael Levy's, so we set off, and I could tell he was going into the low phase he always seems to get before a big speech. It was all terrible, he wasn't confident in the argument, we had no great lines or moments, blah di blah di blah. I said it was not as bad as that, we just needed to work on it. Philip G had taken the last draft and tested sections of it, and he felt we had gone backwards. I said for God's sake don't tell TB that. He's already losing confidence in what we've got. Philip told me that the Phoney Tony line was beginning to break through. All in all it was a bit of a disaster. Liz and I had successfully married TB's Devon draft and the latest AC/DM draft and it was OK without being brilliant. He was agonising about whether we had a central argument. Then he would go to work in the sitting room while we worked in the dining room and he would come through with a few pages he'd done and at one point it was absolute drivel. Liz was tearing her hair out as she typed it, saying he can't say all this, it doesn't mean anything. There was always this point in the speech preparation where he slightly lost the plot and I was hoping to God this was it and that we would be fine by the time we got to Blackpool. I said to TB he was just producing a stream of consciousness. He had also taken out most of the really personal moments in the speech and we had to fight to get them back in. I sometimes think he would be happier giving a lecture than a political speech. The two of us went for a walk around Michael's garden and he was really low. He said he was beginning to panic and lose his nerve. I said by Tuesday night he will have delivered a great speech and all this nerves stuff is part of the process. But we have to work on it as it is, not start from scratch again.

The *Sun* had done an article on Jonathan asking Rory Bremner for jokes, and I got a call from Roy Hudd saying 'the lads' were disappointed, and didn't want to do stuff. I explained this was Jonathan on his own initiative and I was really sorry but I could tell he was fed up. We had dinner up at Michael's and at one point TB said maybe he should just stand up there and do the speech extempore, no notes. We were so down on ourselves at this point that I found myself saying what a great idea it was. I even started to phone round e.g. Peter M, PG to see what they thought. They rightly assumed it was a way of running away from the fact we didn't like the speech as it was. But I was reasonably keen and I did him a note setting out ten points why it would be a good idea. The main point for me was the sense of drama it would bring to the occasion. It would help with the Phoney Tony stuff if he was seen to be speaking from the heart.

Friday, September 27

After four hours' sleep I was back at the speech, working on a new beginning and a new ending. Peter H called with a very good note on how to make the week belong to JP as a means of getting him on board more long term. It was a clever idea. I called Rosie and went through it with her, and then spoke to John. I said the key to it was that he did something surprisingly New Labour, that really made people sit up and think, and on the back of it the mood music and the body language would be very pro JP, TB/JP team. JP and I were back on good terms after the recent fallout and he was up for it. He asked me for help on his speech and I said as soon as Tuesday was out of the way, I'd work on his with the same intensity. He also asked if we could discuss something personal. He said rumours had been doing the rounds about a personal story involving him, and he had found out what it was. It was the fact that Pauline had had a child when she was sixteen, which she had given up for adoption, and never seen since. He said he didn't know how to tell Pauline the rumour was around, and she'd be devastated if it all came out and

it was made to look bad for him. I said she should come to conference as normal, and we can just keep tabs on it. If it broke, or looked
like it was going to, we would get TB up condemning the way that
families of public figures were targeted and make it a press issue not
a JP issue.

Roy Hudd sent through some jokes which cheered me up no end.
I'd assumed from last night's call that he would not be helping but
he sent through some good material. TB was worried about what JP
had told me, not for any political effect but how it would effect
JP. He agreed he would go out on the offensive if it happened. The
speech was coming together. He had gone from the near suicidal of
yesterday to something approaching manic today, full of vim, firing
out ideas, saying obvious things as though they were great revelations,
asking for this, that and the other and saying he was a lot happier. I
wonder if all politicians at this level go through this process for every
big speech. I stayed there for dinner and CB was very frosty because
there had been an argument about whether André the hairdresser
should go to Blackpool.

Saturday, September 28

Grace was playing up because she knew both of us were going to be
away for the week, and she wasn't happy. TB was in the bath when
I got there which was always a bad sign. It meant we'd be rushing.
He then discovered that CB had sent to the dry-cleaners the suit that
had in his pocket his lucky ribbon Sam McCluskie [general secretary
of the National Union of Seamen] gave to him, which he showed me
on the day of Sam's funeral. But he calmed down and said right, let's
get down to it. I had been up at 6 to draft his words for the youth
event he was doing later and we agreed those. The problem was we
didn't have a strong story to take us through the Sundays and into
the start of the week. Then David Blunkett called to say he'd heard
the *Observer* were leading on Robin C saying New Labour was in
danger of forgetting the poor – bang on message for Central Office
and the betrayal thesis. Peter M was in Blackpool and I asked him to
get on top of it while TB and I travelled up by train.

Liz [Lloyd] and I were working late in room 223 and after 11, all
of a sudden TB storms in, livid, having caught the eleven o'clock
news and he says 'What is wrong with these fucking people? Do they
have a death wish?' He meant Robin, whose words were going fairly
big. 'It is all about how the party sees them as they strut around the
conference, and got fuck all to do with whether we ever actually get
the power needed to do anything for the country.' He said what drove

him really mad was that it was all playing into a Tory strategy. 'Their plan is to say I'm unprincipled and all I'm interested in is middle-class votes, so what does Robin do but come along and reinforce their message? It is weak and pathetic.' He was really storming and eventually I thought I should bring the mood back a little and did a big calm down, calm down number, some of us are trying to work on the speech. The storm passed very quickly and we chatted a bit more about the speech before he went off back to his room. I found Robin downstairs by the press office. 'Another fine mess,' I said. 'Fuck off, Alastair, I have been totally traduced on this.' Eventually we got a transcript and to be fair to Robin, he had been. The words had been distorted through selective use. He was genuinely pissed off so we went upstairs and together knocked out a statement for instant release, along with the transcript showing he had been traduced. RC was in full 'pause and sigh' mode, and playing really hurt. But of course on one level it wouldn't harm his street cred for the week.

TB had been to a couple of functions with JP, and Cherie said there was a lot more warmth for JP and he was of course milking it. I said to TB that the worst-case scenario was a sense at the end of the week that the Big Three were offside to greater or lesser degrees and he was isolated and therefore New Labour weakened. It was not hard to see how that might happen. JP was always just one moment away from explosion, which is why we had to build him up through the week. RC was clearly in a position to be identified as being offside, whatever the denials. And if GB combined continued disengagement with an Old Labour speech on Monday, it could all get tricky for TB. I also learned second-hand via Liz that GB had done a 'Labour's coming home' section in his speech for Monday. It was a bit of a coincidence that within a day of them seeing a full draft, we then hear that. I suppose it's possible they thought of it, in that it is a fairly obvious thing with all the football hype we've been having, but I was still very suspicious, and we would have to get it removed from GB's speech. Ed Miliband said GB was very loath not to use that section. I said I saw our 'Labour's coming home' section as possibly the single most important passage for the tabloids and there was no way GB could pre-empt it. I could tell we were in for a battle over it. I suggested to TB that he invite RC up to his room for a drink, not least to remind him it was there that RC told him a couple of years ago this week that getting rid of Clause 4 would split the party and possibly destroy his leadership. He should tell him he was wrong then and he was wrong again now in saying that pursuit of middle-class support meant any weakening of commitment to the poor. Sally said she spent two hours with Clare who was totally offside, not least when she was held up by security and her 'Don't you know who I am?' act didn't appear to impress.

Sunday, September 29

JP was doing *On the Record* and I went up to see him and said this was the moment he could really make an impact by surprising people, and being New not Old Labour. After the recent ups and downs, he was totally up for being seen to be onside, and I said if he and TB worked in tandem, the others would move in and by the end of the week people would be stressing the unity of the whole thing and the Tories would be scared stiff. I could see he was up for it and instead of the usual round and about conversation, in which he needed to go over every point in detail, he just went for it. I said you need to say something that people don't expect you to say, like Labour is the party of enterprise, the party of ambition, the party of aspiration, the party of change. He did it, and it was a real barnstormer and at the end of it people watching in the press office burst into a round of applause.

Still arguing with GB over 'Labour's coming home', and he said he was really pissed off about it. I said it was central to TB's speech and I saw it as probably one of the main headlines out of it, whereas in GB's speech it would not have the same impact. I didn't mean it to come out like it did and I could tell that he hated it. It was as if I was saying because TB was leader he would get more out of it than GB, which was of course true but he didn't like it. I said that the line was more central to the overall strategy of TB's speech than it was to GB's, which should surely be getting the focus on economy/social justice, rather than an overall political positioning. I don't think he liked that point either but eventually he reluctantly agreed, and made clear we owed him one.

There was a bit of a news vacuum so we needed to get going on briefing. Fiona arrived which was nice, but she said CB was being very tense and difficult, and she thought Lyndsey, CB's sister, was winding her up the whole time. Fiona said she was shocked by how the pair of them were on these alternative medicine pills, and talked about them the whole time. Fiona ended up having an up-and-downer with CB re Carole, and saying all this alternative stuff would become a problem if it got out there publicly. The Tories were briefing that they were going to play JM as the Brixton Boy up against the Fettes schoolboy so I briefed one or two on the idea of them launching class war as the last throw of the dice.

The BBC were in full hype mode on *Panorama*'s programme on spin doctors but they made a classic mistake, responding to our pre-emptive stuff by saying they had a big surprise in there which would justify the whole idea, but it never came. We had basically fucked them over, and won the battle of expectations so that when the programme came to be shown, the overwhelming reaction was 'What was the point of that?' When I went back upstairs the office said it was crap. GB had sent round his latest draft for tomorrow and 'Labour's coming home' was back in there. I called Ed Balls who said GB still wanted to do it, and if we wanted to change that, TB would have to speak to him. This was fucking ridiculous. I told Charlie W to get GB to call TB. He came back half an hour later. CB and I were both in the room and TB said to him the same things I had said – that it was more central to his speech than to GB's, that it was an important part of the ending and he'd be grateful, etc., etc., etc. But it was a real struggle, and when GB finally agreed, he just slammed the phone down and left TB looking at the receiver and shaking his head. 'I can't believe we can end up having a shouting match about a line in a speech,' he said. He said it was tragic what had happened between them. 'I sometimes feel he absolutely hates me.'

He read GB's draft and said he was trying to do a leader's speech. TB went to the conference and to be fair to GB, his speech went down a storm, though it was a bit Old Labour. I went down to the hall to get a feel of things but I was being photographed the whole time because of the *Panorama* thing so I went straight back and Liz and I worked through another draft. I went downstairs for dinner while the *Panorama* thing was on. We joined Glenys and I was chatting away with Sinead Cusack [actress] who was very flirtatious and quite a laugh. I'd drawn up another overnight briefing plan and Tim was briefing the papers while I did Oakley and Brunson who both did decent pieces. *Panorama* was widely felt to be useless. I started to watch a video and gave up after five minutes. It was a not very well executed hatchet job but I couldn't be bothered with it.

TB was not very happy about GB's speech. Robin C asked me what I thought of it. I said I never say anything bad about Labour MPs. 'Ah, that bad, eh?' he said, looking very happy. TB was doing a few receptions and when he came back he suddenly said he wasn't happy with the speech and we would have to start from scratch. Oh don't be so ridiculous. He tore off his clothes, got himself a dressing gown, then sat down on the sofa with the look of a man who had just been told the world was about to end, and it was his fault. I said the speech was fine. 'I'll have to do it myself,' he said. 'Leave me now and I'll call you when I've done it.' One year, we'll get a decent speech without all this nonsense. He called us in at 2.30. He hadn't changed that much. It was almost there.

Tuesday, October 1

Up by 6 and in to see TB who was already at the table in the window, and in full flight. He had decided on the 'age of progress' and 'achievement' as a driving theme, which everyone but him thought was crap, and the first thing to do was persuade him to go for one or the other, and achievement it was. It was more aspirational and more in tune with the way the policy sections were done. We had to get the speech pretty much done by 11 so that he could do autocue rehearsal and we just about did it. I was running up and down the corridor the whole time as he kept wanting reassurance that this didn't need changing, that didn't need changing. It actually hung together quite well. I could tell TB was emotional and so was I. I felt emotionally drained and went to my room, sat down and started crying. Fiona came in and was worried something terrible had happened. I said it's fine, I'm just totally drained. A lot hung on the speech and it really had to be good. The ending was better now, as long as he paced it right. We got to the Winter Gardens and he paced up and down while they were playing the video about him.

TB started slowly, and I was trying to work out whether people would be able to spot how nervous he was. The jokes went fine and it was clear the audience was with him. The middle section flagged a bit. He got a huge cheer for Dunblane. He did the commitments well. 'Labour's coming home' got such a good reception first time, better than I thought it would, which meant that the crescendo effect never happened. And the ending became a bit complicated, like there were too many endings within the ending. But the mood was good and they were with him. Some people thought it was tacky to use Dunblane in the film, but as a performance it went down a storm. The buzz around the place was terrific. The general feeling was that it was a government-in-waiting speech. Back at the hotel both TB and I weren't really happy. We had worked so hard at the ending and it wasn't as good as it should have been. He was a bit down, despite everyone saying it was terrific. He said, sometimes I think they don't like me that much. They certainly don't like me like they like JP. I said it was a different kind of thing. JP produced an emotional response because of his passion and his history. But they see you as a leader, they think you're smart and you're the key to winning. It is not a bad combination.

Several MPs told me their constituency phones were jammed all night with supporters and people wanting to join the party, so the speech had certainly broken through. We did the morning media rounds and he was very up and confident. I felt absolutely shagged out. We had been working pretty flat out on the speech for days, more than thirty drafts and maybe three to four hours' sleep a day for the last week. The BBC had some story about our pagers being intercepted which was a bit of a worry. The one they were excited about was Anji paging me to say DO SOMETHING ABOUT HIS HAIR!! But if they had access to all the messages of all the office and the other frontbenchers that was potentially a real problem. We got advice from Derry and the party lawyers and it seems they were not covered by the Data Protection Act.

The *Mirror* lunch was the usual rather embarrassed waste of time. I did at least get Montgomery to agree David Bradshaw could come to us from November 1. I went back to the hotel and tried to start working on some stuff for JP's speech, whilst the pensions debate was on TV. But I was knackered and needed a sleep to get some energy back.

I went out with CB to some of the receptions later. We were getting on a lot better now the speech was out of the way. There was a buzz that Phil Webster had a big story and did I know what it was. I didn't. I called Phil who said he was writing that we had ruled out joining the single currency in the first wave. I was taken aback but said nothing either to stand it up or knock it down. I mentioned it to TB who said he feared he might be the source. He had kind of intimated that to Murdoch when he last saw him, and he guessed Murdoch had fed it into the paper. He said he had not been definitive but he reckoned that could easily be the route. I made the mistake of mentioning it to GB, without the TB/Murdoch bit. He said his first suspicion was Cook, but I could tell by the look in his eye that he thought it was me, and that I was telling him directly as a cover. He had suspicion written all over him. He said the rest of Europe will be really pissed off. He and TB had a session about it and we agreed we had to try to kill it. I said the line should be this was *The Times* pushing their own Eurosceptic agenda and no such decision had been taken. It was going to sour TB/GB relations even more though. We went out for dinner with Richard and Penny Stott. Richard told me about the time [George] Bush [Snr] said it was 'not over till the fat lady sings' so the Democrats hired a fat singer to follow him around. We needed a bit more humour in our campaigns. I said later to TB maybe in JP's speech he should say old and new have come together. TB said fine, as long as it's clear the new has won the battle of ideas.

Thursday, October 3

Met Alex Ferguson who was coming to do a school visit with TB. He went through some of the sponsorship deals the Man U players were involved in, saying the money was becoming unbelievable. He said he was up for helping us but he had to be a bit careful with the club, and also maybe some of the fans wouldn't want him to be too political. TB came out and did some penalties and the best shots were a load of kids whacking balls at Alex and TB in goal. Jonathan, Fiona and I went to Harry Ramsden's [fish and chip restaurant] to talk about Number 10 planning. We had to start getting some decisions on e.g. where they were going to live. Rod Lyne [private secretary] had said to Jonathan he didn't think they should live there. Jonathan said there would be some Civil Service resistance to him and me.

Friday, October 4

The office in the hotel was a total tip. Smelly and dirty, and everyone seemed to have a hangover. It was definitely time to get home, but I was still working with JP, which was pretty exhausting. Late last night, with Pauline asleep next door, he had been literally bellowing the speech out to me, Rosie, Brian Wilson, Rodney Bickerstaffe and one or two others, as if we were a real conference audience. Today I did a bit more on the old and new coming together, and on tough choices, and he was absolutely fine about it. We then had a meeting on how to handle the Tories next week, with the press already gearing up for trouble. TB did a round of broadcast interviews, pushing the line that this was the week the party and the public saw that New Labour is a reality. Peter Cunnah of D:Ream [writer and singer of the song that would define the 1997 election, 'Things Can Only Get Better'] came up to see TB and I then took him to the press room to do some interviews saying why he was backing us.

We set off for the helicopter ride back via Bury, Telford, Northampton and Harlow. It was brilliantly organised, in each place landing where the event took place, quick speech, quick pictures and out and the reception was terrific everywhere. There was a real buzz around TB now, and I sensed we had made a big breakthrough this week.

I got back to lots of messages to call Alan Rusbridger. He wanted to send to JM, TB, Paddy Ashsdown and Betty Boothroyd a memo from [David] Willetts when he was a [Conservative] whip which suggested the government conspired to stop Neil Hamilton being properly investigated.¹ Alan sent them letters 'on Privy Council terms', no less, and was unutterably pompous about the whole thing. TB did not particularly want to get involved, and I said to Alan that TB was the Leader of the Opposition, not some rentaquote.

Saturday, October 5
There was a great poll in the *Telegraph* showing TB's ratings had rocketed after the speech. The press generally was excellent, both for JP and for the party as a whole. I had a nice day with the kids, then got the papers which were dreadful for the Tories. The press had basically decided their conference was going to be a sleaze fest.

Sunday, October 6
Three of the heavies splashed on the Willetts memo, which was a pretty grim start for them. Frost gave Major a pretty easy ride. He didn't press him on the detail and JM tried to do a little smear number of TB over Concorde.² There was something unbelievably small and unpleasant about him when he did that kind of thing. It showed up his big weakness – he had no agenda for the country so he became rather nasty and personal and did things best left to people down the food chain. The *Observer* led on a story that [Peter] Temple-Morris [Conservative MP] was going to support a Blair government. JM said it was obvious we had planted the story and Temple-Morris appeared to be saying the same. I called him to assure him I had talked about the possibility of defections but named no names. The Tories were arriving with sleaze and Europe splits the only shows in town. I almost felt sorry for them.

Monday, October 7
The press was grim for the Tories. Sleaze and Europe. [Lord] McAlpine [former Conservative deputy chairman] was saying he would defect to the Referendum Party.

Tuesday, October 8
After a couple of quiet days I was pretty much back in the swing and beginning to worry about the South Africa trip. It had the potential

---

¹ In 1994 the *Guardian* alleged that Conservative MPs Neil Hamilton and Tim Smith accepted cash to ask questions in Parliament. The Conservatives sought to delay a report into the allegations until after the election.
² The Tories were trying to create a scandal around TB's Concorde fare being paid by lobbyists, but he had in fact travelled as part of an all-party delegation on behalf of the government.

to be terrific for us but we heard that Mandela was ill. Then word came through he would definitely be OK to see TB on Friday so we brought forward plans for departure. He was quite keen on making 'the Open Society' a theme, as a way in to doing the basic New Labour message. Seemingly the idea came from George Soros.

Jonathan and DD were working on a joint TB/Paddy letter to JM saying they didn't believe [Sir Gordon] Downey was equipped to investigate the Hamilton/Willetts situation. We were pushing for a Tribunal of Inquiry but DD was worried it was too easily dismissed.

A key meeting on women at Millbank. Peter M, Peter H, Sally M, Anji, Jo Moore, Deborah Mattinson, Tessa [Jowell] and Janet Anderson. We agreed we had to do more to get through to women who were not immersed in the political debate. We should be looking for far more major tie-ups with the [women's] magazines. There was definitely a gender gap and a lot of it was about language. They just felt alienated from the language of modern politics. The family was still seen as a Tory area, and there was no reason why we should not swing that right round but it required a lot of work with people who were not normally listening. We had to go out and reach them.

TB called to say Paddy had told him Peter Thurnham was defecting from the Tories to the Lib Dems at the weekend and Paddy would welcome my advice on how to handle it.

Wednesday, October 9

Thatcher was getting a lot of coverage backing JM which on one level was good for them. But TB felt it was ultimately a bad image for JM to be seen to need her support. I also felt she was doing the absolute minimum and between the lines you could read a bit of undermining. But yesterday had not been bad for them, they had done some heavy overnight trailing of anti-union laws, so they were in better shape than we wanted them to be.

I was working through a plan for the Thurnham defection and sent a note through to his office. I got a message to call Paddy who said he wanted to do it Saturday for Sunday. I said we could build all manner of things around it. The key was to use it to detract from any sense that the Tories had ended the week well.

I went up to see TB who was about to do an interview with Lynda Lee-Potter [*Mail*]. He was with Ros the nanny discussing whether Nicky should go to Cardinal Vaughan [Roman Catholic comprehensive, former grammar school] or the Oratory. He was wondering if it might be better for Nicky to go to a different school and so get out of Euan's shadow a bit. I wondered if the real reason was that he had realised the Oratory was a mistake, not least because of the profile it gave McIntosh.

Lunch with Brendan Barber to try to get things in a better place after the recent hoo-has. He said TB's ruthlessness was a weakness as well as a strength. He was strong and forceful and tended to get his way, and often for the right reasons, but he didn't take enough care with relationships. He asked for my help or advice re the unions getting a more positive profile and I said there were lots of things they were doing that were good but they were lost because the big boys just saw themselves as being in competition for coverage and that meant whacking us. I liked Brendan but he and John [Monks] were both too prone to seeing the worst and being defensive. They had to have a clearer strategy and fight for it not against us but with the others.

I got back for the Lee-Potter interview. She was pushing him to be very personal and he hated doing it, but he was again terrific talking about his mother. He saw JP afterwards and I interrupted with a story being put to us by the *Mail* that he and Major had agreed not to mention Dunblane at the conferences. News to us.

Thursday, October 10

The Tories got another good press but TB still felt they were doing the minimum. They were not breaking through sufficient to really turn things. We had a few hours on the plane to South Africa. TB and I had been upgraded to first class. Some bloke complained when Anji came up from Club to see how we were. What a twat. I was working on a crime section, TB on economic stuff, and we got some half-decent work done.

Friday, October 11

Cape Town. I woke at 5, the plane landed at 6, and TB was fairly chipper about the work we'd done on the way out, and thought we had the makings of a decent speech for the business event. We went off to the residence, which was in a beautiful setting, and like a very comfortable Home Counties six-bedroomed house. TB had a kip while Jonathan and I worked on knocking what we had done on the plane into shape. We then headed into town to see Mandela, who for most of the meeting was on his own. His eyes were still as clear as ever, big smile, bright shirt, and firm, firm handshake. There was something almost mesmeric about the lilt as he spoke. You wanted the next sentence to begin as soon as one had ended. He was a lovely man. His office was immaculate, and that was more than the fact that someone kept it tidy. Everything was in its place, and I guessed it was the order and the discipline of his decades in jail that made him as tidy as he was. He said as much. He told a couple of Thatcher stories which showed her in rather a good light. But he said he was happy to go out and say Labour were his friends. He would have to be careful not to stand accused of getting involved in UK politics, but it would be clear where his heart lay. And it was. TB raised the idea put to us by Rick Parry of the Premier League of a PL team going out to play in South Africa. Mandela took a pen and paper and made detailed notes, and said he was really keen on it. TB asked him to sign a book for Michael and Gilda Levy, which I thought was a bit naff. He wrote in an immaculate, old-fashioned style, very, very slowly, then looked at the ink drying before closing the book and handing it back. He did everything slowly, thoughtfully, and with impact. We had lunch in the room where [Harold] Macmillan [Conservative Prime Minister 1957–63] made his 'winds of change' speech [in 1960]. I feared we were not going to be making quite the same impact but we were nonetheless in OK shape.

Cherie had arrived, and was saying someone tried to grope her on the flight out. I was on the phone to the office the whole time re JM. He had got quite personal about TB, and both TB and I felt that was probably a mistake. He should not be doing the real boot stuff himself. But it was clear they were going to go for a Brixton vs Fettes strategy. TB was confident we could turn his ordinariness into a weakness, because people actually wanted their leaders to be a bit special. In touch, but a bit different. Liz had the idea of calling a Brixton organisation to invite both TB and JM to do a debate. We would accept, hopefully JM would refuse and we could say he was running away from Brixton.

Saturday, October 12

Over breakfast at the high commission I talked TB through the coverage of JM's speech. They had gone big on the personal stuff, and it was obvious they were going to make an issue of TB's background, and do Brixton boy vs Fettes public school toff. The general view was that Major had put them back in with a shout, but in some cases I thought they were going through the motions. TB said it could have been a lot worse for us, and he had read the speech and there was nothing in it he feared at all. We talked about the class stuff and agreed that we had to turn it on him, and get it to back-fire, à la Back to Basics. I wrote a note and sent it back to the office, emphasising we should be totally bullish, communicate a sense of confidence that it was one more Majoresque tactic that would backfire, and point out the Tory figures past and present who would have been disbarred from office on the grounds of public school education. The other point was that it could be made to make JM look small-minded and petty, no vision for the country. Allied to it all was the dividing line that he was fighting for a job, TB was fighting for a modern vision of the country. It was one of those situations which if we showed confidence, they would lose confidence and think they had made a mistake. And we had to do it before it became a given and started to enter the debate as a given – JM good bloke, TB toff.

We had a short internal flight from Cape Town to Jo'burg, and TB and I worked on the speech while CB and Anji ignored each other. TB moved from absolute conviction and certainty that the Tories had got nothing out of the week to a bit of fretting that they had. To Alexandra township, and the contrast between here and where we had just been, beautiful setting, nice food and drink, well-dressed people, then real destitution but so many smiling faces, was powerful, and upsetting. Then off to Pretoria to see Thabo Mbeki [deputy president] at his residence and again you were back into this world, driving past big houses with big gardens and huge fences and signs warning of dogs patrolling the premises, then Thabo's place probably the nicest of them all, well laid out, comfortable, people on hand to serve whatever food or drink we wanted. I worked in his wife's office while they settled down to talk. I briefed Andy Grice very hard on the 'class war' idea out of Major's stuff and the *Sunday Times* were planning to splash on it as a 'Blair fury' story. TB was sure we could make it backfire on them. Paddy A had been on, very excited, saying it was all on with Thurnham's defection, and worrying that his call would be tapped. Very Lib Dem thing to say. Even if it was, what does he think is going to happen? The South African spooks tip off the BBC or something and screw our well-laid plans? We had agreed to get the story up through the *Observer*.

In the car on the way back to Johannesburg I spoke to Paddy who said it was all systems go, the *Observer* would break it at 8pm. I said TB would react at 9pm our time. Paddy was unbelievably excited, talking all hoity-toity and like it was the biggest thing to happen in yonks. I shared some of it though. It would not be a happy situation for the Tories, just one more thing to knock them back, and of course it would allow everyone to emphasise the reasons, which ultimately were policy- and direction-based. Paddy read me the Thurnham statement which emphasised sleaze and weak leadership, so they

October '96: Tory MP defecting to Lib Dems

were really going for Major where it hurt. TB said he didn't want it to overtake his business speech. No chance, I said.

Liz Lloyd's idea of getting a Brixton group to issue invitations for a JM-TB debate was going fine. A Stockwell [near Brixton] community group was up for it, issued the invite and we accepted straight away. JM said no, as we knew he would.

The moment Thurnham was announced, it led all bulletins and Hilary C called to say it was running as a disaster for the government.

Sunday, October 13

Thurnham was the main thing all day. It couldn't have been a worse end to the week for them but the papers were not all grim and the *Sunday Times* leader showed Witherow [editor] was disappearing right up their arse. I called Fiona who said she thought we were in danger of overreacting on the class stuff. But TB felt we had to push it hard and make it backfire for them. I asked Hilary to get a backbencher to write to every member of the Cabinet asking why they send their children to private schools. We were up early for *GMTV*. Who on earth watched these programmes at this God-awful time apart from a few political hacks hoping for an early page lead and the rest of the day off? TB did perfectly fine on JM's chip on the shoulder, and on policy stuff. But he accepted he would have to improve the language used to connect. Headed for Cape Town, working on the speech on the way. Worked on the speech and then we met up with TB/CB to head for Nazareth House, an extraordinary place run by nuns to look after child victims of AIDS. It was pretty heart-rending. The nuns were fantastic. You could feel the goodness in every word, and every gesture. We walked slowly around a room for babies, most of whom would be dead within two years. There were lively, happy-looking young kids following us around, and most of them would never see adolescence. They gave TB and CB a fantastic reception, and they were both embarrassed by it. One child in particular attached herself to TB and just would not let go of his hand, so she became like part of the entourage.[1]

The press wanted a new clip on Thurnham and I could see TB was really uncomfortable doing it here, but we did it and then headed back. The *Independent* wanted a TB article on Major getting personal. I said we would not do an article as such but would do a 'TB was talking to' piece. I drafted it, TB made a few changes and we put 'TB

[1] Blair later enquired about the girl, who was named Ntombi. She became a penpal, including when he became prime minister.

was talking to [political journalist] Colin Brown' at the bottom. Colin Hughes [executive] came on and said he would say 'TB was talking to Colin Hughes, to give it more authority'. What a wanker. Desmond Tutu [Archbishop of Cape Town and political activist] was round for dinner but sadly I had to duck out because we were still finishing the speech. TB came in at the end and made loads more changes. On the crime and antisocial stuff, he said 'You are even more right wing than I am.' I didn't see it as right wing. I was totally of the view, which he was really the first to articulate, that a tough crime policy, and a tough antisocial behaviour policy, should never have been seen as right wing. It was one of our biggest failings that we allowed them politically to colonise crime.

Monday, October 14

TB got his funny bone hit again when a radio interviewer asked questions and then said 'Unbundle that one for me,' or 'New Labour – unpick that one for me.'

The speech went OK though TB was nervous in his delivery once he got to the morality section. The Tories took ages to decide what to say, which was a problem because John Pienaar [BBC political journalist] told us the BBC were becoming more and more 'stopwatch conscious'. Eventually they went on the line that he was a 'phoney TV evangelist', so they were still running the Phoney Tony line. He was determined that we really make an effort to expose the nature of the campaign against him. The problem was that as ever parts of the left were echoing what they were saying about him. He had a meeting with [Frederik] de Klerk [last president of apartheid South Africa] who was very clever, though very right wing by our standards, and even TB looked a bit embarrassed when de Klerk said at the photocall that he agreed with a lot of what TB said. Also there was a question about TB's left of centre being no different to de Klerk's 'centre right'.

There was a bit of an incident on the plane. TB, CB and I were travelling first class and Anji tried to get upgrades for her and Jonathan. Some Tory wanker was in there clocking it all and harrumphing loudly about how awful it was to have the leader of the Labour Party in first class. I was worried he was a Tory plant, trying to create a scene, or at worst to feed back details of the flight. TB spent a bit of time placating him but my alarm bells were ringing. TB, CB and I had dinner together and we talked over whether it had been worth CB going. She was not sure. I said the problem was whereas when they were out and about, JM and Norma looked like a couple, TB tended to look like a man out on his own who occasionally remembered he had someone with him. She thought there should maybe have been a more separate itinerary which came together at points. He looked strained talking about it, said it would all work itself out during the election, but I said we had to have it worked out before that. During an election, people are going to get tired and fractious and everyone needs to know what will be expected of them.

Tuesday, October 15

I slept a lot of the way back, while the others went through Jonathan's agenda for government paper. He showed TB a new 'map of government', which had a new chief-of-staff position. 'Who would that be?' said TB. 'Me,' said Jonathan. Anji said she felt too much had been decided without proper discussion. I took a look at it as we landed, and it seemed to make a lot of sense. I think TB felt the Civil Service would be tricky, on the one hand welcoming a new government with a proper agenda, on the other with some of the stereotypical attitudes to Labour.

I got home for a bath then straight round to TB's to prepare for PMQs. He was sitting in the big chair near the window in his dressing gown. Peter M had done a note on the Phoney Tony stuff, which was worrying TB. He felt if the Tories really sustained it, and the press got behind it properly, it could damage us. It was a fact he went to public school, spoke a bit posh, etc. At PMQs I got Ronnie Campbell to ask Major 'as a fellow working-class warrior can he confirm he sent his children to private schools?' which went down well on our side and again showed we were going to fight back on this Brixton Boy strategy. TB felt we should get a woman, maybe Mo, to motor on the exposure of the strategy. As they came out of the chamber, JM said to TB he would like to see him privately later. I smelled a rat. I reckoned it would be to agree with TB that we should start to cool things, which the leaders would do, but then he would get his heavy mob to carry on in the same vein. Back for a meeting on Dunblane/guns. There was a bit of anger that we were not going to see [the] Cullen [Inquiry into Dunblane] report in advance. They agreed to go for a total ban and DH briefed that unless Cullen gave compelling reasons not to, that would be our position. I was a little bit uneasy about the working-class shooting fraternity, but then again clarity was a much better position to have. I left early for parents' evening and by the time I got home the word was the government was moving to a total ban too. And they accuse us of opportunism.

Wednesday, October 16

Guns was running big and the Tory line was they would go for a 'virtual ban', whatever that meant. Dunblane parents were up saying it didn't go far enough. TB and I were a bit squeamish about the whole thing, but it still felt like the right thing to do. The Willetts debate was on today, so sleaze was back on the agenda.

At the end of the morning meeting, DH took me and DD to one side, into Peter's room, and told us a story was about to break about Clare. He said she had done an interview with the *Independent* in which she revealed she had a 31-year-old son called Toby and the two of them had done an interview together. Clare had told David's office 'out of courtesy' but said she didn't want me to have anything to do with the handling of it at all. On one level it was a great human interest story, even if it would add to the sanctification of CS. On the other it was a bit too close to TB's speech. It also begged a lot of questions.

I said we would indicate to the *Indy* that TB was perfectly happy for her, and then at 9, too late for the first editions, but early enough for them not to find out from the *Independent*, we would ring round the editors and warn them. Unbeknown to Clare I was dealing with people from her office re her statement which was the usual self-indulgent me, me, me stuff. She even had a line in there about how she used to dream about the adoptive parents being dead. No matter how hard I tried, which was probably not very, there was something in Clare I found totally repulsive. I saw her after Shadow Cabinet, said I know you don't want me involved, but she had to be very careful how the other people involved in this were going to deal with it. She had been exposed to a bit of media pressure, they had not, and they needed to understand what it was like, and she needed a plan for them to get through the next few days. She said she was confident. I was not. I felt they were stumbling into it and it could end up anywhere. I called the editors as planned and the *Mail* were straight on to the 'What about morality?' line.

TB had seen JM yesterday. He didn't want to go into detail but it had basically been Major wanting to calm the personal stuff. As I thought. PG had done some groups on the conference speeches and though we were still well ahead, JM's speech had gone down better than we thought, particularly with women.

Thursday, October 17

The government got a terrible press out of guns. They had fucked it up big time. The Clare operation went fine and by and large the coverage was straight, even the *Mail*. I suppose it was quite a moving

October '96: Clare Short's secret son revealed

story but I felt totally nauseated watching her parade herself. Meeting on TB/women. AC, Fiona, Liz Lloyd, Sally M, Philip, Hilary, Anji, Peter Hyman. We had a good brainstorm, a lot of it was about TB himself, the way he spoke, the use of abstracts rather than words that conveyed pictures. Clinton in the TV debate last night had been a model of how to do it. He was communicating big thoughts and ideas but they were rooted in people's lives and language. Even his put-downs had a real power and eloquence. 'I don't think Bob Dole [Clinton's elderly Republican opponent] is too old. It's the age of his values I'm not sure about.' Clare was leading ITN, and the whole thing was going fine.

Friday, October 18

Very jolly lunch with David Frost at Bibendum. He was pushing again both for a TV debate and for an interview with Cherie. He said the Tories were paranoid about me and Peter, and felt their basic weakness was they had nobody to match us. But we should not underestimate JM. I spoke to TB a couple of times and he was still reluctant to talk about his conversation with Major. But I discovered from Anji that TB had said JM was really hurt about some of the personal lines run against him, and had tried to persuade TB that Peter and I were 'too nasty for you'. TB claimed to have been robust in defence, but JM was playing a clever game on this. The truth is that TB has nerves of steel and all the rest of it, but JM is probably a tougher street fighter. This was about getting TB to lay off whilst he could get his people to carry on. I told TB of the *Sunday Times* poll, 52–28 had become 47–33, so he was in a bit of a gloom about that. PG felt it was the economy translating into votes. It was still proving very difficult to get GB to do anything at all. PG sent over a note which concluded re the conference season that basically JM beat us. TB said it is incredible that we can have such a good conference, but then it is just forgotten, it disappears.

Saturday, October 19

I briefed one or two of the Sundays on our worries about a low turnout in the *Road to the Manifesto* ballot. It was one of those stories where for once we wanted it presented as a real problem for us, because we had to jolt people into voting. On the poll, I said that it was far nearer the real position than these polls that gave us ridiculous leads.

Sunday, October 20

I had pretty much lost Rory to the Man U cause and with his birthday a few days away, I'd asked Jack Cunningham to organise tickets for the game at Newcastle. I got the boys up at 8 and said we were going on a magical mystery tour. They thought it was Hearts vs Celtic because we were on the Edinburgh train. I told them at Doncaster and Rory's face was a picture of joy. Jack met us at the station and we went for lunch with Freddie Fletcher [Newcastle chief executive] who took the boys down to meet [Kevin] Keegan, [Alan] Shearer and the rest of the Newcastle lot. I met Alex [Ferguson] who said he got a fair amount of grief from the club over the Blackpool visit, but it was fine. He then took the boys to see the Man U players so by now Rory was on a different planet. I enjoyed Calum's studied indifference and his telling me he still preferred Burnley. But he was also going round collecting autographs and it was like they were in a dreamworld – [Ryan] Giggs, [Roy] Keane, [David] Beckham, [Peter] Schmeichel, [Eric] Cantona. Alex said at one point 'That's the first time the kit man has ever been asked for his autograph.' Newcastle won 5–0, the biggest defeat of Fergie's career so Rory was miserable by the end.

Monday, October 21

TB on the *Today* programme, a bit of a disaster area. He was hopeless at listing three policies that would make a real difference and he got a bit caught on gay couples and whether that constituted a family. It was a classic case of us going into something because nobody else wanted to do it, and we had not done the usual in terms of preparation and thinking ahead. Sally and Liz said they heard it with mounting horror at his seeming inability to use language that would connect with people.

TB got an amazing letter from the staff in Clare's office on the lessons to be learned of co-operation between her and the Leader's Office. It was a pretty remarkable letter, like a researcher to a front-bencher seeing himself as on the same level as the leader of the fucking party. That office must be a total madhouse, though today they would be loving all the coverage of brave, principled Clare and doesn't she deserve this happiness?

Fiona and I then left for Peter M's forty-third birthday party which bizarrely was being hosted by Carla and Charles Powell. The tables were way overlaid with flowers and plants so it was almost impossible to see anyone other than the people next to you. Charles and Peter both made rather embarrassing speeches. I kept a running gag going about Peter's absent friends, the ones he used to have before he entered a new magic circle, which he took in good spirit but at root there was a serious point. Carla is very funny and engaging on one level, but she is basically a social-climbing Tory. Peter of course said – and he has a point – that my problem is I do work or home and that is about it, because I can't stand socialising any more. I certainly can't stand the kind of small talk that these people engage in as though it is the biggest talk in the world. Apart from us and the Goulds, Gavyn [Davies] and Sue [Nye], the Birts from his pre-politics life, this was basically Peter's new set – the Powells, Jon Snow and Madeleine, Robert Harris, David and Janice Blackburn, [architect] Richard and [restaurateur] Ruth Rogers, [David] Puttnam, the Mortimers [author John and wife Penelope], Waheed Alli [TV entrepreneur], etc. TB and CB turned up for a few minutes at the start, and Carla was all over them, first him, then her and before we knew it, she had Cherie in the bedroom looking at all her clothes. TB looked a bit embarrassed by the whole thing, and could tell I was, but it meant a lot to Peter that he came. I got the feeling that Jon and Madeleine felt pretty much the same as we did about the whole evening. We gave Gavyn and Sue a lift home and they were lamenting that Peter was becoming a bit remote, losing his old friends and mixing with this set, basically just interested in him as a way of getting to TB. Sue said he was more interested in social networking now than being the election supremo.

Tuesday, October 22

The Tories were now pushing the idea of a Philip Lawrence[1] citizenship award and getting away with it. Yet the *Independent* was talking about *us* leaping on bandwagons. I called Andy Marr to say I thought it was very unfair. He said he just hated all this morality debate. At the morning meeting, I said we had to engage more politically on this. We agreed to get Jack Straw, who was speaking on parenting, to challenge the Tories to say why they weren't banning combat knives. I called Gavyn Davies re something he had said in the car, namely that Major had seen debt rise more than all PMs in history, put together. It was a fantastic fact, and like me he could not understand why GB didn't motor on it. At 10.30 I went to a GB Budget meeting at which Ed Balls presented a strategy paper. The whole thing was awful. The meeting had been called not for a discussion on the Budget strategy but because they had an STV documentary crew following them around. I thought the whole project was ill-advised and couldn't see how a documentary crew making a film to go out when we were in

---

[1] Headmaster of St George's Roman Catholic School, Maida Vale, London, who was stabbed to death outside the school gates in December 1995 when going to the aid of a pupil who was being attacked.

power would help us get there. Ed's big point appeared to be that the Tories couldn't be trusted and we had to put forward our own positive initiatives. Hardly rocket science. GB kept looking at me, and inviting me to join in like I normally do, but I was making clear I thought the TV was a bad idea and said nothing, and he did his hurt, looking down look, then shaking his head gently while his tongue rolled around his mouth. I was very glad to be out of there. As to what the positive economic message was, I was none the wiser.

Peter M said afterwards he was really worried. He said clearly the economy was where much of the political battle had to be played out and even we did not really understand what the economic message was. GB had said endlessly it was about Britain being fit to face the future, but that was a slogan not a message. The Tories would say they would make Britain fit to face the future. What were we saying about our approach to the economy that differed from theirs and that made it a distinctive economic message? Every time I had tried to ask GB before, he came back either with the mantra or with a look. It was hopeless. PG was trying really hard at the moment but with GB and Peter disengaged things were not coming together. TB wrote GB an angry note re strategy and said that things could not go on as they are. PG called from Bolton, and said the groups were pretty good for the Tories. The men were on the line that the economy was coming good and there was a lot of 'better the devil you know' in the women. The lack of cohesion at the top was not just depressing but debilitating because it worked its way down. There was a classic example tonight. Belatedly GB alerts us to a speech he is doing on the work ethic, but it is the usual last-minute thing, we couldn't push it properly and then he complains about lack of coverage. In fact if we had known about it, it was a perfect fit for the general strategy we had been pursuing but the usual possessiveness and last-minute-itis meant it was a wasted opportunity.

Wednesday, October 23

I was woken by David Hill and told there had been a helicopter crash involving people coming back from the Chelsea match and the rumour was that it was David Mellor and Ken Bates [Chelsea FC chairman]. It turned out to be Matthew Harding. I told TB who was really shocked, as was I. He was such a bundle of laughs and energy and it just underlined how thin was that thread between everything and nothing. We then learned it was the same helicopter we had used to come back from conference. The government were briefing all day yesterday and again today that the stalking and paedophile bills could only be done through private members' time so we had said we would help get them through straight away. To our amazement, JM accepted the offer after a fairly cursory chat with the Home Secretary [Michael Howard] on the bench. It became pretty much the only story in town, blew out a lot of the rest of his package and we looked like the white knights. TB saw GB after his note of yesterday, and complained about his disengagement. GB said the problem was he felt Peter and I didn't really want to work with him. I was beginning to feel really sorry for TB. Everyone was blaming everyone else. Harding was huge on the news, and really sad, and we were getting lots of questions about whether his full million had been paid to the party.

Thursday, October 24

In his discussion with GB yesterday, TB had gone on about the need for a clear economic message and GB was insistent that there had to be a different way of doing this, through policy rather than message. This was a total non-argument, as the two had to go together. All we were saying was that people doing interviews and speeches need a clear and basic economic message. GB felt we should be trying to get sleaze up at the weekend. He appeared more engaged today. I walked back with DD who said that despite what he called GB's 'Heathcliff wounded animal act', GB was the best thing we had. We both felt the rift between Peter M and Gordon was so deep that it was impossible to do anything much about it. Bevins had the idea of TB writing to Major, who had said he was interested to see what other offers we might make in terms of legislative support, to say we would do the same on combat knives. Mike Brunson loved it. 'You are wicked,' he said. He said it was a sure-fire lead. Brunson told me that after his interview, which Mike had felt was a mistake, Major was vitriolic about TB, saying that he could not be trusted and we stitched him up on Dunblane. I told TB, and I knew that when it came to Major, the iron was entering his soul, but still he said he didn't want me to go too hard on him. We agreed that re JM the basic line was weakness, damage and drift. I later put out some vicious words from JP, including a jokey reference to Major being rejected by *GMTV* for an item on *Tom and Jerry*.

We had a strategy meeting, the usual preposterous nonsense. Ed Balls just sat there with that smirk on his face, beaming whenever GB spoke, then nodding, then shaking his head whenever anyone else said anything. The *Express* and *Sun* were doing tax, saying TB had won the battle to rule out a new top rate. Fuck knows where these things came from.

Friday, October 25

Today was a classic, exhausting day, even though I was not really overwhelmed by work. Charlie W called before 7 to say that Nick Jones [BBC] had done a two-way on the *Sun* and *Express* tax story, and there was a TB/GB row on the top rate. Coincidentally, TB called to say he felt there was a briefing to Jones by CW that GB wanted to raise the top rate to 50p. TB, on his way to Sedgefield, wanted the story killed, which we tried to do. The knives story had gone really well for us. Major's reply was the nose in the Tory press but it was pretty much a win-win. The highlight of the day was the ITN lunchtime bulletins when Howard was interviewed live and was literally only asked about knives before Dermot Murnaghan's 'Michael Howard, thank you.' He had to keep going and protest publicly he was meant to be on talking about the Criminal Justice Bill. We agreed to get JP out, showing how easy it was to buy a kitchen knife and then a combat knife. I called GB to see how we were doing on the sleaze story they had mentioned and he was straight off, how did these tax stories get out? I said I resented the way he always put these questions as though somehow I would know the answer. It was a bad conversation.

We had one or two papers on about Sainsbury's donation, which he had made through a company of lawyers, because he didn't particularly want people to know how much he had given to the party. Just as we were leaving for home, Carole Walker [BBC] called and read me an *Everyman* interview with Cardinal [Thomas] Winning in which he said our handling of the pro-life conference stall issue two years ago was 'fascist' and that TB's refusal to condemn abortion meant his Christian faith was a sham. The guy was unbelievable. My instinct was really to go for him, but TB calmed me down and was instead blathering on about why the BBC were running it. I said it was a perfectly legitimate story if Scotland's top Catholic Church man was calling the would-be Labour prime minister fascist and saying his religious beliefs were fake. We agreed a statement in which we simply said he disagreed with Winning on abortion and it had always been a matter of conscience for MPs. It was a good measured statement, which we hoped people would contrast with the over-the-top way in which Winning had expressed himself.

Saturday, October 26

Winning was still leading the news. I had briefed John McFall, who was billed as a Scots Catholic MP, and he did a very good job saying Winning's remarks were offensive and he should apologise. The Scots said this was all about Winning wanting to be Pope. Rory was playing a five-a-side [football] tournament and it was his birthday party later but I spent the whole time on the phone dealing with this wretched thing. The BBC were looking to keep it going. Carole told me that in the *Everyman* programme he also said left-wing people were more likely to be permissive and therefore not religious. I called Jack McConnell and organised a number of Labour MPs to attack Winning and demand an apology. Major called a doorstep and gave a little speech on how well the economy is doing, which, ridiculously, led ITN news. I made the mistake of telling Tim to complain to them, which probably had the effect of making them stay with it as the lead all day. We just about got the upper hand on the Winning story, and I felt there was a chance that he would apologise. He was in Rome, unavailable for comment. We heard the *Sunday Telegraph* were doing a big leader, based on them backing Winning and attacking TB and I called TB to get him to speak to Matthew d'Ancona [*Telegraph*]. Another mistake. I should have known that once he got on to another big God man, he would present himself as basically anti abortion which, deep down, he probably was. We should have just let the thing blow over.

Tom Clarke [Catholic Labour MP], who would normally defend whatever Winning said, called to say he had put out words backing TB on this. So it was going our way until I heard from media monitoring that the *Sunday Telegraph* headline was 'Blair – I am against abortion'. It would play totally into the idea of somebody who wanted everything all ways, depending where the wind was blowing. He would say one thing, then get a backlash, and say another, that was the charge they would make run out of this. I was really dispirited by it. Why was I having to deal with all this, selling the kids short on a day like today to deal with all these fucking people and then the one I do it for goes and does this? I said why did you say it? And of course he said he didn't, but I know what he'll have done, he'll have left an impression which he didn't think would be turned into a front-page story but which might have softened criticism. He had said that personally he didn't like abortion but he supported the woman's right to choose and he felt it should not be party political. Then he told me this line came courtesy of Paul Johnson [right-wing columnist] of all fucking people. *Scotland on Sunday* said Winning's people were saying they should have a meeting. I said they met recently, and that they firstly should explain why it was only TB who was singled out for these attacks, and whether there was agenda here that had more to do with papal ambitions.

The abortion story was all they were talking about on the Sunday religious programmes. Jonathan told Fiona that Kate and Anji felt they cannot really work properly with Cherie. They thought Fiona and Roz [Preston] should share the work, and effectively be around full-time. I felt we subsidised the Blairs enough as it was, but Fiona said she felt uninvolved and maybe this was a way of involving her more in what I did and at the same time would genuinely help CB too. Jack Straw and I dreamed up the idea of a national petition on combat knives, which the BBC went for.

Monday, October 28

The press was not nearly as bad on Winning as I thought it would be. TB was getting hit as a bit of a hypocrite but it was low-key. RC was big news after an interview he'd done, some saying he was making it clear we would delay EMU entry, others that we would go in without a referendum. GB called, furious, and giving the impression he thought we were behind it. I said if we wanted a message out of his interview, we would have made it clearer. He said, why is he talking about this anyway? It was classic GB. You were either for him, totally in every argument, or against him. So because I was not prepared to say RC should not talk about EMU, somehow I was pro RC and anti GB.

At the morning meeting, GB would not even allow discussion of the RC remarks. 'We just say the policy is as in the RTTM [*Road to the Manifesto*] document,' he said. He and DD also obviously felt I had gone OTT re Winning. GB said we should have seized on the remarks of the spokesman as an apology. I said it wasn't and nobody saw it as such. 'Doesn't matter,' he said. Peter M and I went off for a chat afterwards. He said it was getting worse. GB was barely engaged and TB just said 'I'll leave it to you guys to sort.'

I went back to see TB who was furious at the way the *Sunday Telegraph* came out, and the accusations of flip-flop, which he hated. I said it was because he tried to have it both ways and we were not clear. He said the position he had enunciated was perfectly reasonable but I said it lacked clarity and it suggested he couldn't bring himself to say what he thought. SM and Liz were in a bad mood with him, thinking he had gone anti-choice just to appease a right-wing newspaper. Sally said a combination of this, plus Robin on EMU, would put the PLP into a state. I was pretty irritated with TB after the weekend and after the others left we had a bit of a set-to.

Our other problem was Lib-Labbery. TB had for some time been asking RC to set up talks with Robert Maclennan [Liberal Democrat MP and party president], which had happened, and tomorrow would involve others, on how we might co-operate on the constitutional agenda. I told TB I was worried about it in the present climate, that it might just push the party off the deep end. The combination of RC, Libs, EMU was pretty potent. He said we had to keep the Libs involved if we wanted their support for other things and we may end up needing it.

Tuesday, October 29

There was still too much a sense of the crime/morality issue being played as a game rather than on real issues and dividing lines. Blunkett was terrific on the *Today* programme. Of all of them, I think he got this stuff instinctively and was able to root it in the lives of people from his constituency. We then had yet another Tory cock-up to help us. [Gillian] Shephard was on and was asked about a story in the *Sun* that she wanted to bring back the cane and she appeared to stand it up, which was followed a few hours later by the revelation from Number 10 that Major had called her personally to say it was the wrong line. What on earth was she thinking of? What was he thinking of? At the 9am meeting, I scribbled a note to Jonathan asking whether he thought I should mention the Lib-Lab meeting which was starting at 10. He nodded, and I did, not least because TB had told me he had squared it with GB. It was clear this was the first he had heard of it and he was on the rampage, so much I eventually said for Christ's sake calm down, and let's agree how we handle it. He said it was none of his business and I could sort it out. I went back to find GB in with TB, complaining not about this but about RC on Europe. Tony had one of his 'help' looks, and GB was going at him like a machine gun, pausing only to take breath, look at his papers and then find some other issue on which to unleash a rant. TB eventually said he would have to leave because he wanted the next meeting to start on time.

I persuaded RC not to do a big briefing on the Lib-Lab malarkey, but then he said I would need to speak to Bob Maclennan who had his heart set on doing a joint briefing with Robin. I spoke to him, tried to persuade him, but he bored me into submission and we agreed they should do a background briefing, no cameras, and push it as a development, not a big departure. He was very hoity-toity, clearly resented me telling him what I thought, so I emphasised this was very much TB's view. He said he and Robin were 'very senior parliamentarians' and the media would find it odd if they did not do a briefing. I hesitated in saying what I thought – which is that they would probably be relieved. He droned on and on at me and eventually I gave up and said fine, do whatever. I called Robin who for once by comparison seemed gloriously unpompous. I told him the outcome and said I didn't envy him having to negotiate with Big Bob. 'You've bought the lot,' he said, laughing. I had. The whole thing led to TB and I having a rare semi-public shouting match when I explained what they were doing and he said he wanted it stopped. I said it was too late and he should have thought of this before he dreamed up the whole plan without talking to anyone but Robin. He stormed into his office, and I stormed off upstairs and that was that, though it blew over in minutes and he called me down for a chat and just said he and I shouldn't argue like that in front of the others because it will unnerve them.

Later we had an election meeting. TB wanted a campaign heavily focused on policy and serious speeches and events. We needed a bit of glitz here and there but not too much. He felt he should be seen as a persuader who was going out there making big arguments and winning people over to our side. He said he thought I had done brilliantly in the last few days, particularly on the knives and social issues, but he felt I had a real downer on him. I said I was pissed off at the *Sunday Telegraph* thing, but it was over. We got feedback from the Winning press conference that he had pretty much stood his ground. We took his line that he never meant it as a personal attack as the closest we would ever get to an apology and said that was the end of it.

Wednesday, October 30

Caning chaos was the main political story and the Lib-Labbery had gone pretty big in Scotland but low-key elsewhere. Anna [Healy] said Maclennan had looked really hurt yesterday when it became clear the broadcasters were not that keen. The *Sun* had some ridiculous story that I was going to go to the Lords to become a minister if we won, which for once led to a moderately jolly and good-humoured morning meeting. Also GB had been on the *Today* programme and had been absolutely brilliant, on his best message-machine form. He said we would be able to cut VAT on fuel and it would go in the manifesto. Major and Shephard were doing a visit to Cardinal Vaughan School which had obviously been planned, in a classic piece of Majoresque small-mindedness, to embarrass TB over not using it, but because of the caning fiasco it was another grim visit for JM. Tim had got hold of [Alastair] Goodlad [Conservative chief whip] and [Goodlad's private secretary] Murdo Maclean's diary which showed Murdo was seeing Willetts tomorrow and tipped off George Jones [*Telegraph*] and Ewen MacAskill [*Guardian*]. A *Times* poll tomorrow showed us back up at fifty-six and TB's figures had soared again, without any clear reason I could think of.

Thursday, October 31

JP was incessantly interrupted by Humphrys [on the *Today* programme] and DH and I agreed we should get an article placed about the way he made it impossible for politicians to express a view. JP was going to Matthew Harding's funeral reluctantly, because he didn't know him, but TB felt there should be someone senior from the party. JP did a doorstep in which he appeared to forget his name.

TB wanted to do beef at PMQs. I said you can't on the one hand say to the Shadow Cabinet they need to use the 'Enough is enough' mantra and then avoid it yourself on the day of the launch. He said it sounded naff if it was over-prepared. I know, but we do need to make sure people know that is the message. He agreed to do it as part of the wrap. It worked fine, and even better JM had worked out an attack on it and made the classic mistake of mouthing your opponent's slogan, which cheered our side up no end. We had some of the backbenchers on 'Enough is enough' too. It sounds silly on one level, people going round repeating a slogan, but that impact on morale is important. It is also important we get the idea fixed in the media's mind. It is the negative side to the 'Time for a change' argument. The positive side comes from TB, the vision thing, and detailed policy. But establishing 'Enough is enough', with the overtones of these people have had long enough and done enough damage, is important. I did a note to go round the Shadow Cabinet. GB was reasonably good-natured and engaged. He and Peter were even talking to each other like human beings, which was a bonus. Denis Healey [former Labour Chancellor of the Exchequer] had said something yesterday which was taken as a whack at GB. GB spoke to him and Healey insisted it wasn't meant that way. I then spoke to him and he agreed we should put out a statement in which he made clear he responded to a misleading statement put to him by the BBC about what GB had said. He said he felt such a chump.

Friday, November 1

TB felt we had a real problem with the BBC at the moment because they were coming up for charter renewal and they were very sneering about anything to do with us, and dead straight with the government. I'm not sure it was any worse than usual, but I did feel we were being judged by very different standards. Oakley called to say he hoped last night's report was OK, but he felt we had to avoid situations where it could be felt we were trying to bully them. He felt he got very fair treatment from us but it was sometimes difficult when we were going for the management.

Peter M, Anji and I went up to TB's to go over various things. He said when it came to basic strategy he felt in GB, Peter and me he had what he needed but he needed us to work together. If we did, he felt we were unstoppable. If we didn't, he was worried. Peter as ever said GB was the problem. If TB felt it was six of one and half a dozen of the other, I felt it was more 8–4 in Peter's favour, in that he felt thwarted by GB at every turn but did still keep trying in fits and starts. He was not yet sure about MB being our main woman. He said he sometimes worried about her judgement. I said she was a real pro and she had a great manner with the media which forced them to treat her with respect. He said we should also try to bring on Ann Taylor but he wanted Anji to talk to her. Re the economy he said he was still trying to get a paper agreed with GB but he kept coming back with different arguments against different bits. He said if we got into government, he would advise GB not to take Balls and Whelan with him. They gave him bad advice, and made him less popular in the PLP.

Saturday, November 2

My asthma was dreadful. I was worried it would be too obvious the Major stuff in the *IoS* came from me. There was plenty to chase in the Sundays, and I got Tessa out on the NHS cash crisis, and got Charlie chasing the story that Ken Clarke was not to be a 'key campaigner'. Blunkett was on *Frost* and we agreed he should try to get up the line that the positioning on caning was nothing to do with policy, and was all about post-JM succession.

Sunday, November 3

TB didn't like the *Indy on Sunday* stuff on Major. He said though Cherie said it read like a lot of it came from the Tories, there were details in there which Major would know came from us. He said you have to be careful with this stuff, I have to be able to have some kind of relationship with him. We went round to TB's for a strategy meeting, joined by Jonathan and later Chris Powell. TB had been working on a new strategy note based around 3Rs – Remind (Tory record), Reassure (NEW Labour, change on tax, unions, past, etc.) and Reward (the positive benefits of New Labour policy positions). It was pretty good. He said the economic message was central to it all and we just had to work away at that. The economic theme should be prosperity that lasts, and it should be linked constantly to social renewal. Opportunity plus responsibility equals community. He explained it in a very clear, simple, coherent way. Peter said even the thickest of the thick would find it quite hard not to follow that. TB said the Tory strategy was becoming clearer – it was basically economic success plus fear of the unknown. He said if they could get both of them up in equal measure, we could still be in trouble.

Monday, November 4

I went round to TB's and he was still telling me I sailed too close to the wind on the Major briefings last week. Arrived for the press conference. GB was getting some make-up put on as we arrived and there was the usual non-welcome, a kind of nod and then silence. I wondered what on earth the make-up girl made of it. TB said on the way in he was alarmed yesterday by GB saying he wasn't sure we needed a Budget strategy as the Tories were in such trouble on health spending. TB saw GB and said it was 'Très difficile.' TB was getting more and more exasperated but he said 'Anyone who thinks we can do without GB is plain wrong. He is the best we have and we must not forget that.' He was worried though, felt Ed Balls had become too big an influence over GB and spent the whole time winding him up. While TB was seeing Bill Gates [US businessman], who I met briefly and struck me as a bit of a dork, though clearly a very clever one, Jonathan, Anji and I met to go over how Jonathan should approach his meeting with Robin Butler. It was important they understood from the word go that change was the central theme. We had to get it established that Jonathan would have significant say over the machine and I would be able to run communications across the board.

I got a lift home with TB. He told me that DD had told him of a complaint from Betty [Boothroyd] that one of our MPs had shown a group around the House that included two IRA people. TB asked DD to get written assurances it wouldn't happen again. He was also ruminating on how he must surely be a bit of a security risk. I'm sure he was and we sometimes felt a bit exposed travelling around with no security at all.

Tuesday, November 5

At the morning meeting I got GB to agree we should get up health pre PMQs and he immediately put Alistair Darling on the case. GB could not see beyond the worth of a very small number of people, usually Scots. There was a wild mood to the whole meeting, not least because the windows were open and a fierce wind was howling through the room. DD said – as Bruce had yesterday – that a lot of the MPs found it hard and 'distasteful' to mouth slogans. I said there was no point having slogans unless we communicated them. I had a good meeting with Alan McGee and Andy Saunders of Creation Records. They could get Noel Gallagher [of rock group Oasis] to do stuff for us, but also wanted us to take the music industry seriously as an industry, and agreed to organise a business meeting on that theme. They felt it was better to 'Keep Liam [Gallagher, of Oasis, brother of Noel] away from Tony, but Noel has got his shit together.' I was also talking to Brian Moore [former England rugby international] about coming out for us. CB had met him at some lawyers' do and he was very onside. He said he was happy to be a donor, and had no qualms about public support. He said work was fine about it and he wasn't worried about the rugby administrators. We thought maybe a 'New Labour, New Britain' mag front cover with the famous picture of him looking like a total animal.

To dinner at Wingfield House [US ambassador's residence]. Ken Clarke and I spent most of the time talking about football. Peter Lilley asked me if I thought he would be able to buy his *Spitting Image* puppet. Later at the embassy for the [US presidential election] results coming in. There was a real buzz about Clinton winning again and he was on great form. I was standing talking to Bevins who got a pager message saying the *FT* and the *Sun* had run a story saying TB had changed his hairstyle to woo women voters. I got Tim [Allan] to put out a line saying it was a black day in the history of *FT* journalism, but it was one of those pieces of nonsense that would run. The *FT* of all people, for crying out loud.

Wednesday, November 6

The phone went early and I knew it would be TB and I knew it would be about the hair. I said we just had to make light of it. But it was one of those irritating little stories with the power to connect and damage. He said he would kill whoever was responsible. I guess what had happened was that someone who was aware we were looking at the gender-gap stuff had noticed a new hairstyle and put two and two together and made seven. More likely, a journalist had done the sums for them. Our suspicion fell on Harriet, Tessa or Margaret Hodge, because people had been talking to them about the strategy. Then we learned Margaret had recently had lunch with the *FT* and the *Sun*, so probably from that. So there I am, having to deal with some nonsense about TB's fucking haircut. He and CB were due to visit Great Ormond Street hospital so I went over there and he was seething. He said, all anyone will want to ask me about is my bloody hair. 'I cannot believe the *FT* can run a story like that.' I said the last thing we should suggest is that we were remotely fazed by it. But all the way there, in the car, he was fuming. There was a bit of a scene at the hospital because the team doing the CBS *60 Minutes* profile couldn't get in. I told them they were too pushy and they were going to get on people's nerves. By the time we got to the office, the hair story was all anyone was interested in. I said humour was the only way out of this and we put together a press release saying the *FT* had gone mad. We put the same picture of TB on twice and did a 'before' and 'after' heading. We did quotes from friends of the reporter who wrote it saying they were worried about it and then changed everyone's name to have a hair connection – Trim Allan, Hilary Cropman, Tony Hair, etc. It went down well upstairs but of course what it all meant was on the day the US president was re-elected, the focus on TB was on his wretched hair. TB agreed to a quote saying his problem was not changing his hair, but keeping it, which by my reckoning was his first admission that he was beginning to lose it.

Another economy meeting. Dire. Absolutely dire. I can't even begin to express how dire. Two weeks on from TB writing his economic note, we still could not get it agreed. We were asking for amendments and suggestions and what came back was either monosyllabic or a moved goalpost to a different question. TB's note was clear, cogent, coherent. No doubt it could be improved. But they simply hadn't engaged on it. GB said he would do a speech on new initiatives on investment, the infrastructure, skills, etc. I said a speech is not the same as a core script on the economy that we can circulate to MPs and members. He would then deliberately seize the wrong end of a stick. Ed Balls spoke drivel, a never-ending collection of words that just ran into each other and became devoid of meaning. I caught Gavyn Davies' eye at one point and his face was a mix of bemused and shocked. He said to me later he found the whole thing baffling because they actually didn't disagree on the substance, but GB seemed to want to keep the argument going and avoid agreeing. Eventually TB clapped his hands and said 'Right, not much point going on with this.' And he asked GB to stay back and they had another hour going at it.

Thursday, November 7

The hair story was mega in the papers. *Times* page 1, the *Mirror* did lots of different TB hairstyles. Several papers did him bald. Most of us still felt we did the right thing in making a joke of it but Donald, who yesterday said he thought the press release a good idea, now felt it wasn't, and that we had made it worse. But the reality was the moment the *FT* of all people did the story, it was going to go big and taking the mickey out of the authors seemed to me all we could do. TB was reasonably good-humoured about it all. There were a number of issues to sort at the morning meeting but somehow we sorted none of them. It was probably the worst meeting yet, brick-wall time. As we left, GB went into a huddle with Charlie and Donald, emphasising the sense of division within what was meant to be our main strategy co-ordination team. I did TB a note setting out in graphic form where the weaknesses were in our structure and it made for an alarming picture. It was not a healthy state to be in as an election got nearer. I met Molly Dineen [documentary-maker] who had been suggested as a person to make the personal TB election broadcast. She asked me what I wanted this film to do. I said show something about his background that related to his politics, convey a sense of humour, real conviction, and a sense of knowing what the real world is about.

GB did not turn up for the pre-strategy meeting, so Peter M and I took the opportunity to spell out just how awful things were at the moment. The thing that was crippling us was lack of agreed economic message and strategy, and GB's general disengagement. TB said persuasion hasn't worked. Ordering him around hasn't worked. We will have to work round him until he comes back into the fold. But understand that even with his faults, which are many and difficult, he is a huge asset and we must never think we could do this without him. GB then arrived late for the subsequent meeting where we had another argument about a non-issue. If anyone who knew nothing about it walked into the room they would think 'What on earth are these people arguing about? They are agreeing and yet arguing.'

Friday, November 8

A story that GB's mum was denying his description of her as a busi-nesswoman. He looked a total chump and it was another example of not covering the basics and not taking soundings first. TB said he was worried about Peter M and GB in equal measure – Peter because he was not really in charge at Millbank and GB because he was so disengaged and difficult. He was getting more and more exasperated. From a good meeting at the weekend we had gone back to total disasterville, with GB throwing both TB and Peter and no decisions of substance being made. TB was seeing Murdoch with Jack C and said afterwards he had to stop Jack being too 'Jackish', and talking too much about the old days. TB said he thought there was a 'good chance' of *Sun/Times* support.

CB and I were getting on a lot better. TB was asking why he was having to do the Brixton thing. Because it's a good idea and because you agreed to it. It was held in a pretty grim community centre but run by terrific people. Julie Fawcett [South London tenants' campaigner and anti-drugs activist] was chairing it, and afterwards she told me she thought TB had been a bit patronising, didn't speak their language or answer their questions. The problem was there were too many media there, it felt stage-managed and he hated it. He had not been on form and it was a bit of a wasted opportunity. Some days he just wasn't up for these kind of things. I felt the people felt a bit used. Most of the questions were about education but one boy asked about sport and TB gave a real politician's answer – no connection at all.

Saturday, November 9

PG called and said he felt we were in a vulnerable position re our campaign strength. I had a big argument with Rosie Boycott and Steve Castle [both *Independent on Sunday*] because a poll on women that was actually good for us was being spun by them on the line that TB was seen as 'smarmy'. More and more polls were now being done with the headline in mind rather than really trying to find out what people thought. I said it was junk-food journalism, and played straight into an agenda written in Central Office. TB/CB went to the Festival of Remembrance at the Festival Hall and he was mobbed on the way out, and it took him twenty minutes to get to the car. It was a classic traditional, probably conservative-leaning crowd but they were really warm and positive.

Sunday, November 11

PG and I went for a walk on Hampstead Heath pm. He said the Democrats' operation was far more professional than ours, largely because the people at the top stayed on-message. Clinton and Gore said the same things and they did it with real discipline and vigour. Our people were all saying slightly different things. He felt the women stuff was pouring out because we had too many people who were too gabby. They thought aloud to journalists about strategy as it was being devised and our opponents then exploited that. He also shared my concern that TB was not relating well to people at the moment. His language was strangely disconnected and almost academic at times. Marje Proops [*Mirror* agony aunt] died and I put out a tribute from TB.

Monday, November 11

Clare was in a rage at Anji because we had said no to TB seeing UNESCO in Paris. 'I get the picture, business is more important than aid,' she said. TB was worried about the press again – *Sun* hot and cold, *Mail* basically offside, *Telegraph* reverting to type, *Times* unfriendly, *Guardian* and *Indy* singing the right's propaganda from a left-of-centre perspective. We had a post-mortem on Brixton and agreed there had been too many media, not enough planning, and not enough engagement by TB. We were doing OK but we were feeling pessimistic. Meanwhile GB's office were briefing against me for 'dropping a clanger' on the windfall tax, by referring to 'privatised monopoly utilities' in my letter to the *Independent*, who were obsessed about the subject. TB said he would have words with GB, who would deny all knowledge.

Tuesday, November 12

Had a little spat with Charlie over the 'Campbell dropped a clanger' briefing in the *Indy*, but GB and Ed B fell over themselves trying to apologise. TB was feeling different pressures on the [EU] 48-hour working-time directive.[1] On the one hand, people would like better conditions, shorter hours, better holidays. On the other, they don't like the idea of Europe pushing us around. He felt we had to expose it as a political ploy unrelated to the substance. I felt we should be saying vote Tory for no holidays, and reminding people of his failure re beef. As a Commons event, TB won, and JM looked defensive but TB said afterwards it is possible to win in the Commons but lose in the country, and it was clear to me the way the right-wing papers were coming at me afterwards that as a political ploy, it had worked for JM. The *Mail* were doing it as 'Who governs Britain?' TB said 'You think this is a defining moment, don't you?' I said it could be, if they really manage to turn it into Britain vs Brussels and paint us on the wrong side. JM had for the first time in ages united his party and got his traditional press supporters onside. Low tax, improving economy, national identity, fear of Labour, they still had some cards, and our rebuttal was still weak. PG called from the Wirral and said it was good up there and we could make the 48-hour directive work for us. GB/Peter M was getting worse and TB had them in again to try to knock their heads together. I'm not sure it did any good. I went with Fiona to [newly ennobled Labour Baroness] Meta Ramsay's party. GB

[1] Introduced in 1993 with the aim of improving employment conditions. Member states were able to opt out of the 48-hour maximum working week.

was there and I asked him if it was only me that felt things were moving away from us again. TB and I agreed it would be good if he made the speech in Paris on Friday in French.

Wednesday, November 13

There was a definite shift in the press. *Mail, Express* and, massively, the *Sun*, all got up the 'Who governs Britain?' notion as now being central to the election. TB said the problem was the papers only took pro or anti. If you were pro some of it, you were pro all of it. The *Sun* was back to real misrepresentative journalism. I said we had to get the debate on to withdrawal from Europe. TB spent much of the day telling me to cheer up. GB was more communicative at the morning meeting as we went over the plans for the next few days, followed by a Gavyn Davies meeting where he and TB went round the same arguments as before. TB felt we could turn Europe to our advantage by making it part of the argument about the future. I was working on an article for the *Sun*, trying to get them straight on some of the facts re the 48-hour week, and get the message on In or Out. There was a lot of press interest in TB's trip to Paris and we didn't really have a story. It was all very last-minute again. Greg Cook [Labour official, pollster] did a polling presentation to the Shadow Cabinet, showing JM moving up and the economy improving. A *Times* poll too showing our lead shrinking, from twenty-seven to eighteen. We left for the beef vote in the House which we lost by one. TB and I discussed the Paris speech which was tricky. He had to be pro-European but not so much that we fall into the Britain/Brussels trap they're laying.

Thursday, November 14

I suggested we go for a strong hint on the EMU referendum in Paris, but he was against that, though later he said maybe GB could do it for the Sundays. On the way in, I had the idea of a visit to the bar where TB worked more than twenty years ago. He could remember the name. Tim tracked it down, and we asked someone from the embassy to recce it. The manager was thrilled. The tabloids were keen as soon as we told them, and it would make good pictures. GB was a new man at the moment, polite, conversational, getting on with TB. TB and I were working on the speech for Paris, and he wanted it to be on a 'Third Way' between regulation and laissez-faire, with a focus on education as an economic policy. I briefed a group of French journalists, went hard on the In or Out argument, then did a briefing note for a ring round of the press who were coming with us. Left for

Eurostar, talked to some journos on the train, worked on the speech. We arrived and went straight to the bar. Terrific pictures. Mike White [*Guardian*] was laughing, said you really are a wicked man. Why? Because this is meaningless but irresistible, and your man comes out well. Excellent. There was a guy there who claimed he remembered TB serving him. We went out for dinner with some of the embassy bods then back to the residence. I had a chat with Michael Jay [ambassador] who felt that on the economy, the speech was to the right of [Jacques] Chirac [French President]. When I mentioned that to TB, he said yes, I thought he was a bit Old Labour. Robin C arrived about 11 and I showed him the draft. 'It really is quite right wing on the economy, isn't it?' he said. 'I hope he knows this will mean a government with very high unemployment.' He was very spiky and sniffy with the FCO diplomats, signalling he intended to be master not servant from the word go, and maybe trying a bit hard.

Friday, November 15

We were up early and TB did French TV. The interviewer ended 'Thank you, John Major.' Alain Juppe [French Prime Minister] was the first meeting, and on labour markets, he obviously thought TB was to the right of him. I slipped a note to Jonathan saying that the right in Europe were obviously looking at TB as their new leader. RC looked a bit pained and alarmed at the whole thing. As we got up to leave, RC said to me 'I hope Tony realises how many jobs will be lost if he applies these economic views in practice.' We left for the Elysée. The entrance was less grand than I expected, the rest of it more so. Chirac was friendly, personable, and fond of looking around himself the whole time, smiles mixed with occasional angry flashes for no apparent reason. He did a wonderful diatribe against the US, saying the most outrageous things as though they were statements of fact blindingly obvious to anyone. Chirac pressed on the euro, and if we met the Maastricht conditions, and RC stepped in very quickly – no, not on the deficit – and Chirac raised an eye at him. He had a wonderfully expressive face. He was either saying that is interesting and surprising, or he might have been saying 'I'm surprised that you should answer a question I asked of your leader.' Either way, he made RC feel uneasy. TB did a good doorstep, quite sceptical on the single currency.

At the lunch, I was sitting next to some French guy who said he thought TB was brilliant. 'You're going to win by a landslide.' Maybe. TB was doing the rounds of the politicians and then did *Le Nouvel Observateur* in the back of the car and they were trying to set him at odds with [Lionel] Jospin [first secretary of the Socialist Party], who had just launched very different ideas, e.g. 35-hour week. TB did more interviews at the residence, then off to see Jospin, who was very Old Labour and the body language between them wasn't great. I could remember him being quite a big fish when I lived in France, and yet there was something non-politician about him, quite cerebral, a bit prone to depression I would reckon. He was a big football fan, and knew what he was talking about. Robin was clearly a lot more at home here, whereas TB looked a bit uncomfortable. RC was on good form, and clearly enjoyed being with TB. He was not averse to a bit of decent banter.

On the train back, TB said the Tories were starting to get their act together and we had to regain the initiative and get them back on the defensive. A move on the euro referendum might be the answer. We told RC we might be doing it this weekend. He said it was important GB did it – otherwise it would be seen as 'Victory for Cook'.

Saturday, November 16

The referendum plan was on. GB had done an interview for the *Indy on Sunday*, in which he said we were coming out for it. They were both pissed off at the Paris coverage, TB because it was small scale, GB because it was all very sceptical re the single currency. He was worried that announcing it now would look like a response, trying to outflank the right. GB wanted to be the one to announce the referendum; otherwise it might be thought it was being done against his will, and also, to quote TB, because he had his own agenda on it. I told Charlie Whelan I was worried at the idea of GB giving it to one paper. The others would be pissed off and there was a danger when they found out they would do it as 'Brown caves in' and the best way to avoid that was to give it to the other papers. I tipped off the other heavies and emphasised this was making explicit what had been implicit for some time. The next thing I had to deal with came when Ian McCartney's wife Anne phoned and said he had been beaten up by a bouncer, and had his nose broken, because of his anti-nightclub bouncer campaign. I spoke to Ian, did a kind of interview, gave the quotes to PA and it was running straight. 'It'll be the making of you,' I said.

Sunday, November 17

Charlie W called early to say RC was due to do *World This Weekend* and GB thought it was better if he did it. I called RC, who was already pissed off at not really having been in on devising the strategy, and pissed him off even more. Headed to TB's. GB arrived a bit late and first off there was a row-ette because GB and I both complained we had not seen the last party political broadcast in time to make any real input. TB had said he was going to give everyone a piece of his mind but he didn't really. We went over the main strategic messages for the next few months – future not past; many not few; leadership; Tory fifth term. I still felt their key strategic lines were harder than ours but at least we were making progress. I asked who should go on the *Today* programme re Europe and said it was ridiculous to think we could go on for ever without RC once giving an interview on the subject. I said the more we kept him off the more troublesome he would be. GB said Robin had already been briefing against him. I had no way of knowing if that was true and I'm not sure Gordon did. I could not help thinking, but didn't say, if only GB spoke to him every now and then, their relationship might be more productive.

Monday, November 18

Despite all GB's fears, the referendum plan was going fine for us, and though some of the editorials were sniffy, very few people could be unaware we had made a move. GB had worked hard on the *FT*, which pushed it as a pro-European move, but for the rest it was mainly Cook the winner. The government were doing well presenting the new school tests as a good thing and we spent a lot of the morning meeting on that. We got DB to ring round some of the hacks to make sure the right questions were put at least. We had a not very constructive TB, GB, Peter M, AC meeting talking about the VAT posters, which weren't great. TB was moving to the view the Tories would go for a bigger tax cut, 2p plus a wider band. Michael Levy called me late, and said he thought the *Jewish Chronicle* were doing a story about his involvement and maybe we should try to get it out as a positive story.

Tuesday, November 19

Hilary [Coffman] and I were working on TB's *Desert Island Discs*, doing a note for him pointing out it was not just the records he chose, but the stories he told and the way he told them. It was interesting that someone who in a sense was trying to be the ultimate public figure, in the age we're in, does not like talking about himself much. HC had been with him and the programme's researcher, who said that apart from GB, he had never known a politician so reticent. HC and Anji dragged a story out of him about running away from school.

CBS were in setting up for the *60 Minutes* interview in the Shadow

Cabinet room, and they took an age and a mountain of equipment. They had been a total pain in the arse, and I had been a pain in the arse to them, but I suppose we just about got there, though I wish we had never bothered. TB was on good form. He told them a story I had never heard before about how the cops once helped him get back into Fettes after he had been out seeing a girl, which I told them would run big here.

William Waldegrave [Conservative chief secretary to the Treasury] was planning a big tax and spend attack on us and we did not get our act together quickly enough. Michael Levy was driving me crazy calling and pressing me to announce something about his role. I felt that it was a no-win situation, that the press and the Tories would not allow us to do it positively.

Wednesday, November 20

Tax was the only story in town. The Conservatives' leak to the *Telegraph* had worked and it was the lead on the broadcasts. Waldegrave and Alistair Darling were on at 8.10 so I called AD and gave him a Boris Johnson [*Telegraph*] quote saying the Tories could not be trusted on tax, which he used three times. I paged him to say I thought the interview was terrific. So began the first real rebuttal day. GB chaired the morning meeting well and we felt we were into real election territory now. The story was given spurious cover by the BBC pointing to the line in the *Telegraph* that Robin Butler had sanctioned the costings exercise. I got Jonathan to call Butler and object, but Butler said he had not been consulted and he was sending an internal minute making clear he had not been involved. I immediately called PA, the broadcasters and the *Standard*, who splashed on it – Tory tax bomb lands on Tories. It was a straight hit, a triumph, for which GB and AD, to my and Jonathan's amusement, took the credit at Shadow Cabinet. I called Tony Hall to complain about the way the BBC regularly ignored our stuff but fell every time for Tory propaganda fed out through the papers like this was. He said, like he always did, that he would look into it. It was like talking to a bowl of jelly.

We now had Rachel Sylvester [*Telegraph*] as well as the *Jewish Chronicle* chasing re Michael Levy and he was flapping, calling the whole time, and going on as if it was the biggest story we had ever had to deal with. I still believed it was better to wait and try to make it a part of a bigger story about business, but I sensed he wanted his moment in the sun.

I had a quick lunch with Mike Habib at the US Embassy, who said the word going back to Washington was that we were definitely going to win. He told me that last year the [American] Embassy sent a minute to the Pentagon saying the UK would not be able to do a Falklands or a Gulf War and the British Embassy [in Washington] heard of it and protested. I wondered if we might be able to do something with it at the election.

We were doing a 3pm GB/AD rebuttal press conference and Peter M was rude to George Jones [*Telegraph*] on arrival, 'Ah the man from Central Office and *Newsnight*,' and George stormed out. Despite the policy and rebuttal teams working flat out, we were late with the rebuttal dossier and the briefing didn't start till 3.15. GB and AD did well when it got going and I think people got a sense that we were not going to take hits without fighting back and there was no ground where we did not feel confident about the basic case. The *Standard* having splashed on it all going wrong for the Tories, I got Tim to get a few dozen copies and hand them out as the press came in. We organised some sandwich boards on Tory tax rises to go round the CCO. The press was easier to turn than the broadcasters, who were taking the Tory claims pretty much at face value. We had a real problem with the BBC and I wasn't sure how we dealt with it.

Thursday, November 21

Tax was a messy draw, which was about as good as we could have hoped for. The worst paper was the *Express*, two pages totally buying the Tory line and I wrote to Richard Addis [editor-in-chief, *Daily* and *Sunday Express*] saying it sat oddly with what he had said to TB. The story was moving on to the windfall tax, and a report on youth justice shambles. The *Sun* was bad at the moment and TB said it was all about the black box.[1] Re PMQs, TB wanted to go on Europe and ask why they would not have a debate on the floor of the House. The rest of us couldn't see it, but he followed his instincts and it paid off, both in terms of his performance, but also the impact on the Tories – [David] Heathcoat-Amory [former Paymaster General] came in on it, there was a row at Business Questions and at the 1922 [Committee of Conservative backbenchers] later, who were determined to force a debate. So we had their splits up again. TB said JM looked petrified. I was working on a briefing note for tomorrow re the other leaders writing to JM saying party funding should be referred to Nolan. I briefed our donations from Alec Reed [businessman and

[1] The black box was a piece of TV digital technology that would enable access to interactive television and the internet, therefore important to BSkyB. TB thought the *Sun*'s hostility could be due to the decision a future New Labour government would have to make regarding digital television.

Labour donor], [Greg] Dyke [TV executive], [Clive] Hollick, and slipped in a line about Michael Levy, who was continuing to call the whole time and push for some kind of announcement. He didn't like being part of another story, I could tell. I urged him to calm down, said he was going on as though there was something terrible to hide, and there wasn't, just calm down and we'll do it in an orderly way.

Friday, November 22

Europe was going big and bad for the government. I left early for TB's where he was preparing for *Desert Island Discs*. 'Is this really wise?' he said. 'I'm not sure.' We went over the stories he might tell, e.g. the lunch with CB at Luigi's [restaurant, Covent Garden] that went on and on and became dinner. He also wanted to talk up what a brilliant lawyer CB was. He was very nervous and tense. We left for the BBC and were met by Sue Lawley [presenter] and some suit from the programme. I didn't take to her at all and I could tell that TB didn't either. She felt like a Tory to me. She had very spindly legs and a brittle smile that looked like it would disappear as fast as she put it there. I could sense that he wasn't happy to be doing it. HC and I sat in the cubicle and it felt like it was getting worse and worse. He allowed her to put him on the defensive. She went big on the Harriet/Oratory stuff, and she did the smarmy question too. Central Office would have loved it. At one point she said 'You don't really like talking about yourself, do you?' TB hadn't taken to her at all. Lots of press and TV came in at the end and I said to her 'Sorry he didn't open up for you, like he has with other interviewers.' She got the message. I felt the whole thing had been a lost opportunity on both sides. TB knew he had not been on form but he said there was no point him going hard on her because of the sort of programme it was.

The *Telegraph* were doing a profile of Michael Levy and he was calling every fifteen minutes about it, driving me crazy. Tim said Rachel Sylvester had been close to tears because she had been working on the Levy story and got nothing, then saw it slipped into a line in a story in *The Times*. She felt she had been stitched up. I said she was being paranoid. The *Sun* and the *Mirror* were desperate for *Desert Island Discs* stuff. We resisted, but eventually gave them what he said about being crap on the guitar. Coincidentally, we were due to be going for dinner at the Levys. Andrew Hood [foreign affairs adviser], Ronnie Cohen [venture capitalist] and his wife, and Gale, Lindsey and Chris [CB's mother, sister and brother-in-law]. It was the full Jewish number. I liked Gilda [Levy's wife] who seemed to me really down to earth and very different to Michael, yet clearly they adored each other. The dining room had so many bad memories of painful moments in the conference speech-writing process. I got the *Telegraph* profile faxed over and he seemed happy enough.

Earlier, Barclays Bank investigators called Jonathan and said that someone called the bank recently, pretending to be [Lord] Merlyn Rees [former Labour Home Secretary], one of the trustees of the [Leader's] Office fund, and a clerk gave this person the names of people who had put money in recently. It was obvious that was where the story came from.

Saturday, November 23

Someone in the BBC had given TB's *Desert Island Discs* records to the *Independent* and they did it on page 1. The *Mail on Sunday* were writing that the BBC were accusing me and HC of leaking it. I spoke to Clare Garner [*Independent*] who said she was happy to put it in writing that we were not the source and the BBC was. Nick Rufford [*Sunday Times*] was doing a story on Levy and we discussed the idea of a steady stream of announcements on donors as a way of wrongfooting the Tories and emphasising we had business support. He said there were some who would definitely not want publicity and he had raised the money from them on that basis.

Sunday, November 24

TB called, not happy about the stories re Michael Levy. He also felt, as I did, that there was too much spin-doctory in all the Labour stories. I didn't know how to deal with this. It was like the meetings we had to plan *Desert Island Discs* and someone from the BBC even managed to get diary stories out of the fact I ate biscuits and had a haircut. I went up to see TB later and he had a black eye, quite a bad one, from playing tennis with Michael yesterday. I said it would be quite a story if it still looked like that on Tuesday. I called Anji and said she should organise some make-up on it before he left for the office tomorrow. On Europe, he said the Tories were now doing real damage to themselves and we had to really press the advantage. HC was dealing with all the *Desert Island Discs* enquiries, of which there were lots. Mum called to say TB would have picked up a lot of votes from older people because of the beautiful way he spoke about his parents.

Monday, November 25

The *Desert Island Discs* coverage was OK, but there was far too much about spin doctors and whether we actually chose the records, which we didn't. Some of them I'd never heard of. It was becoming a problem, and TB said we had to work out a strategy to deal with it. It was about painting him as someone incapable of exercising his own judgement, being someone else's creation. I had lunch with Brunson, [John] Sergeant and Elinor Goodman [political editor, *Channel 4 News*]. Elinor basically supported my argument that the media was becoming too much about journalists' interpretation and not enough of the politicians speaking. We had a meeting on the latest crap party posters. They were about tax rises, 1p or 2p with fingers used for 1 and 2. I said I thought it was crap, visually and message-wise. Peter M got very defensive, but TB (with so much make-up over his black eye it was obvious) agreed, and said it should be clearer, and we were better off going for better off/worse off territory.

I was going to bed when Jon Sopel called saying what was all this about the *Mirror*? *News at Ten* had just confirmed that the *Mirror* had got hold of the Budget. I didn't know anything. There was a PA snap saying details of the Budget had been leaked. I called Piers [Morgan] who said it was a 1p tax cut. TB called on his way from the Speaker's reception to say Prince Philip had told them all about it. TB said he was amazed Piers had given it back and so were most of the other papers who were now frantically trying to find out what the details were. GB spoke to Piers. He too thought it was a crazy decision by the *Mirror* but the right outcome for us, because the Labour Party would have been blamed for the leak by association. TB was clear we should not get involved in briefing any of it.

Tuesday, November 26

TB was regaling us with stories about Robin and the Queen at the Speaker's Dinner. He said even with the Queen, Robin was 'Robinesque'. She said she was due to speak to a Church conference but couldn't seem to get the media interested. 'I can't say I'm surprised,' said Robin. Then the Queen said she was amazed the Speaker could remember all the names and seats of all the MPs, and Robin said 'Oh, I don't think it's that difficult.' TB was working away on his Budget speech and said he felt confident. When we got the press releases from the government, we worked out that health spending would eventually fall. By the time TB was up on his feet, we fed in the line that the typical family was going to be £2,120 worse off as a result of all the changes. TB was at his best, on top of the arguments, witty, clever, confident. Everyone was saying he did well. All in all, a good day. The Budget didn't give them the bounce they wanted, our response was good and we could lock horns on the economy with confidence. I went for a meeting with GB to plan the follow-through for the next few days. We agreed we needed to work up to 'better off with Labour'. If we establish this as a tax-raising government, taking with one hand and giving with another, then do the VAT cut ourselves, we will be in a strong position.

Fiona and CB were seeing the Home Office and intelligence people who said that if we won, TB, JS, RC and Mo would be properly protected, but not CB and the kids. They felt there was no security need. They felt the house in Sedgefield was not safe and would need a lot of work done to make it safe. Fiona said CB was getting more and more anxious re what would happen to the kids.

Wednesday, November 27

TB got a good write-up and the Budget didn't. GB had gone back on yesterday's agreement that TB do the VAT cut in his interviews, because he wanted to do it himself in his Budget broadcast tonight. Fine. TB was excellent on *Today*, and was confident they were not going to get much out of the Budget. It was all now moving on to huge new council tax bills. A Budget poll said it was thumbs down for the government. People didn't believe them on tax and we were ahead on living standards, which was great news for us. I really felt the economic argument moving in our favour. Gavyn [Davies] said we should start calling it the tax-raising Budget, which we did. GB's broadcast was excellent, in terms of tone, substance and overall impression. PG called from a focus group in Huddersfield and said the Budget had flopped but women were still very resistant to us.

Thursday, November 28

The press was even worse for the Tories today than yesterday, with lots of analysis showing people were worse off. DM and I had a session at the *Independent* where their main line seemed to be that we were not bold enough, not interesting enough, and too obsessed with the right-wing press, and particularly Murdoch. There was a real lack of intellectual confidence about their own positions, and they could only define themselves against the right. We put up an OK fight, talked up TB's radicalism, and how it would make a real difference. They were a difficult lot, a bit Lib Dem for my tastes. On the way back I saw the Tory poster for the first time – as promised, lower income tax. They had obviously misread how the Budget was going to go down and I felt we had a real opportunity to make inroads on the 'Honest John' part of the image.

We'd got Tessa [Jowell], at TB's request, to do a piece on the [Conservative] strategy re TB and exposing it, and now he was worried that it was too personal and would backfire on us. I said it wouldn't but it had to be hard-edged for anyone to notice. At PMQs, TB asked JM three times whether the tax burden was rising and he wouldn't answer at all. They were running scared. At the strategy meeting GB said we had to brand it as a tax-raising Budget, and that meant going at it again and again. TB felt we could link that to the economy generally. We had to neutralise them on tax and then undermine their claims on the economy. JM had said that dogs bark, cats miaow and Labour puts up taxes and I got Margaret McD to organise barking cats and miaowing dogs at the Tory press conference tomorrow. David Hill and Jo Moore clearly thought I had gone mad but it would give everyone a good laugh and it was time we had a bit of humour in all this.

Friday, November 29

TB was out at a Nexus conference for brainy people, then a visit in Lewisham where he did some hard-hat pictures which threw him into a terrible wobbly later. He hated hard hats because they left his hair looking ridiculous and all over the place when he took them off. DH and I did a Sunday briefing to try to get over the idea that the Budget had flopped and we had neutralised them on tax. I saw James Blitz who was doing a profile of me for the *FT*. Nice enough bloke, and I sensed he shared some of my views about the Westminster press. He was interested in whether I thought I would get on with the civil servants and whether I would change the way that I worked. I said I think people would find it odd if I suddenly became non-political. I got to TB's for a meeting. GB and Peter M didn't acknowledge each other, or address each other. The discussion centred on our fifth-term attack. The question was whether we should be making direct policy accusations – they'll put VAT on food – or whether we should be using it to get up their record, factually. TB/GB were more cautious than everyone else. TB had been happy at the way the Budget came out for us, but seemed nervous about going much harder. He was also not sure re the wisdom of a separate business manifesto, and went on about it so often that Peter got a bit hoity-toity, and the more TB pushed it, Peter moved towards that near-hysterical pitch of voice he gets, so close that I said 'For fuck's sake, Peter, calm down a bit,' and for a while he did. Then we just went round in circles and eventually he disappeared. One moment he was there, the next he was gone. CB popped her head round the door and said she could hear Peter's voice from downstairs. I said if you see him, just ask him to come back in.

Saturday, November 30

Whelan had briefed Andy Grice that 100,000 people were now paying the top rate as a result of the Budget and this became 'Labour to cut tax for middle classes' as the splash, which was frankly absurd. Tessa's article got front-page treatment and TB was not at all happy about it.

Sunday, December 1

TB had done the British Comedy Awards on Saturday night and Jonathan Ross [host] said if you come back next year and you've lost you'll have to show us your arse. Fiona watched it and said it was truly awful. TB did his Prince Charles look. Then there was [the World] AIDS day [event] which Tim said was a total disaster, completely disorganised, reporters and photographers from the *Mail* all over him, trying to earwig. Cherie wore a red ribbon and TB didn't. TB said the most cringe-making of the three was Tessa's article. He said I never want to wake up on a Sunday morning and feel my stomach turn like that again. Too personal, he said.

Monday, December 2

I told CW to tone down the briefings on us taking people out of the top rate of tax. The *Sun* had a phone poll pushing for withdrawal from the EU. TB was convinced the *Sun's* hardened line on us was all about regulation of Sky. He said our position on Europe must not change. He said the same at the *Economist* lunch, where he was very pro-Europe in substance and language. *The Economist* had most of their big players out for the lunch. They were a mix of arrogance and naivety. Their main differences with us were lack of detail on a few policies and lack of candour on tax. TB said that we were judged by far tougher standards than the Tories. Why can they say they have an aspiration to cut capital gains or inheritance tax, and it's taken at face value, but if we say we have a long-term goal of a 10p starting rate, it's torn to shreds? At one point I said their suggestions amounted to a very successful election losing strategy – all-out pro EMU, more liberal on crime, promise more tax and less spending, greater powers for the Scottish Parliament, etc. TB handled them pretty well, was at his best when he was setting out the central objectives, e.g. how he had shaped New Labour through big moments and ideas relating to ideology, culture, membership and the key policy areas, and how we would do the same through the major pieces of legislation. He felt we did not get sufficient credit for the boldness of the thinking we were putting forward. As we left, TB and I agreed they were even more breathtakingly arrogant and up themselves than the last time, particularly [the editor, Bill] Emmott. He had smug tattooed on his forehead. TB was getting very jumpy re doing Des O'Connor and Frank Skinner [chat show hosts].

There was a bit of a flurry earlier when Alex Allan [principal private secretary, Number 10] called Jonathan to say that according to the security people, CB had been demanding to see floor plans and visit the flat in Number 10. This was total balls and I smelt a stitch-up. You could just imagine the 'Cherie measures up the curtains' coverage it would generate. Fiona said it had been the security people who had suggested the idea of a visit and she had said no. Fiona had made a big difference to the whole CB situation, but this just underlined again how difficult this stuff was going to be.

Tuesday, December 3

While TB was seeing [Sir Robin] Butler, and the head of MI5 [Stephen Lander], I wrote quotes for what the *Record* would present as an 'interview' on his dad's family and his Scottish connections, based partly on the stuff he told Lynda Lee-Potter. There was a lot in that interview to get out in other places. TB was nervous about Europe, agonising over how to tackle it. On the one hand, we could get their splits going. On the other, he might give JM the opportunity to reposition himself in a cannier position. Peter M picked up that JM was going to say it was 'unlikely we would join in the first wave', and that set off another bout of TB agonising. But it worked out fine. TB didn't perform particularly well but the significance was that we got Major pinned down on EMU, in a position he would now find hard to move out of this side of the election, with options open and the chance for us to widen their divisions as we went. I briefed hard that it was a disaster for JM because he had devised a strategy aimed purely at winning back some of the Tory press, and Ken [Clarke] and Hezza had blown his strategy out of the water. The Tory line was that TB had been wrong-footed but though he had looked taken aback, the reality was pretty clear – JM had been forced to recalibrate under pressure from the pro-Europeans.

Wednesday, December 4

I didn't think the press was as bad for JM as it should have been and some of them went on the line TB had been wrong-footed by JM's straight answers. Peter M took me to one side after the 9am meeting and said he was really anxious about January. He felt that the Tories were going to be in a stronger position and we were not clear how we were going to deal with that. He and GB didn't speak to each other at all during the meeting. TB told me he had asked GB if he was speaking to Peter again. 'Yes,' said GB. 'But are you speaking to him properly?' asked TB. 'What do you want me to do – love him?' asked GB. TB said he was getting more and more exasperated. Jack McConnell called me to say BBC Scotland had got hold of a focus group report which had a lot of stuff about doubts about TB. He sent it down and it could have been written by a committee of Trots, Tories, Nats and Libs because it had all their favourite lines about Tony in there. It was clearly written to be leaked. GR called to say it had been stolen from Tommy Shephard's [Scottish Labour Party] car on November 13.

We had a meeting re Frank Skinner and Des O'Connor. Because of Jonathan Ross's 'If you lose will you come back next year and show us your arse?' TB was getting nervous about doing these more show-bizzy type interviews. He said he was a politician not a celebrity and he didn't like doing the personal stuff they pressed for. I said he had to broaden his appeal and start connecting with people who normally would not follow politics at all.

TB said we should start getting our heads round the possibility of a March not May election because of mortgages, general decay and the need to avoid the Wirral by-election. TB was a bit of a pain at the moment. He wasn't up for doing much out of the run of the mill, and he found reasons to moan about lots of things that normally wouldn't faze him. We went to St Martin-in-the-Fields to do a homeless pre-Christmas visit and Jeremy Vine [BBC] tried to doorstep him on the Scotland leak and this became a great moan about why we were there. Maybe we were all just tired pre Christmas. At the Shelter [homeless charity] visit, Anji said she was being undermined on three fronts – TB, CB and me. 'That is a pretty formidable trio to contend with,' she said. I didn't feel I was undermining anyone but she said she felt got at and down. I think everyone did. We needed a break.

Thursday, December 5

Very little coverage for the speech to Shelter. The leak of Scottish focus group reports, and negative remarks re TB, was massive up there but apart from a piece on the front of *The Times*, it didn't fly much in the London media. TB was livid at the leak. He said only the Labour Party could whack the ball into its own net like this. It emerged during the day that as well as Tommy Shephard's briefcase being stolen, so was his mobile and there had been a number of calls to Nat-supporting journalists. Donald [Dewar] clearly thought TB was just looking for things that showed him to be strong. TB said

'I'm not doing this to be strong. I'm doing it because I believe these people could cripple a Labour government.' TB did STV, which was all about 'smarm' post the focus group leak, and he was getting nicely boiled up re the Scottish media. He did a very good 'I am what I am' passage, and indicated a lot of scorn and a bit of steel, and gave as good as he got. Jon Sopel [BBC] was saying [Kenneth] Clarke had threatened to quit, had also said to Major others would quit if the Europe policy changed, and that he might even defect to us. Dobbo [Frank Dobson] called me and said he was at Cafe Nico yesterday and Clarke was having lunch with Sopel so the source for this stuff was probably Ken himself.

We moved into overdrive on it just before PMQs. Clarke put out a statement denying he'd threatened to resign. TB was terrific at PMQs, best ever, and he got JM on the rack, asking detailed questions which JM answered with waffle. TB was cheered massively twice and our side was really up and buoyant at the end, shouting at Major 'GO, RESIGN,' etc. As we came out, I was engulfed and they were desperate for any detail re Clarke – who saw him with Sopel, how did we know, blah. I went with TB and CB to the airport, DD in car two with Pat [McFadden] and Roz Preston. The flight was delayed so TB and I wound up Pat re the Scottish press and party. TB said our entire programme could be fucked because of the commitment to the Scottish Parliament and still they whine that we're not doing enough for them. 'I fully understand why Thatcher got to the moaning minnie stage.' We got to the Hilton, Tim [Allan] called to say there was a real sense of disintegration around the Tories re pensions and Clarke and he thought we needed new TB words to push it on. I knocked out a short passage which we got out in time for *C4 News*. I had a very nice chat with GB. Maybe it was because we were on his home turf, and at a jolly Labour event, but he was a lot more relaxed than usual and we talked to each other rather than at each other. Donald [AC's brother] came up and met TB. I met Billy McNeill and Jim Baxter [ex-footballers] which was nice. DD did a great warm-up, and then after a slow start TB did a good job too.

I got a call to say the latest Gallup had us at 59–22, a record lead. Yet another Scots trip was ending better than the build-up had suggested and time was running out for the Tories.

Friday, December 6

The papers were disastrous for the government. The Scottish press had done TB's speech reasonably OK but the *Express* – 'Blair blasts back at Scots' – and the *Mail* – 'I may be smarmy but you lot are a joke' – tried to turn his attack on the media into an attack on Scotland. His exasperation at the Scottish press then had unintended consequences at the breakfast for Young Labour when he was talking to a group of people he thought were basically with us, one of whom was in fact John Arlidge of the *Observer*. He looked across at a little gathering of Scottish hacks and said what a bunch of unreconstructed wankers they were. I said to him afterwards that was the kind of thing I could get away with but it was probably a mistake for him to say it. But he was right. We drove to Ayr, an excellent school visit, TB saying how he had seen the groups of screaming girls at the entrance to the hotel and thought things were looking up, only to be told Boyzone [pop band] were also staying there. Our candidate [Sandra Osborne, who would become Ayr's first Labour and first woman MP] was with him, the mood was definitely turning our way and he got a terrific reception, with people honking their car horns, waving from buses and crowds gathering round him without a hint of aggression or nastiness. 'It's like Elvis has come back,' one woman said to him. He was still a bit stilted with people and he continually forgot to look out for CB as she worked a crowd behind him.

We flew home to the news that John Gorst [Conservative MP] may be about to resign the whip. In fact he announced he was no longer co-operating with them. I put out TB words that the government was now disintegrating and it simply could not go on like this.

Saturday, December 7

TB was in a bit of a state at Michael Howard's interview on the *Today* programme, when he said that because TB had said he would never be isolated in Europe, that meant we would sign up to everything. Peter M meanwhile was pushing for us to change our line on EMU and say we would probably be in the first wave. GB was adamant that we had to keep options genuinely open. GB was much more engaged and TB said I should talk to him to agree how we handle this in the next stage. We went to the Kennedys' [friends] thanksgiving. There was a psychiatrist there who said most psychiatrists were appalled at Leo Abse's attack on TB.[1] 'He strikes me as very well balanced, for a politician!'

[1] Abse, who had been a South Wales Labour MP for more than thirty years, had published *The Man Behind the Smile: Tony Blair and the Politics of Perversion*, a psychoanalytical critical study.

Sunday, December 8

Tebbit was on *Frost* saying there were up to a hundred Tory MPs who would sign their own manifesto against the single currency at the election. This allowed us to get up the line that there was now a party within a party. Major was doing *On the Record* and there was huge interest in it. He did not have any surprises and he did not bow to the sceptics. On the contrary, he said he would not be held to ransom. He was very relaxed and showed yet again that under pressure he is able to exude a certain calm which in turn conveys a sense of strength. So though he changed nothing in terms of substance, it was probably the right thing to do the interview. The only question was whether people would ever turn back to him. TB doubted it. I still felt that there was something unreal about our support and also that JM had strong powers of recovery and reinvention. I felt JM did pretty well but TB said he was relaxed about it. He was in the exact box we wanted him to be on EMU – namely the same place as us – options open, the referendum, and it was going to be much harder for him to play the sceptic tunes he probably wanted to.

Monday, December 9

JM got a reasonably good press re his interview but the airwaves were full of the sound of Tories rebelling. I went round to collect TB. Despite Major's problems, he was still worried re Europe, felt we had to be ultra careful that with the Dublin summit coming, they didn't manage to turn the spotlight on us and paint us as pro come what may. On the train to Doncaster, we agreed that perhaps the best argument to deploy was that on the substance there was not much difference between the two leaderships, but the big difference lay in the governability of the parties. We started to deploy it when he did a doorstep in Barnsley on the by-election visit. 'Do you get a good deal out of an ungovernable party?' I liked the candidate, Jeff Ennis, a big bluff bloke with a cheery red face who said his ultimate hope was for every other party to lose their deposits. The BBC ran a piece on Barnsley but very downbeat re TB and the usual suggestion that he didn't connect with traditional voters, which was becoming a London media thing. In fact, as in Scotland, TB was doing far better with working-class voters than anyone else.

Back for a meeting re EMU/IGC [Economic and Monetary Union/Intergovernmental Conference]. The most instructive moment came when both JP and RC came in pressing GB on whether we were ruling out tax going up. JP admitted to me later it was just a piece of pre-government swordsmanship, but it indicated an argument still to be settled for the election, though it was pretty clear which side TB would fall on. GB said 'I am quite sure none of us would want to make promises we don't intend to keep,' which they took to mean a pretty hard line on tax. First JP, then RC said you cannot possibly go into the election ruling out the possibility of tax rises. It was all fairly light-hearted at one level but markers were being put down.

Tuesday, December 10

Breakfast with Robin Oakley. He agreed with me that the BBC was far too influenced by the press, but he did try to stand back from it. TB saw a group of *News of the World* magazine readers who had already seen JM. It was bizarre at times. One of them said she was a psychic and another asked if he had ever had supernatural experiences. He handled it well enough but it sometimes irked, the stuff he had to do for the sake of 'connection'. Asked which actor he would like to play him in a film, he said Liam Neeson or [Humphrey] Bogart. JM had said John Hurt. The Willetts committee[1] finally reached an agreement and everyone was trying to find out what it had decided. As ever Ann Taylor [Shadow Commons Leader] wanted to play it by the book but the Tory whips were out saying it was strict but he would not have to resign, and getting their line out first. Our lot would not divulge content. DH went to see them but had no more joy but we were still indicating we would be calling on him to go. I went with Jonathan to the BBC party. Birt was bending our ear re Murdoch and the licence fee. Virginia Bottomley complained that I wasn't nice to her any more. Frank Skinner tried to assure me he was not intending to make TB look daft [on his chat show]. He said he was interested in working-class Tories and what we had to do to get them back. He said he wasn't political himself but his dad was a miner and he was interested in politics and the working class.

Wednesday, December 11

I took Frank Skinner and his team on a tour of Parliament, with a terrific guide in the Royal Gallery. We went for a cup of tea and ran over some of the anecdotes he might want to get into. He struck me as a pretty straight, decent kind of bloke and I was less worried about TB being stitched up. Hilary was at the other side of the tea room

---

[1] David Willetts, Conservative MP, was found by the Commons' Standards and Privileges Committee to have 'dissembled' his evidence to a select committee investigation into Conservative MP Neil Hamilton. Willetts had been a whip at the time. He would resign as Paymaster General.

with Des O'Connor's researchers, and I wondered whether we weren't doing showbiz overkill. I'd only just persuaded TB to do them and he was less worried about Des than he was about Frank. The Willetts report arrived and it was clear he would have to go, and did straight away. We had to now get it focused on Hamilton and the others in the frame. The media was inclined to see it as Willetts doing the honourable thing rather than another piece of disintegration. JP did clips and went OTT, saying Willetts should resign his seat. He came back to the office and knew he had fucked up, and was beating himself up over it. In the Europe debate, Clarke put up a robust defence on the single currency. TB believed he and Hezza were actually making sure the option remained open for us. TB had had lunch with Paul Johnson [right-wing columnist] and came back convinced that Europe was a big problem for us. We had the summit coming up and the Tories were cleverly getting up the idea of Europe 'waiting for Blair', which JM launched at PMQs yesterday.

Thursday, December 12

We arrived in Dublin and straight out to meet President Mary Robinson, a really impressive woman who seemed to mix a genuine warmth with a hard-headed assessment of issues. I got a message that JP did not want to do tax but Willetts at PMQs and I had to get TB to talk to him as we drove from the president to lunch with Dick Spring [minister for foreign affairs and Tánaiste – deputy prime minister]. Neil had said he was one of the loveliest men in politics and he was, but he gave a very gloomy prognosis of the peace process, and he was pretty sure violence would resume before the election. He was gloomy on Europe too. His finance guy, Ruairi Quinn [minister of finance 1994–97], came up with the quote of the day at lunch. 'Every Labour government has foundered on the issue of a sterling crisis – so why not just get rid of sterling?' TB said he was determined to be pro single currency but they had to understand just how awful our press were. JP having been sorted he then got angry because someone was putting it round that he had to be forced to do tax not Willetts. I asked Spring how we dealt with the 'waiting for Blair' and he said the best line was that Europe wanted a British government with strength and a clear position. At the press conference, TB had to deal with the charge that Northern Ireland was not a priority for him, and also an attack on him for marrying a Catholic.

Then bad news – Kevin Maguire [journalist] called to say the BBC had said someone had been trying to rig the *Today* programme 'personality of the year' for TB. Peter M and David Hill had known all day and decided to be robust, say it was what the Tories did last year, big deal, etc. I was not so sure and TB was in a real spin about it. I spoke to GB, who felt we should admit someone had done something wrong and apologise. Peter and DH didn't agree and said it was a case of the BBC making a huge fuss about nothing to get some publicity for their poll. I was moving towards agreement with GB as it became clear some of the papers were going big on it and I felt we had to have some humble pie/apology in the mix.

I called home and Fiona was in tears because the kids were being difficult, and I felt like shit for a while. We left at 10 for a round of interviews – John Sergeant for the *Today* programme, *GMTV*, Irish radio. We got the Barnsley result[1] about 12 – terrible turnout not least because of a power cut but I put out a few TB words anyway. We were back just after 12 and I learned that even *The Times* had splashed on the *Today* programme poll. Higgins [*Sun* editor] had said to me earlier 'This is a great story because it means we can get our teeth into you.'

Friday, December 13

A new record was set for a TB call waking me up. 5 am. He said he woke bolt upright, worrying whether he had been too dismissive about John Sergeant's question on the poll-rigging. I said Tony, it is 5 am and even if you were, which I can't remember, there is nothing I can do about it, so go back to sleep. OK, he said, and put the phone down. Then I couldn't get back to sleep. The papers arrived and several had splashed on the wretched *Today* poll. It was a sign of how they would get into us if they could. It had the feel of a one-day wonder but then it emerged the woman who wrote the note was a civil servant on unpaid leave working for us. She had sent a note on the party system and then it had got out on the usual network. We did a doorstep on the by-election then set off for the [Northern Ireland] border. We met up with Jonathan Powell and Mo who although she could be a bit OTT was incredibly good at the touchy-feely, chatty, meeting and greeting.

To Portadown to meet the troops and a briefing from the RUC [Royal Ulster Constabulary] deputy chief constable [Colin Cramphorn], who was very gloomy and said he expected a major IRA bomb before Christmas. Then to meet David Trimble [Ulster Unionist leader]

---

[1] Barnsley East by-election following the death of Terry Patchett on October 11. Jeff Ennis held the seat for Labour with an increased majority. The Liberal Democrats forced the Conservatives into third place.

on a farm. There was huge media interest and they did a joint doorstep standing in front of the cows. TB drove with him to his office and said afterwards he was a difficult guy to talk to, very internalised and hard to probe. We had a rather more rumbustious meeting with Peter Robinson [Democratic Unionist MP] in Belfast. Lunch, then to TB's speech at Queen's [University]. It was striking how few women there were wherever we went compared with audiences in England. We were promising support and continuation re the peace process and trying to put pressure on JM re the beef ban for the summit. The main summit story was agreement on the stability pact and publication of the new euro notes. I was briefing hard against the 'waiting for Blair' line saying that what they were waiting for was clarity, coherence and leadership, the qualities sadly lacking with the current lot.

Saturday, December 14

JM looked pretty weak and isolated but I was still anxious about the 'waiting for Blair' line, which I felt had the potential to damage us. I got TB to speak to one or two of the Sundays with a hardened version of the line I did yesterday. Both the *Observer* and *Sunday Times* led on a TB angle, hitting back at JM's soft-touch jibe.

Sunday, December 15

TB was very strong on *The World this Weekend*, saying Europe wanted a strong Britain offering leadership in Europe and we were now the weakest in Europe since we joined the Common Market. As a short-term exercise, the interview was fine and ran second on the news most of the day. Meeting to go through the 'war book' [internal general election plan] draft, pretty much page by page. It was getting there. GB felt there was not enough about opportunity, but that was easily fixed. The main argument was still about how we handled the concept of a Tory fifth term – did we make specific claims or did we generalise? – e.g. they *will* put VAT on food, as opposed to, given their record, they *might*. Chris Powell was adamant that equivocal statements would have zero effect. I said there was a way between the two – VAT on food, the next tax bombshell – with a question mark. Or 'If you don't want VAT on food, don't vote Tory.' Or 'Twenty-two tax rises – what's next, VAT on food?'

GB was arguing against TB's idea of another new positive campaign document, as being drafted by Roger Liddle. He said he knew nothing about it. Peter M said that was not so, that he had sent TB and GB notes about it at every stage of its preparation and it was exasperating that he did not get replies, when we were just weeks or months from a general election. He said he did not want to keep sending memos into the dark and then be told he had not told GB about what was going on. TB was exasperated that we were nothing like on an election footing yet and he said he was worried that for all their troubles, he still felt the Tories could get back. GB then said he was not yet in a position to do the tax speech planned for January 6, and there was still the argument with TB to be had about the top rate. Peter said later it sometimes felt as if the man meant to be in charge of election strategy was on strike. We also had a discussion about whether to stick to the five pledges or develop them. GB was worried that whatever we did in the campaign document he claimed not to know about, it would all become embroiled as a tax-and-spend argument. He cited DB as someone whose speeches and statements were full of spending commitments.

TB felt there was not enough real argument in the war book. PG and I agreed we would go over it page by page and get a new version done by tomorrow. But the real problem was that GB and Peter still were not co-operating and so there was no cohesion or shared and agreed approach. Peter called me and said he was very dispirited by the meeting, that it was intolerable for GB to claim he had not seen his memos, and he felt it was my job to get GB on board for a proper fifth-term strategy.

Monday, December 16

TB's Euro interview went well, apart from the *Sun* which headlined it 'Blair vows – I'm backing Brussels'. It was, following the poll-rigging splash, another sign they were ready to do us in if they could. I raised it with the *Sun*, pointing out that when JM said there were some areas where they would extend qualified majority voting, they did not handle it the same way at all, and that there was nothing new in what TB said on that. I told Kavanagh there was malice in the way they reported our position on Europe, constant misrepresentation of the position, designed to do damage. I lost it with him and with George Pascoe-Watson [deputy political editor] and later Higgins called and said he would not tolerate my calling his staff malicious wankers and if it happened again he would put it in the paper, which would be no good for anyone. I said if a paper misrepresented our position, it was my job to fight our corner and that is what I would do. Later he called to cancel his meeting with TB planned for Thursday. Ludicrous.

Peter had boycotted the morning meeting after yesterday but I knew he was next door and got him in too. It quickly became another GB/Peter spat. GB asked how the *Today* business happened and Peter said 'You know how it happened because I told you from my own mouth, with my own tongue.' DD and I both looked pretty aghast. GB stood up, said there was no point having this kind of conversation and went to make a phone call. Peter carried on talking to DD, said that on the wider questions relating to chain of command, that was a matter for GB, and off he went, leaving DD and I looking at each other, shaking our heads. DD said the chain of command point was important.

TB admitted that he was more worried about the Des O'Connor and Frank Skinner interviews than any of the big political interviews. He said you had no way of knowing where they went, or the impact they would have. We said the key was to relax and imagine he was talking to a passer-by not a political interviewer.

Tuesday, December 17

We agreed early on we should do beef for PMQs. TB was running late and in a bad mood. He was virtually silent on the way in and when we got into the office I said for God's sake get a grip and stop behaving like a two-year-old. I don't know if he had had a big scene with CB or whether it was just general grumpiness but when he did speak it was to complain that he was doing Des O'Connor's show and I had to start the whole process again of explaining why it was a good thing to do. We had had very friendly conversations with Des' people and the aim was to ask friendly questions and get TB to deliver a few anecdotes, e.g. running away from school, about the time when he failed to recognise Queen Beatrix of the Netherlands talking to him in a queue, etc. DD and Jonathan came in, DD having discovered that last night in the fisheries vote won by the Tories they had paired three MPs with us and the Lib Dems [the same three Conservative MPs had been paired with three absent Labour MPs and three absent Liberal Democrats]. In the climate it was a great story which would go big.

TB was in a round of meetings and I popped in and he was still moaning about having to do Des O'C. I said I could not believe he could not lift himself into a positive mindset about it but by now he had the hump with me. I had a row with Anji about it too, but that was probably more because she thought I was taking CB/Fiona's side in their argument. She said I was mishandling him. He was nervous about it and I had to understand that. I said it had gone beyond that, he was behaving like a child about it. I stayed out of his hair for a while then we started talking again in the car to the studio, first re JM, then trying to get him to focus positively re Des. We met Barbra

Streisand [singer] in make-up, which cheered him up a bit, then Des came through. He was much more charismatic than I imagined, had real presence. In the end, TB did fine, well even, and the audience really went for it. I said to him in the car it would connect with more people for longer than anything else he had done in ages. We left on better terms after a pretty fractious day.

Wednesday, December 18

The [Conservative whips] cheating story was the splash in most places. The first task was to set up a DD press conference and it led to a rare spat between me and him. He was very iffy about my line 'Yesterday caught out cheating, today caught out lying' and instead offered an academic treatise on pairing, too detailed and dull to rebut the charge that fourteen Labour MPs broke their pair. Jo Moore and I were getting very agitated. I gave DD a short, tough script on lying, cheating and challenging JM to say why he was in the Whips Office at 9.50. He wouldn't do it so instead I slipped it to Janet Anderson [Labour MP] at the last minute and asked her to read it. She did so after DD and JS had done their statements and Donald looked like he had swallowed a lemon. We made up afterwards. I said it was too good a hit to miss. He said you're a hard man, rolling his 'r's more than usual.

Meanwhile, the story that Anne Campbell [Labour MP] gave her car park pass to CB finally appeared in the *Guardian* diary. I got Tim [Allan] on the case. There were problems with the Des O'Connor fallout too. Andrew Pierce [*Times* columnist] called Leo [TB's father] who, thinking he was defending TB, said the running away from school story wasn't true. Why on earth we hadn't spoken to him and warned him people might phone him about it, I don't know. He obviously hadn't seen it and he told me afterwards he thought they were trying to get him to say something bad about Tony. He was a lovely old bloke and he said I hope I haven't done anything wrong, anything that might hurt Tony. I got Hilary to agree a statement. Then TB's old [Fettes] housemaster, Eric Anderson, called out of the blue and said he could remember the incident and we put out words from him too, saying it was true.

The other developing drama was the Millennium Exhibition. Jack C, GB, Jonathan and I had all told TB we thought a dome was a waste of money and would be a disaster in government, but TB was very cautious, and very reluctant to be blamed for scuppering it. He spoke to Virginia Bottomley, Bob Ayling and others, but was getting conflicting advice. The media view was sceptical, that the whole thing was a great ego trip for Hezza, but TB felt it could be good for Britain and he didn't want it to be done in by us. The government was having to get our support because lots of the businesses were saying why should we put money into something the next lot might scrap, and he was worried about it.

At the Shadow Cabinet, TB did yet another no-complacency pep talk. They were all on board for the no-pairing decision. We had the office party, where Tim did his Oscars. I won the Clare Short Award for upsetting the most people. I made a rather dull, not very funny speech. I'm not sure Bruce Grocott took too kindly to getting Tim's Unreconstructed Wanker Award for continuing devotion to left-wing policies.

Thursday, December 19

Jim Callaghan's interview in the *New Statesman*, saying the link with the unions must stay, was getting a fair bit of coverage. TB wanted us to use it to get up the already changed relations with the unions. The Des coverage was fine, though there was the odd pompous editorial that he shouldn't be doing programmes like this. But the feedback from people who saw the interview itself was good. I went round to TB's, and Cherie was very nice, like her old self, and gave me a pair of silver cuff links with the red rose painted on them. TB was doing *Breakfast News* and though the interview was a bit trivial, he did fine. He was really on good form on the interview front at the moment. He was worrying about GB still pressing for leaving open the option of a new top rate of income tax and later the two of them met and were both pretty much immovable. TB said to him he knew of nobody whose judgement he trusted who thought it was a good idea, and he was not going to have it. GB said the public finances were such a mess that we could not rule it out. TB said that was a terrible argument. I said my concern was that at a stroke it would wipe out the good job GB had done repositioning us on tax. TB said to him I know why you want to do it, it is all part of the fairness agenda, but it is not the right way to do it.

TB saw Dacre and English [*Mail*] and was on good chief executive form, promising more party reform, dropping hints on welfare reform. Dacre said he liked TB, liked his freshness, admired his commitment to education, but was worried about the party and about our position re Europe. He was basically an offshore island merchant. It was clear English would be happy enough to support us and virtually said he would vote Labour, but Dacre would need an awful lot of pushing. We were preparing for Frank Skinner and again TB was nervous and we went over all the stories and anecdotes we had talked about. Skinner was fine, though the recording went on and on, Terry Wogan [radio and TV presenter], a child prodigy, some US psychic who said TB was going to win big. TB was fine. Skinner asked if there was anyone there who was not planning to vote Labour but having seen him had changed their minds, and three hands went up.

Friday, December 20

A historic first. At the end of today, TB called to APOLOGISE. He said everywhere he had been today, people had come up to him and said they'd seen him on *Des O'Connor* and he was terrific. 'I owe you a big apology,' he said, 'for doubting your judgement and being a pain in the run-up to it.' It had definitely cut through. Grace Gould [Philip's daughter] said some of her friends had been talking about it. Victoria [Bridge, neighbour] said he was brilliant on it. Andy Grice [*Sunday Times*] appeared to know about the tax discussion, which given how tight it was was ridiculous. TB, so far as I knew, had only spoken to me about it. I was bounced a bit by Andy and probably went too far in trying to rebuff the idea of a division, and he went away with the line that GB had fallen in line with TB. GB would be furious. I raised it with TB who said he had already said to GB that his big worry now was not the policy but 'Blair beats Brown' headlines. I was briefing some of the Sundays on the idea of a fingernail government clinging to power without any purpose. Jonathan told me that Jack Straw's discussions with Hugh Dykes [Conservative MP] were coming to fruition and he was minded to give up the whip in the New Year, possibly timed to the Tories' campaign launch.

Saturday, December 21

Peter M called from the States. He said the big difference between the Clinton operation and ours was (a), cohesion and (b), attention to detail. He said before a big interview Clinton would video rehearse four or five times. The people at the top got on together in a way that ours didn't. I was starting to get worried re tax. I told TB both Grice and John Kampfner appeared to know about the TB/GB top rate discussion and it was clearly going to come out. Grice told me the story was that TB 'persuaded' GB against the idea of a 50p rate. He said he had spoken to a GB person who had said GB had decided it was not something worth going to the stake for. That sounded pretty implausible. My heart fell when he said it was going to be the splash. I told TB who assured me he had not told Peter re their discussions.

He said his hope was that this was GB positioning himself to be the person who announced it and seemed to be in charge of it. We tried to get hold of GB because if the first he knew of it was seeing it in the paper he would be furious. Clearly they would think it was Peter but I had a horrible feeling it was me who had turned a possible into a probable with the way I answered Andy yesterday. I spoke to Ed Balls as Fiona and I were driving to Philip's for a drink with George Stephanopolous [ex-Clinton spokesman] and after hearing my end of the conversation explaining the story so far, Fiona said it was obvious it came from me. TB and GB spoke later and TB called, and told me GB was 'fit to be scraped off the wall'.

George was less than flattering re Peter, who he had met in the States. He said he was surprised how insecure he was. PG made the same point Peter did, re the greater cohesion of the US team. I said the problem was we all had big egos and sometimes competing interests. I got the sense the US people were much more subservient. George thought Peter was a particular problem because he was seen neither as politician nor as spin doctor. James Carville [pollster, Clinton adviser] had told PG that TB was clearly our biggest asset and we had to play the leadership line for all it was worth. On the way out, a scene that would have made a great story had it been filmed. I was walking down the stairs behind GS, tripped, landed on his back and flattened him to the floor. He was not much more than half my weight and yet got up and was almost apologetic, as if he had landed on me. I liked George. He was sharp, clever, engaging and he later sent PG a message saying he got the sense TB's campaign was in very safe hands. I got the papers on the way home, tax splash in *Sunday Times*, horrible piece about me in the *Mail*, story in the *Observer* about Tory MPs working for MI6, something about Peter having a car from James Palumbo [owner of Ministry of Sound club and friend of Mandelson]. Then I remembered something PG had said about their meeting with Carville, namely Peter M saying how awful it was to be attacked for having a chauffeur.

Sunday, December 22

GB was incandescent re the *Sunday Times*. TB reckoned he just about persuaded him it was not down to me, but GB still thought it was done for TB. There was less follow-up than we expected but I did make clear to people where TB's instincts lay, whilst denying some of the specifics of the story. On the policy, we were moving in the right direction, but TB/GB's relationship could not possibly be helped by all this. TB felt Tim may have told Peter and I felt pretty shitty at blame being passed around because I reckon when all was said and done Grice took a punt and got lucky through the way I answered him. I took Calum out but every time I thought we would get a bit of peace and quiet, the phone went, usually Ed Balls. A car bomb went off in Belfast, signalling the end of the longest ceasefire in recent history.

Monday, December 23

Peter M came back from the US, having ended the 'official' part of his visit with a little trip to Aspen [Colorado ski resort]. The papers were doing him over pretty badly re his Palumbo car. The papers were starting to fill up with Tory briefings on their New Year campaign, going on tax, TB, Europe, negative advertising. *The Times* were doing a story that JM was up for a £1m negative ad campaign. TB did not think we were geared up for their New Year attacks. Dykes was continuing to move. We were confident at the least that he would serve on a Lib-Lab constitutional committee and stop taking the Tory whip. I thought it was better he join the Libs, because he was basically defined as a federalist.

Tuesday, December 24

The Guardian had a splash, clearly briefed by GB, about his 'fair tax' plans, in which a focus on loopholes and abuses were the alternative to a new top rate. We went to Michael and Alison Farthing's party but had to leave early because Rory had a bad allergic reaction to something. I had a brief chat with a psychiatrist who said twenty-five per cent of all stomach complaints were psychological.

Wednesday, December 25

After Christmas lunch, we went to PG's, then Peter M came round and we were all drivelling on about the usual stuff – division at the top, Tory discipline at the top, laziness (half the Shadow Cabinet were away), DD being so cautious, GB disengaging. PG was recommending we take on someone from the States. I was reading a JFK book that was so Camelot it became a bit sickly.

Thursday, December 26

Telegraph did a story on Fiona being CB's spin doctor. We said that as CB didn't intend to do media, it was balls as she did not require a spin doctor. The main story was JM winning the 'personality of the year' award. The BBC said that was despite 4,000 JM votes being discounted because of evidence of double voting. We went to Helena

Kennedy's party pm. Peter there and Tessa Blackstone, fulminating about Jack Straw who bollocked her for talking about prisons on the radio. I sensed quite a lot of pessimism around the place.

Friday, December 27

There was lots in the papers about Fiona, following the *Telegraph*. The *Mail* did a full page, reasonably straight, but it was all still a pain. I don't think I had been strong enough dealing with Rachel Sylvester [*Telegraph*] when she first came on about it. I should have done more to ensure it did not become a spin-doctor story which was exactly what we had. TB called and Fiona got really cross because he seemed to think we had put the story out, which was ludicrous. He had not worked on the campaign document or on the New Year message. I was suggesting he focus on leadership. The Major 'personality of the year' award was a damp squib because it was surrounded by so much scepticism. I sensed TB was not motoring at all on the NY message so I worked on a draft. We also discussed JM. TB said he was not worried about him. He said the only thing that worried him was that Peter M and I said we were worried about him. I felt JM had greater powers of resilience than we thought, was good at reinvention and he had a basic set image founded on decency that gave him strength. TB feared that a public sense of those concerns would play up the idea of JM as electoral asset. He felt it was better we were relaxed about it, and developed the basic line that he was a decent bloke but not up to the job, and that Britain was suffering as a result of weak leadership.

Saturday, December 28

I put in the changes to the New Year message which TB had phoned through from Ireland, which were mainly about fleshing out economic message based on the government's failure to address fundamental weaknesses. I tried out the lines we had been working on re clear aims and sticking to them. I got the final edit of the Skinner interview, which wasn't great. The *Sunday Times* were going big on a story re the Tories' New Year campaign, going back on earlier reports re negative campaigns, and setting out positive messages/agenda. I tried to get the others on to a 'disarray' wicket, but the truth was the Tories were getting up strong political stories at the moment and we weren't. Number 10 announced JM would do his message tomorrow, so we would have to wait another day to get a clear run. The day ended with a dreadful row with Fiona, usual stuff, her saying I was so distracted when I was there I might as well not be, me saying I worked hard at being there more often, working less, but it was hard. She said she felt like I was on the point of explosion any minute the whole time.

Sunday, December 29

Tim thought the papers were a bit of a disaster area. *Sunday Times* splash on GPs not liking our health policy and a few bitchy pieces re Fiona. Peter M called to suggest words for JP on JM. He said could I speak to him because he felt JP didn't get it when he spoke to him, and missed the point. He said he was really anxious about next week. GB was not even returning his calls and would not say what he expected of next week's campaign. TB was not really focused on it either. Tim called later to say the *Mail* had tracked down where TB was staying in Ireland. Dinner at the Foots', with Will Hutton and Jane [wife], Salman Rushdie and Elizabeth. Salman said he didn't have a vote. He was broadly supportive, but critical re our stance on arts and culture. He was a very good example of someone whose image as set by the press had heavily influenced expectations of him. Most if not all of my meetings with him were through Michael and Jill, and he was very different to the image, much friendlier, probably more insecure, funnier. Michael was on great form, and so was Jill. They were nice to us and about us, and given in fact they probably disagreed with some of the things TB was saying and doing, their support was really warm and strong. Both Jill and Jane seemed to share my general thesis of the press and its snideness. Salman said we were victims of our own success. Michael said 'Not often people have said that about the Labour Party.' HC called to say that Peggy Herbison [former minister in the Attlee and Wilson governments] had died, and we put out some TB words. I went down and told them the news. Most people went through the 'oh that's sad' motions. Jill said, without any emotion but real force, and that wicked glint in her eye, 'She was a dreadful right-winger.'

Monday, December 30

JM got pretty uncritical coverage. As if proving my point to Will Hutton last night re the *Guardian*, their splash was 'Major, I stand by my record'. It would have been news if he hadn't. TB wanted to make late changes to his own message but it had already gone out under embargo, was going down well with the press but we had problems with the BBC, who wanted to make it part of a story about Klaus Kinkel [German politician, former chairman of the Free Democratic Party] who in his NY message seemed to be indicating he was hoping for a Labour government. It was potentially difficult, but no excuse for the BBC not to treat the TB message the same as they had JM's. Tessa [Jowell] and David [Mills] had gone to Jamaica and had given us their house in the Cotswolds but the kids were all under the weather and a bit miserable when we got there. Fiona and I were still not really speaking and the kids were all going down with the same bug.

Peter M called and said he had finally met GB for a proper discussion and it had been a disaster. He had complained there was no point him continuing to communicate through Ed Miliband and must see him. GB eventually agreed and started by saying Peter had 'no right' to proceed with the VAT on food campaign, as GB had expressed his doubts about it. Peter said he had sent him notes, letters, faxes, asking for a decision and he heard nothing, so felt we had to proceed. Peter said it had been a bloody conversation and he now had no idea how we were supposed to proceed. We had a major campaign ahead, high media expectations of it, and yet no real detailed plans in place. Worryingly, we also had a clear security problem. A pretty near-accurate version of the 'five Tory pledges' plan [Labour's claims about Conservative policy intentions] had found its way to the Tories and was part of Mawhinney's response to TB's NY message. TB was also concerned we had a mole pretty close in, because too much stuff close in was being aired in public.

The coverage of the message was fine, with lots focused on the leadership sections. TB called, said he was getting his mind focused for the next stage. Said he was relaxed about JM, relaxed about Europe, not fazed by Kinkel, saying people would think yes, we don't want the Germans telling us how to vote, but is there nobody this lot can get on with?

Tuesday, December 31

TB called and said I had to get a grip of the Straw/Hugh Dykes situation. They had been talking for some time about Dykes maybe giving signals of support to our constitutional plans and they had agreed TB and Dykes would exchange letters and through that Dykes give 'evidence' to the Cook/Maclennan committee.[1] I wasn't keen for TB to get directly involved at this stage and agreed with Jack it should

---

[1] Robin Cook and Liberal Democrat MP Robert Maclennan co-chaired a joint consultative committee on constitutional reform. The 'Cook-Maclennan Agreement' laid the basis for New Labour's general election manifesto plan to reshape the constitution.

be him or RC for now. The aim was to have something to derail the Tories' negative campaign against us which we thought JM would kick off on *Frost* on Sunday, followed by a poster launch on Monday. We agreed Dykes would do nothing until Monday. I didn't think it was enough to have some arcane story about a constitutional committee – it had to move quickly into the field of not supporting the government, maybe by saying he would vote against JM in a vote of no confidence. I said to Jack without real hard edge, anything involving Dykes would become a story about Europe. We stayed in, and with the kids all feeling very down, it was not exactly a happy New Year's Eve. Fiona and I were at least talking.

Thursday, January 2, 1997

GB had made it clear he would not allow a campaign stating that Tory VAT on food would cost £8 a week. The most he would allow was the suggestion I had made earlier – 'VAT on food – the next Tory tax?' But as Peter M said, half a million quid on a question mark did not seem the best way to spend what campaign money we had, but if that was all we were going to get, so be it. Peter said he was now only dealing with GB through Ed Miliband and it was becoming more and more ridiculous.

Saturday, January 4

Burnley at Liverpool but I didn't feel at all well and would have pulled out if Rory hadn't nagged me into going. Peter Kilfoyle met us at the station and we went up to his place for lunch. He said he was not sure what New Labour was and he was worried that if we won, we would find it hard to hold on to the support. The game was OK but we never really looked like doing it. We lost 2-0. A lot of Lib-Labbery in the Sundays, *Observer* doing TB changes his mind on PR, *Sunday Times* some story about a 'secret' TB/Ashdown committee. Peter M denied briefing them and they looked Liberal-inspired to me.

Sunday, January 5

JM was hard against constitutional reform, which would help the Hugh Dykes situation, which Jack S and I had been discussing endlessly in the last few days. Jack had got him to agree that we would publish exchange of letters Monday morning. His feet got a bit colder later, and he didn't want to get caught in the JM fuss, but he did say his letters were in the post to the PA, so there was really no going back on it now. I alerted John Sergeant to what was going to happen and said he could run with it from 6am. Jack called a bit panicky later saying he hadn't heard from Dykes but then it all came good.

Earlier I had a bit of a shouting match with RC who came on all very hoity-toity about who put in these stories re Lib-Lab talks. It was obvious from the tone of his voice he thought it was me, and I gave back with both barrels, saying I had a lot less interest in the Libs than he did, and I had better things to do. If TB wanted me to brief out on this stuff, I would. But he didn't, and I didn't, and that was that. It ended up a bit nasty and we both slammed the phones down. RC called later and was apologetic. 'We have done a lot of good work together. Let's not let one cross phone call spoil it.' I said he was justified at being irritated but I had more experience of things being briefed out against us than anyone, and I resented it when he tried to intimate I had done something I hadn't. If I had done it, it would have been for a purpose and I would have told you.

Took campaign document up to TB's house. The house was absolutely freezing but it didn't seem to bother him. He thought the document was better but, like us, he was not sure what we would get out of it. He was fairly relaxed, feeling the Tories had not managed to get the initiative back. I felt we could get coverage for it simply being an explanation of our positive campaign themes. GB and Ed Balls arrived later and there was another row about the top rate of tax. We all felt that it had been allowed to develop in a way that TB could not back down on it now. TB said he didn't mind changing his mind if he thought it was the right thing to do, but he didn't. The more he thought about it, the more persuaded he was it would be the wrong thing to do. I clocked Murdoch's Christmas card to TB/CB. The family on the front and inside – good luck for '97. I got home and lost a bloody crown eating a fucking jelly baby.

Monday, January 6

One of those rare moments of pure political pleasure. I was in the bath at 6.30 when John Sergeant came on with the Dykes story. Another Tory relaunch, another total flop because we had managed events to turn against them. Sergeant did us proud and later paged me to thank me for putting the story his way. It pretty much led the bulletins all day. Dykes did the 8.10 slot and was fine. JP was a bit all over the shop but it didn't really matter. The thing was running perfectly for us. GB was at the morning meeting. He wanted JP to carry on. I noticed for the first time that he referred to Tony as 'Blair'. I wasn't the only one to clock it. He was not at all happy and didn't contribute much. TB's *Big Issue* [magazine sold by the homeless] interview came out, in which he was strong on zero tolerance and said he didn't give money to beggars, which was the big story in several places. The news was going fine but we had a real problem with the way the BBC were giving soft coverage to launches the Tories described as policy launches which usually were anything but. JM's visits were being treated as news regardless of content. I got home at 11. Fiona said Maggie Rae[1] had been on saying that she was fixing a dinner for TB/CB, me and Fiona to have a proper session with Diana. Maggie said she had said to Diana she was thinking of inviting me. 'Oh yes, I do like Alastair,' Diana said. God bless her.

Tuesday, January 7

The *Big Issue* stuff went far bigger than we expected, splash in several places, and running big on the broadcasts. We managed to get the *Guardian* to change the headline from 'Blair lurch to the right on crime' to 'Blair backs zero tolerance'. It is amazing how they still see anything strong on crime as automatically right wing. The Dykes stuff, which seemed days ago, was still ticking on. JM was doing the *Today* programme and was pretty ratty, and short-tempered. He said he never said he was 'the boy from Brixton', so that was something else he was getting defensive about, and I put out some words on that. We also had to get up a positive message tomorrow for the launch of 'Leading Britain into the Future'. It all boiled down to leadership and education. I felt the basic message was strong when I was briefing around the gallery. They all seemed to have pretty much bought the guff from Major today. He still had an ability to make not much sound like quite a lot. I could tell we needed something to move it our way and I gave Mike Brunson the cover of the leadership document so he could start to flag that up, which he did. TB said it was important we broaden it from TB vs Major and weak vs strong. This was about the parties. They were ungovernable. We were not. The changes we have made to the party make us fit for the task of changing Britain. I used it as the main message in a TB piece for the *Sun*, including the line 'in an uncertain world, Britain cannot afford an uncertain prime minister'. I had a go at Nick Robinson who had relied on the *Guardian* coverage and admitted he hadn't read the whole *Big Issue* piece. I

[1] The Blairs, AC and Fiona had been invited by Alan Howarth, secretary of the Parliamentary Labour Party (not the Conservative-turned-Labour MP), and his partner Maggie Rae, to dinner with Diana, Princess of Wales. Maggie Rae had been a legal adviser in her divorce from Prince Charles.

thought the deliberate misreporting of the *Big Issue* on the Beeb, and them falling for JM's guff was too much. I got home and Fiona had had another big scene with Rory, and I was worrying now that even though I tried to put the time in, it just wasn't possible to do enough because of the demands of the job.

Wednesday, January 8

JM did well out of yesterday. I got to TB's where he was fiddling with the draft press release. There was a danger the story would be seen as a personal attack on Major, around the leadership theme, which is why he wanted to make the issue the governability of the parties. We got in for a meeting with GB who wanted to chair the event and make an opening statement about tax and spend. JP wasn't happy about it. TB said GB should chair it and make his statement sitting down. JP told me that he was fed up with all the performing rubbish they had to do. GB and Peter M had a bit of a spat because Peter said Darling had dealt with the same stuff yesterday and GB took that to mean he should say nothing today. Margaret Beckett looked on with a bit of a smile but the atmosphere was not good and in the end we were all arguing about nothing. We had a strong document, the themes we wanted from it were clear, and everything should be put behind that. But GB wanted to do his own thing, and JP felt slighted. Peter M came in and said change of plan, TB will chair it. He said to JP – let's put the row behind us, and JP was off again, saying put yourself in my place, constantly being told one thing and then another. Then Peter had a go at me, saying I shouldn't have told JP of the changing plans. As we went in, I heard Kevin Keegan had quit [as manager of Newcastle United], and we also had Branson's[1] collapsing balloon so we would be down the bulletins, but it went well as an event. Most of the questions were on tax and spend, and both TB and GB were clear and strong, saying that any proposals here were properly costed and fundable and there was no need for tax rises. So they all pretty much went for that line, which was fine.

We left for Mitcham and Morden meeting with switchers. It went fine, but I didn't like the way that afterwards one or two talked about 'better the devil you know' being the thing that might hold them back. GB called not happy with the way it was going, and clearly felt

[1] Richard Branson, the Virgin tycoon, was forced to land in the Algerian desert only twenty-four hours after beginning an ill-fated attempt to fly non-stop round the world in a balloon.

we had bounced him. In fact I had been emphasising to everyone not to see this as Brown vs Blair. It was GB who had won the big argument on tax and spend with the Tories and in the party. But he was worried a ruling out top rate story would be bad for him. TB was unsympathetic. He said GB should not have got himself on to that hook in the first place, without being clear it was where we wanted and needed to be. 'Are we really going to say we have costed everything and we don't need tax rises, and then say but despite that we are going to raise the top rate?' We got back, and I went upstairs while TB was seeing GB. Kate Garvey said it was terrifying. She was at her desk and they were shouting so loud at each other she could hear virtually every word. Both had purple faces when they left. She said it had never been so bad. TB had to leave early for a meeting at home with CB and the security people. I asked what had happened. He said it was too dreadful for words, but the bottom line was GB said he would not be doing the press conference on VAT and food. TB said he was worried about us seeing Diana, with or without CB and Fiona. Anji was against, and worried it would get out. I was dead keen, and probably for the wrong reasons. It would be fascinating and I'd love to know what she was up to.

Thursday, January 9

I got Tim to start compiling a paper on the BBC's respective coverage of our and the Tories' recent events, to send to Tony Hall. The papers did yesterday pretty big, mainly on top rate. GB was furious and went home to Scotland. I had breakfast with David Frost who was obviously pushing to chair any TV debate. He felt TB would do well but he agreed that JM was a better communicator than people gave him credit for. At the 10am strategy meeting, TB was worried we didn't have enough clear campaigns planned. We talked with JP about the need to get up party funding, and how the Tories were getting the money for all these posters. We agreed to aim for Monday and TB would say on *Frost* that we would not take money from foreigners. TB and I left for lunch with the *Telegraph* at the Savoy. Even Charles Moore seemed resigned to us winning. Mawhinney seemed to get wind of our plan to force a vote on the Wirral by-election timing. He announced it would be held in the normal time frame. TB was still fretting about Diana. I spoke to Maggie Rae, who said she had said she was terribly excited about seeing me. I said she said that to all the boys. TB said he was at a loss to know what more to do to get GB and Peter M working better together. I said it could not go on like this. CB called and said TB was going to be asking GB if they could have the Number 11 flat if we won, as it was bigger and more family-friendly than Number 10. I imagined this came out of the security meeting. I said I thought now might not be the time to ask.

Friday, January 10

We were going through a bit of a *Boy's Own* media phase – yacht rescue,[1] Branson's balloon, Keegan – so politics was a bit dead. PG was hilarious about last night's groups. They knew 'absolutely nothing, sweet f.a.' about anything that had happened in the last three days. They had not heard a word either JM or TB had said. He said we really had to break out of the press conference format and get TB out and about with people.

TB wanted a strategy meeting – his big concern was tax, and the need to get our explanation clearer. He felt there were three points to put over: 1. our spending proposals were costed and did not require tax rises; 2. because of the misleading charges laid against us we were making it explicitly clear that we would not raise the basic or top rate; 3. other taxes would depend on economic circumstances and be up to the Chancellor of the day. TB was on good form at the moment but he took me and Anji aback when he said he thought 'street parties' should form part of the election tour. After the others had gone, TB took me aside and said that he felt at the *Telegraph* lunch I had been a bit tense and ratty, and it was beginning to show that I had very little time for them. I needed to hang loose a bit more. Peter M stayed on too, and TB said to him 'We have to make it work with you and Gordon.' 'How?' said Peter. 'I don't know,' said TB. But he was getting exasperated and he was worried about the possible impact on a campaign. He said he had told GB he might ask Derry to have an overseeing role of some kind and GB said 'I'm not going to be told by some fucking lawyer what to do.' On tax, the plan now was for GB finally to rule out rises in March and meanwhile make a series of speeches on the state of the economy. On advertising, his concern was that the sheer weight of the Tory campaign was bound to have an effect, and we didn't really have the resources to counter it. If people were not watching news, then posters were maybe having more of an effect than we thought. He felt their language was crisper and clearer and wanted me to have a brainstorming session with the agency to get our language better.

I called Ruth Harding [wife of Matthew Harding] to sort out what was happening re Matthew's million. Not all of it had been paid before

[1] Five days after capsizing in the Southern Ocean, yachtsman Tony Bullimore was found alive on January 9.

January '97: TB exasperated by team not working together

he died and I was keen that we could make something of the rest being paid with her full agreement and blessing. It would help deal with questions on Monday, about where the money came from for the posters, in a positive way. She was really nice, talked about how the kids were dealing with it and how he would have been around for these final months of the run-in to an election. I went back to the office for a meeting on the lessons of the Clinton tour. The real lesson, so far as I could see, was that the preparation had to be detailed. In particular, they worked hard at ensuring the right kind of pictures. I was looking to get stills and TV professionals in to help us with that. They also got the right mix of planned and spontaneous, or 'planned spontaneous'.

Saturday, January 11

Tim put out the Matthew Harding story which had a bit of pick-up in the tabloids, but generally it was a quiet day. I was working on the script for *Frost*. We both knew it didn't actually mean much to say the first bill would be education, but it allowed us to get up content and substance on policy. I briefed on it during the day and could tell it would go fine. We even had some of them saying 'TB will say on *Frost*' with quotes, which Frost was laughing about when I spoke to him. We were also intending to use the interview to say we would ban foreign donations. Andy Grice got hold of the *Party into Power* document, which I was angry about, because it would detract from the education story. I assume it came from Peter. TB called a few times re *Frost*, but said he didn't go for that Clinton idea of '100-minute rehearsal for 1-minute TV'. The papers were fine, apart from Grice on *Party into Power*, and another *Sunday Times* piece of crap about us keeping files on personal information and sexual preferences of candidates – probably put there by the Tories, as a way of getting into Peter M.

Sunday, January 12

The education briefing was leading the news from early morning, so the thing was perfectly set up for when we got there. Frost was very funny about the whole thing, joking that he would start by asking him to confirm the quotes we had briefed to the Sundays. The interview was strong and afterwards I briefed Sergeant and Tom Bradby [ITN] that the public were tired of electioneering stories and wanted to hear about actual detailed policy proposals. TB was on after Glenn Hoddle [England football manager] and he got up the education stuff brilliantly. It looked and sounded natural. There was empathy and determination. It led the bulletins all day, on exactly the line we wanted, with exactly the clip we had planned. There was one hard-ball moment when he confirmed we would keep Chris Woodhead [chief inspector of schools] in the job. DB had not wanted him to do that. but he accepted that any other response would probably have led to 'Woodhead sacked' stories. Woodhead later did *World at One*, all sweetness and light. He sounded very creepy though. TB was pretty sceptical on Europe and on PR, but on the whole people thought it was a very powerful performance. Jill Craigie and Michael Foot both called to say he had been terrific, which was nice. A good day for us.

Monday, January 13

Education went OK, though less well in the papers than it had on TV and radio. Prince Charles was doing something on homework later on today, which in a funny sort of way would help too. At the morning meeting, GB was in bark mode, and cutting short any attempt to discuss anything. He had no interest in how we pushed through on education. He was clearly fed up about the coverage of him and Sarah Macaulay [PR executive and GB's girlfriend].[1] The meeting was pretty much a waste of time. At the election planning group, we agreed we had to do some real 'towels on heads' work on TB's tour. It had to be really good. The outline plans weren't great. We went through what we envisaged as a typical day in the life of a campaign, and I felt it all lacked innovation and creativity. If it was to be a long campaign in particular, we would need more than we had. TB mean-while was still worried about the weight of the Tory posters on tax and he wanted us to work up plans to get more money for heavy-weight posters of our own.

I had lunch with Charles Anson and Geoff Crawford from the Palace, at Shepherd's. Both thought we were going to win, and I got the sense they were all pretty relaxed about it. We mainly talked about the difficulties of dealing with the media, the way the BBC was changing, etc. I had talked to TB beforehand, and he said to make clear there was no question of him letting the issue of the monarchy get on to the political agenda while he was in charge.

There was then an awful meeting with TB, GB, Peter M and me. GB was at his most monosyllabic. We had agreed he was going to make a series of four speeches on the economy, and we were trying

---

[1] Gordon Brown and Sarah Macaulay had kept their relationship a secret since they began dating in 1994.

to establish what they would say, one by one. It was like drawing blood from a stone. Asked a direct question, he would answer a question that was never asked. At one point, he said nobody but his office should talk to the press about tax. He was still angry about last week's coverage. I said was he saying that if TB was ever asked about tax, we should simply say – that is not a matter for me? It wasn't realistic. There had to be an agreed approach. He said all enquiries should be referred to him. The whole thing was ridiculous. We ran around the block on how we got here. Where he had a point was in commentators thinking we had said no taxes would go up. But we hadn't. Then he said there was a credibility problem if you could not say where extra investment would come from. But we could. It was ultimately a non-conversation but it meant we made no progress. TB kept trying to get him back to his planned four speeches. But all he would do was pick on something someone had said earlier, and go on about that. At one point, TB just laughed out loud, obviously suddenly struck by the comic nature of the whole thing, where a Shadow Chancellor was refusing to tell a Leader of the Opposition what he thought of the economy. TB called him back in later and they had another voices raised meeting, just the two of them. CB told Fiona that Tony was actually now not sleeping well, because he was worried that if he could not get GB working with me and Peter, we would not really have a campaign.

Tuesday, January 14

The day started with another dreadful 9am meeting. Whelan arrived to say the *Standard* were splashing on a piece whacking JP for going away [to China] – so much for the big fight against the Tories, they were saying. I wonder how that got there. You had to admire Charlie's cheek. I was even more suspicious when GB said it would only be an issue if we made it one. There was no discussion of education, no discussion of BSE, which were meant to be the two big issues of the day.

Meeting with TB and Chris Powell from the agency. PG had said to me on the way in I could complain all I want about the agency but what were they to make of the fact that we would not get TB and GB to agree to a two-sentence statement to give them as a brief? So it transpired. GB wanted to focus on trust. TB agreed but wanted it centred around economic messages. PG and I argued that if we were thinking posters we had to focus on fifth-term messages for now. So Chris sat there looking a bit bewildered, and we couldn't really blame him.

We then had another meeting on TB's tour. I said the answer to 'smarm' was actually for people to get more direct exposure to TB, and the media to see that was happening. TB had to look like he was hungry, up for a fight, really out to persuade people. I wanted words for the sides of the three buses that would make sense whatever order they were driving in. I liked the idea of the press sitting in a mobile convoy advert, and I was busy scribbling loads of options. We'd now agreed that the basic spine of the campaign would be four serious lectures, three 'shows' – i.e. more rallies than big policy speeches but big message opportunities, and eleven Q&A meetings. We agreed that some of them should be specialist audience – e.g., all young, all pensioners, all women, all public sector, whatever. Others would be open to all. We had to be more accessible than Major. We also discussed CB, whether they should be together all the time, how we handle clothes, interaction, all the stuff that he hated to go over but which would get annoying attention if we got it wrong. Someone sent out for takeaway curries and we worked through till late. I felt at last that the shape and tone of the campaign was becoming clearer, and I got fired up by the enthusiasm of the people who would be taking what we decided and trying to make it happen. Peter H was still banging on about TB visiting what he called 'British icons' – golf clubs, balti house, even a bloody launderette.

Wednesday, January 15
I had a terrible dream about election night. The exit polls had us way ahead, and there was lots of celebration, etc., and then the real results started to come in and we were losing seat after seat. I told Fiona, who said she had dreamt that we were made homeless. The main story was Diana visiting Angola, and doing landmines and being accused by an unnamed defence minister of being a 'loose cannon'. Everyone assumed it was Nick Soames but it turned out to be Earl Howe.[1] The other press story running was re the Millennium Exhibition. The *Sun* had a leader today saying we should pull the plug. TB had been worried we would get badly hit by serious opinion if we didn't commit to it, but I was not so sure. I suggested we get out now and say we were unconvinced it was a good use of public money. GB was adamant we must not support it. Only TB and Hezza seemed to support it. Peter M suggested TB use his PLP meeting to speak

[1] Geoffrey Howe, parliamentary secretary at the Ministry of Defence, 1995–97. Called Diana a 'loose cannon' who knew nothing about landmines when she called for an international ban during the visit to Angola.

about the fifth-term campaign launch tomorrow. He didn't want to do VAT on food. We were heading for a problem on this, and a bit of GB sabotage. He had ruled out VAT on food in '94 but told DH it only applied to the European elections. JC called after his meeting with the Millennium Commissioners, which had ended in impasse. He had stuck to the line that we had to be able to review it if we were not happy with the plans.

We had a lunch at Shepherd's with the BBC to talk about election coverage. Peter went through how we envisaged operating during the campaign. we went over some of the concerns we had raised recently – JM got far bigger coverage for events without real news. We were worried that their reporters were far more focused on process than policy, spin doctors not strategy. Tony Hall said he encouraged us to complain. I said we had a feeling the complaints went nowhere. Peter slipped me a note saying he would have to leave because he had a migraine. After an argument, they accepted that TB's launch last week should have had more coverage.

We had the poster launch tomorrow without a politician to launch it. They were all running for cover. I started to brief people overnight on the launch. Word got back to the Tories and Mawhinney put out words saying it was a lie. I got out Clarke words where he had said his instincts were to put VAT on food. Then, according to Roland Watson, JM and Clarke met and KC put out a categorical denial of any intention to put VAT on food. I briefed on previous denials of other rises before they happened. I said this was a campaign predicting a fifth-term agenda based on the record of the previous terms. It had taken off sufficient for me to think we should get the pictures of the poster out now. They liked it as a story, and sensed we were really playing hardball. Some thought it was really unpleasant negative campaigning. At Shadow Cabinet, Jack C briefed them on the Millennium Exhibition meeting, and TB asked them not to discuss it outside. Needless to say, the press knew in no time. I worked late on the final document for tomorrow. We were in for a bit of a rocky ride because the politicians felt uneasy.

Thursday, January 16

The VAT row went big, and we came out of it OK. There was a difference of view about whether the Clarke denial had helped or hindered. I feel it helped, gave the whole thing far more attention, got the Tories on the defensive. Alistair Darling did the media and was excellent, using all their past statements effectively. TB hated the whole thing, said he really wished we weren't doing it but reluctantly agreed it might be the right thing to do. I agreed with GB that the line to take, if we were asked whether we would also categorically rule it out, was that we were hardly likely to mount a campaign like this if we were thinking of doing it ourselves.

After a fifth-term press conference Mike White called 'brutally effective', I got back to the House for an interminable meeting on the millennium. Heseltine had asked to see TB. His people then briefed the *Standard*, who ran it as a challenge to TB, slanted in a very pejorative way. I briefed that he was being 'silly and improper', and repeated that we had supported it but would not do so at any price. PMQs was easy enough. We had every single backbencher lined up with questions on VAT. JM really didn't like it, particularly when his past statements were being put to him. Hezza came in and I was pissed off to learn he had asked to see TB one on one. It meant Jack (totally opposed), me (a student of Hezza) and Jonathan (who would probably have to negotiate afterwards) were not in there, and we were worried TB would just sign up. I listened at the door. TB said that he was worried that the contingency money was not really contingency money but part of the indicative budget. Jack was in the background going on and on about the *Standard* attacking him, a bit thin-skinned about it. TB was saying we could not give a blank cheque. They agreed we would have to work on a new form of words about what actually we were agreeing. But it was clear from the first effort that we were miles apart. To be fair to TB, he had not conceded too much, but Hezza basically sensed TB wanted to do this, and that put them in a stronger position than they needed to be. We then heard the Tories were briefing that Hezza had really torn into him, gone nuclear, blah. I briefed that silly words would not help. TB called him and told him to pack it in. Hezza played innocent. TB said to him, and this time I could hear it clearly, that there was no shifting on the budget – no extra funds – or on the review. He was pretty firm and said he was alarmed that people on the MC were saying the extra lottery money was already committed. TB said that meant it was a fundamentally dishonest budget and should not be sanctioned. Hezza and Jennie Page,[1] with [Bob] Ayling[2] on the phone, were constantly coming up with new suggestions. Simon Jenkins was desperately trying to be involved, and did some not very clever interviews. Eventually JC and I did a briefing, which was taken as a dump on

[1] Chief executive of English Heritage and soon to be chief executive of the New Millennium Experience Company.
[2] Chief executive of British Airways and chairman of Millennium Central Ltd.

the whole thing. We could have steered a neutral line but Jack probably went on a bit, and gave them too much body language to read. So the headlines would be pretty negative. TB still did not want to scupper it unless there was genuine and insoluble difference over a point of substance. The latest draft conceded all the points to us, but then Simon Jenkins went on *Newsnight* and looked so smug, even more than he naturally does, that people clearly felt we were going to back down. It meant I had to embark on a new round of briefing making clear we were likely to agree because they had conceded every substantive point. We were definitely winning on VAT, and just about winning on Greenwich, though it would have been far easier if Hezza had pulled the plug. My natural instincts were to fuck Hezza over, and he was clearly playing hardball on this, but TB really didn't want to be seen either as party-pooper, or as having been won round by Hezza, or as acting out of party interest alone. There was no doubt in my mind the party would prefer we just dropped it. It was their plan, and not our fault they would lose power before its time came. Jack C was clearly not happy. He felt TB should just pull the plug.

Friday, January 17

TB was on the phone at 6.30, wanting to know how the millennium stuff was playing out. We had toughened the line overnight, saying we had started from a position of right to review, but were now very much emphasising the budget issue. TB did not want to kill it off, but he did want to save the extra lottery money. The politics were pretty clear too, with several of the front pages basically depicting Hezza as going cap in hand to TB. As the day wore on, it became clearer that though Hezza saw the £280m lottery money as contingency, the Millennium Commission did not. They saw it as part of the project itself. When Jennie Page and Jenkins came over to see me and Jonathan later, that much was clear. She basically said it in terms. Meeting with Anne Sloman [political adviser, BBC] re TV debates. Sloman was extraordinarily unimpressive. She started by saying her 'bottom line' was that the BBC would have to broadcast any debate. Like we were going to her begging for it to happen. She said it would be Dimbleby, sixty minutes. Every time we raised a question of detail – audience? Clapping? What to do about Ashdown? Relationship to other channels? – she pushed it aside and went back to waffle. You'd imagine for a meeting like this they might have worked out a few answers to a few questions. I said I thought the Nats would turn out to be a real stumbling block. The whole thing was typical BBC – if there is a big event, obviously we will decide how to do it. Mmm. I said they would have to start thinking through a bit of detail, and in any event it would in reality be up to us and the Tories to decide. Partly for the fun of it, I floated the idea of doing it with ITV or with Frost's company. The medium is in the end not so important. As an event, there would be interest in it wherever it was. She looked terribly hurt. The Millennium Exhibition discussions were going on endlessly, and we were refusing to concede the main points. Eventually we agreed a tough statement. Bob Ayling and the commissioners wanted to be able to write to Hezza and TB saying they clearly expected it to over-run. It was clear there were tensions with Hezza and he was insisting they sign up to it but they were covering their own backs, given they and not Hezza would be in charge of it. We were probably moving to a deal but there was no way we could sign up to something that made clear the lottery money was already assigned to the main project. JoP was coming in and out with different wordings of this and that, but none were satisfactory. Then Major did an interview somewhere saying he was surprised we were 'creating difficulties'. We should have seized it as the opportunity to say sod it and pull the plug, but TB still didn't want to scupper it and instead I briefed that JM's remarks were silly, unhelpful and inaccurate and that the real problem was the wrangling between Heseltine and the commissioners.

I went back with JoP for a meeting in the Shadow Cabinet room with Jennie Page, Simon Jenkins and Mark Gibson [Heseltine's private secretary]. Page was very emotional. At various points I thought she was going to start crying. She claimed JC had always known that they envisaged the extra money being required. We went round in circles and eventually had to accept there was a real difference between us. We did not want to commit the extra money beyond £200m, whilst they said if it was not clear they could go to that extra money, they would not be able to attract the extra investment. They kept saying let's have another go at the words. I said there was no point. It was a difference of substance not words. That is why we could not get agreement on the words. I said we had been given different signals. Heseltine said one thing. They said another. If they briefed up the contingency fund, it would look like TB was saying one thing in a public statement, but essentially agreeing to something else privately. JoP and I put together a very bald, tough briefing note, short and to the point and clear on review and funding. They said it made their blood run cold. They wanted to write into their letter that we should talk specifically about the extra lottery money and we refused. Jennie Page went to phone Ayling, who was in Rome with his wife on a wedding anniversary trip, while

JoP and I spoke to TB, who was travelling round Sedgefield. TB agreed we should not say anything that suggested we were prepared to go beyond existing budgets. JoP spoke to Bob Ayling who said he could live with a toned-down version of our note. TB spoke to Jennie. Back in the Shadow Cabinet room she said it was clear he understood there may be the need to go over budget, but there had to be a clear understanding everyone would do their level best not to. It could not be thought to be part of the plan. We were getting there and all that remained was logistics. As Jenkins had to square the commissioners, I said we should say that we intended to make an announcement tomorrow and that TB and Hezza were both now confident of agreement. We agreed that I would put that out. While Jennie was out of the room, Jenkins said what was important was that she and Ayling would make it work but they had to be in it to stay. Jenkins struck me as a total wanker, very self-important, who worked very hard at gravitas but had very little. Now it was his turn to be emotional. He kept saying 'Thank you, thank you, so much,' very quietly under his breath, as though we had just saved the fucking crown jewels. 'You won't regret this. It is a very brave decision but you won't regret it.' He struck me as a total wanker, very self-important. I said it was important that we led on the briefing, and that they briefed similar tone and emphasis.

Mark Gibson called Hezza to tell him what the line was and that I would be briefing it, rather than the government. What a splendid moment that was. I did a ring round and Mike White was the one who got the significance of what had been going on. 'Congratulations,' he said. 'You've made it – you're in government.' The feeling was that TB had held firm, and Hezza looked a bit foolish. I'm not sure I can bring myself to believe that any of it really mattered. All that energy and time, and in the end what were we talking about? TB called and was effusive in his thanks to me and JoP for having seemingly sorted it after all that. Burnley vs Bury was on Sky so I took the boys to Philip's to watch it. Great game. 3–0. TB called late to say he would still pull out if he sensed they were fucking us around. JoP and I suggested we put Hezza in charge of the whole project and make him liable for the losses.

Saturday, January 18

We came out OK of all the millennium coverage. 'Hezza caves in to Blair.' I was trying to get the Sundays going on next week's business plans. What I didn't know was that Whelan, on GB's instructions, was giving Paul Routledge a briefing on the windfall tax, saying it would go far wider than previously expected, raise £10bn, and take in BA and BAA. All Charlie had said was he was going to brief some general lines about the public spending speech but nothing about this, and we knew nothing about it until we got the papers later in the day. It was a typical piece of GB-ery – worried about how the left would react on a tough message on spending and public sector pay, he wanted a little sweetener out there and fat cat profit-making companies were the best target. But it had not even been discussed let alone agreed.

There was a bit of follow through on the millennium stuff. I briefed that Heseltine had pissed off his colleagues by conceding too much. His job as deputy PM was: 1. to ask where the money was coming from; 2. to point up TB's inexperience as unfitness for office; 3. to enthuse his own side with certainty to win. And yet 1. he had shown himself not to care about where money was coming from as long as he got his way; 2. he had had to beg TB for help because 3. he joined in the general acceptance that the Tories would not be in power at the time of the millennium.

Sunday, January 19

TB was livid at the windfall tax story. 'To get this up at this time, as we are about to make a concerted push on a business strategy, is frankly suicidal. God knows what he is playing at.' I had been hoping for a quiet day and had planned for Anna to do the ring round of the Mondays, but it became clear I would have to do it myself. George Jones, for example, said he had been told by Ed Balls that £5bn was a 'conservative' estimate and he had given him very strong hints that a wider net would be cast. So he quickly picked up on the differences in what we were saying. I said it would be for the specific purpose of the jobs programme, stressed the limits, said final decisions would be made in government in discussion with the regulators and the companies, and tried to steer people back on to the business strategy launch. TB said to tell Whelan that unless he reined back, he would ask me to dump on the story big time, with his clear backing. I had pretty much done that already. I said to Whelan I could not begin to understand the logic of getting this running as we were about to do a business launch. It was a blatant and not very clever piece of selfish positioning. He kept saying 'I'll talk to you later,' saying he had GB or someone else on the other line. 'I'm quite relaxed about this,' he said. Well I'm not, I said, I think it is dumb. 'Well Gordon wanted it up so you'll have to speak to him.' 'I can see why he wanted it done for his own internal reasons but the external reasons are non-existent.' TB finally spoke to GB at 1.30 and GB assured him he would rein back. But he could give no explanation as to why he did it, and without any discussion with anyone. What was extraordinary was that he was making a major speech tomorrow and nobody outside his own inner circle had a clue what he was going to say. I was giving out more names of business people who were advising and supporting us and trying to push that ahead of the windfall tax story. The Tories helped again when they came out with a big number on why business still backed them and didn't like our policies. Later Sheree Dodd [*Mirror*] said Charlie had briefed her on the speech and said he had pushed the two-year pay freeze, as expected, and also rubbished the Routledge story. So we were making progress.

But then came a quite extraordinary development. Peter M called me just before 10pm. He said, are you aware that GB is going to announce there will be no rise in basic or top-rate tax tomorrow? I said I wasn't. He said he had only found out because Sue Nye had called Margaret McDonagh to say they would be needing a major operation processing the speech tomorrow, and Margaret had pressed her, put two and two together and made four. I called TB, who was having dinner with Roy Jenkins. CB answered and I asked if GB had sent his speech to TB. She said Ed Miliband had sent something through earlier but because TB had been speaking to GB, she was not sure if TB had read it. It turned out that he hadn't, and it had just been lying there on the floor. I said could she find it and fax it through to me. She did so and after pages of guff, there it was – no rise in the basic rate, no rise in the top rate, clear as a bell. It helped explain why he had been so monosyllabic and protective at the meeting of the four of us last week, and why he had talked about an element of surprise. But what a way to operate. I called Peter and we were almost hysterical with laughter. It was such a ridiculous way to go on. GB was doing what TB wanted him to, and having conceded on the substance, he was making sure he was as difficult as it was possible to be on the process. So on the one hand, he had delivered what TB wanted and he didn't, but on the other was doing it in a way designed to damage further the relationship of trust between them. The whole thing was ridiculous. Then TB called and said he had spoken to GB and I must not tell Peter M. I said he already knows, he is the one who found out first. And I said 'Can you really imagine a campaign being run by GB and PM together?'

Monday, January 20

GB had an enormous hit. The overnight briefing was leading the news and then, bang in the middle of his interview with Jim Naughtie, he dropped it in. He did it very effectively. It was a big hit, one of those moments that you knew mattered. At the morning meeting, he was firing on all guns and now seeking to be inclusive – what did people think, what should we do now? He talked as if we had been planning it all along. You had to admire it in a way. He still had the film crew trailing around with him and he knew I wasn't happy about it, and at the end of the meeting he asked for a private session with me and Charlie. We went into Jonathan's room. He said it had been vital to have an element of surprise. He had set up the windfall tax story to give the Tories something to be angry about, and be commenting on so that they would have no hint of the tax announcement. I said that was all fine, and I totally understood a strategy like that, and he had to be in charge of strategy on tax, but it hardly helped engender trust if they operated as they had in the last few days. He said 'Come on, there have been briefings going out on tax from various places. Nobody can claim to be innocent.' I said I had briefed nothing other than agreed lines between us. He said 'There are others,' by which I assume he meant Peter. He said it was important that he wrest back control on tax, and that the briefings went through his office. I said fine, but it was unrealistic to think TB and I would not be asked about it all the time, and there simply had to be agreement about what we all said. Also, I was concerned about the issue of trust between them. He said things should improve now.

At the election planning group, we went over plans for the first forty-eight hours and the last five days. Re the last five days, we intended to rebrand the campaign in some way, give it a final sense of energy, and that probably meant holding some of our good people back specifically to plan for that. One possibility was simply to leave central London behind and trail one by one through the key marginals. I also liked the idea of maybe one night focusing on campaigning through the night – all-night factories, motorway cafes, really show hunger for it. TB was a lot calmer about GB than I thought he would be, because he was happy with the outcome. He told me something of their conversation yesterday. 'Gordon, as leader of the party, I think I am entitled to be consulted when you are announcing something as important as this.' 'I'm consulting you now.' 'Yes, half an hour after Charlie has started setting up the briefings on it. You are not consulting, you are telling me it is a fait accompli.' He said that today GB said 'You ought to be pleased – I discussed it all with Peter and Alastair.' Which he did – after the *Today* programme.

Tuesday, January 21

GB got the kind of coverage – in terms of scale – you don't normally see outside of party conferences. We now had to focus on his IPPR speech, and on Hezza's appearance. Back at the office, I got a message that Hezza had already arrived. We spread the word and it gave a booster rocket to the event. TB was in confident mood and delivered the speech well. He saw Paddy Ashdown, who told him he had a real problem without TB being warmer on PR. Another election planning meeting – me, Fiona, TB, Peter M, PG, Anji, JoP, MMcD. We had just about agreed the shape and key themes and we were now building in greater detail. Leadership and the future were the themes that best played to our strengths. TB felt the concept of the future was not hard enough. PG felt it was, provided we stayed focused on education. The mood was good. Peter M and I were both motoring, and he was terrific when he was like this, focused, but really insistent we fix down detail. When we started to go into the detail for Day One, I felt a real sense of excitement. TB was happy to delegate a lot of the planning, was looking to Peter and me to shape the campaign, Anji etc. to fix the detail. Peter had a real look in his eye today, totally up for it, and I think we gave each other confidence. On Major, TB felt we had to have someone who made it their job to be highlighting his weakness. 'Weak, weak, weak,' was the charge that really hurt him. He hated it. He said he didn't want personal attacks on JM, because that would rebound in his favour. But the theme of weak leadership, and the damage to the country, was the best way into him. I said we had to get his views on who should be covering the main TV bases during a campaign. He said I could decide that, but I said it was ultimately a political decision, and it involved a fair few egos, so I wanted his view and I wanted to be able to tell people this is what he wanted. Re Day One, as things stood the plan was that the moment JM left the Palace, TB would be lined up in a school, do a visit and then hit all the main programmes live. GB would do something on tax, we would get a major business endorsement and by the evening we would be out in a key marginal doing a Q&A. It felt like the right balance. I spoke to Alan Sugar who was clearly still thinking about whether to come out unequivocally. He said he expected to get a load of shit for it and he had to be sure, so we would just have to wait, and he would not let me down.

Then off to collect Cherie and head for dinner with Diana at Maggie and Alan's. I think Cherie and Fiona were resigned to me and TB behaving like a couple of teenagers, but TB was in a very jumpy mood on the way, really worried that it would get out, and that it would spark a whole host of enquiries we wouldn't be able to deal with. Most of all, probably, what was I doing there? Maggie's answer was that she wanted me there, and I'm not sure he liked that much. We arrived, and he wanted the door to be open so I got out while Terry drove a little bit down the road and turned back. I stood at the door while they got out and he raced up and into the house. It was a very ordinary house in an ordinary street in Hackney and I was confident nobody had seen him arrive. She was already there and looking more beautiful than ever. She had a magical quality that was almost there in pictures, but strongly so in the flesh. She was wearing a lightweight black trouser suit, almost like a man's dinner suit, and a white silk blouse, quite high heels, white pearl earrings, lips heavily glossed, hair looked a bit longer. We discovered we shared a loathing of cats and Maggie's five cats running in and out and always making a beeline for one of us became a running joke. The atmosphere was a little bit forced at first and I think we were all struck by what an abnormal meeting it was, and I resorted to humour early on, telling her about TB's paranoia about the neighbours spotting anyone, and saying I had tried to assure him we were now in the hands of the best media operator in the world, that our operation was hopeless compared with hers, and if she wanted it quiet, it was quiet, so he had no need to worry. TB couldn't work out whether to flirt with her, or treat her like he would a visiting dignitary. He ended up doing a bit of both, but was not comfortable.

We started off upstairs in the sitting room, and she was very much the centre of attention. He said how well she had done in Angola, and how impressed he was at the way she had redefined her role. There was a fair amount of small talk about her life, what she did when she stayed in, the kind of mail she got, likes and dislikes. She said she had made lots of mistakes and tried to learn from them. She was over-whelmed by all the media attention at first, and shocked at some of the cruelty, but said she decided to take them head on. She had met just about every editor now. She said some of them were quite likeable, but she hated the rat pack. She then said 'Of course you used to say one or two not nice things about me,' and there were mock gasps around the place, like Cherie saying 'Oh, Alastair, how could you?' I remember Charlie Rae [royal reporter] telling me she used to get upset by things I wrote and I thought he was just winding me up, but clearly she did. I said I don't know if it helps, but I feel very bad about it now, and my only excuse was that I was writing in ignorance. Later, when the two of us were walking down the stairs to the kitchen for dinner, she reminded me I had also had a go at her on *What the Papers Say*. I said is it all forgiven? And she said yes. She was a curious mix of fun (with a lovely girlish laugh, a beautiful smile and the ability to take the mickey out of herself) and insecurity. There were moments when I sensed she felt the conversation was getting too political, or into areas she did not feel comfortable with, and there would be an almost physical reaction, pushing back into her chair so that she literally withdrew from the conversation. She could also, suddenly, look terribly, terribly sad, just look at the floor, or a fixed point on the table, just for a few seconds or so and then, again with some physical movement, she would come back. She was very flirtatious, big on eye contact, though Fiona said later that was less the case with women. At the dinner table, I three times felt a brush against my leg and couldn't work out whether it was accident, deliberate or, on one occasion, one of the cats. Her self-obsession came through too, or at least an obsession about how she was seen. She said to TB at one point 'You have to touch people in pictures. They can take a lot from you, but they can never take away the pictures.' Later, to the astonishment of Fiona and me, who had been at the earlier discussion on campaign themes, he said that 'compassion' would be the key theme of our campaign, and we had a lot to learn from her. I pointed out this was the man who never gave to beggars.

She talked about the boys, said they got very nervous at times, but said they had no trouble from other kids at school. If there was any aggro, it came from parents. She clearly felt something for Charles. She said she had spoken to him today and he had sounded a bit depressed. 'I said he should go away to Italy for a year and paint.' Later, she and I were alone in the kitchen because I had said, as a joke when talking about my teetotalism, how wonderful it would be to be able to say Diana made me a cup of tea, and she said 'Why not?' While she was looking for things in the kitchen, she said she didn't think Charles would ever be King. 'I just have that hunch.' I asked about William, and she said she would have some influence over what happened to him and she was clearly determined he would be King. She didn't quite say they should go straight from the Queen to William, but it is what she was getting at. She felt there had to be a cutting down of the monarchy. Once the Queen Mum died, it should be Queen, Philip, Charles and William as the main people, others less involved. When she did go, it would be like taking a leg from the table. You could make do with a three-legged table for a while, but not for long. She despised some of the courtiers. She said yes, they had influence. But that didn't scare her. What scared her was that people could be so nasty. Over dinner, TB was hinting at her having a more developed role but she didn't bite. He said the monarchy was clearly in a bit of trouble and there would inevitably be a debate on a new modernised monarchy, but it would have to come from within. He was pretty fawning by now. He said the British people are capable of great rebellion. He said 'You tap deep into the psychology of the nation.' I said 'You probably have the power to save or destroy the monarchy.' TB said 'If they do not change and modernise in some way, there is a risk the people will turn against them. They have to be part of a new Britain.' This was the hint about her taking on a new role, but she didn't bite at all.

We asked her for advice on pictures and she said TB should go to meet the down-and-outs on the Bullring, go to the London Lighthouse to meet Aids victims, or visit a hospital and have his picture taken with children with no hair. She spoke, in fairly calculating terms, of how she had 'gone for the caring angle'. But she also saw it as her work, to make people feel happier and better, and to support causes which didn't always get strong support. Fiona, CB and I were now asking pretty direct questions and she was giving pretty direct answers. Did she have an agenda against them? No. Did she think Charles would be King? Cherie asked that direct. No. Did she like Philip? No. She felt they had to change fundamentally and she didn't think they were capable. No matter how many times they 'relaunch', it won't work without fundamental change, she said. 'I'm fascinated by what Charles will do,' she said. 'I'm with the public on that one. I want to know if he will marry.' She helped clear the table, very 'mucking in', she said, laughing, and Alan Howarth said 'Imagine a lad from Blackburn like me having his plate cleared away by Princess Diana.' TB kind of enjoyed himself but I also got the feeling he was glad to leave. On the way out, he said to me not to do or say anything he wouldn't. He said to her 'He's quite clever, you know.' 'You went all the way to France to get him,' she said. 'And it's ruined our lives,' said Fiona.

After he had gone, she and Maggie were talking gyms and colonics and rubbish for a while. She said she never drank. She went to the gym but she swapped times and dates to avoid the press. She had a stalking case coming in court and she hoped she would be able to get in there and pan the press. Fiona said, but isn't it the case that there are times you have used them? And she kind of half bought that but said she was in a no-win position. I said she was brilliant at pictures and I asked her, half in jest, to get in touch with me if she had any good picture ideas for the campaign. She said she might just do that. She said the first pictures of the campaign would be the most important. There was a slight cynicism about the way she talked constantly about her pictures. I told her about the speech I made to the staff, when I said all the pressure was on TB, and our job was to help relieve it for him, and she went 'aaaaaah' in a real mickey-taking way. She ate more than I thought she would, easily as much as the other women – a potato, egg and mushroom starter, poached chicken, bread and butter pudding and fruit. When she left, Cherie kissed her on both cheeks and then Diana looked at me and said 'God knows what this man will do.' I shook her by the hand, and she giggled. I loved her laugh. I loved her analysis of the press. She was funny when she chose to be. TB had gone back to the House, and Fiona, CB and I got a minicab home. They felt she was tragic. She would be laughing one second and then the next her head was pointing to one side, and her face a picture of sadness.

Wednesday, January 22

The quote of the day was from Maggie Rae to Fiona. She said when she was cooking last night, when we were all upstairs, Alan came down to the kitchen, and she asked how it was going. He said 'It's fine because Alastair is cutting through the crap and Tony's behaving like a dickhead, telling her how wonderful she was in Angola.'

Peter M said he had had a call last night from a well-informed source, which I later discovered to be Howell James, who said the election was going to be sooner rather than later. We didn't need to act on it other than to speed up preparation in relation to the detail of strategy. Philip and I went for a meeting with the agency. Often they didn't understand what we were really on about. I tried to explain, in really simple terms. I said TB was a phenomenon. He touched chords in a way few politicians could. He had changed Labour, and could change Britain. I went through basic themes, leadership, social justice, rights and responsibilities, hard-working families. We should be campaigning on very simple things. We were potentially only weeks away from an election, and we had to get in better shape. They were very possessive of their own ideas. The creative director had not even seen the broadcast with the Oxo mum, which, because it had been done outside, they ran down the whole time. They produced a schedule for election broadcasts, which was frankly pathetic. She said she wanted more fun in there. I blew up at that. I said wit was fine, but we are not here for fun. I sensed the message was not getting through. I said to PG afterwards we would have to take it over completely. For the creative director not to have seen a broadcast was not good enough. It was clear to us what the message was, and how to communicate it, so why wasn't it clear to them? On broadcasts, we needed one on TB, one on business, one on the fifth term, maybe education, maybe the pledges and what difference we will make. I left feeling very angry and fed up.

I persuaded JP to do a stunt with VAT on food baskets, and then met with him and TB re the royal yacht [whether or not to keep it in service]. We agreed a cautious, prudent line with GB and said it was highly regrettable that the Queen was dragged into party politics. TB had wanted to go snap on the yacht, and be clear we would support it, but GB wanted me to say we should be consulted, and we could not sign a blank cheque.

Heseltine did a press conference and again attacked some of the business people who had supported our launch. He said some of the people we said had signed the letter of support had not done so. They included George Simpson [managing director of GEC], who later made it clear he supported it fully. There was a growing sense Heseltine was losing his marbles. Yesterday I'd done a letter from JP to Heseltine saying that just because he was losing power didn't mean he should lose the plot. JP was totally onside for this kind of thing at the moment. TB was worrying about the yacht issue.

I went home and watched a video with the kids. I told them a bit about Diana last night. She sounds like a devious cow, said Rory. Not bad for a nine-year-old.

Thursday, January 23

The Heseltine stuff rumbled on, a few more bad stories and leaders for them, while the royal yacht was big, with mixed reaction. We were getting a good press on business and I spoke to Gerry Robinson who agreed to do an interview with the *Sunday Times* in a few weeks coming out for Labour. TB, Anji and I had a discussion about the press. He still felt the right-wing press could damage us. I suggested I try to get him into the *Mail* to speak to the whole of the staff. As to the *Sun*, in the end it was all down to Murdoch, and he was not going to shift on Europe. We had to separate the issues out. TB was due to see him next week. He'd seen news people yesterday and didn't like the signals. He was not worried about the *Telegraph* or the *Express*, but the *Mail* and the *Sun*. The *Guardian* and *Independent* were a pain in the neck and we agreed he needed to go back in to see them too. His other worry was that Peter was using the GB problem as in excuse, and not doing things he should be doing.

It was clear that Ken Clarke was saying one thing, and Rifkind, side by side doing a doorstep post Cabinet at Number 10, was saying another. TB and GB had a long discussion about the best tack, and we agreed we had to push to the idea of separate Tory manifestos for the two wings. PMQs was deemed to be a bit of a triumph for JM because his backbenchers rallied and he seemed to be saying they were ruling it out for the first wave. Got home late and Fiona was on the phone to Maggie, who said Diana had written and called and said she would like to help us if she could. I spoke to Maggie, who said she'd said I was sweet and funny and she would like to repeat the exercise. Maggie said why didn't Fiona and I go and see her at the Palace? I said it might be more fun on my own. Fiona seemed worried about it, but she accepted if she somehow let it be known she was supportive, that could be very helpful. Diana had said to Maggie she had thought about it a lot, she knew it would be difficult but if she could help, she would like to. I said to Fiona 'What do you think she's after?' 'You,' she said.

Friday, January 24

The briefing on changes to lone parents' benefits, to set up the Holland speech, went well, leading the morning bulletins and getting good reaction. The most important thing was that in general we were back in charge of a policy-based agenda. We decided to ignore Europe all day and let welfare run instead. Alan Clark called, thrilled after landing [the Tory candidacy for] Kensington and Chelsea. I congratulated him, said it was one character for another. He said he would have to do a bit of Blair-bashing for a while 'to keep the Central Office runts off my back', but by Sunday it would be 'back to yo-ho-ho'. I sensed he was in it for the mischief as much as anything. 'I don't think Major likes me,' he said, roaring with laughter. Millbank wanted to put out a dossier on Clark, and focusing on the adultery vis-à-vis JM's family values stuff, but I said it was over the top.

PG said we really had to work harder at some of the basic reassurance. He had done some groups in Loughborough and the women were not even aware of the statements on tax. There we were thinking because the news had been full of it the country would be talking about it. He said they had not even registered it. I said the advantage was that it meant we could get into an election and present an awful lot of stuff as though it was new. If they don't think we have policies, we can spend an awful lot of time spelling them out. I drafted a letter to Diana saying how much we had enjoyed meeting her, suggesting we meet again to carry on the discussion, and hinting I was aware of what she had said to Maggie. Fiona was very wary of the whole thing, and TB said 'Be careful, she is very cunning and manipulative.' We agreed it had been quite an evening. He said I didn't have to drop him in it so spectacularly when he was giving all that bullshit about compassion and I said he didn't even give to beggars. He put on a cockney accent, said 'There was I chatting up this bird and my mate drops me in it cos he fancies her rotten. I clocked that one.' By the time we got to the airport, waiting in the Hounslow Suite, GB was on again, this time arguing about a reference in the new version of the pledge card to 'no tax rises'. TB had pretty much had enough by now. He said he had not been involved in it, he did not expect to be involved in it until it had been agreed by everyone else, and he didn't see why he was in such a state when all he had to do was get it changed.

We got picked up at Schiphol then off to the hotel. We did clips for Robin Oakley, who really liked the welfare story, and Aernout van Lynden for Sky. It was so funny to see him there. I first met him when I was a busker in Holland and he was a reporter on the *Haagsche Courant*, and he did a piece on me and we spent days getting legless. Now he was a big-shot reporter and I was working for the man reckoned by pretty much everyone to be the next prime minister. The speech venue was a beautiful museum. It was reasonably formal and I had to fight to get Brunson in. TB did an interview with Oakley, in which he said no Labour candidate would be allowed to stand on a separate manifesto. But the interview went a bit wrong when he went very hard on the 'candidates to be disciplined' line and then in the context of the single currency it sounded like he was saying anyone against the single currency would be punished. It was a bit messy and I had to work hard on Oakley to unravel it, and stop him going over the top. TB was sitting with Wim Kok [Prime Minister of the Netherlands] and I was with his press guy who doubled as press spokesman for the PM and the Queen. What a thought.

Saturday, January 25

TB said to me that the way to really fuck the Tories was to announce during the campaign that we would make the Bank of England independent, and we would not be joining the first wave on the euro. TB liked Kok, who seemed to see in TB the best hope for real leadership in Europe. He said Chirac was less well regarded than he used to be, and people were looking to TB to be a real leading player in Europe. He said the real driving force on the single currency was Kohl. He said that if we won, he would quickly try to help us on beef, and get the agenda on to CAP, common foreign policy, issues that might be better for us. After a general meeting, TB met Kok privately and I went into town to get some football strips for the boys, Lesley White of the *Sunday Times* and Miriam from Kok's office in tow. It was quite helpful to have Lesley hear from Miriam just how TB was perceived by other left-of-centre parties in Europe, the phenomenal interest there was in him now. On the plane home, he chatted to Brunson who came away with the clear impression JP would be deputy PM and with a department of his own, as well as a roving role. I wasn't sure we needed that in the mix right now, so asked him to wait. Whelan called to say the royal yacht story was going big. 'What royal yacht story?' I said. He said 'I thought Gordon had told Tony and Jonathan.' The story was that we had told the Queen a Labour government would not put any money into the new royal yacht. 'What?!!' I called TB who was as surprised as I was. This was classic GB, he said. He said I was there when they had the conversation. GB had come on to the phone to me and was talking about the yacht, and as TB was with me in the car, I put him on to TB. GB then said that he thought the royal yacht story would be going quite big. What he didn't do was say what the story was, or that he was the author of it. He did the bare minimum to be able to say they had had a discussion, but TB said he thought he was referring to a rehash of what we already knew. He said GB had also asked who in our office dealt with routine handling of relations with the Royals. TB said Jonathan. It transpired GB had called JoP and said he and TB had discussed the yacht and agreed we should harden the line. But there had been no mention of saying no more money, and no mention of talking to the Palace, etc.

When I spoke to JoP, he said we had been totally stitched up. He called Mary Francis [deputy private secretary] at the Palace. We were now half an hour from the main bulletins which were planning to lead on the story. Charlie's line was that there would be no more money. I briefed that the stories misrepresented the nature of communications with the Palace, that we had said to the Palace we supported the idea of a royal yacht and we would be looking at other ways of funding it. It was a bit lame but about the best we could do. I could see the Tories getting up big time on 'sponsored monarchy' and all that. It was classic GB – a nod to the left, creating a mess which we would have to sort out and in the process look like we were curbing his great crusading radicalism. Again, on one level it was a very good story for us (many not the few, future not the past, people's priorities and all that), but the way in which they handled it created a whole set of new problems. At the very least, there should have been a proper discussion. TB finally spoke to GB, then called me and said 'Just let them get on with it.' I said fine, but in the end I have to deal with the press enquiries and I can't just say 'Oh, whatever Whelan says, that's the line.' It is a ridiculous way to work. JoP was really angry. Normally, there was pretty much nothing that he couldn't let flow off his back, but he said he felt betrayed, GB misled him, and he got away with it because TB didn't stand up to him on things like this. It was indeed crazy. We had Ken Clarke set up to be asked whether he would let Tory MPs stand on their own manifesto –

whatever he answered was going to produce a story about division – and now we were all talking about the monarchy. Crazy. And no consultation. GB said to JoP 'I told you it would be a big story.' Yes, but you didn't say what it was.

Sunday, January 26

Alan Clark was on sparkling form on *Frost*, talking up Tory divisions. He said the yacht was absurd and preposterous. Alistair Darling gave our line on the yacht, rather than the GB line, which was absurd. I assumed he had spoken to Gordon or Charlie, and indeed CW told me what they had been saying, which was a slight backtracking. A perfectly straightforward story was in danger of becoming a division-and-climbdown story because of lack of communication. GB had been so keen to get any of the political credit that he didn't touch any of the bases needed for a sensitive decision like this. The only way we could bring the two lines together was to say it was consistent to say there would be no public money, and that we were looking at new ways of funding it. TB refused to have anything to do with it all day.

Monday, January 27

JP pissed off at all the GB stuff in the press, which, he said, gave the impression that he was the only one who mattered and in charge of everything. I thought about telling him about TB's private chat with Brunson and making him deputy PM as he wanted, but TB had not yet finally decided, I don't think. At the moment, he was angry with GB, and with TB's tolerance of him. Peter was writing a note to TB to say GB was effectively now running a separate operation, and it was damaging the overall effort. Whelan was either out of control, or Gordon was letting him run out of control. Peter M was getting really bad headaches at the moment and said he was due to see a doctor tomorrow. He said he would be taking a picture of GB to show the doctor because that was the real reason.

Called later to the end of a TB/GB meeting. GB was sitting there with the *Sunday Telegraph* story that contained my later briefing to David Wastell on the yacht. TB said we needed to talk through how all this came about. I said the first I knew the story was there was from CW at 8pm. He told me GB had spoken to both you and Jonathan. I checked with you, and Jonathan. You both said what GB had said bore no relation to what Whelan was telling the papers. GB was sitting doing his hurt look but as the whole thing was of his making, I let out quite a lot of steam. He said I should not be second-guessing them on tax. I said this had nothing to do with tax, it was a 'TB told the Queen' story. TB had done no such thing. If it was to do with this office's relations with the Palace, that should have gone through here. If there's any story involving TB, I should be called. He said, unbelievably, that the stories could have been avoided. I said that these bad stories were entirely his fucking fault, because he had not consulted and in this case because he had misled Jonathan. It was nobody's fault but his that his own deputy had not known properly what to say on *Frost*. He kept saying that as I had been told by Charlie at 8, and I had spoken to the *Sunday Telegraph* at 9, I did know. I said I worked for Tony Blair, not Charlie Whelan. If I have a choice between something TB wants me to say, and something Charlie is saying, which do you think I'll take? TB said to GB, it was all very well to say the story was going to be big, but you could have told me that you were putting it there. It was in many ways a silly meeting but I think it was important to make it clear I wasn't going to put up with this kind of nonsense. We agreed that we would have meetings with me, Charlie and David on Friday, and put any briefings to the Sundays in writing.

I left for lunch with TB at the Berkeley Hotel, Max Hastings and some of the *Standard* columnists and staff. TB was still very positive on the millennium stuff and they were up for it. On tax, he was praising GB a lot. He was very pro on Europe, and said it was awful that the press were so hostile. Max said he would have no difficulty with Labour were it not for the hunting issue. He said fishing was more cruel, he didn't hunt himself but he could not see why we wanted to ban it. My reading of their mood was 'time for a change'.

Michael Levy told me Alan Sugar had admitted he was back-tracking a bit. TB felt the best thing would be to say to him don't do it unless you're really sure, and not put pressure on. The government was defeated on the education bill, but it was on the issue of GM schools getting extra space for children, so would also be presented as a problem re TB. Tim took JP to Millbank to do a round of interviews after the vote, and Brunson told him he was doing a story tomorrow that JP would be deputy prime minister. Oh God. I had raised this with TB earlier and he said he hadn't decided yet whether he just wanted him to have a portfolio.

Tuesday, January 28

The government defeat was big news everywhere but they were (quite successfully) turning it into a GM issue with at least some focus on TB. TB called me because TV were doorstepping him. We agreed he should not get involved in the GM issue but instead talk of the government falling apart and the country needing a general election. At the morning meeting, Peter M said we needed to push hard the sense of government decay. TB was alarmed when I told him Brunson was doing the JP deputy PM story. I got Brunson on the phone and said all TB was saying was that the Heseltine model was not the only one, that it was possible for him to be deputy PM and have a ministry. But nothing had been finalised. TB wanted to speak to him, and did so, but Mike would not be budged from doing it today, so we just had to work on what he actually intended to say. He read me his script and it had enough caveats in it to be OK. It led the 12.30 and was fine, not overly dramatic. JP liked it, the press liked it. Needless to say GB didn't. He told TB he saw it as a deliberate act of retaliation re tax and the yacht. TB could hardly believe what he was hearing. He laughed out loud, said 'If I told you the background, and the efforts we have been making for it not to be reported, you might think different, but you won't.' TB said it was actually quite flattering the way that GB thought that anything we did was carefully planned and brilliantly executed. He cannot believe it might have been an accident.

I met Molly Dineen [documentary-maker]. There was something about her I liked. She was quirky and it was probably a bit of a risk but my instinct was she was basically a good thing, and she would bring an interesting eye to TB. I said we had to be very clear that the only personality that mattered in this equation was his, that she would no doubt get lots of publicity for it, but she should not be looking for it. She said 'Don't you trust me then?' and laughed. I said I didn't know her, but I thought it was best we were clear from the off. She came highly recommended but there was inevitably a risk if we took on someone we didn't know but we were all determined to make it work. We agreed we had to communicate the sense of energy in TB, and a sense of excitement about change, that this guy can get Britain going again, that his convictions run deep, he has always been the same bloke with the same views and convictions which are the right ones for today. I wanted to have a private chat with her and we drove back to the Commons together. I sensed she thought I was suspicious of her and I said I was determined this was going to work, and I would make sure she got all the access she needed.

DD came to tell us that last night's vote, it transpired, had been miscounted. It was a tie not a defeat for the government. I said it was important we get out briefing on it first, and we can use it to add to the sense of fiasco and decay. At PMQs, TB decided to do just one question, calling for a general election. The *Sun* had asked for an article calling for the same thing. TB said it was clearly all because of pressure from Murdoch in the paper. It is actually sick that one man can have all that power to help shift opinion. Anji called after the news because at the end of Brunson's piece on JP, he had said Nick Brown was saying while income taxes would not go up, other taxes might. She said it was 'chilling', because it was fairly obvious GB had put him up to it, and it was his way of saying no matter how much you try to lambast or keep me in check, I will do my own thing. 'It's like war,' she said. 'We put up JP on one line, he puts up Nick on another.'

Wednesday, January 29

The *Sun* didn't run the piece we did for them yesterday. Mo Mowlam was on *Today* re party reform and was absolutely dire. TB had been driving his kids somewhere and said he almost pulled the car off the road. She was all over the place. He said the problem was there were people who still felt happier talking to a few activists than to the public. Mo's basic message was that nothing much was changing. We agreed that TB would have to do the interviews on this. The morning meeting was grim. TB was furious with Livingstone who had said that our ideas were like something out of Hitler's Germany. He had been at the Anne Frank exhibition with CB in the morning and was really seething, wondering if we could not take real action against him. I had a meeting with Nick Guthrie, Huw Edwards and Peter Horrocks [BBC] who wanted to discuss coverage on the Friday morning after the election. It was typical BBC. They would have an army of people just focusing on that, and couldn't understand why frankly I didn't intend to give it much thought because what mattered was making sure we got there, not planning camera angles on the day we did. TB was due to see Murdoch on Monday and said it angered him that the meeting mattered, but it did. Peter M was trying to persuade me to have Robert Harris on the road with us during the election. It fell into the 'no benefit to the campaign' category and I wasn't keen. Peter said we had to think about how we would be seen at the end of it too and Robert would do a good job. I said I could see what was in it for Robert, but I could not see what was in it for us. After I got home, I got one or two calls about Meacher who had said in the *New Statesman* that GB had only ruled out income tax rises and had gone through some of the tax rises he might raise. I heard about it from Charlie as I was driving home with TB. 'What a clot,' said TB. 'It won't run that big because it's Meacher.' Another meeting was arranged with Diana.

Thursday, January 30

The papers were full of CB's haircut and Meacher, which ran a bit, but without anyone taking it terribly seriously. Major gave the go-ahead to MPs standing on their own manifesto. It was the obvious choice for PMQs. I went to collect TB who was due to speak to 2,000 sixth-formers at Westminster Hall. Molly was there sizing him up. I was still not sure whether we would get on. He got questions on God, being right wing, managing change, fairly wide-ranging and he handled it fine. Not brilliant but OK. I had a chat with Alex [Ferguson] who said we needed to start thinking about mental and physical fitness during the campaign. He said he recommended getting a masseur to travel with us. And we had to make sure there were rest periods worked into the programme. If you have physical fitness, you get mental fitness. You need rest for both, he said. There was a meeting of the Big Four plus me and Jonathan, designed to agree answers to all the difficult questions on tax. They were all trying to get on for once. I said to JoP I didn't know what was worse – when they were barely speaking, or when they were full of false bonhomie. We had a meeting with Glenn Hoddle, Graham Kelly [chief executive, FA] and David Davies [executive director, FA] re the World Cup bid. TB was a bit quiet but was clear we would back it. Glenn Hoddle seemed quite a nice guy, and he was a lot more articulate in real conversation than he was on the box. I suppose everyone spoke a slightly different language on TV. *The Times* had a poll. We were up four, with the lead now on twenty-five. Ridiculous.

Friday, January 31

TB, thanks largely to pressure from Sylvie the driver, was doing a big *Motor Cycle News* event, and the big question consuming him was whether he should say yes when, as was inevitable, the photographers asked him to get on to a bike. On balance I was in favour. He got a reasonably good reception but one of them muttered 'cunt' as Tony walked by. He did a few clips on the election and then we headed for the South Bank awards, stopping at a little cafe on the way, where they were surprised and pleased to see him. He made a little off-the-cuff speech at the South Bank for Richard Eyre [director of the Royal National Theatre and BBC governor]. When the photographers came in, Prunella Scales [actress] did a very sniffy 'Do you want us to leave?' saying she understood we didn't like 'luvvies'. He of course blamed me. I had an argument with him about Robert Harris. I said I couldn't see the point. We should learn the lesson of

David Hare who had been given access to Neil on the road and did a play that did Neil no good at all. Come the campaign there should be nothing that adds pressure, and nothing that gets in the way of the main objective. Also things said in one context would be very different in another.

Saturday, February 1

JP called several times to go over *Frost*. Every time he called he seemed to be in a different part of the country which didn't strike me as a very good way to plan for a big interview. He wanted to say that we were planning for a March 20 general election because he didn't think the Tories would hold the Wirral by-election if they thought they were going to lose. David Davies called and said UEFA were basically backing the German bid and would I put out words from TB saying we still backed the England bid. PG called from Manchester where he had done some groups of *Sun* and *Mirror* readers last night. Not brilliant. The economy was picking up for the Tories and we were not really breaking through yet.

Sunday, February 2

I knocked out a couple of TB articles on the World Cup while watching JP on *Frost*. He did fine. I was determined to have a quiet day and spend some time with the kids. I didn't watch RC on *Dimbleby*. He ended up giving us the worst of all worlds. We were well set up on Europe, with a clear line, and their divisions exposed, and a brilliant story in the *Sunday Telegraph* about the twelve different fudges that Central Office were sending to candidates. But RC, in subtly trying to shift the line on conditions for first-wave entry, was drawn into a story that we were likely to join in 2002. So the focus shifted back to us, with the press ire stirred, saying we would definitely 'scrap the pound' and GB up in arms again. It was heading for several front pages.

Monday, February 3

Peter M called early, worried that on Europe we had the worst of all worlds. He felt that we should move the policy and say that we wanted to delay the timetable. It was odd that RC had got us into the position he had, given that he was the big sceptic. TB said the problem was that GB so terrorised them about not ruling it out that Robin had ended up ruling it in. The *Mail* and the *Sun* needless to say leapt on it. It was not exactly the best backdrop to his meeting with Murdoch. RC was discomfited by the whole thing. I spoke to

TB and GB who both felt we should try to park it and not let anyone push it on. We should leave it to JM's speech in Brussels tomorrow, and GB should respond.

I met TB to go for his speech at Westminster Hall. I had a nice chat with John Bird of the *Big Issue* who said he didn't give to beggars either. TB was fretting about Europe, and the FA story was worrying him too. He wanted Jack C to come up with a plan to stop the Tories making the running on this. TB and GB went to see Murdoch, Les Hinton and Irwin Stelzer.[1] TB said GB had been fine, sounded more sceptic than usual on the single currency. TB's sense was that Murdoch wanted to back us, but the senior people at the *Sun* – probably with Trevor [Kavanagh] in the lead – were telling him he must be mad. TB said that he felt we got a fair crack on some issues, but not on Europe. Murdoch said he hated the idea of the single currency, full stop. But by and large TB felt it went OK. They agreed to differ on a few things, but his sense was Murdoch was reassured on the economy, tax, etc., and had lost any kind of respect for Major and the Tories. TB didn't like having to deal with them. He knew they were very right wing and only even thinking of backing us because they wanted to back winners and be in a better position to deal with us if we did win. But he felt there was something unpleasant about newspaper power and influence.

I went to a meeting on posters and PEBs [party election broadcasts] and finally felt we were getting in shape. They said they wanted to use the Snowdon picture for the last positive poster but they had been told it would cost £10k minimum. I called Snowdon and said that was a lot of money for a political party and said what about two grand. He said as a personal favour he would let us use it as much as we wanted.

Anji called later and said she had had a rare spat with TB. She told him he was becoming impossible. He only really cared about himself, and had no concern about how hard his staff had to work for him. Geoffrey Robinson called re the *Independent* profile and we ended up having a big set-to. There was a reference to him being the person who was suggesting £10m for the windfall levy and I said I didn't realise he was involved in that. He lost it. 'Don't lie. You don't need to lie to me. I know you have to lie for a living, but not to me.' I said I resented being called a liar and if he didn't withdraw it, the conversation was over and would not be resumed. He said he was

[1] Rupert Murdoch's economic guru. Often described as Rupert's representative on earth.

happy to withdraw it. There was a sense of someone protesting too much, asking where Paul Vallely [associate editor, *Independent*] got all his information from, as only TB and GB offices really knew about the windfall row. All a bit weird.

Tuesday, February 4

I missed the morning meeting as I was driving in with TB after going round to work on his transport speech. Nick Jones [BBC] did a good piece for us overnight but the big story was JM's speech on the Social Chapter [of the Maastricht Treaty]. The feedback from Irwin Stelzer on the Murdoch meeting was fine, that he was much more positive about us than the people at the *Sun*, where it was un uphill struggle. We got a bad press out of the *60 Minutes* piece, which was all aimed at presenting TB as a Clinton clone. I wish I had followed my instincts and pulled the plug at the start. Also Daphne Barak [American interviewer] was on the rampage. I was furious with Tim, who had let her in to see TB up in Sedgefield. Her NBC stuff was running, and she had done a big piece about how TB looked like a frightened child. The *Standard* diary called to say that she'd said she had been promised an interview with Tony's mother, which would have been difficult considering she's dead. Fiona was even wondering if she was a Tory plant. I suspected she was more one of those journalists who liked to be the story. Anne Sloman [BBC] had sent through their desired plan for JM, TB, Paddy interviews during the campaign. We were too bunched at one point and I didn't like the fact that by and large JM was going last, though we did get the last *Frost* slot. The problem, she said, was the smaller parties. I left early to take Rory to Wimbledon vs Man Utd, then got home to make sure everything was set for TB's Wirral visit.

Wednesday, February 5

The worst thing in the papers was a vile piece by Dahpne Barak in the *Express*. I called Tim and said because she was presented as some hotshot American, it would run further and he had to deal with it, finding out first who the hell she was. I called Piers Morgan and he agreed to check out whether she had in fact interviewed all these people she said she had. CBS was a lesson. So was this. We should go back to seeing foreign crews as NVTV [No Votes TV].

We were out at the crack of dawn and listened to an excellent GB interview on the way to the airport. Again, he was right on the substance but wrong on the handling. TB said GB had only vaguely mentioned a freeze on top people's pay three days ago but their first proper discussion was last night, after he had already briefed the *FT*. It was on that basis GB told JoP they had been 'discussing it for three days'. This was really moving beyond a joke. GB had his own media operation which he was using to bounce TB on policy, and build his bank of personal political credit. What most annoyed TB was that the decisions were right, but he did not want to involve anyone in them, which long term would alienate JP and the rest. We were on a BAe jet up to the Wirral, with Molly Dineen in tow, and TB working on his Europe speech.

The visit was terrific. It looked and felt like a real Tory area but the mood towards us was good. He did a very good Q&A with switchers including one incredibly posh woman who said 'ay hope thet the so-o-cialists get beck in.' There was enough edge in it to show the media it was not staged, but the general mood was incredibly positive. They were asking serious questions about what we would do in government, almost as if it was obvious we would be there. He was on storming form, both on pay, and on the by-election generally. He did a walkabout in a pretty affluent area and got a tremendous response. But I was wondering what on earth we would do to manage crews on walkabout during the election, when there would be dozens more. The local Tories had a few people trailing us and I clocked them and went over for a bit of sport, asking where it figured on their list of safe seats, because wherever it was, they were losing it. David Hanson [Labour MP] said he had been canvassing last night and every second house was a switcher. Molly Dineen was growing on me. She had a real sense of mischief and I liked the way she just got stuck in with all the other crews. Michael Crick was there doing his usual irritating 'look at me' stuff. We got back for Shadow Cabinet, where GB got a rough ride from DB, Chris Smith and others about the pay freeze and the manner of his announcement. They were in the same position as TB – it may have been the right thing to do, but it should have been discussed and properly planned. GB defended the issue without answering any of the questions about the handling.

I left with JP's team for the launch of the JP book. JP did a little speech, at the end of which Peter Oborne [journalist] asked me if there was a story to be done about me meeting Princess Diana! I played a dead bat but where did that come from? I chatted with Andy Marr who was not happy at what he saw as our pursuit of Murdoch and the *Mail* at the expense of the left press. I said it would be easier if the left press were more supportive. Peter Hitchens was ranting about us not giving him an interview. I said he must not imagine that we take him as seriously as he takes himself.

TB was really anxious on Europe. He called from the car and said he felt the Tories were hitting the right buttons and if they became strong on Europe and the economy, things changed. We had to get greater clarity in our position, either by getting out and being very pro Europe, or, possibly, by ruling out a single currency in the first wave.

I did an interview with John Mulholland for the *Guardian* media pages. Fiona felt I shouldn't have done it, but I wanted to get a message to the party about why we needed a proactive communications strategy, and how the press was still basically lined up against us. I probably made a mistake in saying we handled Clare [Short] wrongly and maybe overdid the *Guardian* bashing. Molly said some of the film from yesterday was excellent, particularly exchanges in the street. Irwin Stelzer had a bizarre piece in the *Sun* about our lack of strategy. If he was a supporter in there, God help us.

Peter and I met TB and JP who were both bemoaning the lack of an attacking strategy. The press were beginning to see that they were two rival operations, that GB and Charlie were the only people, apart from us, who could get stories up. I said to David Hill we had to get better control of the overnight agenda. One of the problems was that TB was best at getting up our issues but he didn't like doing the negative attacks, particularly on Major. I drafted an attack on Major's weak leadership, making the case it was damaging Britain, but TB was still wanting to do a positive, visionary One Nation speech, focused on education and welfare. TB got more and more irritated, as Peter put up more and more excuses as to why we couldn't get going properly. He kept saying 'we cannot let Gordon paralyse us. We have to devise a strategy and bind him in as best we can. There is no strategic message at the moment and we have to change that now.'

TB saw Branson with GB. He said he was impressed and he was confident he would come out for us in the end and certainly do some kind of joint initiative. He said that the decision on the top rate of tax was what swung him to us.

Friday, February 7

I woke up with a cold. Andy Marr called and said everyone was getting excited by a Blunkett interview in which he said it was not a priority to shut grammar schools. I then called David Hill, who assumed it was planned and said he was pushing it very hard. I didn't think that was terribly sensible but I was too tired to bother. DB had a piece in the *Mail* announcing new plans for hit squads for bad schools but the grammar issue was clearly going to drown it out. Blunkett was on the *Today* programme and given a hard time by Humphrys whose constant interruption before anybody had answered was becoming more and more irritating.

The agency produced a quite brilliant Mr Men cartoon with Major as Mr Weak. I loved it. I said we should get a whole stack of them, Mr Weedy, Mr Wimp, Mr Wibbly Wobbly. They were so good I felt maybe we could use them. Anne Sloman called to say they were reorganising things so that we got the first *Panorama* and the last *Frost*. I was feeling pretty grim, the cold getting worse, and went home to watch *Brassed Off* with the boys. Blunkett called to say he hoped Tony realised he was not responsible for the fuck-up, and the fact we pushed grammar schools rather than his other stuff on dealing with bad schools. David was always realty sensitive to what TB thought about this kind of thing, and disproportionately worried about how much impact it might have on TB's thinking. I said I'd already explained that it was not his fault.

TB still didn't want to do the big hit on Major, but I just about talked him round. He wanted a phrase for One Nation. I suggested stakeholder society, but said I was tired.

Saturday, February 8

TB was on early re the speech. He was worried it would not fly because there was nothing new in it, but again we found a way to present existing policy as new by saying we would switch welfare to education spending and education was the first point in a ten-point manifesto *Covenant with Britain*. He was worried the attack on Major would go too big. It was leading the radio most of the day. The news had far too much emphasis on the protest outside by so-called 'UNISON people'. There was a very good poll from the Wirral.

Sunday, February 9

TB called at 8, furious at the *Observer* story that he and GB were discussing whether to swap numbers 10 and 11. There were not many people aware of it, and he said if I cannot have this kind of discussion without it getting in the press, what can I talk about? I had tried to kill it without denying outright and Charlie claimed he was doing the same. We had got up a decent story about Steve Hilton, the Tory strategist, which was not good for them, and we were trying to get the broadcasters to cover it. They would certainly have done it if it had been one of us. I called JP who was joking about his new role as beef supremo, who agreed to put out words on it. I also did some weak leadership words for him. Neil and Glenys came round for lunch, and I sensed there was not much real discussion as there was quite a lot of tension simmering away. I took the kids swimming and then went to Peter Hyman's to work on the grid for the campaign. We're getting there. We had the overall shape, we knew what we wanted to put into it, and we were now getting down to hour-by-hour detail. Peter went out for a takeaway which was truly disgusting. He had done an analysis of coverage at the last election in the tabloids in particular and the relentlessness of hostility was really depressing. The truth was the Tories could still get up and sustain attacks on us because of their corrupt relationship with the press. Major's big negative messages were still getting out there. It was fine for us to campaign positively, and we had to do that, but we also had to neutralise their attacks on us.

Monday, February 10

Stephen Dorrell's interview in the *Scotsman*, saying a Tory government would scrap the Scottish Parliament, was leading the news and we piled in. By 8.10 Dorrell was trying to backtrack. When I first heard it, I feared it was a clever scam to get up the West Lothian Question but the minute I heard him on the radio, flustered and unsure of his ground, I realised we were dealing with a good old-fashioned gaffe. So we went on the chaos and confusion line, given that Michael Forsyth had said they would not reverse it.

TB was due to do a small-business visit. I collected him at 8.20 and he said he could not understand why he was doing a visit, why he was doing a press conference, why this, why that, and I said get a grip, do you want to win or not? A woman from IRN [Independent Radio News] wanted to ask him about a *Sun* story about a three-year-old girl who kept a picture of him by her bedside. He looked embarrassed and said he was lost for words. I suggested we did it again, and he should say that she should write to him and come to the House to meet him. In the car, I said can you imagine what Bill Clinton would have done with that story? 'I am not Clinton, I am me.' He was clearly in anti-campaign mode. I was totally fucked off with him and after the press conference, I said so in a meeting with him and Anji. I said he was becoming self-obsessed and did nothing but add to the pressures on people working for him, often needlessly. Why on earth was he complaining at the suggestion that we whack the government over a question that was easy for us, a complete government fuck-up, a free hit? And the press conference had produced decent coverage broadcast and print. I'd planted a question on Dorrell, which TB dealt with well, and on Steve Hilton, which Margaret Beckett did brilliantly. She was really good at the moment. TB and GB had spent four hours together last night but they didn't appear to be any nearer resolving their differences. At the strategy meeting GB sat on the sofa, leaning forward, half his papers on his lap, the other half on the floor by his feet, and he fiddled with them the whole time. We were back on to the discussion about the need for a clear economic narrative to counter the one the Tories were pushing. GB did not believe we had to campaign on the economy as we were suggesting. TB did. GB suddenly announced he was making a big speech about the windfall tax. I said why can't we marry his speech on the windfall tax with Tony's launch on tax pledges, but then we were off into a different non-argument. My speech won't be about that, he said. What will it be about? Not that. It was fruitless. Even people who had seen him like this before were shocked. TB was just not dealing with him. He allowed him to drive this drivel and nonsense through meeting after meeting, and paralyse us. The truth is there are two rival operations, lots of suspicion and lots of trouble ahead unless we can get it sorted. Even Anji was saying she was finding TB impossible, because he was too weak with Gordon. I said one of our biggest successes was creating the impression of strong leadership. He had it, but not with GB, not now.

Tuesday, February 11

The Tories got up another initiative overnight, this time on education, more league tables and broader A levels. As ever, the broadcasters gave them a pretty clear hit. TB and GB were meeting senior people from *The Times*, Peter Stothard, Mary Ann Sieghart, George Brock and the fearfully right wing Rosemary Righter. Maybe it was just because I knew the arguments going on, but I could sense the tensions between Tony, trying to hint that we would be ruling out the single currency in the first wave, but without saying so, and Gordon, making clear he did not think we should. They were both making sceptical noises though in slightly different ways.

Post PMQs, a meeting on the economy, Tony, GB, Peter and me. We had to resolve this argument, TB said. He said he was really worried they had a big economic message up and we didn't. Did we decide that that message was prosperity that lasts? GB felt like that was conceding too much, that we were saying they had already delivered prosperity and we should be making the point it was not sustainable. The media had bought into the idea of recovery and the press was writing up a strong economy all the time whether it was real or not. GB was more relaxed than yesterday, though still very sniffy with Peter.

I had a meeting with Brendan Monks and Tom Stoddart [photographers] and Pete Baker [TV cameraman] re pictures on the campaign. It was a really good meeting. Every time we got down to detail on the campaign, I felt better.

Wednesday, February 12

It was still the case that the government could get stuff up better than us. TB was seized of the point that Europe and the economy were coming together against us. He was trying to persuade GB that we needed a change of tack. On Europe, he wanted to frame it is a choice, in or out. If you're in, let's make a go of it and over time show the benefits of co-operation. But on the single currency, say that there will be a triple lock: 1. conditions must be met; 2. Cabinet must recommend; and 3. there will be a referendum. He said the problem was GB did not seem to think this was a real problem, believed it was a passing phase when in fact it was what a lot of people were talking about. He was fretting over virtually nothing else at the moment and was convinced that if we could move on this, and somehow neutralise Europe without our position being constantly misrepresented, we would be in much stronger shape.

On Mr Men cartoons, it turned out that the [Roger] Hargreaves estate would not let us use them in any event, so I decided we would brief, as originally planned, that TB did not want this kind of negative campaigning against JM. It would mean we get a hit both ways – funny way of doing core message, positive show of TB, and if they overreacted they would look silly. Above all it was a bit of fun that our people would like. Meanwhile Tina Weaver [deputy editor, *Daily Mirror*] called to say a freelance had put a story all round about CB going to Carole's gym. I left Hilary and Fiona to sort it out, after first doing a little bit of 'told you so'. The story was that she was spending £50 an hour on a personal trainer, which on one level was OK, but I was worried people would quickly find out it was Carole and then the lid would open.

Fiona and I had to go to [family friend] Dorothy Fothergill's funeral, and afterwards we discussed CB/Carole. She said she was sure CB was seeing Carole a lot more than we thought, and there was something rather odd about the relationship, and she felt only TB could stop it. But when I called TB after the funeral, he seemed to think there was no problem. He said she was only a personal trainer, did her hair sometimes and helped out with clothes. So what? I said

I felt he was being a bit too relaxed. JP called. He was in a good mood. He said, now that you've put it in the papers that we've got a new beef strategy and I'm in charge of it, can you tell me what it is? He'd been to Brussels, and got a lot more information. He was really fired up on it. I said we could start moving in for the kill, call for [Douglas] Hogg's head and start to build the line this could lead to a vote of no confidence. It ran big on the news, leading the ten o'clock, with JP clips. It had definitely worked putting him on the case.

I went with Philip to Watford, where he was doing two groups of women. PG wanted me to sit quietly at the back but I burst out laughing when a woman introduced herself as Jane and PG said 'My first girlfriend was called Jane . . . she went on to kill herself.' What on earth was he thinking of? It was the usual mix of hopeful and depressing. What was hopeful was the general mood against the Tories. But the level of ignorance and the trivia that consumed them were depressing. They just were not listening to anything political. When he showed them clips of Major and TB, they thought Major was weak and TB strong. But none of them had seen any of it. At one point, a woman called Georgina suddenly said she didn't like TB's smile, and they spent twenty minutes talking about whether they liked his smile or not. They didn't like it when he really went for the Tories, which was interesting, and what he himself had been saying. There was also a feeling that he wanted to be prime minister for himself, rather than for the country. But the overwhelming impression was that they worry more about every detail of how he looks, rather than what he says or does, and of course at the local government conference he had looked washed out. As they left, I said to PG that was really depressing. He said it was far more informed than usual.

I spoke to Julia the researcher who added to my worries when she said a year ago she was Labour, but she felt things are getting better re the economy, and she was worried about interest rates if we came in. She thought TB had energy and drive but wasn't sure what he believed in, what he was about. It was salutary. They barely read newspapers, and just picked up snatches of the news here and there. They might tune in a bit to the campaign, but in general, they will be nervous about change, and the slightest thing going wrong for us will put some of them back to the Tories. There was, on the other hand, a woman called Margaret who said she now hated herself for it, because she felt like a traitor but she hated the Tories and she really felt TB had changed the Labour Party. She also said she liked the way we shut up Clare Short. There was no awareness at all of the tax pledge and the general view of TB was OK but a bit snooty. They thought JM was weak but didn't like TB going for him as weak. They knew very little about CB but what they knew they liked. They liked the bulldog film [a broadcast using a bulldog as a symbol of Britain].

Thursday, February 13

The beef scam went big, leading several papers and JP was on *Today*. The Tories attacked it as a piece of opportunism. All we had done was make the same points but via JP and with a bit of new information. I briefed TB on the focus groups. He was full of 'told you so' re attacks on Major. He was still trying to persuade GB to go for a shift of approach on Europe. He had written a paper setting it out and there was a pretty clear logic to it but GB was still not buying the argument, largely because it was not his idea. TB wanted to make more explicit what any rational judgement of the criteria would lead you to, namely first wave unlikely, and surrounded by his 'triple lock', which again GB could not really argue with, that gave us much greater clarity. At the election planning meeting, he said he wanted us to build into his visits the theme of him being some kind of great persuader, winning arguments and winning people over.

Friday, February 14

Main story was the *Mail* front page saying the scum involved in the Stephen Lawrence[1] inquest were 'murderers'. It was the kind of thing the *Mirror* should have done but all the more powerful coming from the *Mail*. I called Dacre to say so. He said there had been a big reader response, almost all in favour. GB had told TB he would call me with an outline strategy for the next phase, re the economy, Europe, etc., but he didn't. Later Charlie told me that in the States next week, GB plans to make a big pro-Europe speech, make clear we were very much in to stay, but then make an announcement that we were unlikely to join the first wave of the single currency. This was, thought TB, the agreed plan, but we had yet to hear it from GB himself. His last word to me had been he could not see much point moving from a basic 'wait and see' position. I said it would not survive an election. But GB felt he had persuaded him that this was not a passing media phase but something real in public opinion, a hardening against EMU. Lunch with John Williams and Kevin Maguire [*Mirror*]. They were very fed up at how little they got in the paper, and the *Mirror*'s general lack

[1] Black teenager murdered in Eltham, South London, April 22, 1993. An inquiry into the police handling of the case led to a charge that Scotland Yard was 'institutionally racist'. The *Daily Mail* identified five young white thugs as his killers.

of interest in politics. Williams was going to be on the road with us, doing commentaries but also an instant book. They reckoned [Piers] Morgan would get into proper coverage once the campaign was underway but I doubted it. He wasn't really serious about it, just into stunts and quick hits and general abuse.

I met Pete Gatley from the ad agency at 2.45 and he showed me his latest idea for the last five days, or even the whole campaign. It was just 'New Labour, New Britain' in a series of really bright colours. I liked it. It was fresh, clear, new, had a nice positive feel. He told me Chris Powell hated the idea. But I felt if they were up with real weight, they could add to a sense of a mood changing, hope, energy, enthusiasm. I wondered if rather than NL, NB, we could broaden out to contain shorthand versions of the pledges too. Once I'd seen them at Millbank, I then went to the agency and we went through the charade of Pete presenting them to me again, and I had to react as if seeing them for the first time. This time they had one in claret and blue, and said they would put it up in Burnley. Peter M arrived late, and saw them for the first time. I didn't give him any indication of what I thought when he first saw them. He said he really liked them a lot. He went along with Pete Gatley that maybe they could be used for the whole campaign, not just the last five days. Whether the words were right or not did not matter for the time being. The idea was the bright colours, and it was brilliant. Simple and brilliant. Peter said he had never seen anything so fresh for a campaign. I knew he would like them, and with the two of us signed up positively, we'd get it through. It was one of the best parts of working with him – he would decide on a view, with real enthusiasm, and we could get things done. I felt that Pete, PG and I, in actually brainstorming ourselves, out of the executive chain of the agency, had really moved things forward on the creative front, and this was the best piece of work they had produced. I said I felt we were making a lot of progress. The agency had produced some great work on Mr Weak, which would be all over the Sundays, and now I felt a really good advertising idea was being born.

Saturday, February 15

We went to see Burnley at Bournemouth and even Bernard Rothwell [Burnley FC director] told me he could see no way of backing the Tories. Arrogance and water privatisation were his main reasons, he said. I talked to JP a couple of times and between us we were sorting several front pages on it. We also got huge coverage out of the Mr Weak cartoons and the joy of it was it was a total scam and they were happy collaborators in it because it was funny. Walters said this must be a new experience for you – briefing against yourself as having been bollocked by Blair as a way of getting up a story about Major's weakness. The *Guardian* did a big trailer on my interview on Monday, which alarmed me a bit. They said it was because the *Indy* were doing a new media section. We drew 0-0, then home to go to Phil Bassett's[1] five years on from leukaemia party. John Monks' wife Frankie said she would kill herself if we lost. Jeremy Paxman was sure we were going to win. He said maybe there was just a feeling that times were moving away from them, and towards us.

Sunday, February 16

TB called after he had been to church, a bit more relaxed re the Mr Men stunt, but still worried it would be exposed as a stunt. I said the Tories were hardly going to draw attention to it. Even they must realise every time the pictures are published, they reinforce the message. TB was still working on GB, but Ed Miliband called and said Charlie may have given me the wrong impression. TB and I both had the impression that he was going to use the US trip to signal a new line, and indicate it was unlikely we would be in the first wave because of where the economics lay. We had another GB muddle caused by CW. I had lunch with PG and Stan Greenberg who was over to look at our tracking poll. He said the economy was picking up 'by a spectacular margin' but the government was not getting the credit. Europe was moving up the agenda and we were seen as too pro-European. He also felt we were doing badly among pensioners and this group was the one that was most suspicious of TB. But despite all that he felt we were on track for a good win. He said TB remained far and away our best asset. PG assured me he had not primed Stan re economy/Europe. I said it was exactly what we had suspected, but GB was not accepting it.

Monday, February 17

My interview in the *Guardian* ran over five pages, which was ridiculous. Even Anji, who had been basically against it, felt it was effective, but God knows who would read it to the end. I felt I got over most of the points I wanted to, but it was odd that they gave so much space to it. TB feared the GB/Peter M spat was paralysing us. He was buoyed by Stan Greenberg's analysis, but I felt it was too optimistic,

---

[1] Industrial editor of *The Times*. Later joined AC's Strategic Communications Unit at Downing Street.

borne out by Philip's latest groups which were a real kick in the face. There was enough there for the Tories to mount a strong 'and don't let Labour ruin it' campaign. I had lunch with Phil Walker and Henry McCrory from the *Star*. McCrory was clearly a Tory. I tried to persuade them that they were missing out on a phenomenon, that TB and New Labour was aimed right at their working-class readership, and they should be beating the *Mirror* on this. McCrory tried to give me the 'Major nice guy' line, strong leaders didn't always look strong, that kind of bollocks. Their main interest was in whether they could get TB to do the *Daily Star* gold awards. I went to Millbank for a meeting with Peter M. etc. on the last five days. The agency presented a couple of election broadcast ideas: 1. an allegory of a man who forgets to vote and a cabbie going over the reasons why he should have voted, and what might be different, and 2. a film on the difference between the inside of the Tory party conference, where 'Land of Hope and Glory' is playing and everyone is happy and smug, and the reality outside in the country. Both were good, really strong ideas. We lost the beef vote by thirteen, but we had had a good run, and given JM a real problem.

Tuesday, February 18

The *Mirror* ran the Mr Men posters all over again. TB did an early doorstep, this time over the vote at the entrepreneurs' breakfast. We got a poor press on beef today, the sense of the strategy backfiring and TB not even being there to vote, etc. But I felt that was the Tories clutching at straws, that this was a no-win situation for them. The Tote [possible sell-off of the government-run bookmaker] issue was growing as a problem. On the radio, JP had a swipe at spin doctors and Charlie was potentially up in lights. The trouble was it showed up the GB operation for what it was. GB was adamant that he was not responsible for the Tote story and therefore Robin was the problem. Yet I knew Charlie had briefed it because he told me he was doing it at GB's behest. The truth was Robin had had enough of stuff being bounced into the papers by CW and he felt racing was one of his issues, and he should have been consulted. Of course it was even sillier than that. I don't think the story was originally put there by GB, he just saw an opportunity when it was, and then CW mishandled it. I met Charlie to discuss GB's American visit. He said GB was going to get it up that we effectively ruled out a single currency in the first wave, but it had to be done by him on his terms. Because it was thought TB had pushed him into it, he clearly wanted to be in control of how it was presented. Charlie said if RC went out spinning it in advance, GB would pull back. I said but if he was signalling a shift, GB had to have a proper discussion with RC. Later, Trevor Kavanagh called because he had heard something was going on. When Robin called I filled him in, probably unwisely, by saying we were trying to get GB to shift the line but it would not happen if there was publicity beforehand. He was feeling a bit bounced by TB and he wanted to do it on his terms. Peter M and I looked at Molly's latest rushes, which I thought were getting there but Peter didn't like her stuff. He thought it wasn't exciting, it was flat, and TB didn't look or sound good. I said give it time. He needs to open up with her a bit more. I had dinner at Mike Habib's [from the US Embassy] with a few people mainly from the FCO. It was interesting how they talked to us now pretty much as though we were already in government. Some of the papers picked up on JP's attack on spin doctors, including me. JP called saying he had only had Whelan in mind. He had spoken to TB and said it had to be dealt with. He, Robin, Jack Straw, lots of them were losing it with GB and the way he operated. JP was worried that if we didn't get a grip over various weaknesses, it would fall apart in a campaign. RC still hasn't heard from GB.

Wednesday, February 19

Even [Simon] Hoggart [*Guardian*] wrote quite a nice piece about TB, so maybe the attacks were having some effect. Rifkind was leading the news, saying that he would challenge Germany to rule out a superstate. In his 8.10 interview, he said the government was hostile to the single currency, ending the studied neutrality. GB's speech was being presented as pro-European, assuring the US that we would not come out of Europe, whereas the Tories would. TB's instincts had been absolutely right about doing this at the weekend, so any move looked like it was done on our terms not theirs. I wondered if Kavanagh had tipped off the Tories that we were likely to go for a move and that was why Rifkind did this now. TB felt if we cauterised Europe and neutralised the economy, we would be fine. But everything was saying to him that Europe was coming up big time and we were not prepared. I was called by Peter, in a total state. Earlier Charlie had called to say that Peter had briefed Robin Oakley that Gordon was going to harden our line on the single currency. Gordon had gone mental about it. Peter said Charlie had called and shouted and swore at him, and been incredibly abusive and said this fucking story had nothing to do with him and he should stay out of it. He said he could not go on working like this. He was trying to handle Robin Cook and everyone else in this very complex situation which could go wrong very quickly. TB spoke to him, while I called Whelan and said, whether it was right or wrong to do what Peter did, we must all be saying the same thing.

Clarke had described the Rifkind statement as a slip of the tongue. At last, it was opening up for us, so TB did a doorstep saying they were at sixes and sevens. Then Major said something, seemingly siding with Rifkind. The *Sun* and the *Mail* were clearly buying the line that the policy had shifted against a single currency. They were not really interested in GB's speech at all. Philip called, said he'd just done a group which was terrible, Phoney Tony, worried about change. Even him taking his jacket off sent them into a rage for some reason. How the hell do we get through to these people at any level at all? TB reckoned we had lost the *Sun* and I said we just had to do it without them.

Thursday, February 20

Apart from the *Sun*, the papers were not as bad on Europe as I was led to believe last night. The truth was the policy itself had not changed, they had just done a very effective briefing operation to let the *Sun* believe what they wanted to believe. TB remained convinced that if Major said publicly that the policy had changed, Clarke and Heseltine would quit. They could live with briefing, but not publicly announced change of policy. But surely we had to force them to have the argument out in public. TB now felt that if he did not do Europe at Questions, people would think we had run scared because they had successfully engineered change. For PMQs, he decided to go on Ken C's words, and force Major to say whether he agreed with his own Chancellor. It went fine, we got Major where we wanted him and I briefed hard that this has all been done for the *Sun* and the *Mail*, not the national interest. Then we had the constitution debate. The general feeling was that Major was poor, but as ever, the broadcasters liked him on the attack, and the clips they used showed him in fine form. TB was excellent, very funny, though he didn't handle the West Lothian Question terribly well, and I got a heavy going-over afterwards. I said the West Lothian Question was best answered by the fact that the Westminster Parliament devolved power. Ultimately power that was devolved was power that was retained. It was a big event rather than a big story. Some felt that TB had been brilliant, others that he didn't handle the substance well. We just about got away with it.

Friday, February 21

The *Sun* was definitely moving away from us. There was not a line on Major backing the Chancellor, which of course knocked down their story yesterday. I called Stuart Higgins, who was out, and ended up speaking to a very stroppy Chris Roycroft-Davis, who said he didn't take kindly to being told what stories to put in the paper. I asked if they would only print stories that backed up their own editorial line. We both got abusive. I said Higgins had asked for a piece by TB on Europe, and did they want it today? He said no. TB wanted Peter M to speak to Irwin Stelzer to ask what the hell is going on? With or without them, he still believed we could turn the Europe argument. TB was speaking and presenting the awards at the *What the Papers Say* lunch, and we used it to set out basic strategic position, including the two-faced line. GB was back from the US and seemed to be in a much better mood than when he left. He was moaning about Robin and Peter, the Tote and tax. I said I didn't think we quite got over the agreed messages on Europe as planned, because the debate was conducted on their terms. TB was worried that his speech was too political but it was fine, a few jokes, then on to Europe. John Junor [journalist] looked very pissed off to get his award from TB. We got back, TB doing an interview with the *Daily Star* on sport, then a session with Andy Marr and a few other journalists. He was saying he would be more radical than they thought, but we were in a boxing ring against a very good tactician in John Major, and that meant we had to be careful in our positioning the whole time. TB was still worrying away about Europe, and was sure that we could get Clarke to quit, and Heseltine to follow, if we really pushed on it.

Saturday, February 22

There was very little coverage of the speech, though he felt it was good just to have made the argument to all the senior media bods. We were taking the boys to Chelsea vs Man U, and I picked up TB at 11.30. He was still not sure about the *Sun*. 'There is only one eye that matters, and the trouble is that it's not an eye that is always watching,' he said. His brother thought the *Sun* would promote the Tory line without actually coming out for the Tories. We were met by Tony Banks and Ruth Harding, and taken up for lunch. Chelsea was so not Burnley, all a bit celeb-y, Richard Wilson [actor] and Angus Deayton [actor and TV personality], Dickie [Richard] Attenborough [actor and film director] who was supportive as ever. Ken Bates [Chelsea FC chairman] was very Bates-ish. David Mellor wanted TB to do an interview on Radio Chelsea. After lunch, went to meet Molly. She wanted TB to be interviewed with lots of people behind him but he was not up for it. He did a few bad clips and was clearly not relaxed. I said why not just do shots of him walking through the crowd, but I could sense he was tense, especially when a bunch of Chelsea fans started singing 'We'll keep the blue flag flying high', with the cameras following us. Molly was growing more and more exasperated. She asked a few things as they walked along and he gave very clipped, fed-up answers. She said to me afterwards 'Is it me?' I said no, it is just one of those days where he's behaving like a child at a wedding. I said she just had to persevere and it would be fine. The match was terrific, really high quality. Afterwards I had a good chat with Glenn Hoddle about the World Cup bid. Mellor basically felt the game was up for the Tories. It's all there for you to lose, he said. Alex [Ferguson] came up for a drink afterwards, and we talked about what he might do during the general election. He said he was getting 'slaughtered' by some of the board over his political profile. He said the club had had a few complaints about political stuff he had done in the past and he had to be careful. He was down in London during the week and we agreed to meet and go over it. He said he'd love to help, but just had to be careful. On the way home, TB said he had found it an odd experience walking through the crowds with the camera following him. He was now a kind of celeb whether he liked it or not, which meant people had views on him for good or bad, and it took a bit of getting used to. I think he was quite taken aback by some of the abuse, though I hadn't felt it was particularly over the top, and pretty good-natured.

Sunday, February 23

Molly was filming at TB's but it didn't really work. Also, CB lost it with them, because they just wandered down to the kitchen. I said to TB afterwards he was making a real meal of this. We had to make it work because it was one of the most important broadcasts of the campaign. Workwise it was quiet, but we were pushing Ted Heath on *Frost* who had backed us over the Social Chapter, the minimum wage and the Scottish Parliament.

Monday, February 24

We were doing another visit to the Wirral, this time with CB, so Fiona and I left home for their place at 7.15. As we arrived, Cherie was leaving to take Euan to school, so yet another day started with us waiting for TB to get going. We just made the train, but by then TB was in a foul mood. He got Cherie to sit away from him because he said he wanted to work, but in fact he spent most of the time complaining about his diary. Also, he could not get his head around the Molly film. I said we wanted something more natural than he had done before, and that meant relaxing and letting them get more and

February '97: TB 'a kind of celeb whether he likes it or not'

more material that we could then choose from. He wasn't happy with that approach. It was as if he wanted the thing scripted and then we could make it around the script, whereas I wanted something that emerged, naturally, and got a side of him that people don't normally see. At the moment, however, nobody was seeing that side, because he was being such a pain. We didn't do any filming at all on the way up. I was beginning to share Molly's exasperation. We arrived and were driven over to the hospital, where they did a fairly lengthy visit. The press were interested in her as much as him, particularly with the Merseyside connection. They were in such a twitter about her being there, that when it came to TB doing a doorstep, Bevins, taking the piss out of his colleagues, asked the first question – 'What sort of underwear is your wife wearing today, Mr Blair?' It was all very funny, but of course it would allow them greater licence to write about CB rather than the by-election stuff. Some of them thought Bevins was being serious, and were chasing him about his question. Cherie was excellent, really natural with people, far better than TB was at just going up to people and engaging. We had a meeting with the campaign team who felt we were heading for a 5,000 win, which would be pretty good. It felt good, felt like it was going well. David Hanson said he couldn't believe the kind of people switching to us.

We just made the train back and did some filming with the two of them together but then he said he didn't want to do the interview later. Molly said she thought it was getting childish and she had a point. She said this was not what she expected, that she had been hired to do something different but this was becoming a very ordinary film and not really her style. She had a discussion with TB and said she didn't know what she was supposed to be doing and why she was hired if she was just going to get the odd snatch here and there. I tried to assure her we were getting there but she felt it was all a bit ordinary, not bold. Back in the office, the press gallery was all abuzz about Cherie being with TB. She could not win. Having gone on about her being invisible, they were now complaining that she was out campaigning. Fiona and Hilary were not convinced of CB's involvement in the visit but the reality was she was going to be with him during the campaign, and far better that we all got a sense now of how that was going to work. I felt that today she added something very positive.

Tuesday, February 25

There was loads of Cherie coverage and the *Mail* did the Bevins question, suggesting it was fair game because he is my 'favourite journalist'. But there were lots of good pictures and the overall effect was positive. The *Liverpool Daily Post* was excellent, whereas Portillo's visit bombed. I had breakfast with Trevor Kavanagh. He basically admitted that they would pursue the Tory cause without actually endorsing the Tories. Europe was the prime concern and they simply believed that our stance was wrong. He claimed that Murdoch himself wrote the recent line in an editorial about the UK being better off out of a collapsing Europe. They do not believe that we can sort out Europe. He said Murdoch despises Clarke and Heseltine, but he loves the fact that politicians court and follow him. I said we would not move to the sceptic position, because it would be wrong and it would be a disaster. Coming out of Europe would be madness. Our strategy in government would be to show that we get a better deal for Britain by being engaged. But it was like talking to a brick wall. There was something a bit Moonie-ish about it all, Europe was an obsession, and the facts didn't get into the argument. Sue Evison told Hilary she was having trouble getting her piece into the *Sun* because it was too favourable to TB. I called Neil Wallis who said it was going in on Thursday as a three-pager. TB was in a pretty useless mode, slightly panicky. Yesterday TB again said he wasn't happy with the way our overnight briefing operation was running and wanted me to take it over. I said I was doing enough already. He was getting exasperated that Peter was not doing enough, paralysed by GB. Meanwhile, GB was gearing up for another big speech, on inflation, and the wise men, on reform of the Bank, and as ever we knew next to nothing about it until the briefing operation began. There were still two separate campaigns going on.

Met Alex [Ferguson] again, who has a good feel for politics and campaigns. He said it felt like we were 2-0 up, and now we had to sit back, let the others make mistakes, probe their weaknesses. He met TB briefly and said he felt tax was still a problem. He said TB would feel stress levels rising and he had to learn to become vacant, only let those things get on his mind that really have to. He said in positions of leadership the appearance of calm was important and you had to work at it, by cutting out everything that didn't matter. Don't let the peripheries crowd in. Delegate as much as you can, do as little with the press as you have to, leave the rest to AC. Only do what matters. He said both his wife and Brian Kidd [assistant manager] regularly said he was not listening but if someone suddenly said something that mattered, he would be able to click in. I took him down to the Lords where he was speaking to a football dinner. It was the same kind of theme – the importance of leadership, learning as you go, focusing on what mattered. It was a good speech, made totally without notes, a collection of anecdotes about his life as a manager but which included some real insights into leadership and teambuilding: 1. under pressure, never let outsiders sense that you're not in control; 2. learn to be vacant, withdraw into yourself and only focus on what is important; 3. value the people who work for you. He was fascinating about the Cantona incident.[1] He said he hadn't seen what happened at the time and after the game refused to watch a video. When he got home in the early hours, Jason [his son] asked if he'd seen it. He said no and didn't want to. But he couldn't sleep and eventually got up at 5am and watched it on the video. He was worried he would have to sack him. But once he had decided he wouldn't do that, he stood by him. He said he had never criticised his players and wasn't going to start now.

Wednesday, February 26

GB's overnight briefing went big, the splash in several papers with the focus on inflation. There was a big piece in *The Times* on what Number 10 would look like with us, the usual crap. I had a meeting with Jeremy Vine and Carole Walker, who were going to be on the road with us doing the campaign for the BBC. I said to them my worry – and this particularly applied to Jeremy – was they were actually more interested in process than policy, more interested in projecting themselves than us. They all basically wanted the same thing, access and clever ideas, but there were too many of them on our case. Later I met Nigel Dacre and his ITN team, who are pressing for a TV debate. Their idea was thirty minutes of Blair vs Major, thirty minutes with Paddy, then another thirty minutes just the two of them. None of them was thinking through the problem of the smaller parties.

TB came back from the NEC, and went over a few issues and later I lost my rag with everyone in the office because nobody had done any preparation for the special Shadow Cabinet at Millbank, and I said I was fed up doing everyone's job. This is meant to be an important meeting, really going through the overall strategy and binding people in. In the end, I did a speaking note for TB. The cameras were out in force as he arrived, and again it was a sign we were getting closer to an election. I briefed the line hard that we intended to defeat them on economic competence and living standards. TB asked everyone to go through initiatives they had planned for the coming

---

[1] Eric Cantona, legendary Manchester United footballer, assaulted a Crystal Palace fan with a 'kung-fu' kick during a match.

weeks. Some were OK, some were embarrassing. GB was quite good on strategy. Peter M did a presentation to them on the mechanics of the campaign but he spoke to them like they were two-year-olds, including at one point appearing to tell them how to use a mobile phone. Some of them were getting really irritated at his tone and his manner, just too grand by half. TB did his usual anti-complacency message, JP talked about the specific campaign re the key seats. Blunkett was fine. When Harriet spoke, I don't think I was the only one who used it for a catnap. Beckett didn't have much to say but what she said, as usual, was sound. Chris Smith was better than usual, actually made one or two half decent political observations. Clare did her usual thing on cynicism in politics, and how people were joining consumer campaigns rather than political parties. JP was rolling his eyes up to the ceiling.

The briefing on TB on the economy worked well with GB's speech, and TB did clips, and then Oakley managed to wrestle the story from the economics team and turn it into a political story, focusing on Labour feeling they could win for the first time on economic competence. Roy Greenslade called later. He said Kavanagh was due to do a piece on the *Sun* and Labour for the *Guardian* media page. Ten minutes before deadline the *Guardian* were chasing his copy and Kavanagh said he was sorry, but it was too sensitive. Roy felt it meant that Kavanagh had planned to say they were backing the Tories and Stuart [Higgins] would not let it go ahead.

Thursday, February 27

After all her struggles, Sue Evison's piece on TB finally got in and was very gooey and pro TB. She said she had had to throw a real tantrum before it went in, and there was a real pressure within the *Sun* not to be nice to TB. Higgins called me later to ensure I was happy with it. However, the main political story was GB saying we would scrap the pound in two years, which was total balls. Piers Morgan called really angry that we'd given out new pictures of TB/CB to the *Sun*. I said he hadn't asked for them. Lots of people took the piss out of the interview, but I thought it was a total triumph. TB was constantly asking for feedback from the Wirral. It looked like it was going well. Then to a meeting with TB, GB and Peter at which things were no better than before. TB just closed it down, said he had other things to do, let's meet on Monday. I went home, went to bed early and got up for the Wirral result. It was better than any of the predictions. JP was on great form on the by-election specials, called me a few times to say was he doing OK? – which he was – and then he drove through the night to do the broadcasts in the morning. 'If we can win like this in a place like this, we can win anywhere,' he said.

Friday, February 28

Everyone was in good form for obvious reasons. The result was far better than any of us had dared imagine. The press was absolutely dire for the Tories. I went round to TB's, and his mood had lifted too. We worked on his speech for Wales, and I'd persuaded him we should do a visit with Ben Chapman [new Wirral MP] on the way. It would produce terrific pictures, and if we got the words right, we would get another day's bounce out of the whole thing. We worked on the speech on the way to the airport, where I caught one of Major's interviews. He wasn't listening, looked like a man in denial. TB talked to GB and Peter, and said we had to build on this momentum. I was also using it to try to persuade them all that it showed the Tories were gaining very little from the negative advertising, and there is a case for us being more positive. TB was determined not to be triumphalist. We arrived at Manchester airport, and he did an interview with Molly at the Skyline, which was excellent. There was a great mood around us, lots of people coming up and just saying nice things to TB. I saw Major again on TV at the airport and he was really poor. There were a few hunting protesters out to greet us as we arrived, who were pretty nasty. Ben, who can never really have expected to win so easily, looked tired and bemused. There was a fabulous mood around but though TB's speech went OK, he had to go off script to get them going. I held Ben in a side room, and kept him back to the end and then pushed him in towards a standing ovation. Molly was a bit happier, because TB had done a couple of OK interviews with her. I was really buoyed by the reaction of the Tories to the result, real arrogance and making it clear they were going to go on the fear factor the whole time. It convinced me even more we should be going on hope.

Saturday, March 1

TB was on the phone from 7, worried that we were walking into a big tax story. He was worried because the news had said he was going to announce that there would be a Budget within weeks to announce the windfall levy. He feared it was an excuse for the BBC to rerun Major's line from last night in Scotland, that if we were going to have a special Budget within weeks that could only be because we wanted to put up taxes. TB must have called seven times in an hour, so I knew he was fretting. My chances of a day off were gone. Most of them seemed more interested in the welfare-to-work angle than in the Budget line. TB spoke to GB, who said that though the headlines were not brilliant we could definitely turn it around. He sent me an excellent briefing note, saying that we should call it 'the welfare to work Budget', that an interdepartmental committee was already working on job and training schemes, and that the long-term unemployed would have to take one of several options, as with the young. It gave a real crunch to the broad brush that I'd done overnight and it ran big time. It was so frustrating that whenever GB and I were able to work together properly, it just clicked and we could keep the whole show on the road, but these days it was so rare that he engaged like that. I think the media were impressed that rather than just sitting back post Wirral and letting the Tories wallow in it, we were pushing ahead with a policy agenda. I got home late afternoon which meant I only had a couple of hours with the kids. I got the papers later. Disappointed there was not far more post-Wirral doom and gloom for the Tories.

Sunday, March 2

Dreadful Mawhinney interview on *Frost*. His only message appeared to be that he was in charge. He was terrible. There was a potential problem in the *Sunday Times* whose arts correspondent claimed TB was discussing what paintings we would have in Number 10. It was total crap, but exactly the kind of story that could damage if not killed at birth. Dorrell fucked up on the single currency on *Dimbleby*. Or was it part of the deliberate shift strategy? I think it was a fuck-up.

Monday, March 3

Dorrell was big everywhere and there was a real slant against them at the moment. Also, the *Sun* had a poll in the Wirral suggesting that people who have switched were not going to go back to them at the general election. TB said he felt confident, really confident, for the first time, but he was worried about complacency setting in.

We went to the *Guardian* for one of these Q&A sessions with Rusbridger and pretty much anyone who wanted to come along. A lot of the usual were there, wittering on about the need to be more radical, without being remotely clear what they meant. But I got the impression they were pretty impressed. I was sitting at Rusbridger's desk, working on the general election grid, trying to put in more business and economic events. TB was strong on his own central arguments, didn't really take them on on theirs, made a few jokes about

March '97: GB and AC working well on Budget

state-owned media. We went back to Islington and on the way he suddenly said he didn't think it was really in our interests to have a television debate. Bizarrely, Gordon, Peter and I had all come to pretty much the same conclusion over the weekend. I had raised it with GB who felt Major was now seen as the underdog, and therefore a TV debate was likely to help them. Peter and I both felt it would become a massive distraction that would occupy the media to the exclusion of anything else. It was sensible to keep the option open but it wasn't difficult to build the arguments against it. TB said we should not join Paddy in making a big issue of it. We should start to brief that the Tories are just pissing around, focusing on this because it was a process not policy issue, pointing out too that the major parties' campaigns had been planned, and our general view was that whilst we could see it would be good for TV, we were not convinced it would be good for politics. TB said can you imagine how ghastly the build-up would be, all questions of process, the whole focus of the campaign. It is really all balls that it would improve democratic debate, he said. TB was also worried about Lib-Lab stuff. He said GB and he had discussed this yesterday and GB rightly analysed that TB felt he needed these people to be in the position of getting some political support and what TB wanted to do if we won the election was fairly quickly get some kind of merger, possibly get Paddy and Ming in the Cabinet and park PR. TB was opposed to PR and did not want to go that far. I sensed that little chill of excitement that comes with the planning of big, bold things. I said to David H and Peter yesterday that the Wirral created a new appetite for Labour policy stories and this was a classic of its kind – coverage for the kind of thing that the media assumed helped us win, a good way of getting new coverage for old policy. The by-election had delivered a new dynamic and we had to make it stick.

Molly Dineen arrived to film the interview I was doing with TB. I started by asking why he didn't mention getting rid of Clause 4 in the leadership campaign, and he fell about laughing. 'You can't ask me that,' he said. I read Jonathan's note on preparing for government, Cabinet appointments, policy on Europe, committee appointments, etc. He was clearly very on top of it all. It still seemed a bit unreal. I didn't want to focus too much on the post-election stuff because it was like a form of complacency, but I was glad Jonathan was doing it. I went home with David Blunkett and Tessa who were coming round for dinner, doing the usual probing re TB and what he intended to do if we got in. Philip called halfway through from Milton Keynes to say he had done a group, not one member of which was even aware there had been a by-election. It was one of those moments when you wondered if there was any point in anything we did. Bloody depressing.

Tuesday, March 4

There was a good *Guardian* poll, a bad poll in the *Herald*. In the *Guardian*, Kavanagh was quoted from last night's *Guardian* media event as saying Murdoch would decide the line at the election. I saw Donald who had been there, and said that my name had been mentioned again and again and Kavanagh had basically said we were liars and the Tories told the truth. TB had Peter round for dinner and was worried. 'Do you realise he thinks he's going straight into the Cabinet? He said he thought he should be Secretary of State for Heritage.' TB appeared shocked that Peter believed this was possible. He said he basically wanted to be the Bryan Gould of the campaign, the main front man.

His fears about Peter and GB not being able to work together were borne out again at the morning meeting. The aim had been to go over the campaign day by day but for most days they found something to disagree about the nature of the campaign. GB emphasised that it all had to be about the condition of Britain. I said that was fine as the theme, but the grid was meant to be emphasising those issues that played the theme. Our emphasis is leadership, business/economy, and education. Again, we didn't really disagree on much, but disagreements were made. TB agreed with me we had to set up challenges for the election, and then meet them. I sensed GB was worried about us taking the Tories on over the economy on day one. But again, we felt that was where we had to take them on, where traditionally they were felt to be strong and were now vulnerable. As we went through day by day, GB then started to just nod it through, in order, said Peter, that he could come back on it later. We then went down to the structure of the day, times of meetings, who will be at them, and Peter's list largely excluded GB's people from meetings. GB objected, Balls looked a mix of hurt and smug (no doubt observing to himself that he'd not been kept out of this one), and I argued that they should not become unwieldy. GB said he was not going to put forward names only for them to be rejected. TB said of course Charlie should be in some of these meetings as GB's press person. GB also wanted Donald and Darling at Millbank most of the time. I suggested Jack Cunningham and Margaret too, and I could tell Peter didn't fancy Jack being around, because he would see himself in the role I envisaged for JC. We then had the posters presented. TB, finally seeing them in a proper context, liked them and he liked 'Britain deserves better' as a line. It hadn't been such a bad meeting, and we had got buy-in on quite a lot of what we were trying to do, but the mood was still difficult and sour. TB had to leave to do a women's event and talked about his Auntie Audrey's breast cancer.

The news was leading, ridiculously, with Major hinting that the election might be on May 1. Afterwards I started to talk down the TV debate and talk up the Ashdown and smaller parties problem. Then there was yet another meeting on the grid, one of three during the day, to go through pictures day by day. Meeting with TB re *Richard and Judy*. Philip explained that TB was fine when he was being serious and persuasive but not when it looked like him simply grubbing votes. His ratings had gone up by big margins recently. They loved the Snowdon picture. They liked him being serious. I then briefed overnight on Lib-Lab. I spoke first to Robin who was terribly excited about the whole thing. He was holding the report and said to me 'I am a father,' rather melodramatically, and sadly I couldn't tell whether he was expressing pride or taking the mick out of himself. I said I was going to push the fact we had given nothing on PR but that there was plenty of agreement on other issues.

Wednesday, March 5

Excellent coverage, especially in the tabloids, on the 'family friend' breast cancer pledge. The news was leading on reports that the government was going to abolish SERPS [State Earnings-Related Pension Scheme] and that this was their big idea. The other story was the Lib-Lab constitutional report, which was ticking over without going wild. Robin wanted me to be at the launch but I told him TB was doing an interview with the *Herald*, which we were hoping to use to emphasise the commitment to bread-and-butter issues, not just devolution.

The morning meeting was all about pensions, but Harriet was all over the place, taking ages to make points that didn't quite gel, and I pushed for GB to take over. I got back and watched Major's live press conference and his announcement was far bigger than we thought, effectively ending the state pension as we understood it. There was a quick flurry of meetings in between TB being interviewed by Lesley White. Eventually, after a couple of sessions with GB and Harriet, we agreed we should be emphasising it was going to cost lots of money, it represented a tax rise, privatisation, and it would extend risk. Frank Field was in and out offering help and advice and I got him articles placed in the *Sun* and *Telegraph* and he said broadly helpful things. Harriet just blathered. Peter M, who was better at getting on with her than I was, wrote out a simple straightforward clip for her for the lunchtimes, which was fine. The problem was that the press saw it as a big, bold move, that Major was back with the initiative and we were being forced to catch up.

I had a brief meeting with Joe Haines who had drafted a 'letter to Britain' and was clearly chuffed to be involved. Tim did the rounds and said Peter Riddell thought we had made a historic error in not supporting the pensions change, so it was clear that Major was going to get a good press with the chatterers. Philip was convinced it was a disaster for them because we would say they were going to get rid of the state pension. TB was worried GB was gung-ho. He earlier refused to have Frank Field sharing a platform at the press conference.

TB was doing the usual anti-complacency stuff. We had another session on *Richard and Judy*. He was really devoting time to this, and was quite nervous, because it was a different kind of interview, connecting with people who just weren't normally plugging in, the people who were not even aware there had been a by-election. Major did a brilliant interview on *Newsnight*. He was humorous and relaxed, his charm came through, he was subtly apologising for mistakes without looking too weak, and not going for TB personally. I got the feeling he was like this because he felt he had a strategy and it was now unfolding. Get over the sense of a strong economy, harden the line on Europe, then bring out the Nice Guy whilst doing big difficult policy. Perfectly good approach given their situation and you sensed a new confidence in him. Anji called to say she thought he had been transformed. Earlier, JP had said to TB 'I heard the pensions story on the radio first thing and I was half asleep and I thought they were talking about us. I thought, the bastard's kept me out of the loop again.'

Thursday, March 6

TB's first call of the day came just after 7 and he was furious at RC who had said to a *Tribune* dinner last night that we were heading for a landslide. Unbelievably stupid, he said. He wanted me to contact him. I called Anna H and she said he did say it, but in the context of Michael Foot and Barbara Castle being there, and he said they were part of one landslide, and we could be on course for another one. I said it was a pretty silly thing to say and TB was livid. Robin called and said he was probably saying something that was accurate, though is was not necessarily a clever thing to say. He was anxious we did not put him down. Hilary C and I went to see TB pre *Richard and Judy*. I told him that Major had been very, very effective on *Newsnight*, very calm, relaxed, in control, apologetic. TB said it was clear that they were trying to become the underdog again, and we could not let them get away from being cocky and arrogant. That was why it was so silly of RC to say what he did. He also heard that GB began his speech 'comrades', which was part of the same thing, constantly saying what those you are talking to wanted to hear. We went through the various areas which Richard and Judy would want to cover, Leo, Mum, Cherie, the kids. The pensions initiative got a good press for them, and Harriet was pretty badly savaged, but it wasn't as big as I thought it would be. TB did not want to let it go, felt we had to undermine them on the arguments, said if this had been us, we'd have been murdered on the costs. *Richard and Judy* was fine. TB was a lot more relaxed, especially in the phone-in. Amazingly, we were pretty much allowed to choose the questions. They were an interesting couple. He had a touch of the [Robert] Kilroy-Silk [ex-Labour MP turned TV show host] about him, but I reckon that beneath the permatan exterior is a fairly decent bloke. She was very down to earth and friendly. TB was at his best on the phone-in, much more relaxed, lively and frank about Cherie. I picked up a buzz that the *Telegraph* poll had a massive lead for us and so briefed George Jones on TB's warning against complacency, as delivered to the Shadow Cabinet, knowing he would take it as a bit of a swipe at RC. But TB was adamant we had to play down any talk of winning, let alone a landslide, and constantly emphasise no complacency. He was worried about the underdog argument, and at them being seen as the party of big ideas. I was tired and had a bad cold, and was feeling a bit stressed.

Friday, March 7

The *Scotsman* ran a sniffy editorial saying he should not do things like *Richard and Judy*, but by and large we got great coverage for it. TB was seized all day by his 'underdog' worries, and felt we had to rethink how we dealt with the Tory strategy. I lost count of the times he referred to RC's 'stupid' landslide comments. We worked on the speech on the way up to Scotland, Pat working on the Scottish parts, me on food. Based on a briefing, Charles Reiss [*Standard*] told me he was doing 'Blair dares speak of victory', which was OK-ish, but when I told TB, he went into a total spin. He was so fanatically anti-complacent it was becoming a bit ludicrous. We had a poll showing us twenty-six points ahead but we had to go around with long faces saying woe is us. He said this was all part of getting to a dividing line of 'cocky Blair' vs 'underdog Major'. I said 'Blair dares speak of victory' was hardly Sheffield rally time.

We arrived and went straight to Inverness Caledonian Thistle's ground. There was a huge media turnout and good pictures out on the pitch, TB going in goal against a mix of the kids and the pros, and a nice welcome from the club inside. Back at the hotel, we finished the speech, him sitting there in nothing more than his Calvin Klein underpants. I said 'Right, I'll go and get Molly and she can film some of this,' and he nodded, then as I got to the door, he realised what I'd said and shouted 'What? I've got to get dressed then,' which finally he did. The audience liked the speech, the press liked it, I could tell from their reaction as he delivered it, and they were all marking up the right bits. He went right off script at the end, got really passionate and strong, and you could feel the audience getting lifted with him. It just stopped the right side of evangelical. I liked 'have a bit of faith' that we can deliver, because it was a message to the party and the public, and set in a really strong values and policy section. I did the rounds afterwards and the general reaction was good. You had a few of the devolution anoraks looking hurt that it wasn't the main dish of the day, but the bulk felt they had a lot of meat to get into and they liked the strength of the no-complacency message. Molly seemed a lot happier. There was an interesting piece from Peter Stothard tomorrow on how people were suggesting *The Times* back Labour. I doubted he would do that without some kind of encouragement from Murdoch.

Saturday, March 8

TB had said to GB before his Scottish speech that the best antidote to complacency was a big tax-and-spend message emphasising a new approach on the economy. GB said he agreed but then when it came to it he made the crusade against poverty the big thing, and set out the election themes as community, work and society, very deliberately not leadership, economy and education. We were back to the two different languages for the same campaign. Then even GB was upstaged by Robin who said that Redwood and Portillo were breeding racism and xenophobia. TB called when he heard about it, furious. We just had to let it run its course, but it pretty much drowned out GB. It showed two things: 1. RC was a bit offside at the moment, probably because he didn't feel we went far enough on PR, and 2. he would do anything to upstage GB at a Scottish conference. Neither had told us what they were going to be saying. In GB's case, he had,

March '97: TB flies off the prepared script

but he said something different. It was a problem not just because of the immediate news agenda. The main problem was that two of our biggest players, one of whom was supposed to be in charge of strategy, were not properly integrated into the TB campaign plan and structure. We were saved, newswise, by George Gardiner [Conservative MP] defecting to the Referendum Party.

Sunday, March 9

I watched Chris Smith and RC on various TV programmes. Both were taking a bit of a hit at the moment, briefed against, so everyone assumed, by Whelan. I went round to Molly's to look at all the stuff so far. There was such a distinction between the interview he did with me, and the stuff with Molly asking from behind the camera as they walked around, and I was not sure if they could be married. Hers would be better if we could make it work. My favourite bit was pretty much unusable. Cherie saying that when she first saw him she thought he was an upper-class public school twit. We had good stuff on crime, education, health, the family, but God knows how we would use it all. We went through it frame by frame and I was there till the early hours. It was definitely getting there, but TB had to relax a bit more.

Monday, March 10

There were two or three stories in the papers describing us as 'cocky', largely based on RC. Bevins called later and said he was doing a story about members of the Shadow Cabinet complaining to TB about being briefed against by GB/CW. He clearly had chapter and verse, though GB would admit no wrong. The problem was GB/CW aroused such anger among some of them there was no way they would just take it. I spoke to GB. He said 'You have to stop the story.' I said I couldn't do that, because he had clearly been briefed by some of them. He said I had to deny it. I said I was not in a position to say to Bevins that something he knew had happened – i.e. some of them had told him they were pissed off at being briefed against by him/Charlie – had not happened. Then he exploded. 'This is fucking Mandelson.' I said I thought Bevins had this from various places. Whoever it was, it was heading for real trouble. I said the best I could do was say to Bevins that TB had had no complaints, in the sense that nobody had come in, sat down and said I want to complain. But we can't say nobody was complaining because they were complaining to the press. GB denied any involvement in any of the issues Bevins had mentioned – briefings against JP (re super ministry), RC (re Tote, Libs), Smith (being out of his depth/useless), Harriet (ditto), and

Peter M (sidelined in election plans). I didn't like denying it because the truth was all of the above had at some point complained and been more or less convinced they were the victims of Whelan briefing against them, presumably with GB's consent. TB had really bad vibes about it, and so did I.

TB and I were working on his speech to the Newspaper Society. It was a bit of a cock-up. I thought it was a big event. It turned out to be fifteen proprietors and editors of regionals, most of them Tories, I would reckon. It was truly grim, one of those events where the moment we got there we willed it to be over. He spoke to Irwin Stelzer later who said Murdoch was moving towards supporting us again. For commercial reasons, they would probably make clear who they were backing at the start of the campaign. Paul Dacre had been in seeing Major last week and today we had a two-page spread on TB being all things to all men, lots of pictures of him in different guises, trying to appeal to different constituencies. It wasn't terribly effective but it showed the *Mail* was basically going to go for us.

Tuesday, March 11

Bevins' piece was pretty grim, illustrated by a parody of a Tarantino film. GB was of course straight on to TB, as was Peter. GB was claiming that this was the work of Peter, or even me, that one of us had put Bevins up to it. Arrived at TB's to find him more stressed out than usual by the GB/Peter situation. 'What the hell are we going to do? What do we do if we are out on the road and these two are back in Millbank trying to destroy each other?'

Phil Hall (*News of the World*) called to say there had been a sea change in Les Hinton's view; that there was definitely movement to us; and their big fear was more unions than Europe but his view was Murdoch was definitely going to back us. Then to the TB/GB/ Peter/AC meeting, plus Anji, Sue, Ed Balls. It was meant to be more election strategy and planning but it was absolutely hopeless. The meeting started in about as heavy a mood as I could remember. GB didn't refer directly to the *Independent* story but he said, for example, that it would be difficult to do all the things planned for Millbank 'because I'm having a wee bit of trouble with some of my Shadow Cabinet colleagues at the moment.' There was a long discussion about whether DD should be at the main meetings at Millbank. Peter was resistant to GB's staff being at the main morning meeting because he didn't want them to be unwieldy. TB and Peter didn't think we needed DD there, that he should be out as a campaigner on the road. Peter didn't want Jack C because, he said, he was not a detail merchant.

March '97: GB and Peter M 'trying to destroy each other'

As we went through a revised grid, there was endless carping that we hadn't worked out what the specific stories would be day by day. I said it was too early. We would have to be tactical. This was a grid to set out a strategy, a plan, show which issues we wanted to highlight and how often. Story development was ongoing. After they'd all gone, TB said 'This is a fucking nightmare. There is no way they can work together in a campaign.' I said if they were knocked over by a bus, who would he replace them with? He said he would replace GB with RC, but with considerable reluctance. As for Peter, he would expect his role to be filled by a mix of me and GB. He said if he had to choose, he felt GB was pretty much indispensable, Peter less so.

Meanwhile Gavin Strang had received letters from the Association of Meat Inspectors making clear that ministers had indeed been briefed on poor conditions in abattoirs. Tim did a brilliant job getting it up in the *Standard* and then TV and the regionals. It was a total hit, and by the end of the day was leading everywhere. I got JP up doing clips.

Wednesday, March 12

TB met GB at 12 and GB came with a sheaf of cuttings, the *Indy* story on 'Brown the terminator' and all the stories that led up to it. I left them to it. TB said later that GB had finally admitted that the real problem was his feeling that TB broke his promise over the leadership. He had always assumed that he would take over. TB said I never imagined John [Smith] would die but when he did, it was obvious. That was not just his view. It was widespread. GB said they had promised they would work as a partnership but he [TB] had broken his word on that. TB said they were a partnership, and GB had more say than anyone, but GB's definition of a partnership was that he worked with nobody else. He had to work with JP, Robin and everyone else. When I went back in, GB was just sitting there, glowering. TB said Gordon had been told by Andy Marr that the Bevins story was in part briefed by this office. I said I simply did not believe that. I said what on earth would be the point of us briefing against him? GB just pointed at the papers on his lap, as if somehow they were proof of something, whereas in fact, I said, they were proof of the madness of briefing against people. TB said, you two have got to sort it out, because I can't have my best people not working together. GB even had the *Evening Standard* cutting on the briefing I did from TB urging the Shadow Cabinet to 'keep their eye on the ball', and even that was somehow taken as evidence of me doing him in. It was part of a no-complacency briefing, just a few words from the Shadow

Cabinet. I said how can he take that personally? He said he took tough decisions, and he took flak on TB's behalf, but was not prepared to do it any more if this was the result. I said I thought Bevins' story was simply the result of, over time, him picking up moans and groans from Shadow Cabinet ministers complaining about being briefed against. He said he believed that Peter was behind the story, not to Bevins direct, but via Marr, possibly using Tim. This was a new one on me. Tim denied it when I spoke to him later, and with such emphasis that I believed him. GB said he had proof that CW was not involved in these stories. He said it suited me to have a situation where I could blame Charlie for everything. I said I could say the same about him re Peter. But I said I had no interest in briefing against anyone. TB was just sitting at his desk, looking more and more distant. Then it got worse. GB snapped, started jabbing his finger at me, said 'You've always been opposed to me and my political activities.' I said what on earth are you talking about, are you talking about before or after I did this job? Before, he said. I reminded him I used to help write his *Record* column. That we did the alternative manifesto together when I was still a journalist. That I helped with his speeches, that I spent years helping build him up. And in any event there was a difference between me doing this job and me being a journalist. 'You were not just a journalist. You were an activist with influence and you wielded it. And your loyalty is to Tony.' I said of course it is, he employs me. But loyalty to him does not mean disloyalty to you or anyone else. Having a relationship with JP, as I do, does not mean hostility to you. It's the same with Peter. I have to work with you both. He said Robin, Peter and the rest could do whatever they wanted. He didn't start the Tote story. We were back on that now. 'I let it run then Robin was allowed to kill it without TB or you lifting a finger. We were weakened by that. He said I was weakened every time there was a source close to TB that was not me. He suggested I should be named as Alastair Campbell and Peter should be named as Peter Mandelson. Fine, I said.

Dobson later raised all the briefings against Shadow ministers at Shadow Cabinet but TB shut it down, said he had had discussions with people about that. Eyebrows raised all round. GB finally left the meeting with a warning that if we had a briefing war, nobody would win. Later on RC came to see me, said he felt he and GB should do a joint effort, either a press conference or maybe a joint visit to Brussels with a positive agenda. It was a good idea. TB was totally exasperated. He said there were times during that conversation when he thought GB was losing it. At his meeting with JP, JP said nobody really believed Charlie wasn't at it, because he was. He said if GB and Peter could not get on he could not stand by and watch everyone else work hard for victory and see these people piss about. TB did a brilliant speech at the gala dinner, just working from a few scribbled notes. It was really passionate, Britain can do better, why Labour had to change, what we can deliver. Richard Wilson was doing the auction and I gave him TB's speech notes to auction which raised £4,000. There was a nice atmosphere. I was sitting next to Bianca Jagger who was a bit intense for a whole evening. I saw Andy Marr and raised what GB had said. He said he had said no such thing. He said the only time the Leader's Office was raised in any discussions was from Ed Balls saying I had pulled the wool over their eyes in convincing them CW was behind all these stories. Interesting. Me not Peter.

Thursday, March 13

Saw Peter who was worried we did not have an attack strategy against the Tories. Then Charles Reiss called with news that Thatcher said privately that Britain was safe in Blair's hands, which would clearly run. I had a meeting with JP who briefed me on his chat with GB yesterday. He'd said to GB the least TB deserves is that his top people get on. Robin was always going to be slightly outside throwing things in, but we had to get on. He'd said to him he didn't mind admitting that he had tried to break into the TB-GB-Peter-AC group but it's clear TB is not going to do that. He is loyal to you, you are going to be Chancellor, and that's that, and you'll always have an inside track. He said 'I don't mind moving closer to you publicly but it does mean you have to change the way you work, and get involved properly on the big issues.' He said he tried with GB before and he always says yes, but then nothing changes. He said if this kind of falling out continued into government it would be a disaster. He said if GB and Peter could not get on, and they started to do real damage, he would have to do something. He said it meant me and him working closely together, because he sensed we were the only ones GB worried about. At the strategy meeting later, GB and Peter were biting each other's heads off. TB was looking more and more frustrated. We didn't really have a strategy at the moment. We were managing day to day. TB was talking to Sally about whether we could get seats for [Alan] Howarth, [Douglas] Alexander, Alan Johnson and Charlie Falconer. Charlie is a lovely guy but he touches a few buttons, crony, Islington, public school. We had to watch it didn't become the springboard for a hypocrisy attack. We had a rerun of the arguments over Harriet. He said we should have been more robust from the start. I said he was kidding himself. It was a real problem. He later had a meeting with Clare. He said he had concluded she was mad, bad and dangerous.

Friday, March 14

Some of the papers said that GB had pulled out of *On the Record* for Sunday. The Tories were gathering in Bath, and GB, RC and Margaret were due to do press conference this morning on the risk of the fifth Tory term. RC and GB were reasonably friendly. Stan Greenberg and Philip had just taken TB through the latest message poll. It was very strong apart from on Europe. We had a twenty-point lead, trust was strong, TB was strong, leadership was strong, and we were in good shape on the economy and tax. He was also doing better with women. Stan said he had never seen the poll like this anywhere in the world at this time so close to an election. Europe was the only problem. Back in the office, TB wanted me to push GB's line on the social model, rejecting Europe's social model, which I tried to do. Edwina Currie was the big story, saying on the radio that Major should go quickly if he lost. It was a very silly thing to say. It must drive him mad, the way people just open their mouths and cause him problems. I had a long chat with Jonathan about his discussions with [Robin] Butler. He felt, contrary to what Liz Symonds said, that I could be very political in government. Anji told me that when GB left TB's office on Wednesday, he'd been really upset, and TB said GB admitted he could not get over TB being leader but he had decided to be more balanced and friendly.

Saturday, March 15

Most of the papers were leading on previews of Major's speech in Bath. I watched it. It was well written, and he delivered it well. The main line was helping the have-nots as well as the haves. He got a good response from the audience and from the media there. I took the boys to Brentford vs Burnley, and ran into Stuart Higgins who was there with a friend. He said to call him tomorrow about an idea for Monday. He said it would turn out to be an important one. The main development in the Sundays was Major challenging TB to a TV debate. I was surprised how little he got out the speech.

Sunday, March 16

TB called at 9.30, having spoken to GB, and they'd agreed it would be good to do clips on Major's 'challenge' for a TV debate, both to remind people we had challenged him, but more important to get up that the election would be about the condition of Britain. Meanwhile I called Stuart Higgins as agreed and he said, clearly having spoken to Murdoch, that if we gave them a piece on Europe, saying the kind of things TB had said last time they met, they would put it on the front. I spoke to TB and after we chewed it over, we agreed to go for it. TB felt it could be the last thing needed to swing the *Sun* round. So did I. We agreed it was important not to change in any sense the policy, but in tone to allow them to put over the message that TB was not some kind of caricature euro-fanatic. It was fantastically irritating on one level that we had to go through these kind of routines, but with an election looming, we would be daft not to try it.

I took the boys for a swim then went round to TB's to do Pienaar [BBC], ITN and [Adam] Boulton on TV debates. Boulton was the best of the three interviews, Pienaar just a mass of sweating. TB then did a phone interview with Bevins on JM's nerve at presenting himself as the friend of the have-nots. Though publicly we were in favour of a TV debate, privately the mood ranged from neutral to negative. The truth was JM was now the underdog, the one with something to gain from being seen on a level playing field. Ridiculous but true. I'm not sure Major really wanted it either. His insistence that Ashdown be kept out of it was a way of making sure it didn't happen. I felt that not just Paddy but the smaller parties would be able to kybosh it and we'd all waste a lot of time arguing about something the media wanted purely as a media event complete with build-up hype and ballyhoo and which in all probability would not actually happen because the lawyers would stop it happening. TB thought JM DID want it to happen, and felt we had walked into it with our 'any time, any place' formulation. He and I then worked on the *Sun* piece, which was pretty sceptic, certainly up their street.

I went off to play football with the boys on the heath when Pat McFadden called to say Alan Howarth had been selected for Newport East, which was a big surprise. I put out TB words saying it was a significant event, evidence of New Labour depth in the party.

I had to go back to TB's for another meeting, this time with Peter, Jonathan, DM and later GB to go over outstanding policy problems for the manifesto. TB was by now alarmed about the TV debate. The BBC sent round a proposal which met most of Major's demands – no audience, cross-questioning. I briefed that the suggestions we had made to BBC and ITN were not being taken on board. On balance I felt the ITV proposal was both better and more realistic, though the Nats were starting to get uppity. My original fears – that the whole thing would become a gigantic media wank – were being borne out.

TB was intensely irritated by the whole thing. I briefed out more conditions. GB arrived and with the buzz building that tomorrow was a big day, we went through our Day One plans to test them to destruction. If it kicked off, we'd have TB on *Today*, down to the school as soon as it was called, straight to Gloucester, JP heading to Falmouth for Tuesday. The message for the first part was education, work, leadership. Get up the choice. Really hit the ground running then slow down, do the manifesto before Easter, a series of mini manifestos/charters afterwards. I was feeling quite excited now that I sensed the campaign coming closer. The *Sun* piece was on the front, though not the splash. Higgins had spoken to Murdoch. He was clearly not going to back the Tories but they had to be careful in how they went full circle.

Monday, March 17

At last we were up and running. The *Sun* piece ran as the second leg to the main overnight story. It was seen as a significant event. TB and I didn't know just how significant until later today. The papers were focused mainly on election timing, it was clearly, finally, happening. Terry collected me and we set off for TB's. The photographers were already there, and the press clearly thought today was the day. I got in, and TB was worrying, as so often at real pressure moments, about his bloody hair. He was right that it was looking even wilder than usual, all over the place. He scribbled a few points on a scrap of paper – the choice, New Labour, Howarth, the business survey showing that fifty per cent of businesses want a Labour victory. I said a long campaign could benefit us as it was would allow us to do the three Rs – reassure, remind, reward. The *Today* programme interview was OK. We went back to Richmond Crescent and did a few interviews in the garden. Cherie came out and started talking to them and said she was off to Gloucester, but they didn't seem to twig, so were they. She and I were getting on a lot better, which was good as we were going to be together an awful lot in the next few weeks. They posed for pictures in the garden before TB and I set off for the office. Once it was obvious Major was going for it, we hit the buttons for the visit to the South London school and then Gloucester. While everyone was fussing around outside, TB and I had a quiet ten minutes, and he said Fergie was right, we had to play our own game, we know what we're doing, and then we sit back and let them make mistakes. Over six weeks, they will. I thought they would regret such a long campaign.

Once it was clear Major was on his way to the Palace, we set off for the school. TB was very quiet in the car, nodding to himself and he went over what he was planning to say. Occasionally he would tap me on the arm, look over and whisper a few lines and ask what I thought. He wasn't really looking for an answer, it was just part of the process of self-reassurance, rehearsal and memorising it. He was on good form. I always knew when he was going to be. He wasn't fretful. He was just focusing on what he was going to say, how he was going to say it. I said demeanour would count for a lot today. More than possibly any other part of the campaign, people would latch on to what he was saying, so it had to be clear and strong. We arrived, were taken into a classroom and we listened to Major's declaration, me intently, TB almost disinterestedly. He didn't intend to react. He was sticking to what we had decided. I didn't think much of JM's statement. He sounded tired and it felt flat. It felt like lines written for him by someone who had more energy than he did. TB did a round of interviews in front of a group of well-behaved kids. His down-the-line live ITN interview was brilliant, really strong, word-perfect, great body language, confident and clear, pushing the line that we wanted to frame the debate from day one – can Britain be better than this? We believe it can. He pushed it in interview after interview, and I did feel our lines, attack and defence, were stronger than theirs. He did a big doorstep on the way out, lots of nice pictures with the kids then we set off for Paddington. Brilliant, I said. Fantastic start. He said he felt really relieved we were finally into it.

We went to Paddington to meet Cherie, Fiona and Pat [McFadden]. I was by now briefing hard on the choice, and saying a long campaign suited us fine. I was talking to Derry about the TV debate. He was strongly of the view that we should get out our conditions publicly – on the audience, the panel of commentators, and the minority parties. He too thought there was little for us to gain in doing it but we must not be seen to scupper it. We changed trains at Swindon and TB asked if I thought we would win. I said I did. So did he, but he felt six weeks was a long time and he worried about the quality of the Shadow Cabinet and their capacity for making mistakes. He felt tax and spend remained a problem. The main mood around us was one of calm, which was good, and people like Jeremy Vine were commenting on it publicly. There was a good crowd to meet us at Gloucester, then we were driven to a hotel and country club. TB did a round of live interviews before going into a filmed meeting with twenty-eight switchers. Paged to call Higgins urgently. He said they were going to come out for us in a big front page tomorrow. There will be things they criticise us for, but it is unequivocally backing Blair. I said I was really pleased. He said yesterday's article was important and Murdoch had said he was sure. I asked how Trevor [Kavanagh] had taken it, and Stuart said RM was sure, and laughed. I called Peter M to tell him, then told Fiona, Anji and Pat. As soon as TB finished the Q&A session I took him to one side and said I had some good news. I said you remember in 1994 when I said we should try to get the *Sun* on board and you said you weren't sure it was possible, well, they are. He thought it was good news in its own right, but was good in the effect it would have on the other side's morale. I tipped off Brunson. On one level, it was ridiculous that it should be seen as a big event, but the reality is that is exactly how it is seen. I felt it was a fruit of three years' hard work, and there will be many more. TB said later he couldn't quite believe it. His Q&A went well, and we briefed that the format was very much how he would operate during the campaign, taking questions from anyone, seeking to persuade. *Newsnight* was fine, though I felt Paxman's heart wasn't really in it. But there were no dropped bollocks. One of the sweetest moments of the day was phoning Montgomery to tell him 'as a courtesy' that the *Sun* was coming out for us, and so would be the main media story for the start of the campaign. He didn't say much, said he would act on it. He said they clearly thought we were going to win. I felt the *Mirror* had been so lacking in politics of late that it was no wonder the *Sun* felt able to move in. Then Brendan Parsons [*Mirror*] came on and wanted to do a 'Blair backs the *Mirror*' piece. They really don't get it.

Tuesday, March 18

Overall, the press was pretty good. The *Sun* switching was a pretty big story in its own right. Even the *Mail* wasn't too grim. *The Times* was a bit more iffy than I thought it would be. I got round to TB's early and he said the big problem was underdoggery. We were felt to be so far ahead that the press would want to hit us hard. He said 'I can't tell you how much my stomach churns when I think we've got six weeks of this. I barely slept last night. I've also been racking my brains for any skeletons that might still be clanking around.' We left to do the morning TV, and he was OK without being brilliant. In the car in-between times, he was anxious about some of the policy problems, mainly devolution, Europe and tax. He said he didn't feel we had crystal clear answers on them. There was another problem that emerged from the morning though, re the windfall levy. We were clearly of the view that BT and BAA were not to be included. But GB gave us our first big problem. At the press conference, with TB doing the core script, and JP coming in from Falmouth on a video link, which was excellent, GB was pressed on the levy. He would not say which companies were involved. At no time had he mentioned BT, BAA or Railtrack. However, in his body language he indicated they might be and this was confirmed by Ed Balls afterwards. So the lunchtime bulletins showed GB refusing to answer followed by 'aides' being filmed doing exactly that. It was macho bollocks, and incredibly stupid. It was the last kind of issue we needed up on the first full day of the campaign. Later GB saw [Iain] Vallance [BT] who called Jonathan to say GB was fine, but Balls gave a clear impression BT was to be included. Ted Graham [BT] called to say that he had done us a big favour over the information superhighway, and now can I do him a favour too? I spoke to Charlie and Balls and said we had to stick to the line as agreed. We were now walking the first new tightrope. I briefed the *Guardian* and *Times* that BAA and BT were unlikely to be included. The news was going very heavy on it. I didn't much like the press conference, or the coverage all day. Our people looked a bit tense and the problem was that it was as if we were the incumbent. The Tories weren't really put under pressure at all. Ken Clarke got a very easy ride. We went back to do an interview with the *Sun*. Stuart Higgins told me that lots of *Sun* readers were complaining about the decision to switch. Trevor Kavanagh, who was bristling, and Roycroft-Davis were also clearly unhappy. They ran over all the issues from a very hostile right-wing perspective. I'd love to know exactly what they felt on being told they were backing us. Stuart was clearly a bit worried, feeling a bit vulnerable and Jon Sopel did a piece on the nine o'clock news saying 10 Acacia Avenue didn't like it. They could lose some readers but they could possibly gain others. They certainly got profile out of it though. I felt it put the *Sun* on the political map at the right time in the campaign. I went round afterwards and briefed on the utilities, but the news was crap.

At 7 there was a TB/GB/Peter M/AC meeting. We agreed that a six-week campaign meant we should delay the manifesto launch, to give us more time to get some new Tory plans out there, and not have all the questions focused upon us. GB got angry when TB suggested Balls had been at it over the windfall tax. Peter felt we had to define the campaign more clearly. Philip and I felt Gordon and Peter were circling, that neither was taking charge inside Millbank at a time when TB and I will be spending most of the time on the road. I felt we had to lie low for a bit.

Earlier Alan Sugar called and said he wanted to see me to discuss our strategy. He said he would give us money, and come out for us in the last two weeks if we needed it. He would not work for the other lot, he said, but he seemed to know a bit about their plans. He said Major was going to try to take his time, not get too worn out, use the others a fair bit, then have a two weeks' crescendo. They had a lot of money for direct mail. He said my advice is don't shoot your bolt too soon.

Jon Craig [*Express*] said that if I did nothing else for TB, today's *Sun* front page was a total triumph. GB, with Charlie and Ed, had lunch with Rothermere and English and apparently went down well, though Rothermere was only interested in the rabies laws and whether he could take his bloody dog to Europe. TB saw them too and said he felt if it was left to them, the *Mail* would not be so bad. But there was no way Dacre would do anything other than try to do us in.

Wednesday, March 19

I woke up, joyously, to the Tories leading the news on their suppression of the cash-for-questions report. Oakley talked about 'relentlessly effective spin-doctoring'. PG had done an overnight note from the groups saying that TB alone had begun to break through a little. Terry collected me early and I picked up TB before we set off for Birmingham. He felt the Tories were going to get a better deal out of the press because they all thought we were so far ahead and would want to even up a bit. He was still annoyed at his *Newsnight* interview which he felt was a wasted opportunity. CB and Norma [Major] were both at the *Daily Star* gold awards lunch and the word was that Cherie stole the show. The *Star* put out a picture of the two of them laughing their heads off together. The windfall story get very little play, which surprised me because if they had wanted they could have done the contrary briefings going on. The *Guardian* carried my very heavy knockdown. The Midlands lot had organised a terrific visit to a training centre. Great pictures, good local coverage, good atmosphere when he did his doorstep on sleaze and unemployment. GB's press conference was mainly on sleaze/Hamilton, and the Tories were very much on the defensive, but PG felt it didn't do us much good to be seen to be driving any of this, and he was probably right. It was good to get them on the defensive, but TB was strongest when pushing on a positive agenda for the future.

Anji and I went though the grid day by day and moved a few things around. Six weeks was a long time to sustain the kind of pace we had organised for a three- or four-week campaign. There was the issue of tiredness, also of the public getting sick and tired of the same old arguments. We were going to need to be tactical, try to get a bit of freshness and life into it. We had a team meeting at 2.30, most of the people who would be involved in the day-to-day running of TB's campaign, plus the Special Branch. I gave a not very effective pep talk and went over the dos and don'ts. I said that only people whose job it was to talk to the press should talk to the press. I said that once we were on the road with a permanent press presence they would get frustrated at the lack of access to TB and even me, and they would be looking to anyone and everyone to be a source. Don't feed them. Be nice and polite but don't feed them stuff that they could claim to be a story. I said we all existed for the next six weeks to make life as easy as possible for TB, that he would be the one under the most pressure. We had to pay absolute attention to the detail of every visit, so that he didn't have to worry. The advance teams were hugely important. It could be lonely and frustrating because it did not feel close to the action but it was as important as any other part of the job. Good advance work was vital. Attention to detail was the key. They were excited and Anji said afterwards they were a brilliant team, but I didn't feel I'd really fired them up like I hoped to.

PG said of the three days so far, we were winning 3-0.

Thursday, March 20

The *Star* scored a hit with their CB/Norma picture, which played just about everywhere. Cherie was looking good. Sleaze was the main story but the thing bothering TB was his *New Statesman* interview in which he was promising not to do in Murdoch. By and large though the news was about as good as we could ask for. I got round to TB's and CB was flicking through the press coverage and saying it was all going fine. I called Peter M while I was waiting for TB to get ready and we agreed Derry was the best person to negotiate on a TV debate. Anne Sloman and Richard Tait [ITN] were pestering me the whole time and it would be good to have someone else deal with it. The BBC had changed their proposal to take account of some of JM's objections and to steal the best of the ITV idea. Peter M and I had both fed through the view that Sue Lawley was not really acceptable and wouldn't be taken seriously. I think the scale of what lay ahead had dawned on TB, not just the length of the campaign and what it entailed, and all the pressure on him, but also what followed if we won. It was odd, both of us remarked, how just a few weeks from now, he could be prime minister. Yet because we saw it as our job to keep the party totally focused on the no-complacency message we didn't allow ourselves really to think about that, in case the party became complacent, or the public felt we were taking their support for granted. But he was looking more anxious and I said he had to really try to look more confident than this when we were out and about.

At the morning meeting, sleaze was the main focus though I fed in PG's view that the public wanted to see us on the positive agenda. We had a mini post-mortem on the windfall tax. I said we had got away with it but it should be a warning about the importance of saying the same things on difficult policy. Balls looked a bit sheepish. GB was on good form at the moment, full of energy and ideas. PMQs was pretty vicious. TB felt there was a real stench to the Hamilton thing and JM was pretty rattled. We had some good research done which showed it was perfectly possible to extend Parliament to let Downey do his report on Hamilton. JM lost it and afterwards TB said he looked really rattled. He also revealed he knew something about the deliberations of the committee so DH and I went round afterwards stirring that up.

Alex F called and agreed to get involved with our tie-up with the Premier League on Monday. He said I should be making clear to everyone they should lay off drink totally, build in rest time, and some physical training and massage if possible. He thought TB had been terrific on *Newsnight*. He said he was sure we were going to win but he had heard the Tories had some big story on Europe that was going to do us in. We were getting a good steady flow of people who were coming out for us or giving us money.

Meeting with Derry re the TV debate. I loved the image of Derry negotiating with Anne Sloman, absolute intellectual rigour which could mean he would sometimes argue for twenty minutes about where the comma should go, against head-in-the clouds twittery. Derry was starting from the point that there was not much in this for us, and that the efforts of actually resolving the outstanding issues might be too great. But he was clear we should not be the ones pulling it down. He and I were in exactly the same place on it but I was glad he was doing it not me.

Friday, March 21

I slept in a bit, and was worried about tiredness. The *Guardian* tipped me off last night that they were running some of the evidence to Downey showing that Smith and Hamilton were in it up to their necks. DD called to say he felt we should drop the positive anti-sleaze proposals and just let it run, but I said we must always try to put a positive case as well. Sleaze was running big and JM's morale must be low. I took the boys to school, went for a swim and then set off for Brentwood to see Alan Sugar. It was nice to be on a train on my own and have some time just to stare out of the window. I went straight to Amstrad, caught the start of the news and then sat down for a chat with Sugar. He went over the main lines of attack the Tories were planning, mainly on the economy. He said he liked TB, appreciated the fact he had gone to his fifteth, liked the fact he was in charge. He felt we were in danger of being too active too soon, and needed to pace ourselves better. He said he would come out for us towards the end and I agreed to draft something for him. I thought either an all-round statement or an article in the *Sun*. Higgins was desperate for a big switch endorsement. Alan S was giving the party £125,000. He said he was doing it because he liked TB and he liked the changes he had made. He was more relaxed than the last time I saw him, less worried about any attacks he might get.

TB was seeing GB to go over tax-and-spend problems, agreeing no increase in National Insurance ceilings, more health spending and how we would do it. They were getting on better now that the thing had started. JM was up on sleaze and the broadcasters wanted TB to respond. I said no, felt it was better that they saw JM having to defend himself, but keep TB silent on it, not look for opportunities.

I got home reasonably early but it was a typical Friday. Just when you think you can wind down for a few hours, the phone and the pager go berserk. I had all the Sundays wanting background stuff on the *Sun* switching. Started drafting the Sugar article and getting it back to him while our discussion was fresh in his mind. Andy Grice called and said the *Sunday Times* would be grim unless we found a decent story for them. I talked to JoP and we agreed the idea of a separate business manifesto. Oakley said he would have to say the week ended Tories 0 Labour 1. I also felt confident about next week. The grid looked strong.

Saturday, March 22

I had settled into the rhythm pretty well. It was helping that I had pretty much given up reading the papers closely, and was relying on the party's media brief which was all I really needed. It wasn't just a question of time, but there was a danger of losing the perspective of where the public was if you spent your whole time poring over the press. Peter M shared my worry that we needed to get the *Sunday Times* in a better place. I worked on a briefing note on the idea of a business manifesto, and after taking Grice through it said all he needed to do was wind up a few unions or MPs to say we were going too far pro business and he'd have a story. The Tories were working hard to turn sleaze against us, and some of the papers were buying the line. We were hoping to get crime up today but JM went up on sleaze again and it ran all day, with Jack Straw responding.

We went for lunch at Philip and Gail's. He and I had had a difference over the Molly PEB yesterday but when we showed the latest draft to Fiona and Gail, they thought it could be a bit of a disaster. He thought GB was becoming properly engaged for the first time. We took the kids to QPR vs Portsmouth, Calum proudly wearing his Burnley shirt, but I was in and out on the phone. There was also a fair amount of crowd trouble. In the car, PG was arguing strongly we get on to education as soon as possible. Got home to a message to call Alan Clark. 'Congratters. It's going to be a bloody rout. If we carry on like this, we will be lucky to get a hundred seats. I have never known morale so bad. You guys are just running rings round us day after day. There is no other way to describe it.' I told him we were doing our main poster launch in Kent and was there any chance we could use the grounds of his castle? I said I wanted a big field. He laughed away and said 'Why not? I love black humour.' He really felt Major had been stupid to back Hamilton and Smith because they were so clearly indefensible.

I got the papers early. The *Sunday Times* splashed in the early editions on the business manifesto and later on the sleazebuster proposal, put there by Peter M. The read-throughs had lots about how we won over the *Sun*, and there was stacks on CB, including a nasty profile by Sarah Baxter in the *Sunday Times*. But in terms of the media, there is no doubt it was week one to us. I had a fair few calls to say so, including Syd Young and Geoff Lakeman [both *Mirror*]. Paul Keating called TB. He said whatever you do, don't get drawn into a TV debate, because they're a pain in the ass and the underdog usually wins. And don't go overboard until the last two weeks. Keep a lot of powder dry till then. And don't give them the economy.

Sunday, March 23

A couple of new surveys showing business moving to us. I'd mentioned to Higgins the companies likely or unlikely to be covered by the windfall tax and [George] Pascoe-Watson came on, saying 'he'd heard' who was going to get hit by it. I said we had to say all of the privatised utilities could be covered but in practice that wouldn't happen. Then Whelan spoke to him and gave him a slightly different line, and I had to calm George down, say there was nothing inconsistent, just that we could not be as detailed as they wanted at this stage. I spoke to Whelan and I could hear GB chuntering in the background, saying water will be hit hard and so would the others. Peter M's view was that this was all part of the fallout to the tax row. Having lost on the top rate, he would be looking for another area to have an argument and win.

I took the boys for a swim then got back and the news was now leading on Richard Shepherd [Conservative MP] calling for Parliament to be recalled for the Downey Report. I went round to TB's to go to the teleconference thing he was doing later. Then Mawhinney did a briefing on the TV debate saying they were ready to accept all the new conditions put down by the broadcasters. This was a rare case of them doing a proactive briefing unexpectedly and it worked. The broadcasters fell for it hook, line and sinker and it was the main story for most of the day. By the time we got to the teleconferencing, they wanted TB clips on it. I said no, and the Tories were quite successfully getting up the line that they wanted it and we didn't. Peter M was talking to Richard Holme [senior Liberal Democrat adviser] and Paddy was keeping to the line that he had to be fully involved, not just a small part of a sandwich. I called Nigel Dacre at ITN and Tony Hall and the BBC and said that just because Mawhinney did a bit of public negotiation it was not a story to go to the top of the news.

My concern the whole way about this TB debate thing was that their self-obsession meant any time it was raised, that was the story. It communicated nothing to the public about the parties and the differences between them. Anne Sloman called and said the BBC were not playing it up. We'd see. I couldn't wait for Derry to get stuck into it. TB felt we would probably end up with one debate, pretty much on our terms, but there was nothing in it for us but risk. He felt it would probably end up as a draw but there was so much at stake that anything could happen. He was worried that we were not getting over a sense of a clear vision, or any real excitement. TB was also worrying about the economy, and whether the Tories were beginning to get traction on it, and also speculating which of the Shadow Cabinet would not be good at dealing with pressure. On the teleconference, we picked up the clear line that sleaze was damaging them, but not necessarily helping us. Afterwards we got in Mike Maloney [photographer] and Nigel Nelson [*People* political editor] and while I was called to the phone, I got out to find Maloney talking TB/CB into doing a picture rubbing their noses together, which was potentially embarrassing, and certainly not prime ministerial. TB tried to persuade me to have Robert Harris on the bus. I said it was his decision but I was totally opposed because it was just one more thing to worry about, for a project that would have no impact on the result, as it was for publication after. He felt it would help soften the opposition in the *Sunday Times*. I disagreed. It would make no difference at all. I said the last time Peter M fought this hard for one of his posh-set friends was Molly, and now he regretted it. Molly and I were trying to salvage something now, but Molly felt we had picked the wrong person. She was happy to see it through but she wasn't sure she was right for it. TB called after I went to bed, and said he felt what was missing was a sense of vision; something really uplifting and inspirational.

Monday, March 24

The TV debate was far smaller in the press than on the TV. Blunkett was on the *Today* programme and the Tory response was that he was getting into bed with Murdoch to which DB said he didn't mind who he got into bed with. The *Sun* was OK newswise, but there was a leader attacking the windfall tax. Our main problem was the *Telegraph* splash which said, thanks in part I'm afraid to my rather loose briefing of Robert Shrimsley, that union recognition where a majority wanted it would be in the manifesto. The Tories were slow on to it but eventually got it going. It meant it was coming up as a big item, rather than with a lot of other things around it. Margaret was on the radio about it, and TB wanted fed in the fact it was the same situation already in the US. I spoke again to Derry. Derry said we must all speak with one voice, and he must be the sole negotiator. He was clear that TB would do well, but felt it was not a risk worth taking. He went through the points he would make, including that the debate must be lawful and dignified. He said he would fight against cross-questioning, because Major did not answer questions and instead launched into tirades, so he was not going to get into that at all.

I went round to TB's and as ever he was both late and fretful. He thought the Oxford forecasting centre stuff on the economy would alarm people and if people sensed there would have to be interest rate rises, the Tories trying to do the economic miracle would backfire. He wanted us to push it hard, but we could not persuade GB to get going. Peter, TB and I all had a go at persuading him that we should be pushing on the economy, showing that we wanted to fight them on what they thought was their ground. But Gordon was not keen. Peter called us on the train to Chesterfield to say TB had misled him. He thought the policy was recognition where a majority of the workforce voted for it. David M said that was not the case. It was a majority of the vote. TB was being disingenuous, he said. TB was anxious, first, that the story was running when we didn't want it to, and second, JP and others would use it to rock the boat. He spoke to JP from the train and said it was a Tory ploy, which is why it was in the *Telegraph*. But JP was not happy. The idea of extra-tough sentences for drugs sold near schools didn't stack up. George Robertson came up with the idea of drugs czars to co-ordinate the fight against drugs in particular areas. He had the backing of the Grampian police chief, who, we said, would do the job if we were elected. It was a strong story though that would get a lot of coverage.

Molly called to say she really was getting tired of being pissed around. I did feel for her because she was not getting a clear brief. TB was really pissed off that Gordon would not motor on the economy. TB did a pop channel in Sheffield and got stuff on the Spice Girls, and his favourite Doctor Who. He said Jon Pertwee. GB was now moaning because of the *Sun* windfall tax story and not co-operating with Peter again. Peter wanted us to do a Europe press conference tomorrow, and GB was not sure. TB had a couple of ridiculous conversations with GB, who was constantly complaining about being briefed against, when he wasn't. He couldn't imagine that the *Sun* just took their own line. He had to assume they were put up to it. TB said this was going to happen all the time and we just have to say stay calm, not go crazy about it. GB was seeing things that just weren't there. An increasingly offside Robin was insisting that he would have to have his moment on Europe.

According to Philip, TB was breaking through, the only thing that people were noticing, and we had to have him up the whole time being positive. Philip said the groups in Slough felt TB looked really good, confident, while Major looked tired and washed out. We got two sets of very good pictures on the later bulletins, High Peak and Hillsborough, where he launched the Premier League homework scheme. We had a quiet journey back, TB writing the foreword to the manifesto. Peter said he felt beleaguered and GB was close to explosion the whole time. Philip was adamant we had to be on a positive message through TB all the time. He said women were turning off the election slagging already.

Tuesday, March 25

The unions issue was a real problem now. The papers were full of it, negative and grim. I told TB when I got there that we were taking a hit. The Tories switched their press conference from education to unions, and TB was angry that the points he'd suggested we make were not really coming across and GB, Peter and Jonathan were not returning calls. We left for the airport with him saying we had to get a New Labour initiative and quickly. TB was getting nervous about the way the unions issue was playing. I suggested we give the LEA story to the *Mail* on condition they make clear it didn't come from us. JP called TB and apologised at having overreacted yesterday. TB said these kinds of things would happen again and again and we had to stay calm. They agreed things are not as good as they should be in Millbank. GB and Robin were doing a press conference but by all accounts there was not much engagement by Gordon, who according to Peter was more interested in his documentary cameras having access to meetings than he was in anything discussed. TB talked to GB from the airport and explained the way he wanted the union question handled. But by the time we landed, and GB was doing the press conference, he had introduced the idea of a judge to oversee cases on union recognition. Just when we were trying to kill the story, he gave it fresh legs, and we were struggling to keep on our own issues.

TB was pretty agitated by the time we got there, but did an excellent interview with Allison Pearson on the way up for the *Telegraph* magazine. She had just done Heseltine and clearly hadn't liked him much. I got the feeling she was pretty big on God and seemed to like TB. By *Telegraph* standards it should turn out OK. We were met by George Robertson then off to Dyce Academy, and then surrounded by whining journalists who waited in the rain and TB said nothing. The *Press and Journal* asked him if he'd ever taken drugs. It was a good visit though I had far too many rows with the Scottish media, as ridiculous as ever. In the melee on the way out I fell down a set of stairs, cut my knuckles and my knee and got a huge rip in my suit. Amazingly none of the hacks saw me and I slipped off ahead of the pack and got into the car and waited for TB. I went off to get a suit at Marks & Spencer and then back to meet TB. I got Allison in the car with him out to the airport, TB on bigger themes, while I was trying to keep abreast of the union situation. On the plane back, he was working on the manifesto intro again. Most people thought the draft he had done was crap but I liked it. It was fresh and it was very him. I went and sat down quietly and read through the manifesto with a fresh eye. There was a lot in it to bring out during the campaign.

In the car on the way back from the airport I got the clear impression that the unions issue was still developing badly. Trevor Kavanagh was in pig heaven, going on and on about it being a real problem for us. TB cancelled going home and came with me to Millbank. He said provided the policy was explained properly, it was OK but we were not explaining it well. He was worried we do not have enough good people to explain difficult things simply. We agreed to do a TB article in the *Mail* about it, and try to explain this was fair and reasonable, and the Tory response hysterical. We had a meeting with GB who was clearly discomfited about what he'd said about the judge, which TB said was easily explained. In this area, he did at least know what he was talking about. He said we had to get this up on our terms. I said we should be saying vote Tory for no rights at the workplace at all. I could sense the press thought we were in trouble and the Tories for the first time since the off were happy. I said we had to go for them on it, make them feel uncomfortable, try to turn it around. GB was not on form, he was worried about it going wrong. TB did most of the article himself and we got it to the *Mail* by 7. Bruce Grocott said to me 'Keep the ball in the corner flag and don't take too many risks.' The general feeling was we had fucked up on the unions position, and we were to blame for it. GB agreed he had ballsed up re the judge but said he had relied on Byers' advice. One of the problems is that if we weren't in there, Peter and GB were not going over the really difficult questions properly together, and so there was always a risk of saying slightly different things. Philip called from focus groups to say that the unions issue was not yet hitting us, but the news bulletins were pretty bad all round.

Wednesday, March 26

There was a very funny piece in the *Scotsman* on my trousers. The unions stuff was still kicking on. John Humphrys was revelling in it. 'Just like the old days,' he said to Nick Jones. He is such a wanker. They also had some prick on attacking us over architecture. He said we had taken a big hit on this. I said I felt it would only blow its course if he went up on it. I did a sound bite to slip into the draft Peter H had done for today – 'I didn't create New Labour to hand it back to the unions or anyone else.' On the way in, TB said he wondered if I shouldn't base myself at Millbank. He felt there was a problem with both of us being out on the road together, and Peter and GB squabbling back there with nobody who could really stand up to them. Jonathan said that there had been a real sense of panic yesterday, and nobody gripping it. We had managed to get on top of it when we got back but by then a lot of damage was done and it was too much to expect us to do that every day. I had a chat with JoP and Anji about what I should do and they felt for now it was better I was with him on the road, because that was where I could feed in most to him, and feed back to MBT [Millbank Tower]. Jonathan said it was not just the GB/Peter problem, but Charlie/David [Hill].

In the morning meeting we agreed to push 10p tax rate in Basildon tonight, but GB didn't really deliver. Peter M and I discussed the TV debate which was looking more likely. Derry reported that they had agreed to take an audience, Ashdown would get a bit of time and it would be hard to get out of it. Higgins called and said they would like a JP piece on the unions, which, amazingly, I was about to offer, having put the idea to JP. Stuart was still being supportive but we were taking a real hit and he sensed that. TB was on terrific form at the moment, on the detail, on the big message, on fine points, and he was good in interviews afterwards. I worked on briefing some of the background to the manifesto, and also emphasising that whenever TB was in charge, there was no problem, and if there was a hiccup, it was sorted. TB felt we were on top again though there was a dreadful piece on the BBC, that there was a big hole in our plans. It looked like a very good piece of Tory work to me.

Peter M called to say that [Michael] Howard had attacked TB as soft on terrorism, and we decided to go nuclear on it. Jack Straw had been liaising with Howard about how to respond to major incidents and only last week they had reached agreement on this. I had the note, including our discussions on handling with the Home Office about it and liaising with Number 10 about TB's doorstep on it. It was an easy hit for us, no problem out of it, other than Jack wanting to get into too much detail. Tim Smith resigned at 4. Thatcher put out an attack on TB but it wasn't powerful. It felt like she was doing the minimum required by Central Office. I felt much better doing the rounds, unions fading, JP's article a success, Howard's attack largely seen as a mistake and above all manifesto agreed quickly.

TB was doing an interview with David Baddiel [comedian] at Millbank, which was excellent. It was a more reflective interview than usual and TB put a lot more of himself into it. Ulrika Jonsson [TV personality] was doing Major for the same series. TB said to Baddiel 'How come I get you and Major gets Ulrika?' GB didn't deliver on tax, and instead committed us to spend more on health. Mike Brunson said on the *News at Ten* that the *Sun* had a sex scandal, a Tory MP[1] who had an affair with a seventeen-year-old girl. I called Higgins to see who it was. He totally had me for a moment when he said it wasn't a Tory, it was Robin Cook.

Thursday, March 27

Sleaze was big again, with Tim Smith the main story, then more pictures of Piers Merchant snogging in public. Heseltine was not very supportive on the radio, but Merchant was saying he was staying put. His wife was standing by him and they even snogged for the cameras, which was pretty revolting. The *Sun* loved the JP piece. I

---

[1] Piers Merchant, whose liaison with a nightclub hostess (while his wife was canvassing for him) was vehemently denied, but later proved to be true.

was struggling to walk properly because my knee had locked yesterday. TB was meant to be seeing Higgins but Stuart called and said as the Tories are going to try to say the *Sun* was working in cahoots with us over the Merchant story, it would be better to cancel. Anji and I had a discussion with TB about the [Robert] Harris book. Peter was still pushing the usual balls about recording history, and getting the *Sunday Times* on board by getting him on the bus. I strongly disagreed. GB was doing a press conference and we agreed to move from VAT to sleaze. I called in to the morning meeting and said the backdrop should say 'a question of leadership', and we should go through BSE, ERM, VAT, Europe and go for Major's weak leadership. Then word came back that GB didn't want to do 'a big personal attack'.

To a Matthew Harding 'celebration of life' at the QE2. I sat next to his son who cried and cried and cried. The event was brilliantly done, and very moving and I ended up in tears too. There was a very well put together video and the shot of him and his son cheering a goal at Chelsea was incredibly moving. I wrote TB's words and he did them well. Francis Maude was sitting behind me and said he was impressed.

TB had a round of media meetings, and as I was listening in, I had the thought that we should field a single anti-Hamilton, independent, anti-corruption candidate in Tatton. I rang around for a few thoughts and most people were up for it. GB said he had been thinking of the same thing. TB thought it might work. I called MMcD and asked her to check what the local party might think. She came back and said it was doable. It would be a terrific story for the weekend, and keep the Tories where we wanted them. Then a buzz went round the gallery that the Tories had a massive story about us. The phones were going non-stop to see if we knew what it was. It turned out to be a briefing by Michael Dobbs [Conservative official] saying that we were going to pull the plug on the TV debate. As expected, whenever there was bad news for them, they pulled out a TV debate story. In reality, Derry had laid down a deadline and made clear he was intending to end the negotiation if we could not reach agreement straight away. I met with TB, Peter M and GB and we agreed we had to keep open the possibility of some form of debate, maybe even a Frost-style inter- view on the couch kind of thing, with the leaders. I wrote a briefing note on points to make, then a statement and went up to do a briefing on it, while Peter did the Millbank TV rounds. I sensed first, that the story would be lost in sleaze, and second, we had the chance to share the blame for it. We had no real difficulty and I managed to keep a straight face even though as the negotiations and the media ballyhoo had gone on, I had grown more and more opposed to the idea. Derry had brought things to a head very well, Dobbs had made a mistake in going out and saying we were pulling the plug. Because it allowed us to say they were using it for political game-playing, and we were not prepared to waste any more time on it.

Earlier, I discussed Robert Harris with Peter. He said I was being unfair on TB, because this was a moment of history, and it should be recorded. I said history could wait, that it was an extra pressure we would not need and everyone was opposed to it apart from him. That's because you're winding each other up, he said. I said that was not the way I operated. It all got a bit nasty, and I said he was more worried about his own relationship with Harris, it was already taking up too much time and he should stick it up his arse. He stormed out. Yet it was as if it had never happened when we had to meet later to discuss our response to Dobbs on the TV debate. I later wrote a note explaining why I was opposed to the book project; I felt TB shared his view, though, and had fallen for the nonsense about history. I left to see the liveried buses down at the depot where the work had been done. They were good, though not quite as spectacular as I had been hoping for. Maybe there is only so much you can do with the side of a bus. They were fine, though, and at least we would have the pleasure of the hacks wandering around in a moving advert.

I called Derry to congratulate him on the way he had handled the negotiations, and to tell him the plan re Tatton. I was desperate for it to happen, felt it would be a big blow to them.

Friday, March 28

I felt we were ending another week on top. I missed the morning meeting, and earlier I had cross words, because it was mainly about Tatton and the plan, agreed yesterday, to pull out our man and get the Lib Dems to do the same and try to get a single anti-corruption candidate. But I didn't think they were seized of the urgency. I had sensed a bit of a vacuum, and with a fair while to go to the manifesto, we needed something now. The problem was the Lib Dems were unsure. I spoke to Dick Newby, Chris Rennard and Jane Bonham-Carter [the Lib Dems' senior campaigns and communications executives] and tried to get over to them that it was a win-win situation. We would pile the pressure on the Tories, get days of good coverage out of their problems, and if we got the right candidate it would become one of THE stories of the election, run the whole way through and Hamilton would probably lose his seat at the end. Compare and contrast a traditional three-way fight which you might win. I went off to start drafting a joint press release but then spoke to GB and suggested we did it unilaterally, pulled out our man on his own and then see the pressure build on the Lib Dems. He agreed, felt it was a risk worth taking. I spoke to TB, who was fine about it, squared David Evans [Labour regional secretary] and the candidate [John Kelly] to be ready to do media, then went off to do a briefing on it. The moment I said we were withdrawing, the hacks just smiled. They knew it was a stunt but it was compelling copy and they would all go with it. When I said it was the candidate's idea, obviously, they fell about laughing. It went straight to the top of the bulletins. The Tories said it was a gimmick but I could tell on their faces they were worried about it. Margaret had forgotten to tell Tom Sawyer and Co. and Diana Jeuda [NEC] came on and said if the candidate was pulling out, we would have to impose one. Talk about totally missing the point. JP called in a bit of a stew because he had got the wrong end of the stick too and was worried we were pulling out for the Liberal. I said the aim was to have no other candidate but an independent. He said I should have discussed it with him. He said he had talked to GB a minute ago and GB had said 'It's one of Alastair's crazy ideas.' He was fine about it and we ended up having a good chat about anything and everything. I said if we could get the right candidate we can actually force Hamilton out.

Saturday, March 29

The Hamilton scam was a rare total triumph, the splash I think in all the heavies, and a good show in the tabloids, big on the broadcasts today. Peter M was worried it would unravel at the candidate's press conference, but I had a long chat with him and with David Evans before they did it, then set off with the boys for Burnley. I felt bad taking a day off but in truth I was on the phone most of the way up and most of the way back until the phone died on me. John Kelly by all accounts did fine, and while on the one hand he was disappointed not to be fighting the seat, he was never going to win it and this was a way of landing a big blow on them. I felt sure the Lib Dems would have to follow. TB spoke to Paddy, who said they were doing a survey of local opinion before deciding what to do. The problem was many of their people loathed us and loathed the idea of co-operation with us. Worked on a briefing note on areas where we were taking back or taking for the first time labels taken for granted by the Tories – One Nation, prosperity, family. Andy Grice was telling me that they wanted him to do a story about left-wing MPs threatening to cause trouble, so it was important we gave him something better. I didn't like being blackmailed and I said so, I didn't believe these MPs existed, it would be a quote from Brian Sedgemore [Labour MP] then a few anonymous ones. I spoke to TB who was staying at Waheed Alli's place in Kent for the weekend, and he advised against doing anything dramatic. Then we started to get calls that Michael Hurst[1] was about to resign because of a gay affair. That would be another huge blow to them. There was a real sense of decay about the Tories.

Sunday, March 30

The papers were pretty dull. I couldn't wade my way through them, so I doubt many others would be able to. There was just too much blah. The news was reporting mounting pressure on Hamilton to stand down, which was certainly there. Anji called to say Murdoch was in town and wanted to have dinner with TB tomorrow. JP was refusing to do the press conference with Alan Howarth on Tuesday.

Monday, March 31

I slept in because I forget to set the alarm. We got a bit out of the briefing about going positive but less than I thought we would. I got a cab in to meet Pat at the Members' entrance where the new Jag we'd got for the campaign was waiting. Sleaze was still running pretty big against the Tories, and lots of pressure on Hamilton to stand aside but it was clear he wasn't going to, and that was that. So it wasn't hard to get up the issue of leadership again. Pat and I had drafted some strong words for TB to do at the poster launch, and I also worked up some really strong lines for JP on Major being all drift and dither. Today was a day to draw contrasts, between them being negative and us positive; Major being a crap leader, TB being strong. It was a beautiful sunny day, and Pat and I just had a nice, relaxed chat on the drive down. I think we both felt it was happening, but equally that there were lots of problems ahead. Pat was a terrific sidekick to have on the road, because he and I shared the same politics, he was good with TB and he was always calm. What's more, he was the one, with [David] Bradshaw, who could take one of my brainstorm top-of-the-head briefings and turn it into a speech or article. We got to Waheed's, a pretty stunning house set in its own grounds, where needless to say we found TB sunning himself. He was worried we had taken a hit on the TV debate and that people felt we had scuppered it. But Derry had done a good piece in the *Indy* on it, and I felt it was buried as a non-issue with the public; it was a media

[1] Sir Michael Hurst, Scottish Conservative Party chairman. Resigned after admitting to a homosexual affair, alleged by the Scottish *Mail on Sunday*.

thing. He was also worried about Tatton, and felt it could unravel unless we found a good candidate.

We then left for the country house where we were due to launch the posters. We could not have had a nicer setting or better weather. I had been driving everyone at Millbank and the agency bonkers by going on about wanting to launch them in 'a field of dreams', lots of bright colours spread out in a field, but it was definitely worth it. It was a great sight, and the hacks were impressed. Jeremy Vine said he thought it was brilliant. TB and JP went through the running order, with JP cracking jokes the whole time about which party were we saying was lurching to the right, and then out to do the business. TB's words worked well. I tried to imagine watching this at home. You'd have Major dealing with Hamilton – or not – and TB up saying people wanted a positive vision for the future, surrounded by these big bright posters doing just that. I loved it. I did a briefing on the importance of positive campaigning and they just about bought it. JP said as he got back on to his bus that re Tatton 'You can't just pull out and leave it to the Libs.' We HAD to get the Liberal out. I wrote up a briefing note on the nature of the tour, emphasised that we would have a raised platform that came out of the bus and TB would be doing lots of impromptu speeches. For want of a better phrase I called it 'the people's platform'. What a lot of bollocks. JM sent a letter out to all local parties later which kept sleaze going. Another mistake. TB had a long session with GB and I went in later and GB said he thought we should leak pretty much the whole of the business chapter of the manifesto and get it up overnight, as it would get lost on the day. I agreed, and in any event he had probably already done it. Peter and I were up for doing a thing on who was the One Nation party, as we had Alan Howarth up tomorrow. We had to keep pushing on with positive messages, and make the most of the impact of the poster launch, especially as these colours were going to form part of the backdrop for the rest of the campaign.

TB was doing an interview with Kirsty Young for Channel 5. He didn't like it; didn't like the format, the snap, snap questions, and he got stuff on Merchant and he ended up generally pissed off. He went off to see Murdoch for dinner. Peter M called me late and said it was really difficult at Millbank. GB was totally mistrustful of anyone except his own staff, and he didn't confide anything that he had planned, whilst hoovering up the plans of others.

Tuesday, April 1

With Alan Howarth due to do the press conference, Pat and I had done One Nation words for it. We got good pictures in the papers from the poster launch but they were still largely dominated by sleaze. Thatcher's attack on TB was the lead in the *Telegraph*, which had pretty much reverted to being a Tory rag. At the morning meeting, there were varying views on how to deal with the sleaze stuff. Philip said he felt we were better talking about corruption, because most people basically thought it meant we were talking about sex when people said sleaze. GB was worried that the media felt we were off sleaze, because we were emphasising the positive, whereas in fact on one level it suited us to be on it. It was a bit of a false choice. With so many stories coming out of their woodwork, it was inevitably part of the backdrop and that was fine, but PG and I felt strongly we had to keep the positive agenda going alongside that, and keep saying that's what we were doing. That's why the poster launch was important. TB was in good form at the press conference. GB was OK but very lugubrious and he had this habit of looking down at his notes whenever TB spoke, which acted as a bit of a distraction. At times the body language between them was not good. We got tipped off Major was about to challenge TB over a TV debate again, and I organised a clip on that. We were all of the view there was now no point going there. They were using it as a distraction whenever they got into trouble, and we should stop letting them.

To College Green to launch the buses. They looked OK, and I liked the run of messages down the side, but they were better outside than in. Anji had done her best with the bus people but I suppose there is a limit to what you can do. Because the windows were tinted and covered in slogans, and the seats were a kind of dogshit brown, the atmosphere inside was really dingy. The toilet was incapable of being used by anyone above five feet six, and the little kitchen space was poky and every time we turned a corner, cups and stuff went flying. The thought of spending weeks on here was not a happy one, and TB felt exactly the same. 'I know we have to do a bus tour, but do we have to be on the bus to do it?' The TV didn't work but that was probably a good thing. I was more convinced than ever that the last thing we needed on top of all this was Robert Harris sitting up front taking a note of every spit and fart. As we headed off through North London, we both settled into a bit of a despondence. The only way we were going to be able to survive the bus was through black humour. This is our prison, I said. We will be allowed out for exercise periods from time to time. We will get visitors, mainly reporters from local papers, and we will tell them we are happy, and then the powers that be may feel they should consider us for parole. TB said we should form an escape committee. Shadow Cabinet members who screw up should be forced to come in here as punishment.

He did a couple of TV interviews and the interviewers were rocking about all over the place. Jeremy Vine did an irritating walkabout with the camera, saying this is where Cherie sits and this is where Alastair sits and here's the state-of-the-art this and the state-of-the-art that. State-of-the-art my arse. Nothing worked. The Special Branch team seemed a good bunch, and made life a lot easier, both logistically and in dealing with crowds. We got to Northampton, and we used the soapbox/platform for the first time. It wasn't his natural milieu but he did fine, and the mood was good. He did a terrific walkabout and the TV people seemed happy enough. I then went on to the press bus to brief them on TB's speech on the referendum. I briefed the *Sun* and the *Mail* very hard on the referendum, knowing that we had to neutralise this issue before the Tories tried to get it off the ground, and I gave the *Mirror* briefing on the education stuff in the manifesto. By 4.30 we had a statement on the Lib Dems pulling out of Tatton, which was great, and meant another day of that, plus a good running story for the campaign. We now had to find the right candidate. After the meeting, TB and I got driven back by car, thank God. News came through of the *Guardian* poll in which we were down two and they were up two and I briefed it was helpful for the gap to narrow and for people to know we had a fight on our hands. On the drive back, TB said he was worried we were not prepared well enough if we really came under attack. I called Anji and asked if it was too late to get a different bus.

Wednesday, April 2

Tory manifesto launch. Out before 6 and made the 7am Millbank meeting. TB had said he wanted to get to as many as possible before we went out on the road. I had a chat with Derry, who said things were very fragile whenever we came under pressure, and alliances within the building were not strong. The Tories' main initiative was a new tax allowance to let people stay at home. Again, they were trying to look like the party of ideas. We had a run around the block and then agreed that we had to go on trust. Major cannot be trusted because of his record. We had to get up the promises made in '92 that were broken. We had to make trust a central dividing line. By now the days were rolling into one. A few weeks ago the building had been a shell. Now it was packed with people who had fairly quickly got into a rhythm of activity. I briefed the *Standard* that Tory tax plans were dishonest and dangerous. We watched Major's press conference live and it was a bit flat and lacking in energy, and he seemed to be rowing back from the notion that the tax move would help everyone.

We had a good meeting with TB and Gordon in which they agreed we had to be much sharper on our message work, and much more premeditated. GB wanted to hammer the idea that we would take a responsible approach to the economy, and they had not. I said we should release the 'contract' section of the manifesto in advance, as it contained the meat of the main arguments in the manifesto. We needed a device so I got TB to write it out in his own handwriting. We would give that out and get fresh coverage for it. I then tipped off Martin Argles [*Guardian* photographer] and some agency snappers to go round the back and get pictures of TB sitting outside writing it. The lunchtime news was pretty good for the Tories and so were the later bulletins, but the trust line was working through. We were in fairly good shape and we were making a virtue of the fact that there was no big flashy effort, just careful co-ordinated work towards a manifesto that brought together the detailed policy work of the last few years. Some of them were starting to trail the idea there would be nothing new in the manifesto. I briefed that far more important than flashy big ideas, so-called, was to set out clear and limited pledges that people could identify with as making a difference to their lives. I felt comfortable with the idea that we present ourselves as safe, solid and dependable, and them as a risk because they were getting desperate. But TB, who was going off to Michael Levy's to play tennis, was suddenly worried that there was not enough new in it all and was there a case for putting in more pledges? I said no, we had a plan and we had to stick to it.

The Tories had hired a man in a chicken suit to follow TB around, which wasn't a bad idea, and I wrote to [Charles] Lewington, and released it to the press, saying the real chicken was Major in failing to deal with Hamilton. If the Tories stuck with the chicken, it could be embarrassing so we had to use humour to deal with it. It also helped us make clear they were not serious about negotiating over a TV debate, so the debate idea was well and truly dead. Piers Morgan called to say he was hiring a fox to kill the chicken. Philip called from the groups to say there was a real sense that TB had the energy and the drive to get Britain going. That was the same message coming through on the phone banks in the Pennine belt. I said to TB later 'So much of this hangs on you.' He sighed. 'I know, and the only people who don't know it are in the Labour Party.' Then he checked himself. He said JP knew it, and, when he thought about it, so did GB. I got the paper sent round for once. The Tories had not got a huge lift and our briefing operation had made several of the front pages. The chicken was getting huge coverage.

Thursday, April 3

Today was manifesto day. I woke at about 3 and never got back to sleep. I was reasonably confident we would have a good day, and felt more and more comfortable on the agenda, but I was nonetheless really anxious. I got into that terrible state when you start to panic because you think you need sleep, because the day ahead will be tough, but the more you think you need it, the harder it seems to get it, and your mind races and races and races. I finally got up at 5 and worked on TB's words for the press conference. The Tories didn't do very well out of their manifesto, all a bit flat, but the *Mail* was vicious, a piece on five union leaders headed the 'conspiracy of silence', saying the union barons were keeping quiet in exchange for deals in government. It was clear they were going to go for us big time. On the way in, TB agreed we had to make a real virtue of there not being much new in the manifesto, that we were going to do the basics, deliver on our promises. We left for the ICE [Institution of Civil Engineers] with Sylvie driving, and Bob Pugh [Special Branch] in the front, who had a wonderful deadpan manner. He said the advance people were saying the chicken was waiting at the main entrance, what did I want to do? I said use the side entrance. There was a massive turnout, maybe 300 journalists, huge numbers of foreign crews, and a real sense of occasion. I remembered the '92 manifesto launch and Mike White saying to me that it just didn't quite feel right. This time, it felt right. Yesterday had been flat, and there was no real buzz. Today there was a buzz. TB was nervous beforehand, went for a pee a couple of times in half an hour, and both times asked me to go with him and just go over some of the lines and some of the tough questions again and again. Then we sat down with Peter M and GB and did the same questions again. We told him not to smile too much, to look serious, like the Snowdon picture. He felt the tricky questions were unions, tax and Scotland, but he was fine in the answers. We had a quick photocall with the Shadow Cabinet and then in he went.

He looked strong, sounded confident, no trouble with the questions, was very confident, totally in control, and you could sense the room was impressed. We then did the usual round of interviews, and they all said they felt a real sense of occasion, which is exactly what we wanted. We got out through a fair crowd outside and on to the bus and set off for Whiteleys shopping centre. I was doing a piece for the *Sun* on unions and the *Mirror* were sending a fox to descend on the Tory chicken. Whiteleys was good, lots of people there and TB was signing manifestos. He was on form, saying that New Labour only

April '97: TB nervous but commanding on manifesto day 693

promised what we can deliver, accepting the Tories got some things right, and starting to get up the pledges.

Then to Battersea to get a helicopter to Stansted. We flew over the Matthew Harding stand at Chelsea. TB scribbled a note to me – how did I think it went? He knew the answer. Really well. Hard to know how it could have gone better. The plane was fine, much nicer than the bus, and would also be a place of work. Once we took off, he did a few interviews while I went up and briefed the press at the back. I was getting on really well with CB at the moment. We were able to have a laugh, take the mick out of each other, and she was constantly asking how I was, and saying how important it was I got rest and was able to look after him. The flight was fine, though I sensed the journalists travelling with us would get fed up pretty quickly if they didn't get much in the papers, and would end up just writing process crap. I didn't take to many of them, but Ben Macintyre was there for *The Times*. The *Guardian* and *Indy* had wankers on board.

We got to Edinburgh and George R and Jack McConnell were running round like headless chickens, because of the Tory chicken. George said we had to get up a different story, otherwise the chicken would be the story. I said we had launched the manifesto and I suspected that would carry rather bigger. They tried to persuade me to get something up on tourism! As we waited in the VIP lounge, I suggested inviting the chicken to dinner, and got an invite sent to it. Then its minders suddenly said no, he was going back to London, so I put out a line that the chicken was being held against its will, and it was actually a Labour chicken that wanted to switch to us but they wouldn't let us. I'd decided the only way to deal with it was humour, and smothering it with love. If we took the damn thing seriously, as GR seemed to, they would achieve what they were trying to do, unsettle us. TB got a great reception and as the chicken moved in on him, a few of our people turned on it, and were drowning it out with 'Tony, Tony'.

I went for a quick swim at the hotel then Hilary, Lesley [Smith] and Dee [Sullivan] [campaign press officers] came to see me to lobby me to spend more time with the travelling press. I said I know it was difficult for them because they were whingeing at them all the time about lack of access, not knowing what was going on, etc., but they just had to deal with that. We had to get into the mindset that the press were there for us, not the other way round. The main people were the ones left in London and I was talking to them all the time. I would try to brief the travelling team so that they could at least keep their hacks informed, but they were not a priority. The coverage of the manifesto launch was near perfect, and the commentators I'd talked to were pretty impressed too. The Tories went for us over unions and 'black hole', but we were getting points for candour, honesty and minimalism. It was probably the biggest day of the campaign so far, and we had won it. Re Tatton, tried to get Jill Morrell[1] to do it, but she said no.

Friday, April 4

Scotland, as ever, was a disaster waiting to happen. I had only been half listening when TB did his interview with the *Scotsman*, who went on the line that sovereignty would be staying at Westminster and claimed that TB compared the Parliament to a parish council. It was totally dishonest – he had been making a pro-Parliament point, saying that if a parish council could levy taxes, why was it such a big deal if the Scottish Parliament could? But they twisted it against us, because they were determined to portray him as anti devolution, and it was an immediate fucking nightmare. We should never have done the *Scotsman*. I should have followed my instinct on that and not listened to George [Robertson] and Jack [McConnell]. I should have remembered Alex [Ferguson]'s maxim about not taking risks. It was so ridiculous, it was funny, but the trouble was the rest of the Scottish media were now fixated upon it, and the travelling press quickly got caught up in it. TB and I were joking about it with GR and Jack and Pat, putting on fake posh Scottish accents and impersonating the wankers in the Scottish press. But it was a real problem, and we were on the defensive. TB got irritable pretty quickly, and so did I. All day, the questions just wouldn't go away, even though the answers were bloody obvious. It meant that within twenty-four hours of the manifesto launch, we were firefighting on an area TB never really liked talking about, and which wasn't that relevant to most voters in the election. Through the day, the toughest question became – could a Westminster Parliament veto the Scottish Parliament's tax rises? And there was a general feeling that TB didn't answer. He had to all intents and purposes ruled out use of the power to raise tax in a first term, but there was a tension in that. We were saying we believed in devolution, yet effectively deciding what a devolved Parliament would do. We had to emphasise he was still leader of the Labour Party, but it was not easy and George was getting in a real flap. We had had a great day out of the manifesto launch and now we were in danger of losing the advances we'd made.

[1] Former fiancée of John McCarthy, a journalist kidnapped and held hostage in Beirut from 1986 to 1991.

The press conference could have been worse, but it was not easy. TB looked a bit rattled and it was obvious he was batting off the difficult questions. I could sense them moving into near-frenzy mode. TB called me through afterwards and said 'We have a real problem here.' He was having difficulty answering the question because he didn't want to say taxes could go up. He wanted me to go out and brief that we had effectively ruled out tax-rises. George was in a total flap now, because he feared this was all going wrong. I suggested he write to the other party leaders and challenge them to say they would not use the tax-raising powers in the first term. I managed to spin Brunson into saying it was a deliberate attempt to get through a tough tax message but he was less sure later.

Meanwhile, Tom Bradby was doing a JM blowjob from the Albert Hall, where the Tories got a free hit against us. [Mark] Webster told me that Bradby had had to redo his profile because it was so pro-Major. Even excepting the way the *Scotsman* twisted what he said, I felt we had not planned today properly. The worst thing was we didn't have a story so the story became devolution by default. I spoke to as many broadcasters as I could but it was running away from us. The message that Westminster was ultimately supreme and tax didn't go up was not going through. Instead, it just came across as TB being very dismissive of Scotland. As he left, he kept saying we've got a problem.

We flew from Glasgow, where he wasted God knows how long listening to Harriet complaining about Jack Dromey not being selected.[1] He had a chat with GB, and then Peter M, on tax. We flew to Manchester and as we arrived, I listened to the news on the phone and the BBC was pretty grim. Then Peter M faxed through a note that the *Sunday Times* were planning to run a story based on off-the-record stuff from trade union leaders that TB had promised certain things on the union front. TB agreed we should pre-empt it by putting out something in the *FT* that he had specifically ruled these out. He spoke to JP and John Monks and said he was not going to have the agenda dictated in this way. Jane Smith [daughter of the late John Smith] was at the event in Kidsgrove working for the party, so the press wanted pictures of her with him. She told me her mum was going away for some of the election. We got driven down to where

[1] Dromey (Harriet's husband) had been shortlisted for Pontefract and Castleford. The selection meeting chose Yvette Cooper, policy adviser to Labour's Treasury team, 1993–94, columnist on economic affairs and leader writer, *Independent*, 1995–97. Married Ed Balls, 1998.

April '97: Devolution problem lifts Tories

the helicopter was waiting and a group of kids were there. We had a kickabout, and it was brilliant to be able to do something without the press around us, and just have a laugh for a few minutes before we set off for Sedgefield. I had by now taken the conscious decision not to worry about the schedule, where we were, or where we were going. Anji and Kate seemed on top of all that. I needed to focus on what we did, not where we were. But it meant that I was forgetting what day it was, what time it was, where we were. The key was to sleep when possible, eat when possible, but basically work all the time.

TB, his dad and I went to the club in Trimdon for a drink. Leo and I had a lovely chat about things. He is such a nice man, and was effusive, thanking me for helping him and all that. He talked about Hazel and how proud she would have been, how she would never have imagined this was going to happen. 'Her son – prime minister. It's just incredible, isn't it?' He had a little tear in his eye and he said the reason he didn't believe in God in the same way that Tony did was because Hazel was not here to see him win. Tom Stoddart had some fantastic news on the Tatton front. He had bumped into Martin Bell [BBC journalist, particularly known as a war correspondent], who said he would like to be the anti-corruption candidate. It was perfect. I shook Tom by the hand so hard I almost took his hand off. I spoke to Bell, who said he would love to do it if we would have him. He said he had had his fill of the BBC. He was down to do Edinburgh Pentlands on election night, so they clearly didn't think much of him. It was time for him to do something and this would be perfect. I said I thought he would win. He was perfect for it. I got Jonathan to speak to Paddy's people and they were fine, so it was all systems go. It was a real stroke of luck. It would break right through.

Newsnight was awful on Scotland. Philip called and said we had taken a hit today, and we had to get it back by the Sundays. The broadcasters were running the line that we were faltering after a near-perfect start.

Saturday, April 5

I got up very early, went down to make a cup of tea and then Leo came down too. We talked for a while, before I started working on TB's words for his adoption meeting. As well as the obvious, we were hoping to use it to get up health, and some new figures we had on NHS red tape, but when Pat came over from his hotel, the stuff he had didn't really do the trick. The press was pretty grim. There is no doubt we had taken a hit and I felt responsible for having agreed to the *Scotsman* interview which kicked off the whole thing. Even the sensible ones, who could see at first glance what he had meant, felt they had to go with it. TB wasn't too fazed about it, said he certainly didn't blame me, and if it hadn't have been this, it would have been something else. The Tories were now broadening it out to the wider issue of trust, saying TB could not be trusted. The ease with which the Tories could get up lines was shown again when we got to the adoption meeting and TB was being doorstepped by them all asking about trust. We ignored it and went into the little side room, where I suggested he take it head on at the top, and we drafted a line, yes it is about who you trust – the man who said he would modernise the Labour Party and did, or the man who promised tax cuts and put up taxes, promised to sort BSE, NHS spending, etc. It worked well and got straight on to the bulletins.

The speech went fine, and the Sedgefield crowd were always terrific with him. Good pictures with TB and Leo at the bar. As TB toured the hospital, I was trying to sort out Tatton. It had got a bit messy, because some of the party and unions had got a bit grumpy about it, and David Evans said he was not sure it was deliverable. He said we should get Ian McCartney involved but he was pissed off because he had not been in the original loop. I got TB to talk to Ian later and smooth it over. Back on the bus, I was talking to the Sundays for their endless so-called think pieces, and it took far too much time and effort. Tim called to say the *Sunday Telegraph* were doing a bad story on tax and did we have anything to push them off it? On the flight down from Teesside to Stansted, TB was back on whether I should stay at MBT but every time I agreed, he would go back to saying it was better I was with him on the road, as long as we both went in there regularly. We got back to Battersea and in the car home, TB wanted to go over lessons learned – don't do too much, one or two big things per day; don't do interviews without a clear idea what we want from them; be careful of being driven into making statements that can look like policy on the hoof. He also felt we needed to beef up the briefing operation on strategy. At the moment it was all down to me and occasionally him. That was definitely an argument for being at base more. We got back to record the PEB on pledges, which took an age. Went to Richmond Crescent and Jonathan filled us in on a few things going on. Richard Holme was making a complete hash of the Tatton scene. I spoke to Bell a few times and we agreed he would go up tomorrow to see the local parties and then we would put out a statement. I couldn't believe the local parties couldn't just do this.

Major was on *Frost*. They'd trailed he would go for TB for 'slithering', and would do a big personal attack, but he didn't. He was quite effective on trust, and he did a very effective sound bite on our manifesto unravelling. It was fine on one level, but not enough. TB said if all he could do was attack me, it wouldn't help him. There had to be some sense of the future under him, not him going on about the future under us. That was borne out by private and public polls. They didn't really like to see either of them being just nega- tive. We agreed the best line of attack for us was still trust, but we didn't really have an attacking story today. Howard went for us again over the PTA. We were able to say he was desperate but they were still calling the shots more than we should be letting them. John Monks called in a fury about the *Sunday Times* and I put him on to Sally.

I went into Millbank for the 11.30 meeting, and the privatisation issue was causing us problems. The position wasn't really clear. We were against all these privatisations and yet did not want to get into a ruling out game. Neil Wallis called asking for an article on privatis- ation, and I drafted it, with the top line – what matters is what works – but it showed it was driving up as an issue and I didn't feel we were clear on it. By then RC had done an interview saying it was unlikely we would join the single currency in the next Parliament. It went beyond the agreed line but there was not much we could do about it. RC called, a bit flustered, but said Peter M had said to him – make sure you are not outflanked by Rifkind. He was stuck in Aintree, stranded in his car, and did the interview down the line. He said maybe it would have been better if he hadn't done it at all, but I didn't think it was so bad. At the briefing, I was struck by a change of mood among the hacks. Once I had done my prepared opening remarks, they came at me far more aggressively eg over U-turn-ery, privatisation, devolution. George Jones gave me a very hard time on the unions. I didn't feel they were taking the lines on tax or the unions from the speech briefing. They felt we were more vulnerable. Europe was also tricky. I didn't want a 'Cook out on a limb' story, so I suddenly said that as things stood, a single currency was less likely to happen with us than them. I tried to explain it by saying it was obvious there was a struggle going on re the policy, and Ken Clarke was clearly in charge, and he was ideological about this, whereas we were practical. But I felt I had fucked up. I felt ill, really worried, went back and told Peter I feared I had landed us with a disaster. But Tim did a couple of calls and it seemed the press were seeing it not as a huge thing, but an astute political move to outflank JM and Rifkind, all co-ordinated with RC, etc. so maybe they were still giving us the benefit of the doubt.

I'd promised to take the kids out so I met up with them at the Science Museum, but the phone never stopped, mainly about Tatton. Dick Newby said there had been a very bloody meeting of the Libs' local executive, and the vote was won by 6-5. He said Bell was terrific, really hit the right notes. Then David Evans called at 6 and said our people had backed it too. He said Bell had been terrific and won them over after a pretty bloody meeting. Ian McCartney had been very helpful. Anyway, it was a done deal. Newby didn't want to put the name out yet, and felt there were still a few people to be squared. I felt there was little chance of it holding because the circle of knowledge had widened. But I said we should try. I tipped off a few people without the name, said we had an agreed candidate. When I finally gave out the name at 7pm, from an ice-cream van outside the museum, they loved it. PA snap, change of bulletins, Major interview blown out of the water. I briefed on some of the background and again it helped that we had managed to keep it quiet and we were able to shape the story on our terms. Bell called and said he was not intending to go home and was intending to stay at La Gaffe in Hampstead. We arranged to meet there at 9.30. There was an ITN camera outside but I found a way in where I wouldn't be seen. He was having dinner and was clearly very excited. He said today had been like a Le Carré novel. He said before he had spoken to the Libs' meeting, he could hear them arguing through the wall and 'it was worse than Bosnia'. He clearly felt our people were the nicer lot, but he said both meetings were hard, and he was glad he was able to swing them. We agreed he should not do the *Today* programme because he needed to plan all this out properly now. I asked if he had any skeletons they were likely to find. He said he thought not. He was a friend of Bob Stewart, head of the Cheshire Regiment, and the Duke of Westminster. He was a bit batty, and very wandering from time to time, but it was hard to imagine a better person for the job. I said he could easily win. He said he thought he might be a 48-hour candidate, that Hamilton would go. He said it was weird to be the story like this, but I could tell he liked it and would do it fine. 'I'm not really a political animal,' he said, 'a floating voter.' Perfect.

Monday, April 7

The papers and the broadcasters were mainly leading on Bell. He came round to the house at 7.15, then Newby and Jane Bonham-Carter

April '97: AC meets Martin Bell to discuss Tatton campaign

arrived five minutes later. We went over some of the process points – that it was a joint initiative, that he had been put in touch by a mutual friend. We emphasised he had to show some real passion for doing it, and anger that drove him to it. Otherwise it would look like an ego trip. He was convinced that Hamilton would walk, and he would be the shortest-lived candidate ever. The rest of us were not sure, because Hamilton was neuralgic. Today was economic speech day, one of the main speeches of the campaign. We had a strong speech, but because GB had indicated we were looking at privatisation as a way of filling the 'black hole' and because of Tim's briefing to the *Sunday Telegraph*, the only story in town was an apparent 'conversion' to privatisation. It was a problem. I'd tried to use the article in the *Sun* yesterday to set it in context but the mood music had become 'U-turn' and the press scented blood. I went round to TB's, and we made a fair bit of change to the speech, especially on the single currency. He was angry, as was I, that the story of the speech was being lost in this nonsense about privatisation. I wondered whether because I had been so involved with Bell that I took my eye off the ball on this one.

The venue was good, very modern and airy, and the speech was strong, with serious people in the audience. I bumped into Peter Jay, who felt we could not lose. We went back to TB's and as the sun was out, he wanted to work in the garden as we went over the difficult questions for *Panorama*. I said to the 3.30 meeting that we needed to fight back harder on this trust/betrayal and talk of their five years of betrayal, not our so-called two days. There was agreement on this, but I realised GB was still far happier away from anything negative. I spent a fair bit of the day talking to Martin Bell and getting him settled before his press conference. I could not quite tell whether the insecurity was a bit of an act. He did fine by all accounts though the Tory papers were going to go for him big time. We agreed to use *Panorama* to do a simple explanation on New Labour, that it was real, deep, and deal with this U-turn thing as it arose. [David] Dimbleby came at him from the line that he had basically changed all of his beliefs to try to get power. He was sneering and rude but TB stayed calm and dealt with it OK. But the idea that these interviews are the key to healthy democratic debate is ridiculous. They've become a game. There was no real story out of it and I'm not sure it was worth all the preparation, but it was another one ticked off, and basically fine. It would have settled our people down quite well. Seemingly the party got a good response in terms of phone calls, etc.

A particularly good *Panorama* write-up in *The Times*. Bell's press conference was making big news. The Tories were beginning to give up on their 'U-turn' strategy which was good news, because PG said it was beginning to break through last night. I phoned in to the 7am meeting which was concentrating on the GB/DB/HH press conference responding to the Churches' report on unemployment and poverty. GB clearly didn't want TB at the event, but couldn't quite bring himself to say so. I said I'm sure TB can live with an hour extra at home before we set off for Basildon. I said we needed to keep going on the theme of betrayal. We always tended to give up just as lines were breaking through, and we must not stop now. The phone technology seemed to work fine, though PG later told me whenever I spoke, it came over very loud and the others just stopped.

TB was fretting a bit about *Panorama*, felt it had been ragged. Most people I spoke to thought he did well, but PG said later one or two in the groups thought he got a bit flustered. One man said 'If that's what he's like with an interviewer, what would he be like with [Helmut] Kohl?' We stopped at a little cafe on the way and TB and JP got a perfectly good reception. You could often tell more by the mood at these impromptu stops with no press than you could on the planned visits. I said to Pat [McFadden] in the car afterwards that seventy per cent of those people would vote for us, or not at all. There was definitely a growing warmth to TB, though. Then we had a silly little incident when some wanker in a Range Rover tried to cut between TB's car and the Special Branch car behind, and wouldn't take no for an answer. Only when they put on the sirens did he bugger off. There was still a lot of planning to do on Tatton, and we had the Pennington Report on E. coli coming out.[1] I had them all laughing – including GB, according to Philip – when I said we were running Tatton like a military operation, and today the candidate would be accompanied by Colonel Bob Stewart [British UN commander in Bosnia]. There seemed to be more press than ever around TB, certainly more foreign crews and an old lady was knocked over in the scrum as he came out of the meeting. I thought we might have got a bit of grief on the walkabout but it was good, very warm, very few people not interested, none abusive. The mood and the body language between TB and JP was good,

---

[1] Report of Professor Hugh Pennington's inquiry into the 1996 outbreak of infection with E. coli O157 in Central Scotland.

and with Basildon[1] the symbol it had become, good pictures out of here would be good for party morale elsewhere. Bell called me a couple of times, and sounded more nervy than yesterday. I said he was doing really well.

TB and I drove back and listened to a dreadful *World at One* special. GB had read out a list of people and companies endorsing our welfare-to-work programme and Nick Scheele [chairman and chief executive of Jaguar] was one of them, but they got hold of him to say he knew nothing about it. It was a classic unforced error, something clearly not pinned down and double-checked. It got TB back on to his 'you should be at MBT full-time' kick. He was talking to George R and trying to get Douglas Alexander into Kilmarnock, which GB desperately wanted. TB said he was worried at our lack of capacity at getting up big attacking stories. He was also worried that the Tories were making more inroads on trust than we realised. Peter M said our problem was lack of co-ordination. TB on the road, GB in Millbank, and Millbank as a whole were not enmeshed. They were separate entities which occasionally came together.

I got called out to see an encounter on Knutsford Heath between Bell and Hamilton, surrounded by a media circus, in which Bell said he was prepared to give him the benefit of the doubt. It was a big mistake. He must have known that because he called me. I said it was a problem because it had been a struggle to get the two local parties to stand aside and they had done so in the end because they thought he was going to take Hamilton apart. He said he was not prepared to get into slanging matches and he wasn't a Rottweiler. Tim suggested we get Bell to write to Hamilton, at least getting the admitted wrongdoing down in print. We drafted the letter. He took out one line but was otherwise fine. He just had to be coached in some pretty basic politics. He said he felt vulnerable and didn't know where to start. He was staying at the Longview Hotel. He said he needed help from the other parties. I said we could organise Labour and Lib Dem help, but he should also appeal directly for disgruntled Tories to help him.

Meanwhile, Anna Healy took me to one side and said she needed to speak to me about Mo. She explained that Mo had a brain tumour, which had required radiotherapy, and steroids which were making

---

[1] The marginal seat of Basildon had become a key indicator of which party was set to win a general election. Conservative MP David Amess had been expected to lose the seat in 1992, but like John Major's government, he held on. By May 1997, Amess had removed to Southend West.

her put on weight. She had managed to keep it quiet for around three months but she thought people were beginning to notice and wonder. Mo wanted to talk to me about it. I spoke to her for ages, and she was really worried about the whole thing, not just for obvious reasons. She said she was worried if it got out, the Ulster Unionists would somehow use it against her. I said I was sure she was best to get the whole story out there, on her own terms, rather than wait for it to dribble out and she be forced to react. It reflected nothing but good on her and even the UUs would be forced to express some sympathy. Also, if we briefed it, we could accompany it with a statement of absolute support and approval from TB. She said she was fine but it had been a bit of an ordeal. Snowdon called me, angry that one of the papers had said the manifesto picture was Tom Stoddart's.

Wednesday, April 9

The papers were totally dominated by Tatton, apart from the *Mail* which led on 'Labour's broken promises', because of a Keith Bradley [Labour MP and transport spokesman] letter eight weeks ago ruling out air traffic privatisation. We'd landed ourselves in a real mess on this for two reasons – falling into the 'black hole' trap, and Tim's briefing to the *Sunday Telegraph* which made it seem we were shifting on privatisation generally. The *Mail* was now just a propaganda rag. We were getting hit in the party, which didn't like the focus on privatisation, and with the public, which was getting a sense of U-turn and mess. I called in to the 7am meeting and we agreed we have to stick to a very negative message on tax. I'd written a line that JM would not have the gall to stand again having broken so many promises on tax. We got up the Bell letter quite well and when he called, I said he must stay on the central allegations, again and again and again. He could not afford to be nice for the whole campaign. We agreed TB should do a clip on Hamilton, saying he was not fit to be a candidate. The polls were narrowing, inevitably, but it was alarming TB a bit.

Before we left for Paddington, TB and I met JoP and Peter M to review where we were. Jonathan was spending a lot of his time now on post-election stuff, and we discussed the problem of how to get some kind of balance in the Lords without looking like it was just being stuffed full of political allies. We had an enormous breakfast on the train, then TB did a stack of West Country interviews while Pat and I drafted his words, really strong on JM tolerating Hamilton, and on betrayal on tax. The Tories' latest line was that TB was cracking up, and Jeremy Vine wanted a response. Re the speech in Bristol, it was time to show that he was capable of taking the gloves off and landing a blow. He needed to show a bit of fight and passion, and now was the time to do it, with both Major and Hezza going hard against him today. It was nice and sunny in Bristol, and we had the new bus to meet us, then out to do a boat trip. I met Syd Young briefly who felt we were home and dry. On the boat, TB ended up doing a kind of rolling doorstep with crews coming in and out, but it was fine, and I think gave them a sense of us being a bit more relaxed. On the bus to Exeter, he was in a real fury at the privatisation business, felt it had been badly handled by GB and by us. We were still arguing about where I should be. He felt I was best used at MBT, but equally so much of the action was around him, and I felt provided I could phone in to all the key meetings and had time to brief all the key political editors at some point in the day, I was more use with him. So much of this was about him, his words, how he looked and felt, and I think I can get the best out of that. We had very strong words about the Tories in the speech and for once he was up for really going for them.

Exeter was brilliant. Nice weather, nice setting, good crowds, lots of kids and a bit of heckling but he was getting better at the off-the-cuff stuff. He did strong words on JM, Hamilton, tax/trust. Ben Bradshaw [Labour candidate] said he was really confident, it felt really good down there. I had listened to the *World at One*, which was yet another rant about air traffic privatisation, and on the way to Plymouth I caught the *PM* programme, which was wall-to-wall Tory propaganda. I called Tony Hall and said his radio programmes were becoming oral versions of the *Daily Mail*. They simply did not focus on the Tories in the same way they did us. PG felt GB was a problem. Most of the mistakes were coming from him or his team and when we got into difficulties, he lacked strength. He tended just to sink down and expect others to lift us out.

I hadn't realised how bad it was at Millbank until tonight. I phoned round several people and everyone said it was awful. There was not enough communicating or making decisions unless we were there, and the minute we went, it slid back. Fiona's view was that I was a victim of my own success, that they were so used to clearing things with me; if I wasn't there, they just talked and drifted. The problem with GB was different though. He was always looking to play a slightly different game. I was beginning to think I should be at Millbank full-time. The speech went fine. TB was introduced by Patrick Stewart [actor] – who said 'make it so' and got a huge roar – and TB let rip off the script and it went down well. I briefed TB on the full horror of MBT on the flight back, and the latest nonsense, and we had another round of whether I should be with him or there full-time. CB said she really thought I should be wherever he is, because I could keep him calm and take a lot of the pressure for him. She said she would be worried if I was in Millbank full-time.

Thursday, April 10

I spent much of the day agonising about whether I should be on the road or at Millbank. I had a long chat with Derry, who said the factors were these: 1. would it upset the GB/Peter M operation, though his view on that was that it was so poor at the moment that it wouldn't matter if it did? 2. was it a bad media story? – probably; 3. who would replace me on the road? My view was that 2 and 3 effectively fucked it, but as the day wore on, most people came to the view that I should be there. TB, Derry, Peter, Fiona, Anji, Sue Nye. Only Cherie was really against. Derry even suggested himself on the road, but that too could be a difficult story, and I'm not sure he is entirely cut out for life on the bus.

We met GB to go over some of the tough questions. Air traffic control privatisation was still a problem, and they were both fed up with it, but the truth was it was as much GB's fault as anyone's. Robin Oakley asked a question about an interview with a union official who said he'd been assured by the transport team that we would not privatise NATS [National Air Traffic Services]. TB blanked it, but this was a real problem and we spent a fair part of the day trying to resolve it.

Out on the road, I did a note for Peter M and suggested CW and Tim A were both brought on to the central desk to try to improve integration with us on the road – Tim to be permanent link – and GB's operation. Derry said to me that I was the only person in the operation that Gordon was remotely scared of. He said GB considered me to be more traditionally 'masculine' than TB and Peter, and less afraid of fights. He felt I should be there full-time 'bearing down on him'. I think partly because they were on better behaviour whenever we turned up, it was only when you talked to them individually, and cut through the black humour, that you got a proper sense of how bad it was in there. On the way to the Jimmy Young [Radio 2] prog, I said he had to get back on the key messages, which he did at the end of the interview, leadership plus the contract. But on the way he got a big bogged down in the detail of the privatisation. The chicken was there again, and I said hello, and said he was welcome to a lift on the helicopter.

We flew to Redditch, and had a discussion on how to get more passion into the campaign. I said there was a case, other than for the big speeches, for dispensing with notes completely, just letting rip. I think the pilot may have ended the flight more worried than when we started, because we got into one of our slightly bonkers sessions, laughing about the Tories saying he was cracking up, then doing a very good impersonation of having done so. It was a stupid attack, because it drew more attention to how he was performing, which was well. He got an incredible welcome at the school, real pop-star stuff. But the privatisation story had taken another bad turn, a letter from Derek Foster promising to halt any future privatisations. We had landed ourselves in a real mess on this. I briefed Bill Brett [union leader] and tried to calm him down, but the press could smell blood. TB did an OK Q&A with kids, then a stack of local interviews on the way to Warwick University.

The briefing operations for local papers were working better. Oakley called and suggested moving on the agenda to business, and the launch of our business manifesto. Yes, please! I said we would give him the front cover, some of the pledges and a TB clip. The weather was much nicer again. The press seemed more relaxed and more settled, as if they had worked out this was a long campaign, and it was best to get into a slower rhythm. TB was keen to go on the bus with them for a while, and give them a bit of chat and charm. As we left for the helicopter he said he felt the mood was coming back to us, that in the end people thought they were being too cocky. I briefed, and ended up believing, that the U-turns strategy was no real problem for us.

Ray Powell [Labour MP and former whip] had claimed he was being offered a peerage to step down. Ron Davies denied it but with Charlie Falconer and Alan Johnson possibly about to emerge as candidates, Tony's cronies and Labour sleaze were in danger of coming together as a problem. I was also worried Charlie F's private education for his kids would become a real problem when we were emphasising it was the education campaign. TB was getting exasperated at our failure to land attacking blows on them. GB was very defensive about it, argued that we should set up a little group to tear apart the manifesto. I said we already had one but it was producing analysis not stories. TB said the problem was that the Tories had a washing line – Labour cracking up under pressure. They fitted their stories around that. We didn't have a similar line to run against them. We just about turned around the BBC on NATS. They led on a combination of Major attacking TB and the business manifesto. We had a conference call late on, agreeing to switch tomorrow's press conference to GB/RC on Europe, as *The Times* had a story on the single currency, lots of their own MPs coming out against the policy.

Friday, April 11

The *Guardian* ran a story on 'the Millbank wobble', which was deeply unhelpful and was bound to be followed by others. Alex [Ferguson] called, he said he thought we were doing OK, avoiding big mistakes. He didn't think the U-turn line against us was working. He thought TB looked strong and confident, and they were looking desperate. The chicken was great for us. He thought every time it appeared, they looked more and more pathetic. He said it was vital that we stepped outside the bubble and tried to see the big picture from outside. It's all about psychology, staying calm and confident, keeping your enemies worried. It was good to hear from him, because both TB and I were feeling a bit stressed. He had a habit of calling whenever I was getting a bit worried, and giving good solid advice every time.

I went up to TB's before heading to the business manifesto launch. I called in to the 7am meeting, which was all about Europe and how we get it up on our terms. The press conference went well, with GB and RC on the attack. I listened in to part of the Tory press conference, which didn't go too well, though Major was getting credit for being relaxed and good-humoured and cracking jokes. They were not giving him a hard time at all. The media basically wanted a close fight so they were giving us a hard time, and them a fairly easy ride. On the way in, Sally called to say there was a problem re Charlie Falconer's selection. He had been pretty hopeless and admitted to private health and education, which I suppose he had to, but it was always going to be a problem, even though he was so evidently nice and popular. TB told me he'd had his first really sleepless night, his mind just racing and worrying about all the things that could go wrong. I was working on briefing lines for the Sundays, and also a note on Mo, which I got Anna Healy to fill in re the facts. Mo had agreed it was best if I make it part of the Sunday briefing. It was a human interest story but also in me briefing it, it would be clear TB saw no reason why it should affect her future politically. Business manifesto launch went fine, with lots of serious business people there to endorse us. I briefed hard on the positive vs negative, and suggested JM was making a mistake doing so much negative as it was hurting his nice-guy appeal, which is about all he had left. Derry was angry I hadn't flatly ruled out a suggestion made by *The Times* of a TV debate staged by them, which the telly could cover as any other media event. I'd indicated that it was a possibility and we would leave negotiations to Derry. He felt we should just have said no, that we were not going down that road at all. This is a risk we just don't need. We are crazy to get back into this, he said.

TB's visit was good, nice pictures, good mood. I got back to do a tour of the gallery, and I got a strong sense they had not been giving enough message from us, that the Tories were working them harder than we were. Phil Webster, Nick Wood and George Pascoe-Watson all said I should be full-time in MBT. The *Guardian* and the *Independent* lot were very grumpy, just generally not supportive.

TB was doing an interview with Lynda Lee-Potter, and I decided it was best if I was not there. Then he was seeing Dacre but even if Lynda didn't do the bitch stuff, the *Mail* was a lost cause. Dacre told him they were a conservative paper and they had to back them, even if their heart wasn't really in it.

Saturday, April 12

The days are now really rolling into one. Writing this a day after the event, I'm struggling to remember much at all about where he went or what he did. I can't remember much about yesterday's papers, which is probably a good sign. The *Mail* and the *Telegraph* were pretty much just all out now. The BBC was a problem too. The stuff through the day was bad enough for me to call John Morrison [editor, BBC News] at home to complain. Unions, Portillo whacking TB as phoney. I got the usual 'hear what you say' mantra, and I don't know if it had any effect, but the later bulletins were marginally better. The Tories were not really being pushed on forward policy.

TB went to Ilford while I stayed in MBT to see how it worked with him on the road and me at HQ. It felt the right place to be, but I didn't want to stay here the whole time. It's important to be out and about too, and try to get a broader assessment of mood and feeling. Their press conference was Portillo, who said he was not involved in discussions on VAT on fuel – when he was Treasury Chief Secretary. At ours, GB hit them on Europe and VAT and we had Jack [Straw] and Glenda [Jackson, Labour MP] on crime. I did my briefing to the Sundays, big on education and also the Mo story which straight away became the source of rumours around the place. We decided we would have to put it all round, before which point the *Sunday Mirror*, who had been at my briefing, put it out as their own press release, claiming it to be a big exclusive. What vile unscrupulous people they are. The one thing I found quite hard at the briefing was getting them off the notion we had had a 'wobbly week'. Another problem came with the *Sunday Times*, who had McIntosh [headmaster of the Oratory] doing his usual criticism of our policies on education. I said to TB he should blow him out of the water. Even TB, who normally defended him, was livid and called to complain. According to CB, who was in the car listening to the conversation, he left him in no doubt. I called McIntosh and said he had to put out a statement making clear he was not attacking TB or the policy. He claimed the press were interested in his views long before Euan went there.

Neil and Glenys came round for dinner and we had a dreadful scene when I said I'd spoken to McIntosh and Neil snapped 'Why doesn't Tony do his own dirty work?' and I went down his throat and said I didn't expect friends to come to my house and snipe at Tony during the middle of a campaign, and least of all him. He'd made a few other sniping kind of remarks, about CB, about God, about TB being right wing, and I just lost it. We barely exchanged another word after that and Glenys looked really shocked. I knew it must be hard for Neil, which is why in part we'd asked them over, but I couldn't take the simmering anger any longer. He boiled over, and I boiled over at him, and felt bad about it.

The late news was a lot better, TB on law and order, and the Mo story done straight and sympathetically.

Sunday, April 13

I felt terrible about the spat with Neil, but I also thought I was in the right. He of all people knows the pressures of a campaign, and the last thing I needed during the few hours I was at home was to feel like I was some kind of ogre because I happened to support the leader of the party. I know it was hard for Neil, and I guess he was so loyal in public that he wanted to let a few things out in private with people he trusted, which is fair enough, but it was just too much on top of everything else. I got Fiona to get a message to him to call me so I could apologise and talk it through, but he didn't call back.

JP called early because of an AA Gill piece in the *Sunday Times*, which was wall-to-wall propaganda, as was the *Sunday Telegraph*. Gill and JP had an off-the-record discussion in which he claimed JP said you could not always tell the truth and the minimum wage would cost jobs. JP denied he'd said it and I said he must get out a demand for a correction straight away. The Tories were already calling a press conference on it.

Today was about talking up TB going positive and trailing the big education speech tomorrow. I had high hopes of the poster launch on the pledges, which would give us another hit on the bright colours. TB and I both sensed things were turning our way and we had a real chance to go positive. RC and Peter M were doing a press conference to keep the pressure on the Tories re Europe. But MMcD in particular felt there could be a real problem for us if people felt that they had hardened their position on the single currency. TB wanted me to brief that he was determined to inject some life and passion and conviction into the campaign, that he felt we had to bring it to life. I put together a strong briefing, which worked, using lines from him, and also talking up our irritation at the BBC coverage, saying that combined with a negative campaign by the Tories, it was dragging us all down. I said TB intended to rise above it, make the campaign come alive. He was going to get up the 'two elections' idea, the tit-for-tat media election that was a turn-off, and the election the public wanted fought out on vision and policy. TB did a little speech in Milton Keynes before unveiling the posters, which looked great as they were revealed one by one behind him. He hammered positive vs negative, and then I did a briefing. They bought it. They all pretty much agreed we had to lift it, and it ended up being less of a briefing than a seminar. I was keen to make the BBC an issue, because they were so much responsible for setting the tone of the rest of them. I heard later that Tony Hall was calling a meeting tomorrow to review their coverage so far.

Later, I heard the *Today* programme would not take Blunkett because he had been on *The World This Weekend*. I called to say I intended to hold a briefing to say they would not take him. They came back in an hour and said they would take him after all. Richard Bestic [Sky] wanted a TB doorstep on the way out. We said no but he hassled, and I got TB instead to turn to the camera and say 'this is Tony Blair, Sky News, Milton Keynes', which I knew they would use again and again. On the bus, we were joined by Joanna Coles, Ann Leslie and Anne Applebaum, who were all doing different kind of profiles/interviews. Though she was very right wing, I liked Anne Applebaum, because she had the virtues of being good-looking and clever. Joanna wanted more personal stuff. Leslie was just a right-wing *Mail* hack who made my flesh creep.

We arrived at the Hyatt and worked on the education speech. Again, I used it to brief the positive nature of the campaign, and it was well received. Only the BBC were still sticking to the tit-for-tat news formula. HC, Lesley and Dee had worn me down and we had a drinks do for the hacks, which was worth doing in the end. They were moaning a lot less by the end. But Christ, how many hours a day did I have to talk? At one point, I recognised I was in full autopilot mode, just talking total crap about how we were doing. Philip called to say he was in Merton, and women who had turned off the campaign big time really came back to us when they showed them the Sky coverage today. The men's group felt he was crap on *Panorama*, though very few actually saw it. But they felt he was easily rattled. Philip felt we had the makings of a problem if he did too many interviews like that.

Monday, April 14

The press just about bought our line. *The Times* was great, vision, passion, etc. The *Telegraph* described it as a relaunch. The *Express* went on JP's so called 'gaffe.' *The Times* and the *Telegraph* had a story about Lewington complaining to BBC Radio 1 about playing 'Things Can Only Get Better'. TB was in the hotel dressing gown, his balls hanging out all over the place, working on the speech and generally fretting about Philip's focus groups last night. PG said later TB sounded pathetic when he filled him in. He had to get a tougher skin for this stuff. We'd watched the Molly film and he was quite keen on it but felt it could be better if he was re-interviewed. He now understood what she was after. He felt he had taken a bit of a hit in recent days. There has never been a general election in which the focus is so much on one person, he said. This election, when you boil it down, is all about me, and whether I am fit to be prime minister. It's kind of scary at times.

We left the hotel for Birmingham University, and the speech went fine. I liked these big serious set pieces acting as major punctuation marks in the campaign. The press were angry because apparently we asked the hotel to bump up their bills to save us from paying. I was besieged by a few of them, said I had no idea, I was not responsible for hotel bookings and sort it out with someone else. After the Birmingham speech TB did stacks of local press, then the *World at One* in which he said he would never be isolated in Europe, which was seized on by the Tories as another U-turn. They could still react on their feet. The later BBC bulletins went on it, with JM leading the charge. Yet again, they were buying into Tory propaganda. We got a fair bit of coverage for yesterday's criticism of the Beeb. Peter M said Oakley was upset, but everyone agreed their coverage was dull, yet beneath it the campaign was becoming more interesting. For some reason TB and I agreed to get [Peter] Hitchens in for a chat, and he went on in that mad way of his, before we left for Wolverhampton and the school where Lisa Potts[1] taught. The news was now going on a leaflet the

---

[1] Nursery nurse who, in July 1996, defended children from a crazed machete attack at St Luke's Church of England School in Wolverhampton.

Tories were putting out showing that Sinn Fein supported Labour, and we had to deal with that.

We were driven to Sandbach services to meet up with the buses. Again TB had another little impromptu chat with people in the car park and they seemed pretty friendly. Meanwhile he did a stack of local press on the bus before we got to Oldham. I felt sorry for him doing these interviews, the same questions again and again, only the place names changing. But he was mastering the art: three local facts, a story about the last time he or CB went there, and then the main messages. He got a fantastic reception in Oldham. Phil Woolas and Ian McCartney said the north-west was going well. He was absolutely mobbed by kids and the mood was great. He did local television, and then an impromptu speech before we set off for Leeds.

We discovered Major was doing a big attack on the Oratory, which even though it was a bit of a neuralgic issue for us, I felt was a mistake. TB was a bit down by the end of the day. I thought the Oldham reception would lift him, but he said he was just a bit discombobulated. I said he had not been on form today. He said his mind was on GB/Peter M and whether they could hold things together. He doubted it. He was also thinking about what GB was going to be like in government. The truth is he has not really been a team player. He could not let them drag him down. His great strength was that he could get up in the morning and go out with a smile on his face. His optimism was key and he had to get himself back up again. Earlier GB had complained that my briefing yesterday was being seen as a criticism of him. I had heard no such thing from anyone, but GB was using it to wind up TB. I said he had to ignore it, focus on himself, his own words, his own events. He was our best asset by a million miles and he had to stay in shape. TB said the main problem with politicians was ego. By the time we got to Leeds airport VIP suite, he was as down as he'd been since the start. But he had a couple of TV things to do and he managed to rouse himself and did fine. We were beginning to think they were landing blows on us and we were not fighting back properly. We had to get better capacity at fighting them. That was confirmed by Philip, who said that while women liked the TB empathy, men wanted a bit more toughness from him.

Tuesday, April 15

TB had had a decent night's sleep and was in better form when I picked him up to go to *GMTV*. I hadn't had time to read the papers but the media brief looked fine. We got great pictures from the Lisa Potts visit, OK serious coverage on the education speech, and Europe seemed to be growing as a problem for the Tories. Also, the bulldog PEB which Peter M briefed yesterday was getting loads of coverage. On the way into *GMTV*, I said the message from yesterday and from PG's groups was that he had to be both more relaxed, and tougher. That is exactly how he came across in the interview. He was also on similar form at the press conference. Several of the hacks came out and said it was his best yet. I used it to brief that the dynamic of the campaign was changing and we felt people responding to the positive agenda for change. I said that they had made a mistake by going for TB personally, because it made him the issue and the more people saw him, the more they seemed to like him. Also, their politics was unravelling, e.g. on Europe and grammar schools.

TB set off for Crawley for another blast on the people's platform. I worked on the speech for tomorrow on the decent society then briefed it as I was driven down to Brighton to meet TB. There was a lot of interest in it and we were going to have no trouble getting it up. However, the real story was Europe, with Angela Rumbold [Conservative MP and party vice chairman] now coming out against the government position on the single currency, and there were rumours a minister was planning to quit. I was worried we were going to get painted into the pro-Europe come-what-may camp. I wanted JP to do pictures with the bulldog, which Peter M claimed couldn't be done. He was obviously making the bulldog his own thing but it would have worked far better with JP, because of his face. TB's Q&A went fine, then news came from Luxembourg of the Tories agreeing to reduced fishing quotas so I got TB to do a doorstep on that as we left, saying that Mickey Mouse could get a better deal for Britain than Major did. He was back on his kick that I should be at MBT more, but PG felt strongly now that I should be with TB because that was where the story was. He was on the bulletins in three different stories tonight: Mickey Mouse/fish; attacking them on division on the single currency, and defending himself on the Oratory. PG said the more we had him on the better. He was really breaking through now. Hezza launched another big attack on him.

We got a helicopter to Southampton where we met a group of fishermen who said they hated the government. He did a phone-in with Adam Boulton which went well, and then we went out for a little walk to a pub over from the hotel. Even though the cops were pretty discreet it was not easy to go anywhere without being noticed, but for half an hour or so it was almost normal-life time. We got a bit of a haranguing on the way back from a group of blokes who were a bit the worse for wear. TB was working on the speech while

April '97: Attack on Major re EU fishing deal

Jim Naughtie was hanging round waiting to do an interview on Europe.

It turned out that the so-called big cheese attacking the government line on the single currency was John Horam, and then James Paice [both Conservative MPs] followed suit. For some reason, GB did not want RC to go up on it, so I called to persuade him he had to. TB said Horam had very little credibility, which was true, but to anyone following the news, it was just more and more division. On one level, a harder line would play well for them so we had to keep it absolutely focused on division, division, division. We agreed to keep our heads down tonight and then really go for it. TB didn't like the Decent Society draft, felt that we hadn't really worked out the right balance of rights and responsibilities, and I knew we were in for a late night, which pissed me off because Fiona was down for the night. TB was a bit shaken by the yobs haranguing us earlier, and by the fact everyone in the pub had recognised him. He said it was weird when everyone had a view about you. It was only just dawning on him that he had gone on to a different level and was in all likelihood soon about to go on to yet another level. He said rather plaintively, do you think I'll ever be able to be a normal person again?

Wednesday, April 16

TB was in one of his twitchy modes. I was woken by Naughtie who was still after his interview on Europe and I went through to see TB who was really anxious. He feared the overall message coming through was not Tory division but Labour pro single currency. He had barely worked on the speech, and was angry that DM had not used any of the lines Paul Johnson had done for him. I called in to the 7am meeting and GB shared my concern that we had to keep the focus on their divisions rather than our position. Philip said GB did not really kill them on it at the press conference. 'We are just not hard enough,' he said, and had now moved back to the idea I should be there. I got three clips into the speech – on health, decent society and Europe. They all wanted clips on Europe on the way in and I had the idea of them behaving like lemmings, but TB didn't do it well and wanted to redo it. PG watched it on TV later and said he was beginning to get his frightened-rabbit look.

While he was doing the speech, JM did a big press conference setting out the whole position on Europe, which on one level sounded daft, but he was by all accounts very personal and passionate and he was getting marks for being bold and gutsy. Some thought it was mad, others that it was a real tour de force which brought the campaign to life. TB was meanwhile beating himself up, rightly felt his *Today* programme interview and his doorstep were crap and to make matters worse we were not even getting the speech on the news because JM was going so big. I complained to them all and they assured me it would get something on the late bulletins. As ever, they were following JM's agenda, and he was getting far too good a press for this morning. We got to the airport to learn that ministers stepping out of line on Europe were not to be sacked and we put out strong words on that. It was the only way to get it back on our terms. We got a helicopter to Monmouth and whilst airborne heard that JM was ditching the planned PEB to do an 'address to the nation' type thing on Europe. He was clearly trying to turn his weakness into a strength, and we had to make it unravel quickly. I watched his broadcast and he did pretty well. I put out the line that six years of weak leadership will not be erased by five minutes of TV, which I gave to JP (who we were not seeing enough of in the campaign). TB did an OK speech in Monmouth market square, helped by the Tory candidate Roger Evans heckling from his car. He did an interview on Europe in the square but again it was very lacklustre and I was beginning to think something was wrong. He just wasn't on form. I asked what was wrong and he just said he'd be fine. When he was like this, and when we didn't feel that we had a grip of the campaign, it was very easy to get down. We were beginning to get a bit tired anyway and the only thing that kept us going was being in a good mood and being able to have a laugh and have good ideas and keep our spirits up.

I did lots of phone briefing to the main guys in London but it was less easy to have a general feel for the campaign from out on the road. I was trying to undermine their feeling that JM had done well, but of course they had seen it happen and I hadn't. We set off for Cardiff, now working on the NHS speech for tomorrow, which I briefed on the visit and the press went for it pretty well, which was good, because we had a need to get things back on the domestic agenda. As the day wore on, the papers were beginning to say the Tories were imploding on Europe but apart from *Newsnight* that wasn't coming across on TV. We had Robert Harris with us now and I really did feel it was just one more pressure we didn't need. I watched as much of the news as I could, and felt JM came over OK. We got pretty good coverage for the speech, but I still didn't feel we were on top of things.

Thursday, April 17

The tabloids were very taken with Will Self [writer] who got himself kicked off Major's bus apparently because he was taking drugs. What an attention-seeking wanker. JM's 'bold move' was getting loads of coverage, though TB's speech was doing fine too. There had definitely been a change in moving the press back towards us in the last few days. The Tories were still trying to run Europe against us and ran big tactical ads in the papers. It was clear this was the strategy, to hide their divisions by presenting us as pro single currency come what may, and Europe waiting for Blair as a soft touch. I wanted to get up the line that the Tories had a 'licence to kill' the NHS. It was a tough challenge but I was sure it was worth making the effort because we needed a row on the domestic agenda. I called in to the GB meeting, agreed to push health, and on Europe stay focused on their divisions and off the issue of EMU. I was convinced that if they kept going this could be a problem for us.

TB and I drove in, going over the press conference stuff on health. TB was confident that JM would not get as much out of the public as he was getting away with from the press. But PG said last night's groups were bad, that they fell away from us on Europe, that Major spoke well and spoke directly to them. The pre-meeting was fine, and we had good words on health, but the big worry was Europe. Then at Major's press conference, he said the Tories would grant a free vote to their MPs on the single currency. That was clearly going to be the story today. RC wanted to go up on it big time but I was keen that we keep the emphasis on divisions and not the single-currency issue itself.

TB went off to do a visit to St Thomas' while I went to the gallery. The general feeling was Major was not as good today as he had been yesterday, but he was still getting the BBC in particular to buy into him, as plucky, fighting. I pushed the importance of the health pledge, and went back to work on TB's Edinburgh show speech for tonight. He asked me to stay back in Millbank for the day. I got a fair bit done but it was too hot and there was just a never-ending stream of people coming to talk to me and asking for help with various things. The place was not well managed, and I couldn't find GB. He was not terribly visible around the place. At one point, I was getting a touch of cabin fever and even got them to check out whether I could get a jet up to Scotland to meet up with them, but then decided against. On *World at One*, Ken Clarke admitted he was not consulted over the free vote, which was brilliant. Charlie was straight on to it and really stirring it up. Then later Heseltine appeared to be unaware of it as well, and though he tried to wrestle back, we had a line up on chaos and division and the press were up for it. TB called several times, a bit nervy, and at first was reluctant to say the Tories would kill the NHS.

I reminded him that last week we had said that when he next did Scotland, he should really let rip, move aside from the lectern, throw away his notes and speak with real passion. Saying they had a licence to kill the NHS was just the kind of thing he should be saying. I said he had to break out, explain why he was in politics, what he believed in. I started to tip them all off that tonight would be special, then told him I had given it a massive build-up and he really had to deliver. I did another round of the gallery and again, they were really moving in on the Tories' unravelling. I got back to watch TB live on Sky. He started slowly, though the mood was clearly good, and then really let rip. I knew the press would like it, and it would get the dynamic moving in our favour, and give a sense of fresh impetus in the campaign. TB really had done the business, and even Oakley, who didn't like going OTT, gave a real rave review on the nine o'clock news, while *Newsnight* did a special item at the end. I phoned all the guys up there and talked up the idea he was frustrated at his inability to get passion and conviction to fire the campaign, that he had decided just to speak from the heart, speak direct to people, and explain what he was really about. He was on a high when he phoned in, said he felt a lot better, had felt good doing it and we needed more of that kind of thing.

Friday, April 18

We spent a fair bit of time rehearsing for Dimbleby interview in the Millbank press centre with Derry and Roger Liddle asking the questions. Derry in particular was excellent, really probing on Europe and PR, and TB looked flustered. Derry had been locked away, just working out difficult questions, and TB was OK but not brilliant. It gave us the chance to go away and work out more robust answers. The BBC were leading on the Tory ad with TB sitting on Helmut Kohl's knee. It was unbelievable how they would take any Tory crap. I'm afraid even Oakley copped it from me today when I said they just ran with whatever the Tories said was the agenda. TB went off to play tennis while we fought on. Peter M and I had a real argument about whether to go for the BBC. There was plenty of ground. Both felt, as did Derry, that it would make matters worse. I briefed [Tom] Baldwin on some of the focus-group stuff. The private polls showed them narrowing on us a bit. So if they were thought to be doing so badly, why was that happening? Europe, I guessed.

The IRA let off some bombs and TB did a doorstep. His words were fine but he was worrying about his hair which was having a real flyaway day. He was really capable of focusing on the trivial from time to time. He was also pushing for three days off next week, which was ridiculous.

Saturday, April 19

I had a bad night and woke up with really bad asthma, and tried to do as little as possible, though the phone never stopped. TB was doing the pensioners' rally at Ilford with Tim and Pat. He didn't want to say that the Tories would get rid of the state pension so we had to put a bit of steel in him for that. His Edinburgh speech had definitely broken through and was coming over in the media as something that changed the dynamic and gave new life to the campaign. Clare Short gave us a problem with an interview on the Internet where she said something silly on drugs. We just ignored it. TB wanted me to brief hard on passion, emphasise he had found his voice and his stride at the right time. Man United beat Liverpool 3-1 after which I called Alex to try to fix a photocall for the visit to the north-west. We arranged to meet up tomorrow night. Papers dreadful for the Tories, all talking of civil war.

Sunday, April 20

Grace's chicken pox kept us up half the night, but at least I felt we were nearing the final straight. I worked on the leadership speech, drawing a contrast between TB's and JM's leadership and their respective achievements. I was also going for JM, picking up the gauntlet he threw down last week re who could best represent Britain in Amsterdam. TB was keen we work it up hard enough to lead the news. He felt that because JM's Europe ploy had more or less back-fired, we were in an even stronger position on leadership. I called in to the morning meeting and Peter M and I were both keen to push on health but realistically it was going to be another Europe day, especially as Howard said on *GMTV* the future of Britain as a nation state was at stake. Then on *On the Record*, Clarke contradicted him. It was all leading nicely to TB's speech in Manchester tomorrow.

I went round to TB's where he was sitting in the ugly orange chair by the window and going through some of the tricky questions pre Dimbleby. His worries were minimum wage, tax and spend, Europe, devolution. We left for Broadcasting House, bumped into Lesley White, whose piece today was fine, and Ian McShane [actor], who was totally on board. The interview (*World This Weekend*) was fine. He didn't put a word wrong. Then we went into Millbank to prepare for Dimbleby. He was on much better form, more relaxed, had lost the tension and hyper-ness of the last few days. He said what had been nagging at him was the idea that it would just go away at the last minute, like in '92. The difference was that in '92 he didn't really think we would win. This time, give or take the odd bad day or low moment, we thought it was going to happen. We left for *Dimbleby*, and bumped into some of the audience on the way in, and I sensed he would get a good reception. Jonathan Dimbleby came down to see us in the dressing room and said he was majoring on Europe, tax and spend, constitution. TB was barely listening. He was focusing his mind and getting himself more relaxed but also psyched up for it. I said never to forget the camera would still be on him as others spoke and how he reacted to their points and questions was just as important. Don't look peevish. He was OK, though we could have attacked harder when questions re the Tories came up.

Meeting with GB and Peter M on the last ten days. We all felt we had to keep going on the positive but we also needed harder attacks against the Tories. TB and I thought it was time for the two-headed JM poster. GB didn't want to go on VAT on Tuesday. He had positive stuff on entrepreneurs for Labour, and George Michael helping to fund our computer plan[1]. TB was keen we have a positive sense of momentum around him, and the mood for change growing, but we did need stronger attack capacity too.

JP called earlier, anxious that his/RC's meeting with TB had been cancelled. I said it was purely because of *The World This Weekend* but TB agreed to see him later and they went over the next ten days' plan. They also talked a bit more about what JP would do in government. GB had done TB a note about how he intended to beef up the Treasury. It was a pretty naked attempt at empire building but TB seemed fine about it. I said if you are not careful, you'll be left with a few bits of nothing. We flew up to Manchester, went straight to the hotel and Alex F came over for a drink. TB was in room 247 and Alex said, this is where I signed Cole and Cantona. He asked TB how he was feeling. Tired and a bit stressed. He said we were doing great, and he reckoned we were on for a majority of a hundred-plus. 'Just take it a bit easy. You're way out in front, let them come after you more and watch them make mistakes and then punish them for it. Don't be taking risks yourself.' He thought we should lay off JM personally because he did better under attack. He said believe in yourself, know that you're here because you deserve to be and now just stay focused

[1] Pop star George Michael had agreed to act as an 'ambassador' for New Labour's plans to ensure that every child would have access to a laptop computer, emphasising the huge educational potential of new technology.

and calm. He and I went off for a drink and I told him I was getting more and more stressed out because as we got nearer, more and more people thought TB was going to be PM and they were treating him differently. Things they used to hassle him with, they were hassling me so I was dealing with all that on top of what I did anyway. He said you have to be ruthless. Put the blinkers on. Don't let anyone into your space unless you want them there. If someone says only you can deal with it, give them a few seconds and if you decide someone else can solve it, move on. We went out into the street for some fresh air and I could sense in him the excitement at the idea of us winning and the Tories being out. He said you're home and dry, just carry on as you've been doing, and avoid mistakes.

The feedback on *Dimbleby* was strong.

Monday, April 21

I'd really pushed to get the broadcasters to lead overnight on TB's leadership speech. On TV we did, but radio went on their education initiative. We had a real problem with Radio 4, who pretty much followed the Tory agenda. They argued that they did loads on Tory divisions, but even though that didn't help them, it didn't do that much for us unless we had positive policy stuff in the mix too. Even though Clarke/Howard was running as a split, they were still being allowed to position themselves where they wanted – much more sceptic than us. We were still losing the battle of spin on Europe, I felt. TB was back saying I should be at Millbank more, but the last couple of days had persuaded me I was more good out with him, getting him over the humps and being able to react and respond to what he was thinking. For example, today he was pissed off at the *Independent* saying it was basically all over, because 'out there' there were still people going back to the Tories and I was able to turn that into a new anti-complacency note that went round the system, and into the briefings. He said he felt he had taken a hit out of last week and what was galling was that it wasn't really down to him. But he said if the British people put this lot back in power 'they want their heads examined'.

The speech was strong but then IRA bomb alerts shut down Gatwick, King's Cross and Charing Cross and that was clearly going to be the big story of the day. A lot of our press found the speech a bit too right wing, and thought it jarred a bit. Then worse was to come. He did lots of radio interviews including one where he was asked whether he picked his nose a lot and who was his favourite Spice Girl. Alex told us last night that Beckham was going out with one of them. While I was busy briefing Brunson and Sergeant that Europe was not the big vote-winner they thought it was, JM did grammar schools but it was clear he was happy to let Europe run and they were briefing hard that it was bringing people back to them on the doorsteps. We did a visit to a computer-game place which made for good pictures which helped lift us to number two in the news but then *World at One* trailed a Jacques Santer speech in which he went for Eurosceptics. He was the last thing we needed. Though he didn't mention the UK by name it was clearly aimed here, was potentially explosive and would lead the news. I called GB who agreed we should go for Santer. I spoke to Jonathan and asked him to try to get hold of Santer and ask what the fuck he thought he was playing at. TB said he could cheerfully kill him. Peter M was more relaxed. He said he reckoned it would stay as a radio story unless we overreacted. I couldn't believe what I was hearing. It was so obvious the Tories would pick it up and run with it and make it go big everywhere. While we were arguing about it, we definitely missed a trick. I'm sure GB and I were right on this. We should have been straight out after him.

We left for Bury and Bolton and had the creepy Mary Ann Sieghart on the bus, who gave TB a card from her daughter, to CB's annoyance. We watched Molly's film, which was getting there, and CB agreed to maybe one back-of-the-head shot of Nicky but that was it. We got to Chester, where TB did his best off-the-cuff speech yet. Good crowd, good atmosphere, and he was really hitting the right notes. We had Vine on the bus and he did some OK packages later which though full of himself at least had three TB clips, one from Chester, two from Manchester. Brunson was buying the Tory line that Europe was playing well for them. TB felt constantly putting the case for New Labour, in very personal and passionate terms, was what mattered in the next few days. He was quite chipper despite Santer. He said the problem was these guys didn't really understand our politics. I drafted words to go with the 'twenty-first place in the world' press conference tomorrow.

Dennis Skinner called saying he thought there was a problem with the core vote. He said we should send Santer a letter telling him to keep his nose out. He thought we were not making enough of the size of the national debt. Talk in language people understand. Living on tick. Living on borrowed time and money. Credit-card bills ending in tears. He felt we were not hitting JM hard enough on weakness. GB needs to lighten up. We should use RC more because he had a sharper mind. GB comes across like Steve Davis. Needs to be livelier.

And he felt we should be whacking Paddy harder because he bailed out the Tories in 1992. TB would never do that, but there was a lot in what he was saying. There was a danger we were making it too complicated. We had to have a very simple last few days that motivated our core support to come out with the new support we were getting.

Tuesday, April 22

Lynda Lee-Potter interview was in, and really good, the best thing we were likely to get in the *Mail*. The papers were totally dominated by Santer, so TB's leadership speech was relegated pretty low. TB was OK about it, felt it was something we could keep coming back to in the last phase. I said he really had to let rip today, at the press conference, at the press club, at the speech in Stevenage tonight. His instinct was that where the undecideds were was asking themselves if they really wanted the Tories back, and he was sure they didn't. So that was the question he would be framing through the day. Do people want to wake up on May 2 with these people back? Even on Europe, he was more optimistic than I was that the overwhelming sense of division would hit any bounce they were getting by being much more sceptic. And even though Santer was a problem, he thought the Tories were kidding themselves if they thought Europe was turning things their way. That is what happens when you are behind. You start to delude yourself that things are better than they are. We had a good script on Britain twenty-first in the world, and again we could use that to get up leadership.

Peter M and GB were late for the planning meeting. PG said he feared both were getting exhausted and were not really motoring. TB was fine at the press conference, relaxed and on top of the arguments. TB had done something on him being a 'modern man', future not the past, which I wasn't terribly keen on. Sounded a bit wanky. I got a call from Andy Marr who had been positively raving about TB in the last couple of days but who said that today's *Sun* article, all the talk about St George and slaying dragons, had burnt their bridges. He said he was appalled by it. I told him not to be so ridiculous. We swapped a few insults, I felt my gorge rising, said we were wasting time and breath and we both put the phones down. TB said afterwards people like him had no idea what it was like trying to win an election.

He did fine at the press club, a few old faces from the past there – Keith Waterhouse, Baz Bamigboye, John Edwards. I sensed that they sensed they were with the winner. He did the basic New Labour pitch then we set off for Luton. He did a 'people's platform' speech which was OK. There were some young Tory hecklers. I gave him the line – they look twenty-two, one for every tax rise, which made ITN. He did the pledges and the vision thing and it went down fine. I was starting to crank up the press for tonight.

There was a rumour of the lead being down to single figures in a *Guardian* ICM poll. I hassled them for the figures and eventually got them from Rusbridger around 6. Con 37%, Lab 42%, Lib 14% – only five points in it. It didn't feel right. Gallup had us on a 21-point lead, which felt wrong the other way. But clearly the *Guardian* one would get the attention. He was a bit thrown when I gave him the figures at the hotel, wondering whether in fact they were getting momentum on Europe. I felt we had to use it to hammer the anti-complacency, point-of-voting message. Cherie was on good form at the moment, and said we had been complaining at our inability to get up the fifth-term threat. Here was the chance. He had to go out and say this election was not over, there was a choice and a fight. We ended up joking about the poll. He said have you any idea what it is like to be me at the moment, one week or so away from something that will dictate the rest of your life? You end up as prime minister with the chance to change the future, or you end up with nothing. We ended up laughing about it. I said I had signed a book deal – how we blew a thirty-point lead in a month: the inside story. I said he could go into business with Michael Dukakis,[1] set a political consultancy called Losers Inc. Then we started working on some lines for tonight. They will stop at nothing to win, and they will stop at nothing if they do win.

We were met by Barbara Follett at the venue in Stevenage which lacked the intimacy and the acoustics of Edinburgh so he would have to work extra hard to get them going. He was nervous beforehand, pacing up and down, nodding to himself as he went over the lines and the themes. It was hard, but he just about did it. JP went on too long beforehand, despite my pleas. He wasn't comfortable with the idea of just warming them up and introducing TB, and did his own big number. So TB was getting a bit impatient and edgy. He got a good reception, started slowish at the podium, then moved away and really worked at it, let rip, good message, good lines, audience loved it, press liked it, just about worked. The only slight problem was the Tories were straight up with the line that he had not quite pledged a VAT on fuel cut, and this was a U-turn. Vine covered that bit a little, but in general it was fine.

[1] Democratic presidential nominee who lost the 1988 US election, after having had a seventeen-point lead in the polls.

April '97: Poll shows Labour lead down to five points

Andy Marr called to apologise. He said he was wound up this morning. He said TB should do more of what he'd just done. I said he did it all the time but we couldn't get coverage for it. Higgins called, said the whole thing had been brilliant on TV. People needed to see him more like that.

Wednesday, April 23

We got a good press out of last night in the heavies but the *Guardian* poll was going pretty big. The *Telegraph* even led on it, even though their own poll gave us a massive and growing lead. But we were still in good nick and I woke up feeling confident and strong.

I went round to TB's where he was due to do an interview with Trevor [Kavanagh] and Roycroft-Davis for the *Sun*. They were a bit happier than the last time we saw them but their questioning was still coming from a very Tory agenda, not just Tory but right-wing Tory. MMcD said at the 7am meeting we needed a big new endorsement to go with the 'seven days to go' launch tomorrow, where we were due to go big on 'the choice'. I called Sugar, who said he was in Germany but happy to do something by video. I organised the filming, got an article to the *Sun*, briefed *The Times* and arranged for Alan to talk to Piers Morgan. It was all a bit disingenuous because they all thought they had it exclusive and Piers was particularly pissed off because he felt he was partly responsible for persuading AS to do it in the first place. The important thing for me was that they all loved the story. We were launching our lottery proposals today and MMcD's people did a brilliant job with a specially designed set to look like the lottery, and there was enough meat in the proposals for real connection. Having real people in the audience with the press also helped and the media could feel the growing warmth there was towards him. TB was getting into his stride again, and the strength of his position was coming through.

We set off for Brentford where he did a people's platform job to a small crowd. We had Elinor [Goodman] and Jon Snow along for the ride and Jon and I were reminiscing about Neil's bus journey round his constituency in '92 when everyone suddenly thought he was going to win. It brought me up sharp again, made me think about all the things we could do to lose. I'd even taken to scribbling down all the things that could go wrong, winding up TB, instilling more and more anti-complacency. The crowd was too small for it really to work, but the health centre visit was excellent, good pictures and words. We had to get back because TB and Jonathan were due to meet Robin Butler at Richmond Crescent. Again, it brought home how close it all was now, just over a week to go. I went in for the Molly film screening. It had been a real sweat to get something we all liked but the final product was strong and she was great at the press conference, very self-effacing and factual, not too fancy, good about TB and the whole process. She had grown on me a lot since the start and she'd handled herself well considering what a pain in the arse we must be to work with.

We were in a strategy meeting when Huw Edwards called to say the Tories had got hold of our war book and they were going to release it. I told the meeting which didn't seem to react to it at all. I said this is going to go big. It's the kind of thing the press love and they can make anything look bad if we're not careful. GB and Peter M didn't seem to think it would fly. What planet are they on? Peter was panicky and defensive, as if he didn't want to acknowledge it was going on. GB sat down at his word processor and plonked out a really poor line. I said this was going to be huge and we had to fight them on it. I said I was going to go to the gallery and give out copies myself. Philip was the only one who seemed to think it was a good idea. GB and Peter kind of assented but in a 'if it goes wrong, it was your idea' kind of way. I went over to the House, gathered the hacks together and did the best briefing of any so far. It was a real barnstormer. I said they were incompetent and stupid because all they were doing was showing that we had a plan and we were implementing it step by step. It drew attention to our strategy which was working, and theirs, which didn't exist. And it allowed us to get up the fifth-term strategy properly for the first time. By the end of the briefing, they were asking whether we had leaked it to them, and I didn't dissent. I said we had nothing to be ashamed of in the document or the strategy it represented. We hoped they sent it to every house in the country because it set out what this election was about. I felt totally vindicated when I went back, and it had a really good effect on Millbank morale later when they could see we had just about managed to turn it our way. The BBC was still leading on the lottery, which had been a real hit all round today.

I got home reasonably early but all the kids were in a bit of a state. In their different ways they were picking up on the extra pressure, and there was a lot of change in the air. I must try to give them more time but it's going to be hard for the rest of the campaign, and then for the first bit after that even harder if we win. TB said of his meeting with Butler that it was obvious the Civil Service had pretty much given up on the idea of the Tories coming back. There is so much to do the minute we get in, he said, and we'll be knackered. I still didn't want to focus on the day after. I had become almost superstitious about it, as if we would get punished for taking it for granted. I was glad that Jonathan was taking care of the whole business and only bothering me if he really had to. I said to TB that as the day nears, the focus will get ever harsher on you and Major, and it's now shit or bust. We have to be out there the whole time, hammering the key messages, giving a real sense of energy and hope. The press conferences and all the rest would matter less and less. It was about the connection between him and the public out on the road now. 'God, it's terrifying,' he said. 'One week from now, it's happening, and if we win, it's life-changing.' I said it's pretty life-changing if we lose too.

Thursday, April 24

The war book story was big enough, but largely irrelevant and we didn't get a single question on it through the day. Sugar went big in the *Sun* and the *Mirror* and others followed up. Tax and the economy were being trailed overnight and we were OK on that. I went round to TB's and we headed for 4 Millbank [base for TV stations], where he was due to do a stack of local television. I'd done the words for the one-week-to-go press conference at the ICE, with the Sugar video and some switchers. TB wanted to go heavy on One Nation, New Labour bringing the country together. We also intended, on the back of the war book, to get at them with another fifth-term attack. We had agreed yesterday to go really hard for them on pensions. We had a rebranded set for the last-week launch, and it was fantastic – Tory pledges against Labour pledges, dark against bright. I briefed that we were really going to go for it, let rip again, but the questions were largely about us over-claiming, that we had no right to say they would put VAT on food or abolish the pension. TB had been nervous about doing it, and still was, but he was strong in dealing with the questions. They were a bit nonplussed by the shift. It was as if they had decided we were going to win, so why were we hitting them so hard? One of them said it was like being cruel to a puppy. Do me a favour. We were dealing with a proven and ruthless political machine and so long as they thought they had a way back, we were going to make sure the way back was blocked. I was surrounded and asked to justify the charges one by one. I said look at the record. If you vote Tory this is what you're going to get. I thought Paul Eastham [*Mail*] was going to wet himself. TB was looking fit, the press were looking jaded.

Afterwards, we set off for Mitcham, and TB was worried that we had gone over the top, over-claiming, and it would lead to a big row.

I said that was the whole point. A row was exactly what we wanted. Stuart Higgins called in a fury because the *Mirror* had a decent picture spread on family snaps, and he said he wouldn't mind if I was honest and open, but I was devious about it. It was a nightmare, managing the *Sun* and the *Mirror*. Both thought they should get special treatment at the expense of the other. I asked him to understand the pressures I was under from all the papers, but he wasn't having it. I promised him a decent story by the end of the day. Mitcham was OK, lots of people, lots of heckling Tories. I was embarrassed when some women asked me for my autograph and the TV started filming. We got back for TB's *Times* interview at home. He was in great form and I was briefing the Tories had made a big mistake in designing a strategy focused on him. Equally, the publication of the war book had helped us because we were getting up the fifth-term attack. There was a general feeling we were being very heavy on pensions, but we just had to hold our nerve. He did an interview with the *Observer*, in which Will Hutton spoke more than he did, and he had some crazy ideas among the good ones. TB gave them a little chat afterwards about how we were in a fight and needed their help but Will was only really interested in the full stakeholder Monty. Not sure what kind of piece it will be.

I went to see Rory play football and he scored a fantastic goal. It was great getting away for a couple of hours. Then Tim called about a Tory press conference in which Dorrell had really gone for TB, really vicious. I got JP out saying desperate men, desperate measures. Also they had really come back at us on pensions, because they were so upset at the charge. For two days running, they had let us get up fifth-term attack, which was brilliant. They were total wankers, they really were. We briefed that we were thrilled to bits – their attacks on TB were not working, the war-book plan backfired, we could really hit them hard from now on in. TB was a bit panicky, worried that the charges did not stack up. I said we were in a fight and we had to be tougher about this. They didn't baulk when they launched attacks on us and nor should we back down now. I caught the news which was terrific. I had no doubt we were winning the argument and lots of undecideds would be coming our way.

We set off for *Question Time*, on the way going over the difficult questions, but we had done it so often we were almost on autopilot. I was playing interviewer. I said 'If you lose will you resign?' He did his rabbit look. 'Fuck, what's the answer to that?' I said don't worry, if you lose, we'll put you out of your misery before you have to decide. He asked if I thought we could lose. I said I didn't, but it was important we worked like our lives depended on it. He had to be really tough, really go for them, attack the best form of defence. He was great, played the audience well, and Mark Lawson [broadcaster] who was sitting behind me said he was 'totally awesome'. It was his best interview yet. I could sense the audience changing. Then we went to ITN where he was just as good and I could feel things turning our way. PG said the private polls had us eighteen ahead. Sally and Anji had been working on the last five day plan and I was a lot happier with it now. More energy. More excitement.

Friday, April 25

It was another incredibly early start. Pensions was running big. *The Times* interview didn't come out terribly well, and TB was worried about it, saying he felt he'd been on form and there was clearly something else worrying Stothard and *The Times*. I called in to the GB 7am meeting, saying we had to keep going hard on pensions. TB was not comfortable with it, but he had done fine yesterday, and we had to keep at it. The minute we were defensive, they would be after us. Harriet was at Millbank when we arrived and was demanding to be involved in the press conference. I said it would look like opportunism, that it was running fine, but if it looked like we were now advertising pensions as the issue, it would be a step too far. We were doing crime, but we knew TB would get asked about pensions, and that was the best way to deal with it, let TB/GB handle it, and get both issues up that way. TB did fine, though the broadcasters were pushing on us going too far and over-claiming but we stuck to our ground. They were less interested in the issue than whether we held our nerve. TB was buoyed up by *Question Time*, knew he'd done well, but was constantly asking whether he was in good shape. Oakley asked if our canvassers were saying that people would lose their pension if the Tories came back. I got [Adam] Boulton to ask Major if he condemned push polling. It hit a nerve because JM went mad, especially because Boulton said he didn't always say the same thing. TB was worried but we had to keep going on it. JM was not brilliant at his press conference, though he did one of his big emotional attacks on us.

TB set off for Kent while I stayed back to brief the Sundays on the campaign for the last five days. I was a bit silly at the end, did a throwaway line about Sugar being offered a knighthood to stay with the Tories, and had to row back. I gave myself a mental bollocking. Don't get cocky. Don't make mistakes. Stay on the strategy. TB called a couple of times worried we had gone over the top. I said we'd been trying to get up the fifth term. They had given us the chance and we had to seize it. Around the gallery, most people thought we had done the right thing on pensions. It became clear who the real Tories were, the people at the *Mail* in particular absolutely raging about it. Matthew Parris' secretary had a right go at me. I said you lot don't like it up you. The truth was, as Joe Haines said when I called him, we would be better to be off it now, but it certainly wasn't helping the Tories.

I went to the heliport at Battersea to meet TB and CB, then up to Richmond Crescent to do the *Mail on Sunday*. Also, the *Sun* were not running the Saatchi story so I gave that to them too. Word was out that we were doing something with Richard Branson tomorrow. Higgins wanted to splash on 'Branson backs Blair'. Will Whitehorn [Branson's PR] was worried that we would over-egg it and so would end up with a snub story. Margaret McD had got them as far as saying Branson would support us on tobacco advertising, lottery and consumer protection but he didn't want to go the whole way.

Saturday, April 26

We were holding up really well in the polls. Richard Branson was going to be the big thing today. Again, it would help in terms of mood, the sense of things going in our direction. My favourite story was 'Major takes charge of campaign'. Where the hell had be been up to now? Meanwhile, TB was getting stronger all the time. He was a bit tired after last night's *Sunday Times* Q&A marathon. I got there just before 7 and he stunned me straight out with the boldest plan yet. 'How would people feel if I gave Paddy a place in the Cabinet and started merger talks?' Fuck me. I loved the boldness of it, but doubted he could get it through the key players. He had the Clause 4 glint in his eye. He'd hinted at it a few times in the past, but this sounded like a plan. He was making a cup of tea, and chuckling. 'We could put the Tories out of business for a generation.' He felt if we won, we would never have a better chance. Jonathan told me later he'd sat in on his last Paddy meeting, and Ashdown was 'moist-eyed' about the prospect. First, we had to get through the Branson event. It was being seen as a great coup, but we had to watch him. We travelled down to Euston with TB and CB, a great media crowd on the platform and they walked to the podium. Branson spoke first, though TB was meant to. He said all the things he was meant to say, support re the lottery, tobacco ban, consumer protection, but then slipped in that obviously he supported rail privatisation. He was wanting still to point a little bit in two directions. I could see TB tense up. I think we got the media expectations in about the right place, in that we had made clear we were not expecting the big endorsement. As we travelled up north, TB asked me several times if I thought Branson's words had been a problem. I thought they were just about OK and association with him was still broadly positive. Branson himself made me feel a bit uneasy and I felt there was a side to him that his image and marketing managed to hide. TB was not sure about him either. 'I thought today was meant to be about promoting me, not him,' he said. Never mind, onwards and upwards. I called Richard Addis to work on him re the *Express* leader. Phil Hall [editor] called at 12 to say the *News of the World* was coming out for us, which was great. I got TB to give him a call.

We stopped at virtually every station on the way to get up the sense of a whistle stop tour. Off the train, quick pictures with the candidates, quick clips, stressing One Nation messages. It all gave the sense of energy. Milton Keynes, Stoke, Macclesfield, Stockport, on we went, then Manchester, drove to Albert Square where the main buses were ready. He did a little speech in the rain, One Nation message again, then Oldham, then Rochdale, the same message. There was a great atmosphere in Rochdale in particular, really nice young kids came out, chatting away to TB about football. We went to a school in Rochdale, and I did feel strongly that these were the kind of people we were in it for, ordinary decent working-class people who play by the rules. There was a real look in people's eyes, something good was happening. It felt great. TB was on good form and the crowd was responding. Then we set off for Bradford airport, did a few more local interviews on the way. TB was in incessant 'where do we stand?' mode, a bit nervy and jumpy when it was just him and me talking, but on great form when he went out there with people. I worked on a *Sunday Express* piece, did words for the *News of the World*.

We flew back in a little jet. TB was visibly relaxing, said he felt the end was in sight. He said to the Special Branch guys that he was now thinking as much about Friday as about Thursday. I imagine they were too. Some of them were now likely to be staying with us, and it was amazing how quickly we had got used to having them around. Clare had fucked up over Ireland, and he said he was moving towards getting rid of her. Cherie and I were getting on better than ever. I got home about 6. Rory was being really difficult about me being away so much and Calum and Grace were very discombobulated as well. Alex [Ferguson] called for a chat. He said 'Tell Tony from me, you climb to the top of the mountain on your own, and with a few people you trust. When you reach the top of the mountain, the world claims to have been with you all the way. Stay with the people you trust.' He said he was really excited, he couldn't wait to Thursday, he was praying it would all go well. I said his advice had been invaluable, particularly on pressure and fitness. I watched the late bulletins and Major looked very tired to me.

Sunday, April 27

We had the last slot on *Frost*, and I was keen to get up education again, but it was bloody hard trying to keep finding stories for these big interviews. TB didn't really hammer home the message, which was a shame. He was fine but not brilliant. Interestingly enough, though, JP called and said he thought it was the best he'd ever seen him. Joe Haines had given me a line on grammar schools being the politics of rejection not the politics of selection, which he used without much conviction. Joe had sent me unsolicited a really helpful note about Downing Street and even though it would have changed since his day, I was sure a lot of the lessons still apply, most importantly that they got a sense of authority straight away, and that the system understood quickly who TB relied on. We left *Frost* straight away for an education 'summit' so-called, with forty or so top education people. David M had got a good crowd together and TB introduced it with a little speech, which again I hoped he would use to get out a decent clip on grammar schools, but he murdered it and it didn't really work. We left for Battersea heliport and I complained he hadn't delivered. He said he was a bit tired. I suspected it was more he didn't want to hit the anti-grammar school button. We flew to Derby in what was apparently Al Fayed's helicopter, which was the most comfortable we'd had. Cherie was looking good, all in white. I had to hand it to her and Carole C on the clothes front. Fiona was making a real difference to keeping CB on an even keel. Cherie has some terrific natural campaigning skills. I think both TB and I did better when our other halves were around.

We did a school and a hospital with Margaret Beckett, who said things were looking pretty good in the Midlands. Driven to Nottingham. TB said the last six weeks had been a living hell. Good venue, 2,000 people in there. Mum and Liz [Naish, Campbell's sister] came over and I got them in for a chat and he was really nice to them, joking about how people as nice as her turned out someone like me. Then he took her aside and said I was doing a fantastic job for him, and he was really grateful and she liked that. Ross Kemp [actor] was introducing him. TB started out a bit more subdued than Edinburgh or Stevenage but he got fired up as he went on and they loved it. In some ways it was the best yet. One or two of the press said so too. Mum and Liz came back for a drink then we had dinner with Ross and Rebekah Wade [deputy editor, *News of the World*, and fiancée of Ross Kemp]. He was a nice bloke, very down on a lot of his fellow stars, big against drugs.

Monday, April 28

I was now barely looking at the papers, just flicking through the media brief first thing and picking up a general sense of where they were. I was a bit startled to see a big picture of myself on the front of the *Indy*. The media seemed to be moving on to Tory leadership issues as if they had pretty much given up on the result. It meant we had to keep hammering the anti-complacency message, and getting out the message that every vote counted, but it would be hard. The Moat House was a peculiarly depressing place to be. We had managed to get home more nights than not, thank God. I didn't much like staying in hotels, and felt sorry for people who stayed in them the whole time. I was also conscious of the palaver we created wherever we went now, needing stacks of rooms, office space, extra privacy, security, etc.

We left for Carlton TV studios where TB was doing John Humphrys for the *Today* programme. It was a really boring interview. Humphrys had decided to go on TB mind changes down the years and it was dull as dishwater. We had the press conference up in Nottingham, but linked into Millbank where they could also ask questions and it worked fine, even when the backdrop behind him fell down. He was very relaxed and jokey with the hacks at the end. I'd mentioned the help Alex F was giving us to Piers Morgan who wanted a piece from me on it. Alex was fine, and I worked on it on the bus, and sent a draft through to Morgan who said he would do it as a splash and a spread. Alex called me when we were at Loughborough University, where TB was doing an event with Tessa Sanderson and Brian Moore and where again the atmosphere was superb. He said he was due to be at the Caledonian Club in London later today and could I fax it to him there. He phoned me back at 5.45, when we were at the ITV 500, and said when he got to London he was asked to go and see Roland Smith [chairman, Manchester United] who told him that the board was concerned he was doing too much for Blair, and the feeling was that it had to stop. I felt bad that we'd got him into what sounded like fairly serious trouble. He sounded very down about it, and yet was still wanting to help. He said Smith was a decent bloke who would have been doing it at Martin Edwards' bidding, because Edwards was basically a Tory.

At Leicester, we had a fairly big crowd out for the 'people's platform' effort, and a group of *Socialist Worker* hecklers, which allowed him to go big on New Labour, and did we want to be a party of protest or a government that could do something? We flew back by helicopter. He asked me repeatedly if I thought he could put Ashdown in the Cabinet. 'It makes sense politically,' he said, 'and it stops them peeling off.' I couldn't see it happening, in either party. He said 'You imagine two years in if we are getting hammered by both Opposition parties.' CB was getting worried that he was tired and wanted us to see if we could cut some of the stuff out of the diary. But I felt we had to be pretty much flat out now. The slightest sign of coasting would be punished. There was a good mood in MBT though GB looked exhausted and Peter M was very subdued and withdrawn. Robin Butler had done a selective briefing, to the *Mail*, *Express* and some of the heavies, in which he appeared to have given up on the notion of Major coming back, he'd talked about the process of the transition, the children moving in, etc. David Hughes [*Mail*] said it was absolutely extraordinary. It was also deeply unhelpful. What on earth was he thinking of? I got Tim to put out a line that it was inaccurate, unhelpful and inappropriate. Peter and Jonathan thought it was OTT but I would rather have at this stage a row with Butler than a story about TB/CB measuring the curtains. We already had a problem with a *Sun* story about Cabinet sackings, etc. When I told TB what Butler had said he described it as asinine. 'It reveals a political naivety that is breathtaking.' I was a bit alarmed at the extent to which JoP didn't want a row. TB was sure that it was the right thing to do, rather than feed the idea the thing was all over, and he said so pretty strongly to JoP and Peter. Butler later complained when he heard that the papers were reporting TB as furious.

I had to go home for a while because Rory had been kicked out of football club for being rude to the guys running it. Then I got collected to go with TB for his nine o'clock news interview with [Peter] Sissons. I was back in the make-up room I used to use for *Breakfast TV* and I would reckon every one of the people in there was going to be voting for us. The interview was fine, again no story but strong on message. Major was getting a hard time on tax on *Dimbleby*. In the car home, TB said he felt really fucked. So did I. The travel was the worst bit, but we were nearly there. Two full days, polling day, then a new job. I wished I could will the next few days away.

Tuesday, April 29
He was doing *Election Call* so I had a bit of a lie-in and called in to the morning meeting from bed. I felt really tired and lacking in adrenaline. Reading the media brief, you sensed the press had given up on

it being much of a fight. The Alex [Ferguson] piece was in and he called later to say he'd heard nothing from Roland Smith, and he sounded a bit more up than yesterday. The traffic on the way to *Election Call* was pretty grim and TB was getting stressed out. We were followed the whole way by ITN who were doing a 'day in the life of'. He was on no complacency and basic pocketbook issues. Jon Sopel was in and he said his feeling was Major's aim was to go down with dignity. We had a pre meeting with GB and MB before the press conference to go over difficult questions, e.g. Butler. I called Butler. 'I must be in trouble,' he said, laughing. I apologised for the harsh words yesterday but said there were strong political reasons. I said I had not initially been aware he had done the briefing himself. He was apologetic but the more he talked about the reasons for the briefing, and what he had actually said, the more I doubted his political skills. He was unbelievably naive about the press, thought he was just being helpful to give them a sense of what would happen if. It all ended fine and amicably. TB had backed me yesterday but said I would have to get a new modus operandi with the senior civil servants. I couldn't just expect them to jump when asked as I did with party staff. The press conference was OK. TB looked tired but did fine, and the new set looked great. Afterwards, he had a little nap upstairs while I had a meeting with GB and Peter M, who seemed to be getting on better now.

We got a helicopter down to Gloucester and on the way we were working up new lines for his speeches today, scribbling them on scraps of paper and passing them to each other. There was a lot of mileage in Hezza's warning the country it was 'sleepwalking to disaster'. We got driven to a barbecue and again there was a really good atmosphere. Sinead Cusack [actress] was there and she and I had a nice chat. TB did a little speech and some clips and he was totally on-message now. We drove to Bristol. CB was in a terrible mood, said she didn't want to go to Sedgefield and why couldn't they vote in Islington, which was ridiculous. I got the feeling they had had a row about what Anji would do in government. CB didn't want her there at all, and I was not sure if TB had confronted it. Anji had been told at one point by CB that only one of them would be going to Number 10. She told me she could live with it but she would look to us to help her get a job. I felt in the end it would be fine. TB would want me, her, Jonathan, etc. around. Tim and JoP were in Downing Street discussing with the press people what we might want to do on Friday if we won. I was a bit worried all that would get out too but it did have to be planned. Tim said they did not exactly seem pleased to see us. We wanted to get party and public into the street. They had said they would not allow crowds on both sides of the street. I insisted there should only be one pool camera following TB/CB up the street and the rest should be penned. The Bristol speech went fine. There were big crowds outside the Council House, and the mood was overwhelmingly positive. We had another round of interviews, including Jon Snow. Jon said JM wouldn't be interviewed in Downing Street because he wanted to stay in Huntingdon. He said the feeling was he had given up. He said TB was Prince Hal becoming Henry V and he would be a great leader.

We got a helicopter back, and we all slept most of the way. I had lost count of how many different journeys we had made. I was finding it very hard to stay awake whenever we got on a helicopter now. There was something immediately hypnotic about the sound and feel of it, but I hated the half-dead feeling when waking up. TB looked really tired. But as CB said, just imagine how bad the Tories are feeling right now. In MBT there were lots of silly arguments going on about who should be in Sedgefield doing what. Christ knows how many people would be there. It was hard to avoid the feeling that it was all over. I sensed a real problem on the CB/Anji front and CB at one point seemed close to tears. She said she didn't want to go to Sedgefield and in any event 'she' would be there. TB was just ignoring it.

Wednesday, April 30

I was up at 5.30 to get round to TB's and do *GMTV*. There was a real last-lap feeling. It wasn't a great interview. He was tired and slightly going through the motions and I said afterwards we had to force ourselves, lift ourselves for one last push. The problem was everywhere you went it was being taken for granted we would win. There was a good feeling at MBT and we had a job to do to keep people's feet on the ground. Just as yesterday GB tried to get into the middle chair, and Peter and I had to indicate to TB to move over, so today GB's press conference preamble was far too long. Mary Ann Sieghart had taken to bringing her daughter to the press conferences and she was trying to ask a question. GB ignored her though the two of them went over to talk to her afterwards. JP was a bit too jolly and jocular. I said to TB I thought we came over as a bit cocky and in the bag, and he said it was hard not to be jocular today because it would have been po-faced not to have been a bit more up than usual. It was a beautiful sunny day and the feeling in the press was we'd run a good campaign. He was due to do the *Guardian*, but I left it to Hilary to sit in. They had not been much good for us through the campaign, and I sort of felt we were winning despite a lot of people who traded on being supportive, but whose support was so qualified as to be piss poor.

We set off for Scotland. We had to avoid complacency though. Today was as important as any other, probably more so. We were aiming at the last-minute undecideds. We got a helicopter from Prestwick to Dumfries, landing in the grounds of a mental hospital. George was going on about [poet, Robert] Burns, and Jack McC was saying only mention the British Parliament in passing. I said it was the British Parliament that was being elected. He said you know what I mean. TB spoke at a bandstand in a little park, good crowd and he did the pledges, said we were going for every vote, working to the last minute. We got a helicopter to Stockton, with Irwin Stelzer, who said one day he would tell us the full story of how the *Sun* came on board. He said Anna Murdoch and Higgins had been against and he had to fight for it! I sensed more of them would be claiming authorship soon. We met up with JP at Teesside and drove into Stockton. JP and I had a long chat at the airport. He didn't look tired at all, which was amazing because normally he did. He was handing out Prescott Express badges to passers-by while talking about the day after. He said he was worried the *Guardian* had overwritten his role in government and that when it came to it, they wouldn't think it was as big as they had trailed and it would look like he was downgraded. His ideal was DPM [Deputy Prime Minister] including transport and environment and he wasn't too bothered about chairmanship of the key committees. He feared Robin would be a problem, and TB needed to get hold of him straight away and warn him about messing around. He said Robin was at it the whole time. He'd tried to get Ian [McCartney] to brief against GB's and Peter's roles in the campaign. He was already getting worried about the post-election briefings. I said I would do a briefing note that gave credit to all the key players and I would put it around so that we tried to get one narrative. He said shall I arrive on the bus on Friday morning? I wasn't sure if he was joking but said no, come by car.

We got great pictures in the marketplace, really warm and enthusiastic crowd, then to a school where the kids sang 'Jerusalem' and TB made another little speech, same messages, surrounded by the kids. We then picked up Helen Mirren [actress] and did a visit to Cleveland police. There too the mood was good. A copper said to me 'People like winners and you lot have won.' It was a bizarre feeling, almost flat, certainly a developing sense of anticlimax. I was trying to catnap as much as possible. Most of the calls I was getting now were for the big post-election analysis pieces and logistics for the weekend. I wanted it to feel closer than this. CB was worrying about what to do with the kids. She said she might stay the weekend at Richmond Crescent and then move in a few days after once the fuss had died down a bit. She was worried the kids would get in there and hate it. She said TB had never really listened to her on this, just as he hadn't really let her speak to Butler properly, but these were going to be real issues and if they weren't handled properly, would just add to the pressure on him. It was true that TB had been as obsessed as I was about not giving out signals to the Civil Service that we felt it was in the bag, so it meant some of the family preparations had not been done.

We finally got to Myrobella [the Blairs' constituency home] and everyone was totally whacked, almost in a state of collapse. But we still had a few hours to go. TB went for a nap while I watched the news, which was terrific. Fantastic pictures from Dumfries and with JP in Stockton, and the messages we'd planned weeks ago were the ones they were focusing on. TB had campaigned bloody well in the final five days and we were nearly there now. Maybe there were things we could have done differently but it felt pretty much like we had done what we set out to do. Jeremy Vine did a piece in which he said his overwhelming memory was of our professionalism and the flawlessness of our campaign, that we were always on-message and on-strategy. It hadn't always felt like that, but it was about right. We'd known what we needed to do, we'd had lots thrown at us, but we'd pretty much kept to the plan. Jonathan arrived. He had a draft of the Queen's Speech and it was weird to see all the things we had been banging on about for so long set down on paper as a legislative programme. JoP had his critics, and he wasn't the most political of animals, which meant he got whacked in the party a bit, but while we had been campaigning he had been steadily getting the whole thing in place ready for government, and done a bloody good job. TB's last event was at Trimdon Labour Club, where the atmosphere was buzzing, and he did a brilliant little speech, bringing together the story of them, New Labour, the campaign, and change for the country.

We got back for dinner, TB, CB, me, JoP, Leo and Olwen [his wife], Gale [Booth, Cherie's mother], Ros and the kids. The mood was fantastic. Kathryn was joking and constantly sticking her tongue out at me. Cherie was less fussy and stressed than she'd been. Leo was just looking at Tony with this great beam of pride and happiness on his face. TB said afterwards he would never have been able to do it without me. I said

I'd loved every minute, then said 'That's a lie by the way.' I called home and spoke to the kids and I could tell the boys had a big sense of what was going on. I said life is never going to be the same again, because this is part of history and we're all part of that, our whole family. Calum said 'Are we definitely going to win?' I loved the 'we'. I said yes, I think so, and we might win big. After I put the phone down, I sat down on the bed, put my head in my hands and cried my eyes out. I don't know what it was. Relief it was over. Letting go of the nervous energy. Pride. A bit of fear. It was all in there. But I felt we'd done a fantastic job. We were going to win and we were going to make a difference. I'd felt the emotion welling up in me for days and had been keeping it in check for fear it spilled out in the wrong direction, maybe going OTT with the press. I'd been worrying about Dad's health and was glad he and Mum would both see this happening, but sad that Bob [Fiona's father], who'd always said one day Labour will get back, wasn't there to see it, or even know that Fiona and I had been involved. And I thought of the visits I'd made to John [Merritt]'s grave and all the questions I'd asked him there, right back to when I was agonising about whether to take the job.

Thursday, May 1

It was a weird feeling. It was as if we had been fighting a fifteen-round fight and as the bell rang for the last round, the other guy just didn't show. I had barely slept, even though for the first time in months, there was no reason to get up early. I gave up trying to sleep just after 6, got up and read through the papers. They could hardly have been better. The *Sun* and the *Mirror* were terrific. The Tory papers didn't really do the business for them. A young snapper from *North News* got the best picture in Stockton yesterday and it made a few of the front pages. It was weird having time on my hands. At Myrobella, someone had turned on Radio 4. I switched it off, said we didn't have to worry any more, there was nothing we could do, and I twiddled the knob to find a music station. I got one, playing Abba – 'Winner Takes It All'. John Burton and I fell about. André Suard was up to do CB's hair, and cut mine while he was waiting for her. TB got up late, then was starting to deal with people re Cabinet and junior jobs. CB had said she wanted the kids to go with them to vote, which was great, but getting everyone ready was all a bit stress-y, like going to a wedding or something, but they looked good walking across the field at the back of the house to the polling station. Carole had clearly chosen all the clothes. Hilary had got them all lined up, good pictures, then TB set out to do a tour of polling stations. The weather was good, the mood was good. I went round with him for a while but then went up to the hotel for a swim. I was starting to get inundated with calls re logistics, etc., and also editors and Number Ones who seemed to think I would have some magical insight into the result. TB was fretting on the Ashdown situation, and spoke to him later. Paddy baulked at the idea of the Cabinet post but felt a couple of places on a serious Cabinet committee might be doable. 'Are you sure?' said TB. Paddy said he was. 'He's not really bold enough,' said TB afterwards.

I started to get word of the early exit polls during the afternoon and it looked like it was going to be big. TB didn't believe the figures and nor did I. When he came back from his tour, he said 'Do you really think we're going to win?' I said it looked like it. John Burton told him he had to go and open a factory, and TB was not happy. For fuck's sake, John, do I have to? John was amazing, the way he just fixed things for him to do. I was glad Fiona was coming up, but wished the kids were coming too. I tried to sleep but it was impossible, the phone never stopped. TB had a couple of bad-tempered conversations with GB. GB wanted to know all the junior ministerial positions he was planning, but some of the key ones he hadn't finally decided yet. TB said he did not want Whelan 'rolling round the Treasury'. They discussed the possibility of Whelan working to me in Number 10, but with Tim and Hilary I was already taking two special advisers into the press office. I wrote a long briefing note on the campaign, for the write-throughs, with a big emphasis on TB/New Labour, but also big on JP, GB, Peter M, RC, etc., and the nature of the party operation throughout the country. I went to the Eden Court to do a briefing on the campaign, mainly for their background pieces, and I was still playing down expectations, but was now being met with laughter. There were dozens of them there and they clearly thought we had it in the bag. I went back to the house and had another go at sleeping, again without success. My mind was racing and I was starting to focus on tomorrow.

Fiona arrived with lots of TB and CB's family, and the house was filled with noise. Fiona said the journey was pretty chaotic. TB was locked away in his office. All around us, everyone was incredibly jolly but TB and I were feeling flat. We kept getting updates on exit polls and we still didn't believe them. I went out for a walk and bumped into the BBC lot at the end of the road. I was worried they would see JP arrive, and kept talking to them till he did, engineering them so they were talking with their backs to the road. As he drove in, he was laughing, with two fingers up. He and TB had a long session first to sort his job, then go through the government. By now there was a lot of coming and going, but also problems. Cherie and Anji had had a row, and though both were very calm, they were steely. We watched the exit polls and again TB found it hard to believe. He went back into his office. It wasn't until we got the call from Number 10 later saying JM wanted to speak to him that we dared to believe it for sure. TB sat in the armchair by the fireplace, was very quiet and polite, as Major conceded, said it was clear there would be a considerable Labour majority and congratulations. JoP and I were watching him from the chairs by the door, and I think we both had a sense of the history of the moment, despite the cluttered setting and TB's clothes – he was wearing a rugby shirt, dark blue tracksuit bottoms and his ridiculous grandad slippers. TB paused, thanked JM for the call, said he had been a strong opponent and history would be kinder to him. In truth there was little love lost between them and I could only imagine how much JM hated making that call. There was a little drama before we'd set off for the count, because Nicky was fast asleep and they couldn't rouse him for ages. He went in the car with them and fell straight back to sleep. Alex [Ferguson] called at one point to say they were filming me and TB live through the curtain. I looked over and he said yes, that one, and I went and closed the curtain.

TB got a huge cheer as he arrived at the count. He was meant to be doing some interviews but he said he didn't want to. I did them instead and wished I hadn't. I was still doing no complacency when the votes were already in. I couldn't explain why I felt flat. I'd called David Hill earlier and said TB felt they were being too exuberant when the cameras were on them. David said it is very hard to persuade people that a landslide victory is a reason not to be cheerful. TB said we probably felt flat because we had to start all over again tomorrow. Imagine preparing for a new job by working flat out travelling the country for six weeks and then go a few nights without sleep. There was a TV in the bar and we stood together at one point as more and more Tories were falling. 'What on earth have we done?' TB said. 'This is unbelievable.' We'd decided that he would emphasise the family in his speech to the count, and be very measured, emphasise the party at Trimdon, and the country when we got to Festival Hall. We got to Trimdon Labour Club and they were all watching on a big screen the broadcasters had put up. The mood was fabulous. I really liked the Trimdon people. Fiona Bruce was there for the BBC and she noticed I had a tear in my eye. TB did a speech saying how important they were to his politics and his political journey. I'd said at the briefing earlier that what the media found hard to understand was that he was New Labour out of conviction, that he'd made the changes out of belief, and they were beliefs shared by these people.

We were driven out to the airport and listened to the radio and the fantastic news that after a series of recounts Rupert Allason had lost. Even that didn't lift me out of my flat mood though. Fiona asked what was wrong. I said it was probably the anticlimax and the worries about the future. We got on the plane, TB and CB across from me and Fiona, the cops, John Burton. Tom Stoddart was snapping away and we also had a TV camera for ITN. It was a really comfortable plane, better than the ones we had used for the campaign. There were bottles of champagne there but TB was still not really in celebratory mood. Just after take-off, he and CB had a very private chat across their little table. This was him telling her how important she had been and her saying how proud she was, what a great prime minister he would be, she would always support him, etc. I said to Fiona, it may be tough at times but it's quite something to be here, on the plane flying a new PM to London, to know we helped. He was quickly back into work/focus mode, wanting to discuss tone and feel for the Festival Hall. He was scribbling a few thoughts, as was I. More and more seats were coming through on the pager. TB at one point asked if I should have it on. 'Doesn't it interfere with the mechanics?' Dunno. It was now that the full extent of the rout became clear. Portillo lost while we were in the air. Sue Jackson was paging me all the results and seats were falling that we would never have imagined standing a hope in hell of winning. I would get the result, tell the rest and TB would say 'You're kidding me.' We were working on his speech – One Nation, the extra sense of responsibility a big majority gives.

We landed and I sought out Terry to give him a big hug. How many times had I sat in the back of the car and asked him if he thought we were going to win, and now we had. We headed into London, all quiet really, and then the Special Branch had a nightmare as we got to the Festival Hall. Somehow they ended up down a wrong road and we got stuck, the whole convoy. We could hear them playing 'Things Can Only Get Better', again and again, and on the radio they were saying TB is only moments away, but what they didn't realise was we were stuck, and the whole convoy was having to do three-point turns and get TB's car up ahead of all the rest. Eventually, we got there, stopped briefly at the bottom of the ramp to get TB miked up, then up the ramp to a wall of noise as the cars pulled up. Fiona and I were in the car behind the police backup and I suddenly realised I had his speech notes in my inside pocket. I jumped out while the car was still moving and the wheel went right over my foot. There was a great carnival atmosphere, thousands of people, hundreds of journalists, Peter M, Neil, JP. TB worked the crowd then up to the lectern and 'a new dawn', and they cheered every word. We had been really flagging, but he was in great form now. The only time I got emotional was seeing Peter Hyman and Tim in the crowd and giving them a huge hug. Then seeing Philip and Gail, who said 'You were so, so brilliant.' And yet it was weird. I felt deflated. All around us people were close to delirium but I didn't feel part of it. I wanted to get to a quieter place. We were taken up to a room afterwards, and I said to TB, this is so weird, you've worked so hard for so long for something, it comes, you're surrounded by people who are so happy because of what you've achieved, yet you don't feel like they do, and you just want to get home to bed. He said he felt exactly the same. Maybe it was too big to take in. More likely was that while the crowd were focusing on now, we were thinking about the job ahead.

I got home at 6.30, had an hour's sleep, a shower then to Richmond Crescent. Just a short sleep had bucked me up, and I had a session with some of the hacks in the street before going in. It was another lovely sunny day, and there was a good crowd outside. Inside, the usual frantic activity. Carole was there fussing around Cherie. TB was up in the bedroom working on the speech for the street. 'Practical measures in pursuit of noble causes.' Not sure about that. He got dressed and Jonathan and I went out to be met by Trevor Butler, who I knew from my *Mirror* days when he was looking after Thatcher and Major, and who would be taking over protection. He talked us through what was going to happen, the drive to the Palace, what JoP and I would do while TB saw the Queen, the drive back to Number 10. TB came out, did a little walkabout and then off we went. Jonathan and I were in the car behind the backup and the whole journey was fantastic, people coming out of houses and offices to wave and cheer. Going down Gower Street, it was almost like watching a cascade. We were looking down the street and people following the car on TV were coming out to cheer. I had a surge of emotion almost on a par with the one in Sedgefield on Wednesday night. I said to JoP 'This is unbelievable.' We agreed that expectations were going to be way too high. There were big crowds outside the Palace, huge cheer as he went through. Then he was taken off to see the Queen while JoP and I were taken into a room with Alex Allan, Robin Janvrin [deputy private secretary to the Queen] and Geoff Crawford [press secretary to the Queen]. It was all very friendly and relaxed, and I couldn't quite take in that it was all happening. Alex Allan seemed a really nice bloke. It was odd to see people who didn't look exhausted. I was talking about how hard it had been to be away from the kids so much and then Janvrin said oh, look at those children at Number 10, and I turned round to the TV to see Calum and Grace sitting on the steps of Number 10, looking bemused, Calum playing with some sunglasses. I called Mum to get her to watch, and she already was.

TB was in for half an hour or so, came out and we set off for Downing Street. As we turned into Whitehall, we could hear the crowds. The cars stopped at the bottom of the street and we got out and the noise was deafening. Ton-ee, Ton-ee, Ton-ee. Labour's coming home, Labour's coming home. TB and CB got out, started the walk up. JoP and I followed on behind. The noise was almost like a sporting event. I caught sight of Fiona holding Grace up the street, and Rory and Calum standing there near the door. Tim was in tears in the crowd. It was fantastic to see the party people and the people from the office who had all worked their rocks off and were now able to enjoy this. David Bradshaw and Kerry [his wife], Liz, Peter H. It was brilliant. We got to the top and TB went to the lectern, did his speech, a few more pictures and then inside to meet the staff. Jonathan and I, Sally and David Miliband, followed. I'd been through that door so many times as a journalist. I'd stood in that hall dozens, hundreds of times, waiting to be called through with the rest of the hacks to Bernard Ingham's briefings. But this time it felt very different, walking in behind the new prime minister, knowing that for some years I would be spending more working hours here than virtually anywhere else. I felt a mix of confidence, but uncertainty too.

To be continued.

Index

re TB 497; briefs against Chris Smith 508; his behaviour at strategy meetings 553–4, 555; fails to impress TB 562, 563; talks drivel 565; apologises for briefing re AC 568; at TB/GB meetings 602; and windfall tax 616, 673, 676; excluded from meetings by Mandelson 658; on AC 667; at lunch with Rothermere 674; marriage 696*n*

Bamigboye, Baz 723

Bank of England 152, 158, 200, 202, 250, 626

Banks, Tony 484, 649

Barak, Daphne 635

Barber, Brendan 277, 522, 523, 544

Barclays Bank 576

Barings Bank 154

Barnard, Alan 207

Barnsley East by-election (1996) 585, 588

Barton, John 34

Bashir, Martin 316*n*

Basildon 436, 703

Bassett, Phil 645

Bates, Ken 554, 649

Baxter, Jim 583

Baxter, Sarah 678

BBC 3, 24, 25, 53, 269; and AC's letters 293, 294, 295, 298; gives TB good coverage 484; and Bland's appointment 352–3; Labour's problems with 521, 561–2, 573, 574, 598–9, 603; and Howells' article 526, 527; and interception of Labour's pagers 540; interviews AC on Winning 556, 557; party 586; and TV debate 613–14, 669, 675, 679; election campaign coverage 631, 635, 638, 653, 675, 709, 711, 712; *see also Any Questions?; BBC Breakfast; Breakfast with Frost; Desert Island Discs;* Hall, Tony; *Newsnight;* Oakley, Robin; *On the Record; Panorama; Question Time; Today* programme; *World at One; World This Weekend*

BBC Breakfast 18, 30, 35, 314

Beckett, Leo 30, 486

Beckett, Margaret (MB): and leadership and deputy leadership contests 9–10, 11, 15, 17, 18, 22, 23, 24, 25, 26, 27, 28, 30, 31, 37; on *Frost* 15, 225; calmness 29, 38; interviewed by AC 35; and Shadow Cabinet reshuffle 70, 73, 74; abstains on NEC vote 167; and privatisation campaign 179; NHS speech 182; and health document 207, 209, 219, 222, 228; solid and full of good sense 219; calm in press conference with TB 235; TB's plans for 302, 303; on Clare Short 386; and Private Finance Initiative Bill 391; on Labour's response to JM 453; would have been less trouble than JP 490; in Shadow Cabinet 494; her judgement worries TB 562; and GB/Mandelson clash 604; brilliant at press conference 640; sound 654; and election campaign 732

Beckham, David 552, 721–2

beef: European ban 410, 452–62 *passim*, 469, 470, 471, 473, 477, 561, 568, 569, 589, 591, 626, 646; JP as 'beef supremo' 638, 642, 643; *see also* BSE

Begg, Ann 521

Bell, Martin 697, 698, 700, 702, 703, 704

Benn, Tony 151–2

Benton, Joe 305

Berlusconi, Silvio 469, 528

Bestic, Richard 711

Bevin, Ernest 110

Bevins, Tony: praises TB's speeches 66, 136; briefed by AC 128, 150, 288, 369, 383; leads on public ownership 132; on JM 212; and Howarth defection 292, 296, 297; on Tories' behaviour 300; briefed about Shadow Cabinet meeting 318, 319; wants names of Tory MPs in touch with Labour 383; supports AC in Allason case 436–7; on devolution referendums 479, 480; suggests TB writes to JM 555; questions TB on CB's underwear 651; and further briefing on Shadow Cabinet meetings 663–4, 665, 666; interviews TB on JM 669

Bhutto, Benazir 151*n*

Bickerstaffe, Rodney 156, 157, 188, 190, 191, 192, 200, 285, 406, 541

Big Issue 603–4, 634

Bingham, Sir Thomas 231

Birch, Anna 35

Bird, John 634

Birmingham University 712

Birt, John 178, 185, 295, 352–3, 553, 586

Black, Conrad 239, 313, 374

Blackburn, David and Janice 113, 339, 553

Blackburn, John 86*n*

Blackstone, Tessa 372, 597

Blair, Cherie, QC (*née* Booth; CB)

1994–5

and the children 10; and GB 12; and the media 17, 18; worried about TB 37; confident 40; on Labour leadership day 41; pressures AC to take job 46; in France 48–9, 51; 40th birthday party 58; and Carole Caplin 60, 67, 68, 69, 70, 71, 76–7, 226, 274, 275; relations with AC 76, 98, 113, 126; and media stories 79, 80, 133; sees Queen 85; on TB's Queen's Speech 91; blames AC for Oratory stories 101, 103–4, 106, 107, 270–1; inhospitable 160; makes unconvincing fuss of JP 166; complains about AC to FM 177, 182; has civilised chat with him 185; takes silk 185; her articles on Chiswick women's refuge 194, 198, 203, 205; at dinner with Princess Diana 194, 195; and Queen of Swaziland 196; plans political speech 198–9; worried by press 202; on Princess Diana 205; rude at Sue Nye's party 205–6; rude to JP 207; Irvine's views on 213; and TB's relationship with AC 225, 240, 270; delivers tirade to Anji Hunter 271; and discussions on her role 273, 274–5; to Brighton for conference 290, 291; and the police 290; at *Mirror* lunch 294; jokes with

AC 296; press conference with Clare Short 302; presents prizes at private school 307; and AC's illness 309, 311

1996–7

at Irvine's book launch 357; *Mail* article on 369; at Brit awards 378–9; and Caplin 381, 384, 434, 437, 440; her image problem 384; and the press 413; at conference on women and the law 425; sees homoeopath 433–4; falls out with FM 437; nice to AC about his court case 437; convinced AC is against her 437, 438; wants public role 440; and TB's admission re spanking 460, 461; unusually pleasant to AC 462; and meeting with Robin Butler 462; plans for election campaign 463; and TB's salary 488, 494; rows with Anji Hunter 499; and press story about Norma Major 517, 519; wants to be chairman of Bar Council 520; and TB's lucky ribbon 535; takes alternative medicines 537; rows with FM over Caplin 537; with AC at conference receptions 540; South African visit 545, 546, 548–9; at Mandelson's birthday party 553; anxious about security 578, 581; in Scotland with TB 583, 584; borrows car park pass from Labour MP 592; gives cuff links to AC 593; at Howarth/Rae dinner for Diana 619, 620, 622–3; at Anne Frank exhibition 631; her haircut makes news 632; goes to Caplin's gym 641; and filming of TB 650; visits Wirral with TB 650, 651; on TB as an upper-class public school twit 663; relations with AC 670, 694, 731; at *Daily Star* lunch 674; wants AC to tour with TB 706; and the children 722, 738, 739; and election campaign 724, 732, 734; wants to vote in London 735; hostile towards Anji Hunter 735, 736, 741; and election victory 743, 744

Blair, Euan 9, 10, 40, 51, 71, 80, 101, 104, 113, 127, 270, 328, 491, 492, 650

Blair, Hazel 530, 697

Blair, Kathryn 9, 10, 40, 51, 160, 738

Blair, Leo (TB's father) 18 *and n*, 530, 592, 697, 698, 738

Blair, Nicky 9, 10, 40, 51, 96, 451, 500, 543, 722, 741

Blair, Olwen 738

Blair, Tony (TB)

1994

and John Smith's death and funeral 4, 11, 13, 14, 39; and leadership contest 4–8, 9–10, 11, 12, 13, 14–18, 20–3; and GB (*q.v.*) 4–5; and Mo Mowlam (*q.v.*) as campaign manager 24, 25; and Mandelson (*q.v.*) 24, 26, 32–3; speeches and media interviews 26–30; has TV training session 30–1; at TGWU hustings 31; and dirt spread by Fettes ex-pupil 32, 34; and furore over London Oratory 33, 34, 71, 80, 95, 101–3, 104–5, 106, 114; launches manifesto 33, 34; disliked by *Today* interviewer 36, 37; and

JP (*q.v.*) as deputy 37, 38, 43; meets with Delors 38; BBC interview 38; plans press office 39, 40; his acceptance speech 40, 41–2; education policy 43–4; worries about Tory press 44; asks AC to be press secretary 44–6; in France with AC and family and the Kinnocks (*q.v.*) 47–9, 50, 51–2; decides to scrap Clause 4 (*q.v.*) 50; talks AC into accepting post 50–1; meets Murdoch (*q.v.*) 55; plans for 'New' Labour 55–9, 61–3; tells key people 63–5; successful conference speech 65–6; and Carole Caplin (*q.v.*) 66–7; and Shadow Cabinet reshuffle 71, 73–4, 75, 78; at PMQs 71–2, 74, 79, 81, 82, 96–7, 112; Social Justice speech 75, 76; needs space 75, 76; and sleaze issues 74, 77, 78, 79–80; lunches with women's mag editors 81; wants AC to get on with GB and Mandelson 83; worried by GB 85–6; Queen's Speech debate speech 85, 86, 87, 89–90, 91, 94; and EU Bill 90, 95; and party political broadcast filming 90; and Welsh Senedd 90–1, 92; persuaded to refuse pay rise 91, 92; at *Standard* drama awards 94; and Budget 95, 96, 99–100; at NEC conference 100–1; plans strategy 105–6; his expensive haircut criticised 106, 107; alarmed by allegations against Foot 107; orders election alert 108; and JP's referendum broadcast 109–10, 113; and Tory intruders 110, 111; at meeting with switchers 111; and NEC vote 111; dines with Roy Jenkins 112; irritates his staff 112; in Northern Ireland 113; and dissension and leaks 114–15, 117; briefed by MI6 115; visits the homeless 115; breakfasts with Max Hastings 115; and staff parties 115; angry at filming of radio interview 118; and DB's interview on education 118–19

1995

forces DB (*q.v.*) to backtrack 121–2, 128; holidays in Prague 122, 125; and PMQs 124, 126, 130, 134, 137, 143, 144–5, 149, 154–5, 162, 172, 186, 204, 221, 224, 235, 311, 340; circular conversations with AC 125; BBC interviews 125–6; in Brussels 126–7; and MEPs 126; records Clause 4 video 127; photographed by Lord Snowdon 127–8; and unions 128, 132–3, 143–4; unhappy about coverage of rail policy 128, 129–30, 132, 137; speaks at Stanley Matthews tribute dinner 128, 129; attacks price of soccer strips 130; and 'Reaching out to Britain' campaign 130; back on form 131–2; on modernisation 132; gives brilliant interview 134; on *Newsnight* 135–6; speaks at Trimdon Labour Club 136; and Europe 137, 148, 149, 153, 155, 156, 157; on GB, AC and Mandelson 138–9, 143; in Brighton 139; and Young Labour 139; conference speech goes well 139, 140–1, 142; lunches with US Ambassador 142;

relationship with GB 143; and 'luvvies' 142, 144, 149; dislikes Mandelson profile 145–6; and Scottish devolution 146, 152; meets *Sun* team 148–9; and allegations against Foot 149, 150; attacked by Cardinal Winning 151; supports Tories on Northern Ireland 152; at Eddie George dinner 152; Europe speech his best Commons performance yet 154, 155–6; irritated by Scottish media 156; and minimum wage 156–7; has difficulties with JP 158–60; hosts Clause 4 drafting session in bedroom 160; in Barcelona 160, 161–2; and final Clause 4 draft 162, 163, 164, 165; in Scotland 163, 164, 165; and NEC vote 166, 167; and JP/GB clashes 168, 169, 170–1; on *Dimbleby* 170; gives *Spectator* lecture 171, 172; 'snappy' 174; in Glasgow 174; and unions 177–8, 180, 201, 216, 228; sacks Cousins and Clwyd 178; and Hunter Davies 181; has hero's welcome in Scotland 181; tells AC to take a holiday 183; cheered by CLP and CWU results 185; his 'onslaught on the unions' 187–9, 190–2, 193; and local elections 194, 195, and Princess Diana 195; at VE dinner 196; wants policy debate 196–7; and CB and the press 198–9, 202; in Scotland 199, 200, 204–5; becoming more popular 203; and Nolan recommendations 204, 205, 206; against Heseltine on *Today* 206; and Wilson's death and funeral 208, 215, 216; worries about all-women shortlists 209, 210; praised by Mrs Thatcher 209, 210; and Bosnia 210, 211, 212, 250; meets Kohl 212; and AC's days off 212; used as surrogate by Tories 212; diary diatribes 213; at 'Churches Banquet' 213; and Pete Thompson 214–15, 216; health and education policies 215, 218, 220–1, 224, 228; and religion 216; and Mail Group editors 217; at dire Shadow Cabinet meeting 219; and PLP 223–4; worried by Heseltine 224, 230, 231; on relations with CB 225; his dependency on AC 225–6; on JM 229–30, 232, 233; at Nice summit 231–2; meetings with union leaders 233, 240; toleration of heat 235; grilled by Falconer 236; at *Economist* lunch 237; and JM's 'resignation' 237–8; at T&G conference 241–3, 253, 256; Australian trip 214, 216, 226, 228, 231, 233, 239, 240, 241, 244–51; given surprise party 254; and grumbling in the Party 254, 255, 256; chaotic holiday arrangements 261; hopeful for Howarth (*q.v.*) defection 264; depressed 268–9; does good *Frost* interview 269–70; speaks to union leaders 271; in Ireland 271–3; TUC speech 275, 276, 277–8; and *Guardian* 278, 279, 284; annoyed by JP 280–2; and Lib Dems 281; good reception at Dudley 282; at McCluskie's funeral 282, 283; on taxes 283–4; works on conference speech 284,

285–6, 288–90, 291, 292; football with Keegan 291–2; speech received well 293–4; angry with Meacher (*q.v.*) 294; and JM's speeches 301; and Budget strategy 301–2; Shadow Cabinet reshuffle 302, 303, 304–5, 306; self-doubt 304; at Mandelson's birthday party 305; and AC's illness 307–8, 310, 330; and Clare Short 308, 309; goes to Rabin's funeral 312; at *Q* magazine awards 312–13; CBI speech 310, 311, 313, 314, 315; and Queen's Speech debate 313–14, 315, 316–17; and *Observer* story about Shadow Cabinet 319, 321; fears his relative youth is against him 320; does well at PLP 321; further problems with GB 324–5, 331–2, 333; Budget speech 326, 327, 328; and Clinton's visit 329–30; his 'image problem' 331, 332–3; gives tough speech in Scotland 333–4; good with Stirling students 334; his 'indictable charges' 335; feeling vulnerable 335; Austrian trip 335, 336; and Philip Lawrence's death 336–7; and Jewish community 337; his pro-European statement 339; and the royal divorce 342; in Australia 342, 344, 345–6

1996

Japanese visit 347, 348, 349–50; and letters from JM 351, 380; on stakeholder economy 351–2, 353, 354, 355, 371; in Singapore 351, 352, 353; and Mrs Thatcher 354; drives into dog 355; sceptical about single currency 354, 355; anxious and nervous 356, 358; and Monks article 357; and HH 359, 360, 361, 362, 363, 364, 365, 373, 404, 407, 408; and education 366, 367, 461, 479, 531; at PMQs 368–9, 404–5, 492, 501, 561, 579, 591; and the press 372, 373–4, 375; on key seats candidates 378; at Brit awards 378–9; and RC's affair 381, 382; and CB's 'image problem' 384; worried by GB 384, 385–6; angry with Ron Davies 387–8, 389; wants more party reform 390; and housing 390–1; and devolution 391–3, 397–8, 459; has hopes for *Partnership with the People* 394; and Dunblane massacre 395–6, 398–9; and Tamworth by-election 400, 401, 402, 406; and religion 400, 411–12, 484, 486, 487; lunches at US Embassy 403; and *Road to the Manifesto* (*q.v.*) 405–6, 432–3; and small businesses 407; angered by BBC 408; wants to support anti-terrorist measures 408–9; and euro referendum 409; US trip 410, 411, 412–19; exasperated by Clare Short 420, 421, 422, 426, 427; on gays in the military 423, 433, 434, 440, 441, 443; on need for 'media minders' 423; disagrees with GB over tax 426–7; supports AC over court case 429, 436, 437; rows with CB over Caplin 434; 'child benefit rift' with GB 438–41; and Mandelson/GB rows 442, 444–5, 446;

annoys TB with NEC document 61; becomes Shadow Chancellor 71; and Social Justice report 72–3, 76; chairs election committee 83, 84; his tax reform press release 84; at Clause 4 meeting 91; clashes with JP (*q.v.*) 93, 97; and pre-Budget press conference 95, 96; and RC (*q.v.*) 96, 98; surly at 'Big Guns' meeting 97; wanted by TB for his 'strategic mind' 98; his EU finance bill speech criticised 99; and Budget speech 100; against European referendum announcement 106; and Clause 4 conference 106; has got his confidence back 107; downcast after Clarke statement 108; angers TB at Big Guns meetings 114, 115; angry with DB (*q.v.*) over VAT on school fees announcement 121, 122–3, 124; does excellent interview 125

1995
and 'Reaching out to Britain' campaign 130–1; on cutting taxes 134; in charge of election planning 137; and Clause 4 138; on Europe 139; gloomy 143; presses TB to do education 144; negative 147–8; prevaricates on devolution 149; at Eddie George dinner 152; and minimum wage campaign 154; and TB's disastrous PMQs 155; works on Europe speech 155; at awayday strategy meeting 157, 158; indecisive 158, 159; undermines JP 161, 167; accuses TB of briefing about tax 163; pulls out of *Frost* 165, 166; and Clause 4 165–6, 167; accuses AC of briefing against him 168–70; criticised by Mandelson 169; problems with JP remain unresolved 170–2; further clashes with Mandelson 172, and TB 174, 178, 179, 180–1, 191–2; PG's views on 183; and AC's absence 183; has hidden agenda 184; difficult over union story detracting from his speech 190, 191–2; told to get rid of Whelan 193; weakens TB's resolve 97; and independence of Bank of England 202; annoys TB over Nolan 205; plays positioning game 212, 226, 234; wants to cancel low-pay press conference 216, 217; contributes to Shadow Cabinet meeting 219; and autograph hunters 220; complains about JP/Mandelson in charge of by-election 220; and JM's announcement of leadership election 229, 238; accuses AC of briefing against him 236; comparisons with Mandelson 238; writes speech with AC 238; rows with TB over Mandelson and Nick Brown 246, 252; and discussion re Shadow Cabinet 252; and Joy Johnson 253, 306; at TB/Morris meeting 255–6; relations with Mandelson 264, 265, 267; back in action 267; unhappy with AC's briefing 283, 324; difficult call with TB 286; conference speech 291, 292; and Budget strategy 301, 302, 315–16, 321; and Whips

304–5; welfare-to-work proposals 313; rows with JP and RC 313, 314, 315–16; and leak of Shadow Cabinet meeting 318, 319; in a terrible mood 321; is damaging the Party 323; TB on 324–5, 331–2; loathed by JP and RC 326; helps TB with speech 327; and Tory Budget 328; his 'court' 328; rows with Mandelson 333; against euro referendum 338; complains of not being consulted 340; and Labour Christmas cards 341; and Mandelson's book 342, 343; against Scottish devolution committee 344

1996
responds to Tory ad on economy 347, 348; and Robinson's bid for *New Statesman* 347; opposed to stakeholder economy 354–5, 356, 357–8, 371, 374, 433, 455, 456; and HH 363; and Heseltine's attack on Labour 366, 367; agrees roles with TB 366–7; and MPs' pay 368; on *Frost* 370; difficult behaviour at meetings 374, 376, 380, 381, 403; and RC's success over Scott 385; persuaded to go on *Today* programme 392; body language during TB's speech 392; and election campaign 393; blocks other people's ideas 394, 405; ignores JP 395; rewrites everything to do with tax 395; in USA 395, 400; briefing goes nowhere 403; bounced off *Today* programme 403; and TB 403, 405, 406, 411; threatens retaliation over briefing 405; on beef ban 410, 454; on referendum 410; and Mandelson 411; agrees TB and God is disaster area 412; and briefing on tax 414, 415, 421; worried 423–4; and child benefit 423, 424, 425, 438–9, 441; has different agenda from TB's 425, 433, 508; his views on tax 426–7; his 'Lost Generation' campaign 440, 447, 449, 460, 465; under attack 441, 449; clashes with Mandelson 442, 444–6, 456, 457; and JP 446–7; more humble and conciliatory 447, 448–9; rebuts Clare Short's transport document 450; economic message similar to TB's 455–6; and devolution 459, 471, 479; not known by public 460; on health waiting-lists 461; suggests moving to Millbank 463, 464; grumpy 464; 'off form' 467; previews England vs Scotland match 467; JP wins money off 468–9; on single currency 470; refuses to do economic rebuttal 471, 476, 477–8, 492, 520, 551, 554, 555, 562; sceptical about pledges 471, 476, 478; and labour market reform 472; rude at TB's dinner party 478; angry with Mandelson 485; gives good impression at NEC 486; and New Life launch 489, 496–7; alarmed about MPs' pay 493; and euro row 501; and Field and Smith 501, 502; and Clare Short 503, 504; interviewed by Fiona 508; refuses to admit economy is problem 515, 516; and press stories on tax 519, 533, 556; relations with Mandelson 525, 555, 561,

562, 579, 582; worried about policy 527; has shouting match with DB 529; 'rude and boorish' 529; uses TB's words in conference speech 536, 537, 538; and press story on single currency 540; filmed by STV 553–4; omits to tell press office about his speech 554; angry at RC's interview on EMU 558; brilliant on *Today* 560; and Healey 561; monosyllabic at TB/AC 563; and Budget strategy 563; and Darling 563; continues not to engage on economy 565, 566; his description of his mother denied by her 566; and press story on windfall tax 568; and EMU 569, 571, 572, 584; and RC 571–2; and start of economic rebuttal 573, 574; and Budget 578, 579; on tax rises 585–6, 593; and BBC poll rigging 588, 590–1; claims to know nothing about Mandelson's campaign document 589–90; and 'splashes' on tax 594, 595, 596; further rift with Mandelson 598, 599

1997

and campaign on VAT 601; rows with TB on tax 602; refers to TB as 'Blair' 602; and spats at meeting on economy 604; worried about press stories on tax 604–5; has shouting match with TB 605; and Irvine 606; 'in barking mode' 608; annoyed by coverage of him and girlfriend 608; secretive about speeches 608–9; opposes Millennium Exhibition 610; and VAT 611, 612; briefs on windfall tax 615–18; and royal yacht story 623–4, 627–9; rages about pledges 625–6; and story of JP as deputy PM 630; retaliates with tax story 631; at TB/Murdoch meeting 634; bounces TB on pay freeze policy 635–6; annoys Shadow Cabinet 636; disagrees with TB over policy 637, 640–1, 643; gives pro-Europe speech in US 643, 645, 646, 647, 648; and RC 646–7; further clashes with Mandelson 654, 658, 664–5, 667; sends AC welfare-to-work Budget notes 656; against TB/JM TV debate 657; on pensions 659, 660; speech differs from that promised 662; upstaged by RC 662; denies briefing press on Shadow Cabinet 663–4, 665–6; as 'Brown the terminator' 665; admits to TB his feelings over leadership 665, 668; accuses AC of opposing him 666; at campaign meetings 669, 673; goes down well with Rothermere 674; and sleaze 674, 690; full of energy and ideas 676; getting on better with TB 677; and *Sun* windfall tax story 678, 681; does press conference on unions 682–3; and taxes 683, 684; refuses to attack JM 685; and Tatton candidate 685, 687; and economic message 689, 692; distracts attention from TB at meeting 690; mishandles privatisation 701, 705, 706; does not want TB at meeting 702; makes gaffe 703; not a team player 705, 713; on Europe 708, 709;

complains of AC's criticism 713; and Tory position on single currency 715; meets with Mandelson and AC on strategy 720; 'empire building' 720; and Santer 722; needs to lighten up 722–3; and Tories' acquisition of Labour 'war book' 726; gets on better with Mandelson 735; press conference preamble too long 736

Brown, Michael 433

Brown, Nick 10, 12, 17, 21, 244, 246, 252, 299, 304, 305–6, 494, 631

Brown, Sarah *see* Macaulay, Sarah

Brown, Tina 416

Bruce, Fiona 741

Brumwell, George 271

Brundtland, Gro Harlem 161

Brunson, Michael (Mike) 114, 362; briefed by AC 401, 538; and *Road to the Manifesto* 406; on JM 555; lunches with AC 577; and Labour leadership document 603; tipped off about *Sun* switch to Labour 672; on *Sun* sex scandal 684; and tax message 696; briefed on European policies 722; and Buster Cox story 79; critical of GB 99; on Colvei 313; likes TB's speech 369; and new tone 515; on JP as deputy leader 626, 629, 630

Bruton, John 271–2

BSE 402, 403–4, 405, 408, 456, 609; *see also* beef

Buck, Karen 114

Budgen, Nick 212

Bull, David 18

Bullimore, Tony 606*n*

Burden, Richard 262, 263

Burnley FC 12, 27, 75, 198; matches versus: Plymouth 9; Stockport 19; Millwall 55; Charlton 75, 76; Reading 82; Sheffield United 93; Swindon 96; Chester 105; Preston 118; Liverpool 125, 136, 143; Watford 145; Leicester 282, 283; Swansea 339; Brentford 370; Wycombe 408; Millwall 516; Liverpool 601; Bury 615; Bournemouth 644; Brentford 668

Burton, John 22, 23, 30, 253–4, 739, 740, 742

Bush, George, Snr 540

Butler, Lorraine 36, 37

Butler, Nell 149

Butler, [Sir] Robin 13, 79, 107, 149, 420, 462–3, 563, 573, 581, 725, 726, 734, 735

Butler, Trevor 743

Byers, Stephen 367, 406, 474, 524, 525, 526, 683

Byrne, Colin 39–40, 42

Caborn, Dick 262, 304, 320

Caldwell, Marion, QC 332

Callaghan, James 4, 74, 77, 78, 134, 215, 593

Cameron, Ken 271

Campbell, Anne 592

Campbell, Betty 9, 16, 17, 36, 74, 75, 136, 422, 432, 434, 437, 482, 486, 576, 732, 739, 744

Hewlett, Steve 175
Hibbs, Jon 213, 245
Hicks, Robert 345
Higgins, Stuart: friendly 53; and Caplin story 67; might back Labour 148; and Murdoch 148, 248–9, 250; and closure of *Today* 317, 318; on treatment of CB 401; fed up with AC's continual complaints 422; and rigging of BBC poll 588; clashes with AC 590; and *Sun* piece on TB 654; wants article from TB on Europe 668, 669, 670; and *Sun's* switch to Labour 671–2, 673, 677, 737; wants JP piece on unions 683–4; and sex scandal 684; praises TB's speech 725; annoyed at preference given to *Mirror* 728; and Branson 730
Hill, David (DH) 11–12; worried about Hilary Coffman losing position 46; warns AC re *Mirror* 53; and scrapping of Clause 4 63, 64; on RC 82; warns of Maples memo story 93, 94; role 97, 98; wants more focus on living standards 99, 114; on unions 100; fields questions on TB's choice of school 102; New Year's Eve 119; calls BBC to disown VAT policy 121; takes care of briefing for AC 165; on Mandelson 183; panics over JM's announcement 229; on Shadow Cabinet 253; change of duties 256; at Brighton 290; worried about JP 327; sends AC fake message 342; keeps calm 351; advises HH 359; praises TB for PLP speech 364; complains about number of Tories on *Today* programme 392; dismissive of Central Office document on TB 411; and TB's article on God 412; complains to ITN re JM interview 499; on NEC 507; briefs on firearms policy 549; told of Clare Short's 31-year-old son 550; briefs on Tory Budget 579; and *Today* programme poll rigging 587–8; on DB's interview on education 637; and election victory 741
Hilton, Isabel 15
Hilton, Steve 638, 640
Hilton, Tessa 218
Hinton, Les 317, 320, 375, 376, 382, 634, 664
Hitchens, Christopher 81
Hitchens, Peter 277, 636, 712
Hobsbawm, Julia 34
Hoddle, Glenn 607, 632, 650
Hodge, Margaret 175, 564
Hogg, Douglas 410, 642
Hoggart, Simon 647
Hollick, Clive 42, 205, 495, 516, 575
Holme, Richard 679, 698
Holmes, Eamonn 113
homosexuality 552; and the military 423, 433, 435, 440, 441, 443
Honours Scrutiny Committee 219, 221
Hood, Andrew 575
Horam, John 715
Horley, Sandra 203
Horrocks, Peter 631

House Magazine 17, 307, 508, 517
Howard, John 248, 270
Howard, Michael 55, 157, 198, 230, 408, 433, 450, 481, 555, 556, 584, 684, 719
Howarth, Alan (ex-Tory MP): defection to Labour 264, 284–5, 286, 287–8, 289, 290, 292, 294, 295, 296–7, 298–9, 300, 301, 302; as asset in by-election 340; and other Tory defections 345, 348; as Labour candidate 428, 498, 667, 669; press conference 688, 689
Howarth, Alan (PLP secretary) 425, 603n, 619, 622, 623
Howe, Geoffrey 128, 610
Howell, Denis 463, 481
Howells, Kim 8, 16, 17, 526–7
Hoyle, Doug 448, 492
Hucknall, Mick 379
Hudd, Roy 292, 373, 534, 535
Hudson, Hugh 3, 24
Hughes, Colin 548
Hughes, David 101, 175, 734
Hughes, Robert (Bob) 200
Hughes, Sean 208
Hume, Cardinal Basil 484
Hume, John 53, 272
Humphrys, John 93, 134, 149, 218, 350, 506, 561, 638, 683, 733
Hunt, David 173
Hunter, Anji (AH)
1994–5
on Mandelson 10; on GB 11; on TB's need for support 11, 14; and CB 37; and AC 42, 45, 52–3; on TB's speech 65; watches PMQs with CB 72; suggests DM goes to Sedgefield with TB 75; cut by CB 77; worried about PLP and Mandelson 82; liaises between TB and JP 86; and TB's Queen's Speech 86, 87; and 'Big Guns' meetings 91; and TB's promise of a Welsh Senedd 92; supports AC over Mandelson 95; and TB's criticisms of her 112; gets Christmas presents for staff 115; bets on TB phoning 125; and Clause 4 campaign 130; and Mandelson 137, 140, 141, 183, 184, 268; and Powell 137, 218, 225, 234; wonders if AC has personality flaw 164; reaching end of tether 171; goes to Joy Johnson's BBC farewell 185; has set-to with TB 194; tells him not to bother AC 212; and JM's announcement 229; and Joy Johnson 236; and JP 239; on Australian trip 247, 250; receives tirade from CB 271; depressed about CB situation 273; 'bollocked' by TB 279; lunches with CB 280; and TB's pre-speech preparation 289, 290; unable to stop people wandering in and out of his office 306; and TB's reaction to AC's illness 307–8, 310; tells TB feeling in Walworth Road 332–3; on AC and JP 335; tells AC of Tory defection 345
1996–7
at church with TB 351; rows with HH 365; fed up with TB 373; and Ron Davies's

Manchester: IRA bomb (1996) 468, 499
Manchester United FC 130, 525, 541, 551–2, 635, 649, 653n, 719, 733; see also Ferguson, Alex
Mandela, Nelson 493, 494, 543, 544–5
Mandelson, Peter

1994
angry at AC's *Newsnight* interview 6, 7; devious 7; snubbed by JP 9; and leadership contest 7, 8–9, 10, 11, 12, 13, 14, 15, 16, 17, 18, 19–20, 21, 26; on MB 17, 24; plans to run campaign 24; and AC's tie 25–6; criticises TB's interviews 28–9, 30, 31; unhappy over his position with TB 32–3, 34; and TB's press office 36, 39–40, 42, 52, 53; asks for help with *Sun* article 40; dislikes being called 'Bobby' 42–3; pressures AC to work for TB 44, 45, 50–1; clashes with AC 53, 54; and New Labour slogan 55, 56; and the press 61; criticises TB's Clause 4 speech 63; chucks out *Sun* vendor 67; at Social Justice meeting 70; at TB's 76; and PLP 78–9, 80, 82; and hostile Labour whips 79, 80, 81; wants his role legitimised 83–4, 92–3; relations with JP 85, 86, 88; on TB's Queen's Speech 91; and TB's pay 92; briefs the papers 93, 94–5; wins *Spectator* award 96; wanted by TB for his 'strategic mind' 98; at strategy meetings 99, 114; and furore over TB's choice of school 103; and euro referendum 106; at Blackburns' party 113; has heart-to-heart with AC 116

1995
at odds with JP 129, 131; and AC's campaign pyramid 130; positive and helpful 133; winds TB up 136; wants to chair committees 137; interrupts AC's work in Brighton 139; disagrees over TB's clothes 140; fights with AC 140–1, 143; profile in *Guardian* causes waves 145–6; angry with AC 146–7; at strategy meetings 147, 148, 157, 158; has spat with Joy Johnson 169; bad relations with GB 172–3, 179, 180; wants a break 172, 173; told to apologise to Sawyer 180; and AC's absence 183; suspicious of Whelan 184; too influential with TB 184–5; provocative on *World at One* 191; further clashes with GB 191–2, 200; accused by AC of briefing newspapers 196; and Joy Johnson 204, 212–13, 223; on *Any Questions?* 218; advises AC to involve FM more 225; on Woolas 225; awaits Tory leadership result with GB 238; comparisons between him and GB 238; at Frost's summer party 239; on CB 240; his book a PR disaster 251; and Littleborough & Saddleworth by-election 254, 255; depressed 264–5; 'outed' 266, 267; is a liability 267–8, 269, 274; in discussion about CB's role 274, 275; winds TB up 290; and Howarth defection 297, 298, 299; back from the cold 304;

given surprise birthday party 305; storms out of campaign management meeting 311; refuses to go to meetings 316; on Mo Mowlam 318; and *The Blair Revolution* 331, 342, 343, 347, 348, 381, 383; rows with GB 333; chairs general election planning group meeting 337; against AC and TB going to Far East 340

1996–7
rows with AC over book launch 347; attacks Joy Johnson 354; chairs general election planning group 356; to run media centre 367, 369; and GB 377, 378; 'too imperious' 380; behaves badly at meeting 380; with AC at Wapping 382; his book talked down by AC 383; does interview for *On the Record* 383, 384; on relations with GB 384; book launch party 386; inhibited in briefing press 390; rows with AC over his book 393; 'bollocked' by TB for interview 400; complains about GB 402, 411; criticised by TB 429, 432; and GB's 'Lost Generation' campaign 440, 442, 460; walks out on GB and TB 442; damages party with clashes with GB 443–6; writes resignation letter 445; offer of help turned down 450; leading 'a ridiculous social life' 451; pontificates 452; and JM's statement on beef ban 452; near-physical revulsion for GB 456; author of his own problems 457; annoys JP 460; goes over HH's document on waiting lists 460; and Party poster 473; briefs papers on *Road to the Manifesto* 484, 485; and Clare Short 506; aggrieved at being linked with Brian Wilson 509; holds fort 510; at discussions on Party problems 511, 512; demoralised by TB 512; TB's views on 515, 520; rows with AC 525; at key meeting on women 543; his 43rd birthday party 552–3; worried about GB's economic policy 554; rude to George Jones 574; has 'tantrum' 579; anxious about Tory strength 581; relations with GB 581–2; and EMU 584; and BBC 'personality of the year' poll rigging 587–8; and new campaign document 589–90; further clashes with GB 590–1; on Clinton 594; and Palumbo car 595, 596; complains about JP and GB 598; disastrous meeting with GB 599; deals with GB through Ed Miliband 601; has another spat with him 604; exasperates TB 606; and GB's speech on tax 617; has headaches 628; and Robert Harris 631, 685, 686; worried about European policy 633; bemoans lack of attacking strategy 637; likes 'New Labour, New Britain' posters 644; doesn't like film of TB 647; angers GB by briefing on single currency 647–8; gives patronising presentation on campaign 654; against TB/JM TV debate 657; thinks he is going into the Cabinet 658; further clashes with GB 658,

and HH 366; persuades AC to go to acupuncturist 372; at Brit Awards 379; worried about CB and Caplin 381; worried about *Vogue* profile of CB 384; on GB and Mandelson 384; persuades AC to go to Eric Clapton concert 389; another row 411; and TB's article on God 412; and CB 425, 433–4, 437, 440; supportive over AC's court case 436, 437; at parties with AC 486, 487; supports CB 499; interviews GB 508; ill in France 510; notices new tone in coverage of Labour 515; at focus group with PG 521; row with AC 526; shocked that CB takes alternative medicine 537; finds AC crying 539; on TB/JM 'class war' 547; at Mandelson's birthday party 552; wanted by AC's office to share work 558; sees Home Office with CB about security 578, 581; in tears 588; on AC as source of tax 'splash' 595; accused of being CB's spin doctor 596, 597; further rows 597–8, 599, 600; has scene with Rory 604; dreams they are made homeless 610; at Howarth/Rae dinner for Princess Diana 619, 621, 622, 623; wary of Diana 624, 625; suspicious of American interviewer 635; against AC giving *Guardian* interview 637; and CB/Caplin relationship 641; unconvinced of CB's involvement in Wirral visit 651; on lack of decision-making at Millbank 705, 706; election day and victory 740, 742, 744

Millar, Frank 279

Millar, Gavin 35, 91, 305

Millbank Tower, London 237, 238, 356, 405–6, 458, 705–6, 709

Millennium Exhibition 592–3, 610, 611, 612–13, 614–15, 616

Milligan, Stephen 16*n*

Mills, David 35, 177, 360, 469, 528, 599

Milne, Seumas 146, 276

minimum wage 88, 128, 154, 156–7, 161, 170, 196, 198, 201, 203, 207, 216–17, 241, 255, 267, 269, 271, 275, 282, 284, 285, 292, 479, 524, 650, 710

Mirren, Helen 737

Mitchell, Andrew 319

Mitchell, Austin 17, 487, 513, 517

Mitterrand, François 352

Monks, Brendan 641

Monks, Frankie 34, 645

Monks, John 13, 15, 29, 34, 37, 70, 268, 277, 278, 320, 356–7, 522, 523, 525, 544, 696, 699

Montgomery, David 49, 54, 84, 110, 218, 294, 317, 540, 672

Moonie, Lewis 304, 305, 401

Moore, Brian 564, 733

Moore, Charles 116, 172, 353, 605

Moore, Jo 6, 95, 96, 119, 148, 513, 543, 579

Moore, John 7

Morgan, Gill 34

Morgan, Piers 115, 441, 577, 635, 644, 654, 692, 725, 733

Morgan, Sally: on Bickerstaffe 157; and unions 166, 233, 240, 406, 407; and women shortlists 198; irritated by Jonathan Powell 215, 218; at NPF 220; on NEC 256, 507; 'teacherish' with TB 390; and Clare Short 536–7; at key meeting on women 543; horrified at TB's *Today* broadcast 552; angry with TB 558; warns AC of problem with Falconer's selection 708; works on plan for final five days 729; and election victory 744

Morris, Bill: at Labour conference (1994) 61, 65; wants special conference 85; causing trouble 132; 'pusillanimous' 133, 142; on *Frost* 134; speaks at conference 188; relations with TB 192, 228, 231, 243, 253, 256; angry with Dromey 204, 206; at NPF 217; conciliatory 242; breakfasts with TB and GB 255–6; warns unions will resist ballot 408; 'excellent' 526, 527

Morrison, John 709

Mortimer, John 553

Mortimer, Penelope 553

Mosey, Roger 443

Motor Cycle News 632

Mountfield, Robin 420

Mowlam, Mo: and TB's leadership bid 15; makes gaffe 16, 17; fails to become TB's campaign manager 22, 23, 24, 25; writes nonsense 48; in Northern Ireland 74, 141; and scrapping of Clause 4 113; thinks newspaper stories are part of a plan 118; on TB and PLP 222; bares all to AC 271; discusses Mandelson with TB 272; and GB 294, 314, 318; agrees to defend HH 362; and RC's affair 380, 381; and government's handling of Northern Ireland 407, 410, 496; in Shadow Cabinet 494; good at meeting and greeting 588; 'dire' on party reform 631; brain tumour 703–4, 708, 709, 710

Mudie, George 305

Mulholland, John 637

Mullen, Jimmy 19, 75, 82

Mullin, Chris 15

Murayama, Tomiichi 349, 350

Murdoch, Anna 249, 250, 737

Murdoch, Rupert (RM): and TB 52, 53, 55, 117, 206, 209; and the *Sun* team 148–9; and TB's Australian trip 214, 216, 226, 228, 231, 233, 239, 240, 241, 245, 248–50; Stott on 247; Keating on 241, 247, 248; and JM 317; buys *Today* newspaper 317*n*; meeting with TB 374, 375; is losing interest in Britain 382; his media image problem 382–3; portrait in *Sun* offices 401; opinion of TB 516; and Labour's single-currency policy 540; his Christmas card to TB 602; and Europe 624; puts pressure on *Sun* 631; meetings with TB 631, 633, 634, 635; Kavanagh's views on 652; supports Labour 662, 664, 670, 671–2; dinner with TB 688, 689

Stephanopolous, George 595
Stephens, Phil 245
Steven, Stewart 137, 239
Stevens, of Ludgate, David Stevens, Lord 239–40
Stewart, Allan 174
Stewart, Dave 512
Stewart, Mari 164
Stewart, Patrick 705
Stewart, Colonel Robert (Bob) 700, 702
Stirling University 334
Stoddart, Tom 641, 697, 742
Stone, Carole 113
Stone of Scone 487–8
Stothard, Peter 214, 233, 248, 249, 640, 662, 729
Stott, Penny 200, 540
Stott, Richard 3, 16, 23, 27, 30, 46–7, 53, 69, 70, 74–5, 200, 247, 516, 518, 540
Strang, Gavin 404, 665
Straw, Jack: appointed TB's campaign manager 23, 24, 25; bashes Lib Dems 48; as Shadow Home Secretary 71, 73; his 'slimmed-down monarchy' article 104; at NEC 111; gives bad broadcast 132–3; on *On the Record* 146; accused by Mandelson of briefing newspapers 147; and RC's economic group 216, 217; angry at RC being put in charge of Scott Report 217; Eurosceptic 219; noisy-neighbours plans 227; and PG's leaked memo 277; as butt of jokes by Mandelson 305; and Howard's anti-terrorist measures 408; and Cullen inquiry 444; on their political immaturity 448; at policy forum in Manchester 450; and knives 558; and Hugh Dykes 594, 599–600, 601–2; 'bollocks' Tessa Blackstone 597; responds to JM 677; discusses terrorism with Howard 684; on crime 709
Streisand, Barbra 591–2
Suard, André 739
Sugar, Alan 496, 528–9, 531, 619, 629, 673–4, 676–7, 725, 727, 729
Sullivan, Dee 694, 711
Sun 40, 44, 52, 53, 66, 67, 79; on Caplin 76, 77, 115; and 'Blairgate' 110; AC articles 112, 229, 569; savage about TB 122; lunches 148–9, 401; does 'Gould outs Mandelson' story 266; on TB's bald patch 316; and *Today*'s closure 317; on royal divorce 341; and Labour Christmas cards 341, 342; on TB's public school 372, 373–4; on Waldegrave's number plate 404; alleges AC/Mandelson Stalinist tactics 422; on Kilfoyle's daughter 451; supports JM on beef 457; supports TB on spanking children 461; on 'Phoney Blair' 499; readers meet with TB 500–1; and Clare Short 505; JM's article 514–15; on CB vs Norma Major 519; turns against Labour 522; on Powell asking Bremner for jokes 534; on tax 555, 556; on AC 560; on withdrawal from Europe 580; biased against

Labour and Europe 590, 648–9; on Millennium Exhibition 610; asks for article on general election 630–1; Stelzer's article 637; and Evison's piece on TB 652, 654; TB/AC piece 669, 670; switches to support Labour 671–2, 673, 674, 677; attacks windfall tax 680, 681; JP's article on unions 684; on TB 723, 725; on election day 739; *see also* Higgins, Stuart
Sunday Express 348, 351, 409, 411, 433
Sunday Mirror 218, 709
Sunday Telegraph 7, 8, 116, 209, 254, 401, 411, 438, 490, 526, 557, 558, 628, 629, 633, 698, 701, 704, 710
Sunday Times 54, 110, 137; polls 8, 451, 475, 551; journalists 44, 118, 136, 150, 626, *see also* Grice, Andy; Clause 4 story 93; profile of CB 104; on Tory referendum 113; on spin doctors 131, 133; on 'luvvies' deserting Labour 141; and Foot 'spy story' 107*n*, 149–50; on Ashdown 196; Gillian Shephard on GM schools 227; survey on taxation 425; chases David Mills 469; Howells' article 526; and TB/JM 'class war' 546, 547; on Levy 576; gives TB angle 589; on Tories' New Year campaign 597; on Labour health policy 598; on 'Lib-Labbery' 601; on TB's choice of paintings for No. 10 656; and Labour business manifesto 677, 678; nasty profile of CB 678; and Monks 699; Oratory headmaster on Labour policies 710; on JP on minimum wage 710; Q&A marathon 730
Sweeney, Bridget 242
Sylvester, Christopher 427
Sylvester, Rachel 573, 575
Sylvie (driver) 87, 142, 311, 632, 693
Symonds, Liz 420, 668

Tait, Richard 675
Tamworth (South-East Staffordshire) by-election (1996) 337, 340, 400, 401, 402, 406, 412, 413, 415, 416–17
Tapsell, Peter 212
Tatchell, Peter 443
Tate & Lyle 299
Tatler 78, 96
Tatton: anti-corruption candidate 685, 686–7, 689, 691, 696, 697, 698, 700, 704; *see also* Bell, Martin
taxation 31, 56, 224, 226, 281, 283–4, 288, 291, 301, 302, 306, 315–16, 318, 321, 322, 324, 326, 330–1, 333, 394–5, 413–14, 415, 425, 426–7, 456, 474, 519, 521–2, 533, 555, 568, 572–80 *passim*, 585–6, 593, 594, 596, 602, 605, 606, 617, 655, 677, 683, 691–2, 696; *see also* VAT; windfall taxes
taxi cabs 209, 215, 217–18
Taylor, Ann 11, 368, 448, 492, 494, 562, 586
Taylor, Matthew 478
Taylor, Noreen 110
Taylor, Ron 399, 400
Taylor, Teddy 229

Watson, Tom 140
Weaver, Tina 641
Webb, Sidney 160
Webster, Mark 241, 696
Webster, Phil 172, 443, 533, 540, 709
Week in Politics, A 400, 426
Week in Westminster 22, 34
Wegg-Prosser, Ben 445
West, Elizabeth 373, 598
West, Fred 122
West, Rosemary 122*n*, 321
'West Lothian Question' 83, 391–2, 459, 474, 479, 639, 648
Western Mail 90–1, 92
Westmacott, Peter 410
Weston, John 414
Wheaton, Bob 18, 28, 30, 31, 35, 38, 44
Whelan, Charlie: on TB and unions 4, 5; and GB 96, 98, 161, 163, 167, 169; clashes with Mandelson 192; 'a menace' 193; briefs press on Mandelson policy group 246; a gossip 265; suspected of leaking PG's memo 276, 277, 278, 285; worries TB 287; and Mandelson 311, 325, 442; and Clare Short 419, 421, 508; a 'deeply unpleasant character' 449; briefs on taxes 580, 615 16, 678; briefs on JP going to China 609; and royal yacht story 627, 628, 629; causes another GB muddle 645; attacked by JP as spin doctor 646–7; abusive to Mandelson 647–8; to be included in campaign meetings 658; briefs against everyone 663, 664, 666, 667; has no future with TB 740
White, Lesley 626, 659, 719
White, Michael (Mike) 29, 246, 251, 279, 366, 430, 431, 492, 570, 612, 615, 693
Whitehorn, Will 730
Whyte, Andrew 239
Wilenius, Paul 12, 187
Willetts, David 142–3, 541, 542, 543, 550, 561, 586, 587
William, Prince 621
Williams, John (journalist) 187, 643
Williams, Shirley 48
Wills, Michael 328, 377, 386
Wilmore, Ian 451, 452
Wilson, Brian 4, 75, 164, 165, 188, 393, 481, 506, 509, 541
Wilson, Charles 428, 429
Wilson, Des 284

Wilson, Harold 4, 42, 68, 77, 117, 134, 208; funeral 215, 216
Wilson, Brigadier J. B. 250
Wilson, Mary 293
Wilson, Phil 135
Wilson, Richard 94, 649, 667
windfall taxes 615–16, 618, 634, 635, 640, 672–3, 678, 680, 681
Winning, Cardinal Thomas 151, 152, 556–7, 558, 560
Winston, Robert 214, 215, 219
Winterton, Rosie 26; and Mandelson 86; at strategy meeting 99; at Clause 4 meetings 107, 131, 166; and JP 138, 139, 158, 159, 161, 165, 170, 171; has headache from laughing 179; told by JP not to attend meetings 198; and TB's surprise party 254; at lunch with TB and JP 265, 273; plies AC with sweets 293, 294; on JP's reaction to Mandelson's book 342; clashes with AC 370, 485, 514; at conference 541
Wintour, Patrick 135, 151–2, 233, 276, 324, 474
Wirral by-election (1997) 582, 605, 633, 636, 638, 650–2, 654, 655, 656, 657, 658
Witherow, John 137, 149, 150, 547
Wogan, Terry 594
Womack, Sarah 411
women-only shortlists 198, 209, 210, 265, 308, 353, 355
women voters 543, 642–3
Wood, Nick 709
Wood, Ronnie 312
Woodhead, Chris 608
Woolas, Phil 214, 225, 713
Woolf, Willie 199
World at One 55, 90, 191, 235, 262, 265, 439, 528, 703, 705, 712, 717, 722
World This Weekend 19, 121, 125, 150, 173, 185, 265, 366, 389, 527, 589, 711, 719, 720
World Tonight, The 14
Wyatt, Woodrow 115

Yeltsin, Boris 58, 329
Yentob, Alan 228, 233, 239
Young, Hugo 339
Young, Jim 142, 403
Young, Jimmy 278, 706
Young, Kirsty 689
Young, Syd 678, 705
Young Labour 138, 139, 140, 584